DATE DUE

OCT 1 '98			
DEC '00			

DEMCO 38-296

A MEDITERRANEAN SOCIETY

S. D. Goitein, 1900–1985

A
MEDITERRANEAN
SOCIETY

An Abridgment in One Volume

S. D. Goitein

Revised and Edited by Jacob Lassner

UNIVERSITY OF CALIFORNIA PRESS

Berkeley / Los Angeles / London

University of California Press
Berkeley and Los Angeles, California

University of California Press, Ltd.
London, England

© 1999 by the Regents of the University of California

Library of Congress Cataloging-in-Publication Data

      Goitein, S. D., 1900–
        A Mediterranean society : an abridgment in one volume / revised
    and edited by Jacob Lassner.
        p.   cm.
      Includes index.
      ISBN 0-520-21734-9 (alk. paper)
        1. Jews—Islamic Empire—Civilization.   2. Islamic Empire—
    Civilization.   3. Cairo Genizah.   I. Lassner, Jacob.   II. Title.
    D199.3.G58   1999
    956'.004924—dc21   98-54216
                                                      CIP

Manufactured in the United States of America

08 07 06 05 04 03 02 01 00 99
10 9 8 7 6 5 4 3 2 1

The paper used in this publication meets the minimum requirements of ANSI/NISO
Z39.48-1992 (R 1997) (*Permanence of Paper*). ∞

Contents

Foreword

On February 6, 1985, Shelomo Dov Goitein died unexpectedly at his home in Princeton, New Jersey. It is, I suppose, rather strange to speak of someone dying unexpectedly at a time of life when death can strike without notice and often does. And yet, if we could conceive of any scholar who could have lived until the proverbial 120, as did the biblical Abraham, it would have been Goitein—certainly if sheer willpower and strict regimen were the major considerations. When felled instantaneously by "the sweet kiss of death," he was getting dressed to prepare for his workday. As always, it would have been a day marked by punctilious attention to schedule and to his research on the Cairo Geniza—the unique treasure trove of documents and letters with which Goitein illuminated the social and economic history of the medieval Near East, in particular from the eleventh through the thirteenth century.

Shortly before his death, Goitein had finished and sent off to press the fifth volume of his *Mediterranean Society*, a work based largely on materials from the Geniza. This last effort was seen through press by colleagues. A sixth volume representing the cumulative index, a tome of considerable learning in its own right, was prepared by his former research assistant, Paula Sanders, now associate professor of history at Rice University. *A Mediterranean Society*, a labor of love and learning, is widely proclaimed a prodigious feat of scholarship. Indeed, there are many learned scholars who consider it to be the single most noteworthy project produced by a historian of the medieval Near East this century. There is certainly a broad consensus that it will be read by scholars of wide-ranging interests for generations to come.

It almost appears that Goitein was destined for a life of scholarship. His background is discussed in the moving foreword to the fifth and final volume that he composed, a segment of the text that was added posthumously by his colleague Abraham L. Udovitch. A truncated version of Udovitch's eulogy is reproduced below, interspersed with some additional comments of my own:

Goitein was born in April 1900, in the tiny Bavarian village of Burgkunstadt, where his father served as a district rabbi and leader of the local Jewish community. At an early age, he moved to Frankfurt to pursue studies at the gymnasium and later at the university. His early training, like that of all his contemporaries who studied the Near East, was as a philologian and not a historian. At Frankfurt University he concentrated on Arabic and Islamic subjects under the guidance of Josef Horovitz, whose specialty was Qurʾānic studies. Goitein's curiosity and his studies were, however, by no means restricted to Orientalism. He was an excellent classicist and was even in his later life an active participant in the classics seminar that was held on a regular basis at the Institute for Advanced Studies in Princeton.

In 1923, upon completing his dissertation on the subject of prayer in the Qurʾān, Goitein fulfilled his long-held ambition to emigrate to Palestine and began his career there as a high school teacher in Haifa's famed Reali Gymnasium, an institution that featured a remarkable program of instruction in Arabic. Several of the Arabic teachers went on to be university professors and world-famous scholars. The Reali also trained generations of outstanding students, many of whom, following the lead of Goitein and his Reali successors, embarked on careers as Islamists. Goitein remained an educator all his life. He was a member of the founding faculty of the Hebrew University in Jerusalem, which opened its doors in 1925, and became its first instructor in Islamic studies. While the world of scholarship and the university dominated the rest of his career, he retained his original interest in the education of the young, publishing books on the teaching of Hebrew and the Bible and serving as senior education officer under the British Mandate in Palestine, a post he held from 1938 to 1948 and in which he supervised Arab as well as Jewish educators.

Shortly after joining the faculty of the Hebrew University, Goitein began to do fieldwork among the Yemenite immigrants to Palestine, a research that intensified with the mass migration of the Jews of Yemen following the establishment of the state of Israel. He published works on their Arabic dialect and their way of life. Indeed, this early ethnographic work among what he called "the most Jewish and most Arab of all Jews" would profoundly influence Goitein's study of the life of medieval Jewish communities reflected in the Geniza documents.

Perhaps his most ambitious scholarly undertaking during his early years in Jerusalem was directing the critical edition of Bāladhurī's *Ansāb al-ashrāf*, a major chronicle of Muslim history and biography. In preparation for his own volume in the series, Goitein immersed himself in the study of early Arabic literature and society. The volume he produced was a model of its genre, and the experience garnered on this project stood him in good stead later when dealing with the unique fragments of the Cairo Geniza.

Goitein's serious research in Geniza materials occurred rather late in his career. As he himself testified, it was almost by accident that he discovered their exceptional value for many hitherto poorly documented aspects of Near Eastern history. For the rest of his life, Geniza research was to consume most of his scholarly energies. Indeed, it was to facilitate this research that he moved, in 1957, from Jerusalem to the chair of Arabic studies at the University of Pennsylvania. Upon his retirement from Pennsylvania in 1971, Goitein came to Princeton as a long-term member of the School of Historical Studies at the Institute for Advanced Study. Goitein thrived in Princeton. In the calm and supportive atmosphere of the Institute, Goitein completed the last three volumes of *A Mediterranean Society* and produced three other books and numerous articles, most of which were based on his Geniza work. He continued to have contact with his former students and to serve as an informal advisor to younger scholars embarking on Geniza research. Goitein was not the first to study the Geniza, but he was largely responsible for making "Genizology" an academic industry. While teaching in the United States, he attracted numerous students, each of whom was given different aspects of Geniza research to mine as their own subfield. He was, in that respect, a talent scout who directed gifted individuals into areas that were beyond even his vast erudition. Nor were all those who sat at his feet students of his in a formal sense. He carried on an extensive correspondence with a number of young scholars and sat and read texts with others who were fortunate enough to be within hailing distance of his residence in Philadelphia and later, in Princeton.

After more than thirty years of pioneering Geniza research, Goitein's work, through some remarkable and mysterious symmetry, ended where it began—with the medieval Indian Ocean trade. On the day of his death, the outline of his next major project, a three-volume edition and translation of the Geniza texts relating to the Indian Ocean trade, was neatly arranged on his desk.

A study of the Indian Ocean commerce was his original project. In

1950, while investigating the interplay between Islamic and Jewish law on the basis of Judeo-Arabic court records from the Cairo Geniza, he was able to reconstruct the entire dossier of a series of lawsuits brought against a Tripolitanian merchant who, while traveling to India, had lost part of the merchandise entrusted to him by some of his Tunisian and Egyptian colleagues. As he later wrote, this discovery "electrified" him and changed the course of his research and of his life. "The Geniza treasures had been known to the scholarly world since the 1890s, and I had assumed that their main contents were well known. That discovery showed that the study of their socioeconomic aspects had hardly begun." By 1957, he had assembled about two hundred documents dealing with the trade across the Indian Ocean. These were unique. No other documents concerning that commerce during the High Middle Ages are known from any other source. Goitein's move, during the same year, from Jerusalem to the University of Pennsylvania was undertaken primarily to complete work on his India book. However, as he wrote in 1978, "after a year of great toil it became evident that this was a questionable undertaking: The India trade, as represented in the Geniza, was only one of many activities of a highly developed urban Mediterranean society. One cannot study the branch without knowing the root. By the summer of 1958 I was off India and on the Mediterranean."

For the remaining twenty-seven years of his life, it was the Mediterranean world of the eleventh through the thirteenth century that was at the center of Goitein's research, writing, and reflection. Methodical and disciplined scholar that he was, he formulated and announced the grand design of *A Mediterranean Society* not only well in advance of its completion but even of its composition. The table of contents of the entire oeuvre was confidently published in the first volume when it appeared in 1967, and again reprinted in volume 2, in 1970. Goitein projected a three-volume study consisting of ten major chapters: four to be devoted to economic life (vol. 1); three to be devoted to communal life (vol. 2); and three to deal with the family, daily life, and the individual. As these last three chapters began to assume rather voluminous proportions, Goitein seriously considered some radical abridgments. Mindful of Goitein's unique and intimate familiarity with the Geniza texts and the society that produced them, his friends and colleagues urged him to give full reign to his insights and to his pen. Happily for all, Goitein heeded this counsel, and the projected chapters on the family, on daily life, and on the Mediterranean mind each developed into full, separate volumes. In the end, Goitein adhered to his master plan of 1967; but the three volumes originally projected now grew to five. Neither in Islamic nor in Jewish studies was there a precedent for such an effort. It is a history of the *mentalité* and the soul of Mediterranean man during the High Middle Ages, and Goitein alone among his peers was capable of bringing to fruition an enterprise of this kind.

No other twentieth-century scholar combined both Jewish and Islamic learning with such great breadth and depth as he did. Jewish learning was of natural interest to him, the descendant on his mother's side of a distinguished rabbinical family, a family that included his cousin David H. Baneth, an Orientalist of enormous learning and uncompromising standards. He combined his interest in Judaica with the fruits of a German secondary and university education—the kind of education that characterized German schooling before the darkness descended on that bright world. The rest of the groundwork for his researches, as he called them in English, particularly his work on the Cairo Geniza, stemmed from his studies with Horovitz and his contacts with the learned Islamists that had clustered at the Hebrew University, where he was a pivotal figure.

A man of rigorous and exacting scholarly standards, Shelomo Goitein described himself as a sociographer. By that he meant that he was a describer, a writer about old societies based on their texts. He was particularly sensitive to the importance of documents, and he knew how to read them in depth. In his work on the Geniza material, he exhibited his unmatched gift for recreating a whole society in all its vividness, exposing its many levels and penetrating to the soul and mentality of the people about whom he wrote. From this point of view, the five volumes of *A Mediterranean Society* are a unique contribution to our vision of premodern Jewish and premodern Near Eastern societies, and stand as a model for the study of both.

Twentieth-century historical scholarship has produced two grand visions of the Mediterranean world, that of Goitein and that of Fernand Braudel. These "two Mediterraneans" complement each other. Braudel's Mediterranean is vast, stretching from the pillars of Hercules to the gates of Peking. It is full of plains, plateaus, and peninsulas, of climates, of seasons, and of world empires; it moves with the majestic, leisurely rhythm of the *longue durée*. Goitein was more modest, and his Mediterranean is much more circumscribed. It is the Mediterranean coast between Tunisia and Egypt, with small extensions to the west and east. It is only a part of the Mediterranean, but its shores are teeming with people, their quarrels, their wedding contracts, their dowries, their house furnishings, their tableware, and also their dreams and visions, their religion, and their most intimate feelings. His universe was not on the measure of the sea. Goitein's, like Braudel's, is a total history—but a total tailored to the measure of man.

In summarizing his life's trajectory, Goitein wrote:

I started out as an essentially medieval being, that is, one for whom there exists only one real issue of mind, overriding all others, religion. I have remained, I believe, a *homo religiosus*, but I have become a thoroughly modern man with all that is implied in this change. Finally, there was a constant discrepancy between a particularly happy personal life and a heartbreak or wrath at the sight of so much misery and degradation experienced during this century. Often I asked myself, how was I able to live with all of this? How often did I cry out with Job, "is my strength the strength of stone, or my flesh made of bronze?" and how often did I feel like the Book of Deuteronomy when it said, "you will be driven mad by the sight that your eyes shall see"? As one who was brought up to regard his life as a service to the community, I felt that question of Job, that curse of Deuteronomy, stronger than any satisfaction that I ever derived from personal happiness.

Goitein was always ready and eager to venture on new paths. For the first sixty years of his life he was a philologist. At age sixty, the documents and material he was working on propelled him into new areas, and he transformed himself into an economic historian. In his seventies, when he was working on documents concerning family life, he acquired the skills of a social historian. He read a great deal in sociology and anthropology and applied what he learned to the merchants and craftsmen of the Geniza world—and to their wives as well. In his eighties, Goitein became a historian of *mentalité*. In the fall of 1984, he was a faithful participant in an evening seminar on Islamic and Middle Eastern studies jointly sponsored by the Institute for Advanced Study and Princeton University. He had no hesitation about offering for discussion chapters from his work in progress. He graciously accepted comments and criticism from colleagues his junior in both years and learning and frequently revised his text accordingly. With Goitein one had the feeling that the past was never finished; he looked upon himself as an unfinished product. He had an almost mystical need to keep struggling with himself and to work on improving himself. Next to his radio he kept a list of various musical works. "When I will have the time," he would say, "after I finish the India book, I'm going to buy all these records and listen to them." If Goitein at age eighty-four was still improving himself, then anyone who had any contact with him was made to feel that things were not hopeless. One always left his presence feeling good, feeling that he carried one upward.

As was true of my fellow student and colleague Abraham Udovitch,

Goitein was not my mentor in a formal sense. And yet, as did so many others, I always addressed him as *rabbī u-mōrī ha-yakar*, "my beloved teacher." In this case, this was no mere convention, but a true reflection of his influence on my academic outlook and my scholarly identity. Every offprint sent to him occasioned a prompt reply, always in that illegible Hebrew scrawl and always with words of encouragement, an occasional criticism, and, to be sure, a pertinent suggestion for future research. He also instructed my wife on how to drive an automobile, although he himself did not drive, and how to jog, although he did not—or at least had not for many years. He enjoined me to speak to my children in Hebrew, one day a week, preferably on Shabbat, which to my regret I did not do. And, of course, he urged me to adopt his shortened version of the *birkhat ha-mazōn*, the Hebrew text recited after partaking of a meal, a version which, he calculated in his meticulous manner, had saved him something on the order of four months, ten days, and six hours of research time over the course of fifty years. There are many others, colleagues, students, and friends, who can tell similar stories about this truly remarkable man and scholar.

Reworking *A Mediterranean Society*

Shortly after Goitein's death, the University of California Press considered publishing an abridged version of his five-volume work, the sort of book that could be used in a wide variety of college courses and that would also be of interest to a broad audience of readers. When Stanley Holwitz contacted me on behalf of the Press and asked if I were willing to undertake that venture, I happily consented, thinking, at first, that the task would be rather straightforward, the kind of project that requires mostly scissors and paste. Given the projected audience of the shortened version, I first decided to excise Goitein's extensive annotation and weighty appendixes. Important as it was to specialists, the back matter would not have been of extraordinary interest to the broader group of readers targeted by the Press. That which remained, the main body of the text, was slated for pruning; wherever possible, the technical detail woven into the narrative was to be trimmed, if not altogether eliminated. The plan was to produce a single volume that captured the essence of Goitein's labor of love. It soon became apparent, however, that a more complex and time-consuming plan was required. The very nature of this work, composed as it was over seventeen years, called for a serious reworking of the original manuscript.

From the outset of writing *A Mediterranean Society,* Goitein adhered to a preconceived plan. That was characteristic of his great concern with orderliness; even the chapter headings of volumes two and three were fixed at the outset. Although Goitein never deviated from this conceptual scheme, his writing changed over the seventeen years in which the work took shape. Describing the economic foundations of the Geniza community (vol. 1), he employs a very tight style, his narrative spiced with numerous details, more than we might sometimes wish to encounter, let alone absorb. There are, to be sure, extraordinary insights into the working of the medieval economy, and, because of the wealth of data unavailable from other sources and the implications of those data for understanding the Muslim and Christian societies in whose midst Jews dwelt, the first volume is in certain respects the most significant of all. But because of the overwhelming detail and the highly technical discussions to which the data give rise, volume 1 makes very tough sledding for the average reader, or even the professional historian who is not overly concerned with (or expert enough to digest) the minutiae that elucidate the economic rhythms of medieval Mediterranean society. The descriptions of the various professions and the detailed accounts of how specific business enterprises conducted their affairs seemed to me a less interesting story than communal and family organization, the subjects of volumes 2 and 3. After much labor had been expended on editing the volume on economic foundations, I reluctantly decided to omit most of it from the abridgment. Specialists will always have recourse to the original.

The same held true, even more so, for volume 4, the tome devoted to daily life. After much consideration, the detailed descriptions of housing, household furnishings, clothing and jewelry, food and drink, renting animals, and the like did not strike me as being of sufficient interest to a general audience. And so, that material is also omitted from the single-volume abridgment. On the other hand, the segment of volume 4 dealing with the city was rewritten and subsumed within the introduction under the rubric "The Local Environment." As with volume 1, the reader interested in the small details—in this case, the cost of purchasing and renting homes, types of household lamps, wine cellars, renting donkeys, how jewelry was worn, and so forth—will be obliged to turn to the original.

By the fifth and last volume, there is a noticeable shift in Goitein's style and presentation. The writing becomes more comfortable, the prose more expansive, his thoughts seemingly more philosophical. Perhaps it was the subject matter, perhaps it was because Goitein was by then in his ninth decade when deep self-reflection is not uncommon in unusually reflective persons, a description that most certainly fits our author. In the final volume, Goitein turns to the individual. Here we see how people from all walks of life reacted to their surroundings in a highly personal manner. We learn of their mores and more generally of their attitudes towards life. Put somewhat differently, we see how their expectations intersected with the vicissitudes of their existence. Volume 5 is, in essence, a study of individual musings and stocktaking based on the largest sample of personal documents yet made available for a Mediterranean society. Volume 5 is also an opportunity for Goitein to indulge more freely in discussing his own values, including an epilogue in which he tries to place *A Mediterranean Society* into a wider scholarly framework. But it is not only Goitein the scholar who is deftly embroidered into the narrative. It comes as no surprise to anyone who knew him that his Jewish identity and scholarship are so tightly bound, especially when he muses about leading figures of the past. The last volume contains vignettes of various such persons, including Abraham, the son of Maimonides. Abraham Udovitch was particularly insightful when he wrote: "With minor adjustments [Abraham Maymūnī's career] could equally serve as a characterization of [Goitein's] life and achievement." Or, as Goitein himself put it, speaking of his medieval predecessor, "his life and teaching convey so harmonious an impression because they were in conformity with the best and most congenial elements in the contemporary surrounding civilization, and at the same time represented the most perfect realization of the religion of his forefathers."

It was with the greatest of reluctance that I decided to eliminate most of volume 5 from the truncated edition. That decision, originally made with confidence, is the source of some regret now that I have had time to reflect on it. The original rationale for cutting most of the last volume was that the salient values espoused by the individuals portrayed therein permeate the narratives of all the other volumes, particularly the discussions of communal and family organization. In retrospect, I think that I might have been subconsciously influenced by personal considerations of my own: that is, an antipathy at what I perceive to be an undue emphasis on individualism at the expense of the current family and community, the pillars upon which vibrant Jewish societies have always come to rest. Indeed, the themes which are the skeletal structure of Goitein's magnum opus reworked are those of community and family. Hence the change in order of presentation.

Nor was it enough to simply delete major segments of the original text while changing the order of those that were retained. Other changes were called for as well. For one, there was the question of language. English was not Goitein's mother tongue, nor was it even his second or third language. As someone to whom he sometimes turned as regards diction and, more generally, English style, I became aware of the need to make his correct but at times cumbersome sentences more accessible to readers. Throughout the reworked manuscript, I have attempted to prune Goitein's style; at the same time I have tried to be as faithful as I can be to the cadences and sentiments of his prose. There are occasions, however, when it was deemed necessary to rewrite entire passages for the sake of clarity.

A more serious problem is the weighing of the evidence presented by him. As great a scholar as Goitein was, in *A Mediterranean Society* he is not always consistent in drawing conclusions from his own evidence. Indeed, there are junctures in the text when he is apt to contradict himself without explanation. That seeming inconsistency went hand in hand with his constantly enquiring mind. His fertile imagination, nourished by prodigious learning, was always bringing new material to consider and weave into familiar tapestries. Chance meetings with students and colleagues produced innocuous conversations that soon gave rise to serious reflection about life and scholarship. Observations of how individuals and groups went about their business in contemporary times fueled his imagination in reconstructing the past. No small detail escaped him. As a result, he completely rethought older positions and reconfigured old views in accordance with new perceptions and changed realities. But even Goitein, whose mind was the proverbial steel trap, could not remember discrete passages that he composed somewhat earlier, let alone over the many years that this work was in progress.

Still another concern was Goitein's habit of interjecting his own personal experiences into the narratives of his medieval compatriots, a didactic ploy that he often used to good advantage. He has been likened to a "Renaissance painter . . . identifiable in his oeuvre not only by the signature in the corner of the canvas, but by the auto-portrait he sketches in the midst of his 'Mediterranean People.'" Unlike scholars who mark themselves off from the subjects of their scrutiny, our author favors the personal as a means of illuminating the past. There is an intended sense of immediacy between his personal musings and the experiences of the medieval peoples he describes. Readers will always find these comments interesting, at times even fascinating, but they do raise serious methodological questions, particularly when he uses the experiences of modern Jewish communities in the lands of Islam (in particular the Yemenites) to explain the condition of their predecessors. An earlier generation of biblical scholars sought to understand the peoples of ancient Israel based on observations of contemporary bedouins in the Near East, an effort that, in the end, confused as much as it illuminated the past. No doubt, there is much that one can learn about the past from observing contemporary societies that seem to us, more or less, frozen in time, and even from societies that have undergone significant change. There is, however, the danger that, in using the present to explain the past, we might impose our own sensibilities on circumstances and individuals far removed from us. With that caveat in mind, I have taken the liberty of trimming the text of some of his highly personal observations, however much spice they add to an already delectable work.

I have not attempted to bring *A Mediterranean Society* up to date. That is to say, for the most part, I have not integrated more recent research, although I occasionally refer to it. At some point in a more distant future when the small army of scholars currently studying the Geniza have published their results, someone may wish to undertake a serious revision of the larger oeuvre. I have also not attempted to suggest an analytical framework with which to reorganize the massive detail that Goitein provides in so masterly a fashion. Our author was not one to worry about historical paradigms. His scholarly technique, incisive and always engaging, was to paint miniatures and then follow with broad interpretive comments, always rooted in what one might describe as, for lack of a better expression, a very humane and keen understanding of how people are likely to react when faced with the vicissitudes of daily life. Goitein is at his best when describing the world about which he writes rather than theorizing about it. His understanding of history was shaped by a variety of influences; no single approach or method determined the manner in which he proceeded. As he put it in his epilogue: "I do not remember having chosen any particular book or school as my model . . . [rather] I was guided by the command given to me by my sources [which are] of a very special character."

To be sure, Goitein read widely and also discriminatingly. His reading of other people's history left lasting impressions, negative as well as positive. He admired Jakob Burckhardt, in particular the latter's study of the Renaissance civilization in Italy, a work that Goitein saw as providing the kind of interconnections between political institutions, religion and other accepted beliefs, literature, art, and the formation of the individual and the like—broad-ranging themes that would be useful in his own work. At a later stage of his career, Goitein came to admire Fernand Braudel's magisterial study of the Mediterranean in the age of Philippe II, a work that brings broad sweep to the region in the sixteenth century, much as Goitein did for the eleventh through the thirteenth century. He was, however, not enthusiastic about other scholars who attempted to paint history in broad strokes. He is disparaging of Spengler and Toynbee, grand theorizers whom he regarded as thin and ahistorical, although not quite in those words. In working on the Geniza materials, Goitein was drawn to the then current approaches in socioeconomic history. His guides were Robert Lopez (Byzantium and Western Europe) and Claude Cahen (Islamic Near East), two somewhat younger colleagues who cut their intellectual teeth in the famous *Annales* school of historiography. Both, in turn, very much admired Goitein's work. He was also quite intrigued by social science. As a young man, he familiarized himself with the writings of Spencer, Durkheim, and Weber, and in his mature years, he read Clifford Geertz with much interest and considerable profit, but none of these figures provided him with a ready-made paradigm with which to explain the objects of his scrutiny. He remained, in that sense, very much an eclectic scholar.

Above all, Goitein was the product of a rigorous and broadly based education, the kind of schooling that has seemingly disappeared. He was a superb philologist, a great Hebraist, and (despite his modest disclaimers) an extremely formidable Arabist and Islamist, as were all the students of Josef Horovitz. He was also a strong classicist, having studied with Matthias Gelzer, Herman Dessau, and Eduard Meyer. Although he constantly complained about how rusty his Greek had become, he was a regular attendee and vigorous contributor to the classics seminars at the Institute for Advanced Study. Were that not enough, he cultivated a taste for art and music, subjects that he could and did talk about with considerable knowledge. He was, in sum, a scholar's scholar and a man for all seasons.

Jacob Lassner

A MEDITERRANEAN SOCIETY

Author's Note

Technical language has been avoided throughout. The meaning of a few unfamiliar terms, such as *nagid* (the head of the Jewish community of Egypt) or *qāḍī* (a Muslim judge), is set out at the term's first mention and can be located with the help of the index.

Present-day Spain, Morocco, Algeria, Tunisia, Libya, Lebanon, Syria, Iran, Iraq, and so on, were not in existence as political units during the period covered in this book. These and similar place names are used as geographical terms defining the territories occupied by those states in our time.

Quotations from Judaic religious texts (including the Bible) and the Qur'ān, are translated as they were understood by the writers of the letters in which they occur (evident in the context or known through the general usage of the classical Geniza period).

Biblical names that appear in Hebrew in specific documents are spelled in the accepted English way, such as Abraham, Jacob, Moses. They are transcribed phonetically when the original has an Arabic form, such as Ibrāhīm, Ibrahīm, Barhūn (all standing for Abraham), Ya'qūb (for Jacob), Mūsā (for Moses). In the case of rarer biblical names, where there exists no consensus concerning the English spelling, the one nearer to the Hebrew original is adopted. The Arabic or Hebrew word for "son," when occuring between the name of a person and that of his father, is abbreviated as *b.* (prounounced *(i)bn* in Arabic and *ben* in Hebrew).When introducing a family name, the little word is invariably rendered with *Ibn,* although the manuscripts more often than not write *bn*, and not *'bn*. *Bint* (daughter) is abbreviated as *bt.*

3

In frequently recurring Arabic names, the diacritical marks used to denote their exact pronunciation have been omitted: thus, Fatimids, Ayyubids, Fustat, for Fāṭimids, Ayyūbids, al-Fusṭāṭ. In the latter case, as in that of al-Qayrawān, the article also has been dropped.

Plural forms of Arabic or Hebrew nouns that might otherwise confuse non-expert readers have been rendered as "English" plurals; thus *ḥāshir* (a "rallier"), is rendered in the plural as *ḥāshir*s, rather than the more strictly correct *ḥushshār*.

The Mediterranean in the eleventh century

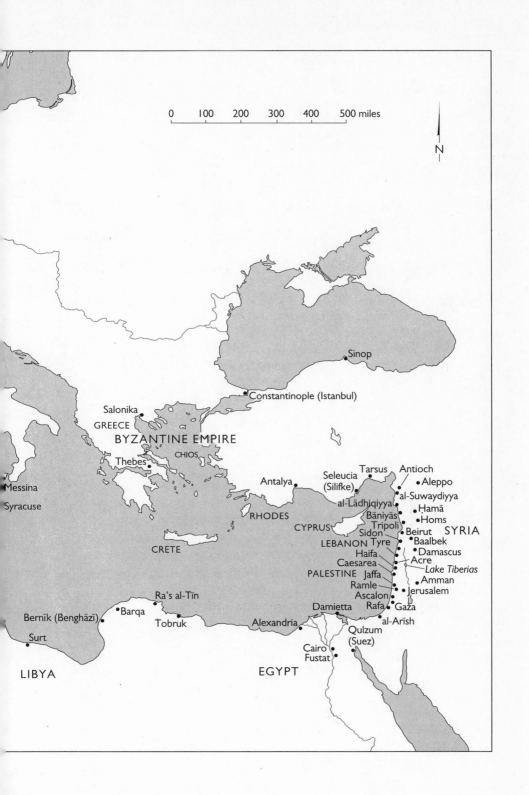

0   100   200   300   400   500 miles

N

Sinop

Constantinople (Istanbul)

Salonika
GREECE
BYZANTINE EMPIRE
CHIOS
Thebes

Messina
Syracuse

Antalya

RHODES

CRETE

CYPRUS

Tarsus   Antioch
Seleucia   Aleppo
(Silifke)   al-Suwaydiyya
al-Lādhiqiyya   Ḥamā
Bāniyās   Homs
Tripoli
Sidon   Beirut   SYRIA
LEBANON Tyre   Baalbek
Haifa   Damascus
Caesarea   Acre
PALESTINE Jaffa   Lake Tiberias
Ramle   Amman
Ascalon   Jerusalem
Rafa   Gaza
al-Arīsh

Ra's al-Tīn

Bernīk (Benghāzī)   Barqa
Surt   Tobruk

Alexandria

Damietta

Quizum
(Suez)

Cairo
Fustat

LIBYA

EGYPT

Introduction

The Cairo Geniza Documents as a Source of Mediterranean Social History

GENERAL OBSERVATIONS

There is for the historian's perusal a wealth of literary sources, monuments, inscriptions, coins, and realia from the medieval Near East. This evidence allows us to reconstruct the broadest outlines of political history and to recapture, however generally, the values of ruling and literary elites. But social and economic history — especially of societal elements not directly represented by these sources — requires written material directly reflecting the transactions of daily life. Historians of the medieval Mediterranean have often complained about the almost complete absence of archives in Muslim lands. In Europe, the Church, feudal lords, cities, and guilds kept their documents as titles of right, as well as for other purposes; nothing comparable is found among contemporaneous Muslims.

Under these circumstances, it is most fortunate that a great treasure of Jewish records, mainly from the eleventh through the thirteenth century and hailing from all over the Mediterranean region, has been preserved in the so-called Cairo Geniza. In medieval Hebrew, *genīza*, or more correctly *bēth genīza*, designates a repository of discarded writings. Jews believe that discarded writings bearing the name of God should be put aside in a special room to await burial in a cemetery, just as the human body, having fulfilled its task as the container of the soul, should

9

be buried, that is, preserved to await resurrection. Similar beliefs toward holy texts were held by Muslims and medieval Christians, but the Jews were more consistent in this matter, perhaps because Hebrew was regarded by Jews as God's own language. The notion of holiness was then transferred from the language to the letters, and scrupulous persons refrained from destroying anything written in Hebrew characters, even if the content was of a purely secular nature and even if the language was other than Hebrew. There existed no uniform practice with regard to this; basically and generally, genizas were used for *shēmōth*, writings bearing, or supposed to bear, the name of God.

The main repository of the Cairo Geniza was a lumber room attached to the synagogue in Fustat, or as it is called today, Old Cairo. Fustat was the capital of Muslim Egypt until 969 C.E., when the Fatimids conquered the country and founded Cairo about two miles northeast of the former capital. During the entire Fatimid period (969–1171), Fustat remained the main city of Egypt and was never really abandoned, even during the days of its decay and destruction. The same was the case with the synagogue to which the Geniza was attached. Although the surrounding area was mostly deserted, it never ceased to be a house of worship. Around 1890, the building was entirely renovated. During these operations, the roof of the Geniza chamber was torn apart, and the extent of its treasures were made known.

THE DISCOVERY AND TRANSFER OF THE GENIZA

Some of the material preserved in the Geniza had been removed earlier, mainly, it seems, through the endeavors of Jewish scholars in Jerusalem. One of them had entered the Geniza chamber as early as 1864 and described it in a book published two years later. In 1890, when Egyptian antique dealers and European scholars visiting Egypt became more fully aware of the Geniza's Hebrew manuscripts, large quantities of its material began to flow into public and private libraries in Europe and the United States. Fortunately, almost all of the Geniza manuscripts that were acquired in and shortly after 1891 by American collectors, mainly from Philadelphia, were entrusted by them to the custody of Dropsie College for Hebrew and Cognate Studies in that city. Other purchased documents made their way to St. Petersburg, Budapest, Cambridge, England, and New York.

Some prominent scholars had doubts about the value of the "Egyptian fragments," as the Geniza papers were called in the early 1890s. One of the skeptics was Solomon Schechter, at that time reader in Rabbinics at the University of Cambridge, England, and subsequently president of the Jewish Theological Seminary of America in New York. Schechter's lack of interest in the Geniza material at that time is vividly demonstrated by the fact that the Geniza papers actually acquired by the University Library from 1893 to 1894 were never even provisionally classified by him, but left in boxes in a state similar to that in which they had arrived.

Then on March 13, 1896, two learned Scottish women showed Solomon Schechter some leaves from the Cairo Geniza that they had recently acquired; Schechter recognized that one of the leaves contained the Hebrew text of Ecclesiasticus, or *Book of Wisdom*, by Ben Sira. This book was written about 200 B.C.E. in Hebrew, but the original had been lost and its content known only through translations into Greek and other languages. This startling discovery electrified Schechter. If the Geniza contained one leaf of such an ancient book in the original language, it stood to reason that a systematic search would retrieve more of the same. Schechter conceived the bold idea to save, with one stroke, the whole of the Cairo Geniza for research. He was fortunate in finding an ardent supporter and Maecenas in Charles Taylor, Master of St. John's College in Cambridge. Equipped with letters of recommendation to the chief rabbi and the president of the Jewish community in Cairo, Schechter arrived in Egypt in December 1896. He spent several weeks perusing the material, then transferred the hoard of remaining documents to Cambridge. As a result, the University Library contains three times as many documents as all the other collections combined.

New Geniza material was unearthed in the Basātīn cemetery east of Fustat at the beginning of this century and was sold openly. Some of the material found its way into libraries and smaller collections. The Geniza documents accounted for, including those obtained from the storeroom itself and from the cemetery nearby, are now scattered in twenty libraries, as well as among private collectors. The history of the transfer of the Cairo Geniza to the libraries of Europe and America explains the scattered state of this material today. Under these circumstances, it is not surprising that pages of one and the same book, indeed, fragments of the very same document, may be found in such distant places as St. Petersburg, Cambridge, and New York. For scholars, the inconvenience of geographical dispersion is aggravated by the fact that only a few collections have published catalogues, and those published are incomplete and insufficient for historical investigation. Moreover, scholarly research on the Geniza, particularly the earlier efforts, is similarly dispersed in journals and works that are not always accessible. Occasionally, they also appear in nonscholarly publications. For example, fragments were published at the turn of the century in a Boston journal, *The Green Bag: An Entertaining Magazine for Lawyers*. To remedy this situation a tentative bibliography of all published Geniza documents was prepared by Shaul Shaked under the direction of David H. Baneth of the Hebrew University of Jerusalem and Goitein himself.

GENIZA VERSUS ARCHIVE

The nature of a geniza hoard of manuscripts can best be illustrated by contrasting it with an archive. The purpose of an archive is to house materials for handy reference; much care is ordinarily taken to preserve individual items, which in many cases are deposited immediately after they are written. The opposite was the case with the Cairo Geniza. Papers were deposited there only after they had lost all value to their possessors and in most cases well after they had been written. Private family letters, let alone business correspondence, would not have been deposited in a place so central except after having lost all relevance to contemporaries. Legal deeds, which conferred rights on their holders, had to be kept by them and their heirs—often for generations—before they could be disposed of in the Geniza chamber.

There was another good reason for holding on to documents for a long time before tossing them into the Geniza: Paper was expensive, and free space on documents was therefore normally used for all sorts of purposes, such as drafts, short notes, accounts, or merely for trying out a pen or writing exercises. Many types of paper found in the Geniza, as well as the ink used on them, were of excellent quality, and the scribes of the courts, clerks of the business houses, as well as scholarly persons in general, for the most part had a clear and often beautiful handwriting. This was generally the case among literate people in the medieval Near East, as can be attested from the numerous Arabic manuscripts in our possession. But time has a way of reducing the readability of clearly written texts, especially when aged paper has been reused. Even in those Geniza documents that are more or less complete, the writing is often partly effaced (by seawater, for example) or otherwise damaged. Many Geniza papers are mere fragments, representing the beginning, middle, or end—or the front or reverse side—of a document. While even small scraps of paper sometimes contain valuable information, the incompleteness of these records, often involving the loss of vital details concerning persons, dates, and localities, is tantalizing and makes heavy demands on the capacity of modern readers to make sense of them.

In an orderly archive, material is normally filed according to subject and kept with similar documents in one place, which makes research on any given topic more manageable. In the Geniza, documents were deposited at random. The helter-skelter transfer of the Geniza material to the libraries of Europe and America did not create the haphazard state of current collections, but it surely exacerbated it. Even in carefully classified collections, the most heterogeneous Geniza material is bound together in one volume.

There can be no doubt, however, that Jewish families and communities kept archives. The Geniza itself has preserved over two hundred letters addressed to Nahray b. Nissīm, a prominent businessman, scholar, and community leader who emigrated around 1045 from Tunisia to Fustat, where he died fifty years later. A considerable number of other persons and families are represented in the Geniza by so many papers that we are forced to assume that they were originally part of carefully kept account books. In many cases, pages from court record books, referring to successive meetings during several years, such as 1027–29, 1097–99, or from notebooks of judges covering prolonged periods, have been preserved. But the remnants of these archives became part and parcel of the larger collection, haphazardly deposited and disturbed by subsequent rummagers who periodically turned the material upside down in their search for usable paper and old prayer books or, more recently, for documents to sell in the antiquities market.

TYPES OF DOCUMENTS

Alongside carefully worded and magnificently executed deeds, one finds hastily written notes, accounts, or letters jotted down in nearly illegible script and in sloppy or ungrammatical language. The very shortcomings of the Geniza, however, constitute its uniqueness. It is a true mirror of life, often cracked and blotchy, but very wide in scope and reflecting each and every aspect of the society that originated it. Practically everything for which writing was used has come down to us.

The largest and most valuable group of the Geniza documents is made up of court depositions—either statements made or agreements reached. They appear in three different forms: as drafts, as court records, or as documents handed over to the people involved. The declarations made by the parties or witnesses are often rendered verbatim, while the case itself is stated succinctly and clearly by the scribe. Almost every conceivable human relationship is represented in these records, and they often read like local news told by a gifted reporter. Of legal deeds proper, the marriage contracts, many hundreds of which have survived, are unusually interesting. They are by no means uniform; rather, they state in detail and with great variety the conditions regulating the future relations of the newly married and thus constitute a precious source for our knowledge of family life. Bills of divorce, of which a great number have also been preserved, are mere formularies; there is little in them beyond the names of the divorced and the signatories, or the dates and places, to interest social historians. On the other hand, the settlements reached between the divorced parties and the lists of the wife's restored possessions are often very instructive.

Wills and deathbed declarations consist almost exclusively of dispositions of property. The Geniza contains no ethical wills (in which the inheritor is enjoined to lead a moral life following the death of the testator), documents that are common in later centuries. Yet very often the last disposition of a person gives a clear idea not only of his possessions but also of his thinking on a wide variety of matters. The wills are veritable mines of information, and so are the inventories of the estates of both the rich and the poor; the many booklists (with or without prices) found in the Geniza are mostly enclosures to such inventories. Deeds of manumission of male and female slaves (only the latter are frequent) are mostly formulaic but not without interest; sometimes, the manumission is included in a deathbed disposition. Some of the most common transactional documents are releases—formulaic declarations by one or several persons renouncing all claims against another or others; many of the longest and best-preserved Geniza documents belong to this category. Another type of document, short in length but most important, is the letter of attorney. These too are mostly formulaic legal compositions. Still, because they normally indicate not only the persons and places involved but also the subject matter for which the power of attorney is given, these documents, of which many have been found, are often interesting. Deeds of sale or gifts of houses (more frequently parts of houses) and female slaves, as well as leases of apartments or of land, are common and always contain useful information. Litigation concerning the sale of goods generally produced no formal contracts in the case record; however, account books might be adduced as evidence, or witnesses might be summoned and deposed in making legal determinations.

The formation or dissolution of partnerships normally resulted in documents rich in detailed information. On the other hand, loans and promises of payment of debts are mostly disappointing because as a rule the reasons and other circumstances of the indebtedness are not stated. Very few contracts of employment have been preserved. The reasons for this are twofold. First, even a poor laborer preferred to enter into a partnership with a richer fellow craftsman than to become his employee. Second, when persons, especially younger ones, hired themselves out as servants or as laborers, normally no written contract was made.

Business letters constitute the largest and most important class of epistolary documents. They are our main source of information not only for commerce and industry but also for various other subjects, such as travel and seafaring. Normally a letter (especially one sent overseas) deals with many topics: receipt and dispatch of goods, lists of market prices, orders for new commodities, actions to be taken on behalf of or against third parties, as well as references to private or public affairs. Business was conducted on the basis of trust and friendship; thus business letters are rarely without a personal touch.

For this reason there is no clear-cut demarcation between commercial and private correspondence. Even in a letter of congratulations to the addressee at his wedding, or in a letter of condolence—again, especially when sent overseas—one finds paragraphs dealing with financial matters. Business letters usually contain shorter or longer references to the receiver's health, social status, family, and friends. There are also hundreds of letters of a purely personal character covering a great variety of topics. Although only a small fraction of the female population knew how to write (for this art was normally practiced only by people engaged in business, administration, or learning), many letters to and from women have survived. In many cases it is evident that letters from women were dictated; we hear the female voice guiding the male pen.

A large portion of the Geniza papers refers to public affairs. There are hundreds of letters addressed to various authorities containing reports, petitions, requests for help, demands for redress of injustice, applications for appointments, and a great variety of other matters. Fewer in number, but still preserved in considerable quantities, are letters emanating from authorities: instructions to communities or public officials, letters of appointment or of introduction or recommendation, correspondence about public charity, and, of course, exchanges between one authority and another. Mention must be made also of endless appeals for funds by the heads of the academies or other institutions of higher learning, or their letters of thanks and appreciation to the donors.

Of particular interest are the documents from communities large and small. We have statutes, public resolutions, and, in particular, many lists of those contributing to a great variety of good public causes, or of those receiving alms, clothes, or loaves of bread. These lists are priceless sources for the demography of the communities concerned. Another most valuable group of documents is composed of the financial reports of honorary treasurers, or of persons farming out the collection of rents, about the sums received from the houses and other property belonging to the community, the expenses on their upkeep and repair, and the emoluments of the officials and other persons on the payroll of the community. Commerce, banking, and industry are further illustrated by accounts, inventories of stores, workshops, and pawnshops, by bills of lading, promissory notes, and orders of payment. Short notes of many types—prescriptions, placards, horoscopes, charms, and amulets—and exercise books written for or by children grant us additional glimpses into daily life.

As it was customary to say a public prayer for a meritorious person—and who was not?—and to commemorate in it his forefathers and their descendants back to at least the sixth or seventh generation, many "memorial lists" have been found in the Geniza. Sometimes the prayer for the person thus honored is attached; most often the names are simply listed. Interpreting these lists often presents no small difficulty; most are scribbled hastily and more often than not presuppose a knowledge of details familiar to the members of the congregation but not to us. While sometimes cryptic or ambiguous, most are nonetheless instructive insofar as they contain detailed information on daily life.

At the present stage of research, it is impossible to state the exact number of Geniza documents in existence. An estimate—albeit highly preliminary—gives some idea of the volume of the material: If we exclude the many thousands of mere scraps of paper, we arrive at about ten thousand items of some length, of which around seven thousand are large enough to be regarded as documents of historical value; only about half of these are preserved more or less completely. (It should be emphasized that these numbers refer solely to items of a *documentary* nature.) The leaves with literary contents—fragments of *books* preserved in the Geniza—are far more numerous: A reasonable estimate would be two hundred and fifty thousand leaves, and this is exclusive of the so-called Second Firkovitch Collection in the State Public Library of St. Petersburg. Compare this figure with the fewer than one hundred thousand Arabic papyri and papers unearthed in Egypt.

The literary remnants assembled in the Geniza are by no means limited to religious texts or topics of specifically Jewish interest. They comprise practically all subjects on which medieval authors wrote, ranging from philosophy and medicine to folktales and the interpretation of dreams. Most but not all of the secular texts come from the orbit of the Islamic civilization. It is not always possible to distinguish "documents" from literary texts, and particularly so for the most common type of literature found in the Geniza: the so-called *responsa*, or "answers," of authoritative scholars on questions of religious and legal matters addressed to them. The Jewish responsa and their Muslim counterparts, the *fatwā*s, were collected in books, which in Judaism and Islam fulfill a function similar to the collections of cases and decisions of the high courts in English and American law. A considerable number of the responsa cover theoretical issues: usually one or more ancient texts are quoted by the questioner with the aim of obtaining an explanation of obscure or apparently contradictory passages. But an even greater number of responsa in the Geniza cover actual cases, and these of course are valuable source material for social history. On the other hand, what we usually find in the Geniza are not the original questions and answers, but fragments of books in which the answers of prominent scholars have been reproduced. Often the authors of these books, who were interested in principles of jurisprudence, omit all the details of a case, such as dates, names of persons and places, and other local color—in other words, those features that most interest the social historian. For this reason, and because so many medieval responsa of this sort have been published and their contents incorporated into other publications, only sparing use will be made of them in this book.

Another type of writing are the so-called *megilloth*, or scrolls, which describe fateful events or periods in the life of a person, family, or community. All the megilloth found in the Geniza are in Hebrew and were intended to be literary works; some are cast in rhymed prose. Nevertheless, the belletristic scrolls also contain much useful information that reflects contemporary society. The script of the Geniza documents, irrespective of the language used, is as a rule Hebrew; this is implied in the function of a geniza, as noted earlier. Many types of Hebrew script, varying according to the region, period, social standing and profession of the writer, are represented, and a careful study of their paleography is prerequisite to any attempt to decipher and interpret them. Considerable quantities of writings in characters other than Hebrew (Arabic in particular) are found among the Geniza documents. Often the reverse side of a document in Arabic script is used for a text in Hebrew characters; in other instances, both sides of a letter or another kind of document are exclusively in Arabic. One may assume that such pieces were kept originally in a family archive or a similar collection together with Hebrew writings, until the whole lot was discarded indiscriminately in the Geniza by a member of a later generation who paid no attention to the variegated material. Although written in Hebrew characters, Arabic is the language of most nonliterary documents; in other words, the Jews, who have left us the records of their daily life in the Geniza, mostly wrote as they spoke—in the various Arabic vernaculars that were then in vogue in Spain, Sicily, and most of the countries of North Africa and western Asia. The use of the Hebrew script for this purpose should not be surprising. The habit of writing in a script hallowed by one's own religion was by no means confined to Jews; Syriac Christians wrote Arabic in Syriac characters.

Nevertheless, many of the nonliterary Geniza papers were composed in Hebrew. European Jews did not have any other means of making themselves understood in the East, and scholarly persons frequently used Hebrew in letters, particularly in those that referred to communal and religious affairs. Arabic was used in most private and family letters— even those written by religious dignitaries—and in most official correspondence; it was used in all business letters as well. In epistles of a more formal character, such as applications, or letters of condolence and congratulations, it was customary to begin with a shorter or longer (and sometimes very long) Hebrew preamble, which consisted mostly of florid expressions and phrases designed for the occasion.

The question of language is more complicated with respect to legal documents. The language of the ancient Jewish courts was Aramaic, the international language of the Near East, from Egypt to Iran, for thirteen hundred years before it was replaced by Arabic. By the tenth century, Aramaic was no longer well known, and the Jewish courts began to change over to Hebrew, with which educated persons had always been familiar. Many deeds and court records from the first half of the eleventh century are composed in Hebrew, and their smooth and rich style proves that its use was widespread. Nevertheless, the need to record depositions made in spoken Arabic forced the scribes to slowly acquiesce in using that language. It is noteworthy that Hebrew lingered on in the smaller towns of Egypt longer than in the large centers. Perhaps the scribes in the smaller towns had not yet learned the relevant Arabic terms, nor the style for making out a proper legal document in that language. But by the end of the eleventh century and throughout the whole of the twelfth, Arabic was used in practically all transactions of the Jewish courts that have reached us. Around 1200, Hebrew words and phrases were inserted only sparingly; these were mainly religious and legal terms, but also proverbial expressions and sometimes certain turns of phrase that are characteristic of Hebrew. Still, the Arabic of the Geniza records may be considered a special language. It was written in a script other than that of classical Arabic by persons who had not absorbed the Qur'ān, the holy book of Islam, from childhood. This made for a language less governed by traditional Arabic grammar and vocabulary. The Geniza papers reflect the living language, and they constitute, in their great variety of styles and local idioms, a first-rate source for the history of the Arabic language. In addition, the Hebrew script often brings out features not detectable in the Arabic script; the pronunciation of many words, as it was in vogue in the eleventh or twelfth century, can be established through their Hebrew transliteration. Needless to say, these documents also contain many riddles for scholars encountering words that are philologically uncertain and linguistic usages unknown to classical Arabic grammar. Certain terms and expressions are known through their use in present-day Arabic dialects; the meaning of others can be ascertained from context.

It is not self-evident why we should have so much material from certain periods and regions and next to none from others. There is, first of all, the question of the Cairo Geniza itself. Since its discovery, it has been commonplace to say that of the many genizas presumed to have existed, that of Fustat survived thanks to the dry climate of Egypt. While it is true that climate contributed to the preservation of the Cairo-Fustat Geniza, it by no means adequately explains why only this single geniza survived. Fustat itself had not one, but three synagogues; a synagogue was built in nearby Cairo shortly after the founding of the city, and many others were constructed later. About seventy-five towns and villages in Egypt are known from the Geniza as places of Jewish settlement. Moreover, certain regions in southern Palestine and North Africa have a dry climate similar to that of Egypt. But nothing comparable to the Cairo Geniza has been found. In Fustat, the Geniza chamber was so large that it was able to hold its contents for a thousand years. A room with no doors or windows and with only one hole in the wall beneath a roof that could be reached only by ladder, the Geniza was constructed in such a way that it could not serve any other purpose than that for which it was intended: This may indicate that those who erected the Geniza and those who used it in its early period entertained strong opinions about the disposal of Hebrew writings; it was due to them that so much ancient material has been preserved.

Who were these people? By 1000, the Jews of Egypt were divided into two groups, the larger group being the so-called Rabbanites — those who followed the teachings of the rabbanim, or rabbis. The Karaites, who professed to rely on the Bible to the exclusion of rabbinic Judaism, constituted the smaller group. The Rabbanites were divided into two branches: Palestinians and Babylonians. Palestinian Rabbanites originated in Palestine and Syria; their service was conducted according to the liturgy accepted in Palestine, and their officials were appointed and communal leaders approved by the religious authorities who had their official seats in Jerusalem. Babylonian Rabbanites had the same relationship to Iraq (Babylonia) and the Jewish seats of learning in that country. All three groups possessed houses of worship in Fustat. The Geniza chamber was attached to the synagogue of the Palestinians. It is therefore necessary to devote special attention to them.

In 882, when the Coptic patriarch was forced to pay heavy contributions to Aḥmad b. Ṭūlūn, the ruler of Egypt, he sold a church that originally had been Melchite (that is, Greek Orthodox), together with some land, to the Jews, who converted it into a synagogue. It has been generally assumed that this was the Geniza synagogue. A careful weighing of the available evidence seems to show, however, that the Coptic church was acquired by the newcomers from Iraq who had no house of worship of their own, while the synagogue of the Palestinians was pre-Islamic, as reported by Muslim historians. Be that as it may, virtually no documents from the ninth century have come down to us in the Geniza, and only a few documents from the tenth; perhaps the idea of a permanent geniza had not yet been born. Around 1012, the Fatimid caliph al-Ḥākim ordered the destruction of the Christian and Jewish houses of worship, including the Church of the Holy Sepulchre in Jerusalem; we know with certainty that the synagogue of the Palestinians of Fustat was demolished and its bricks and timber sold. Had a geniza been attached to it at that time, it could not have survived.

A few years after that religious persecution, permission was given to repair the desecrated buildings. An inscription on the entrance to the synagogue of the Palestinians, mentioned by various medieval writers, enables us to fix the year 1025 as the date of its restoration. There is little doubt that the Geniza chamber was added during that restoration, for from 1002 on we have dated documents for almost every year—and a very sizable quantity by the 1120s. The process of discarding materials in the Geniza continued without interruption for about two hundred and fifty years until 1266; dated documents begin to become more rare from that point forward. The reason for this change in the thirteenth century still awaits explanation, for Fustat remained an area of Jewish settlement even after the majority of its Jews had moved to nearby Cairo.

Dated documents begin to appear again in greater quantity from the second quarter of the sixteenth century on; the paper is no longer locally made, but of European origin; the script is entirely different; it is Spanish-Jewish, and the language, as a rule, is Hebrew and no longer Arabic—in some cases, even Ladino, the Castilian dialect used by the Spanish Jews. In other words, the Jewish East had become completely dominated by the refugees from Spain. Forced to leave their country in 1492, they became prominent in the Ottoman Empire shortly thereafter, just as in modern times the Jewish East has become home to emigrants and refugees from eastern and middle Europe. These later texts reflect another story, one that is not told here. This book is solely concerned with what has justly been termed "the classical Geniza period," that is, documents that appear in a trickle during the second half of the tenth century and become a flood for the subsequent two and a half centuries. The Geniza is therefore a primary source for Islamic social and economic history during the Fatimid and Ayyubid periods, as well as for the history of the region during the Crusades.

Most of the Geniza material is from Egypt itself. At the time, Jews lived not only in the capital and the port cities of Alexandria, Rosetta, and Damietta, but were dispersed all over the Nile Delta, the Fayyūm oasis, and Upper Egypt. Letters and legal documents from many smaller settlements have found their way into the Geniza, which thus is illustrative of life in Egypt in general. Whether the population reflected in these writings was indigenous to the country—that is, whether it represented a continuation of the Jewish settlements in Egypt from Hellenistic and Roman times or originated mainly after the Muslim conquest—has not yet been ascertained.

Since the Geniza belonged to the synagogue of the Palestinians, it stands to reason that it would house many documents coming from or referring to the Holy Land, and this is indeed the case. There are also a considerable number of letters sent from the coastal towns of Lebanon and Syria, but written mostly by foreign merchants and not by local people. Astonishingly little material originates from Damascus and Aleppo, the two great cities of Syria. Considering the close commercial relations of these cities with Egypt and the fact that so many people named Dimashqī and Ḥalabī (Damascene and Aleppine) appear in the Geniza papers, one wonders whether these people were in the habit of disposing of their letters in genizas at all; perhaps many of those bearing those names were simply descendants of Syrian families long settled in Egypt. In any case, the absence of material from Damascus and Aleppo remains perplexing.

The most surprising feature of the Geniza, as far as geographical distribution is concerned, is the overwhelming preponderance of documentation concerning people from Tunisia and Sicily, especially from the time of the Geniza's inception around 1000 until the last quarter of the eleventh century. At least 80 percent, but most probably more, of all the business correspondence during this period concerns trade with these regions. Indeed, one gets the impression that the Geniza originally served the Maghrebi merchants who commuted from the western to the eastern part of the Mediterranean and partially settled there. By cross-referencing some four hundred letters and documents, it has become evident that, in many cases, persons bearing family names such as Andalusī, Fāsī, Tāhertī, or Iṭrabulusī, did not come from the Andalus/Spain, or Fez and Tāhert in Morocco, or Tripoli in Libya, but had their base in the Tunisian twin cities of Qayrawān and al-Mahdiyya. Likewise, most of the people writing during this period from the smaller places all over Egypt where flax and indigo (the staple export crops) were cultivated were Tunisian merchants.

Fortunately, there are documents that enable us to explain the close connection between the Maghrebi merchants and the Palestinian synagogue in Fustat. Shortly after the churches and synagogues in the Fatimid Empire had been destroyed during al-Ḥākim's reign (ca. 1012), he granted permission to rebuild them. We know from a number of Geniza papers, as well as from Christian sources, that the afflicted communities experienced great difficulties in raising the funds needed for reconstruction. In this time of hardship, the leaders of the Palestinian synagogue decided to admit the Maghrebis, mainly Tunisian and Sicilian merchants, to public offices, and showered them with honorific titles, confirmed in florid letters sent from the seat of the academy in Jerusalem. The stratagem was successful: the Maghrebis joined the Palestinian synagogue and soon became its most prominent members. The scope of the Geniza, including the large numbers of nonreligious writings was therefore determined by the link between the Fustat synagogue and the Maghrebis.

As impressive as is the abundance of the Geniza material for Tunisia and Sicily, there is a dearth of material concerning Spain. Apart from responsa and epistles sent from or addressed to prominent persons, only about three dozen letters (and even fewer documents) have thus far been identified as being written in Spain. But the products of Spain filled the markets of Egypt, and there was much direct traffic between the two countries. Moreover, many persons called Andalusī who actually hailed from the Iberian Peninsula are mentioned in the Geniza papers. How are we to understand this seeming incongruity? Given the ancient and lasting allegiance of Spanish Jewry to the Jewish seats of learning in Iraq, we may assume that the Spanish Jews sojourning in Egypt were connected with the Babylonian synagogue in Fustat and left their discarded writings in a geniza there—if they were wont to do so at all. That synagogue, which was still fully in use in the sixteenth century, has since entirely disappeared.

A similar assumption may explain also the almost complete absence of business correspondence with Iraq and Iran, especially since many persons from those lands settled in Egypt—including newcomers, who were likely to maintain contact with families and associates to the East. It would be rash to attribute the scarcity of documents from Iraq and Iran to the political situation. These eastern lands were ruled by the Seljuks, who paid homage to the Abbasid caliphs in Baghdad, whereas Egypt was ruled by the Fatimid counter-caliphs. We have in the Geniza an enormous amount of literary material in the form of private letters, responsa, and other writings from the Jewish academies of Iraq; indeed, this material constitutes a major portion of the Geniza records. These writings were sent from Baghdad to North Africa and Spain and even to Italy and France via Fustat and often were copied there before being forwarded. This explains why we find them in the Geniza. Conversely, monetary contributions were sent from Egypt to Baghdad, accompanied by letters and queries, which also were copied in Fustat before being forwarded. Thus, political barriers cannot account for the paucity of business documents from the Seljuk domain. The volume of trade between these lands and Egypt seems to have been limited, but it was by no means so small as to explain the virtual absence of business correspondence between West and East in the Cairo Geniza. We may then assume that the merchants from Iraq and Iran disposed of their correspondence in the geniza of their own synagogue, if they were in the habit of doing so at all.

There remains the question of dating individual items. Ideally, a document bears an indication of its place of origin or the date of its composition. In the event that these details have been effaced or torn away (or, in a draft or a copy, not filled in completely) we can still, if the document is long enough, gauge its approximate date and place of origin. The handwritings of the prominent scribes of the eleventh and twelfth centuries are known to us, and often the subject matter, names, geographical details, and accompanying circumstances enable us to fix the desired data with great precision. With private letters it is far more difficult. Very often the letter's destination and still more frequently the address of the writer have been omitted; since letters were sent by messenger or with friends, one could well forego these details. If dated at all, the day and the month are indicated, but only in exceptional cases the year. The name of the addressee usually is given in full, but the writer often designates himself solely with a general phrase, such as "your grate-ful friend," "your son," or "your brother"—phrases that in this context indicate a social, rather than a familial, relationship. Formal accounts are headed by a superscription, but very often we have only a second or third leaf, and many of the accounts found—if not indeed the major-ity—are notes made by the writer for his own use. Still, careful detective work and the cross-indexing of several thousand fragments yield both the location and date of four in five documents.[1]

What kind of picture can be obtained from the Geniza records? How accurately do they reflect the society that produced them? Unique and richly detailed as they are, the documents do not reflect equally all as-pects of economic and social life. We learn far less about agriculture and the technical aspects of arts and crafts than we might wish. But the working people themselves are comparatively well represented, and so are the more general aspects of industry. As one would expect, commerce and banking generated numerous legal documents and voluminous business correspondence; therefore, they are richly documented, as is the life of scholars and doctors. Because the Geniza was located in the same synagogue compound in which the courts held their sessions, we have abundant material about legal matters. The Geniza records also reveal how the actions of the Muslim state affected the life of the pop-ulation and how the various religious communities interacted. Above all, the Geniza records are reflective of family life. As regards the trans-actions of daily life—matters pertaining to food, clothing, houses, birth, upbringing, illness, retirement, death, burial, social etiquette, and cus-toms—our information is uneven; the documentation is very rich in some respects and limited in others. As a rule, people did not speak in their letters about mundane things. There is, however, one domain of daily life for which the Geniza provides an extremely rich picture: travel and seafaring. The reason for this is self-evident: when Geniza people were away from home, they wrote. Circumstances forced even experi-enced travelers (who were not in the habit of wasting words on their experiences) to reveal something of their situation. Above all, we are interested in the values and attitudes of the Geniza people—what they believed in and stood for. For that, the entire corpus of the Geniza must be examined—the vast number of literary creations as well as the formal documents. There is also a larger question: To what extent are the Jews of the Geniza representative of the larger Mediterranean society within

1. Card indexes assembled by Goitein contain names of over 35,000 individuals, 200 well-known families, and 450 professions.

which they dwelled? Put somewhat differently: Do our documents also reflect Muslim and/or Christian institutions and practices? And to the extent they do, to what extent can we use the Geniza records to reconstruct the broad world of the Mediterranean basin?

The Jewish communities described in the Geniza documents mingled freely with their neighbors. As the Arab proverb has it, "people are more akin to their contemporaries than they are to their own forefathers." The records make occasional mention of quarters predominantly inhabited by Jews, even of "the Jewish quarter." But these were not ghettos. In all urban localities, whether Fustat, in Qayrawān, Damascus, Jerusalem, or the smaller Egyptian provincial capitals, we find preserved deeds indicating that Jewish houses—even so-called Jewish quarters—abutted houses owned by Muslims or Christians, or both. Non-Jews would lease apartments and rooms belonging to the Jewish community in the heart of areas densely occupied by Jews. Detailed Muslim sources describing the topography of Baghdad rarely draw attention to what must have been a strong Jewish community, suggesting that the Jews were settled among a largely Muslim population and not in an entirely separate quarter of their own. Nor do there seem to have been any differences in the layout of physical space or in the nature of construction. Houses built by Muslims and Christians often were acquired by Jews. This explains also why special women's lodgings, *ḥaramiyya,* required by Muslim but not by Jewish social custom, are sometimes mentioned in documents referring to houses under Jewish ownership.

One might assume that the distinctive clothing prescribed for Jews by Muslim law would serve as a marker, separating them from the larger hegemonic community. But in the Fatimid empire, it seems, not even the canonical rules for the wearing of distinctive badges by non-Muslims were regularly observed. In this respect, the ordinances invoked by the Fatimid caliph al-Ḥākim were extraordinary and soon forgotten. In any case, there is no mention of this discriminatory legislation in the Geniza records for Cairo. Abundant evidence shows that Jewish men and women sported the most luxurious fabrics and colors, the likes of which would please and actually be offered to Muslim governors or sultans. Food was, of course, a distinctive marker given the nature of special Jewish dietary laws: Muslims sometimes chafed when Jews refused their food out of religious conviction, since Jewish foods were permissible for them. But, aside from that, the cuisine of Jews and non-Jews was similar, and Jews were rather prominent as both suppliers of produce and sellers of prepared foods.

Unlike later medieval Europe, where discriminative economic restrictions confined the Jews to a few unproductive occupations, the world reflected in the Geniza records finds them engaging in practically all arts and crafts and in agriculture. To be sure, commercially minded Jews were more prominent in some professions than in others—particularly in dyeing and trading textiles and in pharmaceutical products, as well as in metals and in many other commodities. The attachment of particular ethnic or religious groups to certain occupations has been common in the Middle East until recent times. It is, however, important to note that both the Geniza records and Muslim literary sources show us that non-Jews also engaged in all the ways of making a livelihood that were adopted by Jews. The methods of business, too, cannot have been peculiar to a particular religious group, for commerce was usually between faiths and, to a large extent, international. In certain cases, as with regard to the most important institution of partnership, we hear expressly that it was most often Muslim law that governed contracts, even when the contracts were made before a Jewish court. Partnerships between Muslims and Jews, both industrial and commercial, were hardly exceptional. Even the doctors of law, whose training followed denominational lines, worked closely together, for cases often went back and forth between Muslim and Jewish courts. Sometimes such professional contacts developed into personal friendships.

Jews did not serve in the army, but neither did the Muslims and Christians belonging to the sedentary local population. The Fatimid army consisted of Berbers, Turks, blacks from Egypt, the Sudan and sub-Saharan regions, as well as bedouin levies; the Ayyubids, who were themselves Kurds, maintained a predominantly Kurdish and Turkoman officers corps, with mercenaries drawn from many different ethnic groups. We nevertheless find Jewish physicians attached to the Egyptian army and navy. As with government service, the representation of the Jews was certainly higher than their percentage of the total population.

The entire administration and economy of the country was based on tax farming, an activity in which the Jews, although to a lesser degree than the Christians, were prominent. Entrepreneurs, even with little capital (and often in partnership), paid the government a fixed sum for the revenue expected from the taxes on agriculture, industry, or business, or from a customs house or toll station, and the surplus of the money actually collected represented their profit. This activity brought Christians and Jews into contact with all segments of the population in practically every corner of the country.

On the other hand, Jewish community life seems to have differed markedly from that of the Muslim majority. The generally small Jewish communities, which provided almost all of their own social services, were able to preserve more easily the ancient forms of intensive public life than the Muslims, who had little opportunity for self-government and no real concept of corporate institutions. The Geniza documents' portrait of the Jewish family is similar to that of family institutions found in many corners of the Mediterranean world: an extended family of strong cohesiveness; great reverence for the senior members; prominence in the house of the old woman who presides over a bevy of daughters, daughters-in-law, and grandchildren; tender care of brothers for sisters and vice versa; and, in general, a stronger emphasis on the ties of blood than on those created by marriage. We find that the Geniza society was practically monogamous, although ancient Jewish (like Muslim) law permitted polygyny.

There are, to be sure, related questions that are raised by this discussion of the place of the Geniza community within the larger society of which it was part. To what extent are Islamic civilization and, more particularly, Mediterranean society the sum of many different parts, each distinct from one another? To what extent was the psychology (for lack of a more precise term) of the Jewish community distinctive from that of the others? There is reason to suspect that the people of the Geniza were wont to create markers that set them apart from neighboring cultures and preserved their spiritual and, relatedly, their historical identity. That sense of being distinctive was shared by other Jewish communities until modern times.

Historical Survey of the Mediterranean during the High Middle Ages (1069–1250 C.E.)

There is no specific word for "Mediterranean" in the Geniza records. The ancient Arab expression "the Sea of the Romans" was a technical term used by the geographers of the time, rather than one referred to in daily exchanges. The Mediterranean was *"The* Sea," and as such it is mentioned countless times by the people of the Geniza.

The Mediterranean area was divided into three great regions:

1. "The East," namely Egypt and the Muslim countries of southwestern and western Asia. This term was not often used. Normally, the country or locality intended was specified, even in letters written by western people.

2. "The Muslim West," *al-Maghreb*, comprising all North Africa west of Egypt, including Muslim Sicily, with Andalus, or Spain, forming a subsection.

3. "The Land of the 'Romans,'" *al-Rūm*, originally designating Byzantium, but used vaguely for Christian Europe and its peoples in general well into the twelfth century. There is also the term *Ifranj*, "the Franks," for western Europe, which already appears in the oldest Geniza papers. When the Crusaders made their appearance, the term was applied to them, but only from the second part of the twelfth century were Rūm (Byzantium), and Ifranj (western Europe) distinguished clearly and regularly. From the beginning of the thirteenth century, France proper was designated as *Ifransa*, as opposed, for example, to then Christian Sicily, while *Ifranj* retained its general meaning of western European. Occasionally, especially in reports of the arrival of ships, the Muslim West and European West were lumped together, as in the following passage in a letter from Alexandria: "No one has arrived from the West: neither from Tripoli, nor from Sicily, nor from the Land of the Rūm." The terminology betrays the existence of a deep barrier between the Muslim East and the Muslim West and between both and Europe (including Byzantine Asia Minor). This parallels as well the geographical distinctions found in Muslim sources: When a person describes another as a *Rūmī* or a *Maghrebī* without specifying his city or province, he shows a lack of familiarity with (or interest in) the latter's permanent or original domicile. Besides its geographical remoteness—the desert begins immediately west of Alexandria—the Muslim West differed from the East by being at the time predominantly Berber and subject to a certain kind of religious zealousness. As regards the relations with the Rūm, the contrasts of religion and race were, of course, even stronger, and they were accentuated by the difference of the languages and scripts used by different peoples on the northern and southern shores of the Mediterranean. Yet Europeans are present everywhere in the Geniza records and in the most diverse ways. The impact of the European trade on the local market was overwhelming.

But our story is largely that of Jewish communities in the lands of Islam, communities whose political history changed markedly with the emergence of the Fatimid counter-caliphate in Egypt. The Fatimid conquest of Egypt, in July 969, marks the beginning of the classical Geniza period. The eclipse of their successors, the Ayyubids, in 1250, roughly coincides with its end. It was a time of profound and lasting changes in the Mediterranean basin. Naval superiority gradually shifted from the Muslim South to the Christian North. On the African coast, the center of gravity moved from Tunisia, which had been the nucleus of Fatimid power during the tenth century, eastward toward Egypt. Along the northern shore, the trend was westward: Byzantium, in its role as the protagonist of Christendom, was replaced by the Italian republics, the Normans, and, later on, by the kingdoms of France and Spain.

During all this period, neither the Mediterranean as a whole nor its western or eastern basin was ever dominated exclusively by a single state. As a rule, governments enjoyed only comparatively short periods of strength or were altogether weak. With the exception of Venice, not one maritime power survived with its prominence intact. In the eleventh century and the major part of the twelfth, a spirit of tolerance prevailed — in particular in the Fatimid Empire. The thirteenth century saw the victory of intolerance in the lands of Islam often accompanied and furthered by the rule of alien soldier castes. At the same time, clerical influence and obscurantism became oppressive on the European shores of the Mediterranean. Major changes were underway that would cause Europe and the lands of Islam to embark on different paths. The ancient unity of the Mediterranean world, which was characteristic of most of the period under discussion, eventually gave way to entirely new developments: a Christian Europe, which was beginning to explore cultural and technological avenues never conceived before by the human spirit, and a Muslim world drawing in upon itself and making only limited use of its own vast spiritual heritage.

In the formative period of Islam, as in Roman times, all North Africa was a colonial area with a provincial administration. Egypt had to provide Syria, which was the seat of the caliphal government, as well as northern Arabia, which harbored the holy cities of Islam, with wheat and other victuals, just as it had once done for Rome when the latter was the capital of the Mediterranean world. When the conquering Arabs pushed westward from Egypt through the whole of North Africa, they searched for slaves, gold, and other treasures. At the outset those vast stretches of land were for them nothing but a source for quick enrichment and exploitation. But, as so often happens in history, the colonial areas prospered economically and in due course acquired political strength. The once peripheral territories became centers of power.

Muslim North Africa owed the ascendancy it achieved during the Fatimid period not only to its natural resources and certain favorable trends in world trade but also to the vigorous principalities that sprang up in the region, polities that were founded and ruled by foreigners coming from the East: Arabs, Persians, and Turks. The Geniza records teach us that the new "bourgeoisie" of North African countries, too, had its roots in the ancient centers of commerce and industry of Syria, Iraq, and Iran. This great population movement from east to west was, in the main, complete by the end of the tenth century—the time when the Geniza records begin to appear in larger numbers. It should be noted that the Geniza materials contain numerous family names signifying eastern origins and indeed actual references to the migration westward.

The Fatimid conquest of Egypt was a movement in the opposite direction. The country of the Nile was conquered from the west—from Tunisia—by an army consisting mostly of Berbers of the Ketāma people. From that time on, Ketāmis were found all over Egypt, Palestine, and Syria as military commanders or as private citizens. They appear in these capacities in the Geniza papers. Our sources by no means convey the impression that their presence determined the mold of Fatimid society. The Ketāmi conquest did not convert the Fatimid Empire into a Berber state. For the Berbers, like the Kurds (another militant people who became prominent during this period), had little capacity or inclination to form lasting geographical polities. In any event, the Fatimid caliphs soon counterbalanced the Ketāmis by corps of Turkish mercenaries, black Sudanese contingents, and Arab bedouin levies. For posts requiring loyalty and leadership, they engaged persons from a great variety of ethnicities, including Europeans (mostly former slaves of Slavic provenance). They also availed themselves to a large extent of the services of local Christians and Jews. The very marginality of these peoples in the larger Muslim constellation was a guarantee of their loyalty and obedience.

One should also note that the Fatimids embraced Shi'ite Islam and claimed themselves to be descendants of the Prophet Muḥammad by way of his daughter Fatimah, hence their name. They held to Ismā'īlī views, a controversial doctrine that made them a minority among the Shi'ite as well as a minority within the larger world of Islam. And yet, they managed to create a great polity that rivaled the caliphate in Baghdad and was to last for centuries.

How far the tenets of the ruling sect were responsible for the character of the Fatimid state is a matter of conjecture. As noted earlier, the Fatimid period was one of relative tolerance compared with the period preceding and, in particular, the one following their rule. Because the Ismā'īlīs were organized as a secret society, we know only the literature that was more or less destined for public consumption and cannot be sure what the innermost circle believed. To be sure, the Geniza records cannot help us in this respect. The only express reference to the Ismāʿīlīs found thus far describes them as Jew-baiters, but the document in question refers to some local branch that might have represented an exception rather than the rule of that sect's conduct. It is reasonable to assume that the Fatimids and their Ismāʿīlī followers did not create the comparatively tolerant spirit of the period, but the fact that they themselves constituted only a small minority within the Muslim population of Egypt and Syria may have contributed to their tolerance in governing and to a general leniency toward other minority groups upon whom they came to rely.

In addition to the Ketāmi warriors and the Ismāʿīlī missionaries, the Fatimids were assisted in their rise to power by changes in the orientation of international trade and trade routes. During the tenth century, Fatimid Tunisia and its dependencies (Sicily and parts of Algeria and Libya) enjoyed an unprecedented efflorescence. They served as distributors of Indian and other Oriental products, as well as products from Egypt and Syria, for the flourishing Muslim West and for the economically ascending Christian Europe. It was this economic predominance that enabled Tunisia to conquer almost the whole of North Africa to the Atlantic Ocean, and, later on, even Egypt with its adjacent countries.

The eleventh century, however, witnessed a complete reorientation of the Mediterranean trade routes. The relocation of the seat of the Fatimid government from Tunisia to Egypt was in itself a vital change. The army, the court, and the administration were the largest consumers of imported items and, naturally, contributed much to the shifting of the center of trade from Qayrawān and al-Mahdiyya to Cairo and Alexandria. Even more important, it seems, were various international developments. The merchant cities on the west coast of Italy, in particular Genoa and Pisa, emerged as strong sea powers during this century. As the role of entrepôt enjoyed by Tunisia slowly diminished, Europe traded directly with the Levant, obtaining goods coming from India and the Far East. Moreover, ever larger ships were built toward the end of the century, vessels that were able to sail from Spain or France to Egypt or the Syro-Palestinian coast without calling on way stations.

The economic eclipse of Tunisia was aggravated by political and military disasters. In the 1040s, Tunisia renounced its precarious allegiance to the Fatimids, but had to pay an enormous price for this break. First harassed by Libyan pirates, who intercepted its trade with the East, Tunisia was then devastated in the 1150s, when a Fatimid vizier unleashed against it the bedouins of the Banū Hilāl and Banū Sulaym. Egypt took the place of once prosperous Tunisia in the international trade, and, as such, attracted the more enterprising elements from that land.

The Geniza records of the time illustrate poignantly the spectacle of this migration of Maghrebīs, or westerners, to Egypt. At first, the merchants commute between the two regions; then they set up residence in Egypt, leaving their families in Tunisia; finally they settle in the new land permanently. This process, occasioned initially by changes in international trade, first becomes apparent early in the eleventh century, long before Tunisia succumbed to the devastations of the Hilāl and the Sulaym. The migration eastward was also stimulated by new disasters at the hands of the Normans and later the Almohads. These reverses completed what the changes in the trends of world change had begun: The lively traffic between the mainland of Europe and the Levant, which became even more accentuated in Crusader times, meant for Tunisia (and later on also for Sicily) what the discovery of the direct sea route to India did for Egypt four hundred years later. In sum, Tunisia had become economically redundant.

Conquering the central lands of the Arab world was an astounding feat. That the Fatimids were able to hold them for two hundred years is puzzling. For with the exception of the first two caliphs ruling in Cairo, Muʿizz (d. 975) and ʿAzīz (d. 996), they produced no rulers of distinction, and out of a total of eleven caliphs, three were immature lads and four mere children at the time of their accession to the throne. Despite attempts to "Egyptianize" their regime through symbolic gestures expressed in elaborate formal ceremonies, the Fatimids remained foreigners in the one Muslim land that had a proud sense of a history tracing back to the most ancient times. The Fatimids ruled by playing one corps of mercenaries against the other with the result that internecine conflicts between the various factions were rampant. The history of the court itself was marked by intrigues, executions, and treacherous assassinations. From the second quarter of the eleventh century, leading functionaries were frequently replaced, or usurped absolute rule for themselves. And yet, Egypt was a rich and flourishing country. In any case, it is described as such by contemporary travelers, whose impressions are confirmed, or at least not contradicted, by the Geniza records.

What explains the seeming discrepancy between the economic and political state of the Fatimid domain? For one, the regime hardly interfered with trade, a major source of prosperity; indeed, it stimulated trade through reasonable customs tariffs. These policies allowed merchants to take advantage of an economically rising Europe, with Egypt and Syria serving as distribution centers and largely also as suppliers. In this respect, the Fatimids are to be contrasted with their rivals, the Abbasids of Baghdad, whose rapacious economic policies, brought on by the need to placate their praetorian troops, destroyed the favorable economic climate created by the early rulers of the house.

Although no power was strong enough to dislodge the Fatimids from their territories, there was, from the outset of their rule, continuous fighting along the borders of their empire, especially in Palestine and Syria. For the first hundred years, the Fatimids tried in vain to pacify this region and hold back local insurgencies of a political and religious nature. Among other problems were the bedouin chieftains, a scourge for the sedentary population in turbulent times.

In the third quarter of the eleventh century, the Seljuk Turks made their appearance. Central Asian Turks had been a dominant factor in the history of the Arabic-speaking lands since the ninth century, when they were conscripted in large numbers to serve in elite slave units of the Abbasid state. Many of the best Fatimid generals had been Turks, mostly imported as individual slaves and often remaining slaves even after having been appointed to positions of command. The novelty of the Seljuk invasion was that an entire Turkish people had conquered most of western Asia. In 1055 Baghdad was taken, and when the Seljuks attacked Syria and Palestine, there was no Fatimid army available to defend these countries, for, as usual, order had to be restored in faction-torn Egypt itself. In 1071, Jerusalem was conquered by the Seljuks; five years later, after several assaults, Damascus fell, never to be regained by the Fatimids.

The turbulence of Syria and Palestine during the century preceding the Crusades allows us to appreciate why the local population viewed the newcomers from Europe in a way far different from what we might expect. Having been accustomed to incessant warfare and tribulations by ever new invaders, the average person was unable to recognize the particular character of the Crusader movement. The local populace was not to be blamed for this; the most competent Muslim ruler of that time, al-Malik al-Afḍal, made the same error. He welcomed the Crusaders as his natural allies against the Seljuks and hurried to lay siege on Jerusalem at the time when "the Franks" (as the Crusaders were called in the East) were consolidating their position in northern Syria. Having conquered the city in September 1098, he failed to provide it with an adequate garrison; it fell easy prey to the Crusaders in July 1099. The Crusaders then followed up their victory with an attack on the main Fatimid army, which was ignominiously routed. A quarter of a century of war with changing fortunes ensued. By 1124, the whole of the Syro-Palestinian coast, with the sole exception of Ascalon in southern Palestine, was in the hands of the Crusaders. Finally, in 1153, this last stronghold fell to the Franks, and the way was open for them to attack Egypt itself.

Meanwhile, a new power had emerged in western Asia. Out of the debris of the disintegrated Seljuk state new kingdoms arose, one of which was to play a major role in Mediterranean history: that of Nūr al-Dīn Zengī, the grandson of a Turkish mamlūk (slave-soldier) and originally ruler of Aleppo and Mosul. Taking Damascus in April 1154, he obtained control of all Syria with the exception of the Crusader states. Nūr al-Dīn was the first of the new type of Turkish rulers who made great impact on the history of the Middle East. In addition to being a fearless soldier and great commander, he was a staunch supporter of Muslim orthodoxy and learning.

The conquest of Ascalon by the Crusaders in 1153 and the annexation of Damascus by Nūr al-Dīn in 1154 eliminated the strife-torn Fatimids as a political presence. Both the Turks and the Crusaders now had designs on Egypt and its resources. In general, the Fatimid counselors were inclined to prefer the Franks, assuming correctly that these would be content with some kind of suzerainty, while Nūr al-Dīn's Turks would try to abolish the Fatimid caliphate altogether and occupy the country as its rulers. But they came to accept the Turks when the Crusaders blundered and committed atrocities against the local population.

The commander of Nūr al-Dīn's forces in Egypt, the famous Saladin, deposed the Fatimid caliph and, following Nūr al-Dīn's death, took over both Egypt and Syria. With Egypt, Syria, and northern Mesopotamia in his hands, Saladin turned against the Crusaders and dealt them a crushing defeat. Jerusalem was recovered on October 2, 1187, and, with the exception of Tyre, the entire Syro-Palestinian coast was seized as well. But that did not end the story of the Crusades. It was characteristic of the situation in the Mediterranean at that time that the possession of a single fortified seaport enabled the Christians to resume the Crusades and to again become a power to be reckoned with in the Levant. Under Saladin himself, Muslim sea power went into marked decline. He had started out by making extensive use of naval operations, both in the Red Sea and, in particular, in the Mediterranean. As late as 1180, he had been able to force King Baldwin of Jerusalem to make peace by harassing the Syro-Palestinian coast with his Egyptian navy. But in 1191, he found himself forced to order the destruction of Ascalon, the flourishing seaport of southern Palestine, because he saw no other way of protecting this vital point from attack by European fleets.

Under his successors, Egypt itself was invaded from the sea. In 1219, when Damietta, the great seaport at the mouth of the eastern branch of the Nile, was about to fall, the Muslims offered to surrender the kingdom of Jerusalem on condition that the Crusaders depart from the Egyptian coast. The fact that this ostensibly attractive offer was turned down is taken by some scholars as an indication that a new period of history had begun, when the lust for colonial expansion replaced the zeal for Holy War. This view can hardly be maintained: The papal legate, who was the official commander of the expedition, was the most adamant among those refusing the Muslim offer, and thirty years later, Louis IX of France, the most Christian of all Christian kings, also directed his Crusade against the Egyptian coast. While religious and worldly motives were indeed intermingled from the very beginning of the Crusader movement, in the course of time the leaders from western Europe became more familiar with the strategy of warfare in the eastern Mediterranean and tried to create a broader base from which to protect the kingdom of Jerusalem.

When, in 1250, the Mamluks emerged as rulers of Egypt and Syria, the situation changed markedly. The state was more repressive and the military caste that ruled it was more self-indulgent. The Mamluks failed to grasp the significance of long-distance trade and turned their backs on the eastern Mediterranean. Following Saladin's example, they dismantled and in many cases destroyed the seaports and laid waste much of the coastal region in order to discourage attacks by European navies.

Another great sea power of the eastern Mediterranean that declined quickly during this period was Byzantium. The second part of the tenth century, which saw the conquests of the Fatimids, was also the heyday of Byzantine ascendancy. The island of Crete was taken in 961, Cyprus in 965, and Antioch with its port city of Suwaydiyya in 969, the same year in which the Fatimids conquered Egypt. The maritime bastions dominating the eastern Mediterranean, as well as the borderlands between Asia Minor and Syria, were again in the hands of the Rūm, "the Romans," as the Byzantines designated themselves and were called by the Muslims (although their language was Greek, and they were identified as Greeks by the Christians of western Europe). It was inevitable that the two great eastern powers, Byzantium and the Fatimids, should clash. But these clashes never developed into wars of long duration, for the smaller principalities acted as a buffer between the two. There also seems to have been — at least on the Fatimid side — an element of deliberate policy. When the wise vizier Ibn Killis lay in his deathbed, he was asked by his caliph for political advice. He counseled the caliph to exterminate the unruly bedouin chiefs but to keep peace with the Byzantines, as long as they also consented to do so. In general, the Fatimids followed this advice, and ten-year armistice treaties—a longer commitment is not allowed under Muslim law—were concluded and renewed. Clearly, the two wealthy empires were elements of stability in the area.

There were also other circumstances that prevented Byzantium and the Fatimids from engaging in all-out combat. During most of the eleventh century, neither had competent rulers sufficiently able to organize far-flung military operations; in the second part of the century, both were menaced by a common foe—the Seljuk Turks. In 1071, the same year that the Seljuks captured Jerusalem from the Fatimids, their main army vanquished and captured the Byzantine emperor at Mantzikert. Asia Minor, the heartland of Byzantium, lay open to Turkish invasion. That dramatic event inaugurated a long process of penetration by Turkic peoples making their way to Asia Minor. The erosion of Byzantine power was, however, gradual. Shortly after the defeat of 1071, Byzantium recovered and gained strength. It is indicative of the prosperity and the prestige enjoyed by the Byzantine Empire during the first half of the twelfth century that Jews emigrated there in considerable numbers from the Fatimid lands. The Byzantines were later to lose that prestige when they succumbed to attacks from the West.

In the West, the dominating feature was the rise of the Italian maritime cities on the one hand, and the Norman kingdom of the "two Sicilies" (Sicily and southern Italy) on the other. The rule over this kingdom by the German emperor Frederick II Hohenstaufen (1194–1250), who was himself a native of southern Italy, in many respects marked the end of the High Middle Ages. Even the syncretistic character of Frederick's Sicilian kingdom, in which Byzantine, western European, and Muslim Arabic elements mingled freely, is characteristic of the preceding, rather than the following, period. Conversely, the reign of Louis IX of France (1226–70), Frederick's younger contemporary, although himself an embodiment of medieval ideals, ushered in a new epoch: that of "national" states, which formed the framework for the development of national cultures in Europe.

During most of the eleventh century, the Italian city-states, with the exception of Venice, Lucca, Salerno, and Amalfi, were still outside the horizon of the Geniza records. The Geniza reflects a world where all seafaring was done on ships whose proprietors, whether Muslims, Christians, or Jews, bore Arabic or Arabicized names. In the twelfth century, however, it was common for the people represented in the Geniza records to travel on Genoese, Pisan, or Gaetan ships, as well as vessels of other western powers. (Venetian ships are also mentioned, but apparently were not used by Jews to the same extent.) The struggle for Sicily and southern Italy, in which Byzantines, Muslims, local Italians, and Normans took part, as well as the successful attacks of the latter two on various points of the North African coast, is copiously reflected in the Geniza records. Despite the close connections between the Jews of southern France (Narbonne, Lunel, Montpellier, Arles, Marseilles) and those of the Muslim East, no references to political or other events in that area have been found in the Geniza—that is, if we disregard accounts about hardships endured by Jewish individuals or communities. Only Marseilles is mentioned as a port from which one sailed directly to Egypt.

Of all the countries of the Mediterranean, Spain witnessed the most drastic changes during this period. Near the end of the tenth century, the situation around the sea appeared to be one of great stability: Byzantium dominated the northeast; the Fatimid Empire stretched from Syria to the borders of Morocco; and Umayyad Spain was ruled by the powerful viceroy al-Manṣūr, whose military campaigns had made the Umayyad regime dominant over the Christian principalities of northern Spain and the towns and tribes of most of Morocco. We have already seen how quickly Byzantine and Fatimid power declined. The Umayyad caliphate disappeared altogether within one generation after the death of al-Manṣūr in August 1002. The Christian reconquest of Spain became a menace to Muslim hegemony in the region. Twice, mighty Berber kingdoms of North Africa, the Almoravids (Ar. al-Murābiṭ, "border warrior") and the Almohads (Ar. al-Muwaḥḥid, "a true believer in one God"), intervened and checked the Christian advance; both occupied and protected Muslim Spain. In both cases, however, the Berbers lost their vigor after comparatively short periods of glorious achievements. With the fall of Seville, then the capital of Muslim Spain, in November 1248, the whole Iberian Peninsula again became a Christian domain; even the small Muslim kingdom of Granada in the southeastern corner of the country, which miraculously survived for another two and a half centuries, was under the suzerainty of the Christian kings of Castile, while the various attempts of the sultans of Morocco to renew the attack on Spain proved abortive. The Strait of Gibraltar, the most frequented bridge between Africa and Europe for six hundred years, formed a barrier between the two continents by the end of the thirteenth century.

The history of North Africa itself was characterized during this period by great population movements. The first was the invasion of the Arab tribes of the Hilāl and Sulaym, which ended Tunisia's prosperity. The

invaders finally penetrated into most parts of North Africa and contributed much to its general decline, but also to its progressive Arabization.
At roughly the same time, another movement came into being, namely,
that of the Ṣanhāja (from which modern "Senegal" is derived). Essentially a Muslim religious movement, spawned by missionary border warfare, its adherents, the Almoravids (1061–1147), soon flooded the whole
of Morocco and western Algeria and conquered even Muslim Spain,
fighting Christians and Muslims alike. They were superseded by another,
even more powerful Berber kingdom, the Almohads (1130–1269; ousted
from Spain ca. 1229). Their nucleus was a religious sect of extreme pu-
ritanical outlook and behavior which regarded all Muslims who did not
adhere to their views, including the caliphs of Baghdad, as unbelievers.
This religious movement, which sought the forceful conversion of
Christians and Jews, led to great population shifts: In a land that had
produced St. Augustine, no local Christians were left. On the other
hand, the Jews of North Africa were too numerous to disappear. The
Almohads conquered Morocco, Algeria, Muslim Spain, and also Tunisia
and Tripoli (Libya), from which the Normans were finally driven out.
At the beginning, the movement had a distinct ethnic character, using
the Berber language even for the literary expression of religious ideas.
But Berber gave way to classical Arabic. Consequently, even this greatest
of all the Berber kingdoms did not succeed in making North Africa a
Berber entity. The terrible sufferings endured by the civil population in
the wake of these cataclysms are reflected in the Geniza records. The
upheavals encouraged and then brought to a climax the migration of
enterprising people from the Muslim West to the East.

The Local Environment

The people speaking to us through our documents represent an intrinsically urban population. Their world comprised urban
sites from Samarkand in Central Asia and the port cities of India and
Indonesia to the east, to Seville in Spain and Sijilmāsa in Morocco to
the west; from Aden in the south, to Constantinople, the capital of
Byzantium, in the north. The maritime cities of the northern shores of
the Mediterranean, such as Narbonne, Marseilles, Genoa, Pisa, and Venice, are also mentioned in the Geniza records and were indeed visited at
the end of the twelfth century by Jewish traders, whose letters home are
preserved in the Geniza. There are even sporadic references to faraway

European places, such as Rouen, the capital of Normandy in northern France, and Kiev, situated in the present-day Ukraine. It is, however, the Islamic city of the Middle Ages that is most clearly reflected in our documents. The main information about urban life is derived from Egypt, the linchpin of trade along the southern Mediterranean, and, in particular, from its ancient capital Fustat, where the Geniza papers were discovered.

The Islamic city differed from both Graeco-Roman and medieval European cities by its seeming lack of municipal organization; it lacked a mechanism for local rule peculiar to its local environment and sanctioned by law. Historians have felt obliged to explain this difference and, relatedly, to point out how Muslim urban society managed to cohere while lacking the benefit of legally sanctioned local institutions. Some scholars have argued that Islam itself prevented the emergence of self-governing cities and towns. Others maintain that already in Late Antiquity the city-states of the Near East were subjected to imperial rule that ended their autonomy or, alternatively, that the city-states had become imperial centers too large to function with the "primitive democratic institutions" developed in classical times. Such views do not account, however, for the breakdown of imperial rule that so afflicted the great Muslim polities of the Middle Ages but still did not allow for the development of autonomous cities and towns. It would seem that a more profound explanation is necessary as to why the urban world of medieval Islam was not self-regulating according to established local laws and formal institutions. In any case, the story of urban life in the Islamic lands of the Near East and North Africa ought to begin with the testimony of those peoples who inhabited its cities and towns.

Medieval townsmen, Muslims and non-Muslims alike, saw cities as central to the shaping of their society and culture. Elaborate planning, monumental architecture, and a highly variegated social and cultural heritage all reflected the complexity of urban life. Urban dwellers included great dynasts and local pretenders, merchants and artisans, scholars and sainted individuals, and not least, the flotsam and jetsam of humanity that settled in cities and towns after having drifted in from the surrounding countryside and areas further removed. Regardless of their station in life, residents of Islamic cities generally identified with their native or newly established places of habitation—if not the larger metropolitan area, then certainly its individual quarters. Inhabitants drew attention to the virtues of their native place, be it noteworthy topographical features, salubrious climate, the religiosity of sainted individuals, or the praiseworthy learning of scholars. For urban dwellers, there was the belief that Muslims could live the fullest religious life only in cities and towns. The Jews, most of whom had lived off the land since ancient times, had become a largely urban population in the period of the Geniza. A few reportedly possessed vineyards, orchards, fields, and livestock, but they employed local agents rather than look after them in person.

Despite endorsements of local patriotism, Islamic cities, like the larger regional entities, did not and could not claim formal recognition as autonomous units of the still larger *umma,* or community of Islam. The theoretical Muslim ideal of a polity, united in faith and transcending ethnic, tribal, regional, linguistic, and all local interests, was so deeply and widely rooted in Muslim political culture it did not allow cities and areas contiguous to them to become legitimate self-governing entities. Only the central authority, namely the caliph, or "commander of the faithful," and his chosen representatives could legitimately command the allegiance of the umma and its constituent parts. No charters defined urban settlements as in the Christian West. No city-states emerged as they had in the ancient Near East and along the eastern rim of the Mediterranean. There were no urban republics as in northern Italy. No formal associations of craftsmen or mercantile types regulated the urban economy of Muslim cities. That is to say, there were no corporate institutions — or, in any case, none that resembled those corporate institutions known to us from the Christian West and the more ancient Near East.

The geographer Xavier de Planhol could thus write that the urban ideal of Islam created no urban forms or urban structure and that it replaced the solidarity of a collective community (as in classical antiquity) with an anomalous disorganized heap of disparate quarters and elements. By a truly remarkable paradox, de Planhol argues, Islam, endowed with the ideal of urban life (for the fullest Muslim life could be experienced only in cities and towns), produced the very negation of urban order.[2] This critical observation speaks most directly to the chaotic origins of Muslim settlement — garrison towns, populated initially by tribal warriors from the Arabian Peninsula. It does not follow, however, that lacking formal institutions, Islamic cities remained amorphous and passive communities throughout the Middle Ages.

Regional authorities could and did take license to exercise control over their own affairs. They wrung unofficial concessions from the im-

---

2. "Geographical Setting," in *The Cambridge History of Islam*, 2 vols., ed. Peter M. Holt, Ann K. S. Lambton, and Bernard Lewis (Cambridge, 1970), 2:456–68.

perial core at such times when the caliphs were unable to exert effective power much beyond their capital—if that far. In such fashion, local rulers carved out a niche for themselves in return for lip service to the moral authority of the caliphate and the theoretical ideal from which that authority derived. Similarly, the inhabitants of medieval Near Eastern cities did not need to be granted their own corporate institutions to create an orderly civic life. Market activity was carefully organized. Despite the absence of guilds, artisanal production and standards were enforced. Nor did the lack of a city charter prevent the regulation of urban space and surfaces. Even during the heyday of the caliphate, the central authorities were forced to recognize, however unofficially, the powerful hold that ethnicity, tribalism, and the local economy had on particular elements of a theoretically homogeneous Muslim community and the resident minorities.

In times of relative peace, the imperial authority and its representatives—the local governors and various officials that the caliph personally appointed—could be relatively unintrusive (if not cooperative) in city matters, particularly as regards the economy. Indeed, one might argue that the good sense of the central authorities in preserving order and in stimulating economic growth helped preempt any serious demands for local autonomy, the ideal of the Islamic umma notwithstanding.

Be that as it may, when threatened by external factors or centrifugal forces leading to internal breakdown, the central authorities, power permitting, could quickly reverse course. Withdrawing their much-needed patronage, stiffening hitherto more relaxed attitudes to economic transactions, and turning from progressive to oppressive policies, a harried government could act to the detriment of the merchants and other notables so dependent on the authorities for any semblance of order that they were incapable of mounting a lasting challenge on their own behalf.

Less sympathetic and no doubt less reflective of the delicate balance between local and central authority, particularly in disruptive circumstances, were the various urban mobs. The periodic emergence of loosely organized thugs drawn from the *lumpenproletariat* that had drifted into cities in more vibrant times only worsened local conditions that had turned difficult and created still greater need for imposed regulation. When central authority declined and was unable to intervene effectively, individual quarters often organized to look after their own interests, but this tendency to divide the larger body politic also ran afoul of the ideal Muslim community. Ironically, when the cement that held society together seemed to crack, the idealized concept of the umma, with its call for obliterating disruptive local identities, became a cure-all much sought-after by the Muslim majority. Invoking the idealized community of the Prophet was, however, at best a palliative; at worst, it served to distract the faithful from the structural weakness that beset the Islamic state and its regional and urban dependencies: the absence of a legitimate authority rooted in local society and culture. Whether one speaks of times of vibrant civic life, or of periods of urban decline and disorder, the Islamic city itself did not generate formal—that is, juridically sanctioned—authority. As a result, city dwellers could not summon the wherewithal to resolve deep problems in their own immediate environment. In the Islamic polity that evolved, no local or regional societies or subgroups of Muslim society were granted the privilege of self-rule, self-regulation, or even self-definition. The non-Muslim minorities had their established space and were thus able to rule and regulate themselves, but they too had to answer to the central authorities in matters that extended beyond their immediate concerns. What conclusions ought to be drawn from this assessment of Islamic cities?

The Islamic city was a place where one lived, not a corporation to which one belonged. There were town dwellers but no "citizens" in the legal sense of the word, for there did not exist a municipality that made laws and developed its own jurisdiction. Despite their organizational weakness, however, the Islamic cities constituted effective social mechanisms. As seats of the government or of its representatives they guaranteed relative security; as local markets or international emporiums they provided economic opportunities; and with their mosques and institutions of higher learning, their churches, synagogues, and schools, their bathhouses and other amenities, they contained all one needed for leading a religious and cultured life. It is true that cities as such did not make laws; yet they were highly tangible factors in everyone's life. It was in this environment that the Geniza people—those inveterate city dwellers—were found.

The capital of a large province or district was often identified in terms of the region it dominated. Throughout the Geniza papers, Fustat is called *Miṣr* (Egypt). Only in legal documents is *Fusṭāṭ Miṣr* (Fustat of Egypt) used to differentiate it from Cairo, the newly founded sister city that lay adjacent to it. Damascus is referred to as *al-Shām* (Land of the North, Syria), but also by its old name *Dimashq,* certainly because Syria contained other ancient cities conquered and immediately occupied by the Arabs after the conquest. In *Diyār Ḥalab wa-Diyār Anṭākiyā* (the greater areas of Aleppo and Antioch, both in northern Syria) the district is defined by its capital city. Palermo, the capital of Sicily, is usually called *Ṣiqīllya* (Sicily) occasionally *Madīnat Ṣiqīllya* (the City of Sicily); sometimes it is simply shortened to *al-Madīna* (the City), whereas *Balarm*, the Arabic equivalent of Palermo, is rarely referred to.

In Roman times, provincial capitals such as Caesarea, Alexandria, and Carthage (respectively, the capitals of Palestine, Egypt, and Africa), were situated on the seashore, where they could be easily reached from Rome, the center of the world. Under Islam, the cities chosen or founded as capitals—Fustat, Ramle of Palestine, Damascus, and Qayrawān of Tunisia—were situated inland, where they were safe from surprise attacks by the Byzantine and other Christian navies. A country's main ports, such as Alexandria, Tyre on the Lebanese coast, or al-Mahdiyya in Tunisia, were regarded as frontier fortresses. Alexandria is often referred to in the Geniza letters as *al-thaghr*, "the frontier fortress," and not by its name.

It would be wrong to assume that Alexandria's position as a port city made it the pivot of commerce, or that Fustat, originally the capital of the country, derived its riches solely from its function as the seat of administration. The unmistakable testimony of hundreds of Geniza letters proves that Fustat, the Arab inland city, was also the commercial and financial center of the country, on which Alexandria, the original Greek maritime town, was economically dependent in every respect. Fustat was the emporium of the region, where all the goods were hoarded. For consignments destined to be sent overseas, customs had to be paid first and foremost in Fustat, and no goods could pass through its gate for sale in Alexandria without being accompanied by receipts for the dues issued in the capital. Even commodities from Mediterranean countries, imported by way of Alexandria, had to be obtained from Fustat when they became scarce in the port city. Foreign currency from places with which Alexandria entertained a lively commerce was regularly acquired by Alexandrians in Fustat. Everyday commodities, such as shoes and clothing, implements for silversmithing, or parchment and even ink were ordered for Alexandria in the capital, "for here," as several letters from Alexandria emphasize, "nothing is to be had." To be sure, Alexandria, like other places, had its local artisanal products, such as its world-renowned mats, its *maqta'* textiles, exported as far as India, and its pens, cut from the reeds of Lake Maryūṭ. It seems that it also served as the international entrepôt and bourse of the silk trade. Nevertheless, Fustat was the economic center of Egypt and duly recognized as such.

The situation was similar in Ifrīqiya (present-day Tunisia) and Palestine. Goods were sent to Qayrawān via its port, al-Mahdiyya, but as a rule, the consignments were not opened there; customs were paid in the capital. The great merchants lived in Qayrawān; their agents stayed in al-Mahdiyya. Wheat was cheapest in the capital, where it was stored, and so in times of scarcity one turned there. Naturally, at the arrival of ship convoys, fairs were held in the port city, but one relied on the bazaar of Qayrawān for the winter season, when the sea was closed and the overland traffic from Morocco to Egypt passed through the city. In Palestine, commerce, the dispensation of justice, and communal life were concentrated in Ramle, the administrative inland capital. Its nearest ports, Jaffa and Caesarea, are rarely mentioned in the Geniza papers. The eastern shores of the Mediterranean, however, had an ancient tradition of kingly maritime cities. The Geniza records clearly show that Tyre—then, as in antiquity, the mightiest town on the coast—although it served as seaport to Damascus, was not dependent on the Syrian capital.

Alexandria and Fustat differed also in the composition and character of their populations. Both cities were filled with foreigners. But those who had reached the capital intended to remain there permanently, whereas those staying behind in Alexandria either had not yet made up their minds or were resolved to return home *ba'd qaḍā al-ḥawā'ij*—after having attained their (economic) goals. This may explain why we find fierce clashes between the foreigners and the local people in Alexandria but not in Fustat. Moreover, at least as far as the Jewish community is concerned, the lowest elements of Alexandria seem to have been stronger and more vociferous than those in the capital. They were an unruly crowd, always dissatisfied with their Jewish leadership and making trouble that led to the intervention of the Muslim authorities. We see these authorities, with few exceptions (and in contrast with those in Fustat), experiencing difficulties: the mob of the port city was a ceaseless nuisance and a menace to order.

The presence of numerous visitors from Christian countries, with different social customs, was not without influence. Drinking bouts accompanied by music, anathema to both Islam and traditional Judaism, are reported from Alexandria. Rūmī (that is, Italian or Greek) wine was preferred in that city to the local product. In view of the differences in the lifestyles of the two cities, Alexandrians might not always have felt comfortable in the capital. When a woman in Alexandria learned that her brother, a widower living in Qalyūb, a small town north of Cairo, was about to marry a girl from there (and not as she had feared, from Fustat) "she was happy that you did not become involved with the people from Miṣr." Conversely, a divorced woman from Fustat, who became engaged to a divorced man from Alexandria, stipulated that the couple would live in the capital and that she was prepared to accompany him on his visits to his family in Alexandria—but for not more than one month per year. A month, she apparently felt, was as much as she could bear in that port city.

Besides the inland capitals and their port cities, many other urban conglomerations are mentioned in the Geniza records. It is remarkable that all places outside the capital and Alexandria, including such towns as Damietta (the Mediterranean port on the eastern arm of the Nile and a main entrepôt for trade with the Syro-Palestinian coast) and al-Maḥalla al-Kubrā (a provincial capital and center of production), were subsumed under the untranslatable term *rīf*, "the province." In the language of the Geniza letters *dakhal*, "coming home," meant returning to Fustat-Cairo or Alexandria from a visit to towns of the Rīf; *kharaj*, "leaving," meant the opposite. No doubt, *rīf* originally meant countryside, and beyond that, farmland; *rīfī* came to mean the peasant as opposed to the towns-man. The extension of the term to denote towns other than Cairo and Alexandria betrays a unique attachment to the great city.

This attitude had practical consequences. Marriage contracts stipulated that the husband was not permitted to exchange his city for another place except with the consent of his wife. A defaulting debtor would abscond from the city and try to hide in one of the provincial communities. Exigencies of business or office forced many a Cairene or Alexandrian man to take up domicile temporarily in a smaller town, and bitter complaints about the "wrongs" suffered there—about the "Sodom and Gomorrah" endured from its uncouth people—may be read in the Geniza letters. Under these circumstances it is not surprising that a member of the urban *jeunesse dorée*, appointed to posts in the Rīf, again and again forsook them and returned to the city. Community officials implored their superiors to transfer them to the capital (in order, of course, to continue their education . . .), and businessmen would come to the conclusion that, after all, it was wiser to stay at home in the city than to seek profit in the Rīf. The idea of being forced to pass a holiday "outside" was particularly abhorred.

Indeed, there was movement in the opposite direction. An incessant exodus from the Rīf to the cities can be observed in the Geniza documents. It is illustrated by the large number of persons bearing family names derived from small—even the smallest—villages in the Egyptian countryside. The lists of those receiving bread, clothing, and other help from the community of Fustat are full of such names, indicating the difficulties of relocation. But some of the influential families in the capital also originated in the Rīf, indicating how well individuals adjusted over time.

Despite this contrast, or even tension, between city and Rīf, it is precisely in the Geniza papers that we see the importance of the smaller towns. However one felt about the desirability of living in the hinterlands, there was a tendency to move not only from the Rīf to the cities but also in the opposite direction. Persons bearing the family names of Miṣrī, Iskandarānī, ʿAsqalānī, Qudsī, or Damashqī (that is, originating from Fustat, Alexandria, Ascalon, Jerusalem, or Damascus) are encountered in the small towns of Egypt. In fact, we find there people from all over the Mediterranean, including Byzantium and France.

In more than one respect the small towns were of vital economic importance for the people who left us their records in the Geniza. Flax and indigo, the staple products of Egypt, were partly processed where they were grown and needed supervision at the source. The manufacture of cheese, the main foodstuff after bread, was preferably done where the best sheep were raised, and its processing had to be supervised, since it was subject to ritual taboos of Jewish law. Jews, although to a lesser degree than Christians, were widely active as tax farmers and as such had to live in small towns or even villages in order to collect the taxes in person. They were also employed by the government in other capacities. Jewish physicians and apothecaries seem to have been ubiquitous in the Rīf. The economic strength of the Rīf is demonstrated by the fact that it was regularly visited by traveling merchants and agents to sell their textiles, especially silk, and other wares, and by persons soliciting funds for works of public or private philanthropy.

Still, the majority of the data on urban life refers to the capital, and in what follows, where no remark to the contrary is made, Fustat is meant. Fustat—not Cairo—for although the two cities were only about two miles apart, the people in each urban area lived more or less separate lives. The marriage contract of a wealthy bride from the year 1156 stipulates, "She will live in Fustat [called, of course, Miṣr in the document] to the exclusion of Cairo." No reason is given for this condition, but it demonstrates how strongly the contrast was felt almost two hundred years after the foundation of the imperial city, Cairo. The Maghrebi Muslim traveler Ibn Saʿīd, who visited Egypt in the 1240s, describes the people of Fustat as soft-spoken and far friendlier than those of Cairo and expresses his astonishment that there should be such a difference between two adjacent cities. The reason for the contrast, perhaps, was the fact that Fustat was dominated by a relaxed middle class, whereas Cairo lived under the shadow of a more rigid court. Originally, Cairo "was the seat of the [Fatimid] caliphate and no one lived there except the caliph, his troops, his entourage, and those whom he honored to be near to him." There is, indeed, evidence from the Geniza that the Fatimid court physicians, higher government officials, and other persons somehow connected with the court lived there. When a Jewish government official was fired from his post, he was ordered to leave Cairo and take up residence in Fustat. Maṣlīʾaḥ Gaon, the head of the Palestinian yeshiva, who moved to Egypt in 1127, bore the titles *Jalāl al-Mulk* and *Tāj al-Riyāsa* (The Luster of the Empire and the Crown of the Leadership). His titles, together with the robe of honor bestowed on him (according to an Arabic Geniza letter), indicate that he, as head of the Jewish community, belonged to the caliph's retinue. We find that he and some of the scholars attached to him did live in Cairo. Others had houses both in Cairo and Fustat.

Paradoxically, the Cairo represented in the Geniza, especially in Fatimid times, is for the most part not that of its very important notables, but of a social layer poorer in every respect than many a community in a provincial town. The houses and dowries mentioned in the documents are often of low value; the documents themselves are often of poor quality and signed by persons whose handwriting betrays them as having had little practice in writing. This segment of the population worked as menials, such as water carriers, or consisted of destitute persons who had come to the imperial city seeking help. The Jews connected with the court presumably corresponded in Arabic characters; they had no reason to discard their letters in the Geniza chamber. They left their Hebrew writings in their own synagogue, which disappeared along with its geniza.

The capital of Egypt is one of the most studied cities of the Islamic world. Minute descriptions by medieval Muslim scholars are invaluable, and their modern successors, Egyptian and Western, have continued their work. Excavations were carried out at Fustat at the beginning of the twentieth century and again during the last forty years or so. Ultimately it will be necessary to collect the rich topographic material dispersed in the Geniza documents and coordinate it with the information gained from medieval literary sources and modern archeological research.

The nucleus of Fustat was formed by a Byzantine fortress, situated on the eastern bank of the Nile and called the Fortress of the Greeks, or more frequently, the Fortress of the Candles. The Christian and Jewish elements remained preponderant in this, the pre-Islamic section of the city, and time-honored churches, some of which are still extant, as well as the two main synagogues, were situated there. By the Geniza period, the area had entirely lost its military function. Some of the towers of the fortress were used as apartments and workshops and were owned in part by the synagogue as pious foundations. The Islamic city, founded at the time of the Arab conquest (641 C.E.), surrounded the Fortress of the Greeks on the north, east, and south, and later, when the Nile silted up, also on the west. It was laid out according to the tribes, clans, and groups that composed the conquering army. A section assigned to such a group was called *khaṭṭ* (pronounced *khuṭṭ* by the Geniza people) — literally, "line." That pattern was characteristic of all the early Arab settlements, the so-called *amṣār*, or garrison towns. The area reserved for the high command and its guards comprised a part of the Fortress of the Greeks and extended northeastward to the newly founded mosque of ʿAmr, the conqueror. It was called *Ahl al-Rāya*, meaning those around the (tribal) standard, or al-Rāya for short. Our documents reveal the interesting fact that six hundred years after the Muslim conquest, the main quarters were still called by the names of those ancient Arab groups, such as Banāna, Banū Wāʾil, Khawlān, Mahra, Tujīb, Waʿlān, although inhabited by Jews, among others.

The topographic terminology in the Geniza documents is rather fluid, which seems to indicate that, in practice, the borders between the various parts of the city cannot have been too strictly delineated. Nor were the terms that specified particular kinds of places carefully defined and universally applied. That too is characteristic of other Muslim cities. The word designating a quarter today, *ḥāra*, could refer not only to a large district, such as Mamṣūṣa, one of the quarters of Fustat most frequently mentioned in the Geniza documents, or the even larger Mahra, a tribal sector; it could refer also to a small place, described as a covered alley, a prison, or a little mosque. Two terms designating areas of settlement are found together in a document from al-Maḥalla, which speaks of *khaṭṭ ḥārat al-Yahūd* — the District of the Jewish Quarter (where Christians also lived). The word generally designating a block, or segment of a street — *ṣuqʿ* — also applied to larger urban districts, such as the Fortress of the Greeks, Mamṣūṣa, or the Great Bazaar. Its derivative, *tasqīʿ*, designated a public record that listed revenue from houses in a certain district. In the Geniza documents, it meant rent paid by the tenants living in houses that were communal property. In Alexandria, but occasionally also elsewhere, a quarter was called *nāḥiya* (in modern times, an administrative unit approximately equivalent to a county). As far as we can tell from our documents, it must have been more common in Alexandria to call a neighborhood by name without the addition of a descriptive appellative.

Special mention must be made of the elusive but frequently used term *rabʿ*. Despite its pronunciation in the Geniza papers as *rubʿ*, the word

is not the classical *rubʿ*, "fourth," "quarter," but *rabʿ*, "area," "residence."
Documentary and literary evidence taken together indicate that it represented the smallest subdivision of the *ṣuqʿ*, the urban district; rubʿ
designated a large building, a compound, or a "block" under the care
of the *ṣāḥib al-rubʿ*, a combination of doorkeeper and neighborhood
police officer, the one official with whom the local population was in
daily contact. The blocks containing the "compounds of the poor" or
"compounds of Jerusalemites," that is, pious foundations benefiting
those people, were also called rubʿ. It is indicative of the fluidity of the
terms that the ṣāḥib al-rubʿ is also styled *ḥāmi 'l-ḥāra*, or guard of the
quarter. Presumably, the *darrāb*, or guard of the *darb* (alley, street) was
not much different. (The Geniza documents are most helpful in iden-
tifying the nature of specific locations described in literary sources with
very loose terminology.)

Was there a marked division of the city into residential, commercial,
and industrial areas? As is well known from the works of medieval Muslim antiquarians and richly illustrated in the Geniza documents, many
streets, bazaars, halls, and "houses" were named for a certain branch of
commerce, an industry, or even a product. It is true not only for Fustat
but also for other cities—for example, Damascus. These were residential
as well as commercial areas. Some locations of this sort would retain
their original names even after the original commercial establishments
had relocated elsewhere. Sometimes residential property converted to
commercial use. In any case, living quarters and zones of commerce and
industry were often combined in the same location.

In the Geniza records we find high-priced houses, clearly serving as
living quarters, bordering on busy bazaars; stores are often topped by
an *ʿulūw*, that is, one or several stories used as domiciles. We find a
physician in the street of the wax makers, another in that of the
horseshoers, and a judge in the bazaar of the perfumers. A sugar workshop belonging to a physician is expressly described also as known as
his domicile (*sukn*, which could hardly mean his office). Conversely, a
petition addressed to the vizier Ibn al-Sallār al-Malik al-ʿĀdil (December
1150) with regard to the estate of a *tājir*, or prominent merchant, emphatically makes a distinction between the family's *maṭbakh*, "(sugar)
factory," and *sukn*, "living quarters." An interesting but fragmentary letter says, "People who had been living in their properties give them up.
When you sell the house, they will convert it into a workshop (*maʿmal*)."

Many districts contained both high-priced residences without stores,
including homes with adjoining open spaces, and low-priced domiciles
that contained the ateliers or the shops of the merchants. The truly aris-

tocratic neighborhoods were probably to be found in Cairo. This pattern of aristocratic domiciles removed from the markets and close to the center of government was characteristic of medieval Baghdad, a city comparable in many respects to Fustat-Cairo.

One may assume that, as a rule, the truly aristocratic neighborhoods, whether in Fustat or in Cairo, were settled originally and almost exclusively by Muslims, for example, the Quarter of the Tujīb, so-named after the Arab tribe. Nevertheless, the character of the neighborhoods could and did change. The Tujīb vigorously took part in the conquest of North Africa, bringing immense booty home to Fustat, and later they were prominent in Spain. We may imagine, therefore, that the Tujīb district of Fustat originally was purely Arab and probably also very luxurious. Because of the proximity of the pre-Islamic Fortress of the Greeks, it was infiltrated, however, by Christians and Jews, so that by the fifth Islamic century it presented a completely mixed picture, both with regard to the composition of its population and the juxtaposition of residential and predominantly commercial neighborhoods. The transition from aristocratic to mixed areas of settlement was probably not sudden or clearly marked. In Fustat there is no evidence of the slums of the poor nestled against the palaces of the rich, conditions described by Steven Runciman for Constantinople.

An analysis of documents from two districts at Fustat, the Fortress of the Greeks and the Tujīb shows that there were residential neighborhoods with houses of high value, but they did not form large, independent quarters; they were more like islands surrounded by a network of bazaars and streets, with houses consisting of twin stores topped by modest domestic structures. Even an area of suburban character, such as Jazīra, the Island of the Nile, is represented in the Geniza by store-top homes. One house was worth approximately 660 dinars, a princely sum; another, bounded by the palace of the vizier Ibn Killis and other prestigious homes (one situated in an orchard), comprised also a building of two shops bordering on an open space. Suburban areas tended to be more fashionable. We may assume that the houses there were more spacious and contained adjoining gardens and orchards. The same conditions applied to other cities in the world of the Geniza. It is, however, difficult to generalize about patterns of settlement, because many cities developed in accordance with local concerns.

The general picture emerging from the data seems to indicate that the division of a city into residential and commercial areas was generally not regulated by statute. In practice, some sort of zoning was achieved by private initiative, that is, by the protection that Islamic (and Jewish) law granted a proprietor against any changes effected by a neighbor that might prove harmful to his own property. A characteristic example, taken from a legal inquiry submitted to Abraham Maimonides (d. 1237), the famous Jewish judge, vividly illustrates the problem. A dyer converted a house in a residential neighborhood, *diyyār al-sukna* into a workshop, the smoke from which caused grave nuisance to his neighbor. The latter sold his house; the new proprietor let it fall into disrepair and sold it as a ruin. A third landlord renovated the place and complained about the smoke, which made it impossible "to hang his linen or wool clothing." The dyer moved his furnace from the wall he shared with his neighbor to the one facing the lane, but the smoke still proved to be damaging. Although the dyer had converted his house into a workshop fifteen years before the neighboring house was acquired by its new proprietor, Abraham Maimonides decided in favor of the latter, for "damage has no claim based on undisturbed possession." If it could have been proved that one of the former proprietors had waived his rights, the complaint would have been dismissed. (Islamic law rules similarly.) The case shows that the protection of the property rights of the individual proprietor was not a complete safeguard for preserving the residential character of a quarter.

In certain instances, we know of direct government intervention in zoning urban areas. The development of medieval Baghdad is, by and large, the story of carefully controlled government zoning policies. The same is true for Samarra, the second capital of the Abbasid dynasty in Iraq. However, even in those cases of controlled urban expansion, the demands of the marketplace, combined with official greed, rendered the most carefully conceived plans null and void.

Zoning also involved restrictions concerning the choice of a domicile imposed on the members of a religion, sect, clan, or social group. In this respect, too, the situation of the High Middle Ages was far more fluid than in later times. Jewish houses bordered on those belonging to and occupied by Christians or Muslims, or both; Christians and Muslims lived in Jewish houses and vice versa. Some properties were even held in partnership by members of the three religions. Jews as a rule lived in a limited number of neighborhoods, but none was exclusively Jewish. There is no reason to assume that the situation was different with other segments of the population. On the contrary. By the very injunctions of their religion, Jews were forced to concentrate in certain neighborhoods. Since they were not permitted to ride on the Sabbath or religious holidays, they had to live within walking distance from their synagogues. Moreover, Judaism stresses, more emphatically than Islam, the importance of daily attendance at communal worship. Finally, Jewish (and certainly also Christian) women disliked sharing houses with Muslims because Islamic sensitivities about women were bound to affect them. To avoid the inconvenience for their womenfolk, Jewish authorities promulgated statutes from time to time prohibiting the sale or lease of parts of houses to Muslims. Two letters addressed to Moses Maimonides emphasize that restrictions like these considerably reduced the value of Jewish properties. On the other hand, a recently discovered letter to Maimonides' son indicates that apartment houses inhabited exclusively by Jews may have been difficult to come by and would therefore have been expensive. In the letter, a wife who had the right to choose the couple's domicile insists on renting a floor in a house without undesirable neighbors. She has left the family home of the husband, to which she was brought first according to custom and is now staying with her brother. The writer asks whether the young wife can now be forced by court decision to be content with an apartment in a house in which non-Jews dwelled. All this shows that the seclusion of Jews (and other minority groups) was self-imposed and not dictated by the Muslim authorities.

An additional factor adversely affected the homogeneous character of neighborhoods: the mass of neglected buildings falling into decay. After years, the sites could be used for purposes quite different from those served by the original structures. The abundance of references to ruins in the writings of the Muslim historians of the fourteenth and fifteenth centuries might seem to indicate a general decline marking the late Middle Ages. But ruins appear in the Geniza documents of the eleventh and twelfth centuries as frequently as in pages of later Muslim historians: high-priced neighborhoods, no less than poor environments, were dotted with them. The data also reflect like conditions in cities besides Fustat, such as Damascus and Jerusalem.

Ruins are repeatedly mentioned as adjoining, facing, or being in the vicinity of inhabited buildings, either bequeathed or sold together with them, or, to the contrary, expressly excluded from a transaction. The number of transactions in which ruins are noted bordering buildings, even new ones, is astounding when one considers that only a minority of documents dealing with houses indicate their boundaries. Ruins were purchased, given as a gift, and, of course, rebuilt. It is also not surprising that ruins, in whole or in part, were taken away from their proprietors in a high-handed fashion. Finally, parts of buildings described as *kharāba*, or ruin, were used as storerooms, perhaps even as dwellings; the revenue lists of the charitable foundations note rents paid for such properties. The very practice of describing houses in a deed of sale as being "built up" seems to point to the fact that they often changed hands after having fallen into decay. Contracts of lease for protracted periods during which the rent is waived on condition that the tenant repairs or rebuilds a structure are commonplace in the Geniza records. Consequently, it is not surprising that we find references to a house built on the ruins of another. A widow replies by letter to a suggestion that she sell her house, in which she lives and leases apartments, and buy a new one about whose quality she has doubts:

The old house in the Maḥras [quarter] used to bring [rent of] 60 dinars, and there is nothing wrong with it except the neighborhood. I do not know what would be the price today, whether it has gone up or down. However, its foundations are excellent and its structure is solid, and people say that beneath it is a qāʿa [ground floor] and beneath its pillars are other pillars. I shall pursue this matter until I have certainty about the purchase of the new house, so that I shall have a place where I can put my head down, for in this house I cannot live any longer.

The widow lived in the old house and derived her sustenance from apartments leased. The house, constructed on the ruins of another, was in good condition, but the neighborhood had become insecure.

A property owner could treat holdings as he or she pleased, even to the point of neglecting them, provided, of course, that doing so did not cause damage to a neighbor's property. The constant sight of ruined houses apparently did not annoy excessively the people who lived in the immediate vicinity. It has been suggested that this attitude was, perhaps, occasioned by a certain degree of otherworldliness, which was not disturbed by these constant reminders of human decay and transitoriness. To be sure, the populace, as a rule, cared little about the appearance of public space and probably not much about a neighbor's property. But it is more likely that the "abundance" of ruins stemmed from economic considerations not yet determined.

One may ask whether the ubiquity of ruins was directly tied to with the vexing problem of unoccupied premises reported in private correspondence as well as in the reports of charitable foundations. Empty houses or apartments could be listed by the government as having no proprietor and consequently as subject to confiscation. Action by the interested party to avert a takeover could be costly. A scholarly person from Byzantium or western Europe, installed by his absentee Egyptian relatives as "gatekeeper" of their house, explains in a beautifully written Hebrew letter why he is unable to quit the house: The tenants might move out, the house would remain empty and then be seized by the government, "as is the practice here"; this would subject his relatives to heavy expenses. A woman in a family house in a provincial town north of Cairo asks her sister in Fustat to return, together with her family; otherwise, Ghuzz, or Turkomans will be billeted in her house, or the place will be taken over by the government altogether.

Entries in the accounts of charitable foundations note vacant premises as early as the first half of the eleventh century, when the community possessed only a few houses and the movement of Jews from Fustat to newly built Cairo had hardly begun, if at all. These references in the Geniza documents to empty apartments or houses are not necessarily symptomatic of a decline in population. A decline is palpably felt only when we notice a *sudden* increase in the number of uninhabited premises, so many that the charitable foundations find it expedient to draw up lists of those occupied and unoccupied. It happened in 1201, when the devastating famine and great plague wreaked havoc among the population, a blow from which Fustat never recovered. Another deadly visitation by famine and plague, and a complete breakdown of public order, occurred in Egypt during the years 1063 to 1072. Eliahu Ashtor, who assumes a general decline in the urban population of Egypt by the end of the eleventh century, ascribes the decline partly to that disaster and partly to general socioeconomic conditions.[3] The Geniza does not reflect that change, perhaps because no dated documents of the pious foundations have been found for the years 1060–90, which in itself may be an indication of some disarray in their administration.

The obligatory report to the government of unoccupied premises— namely that they were deserted and therefore fiscal property—was not solely a matter of finance; it was a security measure as well. When in 1124 the vizier al-Ma'mūn ordered the heads of the police of the twin capital to register the names of all inhabitants and not to permit them to move from one house to another without his authorization, he was not interested in statistical data (devout Muslims and Jews shun fixed numbers as bringing bad luck); he did so because he dreaded the infiltration of terrorists from the sect of the Assassins. Vacant premises were a threat to public security; such structures had to be boarded up and a report sent to the authorities.

Besides homes, stores, and workshops, the Geniza records mention a wide variety of other urban structures whose functions are more or

---

3. *A Social and Economic History of the Near East in the Middle Ages* (Berkeley and Los Angeles, 1976), 207.

less self-evident, but whose legal character is not clearly defined. The term "semipublic" may be appropriate, inasmuch as the buildings served the public but were owned by an individual or charitable foundation, or were leased from the government by a private entrepreneur. In the first place, mention must be made of the *dār al-wakāla,* the house of a *wakīl al-tujjār,* or representative of merchants, which could serve as a warehouse, bourse, bank, seat of public notaries, mailing address, or all these functions together, depending on the importance of the individual wakīl. The proprietors of a wakāla might be of widely differing provenance—an illustrious qāḍī, or a man from the Egyptian Rīf, or the son of a Jewish immigrant from Spain. In Fatimid and early Ayyubid times these wākalas, like family firms, were of short duration—at most three generations—and did not leave their mark on the appearance of the cities. The time of the great khāns, as the wākalas were later called, began in the thirteenth century.

The various "houses" named after a commodity, such as jewelry, silk, carpet, threads, sugar, rice, oil, vinegar, saffron, almonds, or apples—all mentioned both in the Geniza records and in the works of the Muslim historians—served a similar purpose, but some functioned also as toll stations. The term "house" in this context is best translated as "bazaar." Money could be changed, promissory notes written, and other financial transactions made in a dār wakāla, or one of the commodity "houses." Two places in Fustat were especially devoted to such activities, the House of Blessing, *dār al-baraka,* and the House of Exchange or of Money Changing, *dār al-ṣarf.* The former was located in the Street of Coppersmiths in the immediate vicinity of the Friday mosque of ʿAmr— a propinquity of temple and money changers familiar to readers of the New Testament. The dār al-ṣarf was apparently so well known that letters could be addressed to it by name without any reference to street or other topographical assignation. The same is true of the *dār al-ḍarb,* the caliphal mint.

Various structures, known from the Geniza records as the scenes of intense commercial and industrial activity, seem to have been remnants from pre-Islamic times. We have already mentioned the Fortress of the Greeks, which contained many Christian structures. The Qālūs market for flax (the main export article of Egypt during the period), as well as for numerous other commodities, betrayed its pre-Islamic origins not only by its name, but also by a Greek inscription on one of its gates, whose meaning was still known to the Arabs (*kalōs,* welcome!). The Greek derivative *qayṣāriyya* has penetrated the Arabic language as an appellative noun meaning market hall. But in a number of Geniza texts it still is a proper name for one particular compound, as brought home by combinations such as "in the Colonnade and in the Qaysāriyya, namely, in the Carpet House," and other references. The original qaysāriyya of Fustat and those under the name of a present or former proprietor appear in the Geniza as places for the manufacture and sale of clothing, carpets, and wool fabrics. Finally, the term *funduq*, in modern Arabic, "hotel," had preserved in Geniza times much of its pre-Islamic connotation of hospice for travelers and lodgings for the needy, as in the Greek term *pandocheion*, from which it is derived. One funduq was situated between the two synagogues in the Fortress of the Greeks; another, named The Small, was in the Great Market. Whether it was identical with the New Funduq, also noted in the lists of the charitable foundations, cannot be decided yet. One may assume that they had been private homes donated to the Jewish community, and were then converted into buildings befitting their new function; in any case, the structural details applied to them are the same as those applying to residential quarters. Funduqs first appear in the second half of the twelfth century. Before then, the needy and the travelers were put up within the synagogue precincts.

Funduqs in the sense of caravanserais — structures providing lodgings for traveling merchants upstairs and shelter for their pack animals, as well as storage for their goods, on the ground floor — are mentioned throughout the Geniza records but seem to have become recognized landmarks only in the thirteenth century. Here too we find specialization according to the commodities traded, such as funduqs for traders in raisins, honey, hides, or mats. But they are rare and cannot be compared with to the "houses" so often referred to in the Geniza that did not furnish lodgings. The multi-function caravanserais belong to the Ayyubid and Mamluk periods.

Conventional wisdom has it that the medieval Islamic city possessed all the elements that later led to the formation of that unique phenomenon, the compact Grand Bazaar, stretching from one end of the city to the other. Under this interpretation, these elements were still disjointed during the Middle Ages — functionally and geographically. Such a reading also credits the great monarchies of Ottoman Turkey, Iran, and Morocco, and the economic boom of the sixteenth and early seventeenth centuries with the development the Grand Bazaar as an institution, its way paved by an earlier period. One ought to be cautious before embracing this view. Both Baghdad and Samarra, the twin capitals of the Abbasid dynasts in Iraq were constructed *ex nihilo* with separate market areas of great size. To be sure, merchants and others lived among the markets, as they did in Fustat, but entire areas of the Abbasid cities were serviced only by small distributive outlets, even in times of great economic prosperity.

The observation has been made that the medieval Islamic city lacked a central public square, comparable with the Greek agora or the Roman forum. The reason: It did not possess the democratic institutions that required a large open space for communal assemblies. That does not seem to be true of the earliest Islamic foundations, the *amṣār*, or garrison towns. Settled by Arab tribesmen, these towns in their early years had caravan terminals immediately outside the city limits that served as places of assembly for the tribal warriors. Individual tribes also had spaces for their own purposes and those of their clients. To be sure, the topographical features of ancient cities inhabited by the Arab conquerors were likely to be different from new structures that reflected the sensibilities of Arab tribesmen with little or no experience in urban settings. In any case, the comparison between the classical and Islamic city as regards public space requires a more nuanced approach.

The Muslims were "brothers through their religion" (Qur'ān 9:11, 33: 5): What bound their polity was their faith; consequently the natural place for their public gatherings was the mosque. Indeed, it was the existence of a Friday mosque—the cathedral mosque of a city, or later, the main mosque of a quarter in a large city—that legally defined the Islamic town or city as distinct from a rural place of habitation; initially, the law did not allow rural areas to build such structures. The obligation to say prayer on Friday in unison was a binding element in early Islamic society, which was beset by fractious tribalism and the integration of disparate peoples who had recently converted to Islam. Nor was the mosque merely a place of prayer. It served many functions, from a place of public announcements to an absorption center for recent arrivals from the Arabian Peninsula and the surrounding countryside. The same held true, and perhaps with even stronger force, for the houses of worship of Jews and Christians within the lands of Islam. The Friday mosque proclaimed this purpose in its very architecture. The early mosques were of large dimensions in themselves and, in addition, possessed a court so spacious that the entire male population of a city, or representative part of it, could assemble there at one time.

Those attending communal prayer were by no means a passive assembly following the recitation of the leader of the service or silently listening to the person occupying the pulpit, whether he was a caliph, a governor, or professional preacher. The mosque was the place where the assembled could vent their grievances and, of course, where the rulers or popular leaders tried to sway public opinion. Moreover, with its shady colonnades and other adjoining structures, the mosque formed an extended compound, sufficient for all the public, religious, and cultural activities with which the community was concerned. Here, as in the temples of antiquity, the public treasury was kept; fiscal arrangements, such as the farming out of taxes, could be made; the qāḍīs administered justice (when they did not do so in their houses); and *muftīs*, or legal experts, could be consulted. Notaries served the public in drawing up their contracts or copying their letters in mosques. As we have seen, mosques, like churches and synagogues, were often situated in the midst of lively commercial neighborhoods. It was a natural association, for where there are people, there is business. It should be noted that the use of church premises for secular purposes was by no means unknown in medieval Western Europe.

In Islam, as in Judaism, study is a prime religious duty. Before the eleventh century, when special buildings, richly endowed by foundations, began to be dedicated to higher education, the mosque was the natural place for study and instruction. Masters and students of all "Islamic" subjects (to which also belonged knowledge of the Arabic language) could be found there, forming circles of different size and duration. Learning was fostered by libraries housed in the premises of the mosques, some of which have become renowned for their treasures. And despite the development of buildings and institutions of Muslim higher education, the mosque, like the synagogue, never ceased to serve as a house of study, especially on a more popular level.

Naturally, the Geniza is not a source for the role of the mosque in Islam, but it is important for what follows to put the mosque's place into proper focus. All that can be said about life in the synagogue applies, *mutatis mutandis*, and to an even larger degree, to the mosque, both to the Friday mosque and to the more modest, but socially no less vital, street or neighborhood mosque, which catered to a limited number of worshipers. The noon service in the Friday mosque endowed the participants with the feeling of belonging to a great urban, and beyond that, ecumenical community and provided opportunities for the discussion of public affairs. The neighborhood mosque took care of the individual and probably discharged welfare services for the needy of its locality. This latter point requires further research.

The synagogue in a city like Fustat served also as the seat of the rabbinical court, as well as the center for the charitable activities of the community. The courtyard of the main synagogue, that of the Palestinians in Fustat, must have been roomy enough to accommodate any overflow during services, lectures, and other events. There are many indirect references to the synagogue court, but no details of measurements. In the thirteenth-century synagogue of Aleppo, the courtyard occupied an area as large as the building itself. In Fustat, with its more favorable climate, the courtyard might have been even larger. In short, since religion represented the social framework of a medieval Islamic city, religious buildings were its most conspicuous architectural creations. This was true with regard to the Muslim majority as well as the minority groups, with the differences inherent in the limitations imposed on the latter by the Muslim authorities.

No government building, conspicuous by its location or structure, appears in the Geniza documents relating to Fustat during the Fatimid period. Nor have Muslim topographers much to offer in this respect. An ancient building named Government House had ceased to function as such long before the eleventh century and had been partly dismantled. It is not mentioned in the Geniza documents. The imperial palaces and their barracks were in the newly built city of Cairo; they served the court and the army. The civil population of Fustat had no business there — commercial or otherwise. This changed in Ayyubid times, when the citadel, *qalʿa*, of the capital was constructed on Mt. Muqaṭṭam in order to defend the city and partly to centralize the various branches of government. Summonses and visits to the qalʿa are referred to in the Geniza, sometimes with unpleasant consequences for the persons concerned. A building called the *dīwān* (that is, government office), is occasionally mentioned, but only very rarely and without any hint as to its appearance or location. It is not even clear that the sparse references concern the same building. Had the dīwān been conspicuous, it would have formed a landmark and lent its name to its neighborhood. But both the Geniza records and the Muslim writers are silent on this point.

All in all, there seems to have been little direct contact between the populace and the government and, consequently, not much need for public buildings. In the great administrative centers of Iraq, this was part of a deliberate policy by which the caliphs kept their subjects at arm's length in order to enhance their own security. No doubt the same was true of Cairo in relation to Fustat. In smaller cities, the government retreated to areas inside walled citadels. Government business with the populace was often engaged elsewhere.

Taxes were usually farmed out and collected in the markets and so-called houses, where the relevant transactions were made. The Nile harbors of Fustat and Cairo, the Arsenal (al-ṣināʿa) and the customs house (al-Maqs), respectively, served international trade, and they, of course, are referred to frequently. Busy government offices, such as that in charge of the poll tax, or the one supervising inheritances, must have had their own premises—possibly even more than one each—but they are always referred to by function, never by location, an indication, perhaps, that they were not buildings of architectural distinction. The government may have used for its offices some of the many houses that had come into its possession by confiscation or another form of acquisition—in particular, estates whose heirs could not be located or were disqualified (for example, under Muslim law, a daughter could never inherit more than one-half of her father's possessions).

A number of buildings, designated as *ḥabs*, "prison," *maḥbas*, "house of detention," or *maḥras*, "guardhouse or barracks," or indiscriminately by all three terms, appear both in the Geniza records and in Muslim sources as landmarks and lent their names to the surrounding neighborhood. These structures are all named after a person, such as the repeatedly mentioned *ḥabs*, *maḥbas*, or *maḥras* Bunāna (or Banān), the *maḥras* ʿAmmār, and the *maḥras* al-Sāriya. Thus it seems that in these cases as well, private homes that had come into the government's possession were used for the purposes indicated by those designations. (The word *ḥabs*, however, also means pious foundation; therefore the word should be taken as meaning prison or police station only where context renders that reading unassailable.)

In the absence of an officially constituted local municipality, the central authority or its representatives supplied all aspects of city administration then in existence. Overall security was entrusted to police, be it on foot or mounted on horses. In addition, the individual quarters, streets, or compounds benefited from special protection, for which a monthly payment, called *ḥars* or *ḥirāsa* (guard or watch), had to be paid. Permanent protection was represented by the *ḥāmi ʾl ḥāra* or the *darrāb*, the guards for a quarter or block, and especially the *ṣāḥib al-rubʿ*, the previously mentioned gatekeeper of a compound; the three titles were interchangeable. The night watchmen, *ṭawwāfūn*, "those who make the rounds," as the title indicates, went about on foot. There is definite information that Jews, too, could be employed as night watchmen; it was not a government appointment but a job like any other. This service was apparently organized by the neighborhood concerned. The difference between the two functions is reflected in the bookkeeping of the community. The *ḥirāsa* was apparently a modest monthly payment incumbent on a building; it is listed regularly in the accounts of the real estate owned by the pious foundations. The emoluments of the night watchmen, however, were a matter of agreement between them and the community; they appear in the lists of beneficiaries receiving cash and loaves of bread and are recorded from the middle of the eleventh through the beginning of the thirteenth century. No doubt the watchmen also received bonuses from the individual inhabitants of a neighborhood. Properties outside the town limits needed the protection of the Arab or Berber clan that wielded authority in the area concerned. This imposition, called *khifāra*, apparently had to be paid in advance.

Similar to the fee for security, another payment, called dust or garbage removal, is listed regularly as required from a landlord. The sums paid varied widely according to size of the buildings, the interval between removals, and special circumstances such as repairs, which were carried out frequently. The regularity of payments for garbage removal, which are sometimes accompanied by a surcharge or tip discreetly called *ju'l*, "consideration," gives the impression that payment was not left up to the landlords. An eighth-century qāḍī is reported as having made a monthly round of the Muslim charitable foundations and, when he found that a manager was remiss in paying up, ordered him to be flogged.

Another sanitary measure, the installation, cleaning, and maintenance of subterranean pipes, was no doubt also supervised by the government. One account notes *'amal qanāt*, "construction of a water conduit," in three different buildings owned by the community; it is hardly likely that such action would have been taken at one time (since the community usually was short of funds) had it not been ordered from above. Charges for the cleaning and maintenance of the clay pipes that drained used water and other waste to cesspools or to the Nile commonly appear in the accounts of the charitable foundations. The system would not have worked without regulation by a central authority. Archeological excavations in Fustat and nearby localities have uncovered sophisticated water supply and sewerage networks.

In countries where the non-Muslim population was intermittently exposed to particularly oppressive treatment, such as Morocco, Yemen, and Bukhara in Central Asia, the Jewish communities were forced at times to supply men who would serve in cleaning the cesspools. (In Yemen, this imposition was still enforced at the beginning of the twentieth century—or rather, was reinstated when the Turks left the country during World War I.) Among the hundreds of manual occupations performed by Jews according to the Geniza, no trace of a cesspool cleaner has been discovered. Had Jews regularly performed that ignoble task, they would have appeared in the lists of the poor receiving bread and other handouts from the community. Payments for the cleaning of the *qanāt*s are noted as such, not as given to specified persons doing the job. Thus it is evident that this operation was under the supervision of the government, which employed the men, probably through a contract with an entrepreneur.

Along with the monthly payment for security, the ḥirāsa, another monthly due called *ḥikr*, an Aramaic loanword meaning rent, had to be paid for houses in the Fortress of the Greeks and its environs. The fortress had been taken by assault (at least so goes the theory); hence, by right of conquest its ground belonged to the Muslims, that is, the government, or as a Hebrew document says, "to the King." Only what was originally the Byzantine part of the city (or what was regarded as such) was subject to ground rent. Nevertheless, the ḥikr is frequently mentioned in the Geniza documents. Wills, deeds of gift, contracts of sale, or rent had occasion to make mention of it, and in the communal accounts it is ubiquitous. The houses donated to charitable foundations probably deteriorated while the ground rent remained the same. That would explain why, early in the thirteenth century, the community would pay the ground rent on behalf of the poor, who, being unable to afford it, probably would have lost their habitations. In deeds of gift, it is repeatedly stated that the ground rent will be paid by the donor or a third party, as when a woman who had donated the house in which she lived "to the poor" gave an adjacent small house to an-other woman (probably her housekeeper), free of ḥikr, since this due was included in that paid to a charitable foundation for the larger house. In another case, a father gives his daughter an upper floor in his house with the stipulation that if she prefers to live elsewhere, she will receive the rent, and he or his heirs will pay the ground rent. In leases for prolonged periods one preferred to have the tenant pay the ḥikr. These examples show that this tax was an imposition very much felt by the people concerned. Like other taxes it was most probably farmed out.

In many cases the government, either referred to as *sulṭān* or repre-sented by one of its ministries (such as that of the Muslim pious foun-dations or that of the mosques), owned not only the ground but also part of a property or the entire property. Jews, like other inhabitants, could be coproprietors of such a place or could lease it. A father in despair over his profligate son even played with the idea of donating his house to the (Jewish) poor or . . . the government. Thus, one had the government as a close neighbor everywhere in the city.

The erection of a building probably required a license, although none is found or referred to in the Geniza. But the government provided surveyors, *muhandiz* or *muhandis*, who supervised the correct demarcation of boundaries between properties in the city. Their expert judgment was sought whenever a dispute over an alleged encroachment arose. In a document dated 1136, two surveyors, expressly described as "generously made available by the government," inspected a tilting house that had caused damage to an adjacent building. The fact that this service, which was provided by the government, was remunerated with approximately the same sum over such a long period of time proves that it was a well-established institution.

Any transfer of urban property was taxed and had to be certified by a Muslim authority. No wonder, therefore, that numerous fragments of deeds of gift or sale written by a Muslim notary have been found in the Geniza. The ends of the documents, as many as are preserved, are co-signed by one or several Muslims whose handwriting betrays them as professional *ʿudūl*, or adjuncts of a qāḍī. A search for a dīwān or other type of central office that would have assembled the information contained in these documents, thus creating a public record of urban properties, produced no results. No cadastre of this sort has yet been found among the Geniza records, but they must have been compiled—and perhaps on more than one occasion. The extremely detailed topographical information about Fustat (and Cairo) from Muslim sources, which largely tallies with the data of the Geniza, cannot have been entirely the random observations of interested individuals; it must have been based on archival material. An order given in 1124 by the vizier al-Maʾmūn to the heads of police in Cairo and Fustat, required the registration of all inhabitants of the capital, street by street and quarter by quarter. It would be worthwhile to inquire whether or not the topographical information provided by the Muslim writers Ibn Saʿīd al-Magrhibī, Ibn Duqmāq, or al-Maqrīzī shows us Fustat mainly as it was in the first quarter of the twelfth century. Studies of the topography of medieval Baghdad based on local Iraqi sources show that the descriptions of the city are not always contemporaneous with the author describing specific locations. Often our authors, basing themselves on unnamed (or named) earlier authorities, will paint a picture of particular places as if they actually stood facing given monuments and streets, when in fact the entire area had fallen into disuse. Needless to say, such accounts, presented without a cautionary word, can cause much confusion for the modern historian. The documents of the Geniza are obviously a useful check on literary excesses.

When modern men or women speak of their native city, it is as the place where *they* were born. In Geniza times, a man's house was originally "the inheritance of his fathers" (1 Kings 21:3) — the town where his father and mother were laid to rest. A merchant from Jerusalem has angrily left his native city after having suffered serious losses there and settled in Egypt. His friends admonish him to return — not because Jerusalem is the Holy City, but because it contains the tombs of his father and mother. A Jerusalem pilgrim from the Maghreb has been impeded from reaching the goal of his journey, first by the struggle between the Fatimids and the Seljuks and the general insecurity of the roads; second, by the civil war over the caliphal succession, which has led to the siege of Alexandria (where he happens to be staying); and finally, by the advent of the Crusaders. But, he adds, after having "seen" Jerusalem, he is resolved to return to his hometown, *waṭan*, and "the inheritance of his fathers."

Using the same phrase, an ascetic who has settled in Jerusalem in order to "mourn" its desolation and "to tear himself away from the world," speaks of his intention to return (where to is not preserved). The term *waṭan* is best translated here as home*town* (and not by its other meaning of homeland), for the intention of the writer is to return to the place where his family lives. When the nagid Mevōrākh travels from the Egyptian capital to another city (Alexandria, apparently), a communal official writing to him expresses regrets that the addressee has been separated from "his dear waṭan and his beloved son." Similarly when Nahray b. Nessīm, in his old age, leaves Alexandria for Malīj in the Nile Delta and then for Fustat (his home), a cousin, anxiously inquiring about his well-being, writes, "May God never separate you and me from our waṭans."

The notion that a man's waṭan was his city rather than his country finds its expression in the blessing "may God keep her," "may God guard her" (the city is conceived as a female being), and similar wishes, which in the Geniza letters, as in Arabic literary texts, are regularly attached to the names of towns, but in the Geniza letters, at least, never to those of countries. Countries were complex polities whose borders often changed and which, by and large, did not inspire personal allegiances.

Although the term "waṭan" originally designated a place where a man's family was indigenous, in an increasingly mobile Islamic society waṭan came to mean also one's adopted city. Nahray and his cousin were Tunisians who had settled in Egypt, one in Alexandria, the other in Fustat. But in the letter cited, the cousin speaks of their "waṭans," which tallies with Arabic literary usage. The renowned Maghrebi historian Ibn Saʿīd, quoting a source contemporary to Nahray, says of the Fatimids that they "took Cairo as their waṭan," meaning their seat and new home (as opposed to their original home, the Muslim West, from which Ibn Saʿīd himself hailed).

This expansion of the linguistic usage betrays a change in social attitudes. Crossing the frontier that separated Arabia from the settled areas beyond, the early tribal warriors could identify themselves by their place of habitation, not by a noble lineage. Al-Aḥnaf, the leader of the Tamīm tribe in the newly founded garrison town of Baṣra, was reported to have said, "An Azdī [a member of the rival tribe] of Baṣra is dearer to me than a Tamīmī of Kūfa." The urban community was on the way to becoming a reality of greater concern than the bonds of lineage.

Towns and cities were not entities with uniform populations. The character of the inhabitants changed frequently with the influx of new settlers from the inlying regions and areas still further removed. Many of the illustrious men of Islamic letters in Cairo-Fustat derived their family names from smaller towns in Egypt where they were born, such as al-Subkī, al-Qalqashandī, and al-Shaʿrānī; not surprisingly, Jews with the same family names left their records in the Geniza. The number of Jewish inhabitants of Fustat named after obscure localities in the Egyptian countryside is surprising; some of them were paupers, but others were not. Smaller towns such as Damīra or Damsīs were the birthplaces of men who rose to riches and to influential positions in the Fustat community. The Mediterranean port of Damietta gave its name to at least ten families or persons in Fustat. Often it is difficult to decide whether a person was a newcomer to the capital or the son of one. Thus, in a document from June 1087, Abu 'l Ḥusayn al-Tinnīsī (from the Mediterranean port of Tinnīs) appears as a well-established representative of merchants in Fustat, but in an earlier letter, showing him in a similar capacity, he is referred to with his full name as Abu 'l Ḥusayn Aaron, son of Yeshuʿā al Tinnīsī. The same ambiguity prevails with regard to persons from countries other than Egypt. In his early years in Egypt, Nahray b. Nissīm of Qayrawān is identified as al-Maghrebī, but in the vast majority of cases this epithet is omitted because Nahray has become a permanent resident of Fustat. The same happens with the often mentioned ʿArūs b. Joseph, who in some letters is called al-Mahdawī (from the Tunisian port al-Mahdiyya), but mostly appears without that epithet. Much research will be necessary before it can be established with even approximate likelihood whether the majority of the Jewish inhabitants of the Egyptian capital represented in the Geniza papers were indigenous or had adopted the city as their home. One wonders how such circumstances of immigration might have affected attitudes to newly acquired residence.

In ancient Israel, where the citizens were mostly agriculturists organized in small urban settlements surrounded by walls, the town was one's "mother" (2 Samuel 20:19); that relationship was assumed and, as a rule, was indissoluble. In the mobile and mercantile world of the Geniza times, the connection of a man with his town should be compared with the bond of marriage. Marriage may be dissolved by divorce, and Muslims, Jews, and even the Christians of Egypt often took recourse to this expediency. Similarly, many Geniza letters speak of the writer's intention to forsake his hometown or report such a step. But once a marriage is successful, it may become a stronger bond than that created by filial piety. The strong attachment of the Geniza man to his waṭan, whether in the sense of his native city or a place chosen for permanent residence, has been illustrated in various ways. In written sources like the Geniza letters these feelings are most vigorously expressed when the writer is away from home and is longing to return.

"Yearning after one's home," al-ḥanīn ila 'l -waṭan, was a well-known theme of ancient Arabic poetry. Al-Jāḥiẓ, the renowned creator of the Arabic essay (d. 869), dedicated a special study to this genre. It is noteworthy that medieval Muslim writers recognize a man's attachment to his hometown as an important sociological factor. The geographer Yāqūt, in describing the town of Zughar (the biblical Zoar) on the southern tip of the Dead Sea, expresses astonishment that anyone could live there given its murderous climate. His answer is one word: waṭan, love of one's native city. (The Geniza letters show that in the eleventh century at least there was another good reason for Zughar's existence. It was an entrepôt for the trade between North Arabia and the Mediterranean.) Ibn Jubayr reports that Muslims returned to Tyre, although the city was in Christian hands at the time and therefore due to be destroyed, and explains their reckless action by man's natural attachment to his native city.

The same motive is found even in official documents. A *dhimmī,* or non-Muslim, from Alexandria has been forced by the adversities of the time to leave his cherished city, his parents and brothers, and to settle in a place where he has commercial dealings with a government office (which one is not stated). He writes that he has been "repeatedly visited by the remembrance of his hometown and longing after it," and he respectfully asks that his affairs be settled so that he may return to Alexandria. Similarly, a Muslim baker petitions the caliph's vizier to permit him to pay a debt in installments so that he may "remain in his native city [waṭan]."

The attachment to one's city is most patently manifested in concern for one's compatriots. *Baladiyya* in modern Arabic means municipality, but in the Geniza letters it designates the feelings and care for the inhabitants of one's town. In a highly interesting document from 1122 an aged man from Tripoli in Libya turns over his possessions to a relative from the same city living in Fustat who, in return, will take care of him until his death. He trusts the man because of "the common bonds of family and city." A Jewish dignitary from the Maghreb, in asking the Egyptian Jewish authorities to inquire about the death of a Maghrebi merchant murdered on his way to Yemen, adds, "He is also my 'landsman' [baladīnā], and I am particularly concerned about him." Such feelings were by no means confined to the members of one's own religion.

While away from home, baladīs stuck together: Maghrebis (meaning mostly persons from Qayrawān and its port city al-Mahdiyya) in Alexandria and Fustat or wherever we find them; newcomers from Hebron and Gaza in Ascalon; people from Tiberias in Acre; people from Aleppo in al-Maḥalla; and groups of pilgrims from Tyre and Tiberias fighting one another in Ramle. Where compatriots are expressly mentioned as groups, a major part of the Geniza correspondence reflects the same urban identity, inasmuch as overseas trade was largely organized in the form of business between inhabitants of a city and expatriates from the same city living abroad. "I did not sell any of the bales that have arrived from Tripoli [in Lebanon]. This can be done here," writes a representative of merchants in Alexandria.

It has often been said that in the traditional Islamic city, a man was attached to his quarter or otherwise close surroundings—not to his city as such. There is much to support this view in the Islamic literature. That sense of local identity is, however, not found in the Geniza correspondence. Perhaps Fustat, where most of the documents come from, was different. A study of the topographic features of Fustat proves that the many quarters and districts mentioned in the Geniza records were not clearly delineated from one another; there was much overlap and seemingly no strict division. The various religions and denominations or sects formed distinct groups, but social separation among them was far less rigid than in the later Middle Ages. Similar observations have been made with regard to Europe. The division of a city into separate administrative units indicates the ever stronger bureaucratic rule of military elites, as was apparent in the Mamluk state and perfected under the Ottomans. It seems also that the population of the capital of Egypt under the Fatimids was considerably smaller than under the Ayyubids and early Mamluks, when the twin cities were united into one large complex with much new space encircled by a wall and defended by a fortress. In short, Fustat was then still a manageable entity, a place where one could feel that one belonged.

In classical Geniza times, Muslims, Christians, and Jews lived in close proximity. There were predominantly Jewish neighborhoods, especially in the vicinity of synagogues, an arrangement made almost necessary by the practice of daily attendance at the public service. Occasionally a contract stipulates or mentions that the property transferred might be transferred solely to a Jew. A Geniza document, in which one party renounces its right of preemption to another, formulates this condition thus: "They may sell the nine and a half shares of the house acquired to any Jew they wish." The house was situated in the Bīr Jabr quarter of Alexandria (which harbored the synagogue of the Babylonians) but was contiguous with the house of a *qissīs,* or Christian clergyman.

In discussing the question of married couples living together, the Talmud states that a husband may not force his wife to follow him from a mid-sized town to a big city, "because life in big cities is hard." Medieval commentators identified the congestion and unhealthiness of cities as the reason for the law; smaller towns, with houses surrounded by gardens and green plots, offered fresh air. (This statement is repeated in a Geniza document with regard to Jerusalem, which was much smaller than Fustat.) The Geniza is replete with stories about illness, and the frequent invitations to places in the Rīf (addressed also to children) seem to show an awareness of the physical hazards of city life. (It should be noted, however, that Fustat-Cairo was not devoid of parks and gardens and other open spaces where one could enjoy fresh air.) Life in a big city was expensive, and not everyone could afford to live there. The city was also a difficult place for a chaste man without a wife. In general, however, complaints about the city are surprisingly rare: one might curse the bad times, but never one's place of domicile. As the Talmud phrases it, life in big cities is hard, but life in villages or in the tents of the nomads is no life at all. Al-Shaʿrānī, the great Muslim mystic, opens his two-volume autobiography with thanks to God "for my 'exodus,' by the Prophet's blessing, from the countryside to Cairo, for God transplanting me from the region of hardship and ignorance to the city of gentleness and knowledge." Similarly, the Geniza man knew well what the city meant for him. It afforded him a measure of security and opportunities for gaining a livelihood; it supplied his religious and other cultural requisites and even some amenities. Above all, he was an eminently social being: "Good company or death" is an ancient Near Eastern maxim. The Geniza man found life in the familiar and variegated environment of the city and in the comforts of his family—the rock of Jewish existence.

PART I

COMMUNAL ORGANIZATION

Christians and Jews living under Islamic rule during the High Middle Ages formed communities of a very specific character. They were not citizens of the principalities in which they lived; rather, they were protected subjects. Their life, property, and honor were safeguarded and the free exercise of their religion was permitted, as long as they paid a poll tax and submitted humbly to the restrictions imposed on them by Islamic law and custom. As they were left to administer their own affairs, they formed a polity not only within the state but beyond the state as well: they owed loyalty to the heads and to the central bodies of their respective denominations, even though these denominations were found in a foreign, and at times even hostile, land. On the other hand, a caliph or sultan ruling over a considerable number of non-Muslims, or even a government official in charge of a city or a smaller locality, might find it advantageous to recognize a representative dignitary or one or more non-Muslim "notables." These representatives would in turn form a connecting link between a subject minority and the ruler and would be held responsible to the ruler whenever convenient. Ecumenical, territorial, and local religious and semireligious authorities of the various denominations thus served, as a rule, also as their official or semiofficial secular heads. In that capacity, they would appoint or confirm the election of local representatives wielding both religious and temporal authority.

The machinery of the state itself was loosely administered; the coercive power of the denominational communities was even weaker. Nevertheless, the cohesiveness of comparatively small groups, living under the pressure of a Muslim majority, and the dedication of their members largely compensated for this weakness. In one important respect—perhaps the most important—the Christian and Jewish communities were even stronger than the diverse Muslims. They had carried over from Hellenistic and Roman times civic forms of communal organization that gave the individual member the opportunity to be active in the life of the congregation. The pre-Christian Jewish congregation grew out of the unique needs of a religion that had abolished sacrifices and offerings everywhere except in the Temple of Jerusalem. Prayer, as well as the study of the Holy Scriptures and the religious law, became a concern for everyone and had to be organized on a local basis. Thus, there arose the Synagogue (lit., the Assembly), the Mother of the Church. When Palestine and most of the Near East came under Greek and, later, Roman domination, the trappings of secular corporation were added to what had originally been a brotherhood of intrinsically religious character. And so, a highly nuanced public institution of enormous vitality developed within both Judaism and Christianity. This asset of a long-standing tradition was enhanced by the rise of a Middle Eastern bourgeoisie in early Islamic times and the effect of that development on the non-Muslim population. Many Christians and Jews belonged to what we may call the middle class of merchants and skilled artisans, of government officials and agents, and to the very prominent medical profession. These well-educated and experienced men took a lively interest in the affairs of their community and competed for the honors bestowed on meritorious members. In addition to this rivalry, there was often a marked tension between the notables, who derived their influential position in the community from their connection with the government or from their riches, and the rank and file, which insisted on having their full share in the decisions affecting the activities of the Church or the Synagogue.

The concerns of the community were manifold. There were questions of religious dogma and ritual practice. Similarly, the upkeep of the houses of worship and the seats of religious learning, as well as the appointment and payment of the various community officials, required much attention. Furthermore, law in those days was personal rather than territorial; an individual was judged according to the law of the denomination to which he belonged. Almost the entire field of family law, as well as cases involving inheritance and commercial transactions, was handled by the courts of the various religious communities. Criminal law was the preserve of the state. Since Muslim juridical organization lacked a public prosecutor, it was left to the officials of the Church or the Synagogue to seek redress when the rights of their coreligionists had been infringed, or when unruly members of their own flock could not be kept in line by the use of whatever powers of coercion were at the disposal of the religious authorities. It is understandable that Christians and Jews often applied to government courts, sometimes even in cases of communal strife or dissensions arising from their own religious tenets or ritual. This turning to government jurisdiction resulted in an interesting interplay of the various laws invoked. In everyday life, however, the ordinary citizen arranged his affairs before the denominational courts, which were more lenient as regards penalties and perhaps less corrupt. All in all, juridical autonomy was one of the most essential aspects of Christian and Jewish life in the countries of Islam during the High Middle Ages.

Finally, the social services—in modern cultures, the responsibility of state and local authorities—had to be provided by the Church and the Synagogue. The education of children whose parents or other relatives were unable to bear the costs, the care of orphans and widows, of the poor and the old, the ill and the disabled, needy travelers and foreigners, and, last but not least, the ransoming of captives were all works of charity, expected to be carried out by each denomination for its own members. This entailed much organization, often transcending the limits of a locality, or province, or even a country, and required a spirit of devotion to the common good, all of which made for closely knit communities despite wide geographical dispersion.

The heyday of the Middle Eastern bourgeoisie of the tenth through the thirteenth century also saw the blooming of communal life among Christians and Jews under Islam. At the end of this period, when the region succumbed to military feudalism and its corollary—a strengthening of the Muslim religious establishment—most of the ancient communal institutions waned or disintegrated altogether. The very detailed information to be gathered from the documents of the Geniza about Jewish public life represents useful comparative material regarding all the numerous and prosperous non-Muslim communities in medieval times. Moreover, it also has some bearing on the history of the Muslim middle class, which has not yet been sufficiently studied. It may well be that a closer scrutiny of all the sources may one day reveal that certain traits of community life, which we are inclined to attribute to the special circumstances of minority groups, were indeed characteristic of the period studied in this book in general. It applies in particular to the question of municipal corporation, to which much attention has been paid.

For Jews, the communal role of religion is well defined in the Book of Deuteronomy 1:13, in which Moses says to the Children of Israel, "Get you wise and capable men, who are well known among your tribes, and I will make them heads over you." It is left to the people to agree on suitable representatives, but the spiritual leader makes the final choice. Referring to this verse, a tenth-century head of a yeshiva, who was also a prominent scholar, wrote a legal opinion that may be summarized as follows:

It has been asked why it is written, "Thou shalt establish judges and officers in all thy gates" (Deuteronomy 1:18)—in the singular and not in the plural. The answer is this: The verse is addressed to the spiritual leader, on whom it is incumbent to appoint judges in Israel, just as Moses has said [citing Deuteronomy 1:13]. Without the appointment by Moses, the election by the people was not valid. Even Joshua's office, although he was chosen by God, was complete only after his investiture by Moses. The same is true of Saul and Samuel. All this proves that installment in an office is incomplete unless it is done by the spiritual leader of any given period. In the absence of such leadership, however, each community is at liberty to make its own choice.

The basic attitude expressed in this responsum dominated Jewish public life during the Geniza period. The local or territorial communities acted largely on their own, but were always eager to receive sanction and approval from some higher spiritual authority.

Modern democracy functions in an extremely formal and legalistic way. The election of representatives or the fixing of a budget, for example, is preceded or accompanied by the exact description of procedures, by the promulgation of laws and bylaws, and by the taking and counting of votes. The society reflected in the Geniza records (much like similar societies not only under Islam but in contemporaneous Christendom as well) was far less legalistically minded, or, rather, it did not feel the need to formulate laws with which to govern itself: it had the Law of God for guidance. The modern historian ought not assume that formal legal procedures were the only way of securing and safeguarding the participation of the populace in the conduct of its affairs. Communal authorities had many ways to make their will prevail. It must nonetheless be conceded that, because of its comparatively limited size, the Jewish community was to a certain extent exceptional. Everyone could be, and normally was, present in the synagogue when public matters were discussed and decided upon. Congregations could and did take action to meet the exigencies of the moment on the basis of discussions involving all the constituents. This ad hoc approach to problems was, nevertheless, common in other medieval religious communities and speaks to the nature of their authority.

ONE

Jewish Ecumenical and Territorial Authorities

The Gaon, or Head of the Academy, and the Head of the Diaspora

The highest authoritative body of the Jewish community was the *yeshiva*, represented by its head, the *gaon*. Yeshiva is conventionally rendered in English as "academy," a convention followed herein; but for the period under discussion, rightly called the gaonic period, the medieval "collegium" would be a more suitable equivalent. The yeshiva combined the functions of a seat of learning, a high court, and a parliament. It wielded absolute authority inasmuch as it interpreted the Law of God, from whose decisions there was no appeal (at least in theory). In view of this, it is strange that there should have been three such Jewish bodies and not one: two in Iraq (Babylonia) and one in Palestine. The Babylonian yeshivas originally had their seats in two different localities, Sura and Pumbedita, but each retained its name after moving to Baghdad, the capital of the Islamic state built by the Abbasid dynast, al-Manṣūr in 762–66 C.E. This tripartite division dated back to the third century C.E., but it should not be compared with the various denominations of the Eastern Church, which also originated in pre-Islamic times. The latter were based on dogmatic schisms, that is, they denied to one another the possession of correct belief, whereas the three Jewish ecclesiastical councils recognized one another as equally orthodox and differed only in matters of ritual and legal usage.

Although the centuries preceding and following the Arab conquest of the Near East are the most obscure in Jewish history, it can be said with reasonable certainty that the Jewish communities of the Byzantine Empire followed the Palestinian academy, while those living under Persian rule were administered from Iraq. The Babylonian yeshivas divided among themselves the provinces of the Persian Empire according to mutual agreement. In early Islamic times, when Egypt and North Africa became colonial areas for immigrants from the East, and when, starting in the tenth century, owing to the beginning of the devastation of Iraq, many members of its middle class moved westward, the geographical division between Easterners and Westerners became entirely blurred. In many towns, there were now two Jewish congregations—Palestinian and Babylonian. This was true not only of cities like Fustat, Alexandria, Damascus, and Ramle but also of smaller towns like al-Maḥalla in Lower Egypt, Baniyas in Palestine, and Palmyra in Syria. In the larger cities, differentiation was made between the large, or main, and the small, or minor, synagogue. We are most probably right in assuming that the main synagogue in these formerly Byzantine cities was Palestinian.

In most of the larger cities there also existed a community of Karaites (lit., Bible readers), a Jewish sect that disapproved of the teachings of the Talmud. They differed from the majority of the Jews, the so-called Rabbanites, that is, the followers of the rabbis or the teachers of the Talmud, as markedly as one branch of the Christian Church from another. As a social group, the Karaites presented a strange picture. On the one hand, many of the richest Jews and many connected with the government belonged to this denomination. On the other, nowhere in Judaism do we find such outspoken condemnation of wealth and the wealthy and of the easy life of the Diaspora as among the early Karaites. These writers preached rigorous asceticism and called for immediate emigration to the Holy Land. This contrast finds full expression in the Geniza documents. In Palestine, militant Karaites and Rabbanites were constantly at loggerheads—a state of affairs that engendered government interference more than once; in Egypt, friendly relations prevailed between the members of the high bourgeoisie belonging to the two denominations. Intermarriage was frequent—indeed so common that the Geniza has preserved not only actual marriage contracts between two such parties but even formularies showing how such mixed marriages should be arranged so as not to offend the religious sensitivities of either husband or wife. The Karaites did not recognize the religious authority of the gaons, since these officials represented rabbinic Judaism, but they felt themselves to be, acted like, and were regarded as full members of the Jewish community. The gaons of Jerusalem and Baghdad freely applied to Karaite notables for help, both pecuniary and other (such as intercession with the government or aid in the settlement of communal strife). That such aid was readily granted is proved by gaonic correspondence in which praise is lavished on meritorious Karaites and God's blessing is called upon them.

It was different with the Samaritans, familiar from the New Testament. This sect, which had already seceded from the main body of Judaism in the time of the Second Temple (indeed, had never fully belonged to it), did not recognize the Jewish religious authorities. Occasionally, an individual Samaritan would turn to a Rabbanite congregation for help or would join it outright. But, generally speaking, references to the Samaritans in our sources are too spotty for a detailed story. With few exceptions, the picture of Jewish communal life drawn from Geniza material is confined of necessity to the Rabbanites, the followers of the yeshivas, and their gaons.

Adherence of a congregation to one of the two Rabbanite rites or, rather, to one of the three yeshivas, was expressed by no means solely by its ritual and law. The yeshiva also had an administrative function. A close relationship existed between the central seats of Jewish learning and the individual communities attached to them. On recommendation by their congregations, the local leaders were appointed by the heads of the academies and were regarded as their deputies. A ḥāvēr, or member of the academy, was usually chosen for the task. Thus, "ḥāvēr" in the Geniza documents is to a large extent equivalent to "rabbi," with the important qualification that, as a rule, he served not only as spiritual leader but also as president of his congregation. During most of the first half of the eleventh century, the leader of the Rabbanite community of Fustat was described as the khalīfa (caliph), or representative, of the gaon of Jerusalem. An official of the synagogue of the Palestinians, writing to the same gaon, constantly uses the term "your synagogue." Similarly, the congregations (the plural is noteworthy) praying in the synagogue of the Babylonians in Fustat, in addressing the head of an academy in Baghdad, refer to their synagogue as "the one that bears the name of your yeshiva." In legal documents of the eleventh century, the court in the synagogue of the Palestinians describes itself as acting on behalf of the High Court of the yeshiva of Jerusalem and its head; we again find the same reference a hundred years later, when the yeshiva itself had moved to Cairo. When a gaon died, the communal officials had to be reinstated by his successor. In short, while it would be incorrect to speak about a Jewish clergy, during the High Middle Ages the Synagogue, not unlike the Church, was organized as an institution marked by well-defined administrative authority and procedures.

Ties linking a congregation to a yeshiva could last for many generations despite the separation of immense distances. A gaon writing from Iraq to Spain in 953 mentions that religious and legal queries sent from Spain to his great-grandfather and to his grandfather (who between them had been in office for forty years) and even to the gaons preceding them were still in his hands. It is no exaggeration to say that in most of the gaonic letters preserved in their entirety the addressees are reminded of the longstanding bonds between the yeshiva and their own forebears or predecessors. Moreover, the Geniza material enables us to actually follow up such relations between a yeshiva and local leaders during two or more generations not only with regard to larger cities, such as Fustat and Alexandria, Qayrawān, and Fez and Sijilmāsa in Morocco, but also smaller towns.

Although the yeshivas recognized the orthodoxy of their sister institutions, they insisted that a community should follow only the guidance of one at any given time: queries should not be submitted simultaneously to two academies. When the scholars of Qayrawān once addressed both Babylonian yeshivas with the same question, they received a stern rebuff. Since decisions depended on legal reasoning, the yeshivas could arrive at different conclusions, with the result that their rulings, instead of serving as a guide, might create confusion and discord. Public appeals, however, were held in one and the same congregation for all three yeshivas simultaneously, with the lion's share going to the one in closest contact with the donors, as evident from various letters. The maintenance of yeshivas, as of other religious or educational institutions, or even of individual scholars, was a matter of religious duty and piety, not solely one of specific indebtedness.

A yeshiva's prestige depended on the scholarship and other personal qualities of the man or the men who stood at its head. When a particularly brilliant and energetic gaon graced a yeshiva, communities might transfer their allegiance to him. References to such occurrences are by no means rare. When assuming office, a gaon would circulate a pastoral letter outlining his own religious and communal program and, where the circumstances called for it, make comments on the situation and needs of the congregation addressed. The first and most tangible bond between the central seats of Jewish higher learning and the widely dispersed communities was the obligation of the communities to contribute to their yeshiva's upkeep. Many gaonic letters contain solicitations, sometimes in the form of urgent appeals or even of more or less veiled threats. Most of the relevant Geniza material comes from the late tenth through the twelfth century, when both Iraq and Palestine were laid waste by almost continuous warfare and other disorders and the yeshivas often found themselves without funds and in distress. A tenth-century gaon writes about Iraq, once the richest of all Islamic provinces: "There is no land in the world in which destitution is as rampant as here in Babylonia." He requests that the addressees, scholars living in Spain, Morocco, and France, send their contributions via the yeshiva's representative in Qayrawān, to its honorary treasurer in Baghdad. The economy of Palestine was in an even more deplorable state, as can be attested from numerous references in the documents.

Glowing descriptions of the splendor of the Babylonian yeshivas also exist, and letters of solicitation were not confined to times of distress. By chance, the Geniza has preserved copies of a dossier of letters sent by a gaon of Baghdad to Yemen and Yamāma, that is, to southwestern and central Arabia. The letters show that the yeshiva had representatives in many small places all over the country, that it was well informed about each of these men, and that the communities sent their donations regularly. They also reveal the different types of donations made, a subject that is detailed in many other letters as well: First, there were fixed yearly contributions that were collected by each community even when, for one reason or other, it was impossible to forward them; we read repeatedly about such voluntary taxes having accumulated over the years. They were called the "fixed charge" or "the fifth"—the same terms used to describe contributions made to Muslim sectarian chiefs. The letters often emphasize that donations to the yeshiva are as meritorious as those made to the Temple of Jerusalem. Indeed, one gets the impression that a very ancient custom persisted in these yearly consignments. In addition, special collections were made in the communities from time to time. Private generosity was another, perhaps no less important, source of income for the yeshivas. In times of danger or distress, as well as on festive occasions such as holidays or family celebrations, vows of donations for the houses of learning were pronounced, and bequests were sometimes conferred upon them. Finally, it was customary to stipulate fines not for the benefit of one of the parties to the contract but for pious purposes, including the maintenance of the yeshivas.

Our documents provide us with considerable information regarding the aid given to the Palestinian academy, first while it had its seat in Jerusalem and then after it had moved to Cairo in 1127. Gifts were made not only to the institution as such, but to its more prominent members individually. They consisted not only of cash but also of precious robes and textiles, oriental spices, and other goods that could easily be converted into money. Letters of thanks have been preserved from which we learn that these presents were sent regularly. It was also expected that each community would address the yeshiva at least once a year. In the early days of their rule over Egypt, the Fatimid caliphs granted substantial stipends to the gaons of Jerusalem.

Most of the letters of the gaons conclude with the admonition that the addressees should submit all their queries to the academy. This standing request had a double purpose. It was intended to assert the prerogative of the yeshiva as the highest authority in all dogmatic, ritual, and legal matters; it also served as a reminder to the local scholars to keep up their studies. The teaching method in the yeshiva required the student's preparation of a given text, on the basis of which he was expected to ask questions that would be discussed in the assembly of the scholars. Since study was not confined to school but was obligatory for a lifetime, the method pursued orally in the yeshiva was later continued in writing. Many of the questions to the gaons that have come down to us are entirely theoretical. They were designed to elucidate the principles of the law rather than to decide actual cases. As such, they should be read with caution by historians arguing that they are (or are not) indicative of juridical practice.

Still, a large share of the questions submitted to the yeshivas were concerned with practical problems—ritual, legal, dogmatic, and communal. These queries were discussed by the member scholars, but as far as we know, unlike the yeshivas in Hellenistic and Roman times, neither the half-yearly conventions of the Babylonian schools, nor the autumnal assemblies on Mount of Olives or other meetings of the Jerusalem yeshiva took formal votes. Certainly, the gaons had to give consideration to the opinions of the other members of the academy and occasionally referred to them. Their responsa were styled, however, in the form of personal, authoritative statements; sometimes heavenly inspiration was claimed ("Thus I was shown from Heaven"). Occasionally, the second in rank, the president of the court, would sign for the gaon, or (in Jerusalem) a reply would be issued jointly by the gaon and the third in rank. But such cases were exceptional and noted as such. Any scholar of recognized standing could be approached for a legal opinion, and the same case could be submitted to several experts, but their responsa were personal judgments, not official resolutions.

The gaons would insist on the strict execution of their decisions, if necessary with the help of the Muslim government. Not elected as a rule, the gaons followed each other according to a complicated system of precedence, the president of the High Court attached to the yeshiva normally being the successor designate. Scions of a number of gaonic families would accede to the office after having served for many years in other capacities. Sometimes, especially in Iraq, meritorious scholars, hailing from as far away as Spain or Morocco, or even a provincial town in Tunisia, would be elevated to the rank of gaon. Naṭrōnay of the Sura yeshiva succeeded his father more than fifty years after his parent's death and after eight other gaons had "ruled" (the term used in the sources) in between. Despite his short term of office (853–58) he has left a large number of responsa, some of which are of lasting importance. Dōsā, the son of the great Saadya Gaon, had to wait seventy-one years until his turn came; he still managed to be in office for four years and was able to report about his good health to his admirers in Qayrawān.

Gaons seem to have groomed their sons for succession by making them clerks (scribes) of the yeshiva, a capacity in which the young men trained themselves in formulating responsa and also had opportunity to correspond with all the leaders and scholars of the communities connected with their fathers. They thus became known to everyone who counted and could prove their mettle within the yeshiva itself. The elaborate system of succession did not always work smoothly, however. Literary sources, as well as the Geniza records, show that sometimes vigorous contests were fought over the gaonate when a vacancy occurred — occasionally even against an incumbent gaon. These contests, albeit sometimes unsavory, with bans and counterbans pronounced and other undignified measures taken, acted in general as a wholesome counterbalance to family rule and clerical sinecures. Scales were often tipped by the lay leaders or by the community at large, whose influence was as pronounced in the Synagogue as in the Eastern Church.

Since the gaon had judicial and administrative authority over the Jewish community, it is natural that the government reserved itself the right to confirm him in his office. When al-Zāhir, the fourth Fatimid ruler of Egypt (1021–36 C.E.), ascended the throne, a gaon of Jerusalem asked his friends in Fustat to obtain for him a letter of installment; the diplomas issued by the preceding three caliphs were still in the possession of the yeshiva. A fragmentary but highly interesting Geniza document in Arabic characters, which was aimed at securing such a letter of installment from the Fatimid government, serves to conclude this survey. The details preserved give a fairly complete idea of the gaon's authority: (1) The gaon has jurisdiction over only the Rabbanite persuasion (to the exclusion of the Karaites and Samaritans). (2) He is the highest authority on religious law and is entitled to expound it in public lectures. (3) In particular, he supervises all matters of marriage and divorce. (4) He is the guardian of the religious and moral conduct of all the members of the community. (5) He has the right to impose or to cancel an excom-

munication. (6) He appoints and dismisses preachers, cantors, and religious slaughterers. (7) He (appoints and) defines the competence of
judges and supervises them, as well as the trustees of the courts (who
were in charge of the property of orphans or litigants confided to them).
(8) His official title is *ra's al-mathība*, head of the academy, and his son
has certain prerogatives. (9) The Rabbanite community owes obedience
to his legal decisions, as well as to his administrative dispositions. (10)
He may delegate his authority over a certain city or country to any
person chosen by him.

While the gaonate was a force that permeated the whole fabric of life
of the Jewish community during the Geniza period, the secular head of
the Jews, the so-called head of the Diaspora, whose seat was in Baghdad,
had only limited importance. Under Roman and Persian rules, respectively, a patriarch acted in Palestine as the representative of the Jews,
and an exilarch, or "head of the Diaspora" performed the same function
in Iraq. Both claimed lineage from King David. The former office was
abolished by the Byzantine emperors early in the fifth century, but the
office of the Babylonian exilarch continued to exist and even attained
new splendor under the caliphs. The Muslims, like the Jews and Christians before them, regarded David, the reputed author of the Book of
Psalms, as one of the great prophets, and, with their respect for lineage,
ranked the scions of such an ancient and noble line very highly, according to one reference, even above the *katholikos*, or head of the Nestorian
Church. By the time of the Geniza records, however, the rule of the
Abbasid caliphs had become confined de facto to a few districts in Iraq—
insofar as they ruled at all—while the homage paid to them by Muslim
rulers theoretically under their control was of a purely honorary character. Similarly, the head of the Diaspora exercised direct control over
only a part of the Jewish communities in the lands of the eastern caliphate; in the other regions represented in the Geniza, Jewish leaders
accepted his suzerainty, if at all, only de jure. As far as they were concerned, the dispensing of honorific titles seems to have been his main
function.

In this period of the primacy of the yeshivas an exilarch could attain
ecumenical status only when he was a scholar of rank or assumed outright the presidency of a yeshiva. It is hardly necessary to mention that
the office of the exilarch was occasionally hotly contested. Since the
caliph reserved for himself the right to confirm the appointment, it was
natural that the Jewish courtiers and higher government officials had a
say in the matter. The family of the exilarchs, which had been prominent
for so long a time, was large and ramified; it is not surprising that some

of its more ambitious members tried to make capital of their dignity as princes (Heb. *nāsī*) of the House of David. We find them everywhere, often trying to assume authority, even in faraway Yemen. In 1051, one particularly gifted Davidite, Daniel b. Azarya, became head of the Palestinian academy; a few decades later his son David tried to establish an exilarchate in Egypt, extending over the whole Fatimid empire. It is characteristic of this state of affairs that Daniel b. Azarya himself, in a pastoral letter, emphasizes that no member of the House of David, and not even of his own household, was authorized to hold any public office except when appointed by himself. In official documents written in Fustat in 1088 and the subsequent years, David b. Daniel was given the title "the great nāsī, and the nāsī of all [the diasporas of] Israel." By the end of the twelfth century we find nāsīs in Cairo, Alexandria, and the Egyptian countryside. Others had their seat in Damascus, Aleppo, and Mosul. Although they sometimes received emoluments from the community, the nāsīs played no significant role in communal affairs, except when they were scholarly persons of renown.

Be that as it may, the Jewish community, as it appears to us through the Geniza records, had more than one communal authority, and these authorities were dependent on their followers in different ways. The allegiance of a congregation to a gaon and other leaders was expressed in public prayer for their welfare inserted into the service. These prayers were by no means mere formularies but contained specific references, for example, to the gaon's family or to his foes; the Church, and later, Islam, followed a similar procedure. When a Coptic priest ceased mentioning the patriarch's name at the Holy Eucharist, he demonstrated that he no longer recognized him as legitimately installed; the Muslim Friday service was the occasion for making a city's loyalties known. The yeshivas, on their side, held public prayers for the welfare of dedicated community leaders at the holy places in Jerusalem or the sacred shrines in Iraq. These prayers had a political connotation as well, for they indicated who was regarded as the legitimate local representative of the gaon. Moreover, any person included in these prayers was mentioned by the official or honorary title or titles conferred upon him by the yeshiva. The public prayer was thus the occasion for the formal conveyance of honors or privileges.

Besides the synagogue service, there were many other occasions for the expression of allegiance to an ecumenical or territorial authority. At a public lecture it was customary for the lecturer to open with an exordium in which he would take permission from the authority to whom he owed loyalty, the reason being that only the latter had the right to give an authoritative explanation of the Holy Scriptures. At weddings and banquets, a similar symbolic request for permission to say grace was pronounced, since the gaon, if present, would have had the honor of giving the concluding benediction. Finally, scores of documents have been found written "in the name of" the leader or leaders to whom communal allegiance was due, for the judges or other persons issuing the documents were regarded as deputies of the individual in power or the institution in place at the time. The common term for all these various expressions of loyalty—whether in the synagogue, at a banquet, or in the courtroom—was *reshūth*, literally, "taking permission." This custom, while conducive to creating cohesiveness, could lead to confusion in times of discord, as is clear from various documents.

Even a cursory reading of the correspondence of the gaons reveals the diocesan organization of the Jewish community. The gaons insisted that all contributions be sent to them through an acknowledged leader in charge of a district or province, that all letters to the yeshiva likewise be forwarded solely through him, and that he be revered and honored and his instructions followed without hesitation. In letters to southern Arabia, Jews in places hundreds of miles nearer Baghdad than San'a, the capital of Yemen, were advised to send their donations and letters solely through the judges in the latter city. Similarly, even queries addressed to the yeshiva by prominent local scholars were scrutinized and screened by the district authority before being forwarded to their final destination.

Two letters written by a ḥāvēr who headed communities in northern Syria strikingly illustrate the myriad duties incumbent on a district authority: He appointed local judges and other community officials, dealt with all public affairs (internal and external), acted both as judge and religious leader, and had the responsibility of collecting all the dues of the yeshiva. These functions were not always combined in one person. The example of Qayrawān, about which we are particularly well informed, shows that the district representation of a yeshiva could be tripartite: a public figure, usually connected with the government, whose influence was strong enough to ensure generous donations and who watched over the proper conduct of communal affairs; a treasurer, who did the actual collecting and forwarding of the sums donated; and a prominent scholar, who presided over the local court and conducted and partly supervised the legal and religious (as distinct from the business) correspondence with the yeshiva.

Whether this diocesan organization developed spontaneously, whether it was influenced by the model of the Church, or whether it derived from an ancient, pre-Christian aspect of Jewish community life, are questions that lie outside the scope of this book. It stands to reason, however, that the institution of territorial heads of the Jewish communities, discussed in the following section, grew at least partly out of the diocesan organization of the gaonate.

The Territorial Head of the Jewish Community: The Nagid, or Ra'īs al-Yahūd

There is hardly a public institution about which the Geniza has provided so much new material as that of the head of the Jewish community under the Fatimid and Ayyubid regimes. There is also hardly one that has been so thoroughly misrepresented by modern historical research. That is because of the role of the *nagid,* as the territorial head of the Jewish community was called in Hebrew, was described by the Jewish authors of the sixteenth and seventeenth centuries in terms suited to the period immediately preceding the abolition of the nagidate in 1517. Their accounts were corroborated by those of Muslim authors writing in late Mamluk times. This double testimony was so impressive that most historians dealing with the subject were inclined to interpret the new material emerging from the Cairo Geniza in the light of the later developments reflected in the literary sources. Characteristic in this respect is this statement of Jacob Mann, the greatest authority of his time on Geniza research: "From the Fatimid regime (969) to the conquest of the country by the Turks (1517) Egyptian Jewry was strongly organized under the nagid, who was the chief of the Rabbanites, Karaites and Samaritans alike, recognized by the government as Ra'īs al-Yahūd [the head of the Jews]."[1]

In reality the situation was far more complicated. Nagid does not appear as a title in Egypt until about 1065, almost a hundred years after the Fatimid conquest, and the term was not in continuous use even after its inception. Only from the beginning of the thirteenth century did the Hebrew title nagid become permanently attached to that of the *ra'īs al-Yahūd.* In general, we have to distinguish between the title and the office, and, as far as the office is concerned, we have to keep in mind that the combined task of representing the Jewish community before

1. *Texts and Studies in Jewish History and Literature,* 2 vols. (Cincinnati, 1931–1935), 1:394.

the government and that of exercising the community's highest legal and religious authority developed in Egypt under very specific historical circumstances. Disregard of these considerations led to a confusion about this most important institution that still prevails in Jewish historiography.

Nagid is a biblical word, usually translated as "prince" or "leader." As a title, it is a constituent of such high-sounding phrases as "Prince of the Diaspora," "Prince of the People of the Lord [or, of Israel]," or "Prince of Princes." As far as we can ascertain, the first to have borne this title was Abraham b. 'Aṭā, physician in attendance to Badīs and his son al-Muʿizz, the Muslim rulers of Tunisia and some adjacent territories during the first half of the eleventh century. Abraham b. 'Aṭā, used his influential position to protect his coreligionists in a period that witnessed a general increase in fanaticism and religious disorders in that country. Moreover, he was a staunch supporter of the Jewish seats of learning in Baghdad. The title nagid was not entirely new; it had already been given by a Babylonian yeshiva to a prominent lay member (a member, however, of a family of gaons) around 900. It was common practice that titles borne first by dignitaries of, or connected with, the academies of Baghdad or Jerusalem were later on bestowed also on meritorious persons abroad. Thus the title "prince of the Diaspora," as a designation for the leader of the Jewish community of a large province, was by no means created in opposition to the office of the exilarch, the "head of the Diaspora," but grew organically from the way in which the yeshivas were used to confer honorary epithets.

Ibn 'Aṭā's, successor, Jacob b. Amram, is called prince of the Diaspora in a legal document written in Fustat in 1041/42 but is simply addressed as nagid in letters—even official letters. As known to us, his activities resemble in many respects those of the later Egyptian nagids at their height. He was a powerful protector of his flock, a stern keeper of law and morals in the community, an administrator of justice whose impartiality was famous, and a shield for the weak. The scholars ate at his table and were honored by him with embroidered silk robes (the embroidery probably contained the nagid's name—like the robes of honor bestowed by Muslim rulers or by the Jewish exilarchs in Babylonia in pre-Islamic times). He personally attended to lawsuits between prominent members of the community, trying to bring about reconciliation, while the rabbinical courts dealt with the strictly juridical issues of the cases. Nevertheless, he and the various other figures designated as nagid in the pre-Mamluk sources shared communal leadership with the other figures previously discussed.

The office of the ra'īs (or *rayyis*, as the word is spelled in the Geniza records) is described by the Muslim scholars of the fourteenth and fifteenth centuries as corresponding to that of the patriarch of the Christians. He was to be selected from the Rabbanite majority, but was to represent the Karaite and Samaritan minorities as well. His function was to unite the Jews and hold them together as legal authority and judge in conformity with their laws and customs. In particular, he had to watch over the proper procedures in matters of marriage and divorce as well as of excommunication. He was responsible for law and order in the community and also for the observation of the restrictions imposed by the Islamic state on its non-Muslim subjects. The wearing of discriminatory badges and the prohibition on erecting new houses of worship are especially emphasized. The rayyis was to be pious and learned and a man of absolute integrity. He was expected to be able to expound the Hebrew Scriptures and was entitled to do so at whatever synagogue he chose. He was appointed by the government after the community had agreed upon the candidate acceptable to it.

Almost all modern historians who have discussed this office seem to assume that it was created by the Muslim successor states in order to make the Jewish communities within them independent of authorities outside their own jurisdiction. According to this theory, the Alid Fatimids did not want their Jewish subjects paying allegiance to the head of the Diaspora in Sunnite Baghdad; when Tunisia was breaking away from the Fatimids, a separate nagid was immediately installed there. Such assumptions conform with the modern idea of the nation-state but disregard the medieval deference to supraterritorial communities based on religion. One searches in vain for a Muslim source that supports these assumptions; the facts reflected in the Geniza records point to the contrary. The strongest bonds of cooperation existed between the Jews living within the borders of the Fatimid Empire and the Jewish academies of Baghdad, and as far as we have documents about the appointment of the heads of the community in Egypt, we see that they were installed by and received honorary titles from the head of the Diaspora, who had his seat in Iraq, and even more from the yeshivas there. The origin of the office of the nagid, like that of the Christian patriarchs with which it was compared by the Muslim authors, is to be sought in developments taking place within the community. It is of course true that everywhere, even in small towns, the Muslim authorities found it convenient to recognize a prominent member of a protected community as its representative. But this was simply a requirement of administrative expediency, not a question of independence from Baghdad. This is borne out by documents indicating that Jews of the Fatimid regime still bore allegiance to the Jewish religious authorities situated in Abbasid Iraq and in Jerusalem.

On the subject of the appointment of a rayyis, it would be inconsistent with the spirit of the age to expect formal elections, followed immediately by an official installation by the government; appointments were far less formal but far more intricate. The rayyis had to seek support from three different sources: the Jewish local and territorial communities that would accept him as their leader; the Jewish ecumenical authorities who would acknowledge him and confer on him a new name and some additional honorary titles; and, finally, the government that was to confirm him officially in his position. The sequence in which these three were obtained depended entirely on the circumstances. Appointment was normally for a lifetime. The office of the rayyis was partly a political one, however, and therefore exposed to the vicissitudes of politics—both state politics and those of the Jewish community.

The rayyis served as the highest juridical authority of the community. It was he who appointed the chief judges, while the appointments of the other community officials were made by the latter with his approval and in certain cases by him directly. As the many relevant Geniza records prove, the appointment and supervision of the community officials outside the capital must have been one of the main concerns of the nagids, as a large segment of the Jewish population was still living in small towns or villages. The administrative districts, although fixed by custom, were by no means rigidly defined. Thus, each new appointment required a careful description of the appointee's district. Encroachments by ambitious community leaders, or *muqaddams*, must have been common. Furthermore, more than one functionary was normally in office in one and the same place; in this respect as well the exact definition of everyone's duties and prerogatives required the nagid's attention. Similarly, the relation between the judges in charge of a district and local heads had to be regulated. There were sometimes complaints about the scholarly competence of the persons appointed or their capacity to guide the community. Often we read about officials leaving their posts because they were inadequately paid or because payments were in arrears; others left in the wake of communal strife. It seems to have been the nagids' policy to persuade the congregations to take their former leaders back. We read about visits of the highest Jewish dignitary to communities outside the capital and even of his spending the High Holidays in one such community and leading the congregation during a part of the service. This was probably regarded by the community as the bestowal of a high honor.

Although the rayyis was the supreme judge, he normally did not give judgments in person. Anyone dissatisfied with the handling of his case by a local court could submit a petition to the rayyis (often through a high-standing person) whereupon he would instruct the court, local community, or both on how to deal with the complaint. This type of legal procedure pervades the whole fabric of community life as it appears to us in the Geniza papers. The same form of juridical organization prevailed in the world of Islam. A party who felt wronged would apply to the caliph (or to a local ruler serving at the caliph's behest) for a rescript in his favor, whereupon a qāḍī, or judge, would deal with the matter in the spirit of the caliph's ruling. It is difficult to say whether the nagid's position in the judiciary system derived from Muslim influence or whether he had simply adopted the role of the gaon, whom he had replaced in the leadership of the Jewish community. Since pre-Christian times, the head of the yeshiva was seconded by the president of the High Court, and, as we learn from the Geniza, the gaon followed the same procedure of giving instructions to the court or courts under his jurisdiction, as was later done by the nagid with regard to the judges he himself appointed. It is not implausible that both the Jewish and Muslim procedures were inspired by Roman precedents.

The nagid's coercive power stemmed from his personal position of influence with the Muslim state. Both the community as a whole and its individual members needed him to intervene on their behalf whenever they were in trouble with the authorities. He was regarded as the savior of a people with little power. He could, as a matter of course, punish recalcitrant offenders with a temporary ban or with total excommunication, but as long as the nagid was held in high esteem by the government, there was little need to invoke this extreme means of disciplinary action. His hayba, that is, the respect paid him, was his most effective instrument of ruling. Only in the later centuries, when the position of the protected minorities—and with it, that of their leaders—had deteriorated irreparably, was the threat or punishment of excommunication invoked even as regards small transgressions.

No police or prisons were at the disposal of the head of the Jews. Whenever we read about raqqāṣīn, or policemen, sent by a nagid, the context implies that they were members of the state police (which also contained some Jews). Normally it was the nagid who ordered or gave permission to turn over a coreligionist to the authorities. Given the legal position of the Jews as a protected minority, this was almost an act of extradition. The nagid's role as peacemaker in his community was not confined to matters of a purely legal character. He had to occupy himself with a wide variety of disputes, which he tried to settle by mediation,

by instructions to his officials, or when necessary, through the intervention of the Muslim authorities.

Matters of religious dogma and ritual are scarcely mentioned in the
nagids' correspondence. To be sure, the responsa of Moses Maimonides
and his son Abraham are filled with religious matters, but they were
often approached in their capacity as great scholars rather than as rayyis
al-Yahūd. In any case, no rayyis had absolute authority in the interpretation and application of the law. After having rebuked the persons concerned for mishandling a case, Abraham Maimonides writes in a responsum, "If, however, anyone, and were it the youngest of students,
would prove that my decision is wrong, I shall accept the correct ruling."
The interpretation of the law was a matter of knowledge and legal reasoning, not of any official authority.

The above-quoted responsum dealt with a case of family law. Matters
of marriage and divorce, as well as of alimony, wills, and guardianships,
were the particular prerogative of the nagid, as is also stated in the Muslim handbooks of administration. No foreigner or other person of uncertain family status could marry without a permit certified by the nagid.
Although, according to religious law, a Jewish marriage or divorce did
not require the presence of a religious authority, again and again it is
emphasized in the Geniza records that only officials installed by the
nagid for that purpose were entitled to perform these functions. As
protector of the weak, we often find the nagid attending to family disputes in person. The material preserved seems to indicate this to have
been his most time-consuming occupation. He was the judge of the
widows and father of the orphans, the hope of the poor and the shield
of the oppressed. Alongside serious matters, such as the neglect or desertion of wives and children, the ransoming of captives, or the education of orphans, many petty requests were submitted to him: A poor
woman wishes to have a new veil for the holidays and asks the nagid to
appoint a man to make a collection for this purpose. "To whom shall I
apply, if not to you?" she writes, as if she were herself uncertain about
troubling the nagid for such a trifle. It is perhaps appropriate to keep
in mind that pious Muslim rulers showed the same indefatigable consideration for small requests addressed to them.

Many petitions submitted to the rayyis contained complaints of oppression by government officials or other torts for which redress by the
government was so sought. With this, we approach another field of the
rayyis's activities (most characteristically neglected in the Muslim descriptions of the office): his role as protector of his coreligionists.
Whether in a large city like Alexandria, or in a small town in the Delta,

the nagid was expected to act against rapacious officials—either by intervening with the central government, or by talking things over with the local authorities on the occasion of a visit. When a Jew was murdered and his belongings taken away, it was not the police who were entrusted with the matter, but the rayyis, who was asked to see to it that the lost goods were retrieved. When pirates from Tripoli in Lebanon captured some prominent persons, it was the rayyis who had to approach the commander of the imperial fleet in order to rescue the captives. Muslim sources emphasize that the duty of the rayyis was to protect the Muslims from Jews—to see to it that the discriminatory laws against non-Muslims, such as wearing distinctive signs on one's clothing, were observed. This again reflects a later and more religiously restrictive time; we read in the Muslim chronicles that the Coptic patriarch and the head of the Jews solemnly undertook to go so far as to excommunicate any member of their respective communities not complying with the discriminatory laws. In the records from the classical Geniza period, however, we find no trace of such measures originating from the rayyis. At most, he warns against any actions that could lead to friction with people of other faiths.

It has often been stated that the rayyis was in charge of the collection of the *jāliya*, the poll tax incumbent on non-Muslims, an assertion not borne out by the extensive Geniza material bearing on the subject. The poll tax was normally collected by government officials, either directly or through tax farmers. In some respects, however, the jāliya presented a major concern to the rayyis. The old rule of Muslim law that indigent persons were exempt from this tax was no longer observed in Geniza times; those unable to pay were imprisoned (and given the conditions in the prisons, this was often tantamount to a death sentence), or otherwise maltreated. It was up to the community and above all the rayyis to guard the poor from that predicament. It seems also that the rayyis, like any other communal leader, was occasionally consulted regarding the estimate of a person's financial capacity. Finally, in the case of a poor community, the rayyis sometimes must have been responsible for arranging the payment of its members' taxes by coming to an agreement with those able to sustain the burden of taxation. Sometimes, it was necessary to raid other public resources. For example, in the fourteenth century, when Fustat had become a desolate place, the nagid ruled at one point that the tax would be paid temporarily out of monies set aside for orphans and widows. At times, it was deemed necessary to force communities to draw deeply on their meager resources. Another letter by the same nagid to that impoverished community warns, "No one from this office will come out to you this time. The tax collection will be carried out by the director of finance, the muqaddam [who ordinarily helped with the estimate], and the government banker. So let every one of you be prepared to pay the tax and the fines [for the arrears]."

One wonders what material benefits a rayyis derived from his office. As in most other matters, we should not expect to find any fixed and formal arrangements; everything depended on the personal position of the community leader. If the rayyis was a physician and a courtier, as indeed most of them happened to be, he would receive a pension from his great patron and probably remunerations from his other patients. Like any affluent person, he would possess land, from which he derived additional income. Several documents to this effect have been preserved; in one, it is alleged that a nagid possessed large stores of grain in a village at a time of famine. As it was usual to send presents to scholars, a nagid would be honored in the same way, and so, incidentally, was the Christian patriarch. When the leader of the community was also head of a school (as was the case with the gaon Maṣlīaḥ and Moses Maimonides), he would receive substantial donations destined for himself and his pupils. A collection made by the Tunisian Jews in Egypt for their nagid (who had gone into exile) was in all likelihood an extraordinary measure aimed at assisting a man in distress, for that nagid had been famous for his riches and his lavish generosity.

As a rule, the rayyis levied no taxes for his benefit on the community. The exilarch at Baghdad did derive fixed revenues from the community, such as fees for animals slaughtered, marriage contracts, and bills of divorce (as reported by an Arabic writer of the ninth century), but nothing of the kind is known thus far for the Egyptian rayyis. Maimonides' insistence on the postulate that public office should be honorary was not mere theory: That he himself suffered under that burden is known from his letters. But he served as head of the Jews for comparatively short periods. His son Abraham, who did so during most of his life, was destroyed by the burden of office: The threefold task of nagid, physician to the court (which included also regular tours at the government hospital), and religious reformer (given to extensive writing) proved too much for him. He died at fifty one, a relatively young age, his important and much-needed work of religious reform (as well as his literary magnum opus) uncompleted. The history of the nagids of the Mamluk period, descendants of Abraham Maimonides and others, falls outside the scope of this book. The Geniza material for these nagids has not yet been studied in full.

TWO

The Local Community

Name and General Character

The mainstay of the Jewish faith and people was a local community, centered in one or two synagogues. It was called the holy congregation, a postbiblical version of "a kingdom of priests and a holy nation" (Exodus 19:6). This designation was already in use in pre-Islamic times and continued to be used during the entire Geniza period—from the few early Hebrew papyri preserved, down to our latest documents written in Arabic. No differentiation was made in this respect between congregations in important cities, such as Jerusalem, Fustat, or Alexandria, and those of the smaller towns in Palestine, Egypt, or Asia Minor. Occasionally, high-sounding epithets, such as "the assembly of God," were employed. Often, a congregation is referred to simply as "Israel," because the local unit represented the whole body of the community.

There was a strong feeling that next to God, as revealed in His Law, it was the people that wielded the highest authority. Bearers of dignities regarded themselves as installed by God and the community at large. Thus, in theory, the community as a whole, not only the leading notables, bore responsibility for its well-being. A man who considered himself wronged could and did appeal to Israel, that is, the local congregation, when it assembled for prayer. This was a custom of deep significance for both legal procedure and life in the synagogue. Local communities acted as judge, or rather as jury, particularly when they were small and without a spiritual leader of higher rank.

Marriage contracts were regularly superscribed with good wishes for the congregation, in addition to those for the young couple (but, strange as it may sound, never for their families). Often we find letters with the community addressed first, while the spiritual and secular leaders are mentioned second or only in the introduction. The practice was followed even when the congregation addressed included a renowned rabbinical authority and a nagid. Such letters were written with utmost care in both script and style and were prefaced by long exordia praising the piety, justice, charity, and learning of the community. As a rule, the various groups of which a congregation was composed were mentioned individually.

An ecumenical or territorial authority, while instructing his representatives about specific matters, such as help for a needy person, a legal case, or an appointment, would extend greetings to the community, often specifying the various groups and classes of people of which it consisted. Everyone, women and children not excluded, was regarded as belonging to the congregation. In accordance with prevailing notions of decency, women were rarely mentioned expressly but referred to in such general terms as "the rest of the people." There are, however, letters in which the public spirit of women (and girls) is lauded together with — or before — that of the men of a community.

Local variations, as well as considerations of style, made for differences in the units described as forming a congregation and in the order in which they appear. The following list presents a cross section from the material preserved: (1) judges and scholars in general; (2) the elders, usually meaning "the renowned elders," that is, the acknowledged community leaders; (3) other notables, normally persons bearing one or more honorific titles; (4) cantors; (5) *parnāsīm*, the honorary or paid officials in charge of the public welfare services; (6) heads of the families (usually praised for their generous giving); (7) teachers and scribes; (8) young men ("in the splendor of their appearance"); (9) the rest of the community, minors and "of age" (i.e., children and women). Sometimes, important professional groups, such as government officials, physicians, representatives of merchants, or the merchants in general, would be mentioned separately.

Unlike Roman law, Jewish (and Muslim) law did not recognize public bodies as legal entities. Even the idea of formal membership in the congregation was alien to the times. Therefore, strictly speaking, a statute or resolution was binding only on persons who had either signed it or attended its solemn promulgation (making a symbolic act of *qinyān*, or purchase, which validated private transactions as well); such at least was the legal opinion of Moses Maimonides and his court, an opinion preserved in the Geniza together with the statute to which it referred. Consequently, documents often are issued not in the name of the community as such, but by the undersigned individuals in their capacity as witnesses either to the unanimous agreement of the whole congregation or to the fact that only those specified were in accord with the contents.

By size and function, three types of local communities can clearly be discerned. The highest juridical and religious authorities had their seats in the imperial and provincial capitals, and only in those major urban centers was a thorough religious and secular education available. Everything was decided there. In effect, the capital was the country—in Egypt at any rate. In Palestine, Ramle, the administrative center, shared certain privileges with Jerusalem, the Holy City. In Tunisia, the seaport al-Mahdiyya stood in a similar relationship to Qayrawān, which it displaced after the sack of 1057.

Second in rank were the communities in maritime cities of larger size, such as Alexandria, Damietta, Ascalon, or Tyre, or in inland district centers, such as al-Mahalla or Minyat Ziftā in the Nile Delta, or Qūs in Upper Egypt. These centers were linked in part to the communities of the third type, located in the numerous smaller localities, which, as a rule, were unable to maintain full panels of religious and communal officials and thus relied on the larger town situated nearby. The geographical boundaries and administrative competence of the various district authorities were by no means static but had to be reapportioned and adapted to the personalities in charge and to the whims of public opinion.

Congregation versus Community

We are accustomed to thinking of a congregation as a group centering in a house of worship; "community" we generally understand as the larger body of people living in a town or district. This ambiguity is unavoidable because Hebrew qāhāl and Arabic jamā'a, the terms used in our sources to indicate congregation, retain both meanings. There was, nevertheless a real distinction between the congregation and the larger community. There existed in most larger towns two synagogues, one Palestinian and one Babylonian. Originally, these congregations had been formed mainly by persons coming from the countries of the former Byzantine Empire, on the one hand, and those from the land of the Eastern caliphate, on the other. By the time of the High Middle Ages, adherence to one of the two rites had become largely a matter of personal taste and decision. As a result, the two synagogues had to compete with each other for new members. The Geniza reveals to us in detail how this was done. The Babylonians, with their centuries-old experience of soliciting funds for their renowned seats of learning, had the gaons of Baghdad shower extravagant honorary titles on the many foreigners who flocked to the capital of Egypt. The Palestinians, albeit reluctantly, followed suit. They boasted of having the most precious Bible codices (some of which are still preserved in libraries), as well as magnificent Torah scrolls and beautiful sitting carpets. In addition, they pointed out that their service was more attractive: their Scripture readings were so much shorter than those of the Babylonians and were chanted by boys, so that parents who were eager to have their children participate actively in the service would certainly prefer the congregation of the Palestinians. On the other hand, the Babylonians tried to impart splendor to their service by entrusting the Scripture readings to excellent cantors.

By the end of the twelfth century, the Babylonian rite (that of the Diaspora) had been accepted almost everywhere. When Moses Maimonides became established in Egypt, he tried, for the sake of unity, to abolish the peculiarities of the Palestinians' rites altogether, but he was not successful. On the contrary: at the time of his son and successor Abraham, the specific customs of the Palestinian synagogue of Fustat were reconfirmed by a solemn pact.

It is natural that such competition would sometimes lead to friction between the leaders of the congregations or even between their members. But according to our documents, the two congregations appear throughout the classical Geniza period as belonging to one local community. For example, the public chest was administered in common. As a rule, donations were made and fines stipulated or imposed for the benefit of the two synagogues in equal shares. Objects such as books, Torah scrolls, lamps, carpets, and precious textiles were donated to the individual synagogues, but the far larger gifts destined for the social services (including the emoluments of community officials) were pooled for the benefit of the local community as a whole. Many accounts show that current expenditure was made for the two synagogues together and often by one and the same official. Property dedicated to charitable purposes was described as forming a part of the *qōdesh* (the holy), in Arabic *aḥbās al-Yahūd*, both meaning Jewish pious foundations. Even when the individual synagogue buildings were affected, as with the renovations undertaken after their demolition under the caliph al-Ḥākim, a united appeal was made, and the funds collected were distributed in equal shares.

Cooperation was not entirely confined to the Rabbanite community. A public fast and united appeal, during which Rabbanites and Karaites were expected to convene in one house of worship, is referred to in one letter, and reports about joint collections actually carried out have been preserved. The title "pride of the two denominations" was given to a notable who, like many others, extended his generosity to both Karaites and Rabbanites.

Moreover, although the Palestinian and Babylonian congregations had their own chief judges and juridical courts, in more important matters the two chief judges and their assistants sat on the same bench. The appointments of puisne judges outside the capital were regularly made by the two in common. In particularly delicate litigations, such as one concerned with a large inheritance, the chief Jewish judge of Cairo would also be asked to participate and preside, if his rank at the yeshiva was higher than that of his colleagues. These orderly procedures operated in full from the time of the nagid Mevōrākh (ca. 1065) forward, but the tendency to have only one supreme juridical authority in a town is evident from the earliest documents at our disposal. Even the beadles, who by their very task were attached to one building, had functions related to the community as a whole.

Finally, the two congregations would gather in a synagogue or other place to listen to a guest preacher or at some other special occasion. We read about such gatherings regarding various cities; occasionally Karaites would also participate. Benjamin of Tudela (thirteenth century) reports that in Fustat the two congregations would join in prayer on Pentecost (the holiday celebrating the promulgation of the Ten Commandments on Mount Sinai) and on the Feast of the Rejoicing of the Law (when the yearly lections were completed and a new round started). According to Benjamin, this was a custom fortified by statute.

In view of this situation, it is not surprising that we find Geniza letters issued in the name of, or addressed to, "the community" of Fustat or of other cities, even though these cities contained more than one congregation. A noble woman in distress writes simply to the *qāhāl* of Fustat. The same term is used in two documents with regard to Alexandria, which also housed a Palestinian and a Babylonian congregation. We have letters sent by the joint congregations of Fustat (one as well by the congregations of Cairo), by those of Alexandria, of Ramle, and of Tyre; others are addressed to the joint congregations of al-Mahdiyya and Constantinople. A statute promulgated by the congregations of the Rabbanites in Fustat has been preserved in the Geniza.

It is doubtful whether the replacement of the congregation by the local community is to be regarded as a sign of transition from a hierarchical to a democratic way of public organization. Both elements, the hierocratic and the democratic, were present in the Palestinian and Babylonian yeshivas. The trend to communal democracy is to be explained by specific historical circumstances. By the beginning of the eleventh century the conflict between the two yeshivas had lost most of its acrimony. The strife around the fixing of the calendar, which was as severe in the Synagogue as it had been in the Church, had died down. A son of a Palestinian gaon could now study under a gaon of Baghdad. Honorific titles conferred by a Babylonian yeshiva were publicized in Palestine with the permission of the gaon of Jerusalem. The Palestinian authorities were quoting the writings of the Babylonian yeshivas as frequently as their own, while graduates of the Babylonian yeshivas living in Egypt were eager to acquire a diploma from Jerusalem. The differences in ritual still gave occasion to bickering, but these are recorded as exceptional cases.

On the other hand, the eleventh century was fraught with emergencies calling for concerted action. It began with the demolition of the houses of worship under the Fatimid caliph al-Ḥākim. There followed a long series of calamities that affected the country as a whole, with the minority groups, as usual, no less hard hit than the Muslims. The Muslim sources have much to tell us about civil war, famine, and the breakdown of public order, resulting even in the pillage of the caliph's palaces. The lists of synagogue furnishings from this period testify that the houses of worship were not spared. In addition, we have direct testimony to the same effect. Events outside Egypt also required that the community exert itself for the common good. As a result of the bedouin invasions of Tunisia and the Seljuk incursions into Syria and Palestine, and, later, the massacres perpetrated by the Crusaders in the Holy Land and elsewhere, refugees were pouring into Egypt. Moreover, the neverending need to ransom prisoners of war or persons captured by pirates presented a major challenge during most of the period.

The newly created office of the nagid contributed much to furthering unity within the larger community. As a matter of fact, the replacement of the congregation by the local community was nothing more than a return to the situation prior to the schism between Jews in the eastern and western regions of the Islamic world. In Talmudic times, our sources speak of no other communal organization except that of the sons of a town, that is, of coreligionists living in one place.

Plenary Assembly and Representative Bodies

Each community or congregation was headed by an official approved by a Jewish ecumenical or territorial authority and accredited by the local governor or chief of police. His authority, although backed by the state and the highest representatives of the synagogue, was by no means absolute. He had to have the approval, confidence, and cooperation of the people; otherwise he faced dissent and even dismissal. With his appointment the community granted him obedience, but it was never forgotten that he was its servant. When the two synagogues of Alexandria were about to choose a new spiritual leader, first the community was consulted about the prospective candidate (who was known in the city), and, after they had agreed, some twenty-five elders convened to decide how to proceed in the matter.

Plenary deliberations of the community were not held solely to decide matters of major importance; they were common even with regard to cases of civil law involving only a few persons. The custom of addressing letters dealing with such cases to the community as a whole was not merely a matter of courtesy. They were actually read out in public, as we learn both from requests made to that effect and from reports that it had been done. Sometimes letters that by their very nature were confidential (for example, the opinion of a higher authority about a community servant), were divulged or, to the contrary, were withheld from the assembly against its wishes.

We have to keep in mind that the population of a town in the Geniza period was comparatively small and that the local Jewish communities were even smaller. The full participation of all members in the discussion of public affairs did not present technical difficulties; on the contrary, it was normal. Since everyone attended service at least on Saturday and many attended during the week as well, especially on Monday and Thursday when the law was read, it was almost impossible not to bring before the congregation matters that were in any way regarded as being of public concern.

It seems, however, that the simple procedure of taking votes, although suggested by a biblical injunction and actually in use in early talmudic times, was unknown during the Geniza period. Decisions were made in such a way that a subject was first discussed in public and a statement then drawn up in writing and read out to the plenary assembly. Unanimous consent was either explicitly stated, or the document was simply made out in the name of the community. Thus, a statute opens with the following words: "Text of the statute adopted by the

community of the Rabbanites living in Fustat." Disagreement was indicated by specifying those adhering to a resolution.

Community finances were not left entirely to the discretion of the
representatives and officials dealing with them. As we learn from one
document, the accounts were displayed in the synagogue for four
months and everyone was not only allowed but obliged to bring any
objection before the court. This procedure explains why numerous accounts of public revenue and expenditure found in the Geniza are written in large and calligraphic characters. All the same, the regular business
of a community could not be transacted by an entire congregation, small
though it might be; rather, it was entrusted to a board of elders. This
important institution, referred to in hundreds of Geniza records, appears
in an early Hebrew papyrus in which the head of the synagogue, the
elders of the synagogue, and the holy congregation are mentioned side
by side. It is hardly necessary to emphasize that this institution of the
elders was not confined to the Jewish communities of the Islamic world.
Just as we find Egyptian elders active in Fustat and Damietta, Palestinians in Ramle and Baniyas, or Tunisians in Qayrawān and al-Mahdiyya,
we find similar groups of elders at the same time and acting in the same
capacity in the German communities of Speyer, Worms, Mainz, and
Cologne.

A statute resolves that a board of ten elders should assist Ephraim b.
Shemarya, head of the community in Fustat, as follows: (a) sit with him
as judges of the court; (b) share with him the burden of all the needs of
the community; (c) support him in the enforcement of religious duties;
(d) help him protect public morality; (e) deal appropriately with those
who live in a way disapproved by religion; and (f) consider the letters
addressed by the heads of the academy to the community and answer
them after deliberation in the general assembly.

The number ten has some significance in Jewish law: a minimum of
ten persons was required for a service to be regarded as communal, that
is, to constitute public body. A board of ten elders, widely attested both
geographically and chronologically, is expressly mentioned as religiously
recommendable in a fragmentary pastoral letter of a dignitary from the
house of David: "We shall select ten elders out of your notables and
strengthen their arms so that they may lead the people, as it is incumbent
on us to appoint elders and judges." We should not expect, however,
that this number was adhered to everywhere and at all times. We also
find boards of seven. "The seven best men of the town" was the standing
designation for a municipal or congregational council in talmudic and
later Hebrew literature, and this might have had some influence on the

formation of these smaller boards. In a responsum, Maimonides states expressly that the number was not compulsory. A committee of three led the two Jewish congregations of Alexandria after the death of their chief rabbi and before the election of another. Because three is the number of judges required to constitute a Jewish court, it no doubt also came to constitute the minimum number of members for a communal committee during a period of transition.

Occasionally we find larger councils of elders. An eleventh-century gaon of Jerusalem appoints, or approves the election of, sixteen elders, each mentioned by name. According to his letter, their duty was to assist the executive as judges "in all matters of Israel" and to strengthen his hand in every worthy cause. The letters issued in the name of local communities bear signatures in widely varying numbers, amounting to fifteen in Gaza and more than twenty in Palermo. Clearly, anyone of consequence who was prepared to exert himself for the public good could become an elder—provided, of course, that he had the necessary following in the congregation or larger community.

Formal appointments of elders by a gaon or nagid have been mentioned. One source speaks of joint action by the plenary assembly and the appointed local or district executive. It is safe to assume that no fixed or general rule was observed. Most likely, the ecumenical or territorial authority intervened only when communal strife made a decision of the higher authorities imperative. In most cases, the bestowal of an honorary title on an elder was sufficient proof of the gaon's approval.

In their capacity as representatives of the community, the elders issued and received letters, signed contracts, made appointments, and promulgated statutes. They did this either alone or, more often, in conjunction with the *muqaddam*. Elders sometimes worked with the larger community in making decisions; their most important fields of activity were the social services and the judiciary. Many elders served as parnāsīm (social service officers), or as assistant judges. Special prayers were said for their well-being on the High Holidays, as for the ecumenical Jewish authorities. When the list of eulogized elders contained names not favored by the community, the latter would not fail to express its dissatisfaction.

Among the honorary officials designated by the Hebrew term *zāqēn* (elder) were the notables, sometimes informally called in Arabic *al-shuyūkh al-mashhūrīn*, "noted elders," or more specifically *zuʿamāʾ*, "leaders." The latter constituted the upper layer of the Jewish (and Muslim or Christian) middle class and probably had the final word in selecting community officials and in other decisions affecting the community. Not everyone, however, belonging to this class acted as an "elder," and the official elders, it seems, were not always rich or influential. These notables often acted as de facto representatives of the community with the central or local governments, using their influence to seek redress of iniquities or to obtain special favors. Many Geniza papers illustrate this situation (which was not confined to the Muslim world and the Middle Ages, as some historians seem to believe).

Age Groups, Social Classes, and Factions

Zāqēn, the word for old man or elder, had in both Arabic and Hebrew a third and rather general sense: a respectable person. Thus, one would speak of "the elder Ḥasan," or "Mr. Japheth, the young man" (the designation is a play on words: *japheth* was regarded as the Hebrew equivalent of Arabic *ḥasan*, both meaning handsome); or a person would be characterized as "the elder, the young man" (*al-shaykh ha-baḥūr*). Similarly, the term "young men" (*baḥūrīm* in Hebrew and *ṣi-byān* in Arabic) designated both an age group and a social class, although it was used more frequently in the former sense. One should be wary of assigning age limits to particular groups. A merchant who had traveled to both Sicily and India, or a silk worker who had been married twice could still belong to the class of "young men"; one letter even speaks of ṣibyān from Aleppo, "young and old."

These young men were active in community life. A congregation in Fustat was divided regarding a guest cantor from Ramle whom the elders of that city had banned; the youth supported him, and many in the community sided with the baḥūrīm, a fact deplored by the writer of the account, for in his opinion the generation of the young is very corrupt, as it is written, "The lad will behave insolently against the aged" (Isaiah 3:5). A letter of the elders of Ramle complains about opposition by ignorant, uncouth youngsters from the lowest ranks of society. According to a report from Fustat, the *shubbān yisrāel*, the Jewish youth, were enticed by a guest preacher who expounded the Holy Scriptures in the manner of mystical allegory, "which should not be listened to, let alone be believed."

In some Geniza letters, the group revolting against the elders clearly constitutes a social class. A judge from Alexandria reports around 1180 that a notable had accused him before the Muslim authorities of having organized dyers, oyster gatherers, and other rabble, of appointing them his helpers (*anṣār*), and of giving them primacy over the elders. Against these accusations, the writer claims that he has always tried to cooperate with the notables, or "the great," as he also calls them, using a Hebrew expression. He distinguishes between "the elders" on the one hand, and the public, the community (*jamāʿa*), or simply the Jews on the other. What is meant here is the common people, as against the "better" people.

Conflicts between age groups and social classes are less prominent in the Geniza records than those between the various factions within the higher ranks of the society. The appointed executive needed the approval and cooperation of the community; for that reason, the muqaddam sought to secure a following for himself among those connected with him by family or other ties. Naturally, this tended to arouse misgivings among those who did not belong to the preferred group. Even in a small town, there would often be found a scholarly person equal to or even exceeding the appointed community leader in learning and religious authority. If that person also possessed enough ambition and fortitude, a faction demanding his appointment might soon rally around him, thereby inviting communal strife.

Local dissensions were often intertwined with contests for ecumenical or territorial leadership. Rival gaons or nagids would seek followers and supporters in each and every town and congregation, giving would-be local leaders and troublemakers an excellent opportunity to become involved in politics. Moreover, because of the mobility of Mediterranean society in the High Middle Ages, factions were often formed by persons hailing from the same town or country who had settled in foreign parts. We should think of these dissensions in terms of party politics inherent in any essentially democratic society. The modern Arabic word for political party, *ḥizb*, is already in use in the Geniza records to designate a faction, and the verb derived from it means organizing, or forming, a party. The term *ʿaṣabiyya*, esprit de corps, appears in our documents in the same sense.

Since everyone of consequence seems to have known everyone else — at least in the countries stretching from Tunisia to Palestine — interest in communal dissension was widespread. We learn about divisiveness almost exclusively through letters sent from one country or town to another. Hearty congratulations were extended when peace was restored, sometimes mixed with the somewhat skeptical hope that it would last. Even more frequent are admonitions to put an end to a situation unworthy of members of the academy (which most communal leaders were), "for bickering among scholars is the delight of the common people."

Where it was impossible to restore peace, the right of secession was invoked. The dissatisfied party would then withdraw from community life and refrain from attending the synagogue, as happened both in large cities and in small towns. While the secessionists could easily satisfy their religious needs by renting a room and forming a congregation of their own, the local community would be seriously affected by their withdrawal, for its financial means—especially funds for charitable purposes—were obtained largely through donations given and vows made in the course of the service. The failure of a considerable part of the community to appear at the service put its finances in disarray. Therefore, in particularly grave cases, strong measures—up to excommunication—were taken by the community, or a caliphal rescript was obtained by the dissenters for their protection. The disruption of the unity of a congregation also affected the proper functioning of its judiciary, an aspect that involved the government and invited its interference. All these factors tended to create a climate of reconciliation. All in all, it seems that such secessions were of an ephemeral character. To the extent of our current knowledge, no new congregations of permanent duration were founded during the Geniza period.

Statutes and Economic Measures

The idea of legislation was foreign to Geniza society. Laws were given by God, and any new problem requiring legislative measures was amenable to resolution by the scholars interpreting the sacred law. Questions regarding communal life were submitted to the gaons and rabbis for decision, just as were those regarding ritual or civil cases. Nevertheless, Jewish law itself, as it had developed during Hellenistic and Roman times, made provision for the creation of statutes (*taqqānā*) either "by individual scholars" or "by the collective community of the learned." The idea behind such expressions of creative lawmaking is that the agreement of men represented the will of God (*vox populi vox dei*), or as the Muslim lawyers formulated it later in a saying ascribed to their Prophet, "My community will never be unanimous in the disobedience to God."

Most characteristically, no Arabic word is found in our sources that conveys the notion of statute, presumably because the notion itself was foreign to medieval Muslim society. Like other documents that were regarded as being of permanent value, statutes were not normally relegated to the Geniza, and therefore few have survived. Still, the material in hand gives some idea of the character and scope of communal legislation. Some statutes took the form of the pronouncement of a ban on anyone not complying with their provisions. Thus, we have a large fragment containing regulations with regard to the tenants of houses belonging to the communal chest. Another statute imposes a ban on men and women dyeing silk materials in their homes and thus depriving the *ḍāmin*, or tax farmer, of his legal income.

In general, economic measures were a major concern of the community. The Talmud discusses the extent to which foreigners are obliged to share the financial burden of the local people. In the Geniza papers, the welfare burden seems to relate mainly to the obligation to contribute to the *jāliya*, or poll tax, incumbent on indigent persons. Since the foreigners had already paid at home (or would otherwise not have been allowed to travel), it was reasonable not to trouble them with the local jāliya at all. There were circumstances, however, that induced some congregations to deviate from this rule. The Jewish (and also, it seems, the Muslim) population of Alexandria, the main port of Egypt, included many indigents. Attempts were therefore made to have the foreigners share the welfare burden. A letter from one Sicilian merchant to another regrets that the addressee was squeezed dry, noting that foreigners normally pay little or nothing. Another very long letter from Alexandria written by a Maghrebi is devoted wholly to this matter: A delegation of thirty-five foreigners, headed by the writer, had approached the Muslim judicial authority and made a certain contribution in order to avoid further molestation. After a second complaint to the qāḍī, the local community took new measures. It lightened the tax burden on foreigners by 50 percent but insisted on payment, and disparaging rumors were spread against the leader of the Maghrebis. Since practically everyone coming from the West arrived in Alexandria, the matter was important enough for the promulgation of a ban by the gaon of Jerusalem on anyone injuring foreigners by impelling them to make contributions not incumbent on them or by otherwise wronging them.

Another question that arose was how to protect inhabitants from economic competition by newcomers. Nothing has been found thus far among the Geniza documents comparable with an institution developed among European Jews, rightly explained as consistent with the general structure of feudal society: the so-called *ḥerem ha-yishūv*, the denial of admission to any newcomer, except with special permission. In general, we see that statutes and formal enactments of a public body, although not frequently found in the Geniza, were by no means unknown. In these matters, as in others, the society reflected in the Geniza records somehow held the middle ground between corporative Graeco-Roman life and the seeming paucity of formal communal organization in the Muslim society of the period.

THREE

Community Officials

The Muqaddam, or Appointed Executive

The main figure of Jewish community life during the Geniza period was the *muqaddam* (lit., the one put at the head, the superior), the religious and temporal head of the community, appointed with its consent by the Jewish central authorities and accredited by the local representatives of the government. Some uncertainty has prevailed thus far concerning the nature of this office and its relationship to other offices in the community. Nevertheless, the Geniza contains sufficient material to enable us to clarify matters somewhat. We have to keep in mind (*a*) that the term "muqaddam" appears in the Muslim East both in the specific sense of appointed executive and in the general meaning of leader, and (*b*) that the post of appointed executive could be held by persons of various professions, such as a *ḥāvēr*, or member of the Jerusalem yeshiva, a judge, cantor, scribe, or even a layman with some Jewish learning. Consequently, we find persons styled muqaddam who do not specifically hold the position of an appointed community leader, while other persons called muqaddam are noted by their profession or by some other marker of identification. In some cases, both the profession and the title of the muqaddam were indicated; for example, the sender of a magnificently written letter from the townlet of Malīj signs thus: "The ḥāvēr, muqaddam of Malīj." Since this fluid terminology has led to a certain confusion, some details are given to explain the situation.

The verb *taqaddam*, "to be appointed as head," could simply mean that an individual was appointed to lead a congregation in prayer. That might refer to an honored guest or a community official taking up his duty in turn. On the other hand, even in our oldest documents we find the verb *qaddam* used in the technical sense of appointing to a post in the service of the community, and by the end of the eleventh century, in the documents issued under the authority of the nagid Mevōrākh, "muqaddam" had become accepted as a term denoting a person in charge of a local community. Since normally any larger community was headed by a judge, the Arabic term was used to designate such a person, as when, in a letter from Aden, around 1130, respects are paid to the gaon, the muqaddams (meaning the three Jewish judges of the Egyptian capital), the cantors, and the scholars of the gaon's entourage. Persons mentioned in a text first as judges, puisne judges (*nā'ib*), or members of the yeshiva are later on referred to as muqaddams. When we find a circular addressed to the muqaddams and puisne judges of the Egyptian countryside, we should not take this to indicate the existence of a judge and a muqaddam side by side, but rather that there were many places in which the latter office was held by persons who were not qualified judges. On the other hand, in a city like Damascus or Fustat, when muqaddams and judges are mentioned together, we have to remember that the former term could also designate the head of a synagogue.

In short, the appointed head of a local community was not always designated by the term "muqaddam." In fact the office was in existence long before the term became common in our sources. It may be that the Arabic title took on this specific meaning in the last third of the eleventh century for the same reason that gave rise to the office of nagid: the eclipse of the gaonate of Palestine necessitated regulating communal service on a territorial basis. Licensing by the nagid's representatives— the Jewish chief judges in the Egyptian capital—gradually replaced the diploma of the yeshiva.

Most of the judges and other muqaddams whose origin is referred to in our sources were foreigners, or at least were not native to the town or district in which they served. Palestine and Iraq, northwestern Africa and Spain, Byzantium, and later also France provided most of the spiritual and communal leaders. In smaller towns we most often find outsiders serving as muqaddams.[1] Many of our records refer to muqaddams

---

1. This suggested to Goitein a deliberate policy to keep the appointee as independent as possible from the local coteries. On the other hand, it may simply indicate that smaller towns did not contain enough individuals with the requisite learning to deal with legal matters.

new in the town; in one letter the local people do not want him to serve as teacher, because they do not regard him as a permanent resident.

The muqaddam of a city or an entire district needed a written certificate by the local governor or the caliph himself confirming his appointment. A man who had been transferred by the yeshiva from Egypt to a district in northern Syria (which included towns as distant from each other as Baalbek in present-day Lebanon and Raqqa, east of the Euphrates) recounts that he had already seen the local governor four times and had been exceedingly well received by him, but had not yet taken from him the certificate of installment because he did not cherish the new place and was not sure whether he would remain. At a change of government a new certificate had to be secured (as was true of all other offices).

A muqaddam's duties and prerogatives depended largely on local conditions, as well as on his own qualities and qualifications. Still, a common pattern emerges from our records. The duties of a muqaddam are well defined in three letters referring to "an excellent member of the academy" who had to leave his post as muqaddam in al-Maḥalla because of the dissatisfaction of his flock. He had to administer all the affairs of the community, large and small, a task that included maintaining peace and unity within the congregation and representing it before the local state authorities; deciding all questions related to religious law and ritual; expounding the Scriptures and teaching the adults; and supervising the education of the young. The muqaddam's most substantial duty, however, was to preside over the local law court and to perform all functions regarding marriage and divorce. He would also normally lead the congregation in prayer, but, unless he was a professional cantor, he would leave most of the chanting and singing to others. Because the liturgy was still fluid at that time, the muqaddam would make decisions in this matter as well or ask a higher authority for guidance. In addition, he would also serve as one of the local scribes, draw up legal documents, and write official letters. The handwriting of many a muqaddam is known to us, since many of their writings have been preserved.

From letters regarding al-Maḥalla, as well as other documents, it is evident that the muqaddam was empowered to make unilateral decisions solely in cases of religious law and ritual, where he was supposed to interpret the sacred writings authoritatively. But in communal as well as in legal matters (which were decided mostly by settlement rather than by formal judgments) he had to consult the elders and the community. In the smaller towns of the Rīf, where muqaddams were chosen on the basis of their ability to restrain the unruly rather than for their scholarship, their religious authority was occasionally challenged. In addition to his legal and religious responsibilities, a muqaddam also had to be a good fundraiser, since communal revenues consisted to a large extent of voluntary contributions. Another substantial and certainly not always pleasant duty was to assist government officials or tax farmers in the assessment of the poll tax incumbent on the members of the congregation.

The emoluments of the muqaddam are treated together with those of other communal officials (see *infra*, chapter 4), since they differed from those of others in quantity rather than in nature. We frequently read of muqaddams (and others) leaving their posts in smaller towns or rural districts because they were not paid sufficiently or were not paid at all. Sometimes the parting official speaks about the area of his responsibility in fond and even loving terms, realizing that poverty rather than ill will was the cause of the community's default. Thus, in a letter to the nagid Mevōrākh, a muqaddam (and cantor) expresses his gratitude to the local community, young and old, and writes that he would have preferred to stay until a substitute was sent by the nagid. He was unable to do so, however, since the income from his provincial post sufficed only for his own maintenance, not for that of his family (which had remained in the city). Another muqaddam, a professional scribe, writes that he cannot remain at his post because he does not derive from it the benefits normally connected with such a position; he will stay on until he completes a Torah scroll that he has promised to write for the community. In other letters, though, the complaints are bitter, and there is a general outcry against the sufferings endured by the more scholarly muqaddams in the congregations of the Egyptian countryside.

Given the conditions prevailing in the smaller communities, the Jewish authorities in Fustat Cairo were anxious to strengthen the authority of the muqaddams. In a letter issued by the two judges of the capital in the name of the nagid Mevōrākh, a circuit judge is strongly rebuked for having given judgment in a town in the absence of the local muqaddam and for having taken other actions without consulting him (and the elders). When a community leader, upon returning from a trip to the capital, finds that the son of a scholar has in his absence married four couples, writing their marriage contracts and performing the weddings, he respectfully asks the chief judge to send him a letter explaining whether or not the action of the scholar's son was permissible—a polite way of announcing that something very improper had been done. In

1187, Maimonides and his court published a solemn prohibition against anyone except the muqaddam performing a wedding in specified provincial towns. A similar ban was pronounced in 1235 for Alexandria, and the nagid Abraham Maimonides restated the position of his father with regard to the provincial towns. It was considered a serious matter for scholars to trespass on the rights of the local muqaddam.

In addition to material gain (when that was actually the case), it was the social position and prestige connected with the office of the muqaddam that made it attractive for both professionals and laymen. To be sure, according to the pious nagid Abraham Maimonides, neither should be the source of the muqaddam's gratification. "It is not proper and it is not permissible," he writes, "for a muqaddam, or for the person who appoints him, or those over whom he had been appointed, to believe that the purpose of his office is to make profit from public funds or to gain an honored position. All this is merely incidental. The basic aim is the gain of the community in religiosity and welfare. This is the essence of a religious office, all the rest is incidental."

The Head of the Congregation(s)

"Muqaddam," as we have seen, was the name of an office, not a title. Therefore, it is rarely found as a family name and is never attached to the name of a person's father. The opposite was the case with "the head of the congregation" (or "congregations"), *rōsh ha-qāhāl* or *ha-qehillōt* (pl.). It is extremely common as a title of honor following the name of a person's father or that of a person addressed in a letter or mentioned in a document, but we hear next to nothing about the activities specific to a person designated in this way. Clearly, at various times and in different places the title was given to holders of diverse positions in the community. Nevertheless, one can venture a hesitant sketch of the historical development of the rōsh ha-qāhāl. It is highly probable that the head of the congregation of the Geniza period replaced the ancient head of the synagogue (*rōsh ha-keneset*), for the latter term is entirely absent from our records. As is evident from the Talmud, the head of the synagogue was a layman inferior in rank to the scholar appointed as community leader, and indeed to any scholar. The new title of rōsh ha-qāhāl could be borne by both judges and laymen. In sum, it had cachet in an age when everyone wanted to be regarded as a religious scholar. In the tenth and early eleventh centuries, the term seems to have designated presidents of the congregations, for we find persons so styled mentioned in memorial lists together with gaons and judges, or using this title regularly after their signatures. In Yemen and North Africa, the diocesan representative of the yeshivas was designated as head of the congregations.

During the same period, however, it had become customary that only a scholar qualifying as a member of the yeshiva could lead a large congregation, while toward the end of the eleventh century, we find that only a muqaddam, that is, an appointee of the nagid or his representatives, could fill this post. We never hear of a clash (nor, for that matter, of an act of cooperation) between a muqaddam and a rōsh ha-qāhāl. Thus, it would be erroneous to regard the latter as a representative of the local people rather than a scholarly executive. We have also to keep in mind that no Arabic equivalent exists for the rōsh ha-qāhāl. It seems, therefore, that by the end of the eleventh century the title "head of the congregation" had become merely an honorary designation, one given to meritorious individuals within the congregation, perhaps to those having some prerogatives in the synagogue, like those held by the ancient rōsh ha-keneset—for example, the assignment to members and guests of the reading of various parts of the service. No express mention of this has been found thus far. Only in small Jewish settlements that had no muqaddam does the head of the congregation appear as the man in charge of the community.

We sporadically find other terms referring to leaders of congregations or local communities. In 1240, the *qayyim*, or superintendent, of the small synagogue in Alexandria possessed a house in Cairo, and, rather strangely, also seems to have lived there. (*Qayyim* is a Muslim title referring to the administrator of a mosque or other religious institution and was in later times transferred to that of a synagogue.) A person called shaykh al-Yahūd, elder (i.e., head) of the Jews of Ascalon, is mentioned early in the twelfth century, and a letter from Qūṣ in Upper Egypt, written about a hundred years later, speaks somewhat derisively of a perfumer who calls himself the shaykh al-Yahūd. By the fourteenth century the title "shaykh al-Yahūd" designated the head of the community in Fustat who was responsible to the government for the payment of the poll tax. All in all, it seems that despite the prominent role of the elders and the plenary assembly in the conduct of the affairs of the community, there was no need felt to formally elect a president as a check against the appointed executive. In any event, the head of the congregation(s), although often mentioned in the Geniza records, seems not to have had such a role.

The Social Service Officers and the Trustees of the Court

The *parnāsīm,* who were in charge of the communal property and the social services, are mentioned in the Geniza documents more frequently than any other officials. The very fact that the Hebrew term is often rendered in an Arabicized form (*firnās,* pl. *farāranisa*) illustrates the popularity of that office. The parnās of the Geniza period differs considerably from his successor in European Jewry. He was neither a leader nor president of a congregation, but rather an official of lower rank who served mostly in an honorary capacity but sometimes received emoluments. As revealed by the greetings extended in official letters to various groups of the community, the social service officers were ranked below scholars, elders, notables, and cantors. A beadle might also serve as a parnās, hence the unitary term "the parnās and beadle." When Benjamin of Tudela visited the Synagogue of Moses, the holy shrine of Dammūh on the southwestern outskirts of Fustat, he found it under the care of a scholarly old man whom he describes as "parnās and beadle," presumably an expression he had learned on his travels. The field of social services was the one in which respectable members of the community who did not excel in scholarship found rich opportunity for making their contribution to the common good.

As far as we are able to determine, the parnāsīm usually came from the upper middle class, not from the wealthiest families; at least this was so during the earlier part of the classical Geniza period. Although many are known to us, none seems to have been honored with the title "head of the congregation." All our sources point to the fact that in each congregation several parnāsīm were active simultaneously, a circumstance that was in accordance with Jewish law which required that no public office involving the handling of money should be held by fewer than two persons. The Palestinians in Fustat at one time had seven parnāsīm, at another more than four (including one physician) and once exactly four, but even in a provincial town the judge would be assisted by several parnāsīm. Numerous social service officers were required because of the many different tasks incumbent on them. The administration and maintenance of the houses belonging to the community and the distribution of the revenue gained from them were sufficient to occupy more than one person. Since the parnāsīm were busy people engaged in gaining their livelihood, they would take turns, one collector soliciting contributions one week and another the next, and so forth. A distinguished visitor, a proselyte, or an indigent person from a good family (especially if he was a scholar) was assigned to one parnās, who was expected to look after him personally. Jews living in remote villages would confide their affairs to a parnās in Fustat, probably because they had no access to a higher official. Occasionally, a parnās had to travel in order to raise funds—for example, for the ransom of captives—or to accompany a scholar for the same purpose.

In a large city, having several parnāsīm originating from different countries was desirable to meet the requirements of a cosmopolitan population. Thus in Fustat we find parnāsīm of the Rūm (Europeans), of people from Jerusalem, from Damietta (most probably after the conquest of that town by the Crusaders in November 1219), and even from the island of Crete (from which Jews might have migrated in large numbers after it fell to the Venetians in 1204). One of the chores of the parnāsīm was to assess the frequently changing needs of each indigent household; this of course could be done more easily by a man closely acquainted with the background of the families concerned. As regards the appointment of the parnāsīm, we find in one document that the ḥāvēr, the member of the yeshiva appointed as executive, chose them in concert with the community, an arrangement to be expected in a society that, as we have so often had opportunity to observe, displayed both a hierarchical and democratic character.

Until approximately 1150, we do not read anything in our records about material gains accruing to a parnās from his service to the community. This lack of information may or may not reflect the actual situation. From the second half of the twelfth century forward, financial reports occasionally contain the item "cost of the collection of revenue," which suggests that honorary social service officials were assisted or replaced by those receiving salary. Similarly, in these later times, a parnās distributing clothing would also receive a piece of clothing for himself—sometimes for members of his family as well. This development is perhaps indicative of growing poverty rather than of a decline in public spirit. In any case, the practice that a person administering public funds should be remunerated out of those funds is already attested as customary in an ancient Hebrew source.

Another public office, often connected with that of the parnās, was the trustee (of the court), ne'emān (bēth dīn). Despite the frequency of this Hebrew term, no Arabic equivalent appears in our sources, which probably means that it was an essentially Jewish institution. Like the parnās, the trustee had myriad duties. Insolvent debtors deposited gold and silver vessels, books, and other valuables with him as collateral until they were able to meet their obligations. With the consent of the depositor and under the supervision of the court, the trustee could safeguard such objects with other persons. Husbands traveling abroad empowered him to cash sums due them or left him money for the maintenance of their families during their absence. The alimonies due separated wives or divorced women with small children would be paid through him, and he was often in charge of the estates of orphans or of foreigners who died far away from their families. In addition, he gave loans to the needy against collaterals deposited with him. The accumulated value of such deposits was sometimes substantial.

A trustee of the court was a highly respected member of the community. Therefore, a person who had such a man as father would be referred to in official documents and in letters addressed to him as "the son of the trustee." In a court record dated May 28, 1207, three such persons are mentioned, two appearing as guardians of orphans, and the third as one of two witnesses to the legal procedure, indicative that the sons held positions of trust similar to those of their fathers. Many functions incumbent on a trustee of the court, such as the payment of alimony to a divorced woman, were also fulfilled by a parnās. Although intrinsically different, trustees and parnāsī in fact often rendered the same services.

The Synagogue Beadle and Messenger of the Court

The synagogue attendant, *shammāsh* (Ar. *khādim*), was not the minor official that a sexton of a church or a beadle in a synagogue is today. As letters of appointment state, the duties of the shammāsh comprised not only maintaining the synagogue property but also servicing the community and, among the Babylonians, the muqaddam as well. He was the community's factotum and in some places was in fact called "the servant of the community." Among his many functions, the beadle served as messenger and assistant clerk of the court and, in connection with this task, as attorney, trustee, cashier, and other functions as well. Therefore, he had an intimate knowledge of all that was going on in the community. It seems also that beadles, more often than not, were rather well-to-do; we see them giving loans, some of no small size. Even the trustee with whom valuables worth ten thousand dinars had been deposited in 1168 was a "servant of the sanctuary." The shammāsh of those days perhaps resembled his Christian namesake (*shammās* in Arabic), who acted as deacon or clerk of the church.

At the appointment of a shammāsh, an inventory of the books, scrolls, and furnishings of the synagogue—gold and silver ornaments, lamps, precious textiles, carpets and mats—was drawn up and all items confided to his care. He was responsible for their maintenance and preservation—a task that, in those insecure times, required both vigilance and resourcefulness. He was also in charge of their cleaning and of small repairs, for which he submitted monthly accounts. In particular, he tended to the illumination of the synagogue during the night to enable laymen and scholars to pursue their studies. In one document this appears as a primary duty.

We frequently find beadles assisting the social service officers or performing some of their functions. In a letter of appointment, a beadle of the Babylonians is required to help the parnāsin collecting and distributing loaves of bread to the poor; in various documents, beadles collect the rents from houses or other property belonging to the community. If he had sufficient means, a beadle would farm out the revenue from pious foundations. In his capacity as messenger of the court, the shammāsh delivered summons and other communications to the parties and had to be on hand during the sessions. In addition, he had to take down the depositions and pleas made by the persons appearing in court as they were repeated to him by the presiding judge. (In one letter of appointment the beadle is threatened with immediate dismissal if he makes any changes in the texts dictated to him.) It is doubtful that this was a common function of the beadles, for most of the rough copies of court records found in the Geniza are in the handwriting of scribes and judges known to us. (We should remember, however, that the Geniza chamber was attached to the synagogue of the Palestinians; the letter of appointment referred to was issued on behalf of the synagogue of the Babylonians, where other practices may have prevailed.) In any case, a Geniza letter shows that even in a small town a beadle would have a good hand—reflecting thereby continuous training. Thus it is not astonishing to find in a city like al-Mahdiyya a beadle (who was writing letters for a woman) serving as an accomplished scribe.

Their close connection with the courts gave the beadles opportunities for many different tasks. From a document issued in Cairo in 1094 we learn that a shammāsh who was charged with the delivery of a bill of divorce to a woman living in Palestine had retained it for three years; as he explained in court, he always procrastinated in order to give the couple the opportunity to reconcile (a rather high-handed way of forcing happiness upon others). In 1098, a husband deposits the trousseau of his wife with a beadle until a settlement is reached. A silk weaver appoints a beadle as executor of his will, a physician makes another his attorney against a debtor, and a rich woman does the same in a matter of inheritance.

In only one example thus far has a beadle been found performing police duties. In Fustat in April 1028, a beadle of the Babylonians caught a man and, because it was Passover week and the court was not in session, confined him in his house. At the end of the holiday, when the beadle was busy in the synagogue, the accused escaped through a window. Perhaps in this respect as well the Babylonians had their own traditions. In the lands of the Eastern caliphate, for example, the authorities of the minority groups were sometimes permitted to imprison their own members or to inflict corporal punishment on them.

In order to best fulfill his duties, the beadle lived in the synagogue compound. One letter of appointment requires him to reside there together with his young sons. Sometimes this led to abuses: we read in a complaint to the nagid Mevōrākh that the beadle of the Babylonians lived in the synagogue with his brothers and their families, totaling altogether about fifteen individuals; they treated the compound as their own property even to the extent of flying pigeons from the roof. (According to *The Arabian Nights*, breeding carrier pigeons on one's roof was a sport of people of low class.)

Needless to say, the position and authority of a shammāsh was more secure if he remained in office for a long time. The beadle of the Babylonians, against whom such strong representations were made before the nagid Mevōrākh, was appointed in 1099 and was still at his post in June 1127, many years after the nagid had died. We have documents dated from 1159 until December 1188 regarding a beadle of the Palestinians; his son served in the synagogue of the Babylonians for a still longer period (documents dated from 1186 through 1223, probably even 1183 through 1227). Since the preservation of documents is a matter of mere chance, the beadles may have served for even longer periods than those indicated in these instances.

Other Officials

Most of these professionals have to be regarded as community officials, since they often received emoluments from the community or derived benefits from it. Scholars and judges, cantors and preachers, the officials connected with the observance of the dietary laws, as well as the scribes, either appear on the payrolls or were assigned other sources of public revenue. There were also classes of employees of minor importance. Medical care was not the concern of the community but was left to pious foundations. Police and other security services were the prerogative of the state. Among the communal appointees of lesser status, only the night watchmen, in Arabic *ṭawwāfūn* (Heb. *meshōṭeṭē layla*), regularly appear as receiving emoluments. It would appear that over time the minorities obtained the right to provide night watchmen of their own in the quarters predominantly inhabited by them. A document from a provincial town suggests that the *ṭawwāfūn* were paid by the proprietors of houses, who sometimes delegated this duty to the tenants. This explains why emoluments from the community to night watchmen were rather low: such payments constituted supplementary income. Similarly, funeral personnel, such as washers of the dead, bearers of the coffins, and gravediggers, were normally paid by relatives of the deceased, but they sometimes appear receiving wages or being compensated with loaves of bread from the community. Occasional payments were also made to the members of the district police, local judges, and the like.

We do not yet know the function of a figure designated in Hebrew as *mashmīʿa*, a herald. He could hardly have been a town crier, since here one would expect the ubiquitous Arabic *munādī* rather than a Hebrew term. Perhaps he acted as a solicitor of contributions to the synagogue who announced the pledges in a loud voice. Persons called *murahhiṭ*—writers, and perhaps also singers, of liturgical poetry—and their families appear from time to time in lists of beneficiaries of the community chest. Certainly, this medieval calling would have been even more conspicuous in the Geniza records had not cantors fulfilled the same task. Our documents also include other officials whose precise function cannot be ascertained.

Public Service and the Principle of Heredity

Public service was seen as obedience to heavenly decree. As the Talmud put it, "Even the ditchdigger has been appointed by God." All the same, the idea of service to the people is represented in the Geniza with great frequency. The Palestinian gaon Solomon b. Judah, in a letter to Ephraim b. Shemarya of Fustat, lauds him as serving the people "with all his heart and all his soul and all his might," using the biblical phrase that refers to service to God (Deuteronomy 6:5). While reprimanding the same leader for quarreling with another, he writes, "These times are not like those that have passed, when each of you was his own lord; now you belong to God and to Israel." Public service was not, however, a voluntary act. Rather, public office was sought as a source of livelihood. "No man does service except for re-muneration," states Solomon b. Judah, the gaon of Jerusalem. In an application to a nagid of Yemen, a writer describes himself as being fit for nothing except the service of the community. Disappointment over not obtaining a steady income from community service was only too frequent. A cantor in a small town complains bitterly about his lack of opportunity: "All my life I have been tossed about serving the Jews. . . ."

Unhappy relations with the community were a common cause of dissatisfaction. A remarkable but unfortunately much damaged letter contains, among other telling passages, the following:

I am most miserable. Some envy me, others despise me; others, again, are hostile. I have trouble with them all. God is my witness! Would that I knew any profitable occupation bringing two dinars a month, I would not have touched the service of the Jews. Now, letters have their pitfalls; so please excuse me for writing this. You remember that I have come here at your advice. "If it displeases you, I shall go back" [cf. Numbers 22:34]. . . . They have torn my honor to pieces. . . . I sit alone in my house, which is empty of everything. "But God is there" [Ezekiel 35:10].

Community officials had to please their superiors and influential lead-ers, but at the same time had to avoid offending the common people. In a letter addressed most probably to Maimonides a cantor excuses himself for being unable to perform a certain service for him, as he had to officiate at a circumcision ceremony for a poor man. It was absolutely impossible for him to absent himself, "lest people say that I was staying away because he is poor. . . . You know how our people are." Many documents illustrate the reciprocal relationship that existed between the public servant and the ecumenical or territorial authorities who had ap-pointed or approved him. On the one hand, when a gaon or a nagid was faced with a rival, he had to secure the allegiance of his appointees. In numerous letters we find solicitations, or assurances of loyalty by officials, or excuses and explanations when the writer has faltered in his loyalty. A document in which officials from six small towns and villages in Upper Galilee reaffirm their support of a certain gaon is headed (with a pun on Exodus 21:5), "I love my lord; I will not go out free." The most characteristic aspect of public service in the Geniza letters was the absence of rigid limits of demarcation between the various offices. A judge, a social service officer, a cantor, a scribe—each had his specific qualifications and duties. All the same, he would often be called upon to do another man's work. Precisely because of this fluidity, we frequently find a muqaddam, a cantor, a teacher, or a ritual slaughterer jealously guarding the privileges derived from his office.

When a public servant had a son who was able and willing to succeed him, it was regarded as proper to give him his father's post. The extent to which father and son were regarded as one person, so to speak, is dramatically illustrated in the complaint of an old cantor to a nagid that his post has been taken by someone other than his son. He lived in the synagogue compound and whenever he heard the voice of the other cantor, his illness grew worse. "It is fitting with your sense of justice that one should retain one's position. If my son is treated like this during my lifetime, what will happen to him after my demise?"

To secure his son's succession, an official would have him work as his assistant and, as he grew older, as his substitute—a practice found in all ranks, from the head of a yeshiva down to a beadle. Prudent persons went even a step further: The attendant of the tomb of Ezra, the most popular Jewish place of pilgrimage in Iraq, obtained certificates from an exilarch promising that his son would succeed him. When opposition arose after his death, these certificates stood his son in good stead, according to the letter of another gaon who confirmed him in his office on the basis of the promises secured earlier. Contracts of appointment have been found for even a beadle and a religious slaughterer. One such contract, however, states with much emphasis that a second son will have no share in the services of the slaughterhouses, not even as a guard, because the community is not satisfied with his demeanor. Thus, succession to a father's post was by no means guaranteed. Moreover, the principle of heredity was superseded by that of seniority and precedence. This was especially the case with regard to the gaons or heads of yeshivas, but it applied also to lesser positions. After an ambitious cantor from Baghdad had sojourned for years in Tunisia and Spain, he was informed by a childhood friend, a gaon, that all the older cantors had died and that it was now his turn to become the muqaddam of the cantors. A similar procedure seems to have been in force with regard to the appointment of beadles. When an official had no male offspring, or had a son who was not inclined to follow his father's profession, he would look for a suitable son-in-law as his successor. Naturally, a son-in-law as well sometimes had other plans and might seek a higher position.

In Jewish as in Muslim society, the principle of heredity was particularly strong in regard to the families of judges. This tradition invites special attention in studying the formation of the judiciary system. As regards lesser community servants, the material at our disposal seems to indicate that the privilege of succession was exercised less often than one would expect in view of its general acceptance by both social custom and Jewish legal theory. Perhaps the wider range of occupations open to Jews during the Geniza period induced younger people to look for jobs other than those held by their fathers. Moreover, society at that time looked down on income derived from service and salary. The great fortunes and reputations were made from commerce and trade.

FOUR

The Social Services

General Character and Organization

Among the Muslim majority, charity was semipublic.
Having drained the community of its resources, members of the ruling
elite or otherwise wealthy people often returned to it a part of the spoils
in the form of pious foundations or other charitable works. Such contributions to the public good cheated the state of its inheritance tax while
providing the donor a favorable outcome on the Day of Judgment.
Generally speaking, Muslim philanthropy was highly individualistic;
Muslim society seems to have lacked incentives for communal cooperation. Interfaith charity, although not entirely unknown, was of little, if
any, practical importance. The religious minorities were responsible for
their own well-being and were therefore burdened with supplying all
the social services provided in modern societies by the state, municipal-
ities, and other public bodies. How the Jewish communities of the Mediterranean area and that of Fustat in particular acquitted themselves of
this noble and arduous task is revealed in detail by the documents of the
Cairo Geniza.

These Jewish communities had no statutory power to impose taxes
on their members. Hence, all charitable work was performed, of necessity, on a purely voluntary basis—and was accomplished with remarkable vigor, scope, and continuity. Because officials, as well as the needy,
depended on voluntary contributions, the members of the community
had a most effective means of expressing their satisfaction or dissatisfac-

tion with the conduct of public affairs. The very character of public finances and social services safeguarded the participation of the community at large and provided it with a broad democratic base.

Our knowledge of Jewish social services is derived largely from lists of recipients and contributors, and from documents relating to houses and other communal property that describe the allocation of the revenues that they brought in. Records of the second type are mostly self-explanatory and are often dated. The interpretation of the charitable lists is far more difficult. Only a few are dated, and rarely do they include a formal explanation of their purpose. Even where a superscription is provided, understanding it correctly is by no means easy, and to do so often requires correlating the data carefully with other relevant Geniza material. Fortunately, the handwriting of the more prominent scribes active in Fustat between approximately 1015 and 1265 is known, and so it is possible to fix the period to which many an undated charity list belongs. Moreover, numerous names mentioned in the lists reappear in the dated records about public buildings or in other dated or datable documents. Finally, the professions of the persons listed or other details given about them divulge the purpose of a list. Only one of these lists has been edited thus far.[1]

Ecumenical Aspects

The most impressive aspect of Jewish philanthropy as reflected in the Geniza records is its ecumenical character. The principle "charity begins at home" (or, as a Hebrew saying has it, "the poor of your town have precedence over those of another") was regarded as a religious injunction and is so referred to in Geniza letters. The very existence of such an injunction shows that at the time much was done for the needy outside the local community. The character of the Jewish community, with its long history of social concerns going back to the biblical period, precluded a parochial attitude to social problems affecting all Jews. We have already noted that the maintenance of the ecumenical seats of learning in Jerusalem and Baghdad was a major

---

1. Goitein scrutinized over four hundred of these documents and tried to define their contents and fix their approximate dates. Details are available in appendixes to volume 2 of Goitein's five-volume *Mediterranean Society*. These should be consulted by readers interested in the larger history and structure of social services during the Geniza period.

concern for all Jewish communities, large and small. Local institutions of higher learning or even individual scholars could likewise count on the support of friends in other countries.[2] Presents made to a scholar were regarded as an equivalent to the offerings on the altar in the ancient Temple of Jerusalem. It was the quality of the scholar, not where he was situated, that mattered.

A similar rule applied to the poor. Gifts were sent to localities in which the need was greatest. It may seem strange that a merchant from Aden—a native of that southern Arabian port—should dispatch to Fustat the very substantial sum of twenty dinars for the benefit of the poor of that city. The capital of Egypt was, however, a refuge for Jewish victims of persecution from all over the world; as such, the demands made on its Jewish inhabitants far exceeded their financial capacity, and others felt obliged to share part of the burden. Ransoming prisoners was a particular concern. The Geniza contains a letter from an individual named Najera in the kingdom of Castile describing what that community had done for a woman who had been taken captive with her two daughters and whose husband had been killed; other congregations were admonished to act accordingly. Similar requests were made in a letter from the community in Granada and another from Arles. Indeed, the largest group of needy people appearing in our lists are the foreigners, particularly persons coming from Europe. Under such circumstances it was proper and natural that the wealthy merchants of Aden, whose livelihood depended on the prosperous trade between the Mediterranean area and India, should send their contributions to Fustat not only to scholars living there but also to the poor—regardless of their place of origin.

To alleviate its burden, the community in the Egyptian capital would send foreigners seeking help on to the provincial towns and villages. We have a letter in Maimonides' own hand in which he asks a notable in a provincial town to arrange for a collection to pay the poll tax for a Jewish scholar from Morocco and his son; another communication seeks help for a young scholar whom Maimonides' son Abraham, the nagid, had sent away to the country with a small sum of money. This procedure was adopted particularly in cases of ransom and for support of persons who had fallen into the hands of pirates or enemies; in either case, great financial sacrifices were required. While Alexandria, the usual port of arrival of such captives, and Fustat, their normal destination, had to

2. In the course of his work on the India trade, Goitein came across a number of letters proving that the Jewish merchants of Aden regularly sent gifts to both local and foreign scholars in Egypt.

shoulder the main burden, we see from reports preserved in the Geniza that the smaller communities also made very substantial contributions. This is all the more remarkable since most of these captives came from Byzantium or other parts of Europe, and those who ransomed them might not have been familiar with their spoken language and some of their social habits.

Another concern shared by all Jewish communities was the support of the poor, the devout, and the scholars of the Holy City. The ever present state of anarchy in which Palestine found itself during the eleventh century and the crushing taxation imposed on the minorities (and perhaps also on other segments of the population) had a ruinous effect on the economy of the country. Financial aid to Palestine's Jewish community, which had always been regarded as a religious duty, now became a dire necessity. The Geniza records indicate the gravity of the situation far more than do the literary texts. Special collections, made for the Jews of Palestine, were called *tafriqat al-maqādisa*, literally, "the distribution [for] the Jerusalemites," and were held, like the collections for the distribution of cash among the local poor, on (or rather shortly before) the holidays. A fund-raiser would be sent from Jerusalem—invariably someone other than the yeshiva's permanent envoy, who, being first and foremost a scholar, was responsible for many assignments, in addition to collecting money.

The amounts collected in Egypt, Sicily, and the Maghreb in a joint Karaite-Rabbanite emergency campaign for Jerusalem—a campaign to repay the debts of the Jewish community there to the Muslim moneylenders—are the largest raised in any public appeal documented in the Geniza records, with the exception of ransoms for captives and funds raised to meet special impositions by the Muslim government. One should bear in mind, of course, that the Jerusalem community had to take care of the many destitute persons visiting or domiciled in the Holy City and to pay fixed contributions even in years when, because of war or other calamities, no pilgrims with means made their way to Palestine. At times a donor would earmark his contribution to Jerusalem for a special purpose.

Popular Participation

The entire community participated in raising funds for social services. Public appeals were of two distinct types. When large amounts were needed for immediate payment, as for the ransom of captives, all in a position to do so had to make an extraordinary effort in accordance with their means. To be sure, the contributions to appeals of this type reflect a pronounced gap between the rich and those less well-off. On occasions such as holidays or feasts associated with fast days, the affluent by far outstripped the rest of the contributors. In cases of special urgency but of limited scope—for instance, when a foreigner had to be supplied quickly with travel expenses—often no general appeals were made; a number of notables contributed the money needed. Nevertheless, the sources also speak of general giving wherein rich and poor alike contributed in more or less equal sums. It is thus evident that for certain types of charity comparatively small sums were solicited, but everyone was expected to contribute. This principle seems to have applied to the weekly collections for the *mezōnōt* or food (meaning bread) for the poor, from which other communal expenses were also paid in later times, and to the contributions for the payment of the poll tax on behalf of those who were unable to pay it in full or at all. We also have the strange case of the appeal for wax candles, which must have been a quite regular undertaking (presumably before holidays, when candles would be needed for ritual purposes). The preamble to that document says expressly, "We shall bear it as if with a single hand" [*naḥmilḥā yad wāḥida*], meaning that the payments were in equal shares.

Popular participation went beyond monetary contributions. Everyone wanted a say in the use of funds and an accounting of how they were used. The aforementioned preamble and numerous other appeals to congregations that appear in our documents illustrate the substantial publicity that accompanied communal philanthropy. Even a nagid giving an order of payment from a public fund would state that it was made "with the consent of the community." Most of the communal accounts and many of the lists of recipients or donors are written in large, calligraphic characters, for they were intended for display in the synagogue, and all members were invited to scrutinize them. One document even states that everyone was not only entitled but religiously bound to advise the court of any inaccuracy to be found in the report, which for this purpose was finalized only after four months had elapsed.

The Community Chest

In cities with more than one synagogue, donations were sometimes made and houses acquired for individual synagogues, but the social services were usually communal, comprising all the coreligionists living in one place, rather than congregational. In Egypt's twin capitals, Fustat and the newly founded Cairo, even the payrolls of the various synagogues sometimes were combined in one list.

The community assets and property were called *qōdesh*, "holy," a designation dating back to ancient times when the treasury of the nation was stored in the precincts of the Temple of Jerusalem. The term conveyed the idea that anything dedicated to the common good was given to God, an idea familiar also to contemporary Islam, which construed *māl al-muslimīn*, "wealth belonging to the Muslims," as synonymous with *māl Allāh*, "wealth belonging to God." The qōdesh was an idea, not an institution; there was no central treasury to which all revenue was paid and from which all expenses were drawn. Organizing charity and other communal needs, such as the payment of officials and the maintenance and administration of buildings, was far more complicated. The income of the community derived from regular collections, special appeals, miscellaneous items such as fines or wills, revenue from the slaughterhouses, and, in particular, rents from the many buildings administered as charitable trusts. While certain types of expenditure were funded regularly by specific sources of revenue—the distribution of bread by weekly collections or the maintenance of buildings by the rent raised from them—many other types were not. Orders of payment on account from the community chest had to be indicated, expressly or by implication. Moreover, it was deemed necessary to keep funds in more than one public treasury in order to thwart rapacious government officials. Religious scruples as well were involved in this splitting of communal revenue and earmarking of its various units for specific purposes: the apprehension that funds donated for one charity might be used to finance another, a practice not uncommon and difficult to control.

The community chest, although not a legal person in the strict sense, appears in the Geniza letters as party to a contract, and orders of payment were issued on it. Its administration varied according to the times and the local conditions. As a rule, it was in the hands of "the trustworthy elders in charge of public property and communal affairs," as the representatives of the community were called. Contracts to lease public property or agreements related to such property were written in the names of the elders, or, like other legally valid documents, signed by three persons, usually including a judge. Occasionally a parnās would appear as the lessor, perhaps an imitation of the Muslim practice.

An expenditure from the community chest required the witness of at least two representatives of the community. Since people were busy with their own affairs, a parnās normally had several elders at his disposal from whom he could choose one to assist him in a transaction. As long as Jewish community life in Egypt was vibrant—as it was during the eleventh and twelfth centuries—there was no difficulty in keeping the executive and legal aspects of public administration separate. The elders and the parnāsīm estimated the requirements of each branch funded by the community chest and took whatever action was necessary. The judges saw to it that everything was done according to the law, gave instructions as needed, and confirmed the transactions of the administrative officials after proper scrutiny. Whenever we have a neatly written document that bears no signature, it is fairly certain that the action proposed by the elders was not approved, and often we can surmise the circumstances that provoked doubts. A long list written around 1100 that enumerates the proposed allocations for clothing, partly in kind and partly in cash, bears the following remark over the signature of three well-known judges: "We, the court, are of the opinion that what is found above needs further examination, although it was written according to the counsel and the dictation of elders." Even in matters of orphans and widows—the particular preserve of the courts—the elders were regularly consulted on the amounts of alimonies and related matters.

It is true that with regard to communal charity, as in all other matters, the official head of the Jews of Egypt, the nagid/rayyis, was the highest decisionmaking authority. His task, however, was not the daily conduct of the social services, but the overall supervision of the charitable foundations, the redress of injustices, and making amends for negligence (no small task given that so many people felt themselves wronged or unfairly passed over). Only when the deep decline of Egyptian Jewry set in around the turn of the thirteenth century did the Jewish judge, like the Muslim qāḍī, become administrator of the public funds, making each and every decision. Yet even in the late thirteenth century and throughout the fourteenth century we find the laity participating actively in the administration of charities. Thus the Jewish community of Fustat faithfully preserved the popular character of its social services—that is, as long as we are able to follow its activities in the Geniza documents.

Sources of Revenue and Types of Relief

The organization of the social services implied that each type of relief had its specific source of revenue. There was, however, one great exception: the income from houses and other real estate owned by the community could be used for any purpose if the donors had not stipulated otherwise. The mechanics of public financing within the Jewish communities were by no means uniform even within Egypt. Alexandria, about which we are comparatively well informed, adhered to a system entirely different from that of Fustat. There, as was common in later times in many Jewish congregations in Europe, the source item of communal revenue was the slaughterhouse—a tax on meat, the food of the more affluent. A letter to Solomon b. Elijah inquiring whether his father, the judge Elijah, would be prepared to become the spiritual leader of the two synagogues of Alexandria promises as his main (or sole) emolument the income from the slaughterhouses, while the orphans of his predecessor will receive ten dirhems a week from the same source. In another letter on the same matter to the same addressee the writer says, "The slaughterhouses are the city," meaning that they constitute the community's main source of revenue. In Fustat, by contrast, revenue from the slaughterhouses was of little consequence. The professional slaughterers there were communal officials inasmuch as they were appointed to their posts by the religious authorities, but economically they were on their own, receiving a fixed weekly payment of comparatively small sums (seven or eight dirhems) against the large revenues derived from their services.

There was another, main feature of public charity in which Alexandria followed old Palestinian ways and differed entirely from Fustat: the *quppā* (*shel ṣedāqā*). In later Hebrew this simply means alms box, and in modern Hebrew quppā is the window of a cashier in a bank or a store. The original meaning of the word, however, like that of its Arabic equivalent *quffa,* was basket—for the Jewish communities of the classical Geniza period, the basket in which bread was collected for the poor and from which it was distributed to them. The long life of this primitive method of relief for the destitute may be explained by the scarcity of small coins prevalent throughout most of the period. Although change was hard to come by, it was easy for a family to prepare at home a few more loaves of bread than it needed for its consumption. Doing so also gave the woman of the house the opportunity to engage regularly in a meritorious work of piety. Technically this was possible because women made two types of bread: flat, soft loaves that were eaten fresh, preferably warm from the oven, and another, hard variety—a kind of biscuit that could stand a long time without becoming stale. It may be that on Friday, the traditional day of distribution (in Fustat there were two such days, Tuesday and Friday), bread of each type was donated, fresh loaves for consumption on the Sabbath and hard biscuits for the rest of the week. The Geniza offers no firm evidence on the question, but the special collections of fresh loaves of bread on Friday night and other nights reported for Fustat may point in this direction. The term "quppā" is never mentioned, however, in connection with Fustat. Since we possess hundreds of records and letters referring to charity from that city, this can only mean that the institution characterized by that word did not exist there.

Contributions to the public chest were made in two stages: the *pesīqā*, the assignment of a certain sum to a certain purpose by the community as a whole and by each contributor individually, and the *jibāya,* the collection of the sums promised. The first term is Hebrew, although it appears often in an Arabicized form (*basīqa* and the like), and carries with it a religious connotation: it was a vow that had to be fulfilled. The second is Arabic, a term often used in commerce to signify a long interval, often two months or more, between the "handshake" (agreement) and the "collection" in commercial transactions. A pesīqā was arranged both for the regular budget of the community and for any particular need requiring attention. The Geniza has preserved a contract with a beadle that provides for the same emoluments as those granted to his predecessors: in addition to the poll tax and "extras," he was to receive two pesīqā a year, which means that twice a year a number of persons would vow to contribute a certain sum for him. A pesīqā was usually made on the Day of Atonement, since charity was regarded as a means of expiation.

No appeal could be made without authorization. This rule is evident from applications to nagids and other dignitaries for permission to solicit funds and from a nagid's note under a solicitation ordering a cantor to read it out in the synagogue. Numerous letters, addressed by nagids and gaons to the community in Fustat, contain instructions to arrange a pesīqā, and there are responsa promising to expedite the collection of funds or explaining why it was impossible to arrange a pesīqā. Pledges were solicited not only in public but also privately, by notables going from house to house and from shop to shop, as stated expressly in some documents. It would be interesting to know whether there was any competition among the various professional groups. In accordance with the spirit of that age, there certainly did not exist any formal organization to solicit charitable funds either in the synagogue or door to door, but unofficial pressures perhaps proved no less effective, to judge by the many standard sums donated by large numbers of people.

Women are occasionally referred to as contributors and even as heading drives, especially for the upkeep of synagogues, but one finds them less frequently than one would expect in view of their far-reaching economic independence in those days. Their charitable concerns were mainly private and personal. Weddings and other family events, besides being essentially religious ceremonies, were also marked by charitable collections. These were of two types: for the needy and for the cantors and other singers of religious songs.

Needless to say, many pledges went uncollected. To expedite the realization of the pledges, and perhaps also to have as many members as possible participating in this meritorious work, several collectors were employed simultaneously; they often took care of the distribution as well. In one document showing the persons in charge of collection each week, a bridegroom heads the list, perhaps as a special honor. In a provincial town (Sunbāṭ), a merchant, while collecting debts outstanding, also collects from his customers their obligations to the community chest, repeatedly called here ṣibbūr, "the public."

Funds raised for the semiweekly distribution of loaves of bread to the poor usually brought more than was needed for that purpose, and the surplus was used for other important needs, such as communal salaries. Since the weekly collection was the backbone of recurring revenue, numerous documents refer to it, but it is not always easy to understand the procedure. The following steps seem to have been adhered to from the eleventh through the thirteenth century: During or shortly after the High Holidays that initiate the Jewish calendar year, the members of a congregation would vow how much they would contribute every week. A number of collectors (documents from the eleventh and thirteenth centuries mention eight to twelve at a time by name) would make the rounds every day except the Sabbath. On Sunday and Monday they would not collect much, but from Tuesday on the payments would be more substantial, and the service on Thursday morning was the occasion for trying to reach the weekly goal of contributions. The sums cashed in would be handed over to the parnāsīm, if they did not do the collecting themselves. The parnās would then draw up a list, either of the individual donors or of the sums brought in by each assistant collector, and he would note—on the left side of his account or on a separate sheet—the sums paid to community officials and needy people or amounts spent for other purposes.

In addition to the weekly collection, whose main purpose was the distribution of bread to the needy, there was a recurrent appeal for wheat, which was also addressed to the community at large. While the weekly contributions were invariably in money, as proved by all the extant lists, the gifts for the distributions of wheat were made either in cash or in kind; gifts of wheat were obviously regarded as more appropriate and more meritorious since they are always listed first. There was another striking difference between the collections for bread and those for wheat. Whereas bread collections consisted mostly in small standardized sums, wheat donations varied widely in amount. It seems, however, that when appeals were made close to one another in time, the same persons made approximately the same contributions.

The amounts required for this charity must have been very large, since the recipients of bread rations appear also in the lists of those partaking of the wheat distributions. We might therefore be right in assuming that everyone who was able to do so was expected to contribute. The Wheat Collection of Av for July and August 1178 lists 110 households making donations during two days, but it is more than probable that the drive was pursued throughout the period of mourning of the first nine days of Av, which culminates in the fast commemorating the destruction of the Temple of Jerusalem.

A third regular collection was that for clothing the needy and the lesser community officials. The lists referring to clothing suggest at least two yearly distributions. In view of the widespread custom of acquiring and wearing used garments, common even among well-to-do people in those days, one is surprised to find no reference to the collection of old clothes for the benefit of the poor. The communal authorities were extremely careful to ensure that persons of like social status received clothing of exactly the same type they ordinarily wore. Any other manner of distributing used garments would have led to endless jealousies and perhaps even disputes.

These three appeals, bread, wheat, and articles of clothing, provided for only the most basic needs. In addition, throughout the year, the congregation (assembled in the synagogue) responded to a vast range of individual requests.

While it was common to will a house or part of a house to the qōdesh, comparatively few documents have thus far come to light in which a sum of money or other movable property was bequeathed for charitable purposes. We have a bequest of two thousand dinars to the community chest, called *quppā shel ṣedāqa*, in a letter from Tyre. A man in Tunisia leaves all his property to the poor; a freedman gives one-quarter of his considerable belongings to the poor of his own town; another individual makes a contribution to the indigent of the Rabbanite community of Jerusalem.

In times of famine or other calamities causing food shortages, the social officers could incur severe hardship and even dangers, as is illustrated by an administrator of charities in Alexandria who complains to the nagid Abraham Maimonides of accusations and even threats against his life. The nagid had instructed the Jewish authorities in the Mediterranean port to store part of the wheat collected to meet impending emergencies. The administrator had acted accordingly, with the result that only meager rations could be distributed. A rival scholar took advantage of the hardships and dissatisfaction of the poor; arranging a collection of his own, he immediately distributed the wheat that he had accumulated. At the same time, rumors were spread that the nagid's administrator had appropriated some of the victuals destined for the poor. The agitation against the administrator culminated in his being accosted by a man who threatened to murder him if he did not distribute the accumulated reserves immediately and hand over the communal accounts to another specified person. The administrator, backed by the acting judge, as well as by prominent scholars and notables, was urged to take legal action against his adversaries, but, as he explains in the letter, because of the precariousness of the situation, he prefers to await a rescript of the nagid or the return of the chief judge to Alexandria. It should be noted that in many Geniza documents the population of Alexandria, Jewish and non-Jewish, seemed particularly prone to discord and violence.

Charitable Foundations (Houses and Other Communal Property)

During most of the Middle Ages—in western Europe and Byzantium, as well as in the lands of Islam—charitable works and institutions of learning were maintained largely by the income from houses and other immovable property donated for that purpose. The Jewish community was no exception. The rich documentation found in the Geniza records on the subject furnishes a good deal of insight on how the pious foundations in Islamic countries functioned, even though the early development of this institution is rather obscure.

A report about the history of the houses belonging to the synagogue of the Palestinians in Fustat up to 1039 makes mention of only eight houses and two stores. A century later, during the second half of the twelfth century, the situation is entirely different. The accounts for the years 1181 through 1184, that of one welfare officer alone, contains details about twenty-nine houses and ten shops, while from other sources we know the names of ten other houses then in the possession of the Jewish community of the city. More than ninety such houses are mentioned in the accounts preserved from the years 1164 through 1215, and numerous new items appear in later documents.

This large increase in the number of charitable foundations might have been caused by specific events, such as the migration of wealthier families from Fustat to Fatimid Cairo, the more fashionable city and the seat of the government, an exodus that precluded the profitable sale of old houses; it would have been deemed a commendable practice to give these properties away as a pious deed. It seems, however, that in the Islamic population as well there occurred—from the twelfth century on—a vast increase in the number and scope of charitable foundations. Thus, the marked changes discernible in our records might reflect a general trend of the period rather than circumstances particular to the Jewish community. As a matter of course, the spiritual and communal leaders took the lead. A house often mentioned in the 1180s was that of the rayyis Abū Manṣūr, the Arabic name of the nagid Samuel b. Hananya (1140–59). His chancellor, the judge Nathan, also left a house to the community. Nathan's wife had bequeathed to him half the house in which they lived and had given the other half to the qōdesh. It is not surprising that the judge followed the example of his wife when his own hour of death drew near. However, lesser figures from all walks of life also donated houses to the qōdesh.

There were also certain types of properties whose acquisition by the community remains unexplained. Such, for example, were the Oil House, the Vinegar House, or the Spinnery, and the hospices called *funduq*s, buildings ordinarily attached to a church or a synagogue and set aside to harbor needy travelers. We hear about "*the* funduq" or "the funduq on the Great Bazaar," as well as about "the small funduq" and "the new funduq" and another located between the two synagogues. Tenants paying monthly rents lived in the funduqs, as well as in buildings named after the commodities that were produced or sold therein. A slaughterhouse and a *misṭāḥ*, an open space for the spreading of materials dyed or tanned, are also mentioned as forming part of the *aḥbās al-yahūd*, or properties of the Jewish community.

The community chest shared many buildings with private persons, including Muslims and Christians, sometimes because a donor earmarked only a part of his property for the qōdesh, but mainly because many or most properties during the classical Geniza period were divided up among various owners. Normally, more than one tenant lived in a house belonging to a charitable foundation—as many as nine according to an account from the year 1040 or so—and twelve to fifteen parties shared the House of the Glassmaker in 1183 and in the years following.

It was not always possible to lease all the apartments available. Vacancies might occur even when the community owned comparatively few houses. In a later period we find vacancies in six out of fifteen houses — in three of them more than one vacancy; in another instance the entire building remained empty. Some accounts contain separate columns for unoccupied apartments. Half-empty dwellings entailed not only a loss of revenue but also the threat of encroachment by the Muslim authorities and special expenses as well. Under these circumstances, it is no wonder that rooms or apartments in the synagogue compound were rented also to non-Jews. Later on, such examples become common; the tenants of one apartment included even a Muslim judge — a qāḍī — who happened to abscond without paying the rent.

Many accounts imply or state expressly that tenants were in arrears with their rent. Tardiness in payments resulted sometimes in a reduction of the rent; sometimes stringent measures were imposed to collect the rents. A late tenancy statute, of which only the last four paragraphs have been preserved, makes the following points: (*a*) No excuse for late payment of the monthly rent is accepted. In case of want, "just as you beg for your food, beg for your rent." (*b*) The price fixed by three Jewish experts is definite, and no unilateral adjustment is allowed. (*c*) The tenants are required to show their contract with the charitable foundation (designated here by the Arabic term *waqf*) whenever requested. (*d*) No one is permitted to use the influence of Muslim acquaintances to obtain a lodging or a rent lower than that stipulated by the experts. In the event of his failure to comply with the statute, the tenant is threatened not with eviction but with excommunication, "which would bring damage to his person and to his property." Both Jewish and Muslim law provide that rents and wages are to be paid at the end of the periods for which they are due. In later times, however, when the community chest was in dire straits, the contracts it entered into show payments in advance for a full year and even for two years. The rent stipulated in these contracts was presumably lower than normal, and in one instance this is expressly stated.

Usually several persons dealt simultaneously with the varied property of the community. The official specifically charged with this task and most frequently mentioned in connection with it was the parnās. The parnāsīm constituted a kind of administrative board that received its instructions either from the chief parnās, where that office existed, or from the communal leader, whatever his rank or title at the time. Cantors and beadles often performed administrative work. Properties were also farmed out to professional collectors, some of whom were not Jewish.

In the spring of 1150, the energetic nagid Samuel b. Hananya appointed a general administrator for all the property of the community—from its synagogues, books, silver ornaments, and precious textiles to its houses, orchards, and palm groves. He even exempted the administrator from the supervision of the courts. This stringent effort at centralization had some salutary effects, inasmuch as the new administrator started to resuscitate the properties that had fallen into disrepair or into ruin. But such plenipotentiary powers were not to the taste of the Jewish public and conflicted also to a certain extent with Jewish law, which granted the courts the highest authority with regard to communal property. The office was abolished, either by Samuel's immediate successor, the gaon Nathanel b. Moses, or by Moses Maimonides during his first term of office. Yet the reforms introduced by that administrator must have been far-reaching: Over a hundred years later, in 1252, his letter of appointment was submitted to Maimonides' grandson, the nagid David b. Abraham, by some of the elders as the basis for all claims by or against the public chest.

Accounts of the collectors of revenue, partly drafts and partly clean copies, are normally divided into one or two months; some cover longer periods—four months or even five. A summary of expenditures and revenues over the six months that coincide with the second half of the Muslim year seems to indicate that yearly accounts for buildings were made, at least during certain periods, according to the Muslim calendar and not the Jewish calendar. These documents should be interpreted with the utmost caution. The predilection of medieval scribes for variety, as well as other reasons (such as a change of tenants), may result in the same building being referred to by two or three different designations. Moreover, in most cases only the actual receipts are listed; there is no indication whether they represent the entire rent due or only a fraction of it, or whether these sums also reflect the payments of arrears.

Since the idea of a central treasury was unknown, each collector served also as a paymaster. His balance sheet showed revenues on the right side and expenditures on the left. (The reason for this order of columns is, of course, that Arabic and Hebrew scripts run from right to left.) Sometimes revenues are written above expenditures. Depending on the purpose of the account, the side devoted to revenue shows the payments of each tenant, or the total payment of each house, or the collector's total monthly revenue. In some accounts the arrears or additional payments of tenants are indicated. On the expenditure side, first place is taken by the maintenance of the buildings concerned, including a small tax called *ḥikr* or lease (the idea being that the land itself was owned by the government), regular payments and gifts to watch-men and the keepers of the compounds, expenses for rubbish removal and cleaning of cesspits and, above all, for repairs. In one half-yearly account, the cost of repairs amounted to almost one-third the total rev-enues.

In addition to these expenses, countless items, changing every month, reveal the varied needs and social services of the community. In the first place, there was the expenditure for olive or linseed oil for the lighting of places of worship and for sundry other purposes. Second, payments for community officials and teachers (the latter received only small sums for orphans and the children of the poor whom they happened to teach during the month concerned). Third, an odd variety of grants to needy of all kinds. Finally, where there was a cash balance, purses of dirhems or dinars, or bankers' notes, were handed over—not to a treasurer, for one did not exist—but to specified persons such as a parnās, a cantor, or a beadle. Usually several individuals acted as treasurers during any given month.

We have very definite information on the cost of the administration of the qōdesh. In various accounts dealing with collection, the collector's fee is invariably 10 percent of the revenue, which seems reasonable given the varied troubles the administrator had to face. Occasionally, when the Muslim authorities were rapacious, or when the revenue was oth-erwise reduced through no fault of the collector, a special settlement with regard to his compensation was made. It is still premature to assess the total revenue from the immovable property of the Jewish commu-nity chest as reflected in the Geniza records. One fact stands out clearly: during the second half of the twelfth and the first half of the thirteenth century, a period for which we have comparatively rich documentation, the immovable property willed or donated to the community yielded a large percentage of its regular revenue. It is somewhat strange to see the dead providing for the daily needs of the living; this phenomenon, how-ever, accords with a civilization in which people were eager to save their souls by special deeds of piety.

The Officials

Despite a certain regularity discernible in the salary scales and other types of income in the Geniza records, each employee of the community seems to have worked under a special contract that also left considerable leeway for correlating remuneration with performance. One benefit, it seems, was granted to all officials, high and low: the community paid their poll tax to the Muslim government. Whether it was the beadle of a synagogue in 1075, or the Jewish chief judge of the capital in 1213, or a schoolteacher in a small town, payment of the poll tax was made or promised for all of them. There are many instances of this payment in our records. (As a matter of fact, this arrangement remained unchanged up to late Ottoman times.) In this respect, the position of the ritual slaughterer was particularly noteworthy. He had to deliver to the community a part of his weekly income, but the community paid his poll tax. The payment of their poll tax by the community meant a great deal to people who were short of cash. It seems, however, that this benefit to community officials had more than financial significance; it dates back to the talmudic precept that scholars — and, as a rule, only scholarly persons were appointed as community officials — should not share the burdens imposed on the public. This injunction was based on the moral idea that learning makes one free: "Whosoever accepts the yoke of the Torah is exempted from the yoke of the rulers."

With respect to salaries, various arrangements are evident in the documents. The differences are accounted for not so much by the change of time or place as by the diversity of the sources from which the emoluments were paid. A muqaddam in Hebron complains that he has received neither a pesīqān or a weekly salary. We often read about both systems of remuneration in our sources. With equal frequency we find a monthly salary, in some cases paid to the same officials who appear in other records receiving weekly wages. The reason for this duplication was technical. The rents for the houses belonging to the community were paid monthly; therefore, when the collector of the rents acted as paymaster, salaries were calculated on a monthly basis. On the other hand, when the wages were paid from the weekly contributions of the community members, the payrolls were made out weekly. Since most of the lists are undated, it is difficult to say whether an official received both weekly and monthly payments at one and the same time, although duplication may well have occurred.

Most community officials, from the cantors down, appear also as recipients of bread and wheat. They normally received larger quantities than the needy persons listed with them. Under Muslim administrative practice, employees were paid partly in cash and partly in kind, an arrangement that applied to a private teacher as well as to a soldier or an army officer. The *dīnār jayshī*, the unit of a Muslim soldier's pay, consisted of a quarter of one dinar in cash and certain quantities of wheat and oats. It may be, however, that including cantors, beadles, inspectors of slaughterhouses and of dairies, night watchmen, and others (as well as parnāsī at times) in the lists of the those that received bread and wheat was not a Muslim borrowing but an old Jewish custom; the idea may have been that these professions ordinarily attracted those who were hard-pressed to earn a living and were regarded, at least theoretically, as belonging to the poor.

No unified practice prevailed, it seems, in the distribution of clothing to officials. In some lists, cantors, beadles, and other lower officials and even the parnās in charge of the distribution, received either an item of clothing or a small monetary compensation. In one list written around 1200, a judge, a cantor, a beadle, and the distributing parnās are allocated the very handsome sum of 45 dirhems each; since the parnās notes in a postscript that he has already received 22½ dirhems for a *yūsufī* cloth, we may assume that the sum of 45 dirhems was sufficient for two articles of apparel. It is noteworthy that the judge and the beadle, although receiving different salaries, are given identical sums for their clothing.

We noted earlier that many documents suggest that community officials — and in particular, beadles and cantors — lived in the synagogue compound. Some references give the impression that free lodging was granted these officials, and one list states so explicitly. Some later records, however, show them paying rents to the community chest like other tenants. Another important benefit to officials was the payment by the community of school fees for their children. In most cases it is not indicated whether the boys referred to were fatherless or not. Although, generally speaking, care for all widows and fatherless children was one of the main concerns of public charity, many of our lists show that particular attention was paid to the immediate families of deceased community officials.

Was there anything resembling a pension for retired officials? Our data, such as they are, seem to indicate that when officials retired (wholly or partly), they received only a fraction of their former emoluments, but this is far from certain. In any case, additional work connected with each office and "honoraria" of various kinds constituted the main source of income for community officials. The dayyānīm, cantors, and beadles had regular functions at weddings and funerals, family events from which they probably derived more monies than they received from the community chest. Judges normally were also notaries and scribes, and for each document they wrote appropriate fees were paid by the parties involved.

Maimonides in his *Code of Law* insists on the old religious concept that public service, such as sitting in judgment or teaching adults, should be rendered without compensation. The Geniza evidence shows that this postulate was not as implausible as it may appear. The salaries paid by the community chest to public servants were no more than "compensation for loss of time"; their true income came from a wide variety of other sources, a arrangement that accorded with both the religious attitude and the spirit of free enterprise characteristic of the Jewish society of the period. Instances of uncompensated service to the community, such as teaching adults, dispensing law, and performing religious functions, continued to exist well into the twentieth century, and not only in eastern Europe, where traditional Jewish life persisted until World War II, but sporadically elsewhere as well.

The Needy

The family was the first recourse for individuals in distress. The loss of face that befell a clan unwilling or unable to support a faltering member was in itself sufficient incentive for coming to his rescue, even where humanitarian or religious impulses did not inspire such action. That protection, of course, did not cover solitary people — foreigners and others — nor indigent families consisting entirely of paupers. The communities that have left us their records in the Cairo Geniza extended many different types of help to these unfortunate people, including cash payments and subsidies of various sorts that covered basic needs for the living as well as burial for the dead.

First and foremost was the weekly distribution of bread, the main food staple. Bread was distributed with absolute regularity during the entire Geniza period and was the conspicuous feature of public charity. Twice a week, on Tuesday and Friday, the Jewish community of Fustat would distribute between 500 and 600 loaves of bread to about 140 persons or households, an average of about 4 loaves for each recipient. Utmost care was taken to ensure that each household received exactly what it was entitled to — no more, no less — a fact made evident by the changes in the rations discernible from week to week and even from a Tuesday to a Friday. Four loaves of bread, weighing a total of about 1,750 grams (approximately 4 pounds) would not, of course, have been sufficient food for one week. But the community also distributed wheat, which meant perhaps that, on special occasions, poor people as well preferred to bake their own bread (or, rather, to prepare it at home and have it baked by a *farrān*). Even combined, however, the quantities of bread and wheat could not have provided more than mere subsistence. Some proselytes, presumably Europeans of noble descent, were apportioned exceptionally high quantities of wheat, perhaps because their eating habits were so different from those of the indigenous population. That view has been confirmed to some extent by a fragmentary text. A proselyte expresses his gratitude in beautiful Hebrew to a distinguished woman who looked after him. He thanks her for the fine bread she has sent and then gives her instructions on how to bake certain cakes (he suggests putting hot ginger in them). In the introduction to his letter he says, "When I was holding an office in the vain religion that I followed before, I was served twelve dishes or more. Every day I partook of [meat, wine, and so on, and] extremely tasty bread. I tried [to obtain such bread] from the day I came to the land of Ishmael [Muslim countries], but was never entirely successful, until I found favor in your eyes. . . ."

Clothing Distribution

There were two types of clothing distribution: one for those who served the community and the other for the poor. Distinguished persons received a *muqaddar*, literally, "something valued," a term which seems to denote an expensive item of clothing. Most of the clothing distributed was, however, modest. The lists mention either felt garments or, in most cases, something known as *jūkhāniyya*. It probably was a robe with a hood, similar to the present-day Maghrebi burnoose.[3] There is also mention of a *fūṭa,* a sari-like cloth, the price of which varied widely in accordance with the material used. Respectable beneficiaries received pieces of cloth, which they would have tailored according to

---

3. It is plausible that the latter was similar to or identical with the fourteenth-century *jūkha,* a kind of cloak or raincoat, which the Muslim traveler al-Maqrīzī (d. 1442) reports being worn by Europeans and other foreigners as well as by poor people in Cairo; only later, when prices for clothing had soared, did respectable persons also begin to wear the garment. Eliahu Ashtor has drawn attention to high-priced jūkhāniyyas made of silk, fine linen, or other costly fabrics; such garments appear in trousseau lists ("Some Features of Jewish Communities in Medieval Egypt" [in Hebrew], *Zion* 30 [1965], 68). It is likely, then, that the term *jūkhāniyya,* although derived from *jūkh,* (woolen) cloth, designates the cut of the garment, not its material.

their own taste. Sometimes a piece of clothing was given to more than one person. Cash was sometimes given as an alternative to direct gifts of clothing, although it is unlikely that the small sums mentioned in the accounts—from one to five silver coins—would have gone very far. (The cash allocation for clothing did not represent the entire amount a needy person received for a certain period, but rather the share allotted by a particular collector during a certain month.) Thus we find Sirb, a freedwoman, receiving a jūkhāniyya in fall 1183 and only a few months later getting five dirhems for clothing. Most of the beneficiaries of this charity were women, in accordance with the talmudic injunction and the conventional wisdom that female decency required proper clothing.

Other Subsidies

As a rule, free lodging in the houses owned by the community was not among the benefits granted to needy people, at least not in later times. Many poor families, however, lived in houses belonging to pious foundations, and many tenants of these houses appear in the dole lists of the community. A closer study of the numerous references to prices of rents found in the Geniza records proves that many indigents were paying reduced rents: thus, although there was no free lodging, there was subsidized housing. After food, clothing, and housing, the most urgent need of a member of the minority groups under Islam was money for the jālīya. Failure to comply with this obligation entailed imprisonment, which, because of the bad state of the prisons in those times, could mean death. It is no exaggeration to say that the largest single group of requests for help preserved in the Geniza is for assistance to pay the jālīya. This charity, which was regarded as nearly equivalent to the greatest of all meritorious works, "the ransoming of the captives," was not left entirely to private initiative; in certain periods it must have been the main object of communal efforts. It is clear from preserved lists that the majority of people requiring assistance were not entirely destitute. Therefore, the community expected them to contribute whatever they could while it made up the rest.

No reference to a Jewish hospital has been found thus far in the Geniza material. This is somewhat surprising, for both the Geniza records and Arabic sources mention many Jewish doctors working in what could be called government hospitals, namely, those established by Muslim rulers; there are no Geniza references, however, to Jewish patients making use of the Muslim hospitals. On the other hand, our records from both the eleventh and the twelfth centuries reveal the existence of pious donations for medicines for the Jewish needy or for indigent sick people in general. Physicians treated indigent patients at no charge — provided the sick could make their way to the physicians. Both Maimonides and his great-great-grandson David b. Joshua gave medical advice and help to poor persons with whom they had dealings in their capacity as heads of the Jews. Numerous disabled persons of all descriptions are mentioned in the lists of beneficiaries of the community chest. The blind, although they do not appear in particularly large numbers, seem to have constituted a special group.

Education, a significant item in the family budget, was provided by the Jewish community to orphans (that is, fatherless children) and the children of the poor. Many references to this are found in our records — in particular, details about payments to teachers noted in monthly or weekly accounts. This educational policy changed over time. During the eleventh and early twelfth centuries, we read about the community providing special classes for orphans — even supplying food there for them; later, orphans and children of the poor were given over to teachers whose fees were paid by the community. This change was attributable probably not to new pedagogical insight, but to the general decrease in the number of children in Fustat. A letter addressed to a nagid suggests that it was customary for the community to provide a minimum education for orphan girls as well, and that books were donated to the synagogue for the use of orphans.

The people of the Mediterranean, and the Jews in particular, were busy travelers. Lack of funds was an incentive rather than an impediment to travel, for the local communities would lodge, feed, and, if necessary, clothe the needy foreigner and see to it that he reached the next place able to take care of him. The Geniza abounds in references to such charitable works. People from outside of Fustat regularly constitute the largest single group in the lists of the needy receiving bread. Although we hear little about lodging, it may be assumed that because the community owned houses that were rarely rented out in their entirety, as well as several funduqs, such houses were used to lodge travelers, wealthy and poor alike.

Having arrived in a place like Fustat, the foreigner might remain for some time. If the traveler took ill, a rather common occurrence, the community incurred serious expenses, especially if the patient happened to be a scholar: He had to be lodged in a private home, and his food, medicines, and other needs supplied. The cantors, often widely traveled persons themselves, usually played host. Finally, the visitor had to be dispatched to the next station on his journey. In the case of a distinguished guest, accompanied by a retinue, this was a large item of expenditure. Sometimes the traveler was in a hurry to catch a caravan, whereupon the community would be asked by the nagid to expedite a collection in his favor. Occasionally, particularly when a person of modest status was concerned, the authority responsible for his travel would see to it that he reached his final destination. For example, after having arranged for the travel of a poor woman and her infant daughter from Fustat to Alexandria, the nagid Abraham Maimonides asked the community in Alexandria to send her on to Palestine, where she had a grown daughter and some property.

When a foreigner stayed on for a longer period or settled permanently, work had to be found for him. The fact that so many teachers and cantors from foreign countries make their appearance in the Geniza documents may be partly attributable to the difficulty of finding other occupations for educated persons without means. In one case, and most appropriately, a newcomer was assigned the administration of a communal caravanserai. The relevant document states that he was given that post in preference to his compatriots arriving with him—but he was a complete failure. Communities also tried to regulate the influx of foreigners. A traveler on his way to Jerusalem from the land of the Franks, stopping in Fustat, was asked by the yeshiva to meet with the "distinguished member" Eli b. Amram, whose report would decide whether the pilgrim would be welcome in the Holy City; clearly, the pilgrim intended to settle there permanently. The same dignitary was approached on behalf of a cantor from Spain with small children, who was exiled from his country (for unstated reasons); the exile had found temporary refuge on his way to Fustat.

Ransoming of Captives

Rescuing captives was the most costly demand on public charity. A person captured by pirates first had to be ransomed, a cost of 33⅓ dinars; he had to be given clothing as well, since his clothes were invariably taken by the pirates, and he also had to be maintained during his stay in the country and on his way back to his place of origin. A poll tax and a port duty (amounting in one instance to 2½ dinars) had to be paid to the Muslim authorities for him, and, of course, the fare of his return journey had to be found. A single captive might cost the community more than the provision of bread for 150 persons during two months. Raising such sums required a major communal effort that involved all elements of Jewish society.

In addition to all these recurrent and often exacting demands on private and communal generosity, there occasionally occurred a disaster, the consequences of which could be overcome or mitigated only by extraordinary efforts. In the Geniza period we first have the destruction of the Christian and Jewish houses of worship in and around the year 1012, entailing decades of rebuilding; then the devastation of Palestine by bedouins and Seljuks and, later, the capture of Jerusalem by the Crusaders in 1099. The Geniza records prove that the Jewish population of the Holy City was not entirely annihilated, as believed before, but that the capture of the city created a substantial refugee problem. When Jerusalem was recaptured by Saladin in 1187, strenuous efforts were made to restore the Jewish houses of worship and learning. Finally, in 1265, when Sultan Baybars threatened to burn the Christians and Jews of Cairo but converted the punishment into an exorbitant fine, the Jewish communities of the Egyptian Rīf exerted themselves to help their brethren in the capital bear a burden they were unable to shoulder alone.

Epilogue: An Appraisal of Social Services

Needless to say, we can recover at best only a partial picture of the social services in the Mediterranean Jewish community during the eleventh through the thirteenth century; our sources are fragmentary and not equally representative of all periods and places. The most striking feature of these services was that they were all rooted in pre-Islamic, talmudic institutions and changed little over the Geniza period. For example, throughout the centuries two loaves of bread were given twice a week. The distributions of wheat, clothing, and cash also remained constant—as long as the impoverished community was able to bear the cost.

In his *Code of Law*, Maimonides enumerates eight degrees of charity, the highest being the help extended to a faltering member of the community through a gift, a loan, a partnership, or employment, which would spare him from needing public assistance. There is ample evidence in the Geniza records that Maimonides' admonition (which is based on a talmudic precept) was followed by many of his contemporaries. It applied, however, mainly to relatives, friends, colleagues, or sons of good families, who had not yet "uncovered their faces" by accepting alms or other relief in public. Those who had, belonged to the mass of 'anniyīm, "the poor." They were almost a people unto themselves, a subgroup that one was obliged to support but that could not expect to be extricated completely from poverty. "God is the maker of rich and poor" (Proverbs 22:2). It was assumed that one helped the poor as much as one could, but there was no obligation to make them wealthy, for poverty was ordained by God; one might mitigate its evil consequences, but one could not root it out altogether. Charity was designed to keep people at a subsistence level. Even if the community had sought to eradicate poverty altogether, the large number of relief recipients as compared with that of breadwinners would have made that impossible.

Although rooted in biblical notions of tribal responsibility, the motivation of charity was largely religious, a duty to God rather than solely to one's fellow man. Gifts to the poor served as vehicles to express one's gratitude to God or to seek his forgiveness; they substituted, in a sense, for sacrificial offerings: the Temple of Jerusalem—the only permissible site of sacrifice—had long been destroyed. This idea, so impressively expounded in talmudic and medieval literature, was taken literally and deeply held. The long calligraphic lists of contributors, which were suspended in the synagogue for public examination and as incentive to further liberality, may well have had an additional purpose: they were destined for God, who, while inspecting his synagogue, would see, black on white, what pious and charitable people had come to pray in His house.

Private munificence competed with communal charity. With the exception of collections, which were made on extraordinary occasions, only relatively small sums were donated in response to public appeals or as regular contributions to a synagogue. Liberality was a virtue best displayed in splendid isolation. While the basic needs of the mass of the poor were satisfied by the social services, special cases of want or misfortune—and how numerous they were—were as a rule directed to private help.

FIVE

Houses of Worship

Architecture

The architecture of the Christian or Jewish houses of worship under Islam cannot be discussed without noting Islamic legal restrictions regarding synagogues and churches. According to a proviso in one of the oldest sources of Muslim law, no churches or synagogues were to be established in the new towns founded by the conquerors, an injunction that soon was understood to mean that no new non-Islamic houses of worship were to be erected anywhere in Islamic territory. In fact, however, numerous churches and synagogues existed in Fustat and Baghdad at a time when the power of Islam was at its height, and even Cairo, which was founded in 969, soon had its own churches and synagogues. Occasional references to the rebuilding of houses of worship are found in the Geniza records. It is misleading, however, to infer from this that the law banning non-Islamic houses of worship was honored more in the breach than in the observance. The more distinguished churches and monasteries in Fustat and Baghdad were pre-Islamic; the new non-Muslim houses of devotion, to the contrary, had to be modest and inconspicuous so as not to arouse the attention of zealots. Indeed, a Geniza letter reports that the renovated part of a *kanīsa* (referring, it seems, to a church and not a synagogue) had to be pulled down because it was higher than a nearby mosque. Synagogue architecture as reflected in the Geniza records should be considered in the light of this situation.

The most striking architectural difference between synagogue and mosque was that the former had a gallery for women. As a rule, Muslims were uneasy about the presence of women in the mosque and for the most part banished them altogether from their houses of worship. In the Temple of Jerusalem, it seems, women were originally separated from men only on special occasions involving popular entertainment rather than during acts of devotion. In the ancient synagogues of Galilee we find structures understood to have been women's galleries; the same is true of the magnificent synagogue of Sardis in Asia Minor. The existence of such a gallery in medieval synagogues is confirmed by the Geniza records. The synagogues of both the Palestinians and Babylonians in Fustat had a women's gallery (called *bayt al-nisā'*, "the place for woman"), as did the holy shrine of Dammūh near Gizeh on the western bank of the Nile. The gallery was reached by a staircase leading up from a special entrance, called *bāb al-sirr*, "the secret door," or *bāb al-nisā'*, "the women's door." The portal faced a side street leading to the thoroughfare, on which the main gate of the synagogue opened. This separation, however, did not prevent women and men from meeting before and after prayer.

Common to all synagogues was the holy ark, which contained the Torah scrolls. During the classical Geniza period, the ark was called the *hēkhāl*. (The word is biblical Hebrew, but it was not used in the talmudic period; it stands to reason that the term was borrowed from Coptic *haykal*, "sanctuary," itself ultimately derived from the Hebrew Bible.) In the synagogue of Hebron, which was rebuilt at the end of the eleventh century, the ark was situated between the two entrance gates. This arrangement recalls the tripartite doorway (one main and two side entrances) found in the wall facing Jerusalem in the ancient synagogues of Galilee, such as those of Capernaum, Chorasin, and Beth Shearim. The orientation of the ark was always in the direction of Jerusalem except when the lay of the land made that impossible. At that time, the ark was still a wooden chest and not a stone structure, and the tripartite portal was, of course, a common feature in Hellenistic architecture.

Another construction detail common to many synagogues was the raised platform in the middle of the building, on which the Scripture lections and certain parts of the liturgy were read. Solemn processions, headed by a particularly holy Torah scroll and moving from the ark to the platform and back, were ancient custom in the synagogue of the Palestinians. Talmudic literature makes frequent reference to a reader's platform, called *bēmā* (a Greek word)—ordinarily a piece of movable wooden furniture. In the Geniza period, we have instead a fixed structure made of masonry, called *anbōl*, cognate with the Latin-Greek-Coptic *ambon(e)*, which still designates a similar structure in Coptic churches. The term appears in a Geniza letter with reference to a synagogue in Ascalon, and a Greek inscription from Side in Pamphylia (southern Asia Minor) mentions a Jewish ambon. The absence of references in talmudic sources to such a central architectural feature of the synagogue building suggests that it was taken over directly from church architecture in a later period (approximately between 400 and 600 C.E.). The Geniza also contains a reference to the *ṭāqat al-anbōl*, "the niche in the platform," which was large enough to harbor a Torah scroll. (It is noteworthy that *ḥēkhāl* has remained the term for the holy ark among the Oriental Jewish communities, while the foreign word *anbōl*, although used throughout the Geniza period in both documentary and literary sources, has disappeared from the Jewish lexicon.) The Muslim term for the pulpit (*minbar*) became the designated term for the elevated platform in the synagogue; the Hebrew term *migdāl* is found only in learned books; *minbar* almost never appears in Geniza records.

Furnishings

Unlike the mosque, where prayer is short and consists mostly of prostrations, genuflections, and other bodily movements, the service of the synagogue is protracted even on workdays and requires that the congregation be seated most of the time. According to the habits of that period, pews or chairs were not used. Instead, the floors of synagogues were covered with mats and carpets; members would bring in cushions on which to sit or recline. Our knowledge of the synagogue furnishings during the Geniza period is derived mainly from inventories drawn up either when a new beadle was appointed or when the pieces remaining after the sack of the city or a similar disaster were counted. Such lists have been preserved from the years 1075, 1080, 1095/96, 1099, 1159, 1181, and 1186. It seems that the compound of the synagogue of the Palestinians—the main synagogue of Fustat—was better protected than that of the Babylonians; it often provided storage for all or some of the metalwork and precious textiles belonging to the Babylonian synagogue. A synagogue usually had more than one beadle, each apparently responsible for particular furnishings.

The lighting of the synagogue also appears as an important concern in the Geniza documents. Monthly accounts of expenditures for olive and linseed oil are extremely common. Detailed lists of lighting devices are also found in the records from the years 1075 and 1080—that is, shortly after the great sack of Cairo by the Turkish mercenaries, when even the palaces of the caliph were plundered and the fabulous treasures of the Fatimids were looted. A remark in a contemporaneous letter indicates that the synagogue of the Palestinians in Fustat did not escape the general devastation. Not a single silver lamp is mentioned in those lists, not even the one that hung in the holy ark according to an earlier document. On the other hand, the number and types of lighting devices referred to in the Geniza records are impressive and include a wide variety of different sizes, shapes, and designs.

Synagogues were particularly rich in precious textiles, which served primarily to decorate walls and columns. Murals, such as those found at Dura-Europos illustrating biblical stories, had been banned from synagogues by the seventh century, and there are references to the whitewashing of the Palestinian synagogue. Hangings, on the other hand, were a common decoration, as they were in private homes. The material especially cherished was *siglaton*, a famous medieval fabric of heavy damask, which in the synagogue inventories is invariably of two colors, such as light green with blue-black, or white with black or red; sometimes it was decorated with stripes of gold and silver. Brocade is also well represented. The covers for the Torah scroll, the Pentateuch, and the Haftara (the lections from the Prophets) were particularly luxurious; a cover was spread over the *tēvā*, the desk on which the scrolls were laid when they were chanted. The inventories include also other utensils, such as reading stools (*kursī*) and a prayer mantle (*īzār*) to be worn by the kohens, the priestly congregants, while pronouncing their blessing.

The most honored possessions of any synagogue were, of course, its Torah scrolls and books. After the sack of Cairo in 1075, there were eighteen Torah scrolls in the synagogue of the Palestinians, some of which belonged to the Babylonians and to the holy shrines of Dammūh and Taṭay. Some lists indicate that the scrolls were stored in plain copper or wood cases; others mention more ornate cases covered with decoration. The synagogues were eager to acquire old codices written by famous scribes—or at least copies of such codices, designated as their "brothers." Utmost care was taken to read the Holy Scriptures with the correct pronunciation and with the traditional cantillation that fixed the tone appropriate for each word (analogous to neumes in Western church music during the Middle Ages); this could be done only with the help of authoritative and scrupulously exact texts. Our lists indicate that book stocks were often depleted over time because of fire, general wear and tear, and the failure to return loaned texts. There is, however, evidence that books were replaced, sometimes from unexpected sources. The synagogue of Fustat was enriched by the most precious treasures: the manuscripts looted by the Crusaders at the conquest of Jerusalem in 1099 and sold by them afterward to the Jews of Egypt. Some of these treasures are still in existence, preserved in public libraries in Europe, the United States, and Israel.

Since the synagogues had no pews or other furniture where one could keep one's own books for use during the service, and since Bible codices were heavy, the weekly Torah lections were copied separately in small booklets that could be carried easily by the worshipers. This custom gave the wealthier members of a congregation the opportunity to vie with each other in acquiring precious copies of holy texts. An outstanding example is the weekly lection of Numbers, chapters 13–15, written in 1106/7, most probably in Fustat, by Isaac b. Abraham ha-Levi, remarkable both for its precious readings and its artistic execution. The talmudic injunction, "beautify yourself before God with good works," was understood also to mean that the objects used in God's service should excel in beauty.

The Synagogue Compound

"The synagogue" was not limited to the place in which the prayers were held, but comprised the whole surrounding compound, all of which constituted the property of the synagogue. We read about a house adjoining, *mulāziq* (lit., "cleaving to"), the synagogue, others adjacent to its vestibule, *dihlīz*, or to its *sukka* (the hut for the Feast of Tabernacles), or to the women's entrance. Also mentioned are the living quarters, *sukn*, of a man, and the apartment, *ṭabaqa*, of another, designating one of the buildings in the immediate vicinity of the synagogue. Some letters indicate a synagogue as the address; since the synagogue complex bordered on more than one street, one would indicate also the street on which the living quarters of the addressee were situated. In a smaller locality, an upper story of the place of prayer might even house a workshop. Asked whether this was proper, Moses Maimonides decided that the room directly above the holy ark should not be used as a bedroom or as a workshop. The synagogue compound had two special designations: *jiwār al-kanīs*, literally, "neighborhood of the synagogue," and *rubʿ al-kanīs*, which, although pronounced thus, seems not to have meant "quarter" (as in classical Arabic *rubʿ*), but rather "area" or "residence" (*rabʿ*).

The clustering of houses around a synagogue or Coptic church served various purposes. It was in the first instance a protective measure, aimed at concealing the building from attack by agitated Muslims during times of religious tension. The general area of the synagogue was also considered a desirable place to live (Jews could travel to worship only by foot during the Sabbath or religious holidays), a fact that may also account for the manner in which the building blended into its general environment. The synagogue itself served many functions: It was the meeting place for sessions of the rabbinical court. Classes for schoolchildren that were not held in houses rented by teachers or in private homes took place in the synagogue. (Schoolchildren were called "synagogue boys" for that reason.) Adults as well studied in the synagogue, especially at night, on the Sabbath, and on holidays. Whether these particular activities took place in the hall dedicated to communal prayer or in adjacent rooms or buildings is not evident from our sources. Synagogues also served as hospices for travelers in need and for foreigners seeking shelter.

Since the distribution of bread and wheat to communal officials and to the needy was one of the main social services, it is natural that the community kept a room for storing wheat in the synagogue. The synagogue compound also included the communal sukka for use during the seven days of the Feast of Tabernacles—a necessity in crowded cities, where many people lived in apartments or possessed no courtyard in which they could put up a festival booth of their own. The communal sukka of Fustat was a permanent building. In addition to its function in the Feast of Tabernacles, it could be used during the rest of the year, especially for weddings, prescribed to take place under the stars, and other festive occasions when accommodations in private homes were not sufficient.

Congregants were obligated to wash before prayer. Unlike drinking water, which was brought by carriers from the Nile, water for washing was supplied by subterranean wells. Such wells would have been an essential component of the synagogue courtyard, and they are expressly mentioned in one Geniza document. Strange as it may seem to anyone familiar with traditional Jewish practices, no reference to a ritual bath has been traced thus far in any Geniza document referring to Egypt prior to 1200. In Palestine, for example, a ritual bath connected with a synagogue building in Ramle is mentioned in a document written shortly after the severe earthquake of 1034; another is mentioned in a letter to a nagid, most probably with regard to Jerusalem, thus showing the practice of Egyptian Jewry to have been unusual. Had there been a ritual bath in Fustat prior to 1200, it would have been mentioned somewhere, particularly in the many accounts of repairs of buildings belonging to the community. This impression is confirmed by the text of a statute issued by Moses Maimonides and nine other scholars in spring 1176. It notes that, with very few exceptions, public and private bath-houses were regarded by Jewish women in Egypt as sufficient for the ritual requirements of monthly purification, a laxity regarded as an abomination by Maimonides, who had come from the far stricter Muslim West. The reforms introduced by the statute were very severe in nature, and their impact is immediately recognizable in the Geniza records. In many marriage contracts issued after 1176, the two spouses promise to observe the so-called laws of purity—under penalty, in the case of intentional transgression, of losing all rights resulting from the contract. The pool of the Babylonian synagogue of Fustat, which appears in an account from April 1234, is evidence of a stricter and more widespread observation of the ritual laws.

Life in the Synagogue

The Geniza synagogue was a house of assembly in which one encountered both God and one's fellowmen. When the holy ark was opened and the Torah scrolls revealed, the devout worshiper felt transported into the very presence of God. A man tells us in a Geniza letter that during a time of great danger, he went to the synagogue, opened the ark, and rolled himself on the floor beneath it, showing in this way his utmost devotion. He was subsequently saved, causing joy among both Jews and Muslims, who congratulated him. "It was a glorious day because God had shown mercy upon us all. He had heard my prayer and had noticed my fasting and how I rolled myself beneath the holy ark."

Taking an oath on the Bible, a mere formality in modern courts, was regarded as the invocation of God as a personal witness and was therefore administered in the synagogue in front of the open ark and Torah scrolls. These ceremonial trappings were believed to be so essential that we find a query addressed to Maimonides asking whether an oath on a codex of the Bible (rather than a scroll) was legally binding. In short, the synagogue was revered as a sanctuary. At the same time, the synagogue served so many cultural and communal purposes that its character as a house of worship became blurred. Unlike the mosque, where all present prayed toward Mecca (that is, to God), the members of the congregation in the synagogue sat along the walls or in spaces in front of them facing one another, enhancing thereby the sense of community. Abraham Maimonides, the pietist reformer (1186–1237), tried to change the seating arrangements to have all congregants facing the holy ark throughout the service and sought to do away with the comfortable cushions and reclining pillows, which seemed to him inappropriate to a servant in the presence of the Almighty. This effort proved unsuccessful, and the seating arrangements in all oriental Jewish congregations remain to this day just as they were during the Geniza period. In Islam as well there were many complaints that the mosque served too many secular purposes, so much so that the prophet Muḥammad was credited with having said, "At the end of the days, people will enter the mosques and sit in them in circles, speaking about worldly things and loving this world. Do not join their circles, for God has no use for them." Nonetheless, for reasons explained below, the difference between Jewish and Muslim worship was marked and caused much soul-searching for pious Jews.

During the classical Geniza period, Jewish services were held three times daily on workdays; the Muslims prayed five times. The Muslim prayer periods were, however, significantly shorter, and although Islam similarly favored attendance at public service over private prayer, Jews were far more insistent in this respect. On Mondays and Thursdays, when a Torah scroll was taken out and a section of the weekly lection read in public, most Jews attended the synagogue. There are many references in the Geniza records to communal events taking place during or after the services on Monday and Thursday. Appeals to the congregation assembled during these morning services were common, and court sessions were regularly held afterwards. One document characteristically speaks of a settlement reached between a man from Baghdad and another from Damascus and an oath given by the latter in the synagogue of the Palestinians in Fustat "after prayer." The oath was administered according to the gaon of Jerusalem's written instructions, which had arrived shortly before and were known to the members of the congregation present.

As to the Sabbath, Saadya Gaon writes in his prayer book, "For about half a day we stay in the synagogue, devoting ourselves to prayer and to the reading of the Torah and expounding the subjects related to each Sabbath [i.e., the contents of the weekly lections from the Scriptures]." Four services were held on Sabbath and holy days; readings from the Scriptures were rather lengthy, all the more so since the Hebrew text was translated verse by verse into Aramaic, a language that had been the international means of communication throughout southwestern Asia before the Islamic conquest. By the Geniza period, Aramaic had been displaced by other languages; even scholars were less familiar with it than with Hebrew. Still, the old custom of reading the Aramaic translation (*Targūm*) was retained, and even boys were trained to recite the Targūm, most likely with breathtaking speed.

After the morning service and before the reading of the Scriptures (not after, as was customary in later times), a sermon was delivered, or more exactly a *derāsh*—a combination of sermon, lecture, and disputation. When time permitted, another derāsh would be delivered, either by a notable guest addressing the general public, which might include people from a number of synagogues, or by a scholar chosen to speak to a select group—an occasion on which special invitations, calligraphically written, were sent to the notables of the community. According to one letter, such a lecture and disputation lasted through all the daylight hours of the Sabbath. The writer, who apparently attended the derāsh, was a fruit peddler, indicating a rather high general level of learning and intellectual involvement. The derāsh of the nagid was, however, not ordinarily subjected to immediate questioning during the service itself.

The most time-consuming portion of the service was the piyyūṭ, the poetical segments inserted randomly into the official order of prayer. (The word is derived from Greek *poet[es]* and is pre-Islamic. In Arabic, these poetical pieces are called *ḥizāna,* because it was during this part of the service that the *ḥazzan*, or cantor, had to prove his mettle.) The biblical exhortation "Sing unto the Lord a new song" (Psalm 98:1), echoed in the talmudic injunction "Everyone is obliged to say something new in his prayer every day," was taken seriously in the Geniza period, thus continuing a tradition of liturgical poetry dating back some five hundred years prior. Tens of thousands (perhaps over a hundred thousand) leaves with religious poems have been found in the Geniza, a reflection of the astonishing output of the more famous liturgical poets of old, as well as the large number of authors, otherwise unknown, who were active in composing these poems.

Linguistically, these poems are extremely elaborate and highly allusive, so much so that they cannot be understood properly without a good knowledge of rabbinical lore and law and, more particularly, a complete mastery of the biblical text; a modern scholar equipped with lexicons and reference materials of all kinds is sometimes at a loss to understand the meaning of a particular passage. One wonders for what audience these creations were intended, particularly as they usually consisted of a circle of poems whose full recitation required hours. It must have been the melodies on which the piyyūṭ was sung that constituted its attraction for the congregation and made the long hours in synagogue enjoyable and edifying. Both familiar tunes and new melodies were received with pleasure, and we often find passages from older pieces inserted into the manuscripts of later creations—no doubt because they were cherished compositions. Innovation was provided by guest cantors from foreign countries; their appearance is frequently mentioned in the Geniza papers. The notation of Hebrew synagogue poetry in Lombardic neumes by the Norman proselyte Obadiah is a case in point.

The apostate Samuel the Maghrebi, who embraced Islam in 1163, found it necessary to explain to his Muslim readers the musical aspect of the synagogue service, a practice utterly foreign to them (although it had a fairly exact counterpart in the liturgy of the Eastern churches). Samuel asserted that when the Persians, who had ruled over Iraq and the adjacent countries prior to the advent of Islam, prohibited Jewish prayer, the Jews invented poems into which they inserted passages from their official prayers; they then composed many melodies for the texts, which they chanted in the synagogues. When the Persians rebuked them for acting against the prohibition on public prayer, the Jews retorted that they were not praying, but merely making music.

This pseudohistorical explanation of the origins of the piyyūṭ was not an invention of the learned apostate; indeed, it was a commonplace in the arguments of many generations of Jewish scholars in the centuries preceding him, particularly among authorities who wished to eliminate this popular element from the service by discrediting its need during a period when there was no need for dissimulation. That they were not successful can be seen by the enormous number of liturgical poems actually found, as well as by direct references in the Geniza letters to liturgical recitations. In an exceedingly eloquent, indeed flowery, letter laced with biblical quotations, a certain group—no doubt in a provincial town—complains about their communal leaders, who have abolished the time-honored chanting of specially inserted prayers on Sabbaths, holidays, and weekdays. The complainants received affirmation of their position from renowned scholars and even a rescript from the sultan approving their view, but the local Jewish authorities remained adamant in their decision to do away with these additions to the official liturgy. The group admonishes the addressee, a renowned physician and confidant of the sultan, to be as courageous as Queen Esther (quoting Esther 4:16) and to approach the ruler with a request to allow them to conduct their service according to the customs of their forefathers.

The letter sheds light on Moses Maimonides' leniency as regards the insertion of poetical passages into the established text of the liturgy. In response to the inquiry of a cantor, newly appointed to a locality in which these additions were chanted, Maimonides, in his usual wisdom, replies that they are indeed highly improper, but their recitation is preferable to the communal strife that will inevitably erupt if a newcomer were to try to prohibit them. This decision, as well as the letter of the disgruntled congregants, shows how enamored those worshipers must have been of those poetical pieces—or at least of their traditional tunes.

The popularity of the piyyūṭ should not be attributed solely to its music, as important as that might have been; otherwise, we would not find the cantors competing with one another so eagerly to find (or produce) ever new texts. Even at the end of the classical Geniza period, there must have been in any large community a considerable number of persons who were able to understand and to appreciate those difficult poems. The synagogue, we ought to remember, was not only a house of worship, but also a place of study; or rather, as often said, study *was* worship. It may be that the piyyūṭ served to titillate the imagination and puzzle the intellect; since almost every line contained a hidden allusion to a Bible verse or a passage of talmudic literature, every new poem must have prompted a vigorous contest to determine the poet's sources and his aesthetic intent. While the melodies were a devotional pastime for the many, the effort required for the full understanding of the texts was an intellectual exercise for a sophisticated and learned audience.

Congregational prayers were not led by one or two persons officiating permanently; instead, both the recitation of the different sections of the liturgy and the readings from the Scriptures were assigned to members or guests present. Selecting them was the privilege of the muqaddam and was indicative of the social status of those selected. The future gaon Solomon b. Judah, while third in line for the leadership, reports to his friends in Egypt exactly which segments of the prayers, which sections of the Scriptures, and which sermons were apportioned to each of the three highest dignitaries of the yeshiva of Jerusalem (plus one prominent layman) during the entire eighteen days of the autumn festival, the period beginning with the celebration of the New Year. The honor of leading the congregation in a section of the service—for example, reading a lection from the Prophets on a certain Sabbath or holiday—could be bestowed for a lifetime and even become hereditary through generations. In a query, possibly sent from an expanding community, Moses Maimonides is asked whether such hereditary honors were lawful, since "the Torah is no heirloom" (Sayings of the Fathers 2:12), that is, every-one should be honored according to the knowledge and merits he him-self has acquired. Maimonides' answer is characteristic: If the persons designated to replace the hereditary readers are more learned or God fearing, their claims should be heeded. Otherwise, the principle of heredity has precedence, since it is conducive to the preservation of peace.

As an exceptional honor, a distinguished guest was entrusted with assigning the sections of the Scripture lections to the persons called up to recite them. Complaints about high-handed procedures in these mat-ters by synagogue presidents were common. Everyone was called up by his honorific title or titles. When a title was omitted, an official com-plaint was often filed with the highest Jewish authority. Reference has already been made to the recitation of public prayers for benefactors during the most solemn part of the service—when the Torah scrolls were taken out of the holy ark and placed down for reading. It was, of course, an occasion of intense social rivalry. As the preserved copies of such prayers show, patrons took no chances but saw to it that the text of the prayer was written down in advance to make sure that all their titles and declared merits were set down properly and that their specific requests to God were backed by communal supplication.

Another opportunity for displaying one's social status in public was the prayer for the dead, for a man's standing was conditioned by the length and quality of his pedigree. The titles and merits of one's fore-fathers were mentioned in the prayer, back to seven or more generations, particularly when they had achieved the virtues of piety, generosity, or learning. The very large number of memorial lists preserved in the Gen-iza testifies to the wide diffusion of this socioreligious custom. The prayer over the dead was called either by the ancient Aramaic term *du-khrān* derived from its traditional opening, "To the blessed memory (*dkhr*) of those who rest in peace," or by the more popular Arabic term *tarḥīm* (taken from the beginning of the Hebrew form of the prayer "May God have mercy [*rḥm*] upon the soul of . . .)." It was usually followed by a prayer for the person whose ancestors were eulogized.

According to a letter addressed to Moses Maimonides, it was cus-tomary in Alexandria (and in other places as well) for the coffin of the deceased to be brought into the courtyard of the synagogue early in the morning. After the termination of the service, the community and the dignitaries would come out of the prayer hall, attend the recitation of the dirges by the various cantors, and then accompany the dead to their final resting place. Maimonides objected to this custom in the strongest terms: The synagogue was a house to worship God, not to mourn for men. Only in the most exceptional case—the death of a very great religious figure—did he consider such a procedure permissible. His answer implies that the custom of praising the family of the dead in an elaborate fashion was not in vogue in Fustat. In any case, we find no attestation of that custom in any Geniza document dealing with Fustat. Rather, the Fustat Jews recited dirges in the synagogue during the seven days of mourning. Maimonides tolerated this custom only on the strength of a legal fiction—when the building had been erected, it had been stipulated that a section might serve as a place of mourning. This legal fiction had no precedent in the Talmud. (The Muslims, it should be noted, carry the bier into the main hall of a mosque, where a special prayer is said over the dead before the funeral.) Oddly enough, wedding ceremonies, as far as can be judged from the Geniza records and contemporaneous literary sources, were not held in the synagogue; certainly, Muslim and Christian wedding ceremonies during the Geniza period were conducted outside of their respective houses of worship.

Jewish religious services, like those of Muslims and Christians, also had political overtones, inasmuch as they included prayers for the ruler and for the Jewish ecumenical and territorial authorities. Whenever there was a rivalry between leaders, the community was obliged to declare allegiance to a particular authority. As a rule, prayers for the ruler were said only on special occasions, but particularly at the service held on the eve of the Day of Atonement—the most solemn service of the Jewish liturgical year. (This custom still prevails in some Oriental communities; elsewhere, Jews regularly offer a prayer to the government during Sabbath prayers.) In addition to the public prayer for the communal authorities, it was customary for readers and preachers to preface their performance with a symbolic request for the permission of the gaon or nagid in office. Even the reading of the Aramaic translation of the Pentateuch and the Prophets was introduced by such a request. The Geniza has preserved a late preamble referring to the nagid David b. Abraham, the grandson of Maimonides (1237–1300). Since Aramaic was no longer generally understood, the preamble was written in Hebrew— and in quite elegant Hebrew at that. The reader takes permission first from God, second from the Torah, third from all notable religious figures and scholars, and finally as head of the Jews, from the nagid himself, whose titles are, of course, enumerated. At the end, the wish is expressed that the nagid be restored to health. Most probably this addition was the reason the preamble was written down and not merely recited from memory.

Whenever a difference of opinion about liturgy, leadership in prayer, or any other question led to communal strife, the dissenting group would refrain from "going down to" (that is, attending) the synagogue, not so much for the sake of public show as out of religious conviction, for it was regarded as unlawful to say a prayer when led by an unworthy person. When a worshiper who was assigned a part of the reading of the lection was suspected of improper conduct by other members of the congregation, he was prevented by them from ascending the reader's platform.

Since everything done by or for the Holy Congregation was hallowed with religious connotation, the synagogue was also the proper place for attending to communal affairs. The letters of the ecumenical or territorial authorities—or of other communities near and far—were read out, discussed, and acted upon; resolutions proposed by the elders or by an individual leader were acclaimed or rejected; bans were pronounced and public chastisements, such as lashings, were administered; collections were solicited; vows for donations were made, and reports about public finances or other matters were rendered during or immediately after the service or between the prayers. When dire calamities called for concerted efforts, a public fast was announced, shops were closed, and all were required to attend the synagogue service, during which each would vow his share to alleviate public distress. In short, all matters of public concern were normally transacted in the synagogue, in conformity with age-old, even pre-Christian usage ("synagogue" and its Hebrew equivalent, *bēth kenēseth,* mean house of assembly).

A letter dated around 1030 from Ramle mentions the meetinghouse (*majlis*) in the Market of the Jews. The house must have been of sizable dimensions, for the writer of the letter, the gaon Solomon b. Judah, says that the whole community, led by its notables, was gathered there, demanding that he pronounce a ban. (Bans were usually given the widest publicity.) The Ramle meetinghouse should not be regarded as a synagogue but rather as the equivalent of the classical basilica regularly found in the central markets of Hellenistic and Roman cities—serving as both courtroom and public hall. Karaite synagogues and Rabbanite private places of prayer are also referred to in the Geniza records by the term *majlis* (lit., place where one sits down), and not by the common Arabic word for synagogue (or church), *kanīs* or *kanīsa* (derived, of course, from the Hebrew term through Aramaic). Since all Karaite places of worship were erected after the advent of Islam, the noncommittal term "majlis" was preferred to avoid a conflict with Islamic law, which prohibited the erection of new churches and synagogues.

While the formation of secessionist congregations was vehemently opposed, small private places of worship must have been common and were tolerated because of their transitory character. A prominent physician kept a private synagogue, probably because his patients were mostly government officials and other persons of high standing whom he usually had to visit early in the morning. It would have been impossible for him to do so had he attended the public service, which naturally was of a longer duration—and breakfast could be taken only after the service. A scholarly India trader who had been away in the East for over two decades and had brought back from there native in-laws perhaps felt more comfortable keeping a small private synagogue for a certain period of transition. In any case, he reportedly kept the place for at least three years before moving on to another town and participating in the local synagogue. As is done today, prayer assemblies in private homes were permitted for weddings or during periods of mourning—but without Torah scrolls, which remained the privilege of communal places of prayer.

One of features most characteristic of Jewish life until this very day was the foundation of synagogues named after the countries or cities of their original members. In the Geniza records, we frequently read about foreigners operating as discrete groups in a synagogue (occasionally as troublemakers): persons from Hebron situated in Ascalon, from Gaza in Hebron, from Tiberias in Acre, from Aleppo in al-Maḥalla—and Maghrebis, of course, everywhere. But these groups never formed congregations with permanent buildings, either because they were not numerous enough, or—and this seems to be the main reason—because the local rites were not as yet so differentiated and their liturgy so rigidly fixed as in later times.

Dissatisfaction with a particular synagogue could be occasioned by a number of vexations—the excessive length of the service; the chanting by laymen of often difficult texts according to fixed and unwelcome rules, personal rivalries, and public dissensions. For some, a synagogue might be compromised as a house of worship because it served also as a social club in which members spent most of their time when not in the bazaar or the workshop. The sources even speak of brawls taking place during worship. Lack of decorum is decried by Moses Maimonides in his responsa and by his son Abraham in his *Complete Guide of the Pious*. Disruptions might, however, also serve a social function. The congregation assembled in the synagogue served as the highest juridical authority. Individuals—even women—who had not obtained satisfaction of their claims through conventional legal procedures could, in extreme cases, interrupt and even stop the service until their complaint was heard by the whole community. Those afflicted by particular hardships were also permitted to address the community assembled in prayer after receiving the authorization of the appropriate official. It was customary for applicants to appear in the synagogue in person so as to make their appeals more effective.

SIX

Jews and the Muslim State as Reflected in the Geniza

Rulers and Their Entourage

During the Fatimid period and most of the Ayyubid period, non-Muslim minorities were represented in the entourage of the
rulers and the state administration to an extent that far exceeded their
position and numbers among the general populace. One would thus
expect that the Geniza documents would be particularly rich in information about the court and the machinery of government. That, however, is not the case. To be sure, many Jews with connections to the
court did live close to the seat of the Fatimids in Cairo, the new residential section built adjacent to but separate from Fustat. As such, they
could easily have observed at first hand the workings of the Fatimid
state. How is it, then, that there is no record of their observations comparable to works of Muslims attached to the court? There are several
explanations. Had individual Jews in the caliph's retinue written about
the administration of government or life at court they would have done
so in Arabic and in the Arabic script; documents of that sort would not
ordinarily have made their way into a geniza. Moreover, some of the
more prominent Jewish families of the Geniza period were Karaites and
therefore had no opportunity to deposit their writings in a Rabbanite
synagogue. There is also the possibility that Jews well placed in the
government and at court thought it prudent to keep their reflections to
themselves and not make them part of any written record. For all these
reasons, it is only in exceptional cases that we find informative descrip-

tions of the court and the administration with which Jews were connected. For the most part, what we have in the Geniza is a description of institutions as seen from outside government circles; it is government as reflected in the minds of those who had little, if any, direct contact with it.

On the other hand, the few "insider stories" preserved are colorful and highly instructive. From a report to a high government official who is often referred to in the Geniza records, we learn that even a lawsuit personally decided by the sultan (Saladin, or perhaps his son al-Malik al-'Azīz) required substantial bribes, which are, happily for modern scholars, specified in the letter. As fate had it, the opposing party was more lavish—"money answers all things" (Ecclesiastes 10:19)—but the recipient of the letter is assured that he will eventually succeed, since the law, that is, Muslim law, is clearly on his side. Circumstances during the early Fatimid period are reflected in a letter of congratulations to a Jewish physician transferred from a hospital in Ramle to the personal service of the vizier in Cairo; the vizier bestowed a robe of honor on him and gave him a munificent allowance. A more critical view of Jews serving the Muslim state is that of a notable writing to his brother. The latter had entered service with the family of Nāṣir al-Dawla, the Turkish commander, who, around 1065, was the de facto ruler of Egypt. According to the writer, the costly gifts made by the rapacious Turkish generals to their entourage were a disgrace rather than a blessing to the Jews; carousing with them was damaging to both body and soul. Still another source indicates that the Jews helping "the Monk"—the Coptic minister of finance who ravaged Egypt in the 1120s—were to be condemned in even stronger terms. These random comments paint a picture of Jews at court less complimentary than presented in other materials.

Intrigues among higher government officials are well illustrated by a letter of "the president of the court of all Israel" in Jerusalem. The letter, dated to between 1057 and 1062, is addressed to an overseer of the caliph's mint in Cairo. It concerned a Jewish official of the *dār al-ṣarf*, the caliphal money exchange, who, after being married in the Egyptian capital in 1050, allegedly intended to marry again in Ascalon. This was not only against the norms prevailing at that time among the Jews but was also disapproved of, albeit for quite different reasons, by the government. The president of the court admonishes the addressee not to use these allegations, which according to the best of his knowledge are untrue, to secure the downfall of that Jewish official, but, on the contrary, to exert his influence to stop any machinations against the latter. Undoubtedly it was dangerous for Jewish members of the ruling entourage to become embroiled in the politics of ambitious bureaucrats — dangerous for themselves and possibly for the community as a whole. The precarious position of government servants in general is illustrated in a number of documents.

Nowhere in the thousands of letters preserved in the Geniza do we find abundant criticism of Muslim rule. To the contrary, when rulers are mentioned in the letters, it is generally in the context of their acts of justice, the favors that they have granted, or their actual or expected victories in battle. Conditions of oppression and lawlessness, as well as military or economic disasters, are never attributed to the government but are accepted as God's will or simply recorded as a fact of life. For, as a Geniza letter puts it, "the hearts of the kings are like watercourses in the hand of God which He may divert into whatever direction He will" (Proverbs 21:1). The breakdown of public order and the imposition of oppressive measures by the government were regarded as natural phenomena like famines and earthquakes. At most, a minister or other high official might be blamed, and this, it seems, only after he had fallen into disgrace — an indication that it was safe to offer criticism. Only the lower officials, with whom the people were in daily contact, were fully exposed to public censure, by writers hopeful that the influence of the Jewish notables would be sufficient to bring about the dismissal of harmful Jewish bureaucrats — or at least put an end to their misconduct.

Minority groups, and perhaps the common people in general, seem to have been loyalists by a long-standing accommodation and deeply held convictions, for a stable though oppressive government was considered preferable to disorder and turmoil. The person of the ruler was regarded as sacrosanct; one swore by the ruler's life or head, as one swore by one's religion or by the Torah, and one might even mention the Torah and "the ruler" in one breath while making a public declaration in the synagogue. Swearing falsely while using the ruler's name was a crime deserving strict punishment. Even in private letters, the name of the ruler would be invariably accompanied by good wishes, such as "may God give him victory and make his days eternal" — not only in Arabic, which might come to the attention of the authorities, but also in Hebrew; the phrase "may his Rock [God] preserve him" is attached to the name of the caliph al-Ḥākim in one letter and to that of a provincial governor in another (ironically, the governor is described in that missive as having done harm to a Jewish scholar). Those in power were regarded as somehow being in a special relationship with God.

Communal prayers for the rulers first appear in Jewish liturgical textbooks at the beginning of the fourteenth century. The Geniza records, however, contain the text of such a prayer two hundred years earlier. Many words in that Geniza prayer are abbreviated, an indication that the custom of praying on the ruler's behalf must have been in vogue even earlier. It seems that the prayer for the government was said at the most solemn moment of the Jewish liturgical year—during the opening of the service ushering in the Day of Atonement—a custom still followed in congregations of Near Eastern origins today. In addition to these regular demonstrations of loyalty, special prayers might be held on particular occasions or Hebrew poems recited in honor of the ruler. Thus the gaon arranged for solemn prayers of thanks in Ramle and Jerusalem when the Fatimid caliph and his vizier acquitted the leader of the Jewish community in Fustat of false accusations leveled against him. The justice of the ruler and his adviser was extolled and supplications for his success in peace and war were recited. When an attack of the Seljuk Turkomans on Cairo was repulsed in 1077, an extended Hebrew poem was dedicated to the caliph al-Mustanṣir by Solomon ha-Kohen, the son of Joseph, the president of the court of the Jerusalem yeshiva.

The entourage of the rulers—the *aṣḥāb al-khilaʿ*, "the bearers of robes of honor"—is frequently mentioned in the Geniza documents, for it included Jewish notables. Normally the notables are referred to only in letters addressed to them or to their friends with requests for intercession, or in expressions of gratitude for help previously given. The most important officials were not the only figures given robes of honor, however; even government agents or physicians received robes in recognition of outstanding service. It is, therefore, not always possible to define the exact position or rank of Jewish persons addressed or referred to. Abū Saʿd Abraham Tustarī, who before his assassination in 1047 wielded extraordinary power in the Fatimid government, is called in Hebrew *mishne la-melekh*, "deputy to the ruler." The epithet is understandable; so great was his influence that some Muslim writers give him the title vizier. The same epithet is attached to the name of the nagid Mevōrākh, who was al-Malik al-Afḍal's physician and, according to the Geniza, also his counselor "from the days of his youth." In addition, the nagid was occupied with affairs of state. It is not unlikely, then, that Mevōrākh held a position of great importance in al-Afḍal's administration, albeit one not reflected in Arabic historiography, which is rather sparse in details regarding the internal affairs of Egypt at the time. What is meant precisely by *mishne la-melekh* in his case is therefore uncertain.

All letters addressed to a Jewish official or court notable express the wish that he should find favor in the eyes of the ruler, his deputy, and all others in positions of power—sometimes even the ladies of the court.

Letters written in Arabic use the same word for "favor" as that applied to a favorite concubine; in Hebrew, the corresponding phrase, familiar from the Book of Esther (2:17, 5:2, 8; 7:3), is used. The gift of being accepted was critical to the success of the courtier. The protection of Heaven is thus usually implored against all those who envy the addressee and intrigue against him. The phrasing of such wishes gives the impression that the writer is not speaking in general terms but referring to specific situations laden with danger. There was no need to remind anyone of the downfall and assassination of the "vizier" Abū Saʿd Abraham Tustarī in 1047, and the same fate of Joseph b. Samuel of Granada in 1066 — events fully reflected in the Geniza records. But even where positions of power were not lost in so brutal a way, royal disfavor frequently terminated the careers of high Jewish dignitaries who combined leadership in their community with service to the ruler. Given their relatively weak position, Jewish notables could be valued for their service at little risk to the authorities, but they could also be removed by those authorities without fear of reprisal.

Families of officials who lost office were affected as well. The Geniza has preserved a large circular urging all Jewish communities to assist a man whose father had been in the service of the king of Granada but fell into disgrace, whereupon his son had to leave the country. In general, the family was held responsible for the misconduct of any of its members in government service or with other connections with the ruling authority. Therefore, as soon as a government official or any other person who had dealings with the government died, all his belongings were confiscated and held under seal until his conduct was cleared. This was a much dreaded procedure, apparently affecting also people of modest means with no connections to the ruling society. The downfall of high government officials, especially those belonging to minority groups, was so taken for granted that it was reported by historians even if it had not in fact taken place.

Government Officials and Agents: Tax Farmers

The usual designation for a government officer was *kātib*, "scribe," applied equally to the head of a department in the central administration and to a humble clerk in a provincial town. Thus, "the Secretary of the State," Abū ʾl-Barakāt Judah ha-Kohen, accorded the epithet "the great prince, the Mordecai of his time" and a dozen other grand Hebrew titles in letters addressed or referring to him, was officially only a kātib. Even a little boy who happened to be born into a family of government servants could bear the proud name Zayn al-Kuttāb, "Ornament of the Scribes." (The Zayn al-Kuttāb referred to in the Geniza was a grandson of Judah ha-Kohen.) Girls from such families would not infrequently be called Sitt al-Kuttāb, "Queen of the Scribes," although it is not quite certain whether they themselves had actually learned to write. The exact position of a kātib in the hierarchy of officialdom would be defined by the honorary titles and epithets conferred on him by his superiors; the Geniza records contain a plethora of them. Lower officials had to be satisfied with an honorific epithet such as "the Sound," bestowed also on physicians. Those higher up were honored with one or more titles lauding the services they rendered to the state. The state kept tight control over the financial affairs of its officials—or rather, regarded the riches amassed by them as its own—often culminating in wholesale confiscation or at least sequestration of the estates they left.

Geniza documents indicate that the government interested itself in the family life of its employees as well. A Sicilian Jew who had married in Damascus was about to receive a government post in Cairo. He was told, however, that he would not obtain the appointment unless his wife followed him to the Egyptian capital (she refused). He then approached the rabbinical court with a request to marry a local (Egyptian) woman on condition that he deposit with the court the indemnity due his first wife in the event of their divorce. The record reporting the granting of this request emphasizes that this policy of the government was well known to the judges. In a similar case, a high official of the caliphal monetary exchange of Cairo, suspected of having married a woman in Ascalon, was in danger of losing his post. The reason for this policy is obvious: When the official's family lived in another country, the government did not have a firm hold on him; if he fled after committing improprieties, there was no one to be taken as a hostage to guarantee his return.

Precise statements about government salaries and emoluments are rare in the Geniza, rarer even than those about commercial profits; the reason for this reticence is the same in both cases: one was reluctant to put these details in writing. We read about salaries only in specific instances, for example, when a person unacceptable to both the writer and the addressee of a letter was appointed to a post that they would have preferred to see occupied by one of their own. Thus, in a report to a high official in Saladin's time (ca. 1180), the writer mentions with regret that an individual was made *mushārif* (controller) of town revenue, for which he was promised 180 dinars and 100 *waybas* (about 2,500 pounds) of wheat per year. As usual, the emoluments were in cash and kind. During approximately the same period, a mushārif of a village received 1½ dinars per month, or 18 per year — exactly one-tenth of the salary just mentioned.

Arrears in the payment of salaries to government officials seem to have been common; even higher officials had difficulty receiving their scheduled allotments. In one letter, the addressee is asked to approach no less a person than the nagid with a request that he induce an important Jewish official in the service of al-Malik al-Afḍal to have the writer pay his accumulated back salary. When an official asked another to substitute for him, he would give instructions to have his salary transferred to his colleague for the duration of his absence.

Lower officials who were in direct contact with the public, such as the messenger of the tax collectors, official money changers, customs officers, inspectors of scales, gatekeepers, and port clerks, apparently did not receive any fixed salary from the office employing them. Instead they were remunerated by the persons involved with a small gratuity for each service rendered. References to such payments abound in all reports of expenses, whether communal or commercial. We read too about persons working in the caliph's mint for *fā'ida* "profit"; they were paid by the piece and did not receive regular emoluments. Whether the same held true for the Jewish official called "director of the mint" is not evident from references found thus far. Since he is called "director of the mint and agent appointed by the government" in one legal document, it is likely that he too was paid by the job. The Muslim official who was in charge of the mint and who bore the title "director of coinage" is repeatedly referred to in one source as "the farmer of the revenue from the mint"; even that high official was an employee with no fixed salary.

One should bear in mind that even a post like that of the head of the police would sometimes be farmed out; the aspirant would promise to pay the government a fixed sum every year and then cover himself by imposing heavy fines on whatever culprits he could lay his hands on. A letter referring to such an arrangement emphasizes that persons committing even a slight offense, such as a Jew (not a Muslim) getting drunk, would "perish." In effect, fines constituted the personal income of the official.

In general, the farming of revenue of all descriptions pervaded all levels of the administrative system and the economy of the time. The conventional term for tax farmer was *ḍāmin,* literally, the one who stands as security (occasionally also *mutaqabbil*). Ḍāmin was used not only in relation to public revenue, but also to designate an individual leasing property from a private person or from a community (such as a Jewish congregation), or for collecting rents on their behalf. The term was used as well with the literal meaning of standing as security for a person's poll tax or any other financial obligation. The term *nā'ib,* "deputy," which we have already discussed as designating a judge, could also refer to a tax farmer, for it was common practice for the larger ḍāmins to sublease their rights.

Research on the subject is rendered even more complicated by the fact that, as a rule, a farmer of revenue is called simply "al-ḍāmin" without any further definition. Only the context of the document or a reference to the same person in another Geniza record enables us to determine more precisely the nature and extent of his contract. On the other hand, references to this institution are so numerous in the Geniza records that a systematic search for them will provide important source material for this interesting and ubiquitous aspect of medieval administration. In this respect, the Geniza has a great deal to tell us about the Muslims as well.

In classifying the different types of tax farming, we find that most farmers of revenue are mentioned in conjunction with the name of a particular locality. Where a village or a small town is involved, it is perhaps reasonable to assume that the ḍāmin collected all the various dues payable by that place, although this assumption is by no means certain. It was common practice to travel to a locality in the Rīf and to farm its revenue, or for a woman from Fustat to join her husband, who was the ḍāmin of a place in the Rīf. The father of a profligate son was afraid that unscrupulous people would induce the youth to stand as security for the collection of tax revenues from a village in the Rīf: "You will eat and drink and your father will pay," that is, the money collected would serve the boy as an immediate source of income, while the old man would be held responsible by the government for the ultimate shortfall in revenue.

Where a larger provincial town or the capital itself is mentioned as the domain of a tax farmer, the reference is no doubt to only one specific type of fiscal income. Thus, 335 dinars as ʿibra, or yearly assessment, for a provincial capital such as al-Maḥalla almost certainly represents only a fraction of the taxes collected there. Most probably it was the tax on silk weaving and dyeing. In a letter concerning Cairo, the context clearly implies that it was this tax of which the ḍāmin was in charge. Even in a small place like Atfīḥ, otherwise known as a center of flax growing, the ḍāmin, as the document goes on to show, was concerned only with taxes on silk work; for an equally small locality, Qalyūb, this is stated expressly. A statute forbidding women to dye silk at home without notifying the ḍāmin takes it for granted that the term referred to the farmer of the silk tax. There are many other examples of Jews farming taxes on silks. Since the Jews were so conspicuous in the silk industry, they were no doubt the best qualified to collect taxes levied on it.

The dues on dyeing and selling silk constituted only part of the revenue "from the market" in general. "The judge of the Jews" in Manbij, a town in Syria, was also the tax farmer of the bazaar (sūq) of that locality. This office had its downside, as did all tax collecting. We read, for example, in a letter concerning a Jewish scholar, "God forbid that he should farm the market, as has been rumored," a task affecting so many coreligionists. When a merchant received a payment, "the master(s) of the market, namely, the tax farmers" would sequester it until any claims on dues from former transactions were satisfied. In at least one case, the tax farming of a locality (without further definition) refers to that of its market. On the other hand, there were such specialized sub-vocations as "farmer of the taxes on the lands sown with Egyptian clover in the district of Alexandria." This would appear to indicate that provisioning the city with fodder for riding animals was the concern of a separate branch of the administration. Tax farmers even collected taxes on revenue from the sale of houses or parts of houses.

It should be noted that in some localities the poll tax incumbent on non-Muslims was also farmed out. Thus in a letter from a village the writer complains that he was unable to come to the capital since the ḍāmin issuing receipts showing payment the poll tax had not yet arrived (and without such a certificate one was not permitted to travel). Another aspect of tax farming was the collection of customs duties. Geniza documents refers to such tax farmers in the Nile ports of Fustat and Cairo and the busy seaport of 'Aydhāb on the coast of eastern Africa. The Muslim traveler Ibn Jubayr reports that customs duties were collected in the Palestinian harbor city of Acre, which was in Christian hands at the time of his visit. Still, it seems doubtful that the farming of customs duties was widespread or permanent during the classical Geniza period. Were duties collected by such officials, we would expect to find more references to the practice in the numerous letters and accounts concerning persons and goods that passed through customs stations.

An appointment to farm taxes (ḍamān) was obtained from a local revenue office, from an official responsible for raising a set revenue, or from the central government itself. In general, the dīwān, the government office concerned with the tax in question, or its director, the *ʿāmil*, or its controller, the *mush(ā)rif*, is referred to as granting the ḍamān. Competition was keen, and a ḍāmin had to work hard to procure and to retain his post. The officials of the relevant departments, local and central, had to favor the applicant, as did the local police and the head of police in the capital, for without the police to back his collection, the tax farmer had no power to enforce payment. Although the amount to be guaranteed by the tax farmer and the term of his office were fixed by the nature of his appointment, it became common practice to force collectors to turn over greater sums than those specified as soon as a higher bid was made by someone seeking to replace him. Indeed tax farming became so rampant a social evil that outbidding a ḍāmin, thus raising taxes still further, was eventually punished with excommunication.

The tax farmer usually stood as security for a larger district and subleased his rights to a host of associates who performed the actual collecting of taxes in areas allotted to them. In a document of 1106, the farmer of the dues from dyeing and selling silk in the district of Damietta subleases his rights regarding a small town to three partners for the duration of one year against a payment of two dinars per month. Conversely, two capitalists who farmed the arrears (or rather the taxes evaded) in the Fayyūm district take on as collector a silent partner registered in a Jewish court but not with the government. The two main tax farmers make substantial profits but cheat their partner of his share; unable to meet his obligations for lack of payment, the Jewish partner is confined to prison. The letter that recounts his misfortunes was clearly written under dire circumstances.

In general, tax farming was a hazardous undertaking, and references to severe losses are not infrequent. We read bitter complaints about the government offices and their arbitrary and ruthless treatment of the ḍāmins. Muslim historians recount the story of a prominent Jewish tax farmer of Basra in Iraq. He was the confidant of Niẓām al-Mulk, the famous vizier (d. 1092), and so influential that all Basra, with the sole exception of the qāḍī, turned out at the funeral of his wife. When the Seljuk sultan Malik Shāh had the tax farmer executed because of an intrigue fostered by Niẓām al-Mulk's enemies, the great vizier refused to appear before the sultan for three days and took up his duties only after Malik Shāh had expressed regret about what he had done. This did not hinder him, however, from appropriating a hundred thousand dinars from the Jew's estate, the sum for which he was annually liable when he was alive. The same amount, together with a hundred horses, had to be delivered annually by the new tax farmer of Basra. Sums of such magnitude are exceptional in the Geniza records.

Tax farming was extremely common in the Roman and Persian empires and, as the New Testament and talmudic literature eloquently testify, it weighed heavily on the population. The system of tax farming in Fatimid and Ayyubid times, to the extent that we are able to reconstruct its workings through the Geniza documents, appears somewhat different. Although pernicious in more than one way, it was generally appropriate to the economy and society of the Geniza period. Most of the ḍāmins belonged to the middle class, and, being themselves merchants and producers of goods and services, they possessed knowledge and understanding of the problems they encountered while collecting taxes. Complaints about overbearing tax farmers are rare. But when the central authorities, for whatever reason, felt constrained to raise increasingly larger revenues, they could and did place enormous pressure on those who farmed taxes to increase the yield. These pressures were, in turn, also placed on the judiciary and security forces, who worked in tandem with the tax farmers.

Judiciary and Police

Biographical dictionaries contain literally thousands of entries on *qāḍī*s, "judges," arranged according to the city or country over which they presided, or according to the year in which they died. In addition, other works of Islamic literature offer considerable information about Muslim magistrates. The Geniza documents add interesting insights to the larger picture of the Muslim judiciary and enable us to compare the Jewish and Muslim judges from the perspective of the minority community.

The most impressive aspect of Muslim juridical organization, as evidenced in our records, is its strict centralization. The lower courts investigated but were loath to decide matters before making sure of the opinion of their superiors. A Muslim magistrate in Qūṣ, a town near the southern border of Egypt, sought the signed instructions of the chief qāḍī of Cairo in a case of inheritance involving Jews. For this purpose, a messenger had to be sent to the capital, an expensive trip that required over two months of travel. Even the powerful qāḍī of Alexandria decided a case about the disposal of a drowned silk merchant's goods only after having received a rescript from the caliph's court. Similarly, it was

thought that two disputes that had come before the qāḍī of Jerusalem—
one concerning the Jewish community of the city and another regarding
a house shared by a Jewish notable and a Muslim—could be settled only
by the chief qāḍī of Ramle, the capital of Palestine at the time. The tenor
of the two letters dealing with these cases shows that this was the regular
course of action. As we have seen, a similar system of procedure was
common in the Jewish courts: instead of deciding a case and then allowing for an appeal, the lower Jewish courts deferred their judgment
until they had received proper instructions and backing from the central
authorities.

This weakness of the lower courts was not without consequences. On
the one hand, people applied, or threatened to apply, directly to the
chief qāḍī. On the other hand, with many cases being referred to the
higher courts, important dignitaries and other influential notables exercised pressure on the court, the chief justices, and the legal experts in
order to obtain instructions favorable to their clients. The Geniza has
preserved numerous letters in which persons engaged in lawsuits make
specific requests to that effect or allude to the manner in which such
requests were made. This manner of trying to influence the judges is
reflected in our records far more frequently than outright bribery. The
issue was not one of moral scruples among those seeking to protect their
interests, but rather of how best to exert pressure on judges. Bribes to
the higher judiciary, such as the qāḍī who had his seat "in the palace,"
were not paid directly, but to a go-between. Buying a favorable judgment could be a heavy imposition. Lower judges were content, however,
with as little as ten dirhems, very likely a kind of fixed fee known to all
seeking to corrupt them.

In general, the chief qāḍīs of the larger cities loom in the Geniza
records as powerful persons whose authority was paramount—to such
an extent that one sometimes gets the impression that regarding certain
matters they were the actual rulers of the area under their jurisdiction.
In a time of tension among the various segments of the population in
Alexandria, a traveler on his way to that city tries to secure a letter of
recommendation to the Muslim chief judge—not to the governor or
head of the police. Likewise, a traveler from France asks to be granted
a rescript from the viceroy al-Malik al-Afḍal to the qāḍī of Damietta,
then the second-largest port of Egypt. (The document was required to
protect the merchant during his stay in that city.) His letter asks the
judge to recommend the traveler to the captain and sailors of the boat
on which he will continue his voyage. The qāḍī in a maritime city often
served also as *nāẓir,* or superintendent of the port. Our documents refer

to qāḍīs who were shipowners, especially in the Lebanese ports of Tyre and Tripoli; they owned not only coastal craft but also the largest ships plying the Mediterranean during the eleventh century, each carrying five hundred passengers. In pre-Islamic times, the patriarch of Alexandria played a similar role in the economy. It may be that such combinations of religious and legal authority and economic power represented an old tradition, dating back perhaps to the ancient Phoenicians and Carthaginians.

Most often we find qāḍīs engaged in mercantile undertakings and, in particular, as proprietors (*wakīl*) of a *dār wakāla*, a combination of storehouse and bourse. A wakīl was originally and essentially the legal and commercial representative of foreign merchants. Qāḍīs, who were themselves charged with dispensing justice, were the representatives most sought after by foreigners. The qāḍī of Tyre, who was a shipowner, owned a storehouse as well, in which he kept precious Persian silk brocade (among many other wares) before it was shipped to the West. He ruled that the merchants who stored goods with him were not obliged to pay certain evaded taxes (or customs) unless they sold their goods locally instead of shipping them to the next destination.

The *faqīh*, or Muslim doctor of law, is also referred to in the Geniza records, where he appears in two different capacities. At a lower level, he acts as a notary, making out legal documents, or as puisne judge, settling minor business such as the approval of the appointment of an attorney. On the higher level, he is a very influential legal expert: he is asked to rule on the level of the poll tax, for example; in a meeting with other jurists, he may have precedence even over the qāḍī. Faqīhs are repeatedly mentioned as belonging to the entourage of the rulers and traveling in their company. The term *muftī* for a Muslim jurisconsult, so common in Mamluk times, is surprisingly rare in the records of the classical Geniza period, although the word *fatwā*, legal opinion, and its derivatives are frequently mentioned.

One of the most characteristic institutions of Muslim legal procedure was that of certifying witnesses of good reputation, the *'udūl*, or "the just," as they were called. Originally such certificates were issued to prevent testimony from being contested because of allegations against a witness's character. By the fourth century A.H., the 'udūl had become an institution; they served as assessors witnessing court procedures, as well as notaries. The Geniza records refer to both functions of the 'udūl. A Hebrew "Scroll," or poetical story, praised the caliph al-Ḥākim, among other things for appointing as night watchmen only "faithful witnesses" (Isaiah 8:2), that is, 'udūl, or persons of certified good reputation. In descriptions of the session of a Muslim court in Alexandria in 1143, the judge is assisted by two "just witnesses" and by the scribes of the government office in which the session was held. We meet a similar pair of ʿudūl witnessing an oath given by a Jewish woman before a Muslim judge. (When Jews make a contract before "four just witnesses," the reference is, however, to a Muslim notary and his assistants.) The facts attested to in such a way were usually accepted by a Jewish court as true, although there are some complaints or reports of ʿudūl giving false testimony.

Shurṭa, the classical Arabic word for police, is almost entirely absent from the Geniza records. It was retained, however, as designation for the office and guardhouse of the police in Fustat. The honorary title *ṣāḥib al-shurṭa* "head of the police," was borne by a number of Spanish Jewish notables but was unknown in the communities of the East during the Geniza period. Both terms were relics of older usage. The head of the police was rather called *wālī*, literally, "governor," but the term's occurrence in numerous Geniza records leaves no doubt about how wālī should be construed in that context. The wālī as head of the police is found in large cities such as Cairo and Alexandria, in provincial towns, and even in mere villages. In urban areas such as Alexandria, Ramle, or Jerusalem, the governor, as a rule, was called amīr. In smaller settlements, the wālī might also be the head of the civil government. In view of the dichotomy that existed between the judiciary and executive power, whenever one required the intervention of the authorities (in a lawsuit or in other circumstances), one applied to both the wālī and the qāḍī. If the person concerned was of low social standing, he might ask a friend to ask still another friend with greater influence to approach the two for him. A fine paid by a community was collected both by the wālī and the nāʾib, or "deputy" (as a judge other than the chief qāḍī was called).

One tried to be on good terms with the custodians of order. When a new wālī was appointed in a townlet of the Rīf, a fruiterer living there was alerted by his brother in the capital that the new wālī was a relative of his predecessor and likely to carry on his vendettas against the fruiterer; the letter notes that it would be good if "a gift of honor would reach him soon." When the Spanish Jewish poet Judah ha-Levi visited Alexandria, a notable of that city was eager to have him as guest for Friday night, an honor that the poet generally refused to grant in order to avert unpleasant rivalries. Undaunted, the host induced his friend, the chief of police, to send a message to the distinguished visitor, whereupon the poet accepted the invitation.

Another very important security officer was the *muḥtasib,* or superintendent of the market. His duties were manifold and ranged from the supervision of commerce and industry to the enforcement of religious law (which partly concerned the non-Muslims as well) and the infliction of corporal punishment. Detailed documents on this interesting office began to circulate towards the end of the twelfth century. A letter from Alexandria, written around 1140, reports that "everyone in the city behaves as if he were a muḥtasib set over us," indicating the office to have been common in Egypt by that time. References to market supervisors in Palestine date from several centuries earlier. It is not unlikely that the institution existed also in Egypt and in the Muslim West concurrently. Still, it should be emphasized that, with one important exception (a case from the thirteenth century), the Geniza records tell us little about this office. This is all the more remarkable in that most of these records deal with economic and legal matters; one expects that they would make mention of the muḥtasib if his presence were felt in the bazaars. The dearth of material in the Geniza records with regard to the muḥtasib is matched by a similar scarcity in the literary sources of the Fatimid period. One explanation is that under the Fatimids the office was often united in one person with that of the chief of police.

Each urban area, compound, or quarter had its own police inspector, called ṣāḥib al-rubʿ, "the supervisor of the quarter." He and his patrolmen were the first to appear at the scene of a public disturbance. The ṣāḥib al-rubʿ also had other functions, for example, assembling the inhabitants of the quarter and leading them to meet the ruler when he entered the city. The supervisor of the quarter appears frequently in the accounts of the Jewish community, for he received gifts of money at the time of the Jewish and Muslim holidays, as well as on special occasions. It was, needless to say, advantageous to be on good terms with him. In one document we find "the supervisors of the quarters" acting as a kind of advisory council to the superintendent of the market.

The police force itself consisted of different contingents. Most frequently mentioned is the patrol. We find them under the command of the police inspectors, or carrying out the orders of qāḍīs, customs officers, collectors of the poll tax, and the director of the mint. In the latter case, they were accompanied by mounted police, because the search for counterfeit money required that they completely encircle a neighborhood. Another common member of the security force was the raqqāṣ, "runner." In modern Arabic the word means "dancer," but in the Geniza period it designated an unskilled laborer and an errand-boy for any government office, especially one who had the task of summoning or arresting a person. In one document, the runners are identified with the patrolmen. Normally they were attached to the wālī — the chief of police.

Summonses to appear at the poll tax office were distributed by the *ḥāshir*s, literally, "ralliers." Upon receipt of such notices, non-Muslims were obliged to appear. (Muslims were exempted from the tax.) Often referred to in the Geniza records, the ḥāshirs were evidently not concerned with the actual collection of the taxes, but constituted a kind of auxiliary police whose task it was to let no one escape from fulfilling his obligation. The royal mint itself was protected by guards of the regular army. Also mentioned is an armed force, called the *aḥdāth*, "young men." They appear in Jerusalem and Aleppo, and perhaps also in Sfax in Tunisia. Their precise function is yet to be determined. (They are not to be confused with the urban mob of that name that is found in Muslim literary sources.) From three letters sent from Jerusalem around 1040, it is evident that the Jewish inhabitants of that city paid a special contribution toward the upkeep of this militia, and it is probable that Christians did so as well. Finally, there were the "messengers" of the chief of the secret police and his "spies"—plainclothesmen to all intents and purposes. Patrolmen, "runners," and "ralliers" certainly did not wear uniforms, but in one way or another they were recognized; the police inspectors and informers remained, or rather wished to remain, unidentified.

As with government offices in general, there was no clear-cut and fixed division of duties among the various branches of the judiciary and the security force. For example, in Damietta the office of the chief of police is reported as dealing with cases of inheritance, normally the prerogative of the qāḍī. It therefore happened that people seeking a legal authority were sometimes at a loss as to whom to turn. In a detailed but incomplete report from Alexandria, an emissary of a Jewish authority describes how he sought to have someone punished physically for a religious offense. After sketching the contents of his charge, he continues:

I did not know to whom to submit it, to the qāḍī or to the wālī. Finally, it occurred to me to send it secretly to the muḥtasib, emphasizing that a light punishment was sufficient. The latter sent his messengers to summon the supervisors of the quarters, who advised him to bring the accused before the wālī. The wālī decided that he should be flogged and pilloried, a decision that was carried out after the messengers of the muḥtasib had brought the man into the presence of the wālī. The public asked that he be put into prison as well. The messengers dragged him around the whole Qamra [a predominantly Jewish quarter], and cried out that he had vilified the [Jewish] religion.

The report concludes by saying that the chief of police was prepared to bring the case before "the great wālī," the superintendent of police in the capital, which was done only in exceptional cases. The writer emphasizes with satisfaction that his appeal to the Muslim authorities was heeded, although he was not known personally either to the muḥtasib or the wālī.

The punishment most frequently mentioned in the Geniza records, and no doubt constituting a major, if not the main, source of income for the police, was the so-called *tarsīm*, "the dues for guardsmen." Originally, it meant that a person would be confined to his house and a guard would be posted before it, for which the accused had to pay.

Imprisonment in those days did not mean simply denial of freedom; it was a far crueler punishment. First, the prisoner was in danger of dying from starvation in the event that no one looked after him, for the prison authorities did not feel themselves obliged to feed him. Thus, a poor woman whose husband was in prison because he was unable to pay the poll tax, asks in a letter for bread to bring to him. Imprisonment, moreover, like any other "service" of the government, had to be paid for. If the prisoner defaulted or was unable to pay, he was cruelly mistreated. "I am afraid to leave my hiding, lest the poll tax collector finds me and puts me into prison, where I shall die, since I possess nothing with which to save my soul," writes a man who lost everything when all his goods were jettisoned from the ship in which he was traveling. A mother from Alexandria, pleading with the Jewish authorities in Fustat to work for the release of her son from prison, remarks that he has to pay the jailer several dirhems a day, a luxury she cannot afford. Even a person apprehended for only one night had to pay the prison guard. It is not surprising then that reports about imprisonment are usually accompanied by remarks about how much it cost.

Corporal punishment and torture were applied even in cases of insolvent debtors. In addition to being flogged and beaten, the prisoner could be put in the stocks; his joints might be wrenched, or he might be chained with a nose ring, or needles driven under his fingernails and into other sensitive parts of his body. The rigors of imprisonment were universally dreaded. Nonetheless those incarcerated by the authorities were ordinarily allowed to receive the visits of relatives and friends, or were at least permitted to see them and talk to them as the visitors stood outside. They were also permitted to send letters from prison, some of which have survived in the Geniza. In one such letter, complaint is made against a particularly vicious jailer who cursed and beat the writer without reason.

It would seem that, in some places at least, the authorities did not tolerate excessive cruelty. Jews were given certain facilities to keep their

Sabbath, and similar consideration no doubt was extended to adherents of other creeds. Thus far, in all the Geniza documents and letters, not a single report of or even reference to an execution has been found. By contrast, the accounts of Muslim historians of the period contain numerous references to public figures of consequence who were executed by their superiors or assassinated by rivals. Among the people of the Geniza, an entirely different climate prevailed: punishment of crimes by the death penalty was next to unknown.

Non-Muslim Government Officials

It has often been emphasized that the Fatimid period was a golden age for minorities entering government service; the same was true later under the Ayyubids. "Government servants," together with judges (who were also to some extent public officials), were the cream of Jewish society. Although there were far more Christian than Jewish government functionaries, a fact fully evidenced in the Geniza records, Jews frequently attained positions of influence disproportionate to their numbers in the general population. An Egyptian poet complains:

> The Jews of our time have attained the goal of their aspirations:
> The honors are theirs and so are the riches. Counselors and kings are taken from their midst.
> Egyptians! I advise you, become Jews, for Heaven itself has turned Jewish.

Long before the tenth century, Muslims attained the same standards of educational and professional experience required for administrative work as their non-Muslim compatriots. Why, then, did they leave the field of government service so much to Jews and Christians? One can attribute the admission of non-Muslims to government service during the Fatimid and Ayyubid periods and even later, as well as the violent reaction ending eventually in their removal, to socioeconomic conditions. In the free economy prevailing at that time, business and industry offered more lucrative and less dangerous opportunities than the often humiliating and precarious service to the sultans. Indeed, the great merchants and providers of goods and services were largely Muslim. From the thirteenth century forward, however, when the economy became increasingly monopolized by the state, Muslims actively sought government posts, and members of the minority groups were forced to give way.

Perhaps it was the initial unattractiveness of government service to Muslims that made it possible for non-Muslims to serve the regime. This explains why the mints—which entailed working with hot melted metals in a hot climate—in most Muslim states remained largely the domain of the Jews, even in later periods. A second reason might be more convincing; indeed it moves our understanding of the role played by minorities in government service to a more complex level: It was not simply economics that brought Jews into the mints, or for that matter into any other government services. No other branch of government work was so exposed to the temptations of fraud and embezzlement as was minting coins; Jews, the least protected minority, were by their very status the most faithful servants of the state, for they knew only too well that in case of discovery of any impropriety no one would shield them from punishment.

We have to allow also that Muslim writers often exaggerate the role of non-Muslims in government. The thirteenth-century verses quoted are a case in point. As late as the 1240s, a Muslim visitor to Egypt reported that most of the Christians and Jews in that country were officials working in the revenue offices and physicians. The Geniza documents enable us to check that statement as regards the Jews. Our sources reveal that there were, in fact, a disproportionately large number of Jews in the medical profession. We may also assume that persons styled *ṣayrafī*, or money changers, were at least partly attached to some government office and that the profession would include many Jews. But there were few Jewish *kātibs*, that is, higher officials. Even if we assume that most kātibs lived in Cairo and not in Fustat, where the Geniza chamber was situated, a survey of Jewish occupations in that period certainly would not corroborate the bald assertion that most Jews were in government service. No doubt, as a traveler, the visiting Muslim had many dealings with customs and other government offices, and he may have been astonished to find far more Christian and Jewish clerks than he was accustomed to in his native country.

The uppermost stratum of officialdom—Jewish and non-Jewish—was formed by the courtiers who had direct access to the caliphs and sultans, or, where power was exercised de jure, access to the actual rulers, whatever their titles. Foremost among this group of officials were the court physicians, about whom we hear so much in the Geniza records. A less conspicuous but still important position was occupied by individuals who controlled the revenue in one capacity or another. The

Geniza refers to two different types of such officials—they are some-times confused in the literary sources. The *mushārif* or *mushrif,* the con-troller of the revenue, and the ʿāmil, or director of the revenue office. The two acting together, with the mushārif mentioned first, fixed the amount of the yearly payments to be made to the government by tax farmers. As in the case of kātib, the term "mushārif" might be applied to the controller of both a whole province and a small village. Numer-ous money changers, bankers, and accountants were required for the collection of taxes and the accounting of expenditures. Such persons were either regular employees—bearing the title *jahbadh al-dīwān* "gov-ernment cashier"—or were more or less loosely connected with the administration. As with the terms "kātib" (official) and "mushārif" (controller), the word *jahbadh* could designate both a powerful min-ister of finance and a poor money changer barely able to make a liv-ing.

Since the Jews were avid travelers, it is not surprising that some of them occupied government posts connected with seafaring. We find Jews acting as superintendents of the port of Alexandria and the port of Denia in Spain, and as controllers of ships, in charge of the passengers and their goods. Like other government officials, the latter were per-mitted to do business on their own account while traveling and could not be sued during the time they were in service. On the other hand, merchants were reluctant to make use of them as agents, precisely be-cause of their connection to the government.

Although it may seem odd at first, the Geniza records prove that Jews served as police and were found in the army as well. Persons working in the *shurṭa* (the guardhouse of Fustat) or as ḥāshirs, "ralliers," night-watchmen, or members of the secret police, appear in our documents at different times. Jews are repeatedly called raqqāṣ, "runner." Since, as noted earlier in this chapter, the ralliers, runners, and plainclothesmen assisted the authorities in the collection of taxes and customs dues, the surveillance of minority groups was facilitated by employing persons of their own kind. That is to say, the government preferred to rule minor-ities wherever and whenever possible through their own intermediaries. The army was composed of foreign contingents, such as Berbers, Turks, blacks from the Sudan and elsewhere, and some bedouin levies, and as a rule, did not admit members of the local sedentary population, whether non-Muslim or Muslim. Still, one army service, the "medical corps," seems to have been popular among the minority groups: letters to and from Jewish physicians serving with the army or navy are by no means rare.

The Poll Tax and Other Impositions

Literary sources—Muslim juridical books on taxation—and the documentary evidence of the Geniza records present radically different views of the *jizya*, or *jāliya*, the poll tax paid by non-Muslims. It is, of course, evident from all our sources that the tax was discriminatory and was intended, according to traditional interpretations of the Qur'ān to emphasize the inferior status of nonbelievers. Literary sources give an impression that the poll tax did not represent a heavy economic imposition, since it was to be paid according to a sliding scale, originally of one, two, and four dinars, that was adjusted to the financial means of the taxpayer. But this impression is entirely misleading, for it does not take into consideration the immense poverty and privation experienced by the larger Jewish community, a fact made clear in the Geniza materials. Jews are depicted in our documents living from hand to mouth and persistently short of cash, all of which turned the "season of the tax" into one of horror, dread, and misery. The provisions of ancient Islamic law that exempted the indigent, the invalids, and the old from taxation were no longer observed in the Geniza period and had been discarded in theory as well by the Islamic school of law that prevailed in Egypt. The payment of the poll tax was the very first consideration in the budget of families with modest income, such as teachers or laborers. A man could clothe himself inexpensively, he could eat at subsistence level, as perhaps a very large section of the population did, but he could not escape the tax-collector—at least not for long. If he was caught, he was liable to be beaten and suffer other corporal punishments, if not thrown into prison, with all that implied for his survival.

A few passages selected at random from a mass of pertinent Geniza letters serve to illustrate the difficult state of affairs. A schoolmaster from Qalyūb who earned some additional income by copying books, complains to a relative in the capital around 1225: "This place does not provide me with [payment for] the poll tax or clothing, and, as to food, the fees suffice only for me alone, for they amount only to five dirhems a week and I need three-quarters of a dirhem a day at least. Thus my income is not enough even for having a robe laundered. . . . The nagid promised me a year ago that he would take care of the *jāliya*, but the year has passed and I have received nothing from him. I am now perplexed and pondering where to turn and where to flee." He sends four books copied by himself, hoping, somewhat faintly, that the proceeds of their sale will resolve his predicament. Even so prominent a teacher as Solomon, the son of the judge Elijah b. Zechariah, requests money for the payment of the poll tax. Nor were orphans exempt. From a query submitted to Abraham Maimonides, we learn that the guardians of an orphaned minor had to pay the jāliya for a full ten years before he was declared of majority by a Jewish court and thus competent to take care of his property. From a document written around 1095 it seems that the jāliya was due from the age of nine. Whether death canceled arrears in poll tax due was a point of theory among Muslim doctors of law; in the Geniza period it had to be borne by the legal heirs. Therefore we find provisions for the payment of such debts in deathbed declarations.

Members of a family were held responsible for each other's poll tax. A silk weaver fled from Fustat and went as far south as Aswan because being such a burden on his father and three brothers was too much for him. We learn this from a letter of one of the brothers assuring him that the members of the family had paid his tax — not, however, without the father having spent one night in prison — and that he could now safely return. Cases of persons who had to account for a brother or sons are cited in our documents. The same applied to brothers-in-law. The poll tax was also assessed on travelers to distant countries — to be paid for them back home. We learn that the brother of a merchant who sojourned in India for nine years and finally died there fulfilled this duty for the whole period — a fact mentioned in the document concerned as in no way extraordinary.

A person traveling within the realm of Islam — indeed anyone leaving his domicile even for a short period — had to carry with him a *barā'a* "acquittance," showing that he had fulfilled his obligation for the current year. In a smaller locality, when the tax collector had not arrived in time, people who had arranged journeys in advance had to cancel them because it was dangerous to travel so without a barā'a. Because everyone paid where he was registered as a resident, one would expect that a traveler would not be held liable to pay the jāliya of the locality where he sojourned temporarily. The Geniza records show, however, that tax collectors found all sorts of ways to have foreigners pay. Even while setting out from one town of Egypt to another, a cautious traveler would provide himself with a letter of recommendation to an influential person asking him for protection against overreaching tax collectors. A letter written in Arabic characters to a notable in Fustat by his brother traveling in the Rīf contains this story: The muqaddam of the little town of Damīra paid his poll tax in the provincial capital al-Maḥalla. While staying in Fustat for a year he paid there as nonresident and received a proper barā'a. When he returned to Damīra, however, the authorities did not honor the receipt and ordered him to pay a second time. It was regarded as necessary to obtain a caliphal rescript for the redress of this oppressive act.

It was not only the government officials and tax farmers whose rapacity was dreaded. The leaders of the local denominational communities, who had a say in the assessment, also contributed to the plight of the "newcomers." A passage from a letter of a Tunisian merchant writing from Alexandria is very instructive in this respect:

I wish to tell you what happened to me with regard to the poll tax since your departure from here. There are many in this city who arrived before I did, but they were not treated as I have been. Everyday they molest me and summon me to the court, asking me to pay the jāliya in full. They want to register me as a resident, whereas my father, as you know, was only a "newcomer." What they impose on me is remitted to others, who do not allow themselves to be molested—you know whom I mean. The benefit that I derived from your intervention on my behalf is that I have to pay almost two dinars this year. I would not have minded, if others had been treated in the same way. The tax collectors [ḥāshirs, ralliers] and the director of the jāliya are not to be blamed; all this is entirely the work of the Jew!

When did a person cease to be a newcomer and obtain the status of a permanent resident (qāṭin)? Owing to the astonishing mobility of the Mediterranean middle class, this issue caused many problems for both the administration and the persons affected. It appears from the Geniza records that it was not easy to change one's status. An eleventh-century Tunisian merchant and scholar who, after having lived in Egypt for years, spent some time in Byzantium and finally settled in the Holy Land, writes, "I intend to pass the winter in Jerusalem, for I have learned about the [bad] Nile [an allusion to famine in Egypt, where the writer expected to travel]. Furthermore, I am registered in the revenue office (kharāj) of Fustat as resident. Originally they registered me as a newcomer, but when my stay in the country extended, I became a qāṭin. By now, I have been away from Egypt for ten years and this is my eleventh." Since the writer wished to pay the poll tax levied in Palestine, his true place of residence, he preferred not to return to Egypt, where he still was registered, and hence arguably liable for its payment.

Were there any exemptions from the duty to pay the poll tax? The ancient idea that those who dedicate themselves to the service of God should be free from the service of men was honored in the Jewish community, which bore the tax burden for its scholarly officials; it was an internal arrangement that did not directly involve the Muslim authorities. Some Jews were technically exempt from the poll tax. The strangest such exemption is that of the poet Yākhīn, who had settled in al-Maḥalla but fled when the superintendent of revenue "harassed him" by demanding that he pay the poll tax. The letter argues that Yākhīn was entitled to tax exemption because he was a Khaybarī, a Jew from a northern Arabian clan that asserted it had received special privileges from the Prophet of Islam. A forged document to this effect has found its way into the Geniza and is preserved in extended form in the popular literature of the Jews of Yemen under the title "The Letter of Protection Granted by the Prophet." References to persons called al-Khaybarī are found in various Geniza documents of the eleventh century. But there is no express testimony that any tax collector honored the Khaybarīs' claim. It is not clear that those claiming to be Khaybarīs were in fact the descendants of the oasis dwellers defeated by Muḥammad in the 630s.[1]

The Geniza records prove that the data given by the Muslim handbooks of administration on the amounts of the poll tax, although hardly reflecting the realities in full, are basically correct. Ibn Mammātī (a Christian convert to Islam, d. 1209) notes as the highest yearly rate 4⅙ dinars. This is exactly the sum paid by a physician according to a document dated 1182. As lowest grade he gives "1 plus ⅓ and ¼ dinars and 2 *ḥabbas*," that is, 1⅝ dinars. We find this amount in Geniza records repeatedly for Saladin's time, but also 120 years earlier. In practice, these rates were adjusted in conformity with local conditions. Such adjustments represented not only increases in the rates (as when the caliph al-Ḥākim doubled the poll tax for a period of time) but also reductions. Where we find that both foreigners and persons native to Egypt registered for the jāliya in smaller towns and not in the cities in which they lived, we may surmise that they did so to take advantage of lower rates. However, it is not possible at this time to determine whether this was in fact the case. The Geniza records for a particular locality may either represent fines for arrears, or, on the contrary, may represent merely installments of a larger payment due. The question whether special rates existed for individual, meritorious cases cannot yet be decided with the material at our disposal. We find many requests addressed to notables to use their influence with tax officials to obtain more favorable conditions for a certain person or community. One wonders, however, whether such interventions were successful. Had preferential taxation been common practice, it is not likely that the Geniza would bear testimony to so much deprivation occasioned by the poll tax.

1. Goitein believed that the so-called Khaybarīs actually came to the West via Iraq, unlike the Ḥijāzīs, Jews of northern Arabia who emigrated directly to Egypt.

There are repeated references to fines for arrears. These were actually payments to the ralliers sent to summon the non-Muslims to the tax office. A man who was thirty dirhems in arrears had to pay one silver piece (*fiḍḍa*) every week. Another writes that he gave the rallier four dirhems at a time (perhaps four ralliers appeared together); to meet the payment, his house was offered for sale by auction. Pressures to pay the poll tax in advance are found in Geniza records only for Palestine and then only for the second quarter of the eleventh century, a period of lawlessness and misrule. According to one report, payment was demanded a full five months before the Muslim New Year's Day—the date on which it was legally due.

It has often been asserted that the jāliya was collected by the non-Muslim communities and their official heads. This assumption is refuted by the Geniza records, which show that each individual was contacted by the state authorities directly and had to find the means of payment for himself. A person lacking the required cash would sell or pawn his clothes, or might even be forced to dip into his wife's assets, which he was not allowed, by law, to touch. Husbands desperate to meet the burden of the poll tax even appropriated material given to them for processing, such as raw silk. When all available family resources were exhausted, he might implore a generous and well-fixed person to assist him—or to introduce him to others who could.

When all efforts to obtain the sums due for the jāliya failed, the insolvent taxpayer often went into hiding, a means of escaping payment that had many drawbacks. As we have seen, the fugitive's male relatives were held responsible for him. Moreover, while in hiding he was unable to earn a livelihood, especially if his income was derived from a workshop or a store that required his daily presence. Finally, such a person often owed money also to private creditors, who would track him down even without the aid of the state police. Imprisonment, the routine punishment for failure to pay the poll tax, was not always limited to short durations: we read about a cantor who had been in jail for two months because he had found no one to pay his tax for him; he was not set free despite a serious illness.

Although the local or regional non-Muslim communities did not collect the poll tax directly from their constituents, the denominational leadership played an important role in the tax process. Direct and indirect references in the Geniza records prove that both the local muqaddams and the nagid were consulted by the state authorities when they assessed the financial capacity of the Jewish taxpayers, and it goes without saying that the same must have been true of the local and regional Christian leaders. The total amount to be levied in one area, like other items of the budget, was fixed in advance (otherwise it could not be farmed out), a fact that explains why the Jewish authorities were so eager to register foreigners as residents—even those sojourning in the city for a short while. Although—in Egypt at least—the Jewish local leaders were not held liable for the total amount of the poll tax to be raised in their communities, they themselves regarded the payment of the jāliya for the poor as a holy obligation and a pious deed comparable with the highly meritorious ransoming of captives.

Nevertheless, it is evident from many Geniza records that during long periods, and in many places, the assistance of the indigent taxpayer was not handled by the community but was left to private philanthropy. But there were times when a local non-Muslim community was charged with a comprehensive communal poll tax, or when its leaders felt coerced to undertake a yearly collection for a segment of the community. Owing to the dismal situation in eleventh-century Jerusalem, the Jewish population fluctuated periodically. Thus, a fixed sum was imposed on the Jewish community, and its leaders were held responsible for its payment by the Muslim authorities. The Jerusalemites, in turn, made desperate appeals for help to their brethren in the Egyptian capital.

The task of collecting the poll tax was assigned to a group of special officials. One called the ʿāmil took care of administering tax collection, while cash payments were handled by a government collector, who was styled jahbadh al-jawālī as late as the twelfth century. Later on, this function was handled by someone called a ṣayrafī, the general designation for a banker or money changer. In cases of "irregularities," the chief of police and even the governor of a city were approached.

The poll tax is a subject that occupies far more space in the Geniza records than one would expect. A considerable section of the non-Muslim population must have been unable to pay it and often suffered humiliation and privation on that account. Whereas in the higher circles, the prospects of appointment to leading government posts acted as an inducement for embracing Islam, the mass conversions in the lower classes might well have been caused in part by the intolerable burden of the poll tax. The express testimony of the Geniza letters to the severe hardship caused by the jāliya is confirmed by implicit evidence of the Arabic papyri. Adolf Grohmann's study of Arabic administrative papyri concludes that the voluminous data about arrears and installments in the payment of the jāliya indicate the dire circumstances in which so many taxpayers usually found themselves.[2] The papyri discussed by

2. "Die arabischen Papyri aus der Giessener Universitätsbibliothek," *Abhandlung der Giessener Hochschulgesellschaft* 4 (Giessen, 1960).

Grohmann refer to Christians, but the Geniza confirms that this was certainly true of the Jews as well.

Taxes and government impositions connected with economic activities were also common. Impositions on special occasions are referred to in the Geniza records. Thus, one letter describes most vividly a requisition, or *muṣādara,* carried out against a whole town, in which Muslims, Christians, Samaritans, and Jews were all affected; the latter suffered even more than the other communities. All the clothing and the provisions of wheat and wine hoarded in the house of the writer's uncle were plundered; even the rope of the well was taken away. In war and peace alike there were occasions when the civil population, both Muslim and non-Muslim, was summoned to perform corvées, enforced and unpaid labor for the central government—or for whomever was in power. The Geniza refers to a similar form of enforced labor about which we are less well informed: the mandatory recruitment of skilled artisans for government workshops.

As did the poll tax, the appropriation of estates by the government caused constant concern to the people speaking to us through the Geniza records. The threat of losing an inheritance was by no means limited to religious minorities, as we know only too well from literature describing Muslim society. Because Muslim law made it easy for the state to appropriate the property of non-Muslims, Christians and Jews had to fight to preserve the right to have their cases of inheritance treated according to their own law and before their own courts. Although practice varied widely in different places and times, it seems that during the Fatimid period the right of Jewish courts to decide inheritance cases involving Jews was generally recognized, although it had to be reinforced from time to time by caliphal rescripts.

Communal Autonomy and Government Control

THE INTERPLAY OF LAWS

In certain cases, Muslim law allowed the government to lay claim on part or all of an estate; in addition, it opened the door for arbitrary and unscrupulous practices. A few examples selected from the Geniza records illustrate the complex situation.

According to Muslim law, a woman is worth half a man. Therefore, a daughter can never inherit more than half her father's estate; if no other heirs are extant, the other half falls to the state. In contrast, according to Jewish law, an only daughter inherits the entire estate of her father. No wonder, then, that the Muslim authorities were eager to apply their own law when Jews were to inherit. Moreover, the Muslim authorities would not investigate too deeply whether other heirs existed or whether or not the possessions left actually belonged to the intestate. Accordingly, any interference by the Bureau of Estates was dreaded as potentially harmful by Jews. The practice of Muslim governments seizing part of an inheritance when only female heirs were left is specifically attested to by Geniza documents for the late tenth or early eleventh century.

By their very nature, most cases of succession are complicated. Since it was taken for granted that the government would appropriate a part of the estate when there were only female heirs, and since the Muslim authorities did not want to be bothered too much with the intricacies of administrative practice superimposed on Jewish law, we read about agreements on flat sums between the two authorities. According to Jewish law, a widow could not inherit, but her marriage contract entitled her to a payment from her husband (in this case, his estate) which was regarded as a debt; as such, it had precedence over the claims of the heirs. Some Geniza documents show that this principle was recognized by the Bureau of Estates. Interference by the bureau was similarly dreaded as regards inheritance by male heirs, even in cases where there was no discrepancy between Jewish and Muslim law. An heir informs his correspondent that no one, the government included, has any claim on his inheritance, but he adds resignedly that, as his case stands, it is only a question of whether the government will take one-half or three-eighths. An old man, supported by his nephew out of the estate of his late brother, loses that support when the nephew dies and the family of the deceased is not prepared to continue the help; the old man is afraid that invoking the help of the state might provoke its direct intervention. (When a son was heir, the decedent's brother had no legal claims to the estate, according to both Muslim and Jewish law. Nonetheless it was assumed that, if approached, the Bureau of Estates would intervene and use the opportunity to appropriate the lion's share of the remaining estate.) With the progressive deterioration of the legal status of the non-Muslim minorities (and that of Islamic justice in general) during the times of general crisis in the twelfth century, estates were confiscated when the legal heirs happened not to be present at the time of a person's demise.

The direct and negative interference of the Muslim authorities in the legal matters of non-Muslims was seemingly confined to inheritance. In other instances of legal disputes, however, there is much evidence in the Geniza records about Jews themselves applying to the state courts. The vast material on the subject can be grouped under three different headings. First, persons might approach a court of the state when the law applied in that venue was more advantageous to them. Second, the government court might serve as a kind of court of appeal for litigants unsuccessful in a lawsuit in the Jewish court or as an enforcement authority when the opposite party refused to appear before the Jewish courts. Finally, deeds would be made out in a state court (or, concurrently in that venue and before a Jewish authority) in order to safeguard their legality and to have them as an instrument of proof should litigation in a state court ensue.

The first point is best illustrated by examples concerning succession. The Muslim and Jewish laws of inheritance differed not only with respect to the status of women as heirs but on many other points as well. The contrast between the two legal systems in this regard stems from their entirely different origins. Israelite law, like Roman and Germanic law, developed in an agricultural society eager to hold an estate together in units large enough to sustain a family. For this reason, Jewish inheritance law, unlike Muslim law, gives the firstborn preferential treatment. On the other hand, the ancient Arabs were bedouins and traders whose possessions — livestock, pack animals, camels, horses, goods, and cash — unlike land, lent themselves easily to division. An inheritance was regarded as a kind of spoil to be distributed among numerous members of a clan. Hence, Muslim law granted many persons excluded by Jewish law a share in inheritance. Jews seeking an otherwise unavailable inheritance might for that reason seek recourse to the law of Islam. For example, if a son and a daughter were heirs, according to the ancient Jewish law the son received the entire estate — normally the father's farm — but was obligated to provide his sister's dowry. In Islam, where legally a female was worth half a male, the brother received two-thirds of the estate and the sister one-third. To forestall a conflict between his children arising from the discrepancy in coexistent laws, a Jewish father would will two-thirds of his property to his son and one-third to his daughter, or provide the latter with a house and other parts of her dowry early in life. Similarly, Jewish courts would compensate sisters, or the families of sisters, with an appropriate share in order to avoid the interference of the state. These precautionary measures must have been successful, for cases of a sister claiming a share in an inheritance from her brother in a Muslim court are extremely rare. One must bear in mind, however, that lawsuits by a sister against a brother are almost unheard of during this period, since he was regarded as her natural protector against her husband.

When a father "sells" half a house to his firstborn, but wills to two others one-quarter each, it is evident that the "sale" was a formality intended to safeguard the rights of the firstborn and to deprive the others of the possibility of claiming equal shares in a Muslim court. When Jewish authorities allot a small part of an estate belonging to a man whose only heir was a daughter to the son of his paternal uncle, they no doubt acted in such fashion because Muslim law granted the nephew this right.

A protracted lawsuit between a father and his son over the latter's inheritance from his mother, grandmother, and great-grandmother was argued before a Muslim qāḍī but was finally settled in a Jewish court on December 31, 1100. The appeal to Muslim authorities against the decision of a Jewish court was no doubt an incentive to have both parties settle quickly.

Such appeals were made even in family matters, normally the prerogative of the denominational judiciary. In Maimonides' time, when a kohen was denied permission by Jewish authorities to marry a divorced woman (a union prohibited by Jewish law), he contracted the marriage in a Muslim court. Conversely, in 1042, a Jewish judge—a ḥazzān in Alexandria—had to testify before a qāḍī that there were no objections to the marriage of a woman who had been denounced as being legally bound to another man. When a settlement was reached in 1052 between a husband and his former wife concerning the maintenance and education of their five-year-old boy, the woman promised not to trouble the contracting partner with appeals to a Muslim court or to the government; she was threatened with excommunication if she did.

Non-Muslims appeared and argued in Muslim courts in person, or they were represented by Muslim attorneys. In the great majority of cases mentioned in the Geniza, Jews made use of the Muslim judiciary not to litigate disputes but to ratify contracts. Even the Jewish community chest stipulated in an agreement made with a tenant in 1156 that a contract of lease should be written *fī 'l-muslimīn* "before a Muslim authority." As regards these contracts, the Geniza records mostly settlements, in which one party hands over to the other "the document written according to gentile [Muslim] law." Such documents at the same time granted some discount or permitted a delay in payment when the other party had fulfilled, or promised to fulfill, the obligations emanating from the new agreement. It was common practice to make contracts before Muslim and Jewish authorities concurrently.

In principle, Christian and Jewish authorities alike regarded any application to a Muslim court by one of their flock as offensive and even worthy of excommunication. In quite a number of Geniza records, the contracting parties undertake not to apply to a gentile court. This was done not only in matters of family law and inheritance but also with regard to purely commercial matters. The very fact that such provisions were stipulated in contracts proves, though, how common the practice of turning to the state judiciary had become, and we are not astonished to find a judge newly transferred to al-Maḥalla stating with relief that his flock applies solely to him and never "transgresses" to a Muslim court. There are many references to Jews seeking justice in Muslim courts in the responsa of the gaons and those of Moses and Abraham Maimonides. These discussions of the Jewish and Muslim courts betray many shades of opinion, which can be summarized as follows: While, in principle, only the denominational courts had religiously approved competence, it was permitted and even advisable to apply to the state authorities when the causes of justice and expediency were served by such a step.

Numerous Geniza records reflect the same attitude. Almost all the powers of attorney made out in Jewish courts allow the appointee to bring the accused before a gentile court. Letters of attorney were written mostly in extreme cases after all other means of achieving satisfaction had failed. It was assumed that only the threat of arraignment by a state authority would bring a recalcitrant debtor to reason. The creditor would then deposit his "Arabic legal proofs," that is, documents written by a Muslim notary and witnessed by Muslims, with the Jewish court (in deference to Jewish jurisdiction) but received permission to make use of them in Muslim court should the opposing party not turn up at the *bēth dīn*. When an Iraqi gaon issued a decision in 1166 in a case of inheritance occurring in Egypt, he instructed the local court to turn to the government if the losing party disobeyed his instructions. By so doing, it could be argued, the Jewish courts did not simply surrender their jurisdiction to the state.

A clause giving the bearer the right to apply to a Muslim court, found in many letters of attorney, was not entirely for inner consumption. The Muslim authorities did not accept a Jewish case indiscriminately and, as the Geniza shows, there was a good deal of cooperation between the state and the denominational courts. The case of a female slave, who claimed to be Jewish, was sent by a Muslim judge back to his Jewish colleague. Two parties, having made a settlement in the Jewish court of Alexandria in 1152, wanted to make a different one before the qāḍī "according to the noble religion of the Muslims." Before acting on the request, the qāḍī sent his messengers to the rabbinate, where a declaration, properly reinforced by the symbolic purchase, was deposited by the parties acknowledging that they had annulled the arrangements formerly arrived at in the denominational court. Similarly, a female heir, who felt herself wronged by a Jewish judge to the advantage of her late father's business partners, applied to the qāḍī of Alexandria; her case was heard favorably by the qāḍī, but it was directed for a final settlement to the nagid Mevōrākh in the capital. Such cooperation prevailed particularly in the realm of family law. Sometimes going to the Muslim courts was apt to present a Jewish judge with a moral dilemma: Should he submit his findings to his Muslim colleague when he knew that this would lead to the imprisonment of one of the Jewish parties? The Geniza records also report gentiles, both Christians and Muslims, making settlements with a Jewish party before a Jewish court, but such cases seem to have been exceptional.

HOW MUCH AUTONOMY?

A postscript to a letter sent in 1016/17 by the representative of the Baghdad yeshivas in Qayrawān to Ibn ʿAwkal, the head rabbinical authority in the West—his seat was in Fustat—describes the following situation: A Jewish merchant from Baghdad had died in distant Sijilmāsa, Morocco. The Jewish authorities there informed the writer of the possessions left by the deceased in that city. In addition, the traveler left goods with merchants in Qayrawān. The writer asks Ibn ʿAwkal to request the Jewish authorities in Baghdad either to appoint a legal representative for the heirs or to transmit their names and claims to the nagid of Tunisia, its chief Jewish judge, and to the elders of Qayrawān, all of whom would take care of the matter.

This case is yet another indication that the non-Muslim communities formed a state not only within a particular Muslim polity, but also beyond its confines. Months of travel separated Baghdad from Qayrawān, and the latter from Sijilmāsa. Several frontiers of mutually distinct and hostile ruling authorities had to be traversed. Still, the disposal of the deceased's estate is treated here as an entirely Jewish affair. No reference is made to the regional governments of the caliphs in Baghdad. Instead, the matter is handled entirely by Jewish authorities, religious and lay, ecumenical, territorial, and local.

The yeshiva was a pre-Islamic institution, and, even during the heyday of Islam, it differed completely from its Islamic counterpart, the *madrasa*, which was essentially a theological college. Thus, the ecumenical Jewish authority and all that was connected with it—in particular, the diocesan organization of the Diaspora, which later gave rise to religious and secular territorial heads—must be regarded as essentially autochthonous. The Jewish local community, with the prominent participation of the laity in all its functions, is age-old; as far as our present knowledge goes, nothing comparable to it existed in Islam. The works of charity described in chapter 4 had their roots in talmudic ordinances and were matched by those practiced by Jews in Christian countries. Similarly, Jewish education grew organically out of the needs and practices of Jewish religion many centuries prior to the rise of Islam, but it was clearly open to Islamic influences because of the close affinity between the two religions. Secular education within the Jewish community was identical with the courses of study in the corresponding social milieus of Muslims and Christians.

The impact of the Muslim environment was strongest where the contacts were broadest: in the economic, legal, and political spheres. Ultimately all power and authority rested with the state. But before the state's influence can be appraised, some preliminary questions must be asked. What was the character of this state? How far was it willing and able to occupy itself with its non-Muslim subjects?

The Muslim state was concerned mainly with security and justice, and, needless to say, with raising the revenues required to sustain a vast bureaucratic apparatus. On the whole, the Fatimid state was inclined to be less intrusive in the lives of its subjects than earlier Muslim dynasties. The minorities in particular were left to administer their internal affairs—subject, of course, to state intervention were that considered necessary.

Still, all who wished to exercise authority among the minorities—the exilarch, the gaons of Baghdad and Jerusalem, territorial and local leaders, and, of course, the Christian patriarchs and other dignitaries— needed the backing of the Fatimid state. But it was the Jew or Christian who sought an appointment, or his followers, who were eager to have him confirmed in office; the state itself had no specific stake in strengthening the communal organization of non-Muslim groups. The assumption that it was the Muslim state that united the Jewish congregations into local communities to serve their own ends is not grounded in the true nature of either Jewish or Muslim society. The vacillating attitude of the Fatimid caliphs toward the controversies of the Rabbanites and Karaites in Palestine, granting privileges at one time to one party and then to another, shows how little the Muslim authorities were concerned with keeping communal peace among the Jews. Certainly there was no set government policy as regards these particular disputes, which fractured the Jewish community. The same occurred during three years of communal strife stemming from a rivalry between the Palestinian gaons Solomon b. Judah (1025–51) and Nathan b. Abraham (1038–41). Once, at the request of one or two of the parties, a high Jewish personage in Cairo, apparently a government official, was appointed to resolve the dispute. But he did nothing, and no further action was taken by the central government. After some time, the crisis came to a head, and the government was again approached, this time by both sides. Finally, the authority of the legitimate gaon was upheld by the government, but, as the document reveals, the settlement between the parties resulted from the intervention of the Jewish laity rather than the sultan. In sum, the state had no intrinsic interest in the internal affairs of the Jews. It therefore had no reason to try to regulate those communities other than keeping them responsive to the needs of the state and the legal demands placed on them by Islam.

Circumstances changed slightly under the Ayyubids. In Saladin's time, a Jewish judge in Alexandria declares having received a letter of appointment from none other than the sultan, meaning from a Muslim rather than a Jewish authority. It seems that Saladin himself, when he was still vizier of the last Fatimid caliph, appointed a Jewish muqaddam in Minyat Ziftā, who was, however, soon replaced by the local man who had held the position before. A French rabbi, chosen by the nagid Abraham Maimonides as one of the three Jewish judges of Alexandria, had incurred difficulties with one of his colleagues and therefore wished to have his appointment confirmed in public by a "gentile writ." In accordance with this situation, Jewish judges received (or expected to receive) a salary or pension from the Ayyubid rulers, but that financial arrangement was not consistently applied.

Dangerous as it might have been, the practice of turning to the Muslim state even in controversies of a purely religious nature became widespread in Ayyubid times. Staunch supporters of strict orthodoxy, the Ayyubids could be counted upon to uphold the preservation of established rites. No wonder, then, that the opponents of innovation in the Jewish community confidently turned to what they perceived a similarly minded government. A case in point is the rescript of a sultan in favor of retaining the time-honored poetical insertions into the synagogue liturgy, which reformers, for various reasons, wished to abolish or at least reduce in number. The Geniza has indeed preserved a query written in Arabic characters and addressed to one ʿImād al-Dīn, who bore the title *muftī dawlat amīr al-Muʾminīn,* "legal expert of the caliph's realm."

It contained the following question: "Jewish prayer on workdays, Sabbaths, and holidays follows ancient patterns and long-established customs. Certain people now want to introduce changes. Are such innovations permissible in the days of Islam? May God make them permanent?" The expected answer was, of course, that any "innovation" was anathema. Indeed the word for innovation in Arabic also means heresy.

More serious was the action sought from the Ayyubid government by the adversaries of the nagid Abraham Maimonides. At issue were his reforms for synagogue worship. Abraham sought to give the service a strictly devotional character. The members of the congregation were to be seated in rows facing the holy ark (and not along the walls facing each other, as is still the custom in Oriental synagogues). Cushions and reclining pillows were to be banned, and, when seated, everyone was to maintain an upright position. Prostration and genuflection, as of old, should underline the character of prayer as "service to God," and numerous ablutions should stress the need for inner purification. The text of the liturgy was also to be reformed. The opponents of these measures, led by Abraham Maimonides' political foes, approached the sultan al-Malik al-ʿĀdil (d. 1218), forcing the nagid to explain that his reforms were a matter of personal religion and confined to his private synagogue; he did not use his office to exert pressure on anyone to make changes in his established customs. How aware Abraham was of the dangerous character of such an accusation may be gauged from the fact that he had "the whole community, almost two hundred persons" sign an appropriate declaration.

None of Abraham Maimonides' religious reforms were implemented. But, once again, it was not so much the attitude of the government as the opposition of the Jewish community of Egypt that frustrated his efforts. How little the Ayyubid government was concerned with the inner affairs of the non-Muslim communities may be seen from the contemporaneous history of the Coptic Church. Starting in 1216, the office of the patriarch of Alexandria remained vacant for nineteen years—that is, during most of the tenure of al-Malik al-Kāmil, one of the most energetic Muslim rulers of Egypt. It is fair to say that while the Christians and Jews shared with their Muslim compatriots a common language, economy, and many social notions and customs, their communal life remained largely their own.

SEVEN

A Social Being

Introducing the People of the Geniza

       The individual encountered in the Geniza documents was eminently sociable and outgoing. Women and men hated being alone and thirsted for congenial company. They cared very much what people said about them and entertained definite opinions about others. A man was an ardent partisan, prone to take sides; his intense preoccupation with his social environment sharpened his eye for human weaknesses and wickedness and taught him to appreciate goodness and nobility. Warmth and compassion were regarded as the most precious human qualities. Women and men, uncomfortable in the company of more than one member of the opposite sex, enjoyed being with relatives and friends of their own gender.

       Bartering a wide variety of objects for equally disparate goods (money in those days was also a merchandise "bought" and "sold") seems to have been the passion and pastime of the populace. It required acquaintance with a wide selection of dealers and craftsmen (often united in one profession). Together with the house of prayer, the bazaar was a person's other home. Conversely, the precariousness of life—economic insecurity, famines, uncontrollable diseases, epidemics, wars, and revolts—forced the individual to create for himself a limited circle of dedicated persons on whom he could rely in both ordinary and adverse circumstances. Exerting oneself for one's relatives and friends was the most highly appreciated virtue.

God could be approached only through the channels created by the religious community to which one belonged. Thus, religion, which formed the basis of a person's inner life, determined also his or her status as a social being. Within the community, down to the lowest layers of society, there were controversies about matters of belief, or ritual, or the choice of a leader; participation in the disputes over such issues was extraordinarily lively.

The attachment was to one's city, native or adopted, rather than to one's region. It was almost universal practice in Islam to identify a person by his city of origin, his city of residence, or even his residential quarter and not by any broader geographical unit. One owed allegiance to one's family, friends, faith, and faction, but the city or native quarter was one's *watan*, the larger unit to which one belonged.

Because of the mobility of the Mediterranean and Islamic peoples in general, the population of a city was composite in every respect: race, creed, occupation, and standard of living. It was a mirror of the world. The very character of a bustling mercantile emporium like Fustat turned its inhabitants into citizens of the world.

A similar polarity between parochialism and openness can be observed in the spiritual world. One belonged to a specific religious group; everyone else was a stranger. Yet the situation was entirely different from that prevailing, say, in central and northern France and western Germany, the countries that most typify Judeo-Christian confrontation in medieval Europe. There, Jewish learning was identified exclusively with religious matters, and Hebrew was the means of literary expression. In Islamic countries like Spain or Egypt, to the contrary, Jews wrote even their theological and ethical treatises in Arabic and participated fully in the study of the philosophic and scientific works of the ancients, which they read, of course, in Arabic translation. The reason for this difference was the openness of Mediterranean society during the favorable times of the High Middle Ages: Jewish houses bordered on those of Christians and Muslims, and there were no occupational ghettos; members of different religions who exercised the same occupation might be more akin to one another than they were to people of their own religion belonging to another class and doing entirely different work. Occasionally one was also reminded that all prayed to the same God, "the Lord of the World," and that one shared with members of the other monotheistic religions more than the clay from which all were formed.

Nor did the "pagan" world remain outside the orbit of a Geniza person. India and China were certainly far away, and Africa was regarded as "another clime," but the products and artifacts of those regions filled the markets and houses. Africans and peoples from the subcontinent of India often served in households or businesses. Daily contacts often revealed that such foreigners were valuable human beings like anyone else, and the attitude toward them was conditioned by their worth rather than by their ethnic background. Servants were often treated as family and after their manumission became members of the community.

The ancient Greeks had long passed from the scene but the value of their achievements lingered on. One consulted a physician or an astrologer with the assurance of being treated or helped by knowledge gleaned from the most reliable books of the ancients. Their idolatry had been forgotten; their scientific attainments were avidly studied. Translations from the Greek formed a substantial part of any respectable library not confined to religious matters, and numerous lists containing such works have been preserved in the Geniza.

In daily life, a Geniza householder used clothing and food, draperies and utensils, medicines and chemicals brought from the four corners of the earth, items often named after the countries or cities where they were first produced. The walls of his house encompassed the world. He probably had acquaintances who had visited foreign places or even hailed from there, or he might invest in business ventures carried on in faraway markets. When he traveled abroad—and not only great merchants but also ordinary people and even beggars traveled frequently—he was not a complete stranger. He was familiar with the money circulating in the country visited and the goods customarily imported from there. He probably had business friends there, occasionally even relatives. In short, as parochial as the Geniza person was, dedicated to his extended family, religious group, party, and native city, he was intensely social and outgoing and could become a thorough cosmopolitan, making contacts in foreign parts and feeling at home abroad.

It is this intimation of an expanded existence that makes reading the Geniza correspondence so pleasant. It was a civilized world, inhabited by people who knew precise rules of decorum, who were considerate and paid proper attention to their fellow human beings. Men knew their station in society but were not unduly deferential to their superiors.

The Geniza letters and documents deal almost exclusively with practical matters; they offer little discourse on the demands of religion, or, rather, since such matters were taken for granted, there was no point in enlarging upon them. The deep theological problems that had occupied the Islamic world and the Jewish community within it during the eighth through the tenth century had been either settled or at least clarified; the battle lines between conflicting views and practices (within Judaism, for instance, Karaites against Rabbanites) had been drawn; one knew where one stood, what to believe, and how to act. The eleventh and twelfth centuries were comparatively sedate. Few new questions were asked, and there were answers to those that were. The most tangible question of all, that of human suffering, found its ever ready explanation in God's inscrutable ways. One was assured that all that occurred was caused by God and that all done by him was to the good. Such teaching certainly had a soothing effect on grieving souls, but it could be fraught with danger, for it left too much to God and too little for the victim.

This acquiescence in fate could lead to disregard for the spiritual needs of both the sincerely pious and the intellectually curious. At the turn of the twelfth century, however, a crisis became visible. The pietist movement led by the two Abrahams—Abraham, the son of Moses Maimonides, the nagid or head of the Egyptian Jews, and his elder contemporary Abraham the Pious (Abū 'l-Rabīʿ Solomon b. Joseph b. Gabbay)—was actively opposed by the congregations in Fustat and Alexandria and seems to have found only feeble following in subsequent generations. Many Jewish thinkers who were given to doubt preferred to join the religion of their hegemonic Muslim rulers, while the spiritually dissatisfied, simple Jews began to listen to the sermons of fervent dervishes. No doubt, a complicated spiritual situation within the faith contributed to religious dissatisfaction, thus weakening the bonds that kept Jewish communal society together. The community lost valuable members, a loss intensified whenever the Muslim state, going against its norm of tolerance, oppressed minorities, as it did beginning in the mid-thirteenth century with the advent of the Mamluks.

It was precisely the physical and educational symbiosis between Muslims and Jews experienced during the preceding centuries that eased the transition to the dominant faith. Another factor was the absence of serious theological obstacles of the sort that the Trinity and graven images of Christianity presented. One was prepared to die on the stake for denying a God who had partners (as the Trinity was misunderstood) but not for refusing to sip a bowl of soup cooked in a dairy pot. Had not Abraham Maimonides himself written that the pious of Islam were truer followers of the Prophets of ancient Israel than many of his Jewish community, which, clinging to its inner security untroubled by theological problems, had little to offer wavering spirits exposed to unbearable suffering?

Yet we should not belittle the inner security of the Geniza community during the Fatimid period, the main object of our inquiry. Theirs was an orderly world. "Fear God and heed his commandments; for this is the whole man." There were many commandments to be heeded, and much study was required to know them all properly. The ideal person was the eternal student, who "pondered over the words of the Torah day and night," whatever the profession by which he earned his livelihood. Only a learned man (or one who had the reputation of being one) could be a communal leader. Rabbinic Judaism was a religion for scholarly minds. It was a great blessing for this type of Judaism that it was codified and canonized — between Saadya Gaon (d. 942) and Moses Maimonides (d. 1204) — within the orbit of Islam, which had similar ideals. Although the generalization may be hazardous, it may be argued that the scholarly person as a religious *ideal* was more widely popular in Judaism than in Islam. To be sure, Islam, with its ample economic resources, was far more able to realize this ideal, specifically, by making learning a salaried profession. The pittance paid to its officials by the Jewish community of Fustat did not enable them to devote much time to study. The students were merchants, physicians, even craftsmen, who had earned (or inherited) enough to find leisure for study. It was this aspect of study, undertaken for its own sake and as a kind of worship, that brought with it so much esteem within the Jewish community.

The erudition of a Geniza person meant primarily familiarity with sacred Scripture and the law codes, together with their commentaries and all that was connected with them — occasionally the ability to evaluate and write Hebrew poetry as well. In Fatimid times, however, pursuit of the secular sciences did not render one's orthodoxy suspect. For a physician, such study was of course imperative; for others, it was an honor to be described as both *ḥākhām* (Heb.), "religious scholar," and *ḥakīm* (Ar.), "student of philosophy and the sciences."

Conspicuously absent from the character of the Geniza person was the glamour of arms and the romance of bloodshed. Weapons were rarely used by the civil population in defense against bandits and burglars. The conduct of war was left to professionals, mostly of foreign origin. Yet the Geniza correspondence is pervaded by an atmosphere of contest and tension. *Everything* is urgent; a statement is often repeated twice or several times. Geniza people seem to have thrived on stress. Clashes in family, occupational, and communal life made for an all too lively environment. Since most of the longer letters extant were exchanged between friends, they also preserve for us the beautiful picture of a type of friendship that may be compared to *Kampfbrüderschaft*, "comradeship in battle," emphasized by a keen observer as one of the binding forces of medieval society. Geniza society embodies the romance of daily life.

Weekends and Holidays

Day began with prayer. Judaism, more than Islam, emphasized the meritoriousness of daily attendance at the public service. The documents are reticent, however, as to whether and how far this recommendation was heeded in Geniza times. There can be no doubt that Mondays and Thursdays, the holy weekdays on which a lection from the Torah was recited and the service was followed by regular sessions of the rabbinical court, were marked by increased numbers at communal prayer. Judges, clerks, litigants, and witnesses would join the congregation, as would the ubiquitous "righteous elders," who always intervened helpfully when a case appeared to be hopeless, and people who wished to learn or to gather news. Tuesdays and Fridays, the days on which loaves of bread were distributed to the needy and other beneficiaries—in times of stress up to one-fourth of the community—were also opportunities for large gatherings.

The Sabbath, "the Day of the Lord," was in Geniza times very much the day of the people: the cherished opportunity for getting together, for visiting family and friends in the capital, or in the countryside, or even in a faraway city. Perhaps the special character of the Sabbath, as it emerges from the Geniza papers, was influenced to some degree by the model of the Muslim Friday holiday, which was not a day of rest, but a "day of assembly"—originally a way to manifest one's allegiance by attending the public service. During the Jewish service (and the Muslim and the Christian service as well), allegiance was indeed expressed by prayers for the spiritual and secular leaders of the community. Everyone was present, for work of any sort was forbidden, but the allegiance created and confirmed by common attendance had a wider, and, at the same time, more intimate application. The members of the congregation, seated or standing close together, could feel themselves as one body, while the hours left free from service and study were dedicated to the attention one owed to family and friends. The prayers and literary sources emphasize the atmosphere of repose and sanctity to be found on the Sabbath.

In addition to the Sabbath morning service, held early in the day, the congregation—often both rabbinate congregations—convened again in the afternoon to listen to and to participate in a public lecture expounding the Scriptures given by a local scholar or an itinerant preacher. After the service or lecture, people did not hurry home but tarried in the synagogue plaza, and no one could pass without being observed.

Even without references in letters to meetings on Saturday, we can imagine what they were talking about on those occasions: One inquired about the health of a relative, invited friends, and even touched upon business matters (although this was disapproved in the Bible and, of course, in Jewish law). When someone had an errand in the capital, he tried to arrive on Friday in order to talk things over on Saturday; he would remain on Sunday — not because it was another weekend day, but because on Saturday he could not formally conclude matters that required writing (forbidden on the holy day).

Mundane pastimes are mentioned in our sources only when they were disapproved by religious authorities or the pious. A beautiful sermon on the love of God emphasizes that the Sabbath is the ideal time for joy in and nearness to God; one should therefore refrain from wasting time by taking walks for pleasure in promenades and gardens. When the Jewish community in the provincial capital of al-Maḥalla was split by strife, its members were scolded for "sitting most of the time in the streets and shops or in the shade of sycamores, thereby spurning the synagogues." Swimming, which was regarded as a profanation of the sacred day, was a different matter: A summons to the court of the nagid superscribed "It is time to act for the Lord" (Psalm 118:126) invites persons claiming to have seen Jews swimming on Saturday to appear and "deposit their testimony." The reverse side, headed by the same verse, contains a list of the culprits, eight altogether, which must have been rather embarrassing for the nagid: it is headed by the names of two sons and one grandson of a beadle and the son of a parnās, both officials of the synagogue. It is not clear, however, whether such writs were meticulously enforced.

Besides service and study, the main social pastimes on Saturdays (and holidays, of course) were parlor games with dice or the like. In the atmosphere of strict observance created by Maimonides even these became suspect. A question addressed to him when he was a judge in Egypt, seeks guidance on the matter:

Question: People get together on Sabbaths and holidays to drink wine and play with dice made of ivory bearing signs. The stakes are goblets of seeds; for instance, one takes three and a half grains in his hand and lets the others in turn guess their number. He who hits the right number, drinks and plays the next game. Are these and similar things permitted on the Sabbath and holidays, or not? Many highly esteemed persons occupy themselves with this. May your excellency instruct us.

Answer: Touching dice on Saturday is forbidden, touching

seeds is permitted. But this is a gambling game [and prohibited for this reason].

It is unlikely that the ban on such extremely popular entertainments was entirely successful. Egypt was not the Muslim West, more familiar to Maimonides.

Invitations to spend the Sabbath in a provincial town or promises to do so have been found in considerable number. A visitor from the city on the Sabbath was an event in a provincial town, and, if the visitor was a distinguished person, it boosted his host's prestige. When young Solomon, son of the judge Elijah, served as teacher in a Bible school while holding other religious offices in Qalyūb, north of Cairo, he reminded his father to make good his promise to visit him on a Sabbath. The judge was expected to perform the sacramental killing of an animal for the local community. The judge would leave his razor-sharp knife to his son, who then would perform this service for the community in the future. When a guest could not stay over the weekend, one grieved over his absence. "I had a very bad Saturday, realizing that you went away, and without a fellow traveler to keep you company." "Since we parted my tears have not dried for yearning after you, on weekdays and even on Sabbaths [when one was not supposed to grieve]." The prolonged absence of a dear relative was particularly felt on Sabbaths and holidays, when one was accustomed to being joined by him at the congregational prayer.

If the Sabbath (ideally dedicated entirely to devotion) included a generous measure of social intercourse, this was even more the case on holidays, which, by official definition, belonged "one-half to the Lord and one-half to you." The lengthy feasts of spring and autumn offered many opportunities for timely and protracted vacations and, in particular, for ceremonial gatherings of families and friends. Other feasts, as well as fasts, were occasions for the display of sociability. People from the provinces streamed into the capital for well-attended services that were embellished by the vocal art of famous cantors. Various branches of the families or circles of friends vied with one another for the honor of playing the host. A letter to Qalyūb, jointly addressed to a father and a father-in-law relates, "All our lives we have passed the holidays with you." Now it was time for the grandparents to favor them with a visit and spend the holidays with them, especially because they would be celebrating their son's betrothal on that occasion. The sender addresses his mother-in-law in particular, imploring her to give her daughter the pleasure of being the hostess. The children greet the mother's brother, who is, of course, also invited. In another letter, a father is asked to spend the holiday in his son's house, as he has been accustomed to doing, although he has urged the writer to visit him. "By the truth of what we believe, your coming to us will be a great merit for you with God, since I enjoy your presence. The children greet you." To be remote from one's mother on a holiday, says another invitation, was "a grave matter," almost a sin. Waiting on one's teacher and parents was comparable to appearing "before God" on a feast of pilgrimage to the Temple.

The great feasts of the spring and the autumn had a specific meaning for the community of Mediterranean traders: some time after Passover-Easter they sailed for the summer season; they came home for the holidays of the autumn. "All the young men are back in Qayrawān," we read in a letter written on the eve of the Day of Atonement, "and celebrate the holidays with their families most happily. Your boy Ṣadaqa has become a big man, an efficient merchant, for whom one can only wish that he follow in your footsteps."

Holidays and fasts, which punctuated the cycle of the year at fixed intervals, were convenient times to fulfill contractual obligations or pay debts. It was the same in medieval Christendom and, perhaps to a slightly lesser degree, in Islam. The three biblical holidays, Passover, Pentecost, and the Sukkot feast of tabernacles, as well as Hanukka, the feast of lights, served these purposes. A clause in a court record reads, "He will not pay these forty dinars on the Passover feast," since a Jew was not expected even to touch money on a holiday, let alone to take any action with it. The extent to which profane occupations should be permitted on the *wasṭāniyyāt*, the so-called middle days between the sacred opening and concluding days of Passover and Sukkot, was (and continues to be) a point of debate among observant Jews, but during the Geniza period people understood that at a time people flocked together, it was practical to give them an opportunity to settle urgent affairs.

Holy Shrines and Pilgrimages

The sacred times of the year have their parallel in visits to sites designed for special devotion. Both unite those who belong together in joint observance, both relieve them of their daily chores, and both are apt to transport the devotee beyond himself to spheres not easily attained otherwise. The frequency of such events, however, has its pitfalls: Repetition breeds neglect. Just as holidays may become degraded to mere pastimes, so visits to holy sites may deteriorate into outings for the enjoyment of company and nature and less desirable distractions. And, who knows, in remote times when such places began to assume their specific character, whether social or even political factors might have been primary and stronger than intrinsically religious factors, as was the case with Safed in Palestine, sometimes revered as a holy city. In view of this, the secularization of some holy sites should not be regretted too much. The end of their life cycle may have grown to resemble their beginning.

Various types of holy sites are to be discerned. The great central sanctuaries, such as Jerusalem or Mecca, are in a category by themselves. They were meeting places, attracting peoples from widely different countries; one tried to visit them in groups, and the visit to the Holy City could and often did give rise to a wide variety of mundane, rather than strictly religious, affairs. The same was, of course, true for the Muslim *hajj* or pilgrimage. Nevertheless, the universally and officially recognized character of a holy city as "the city of God" made a posture of devotion and ethical decorum imperative.

The sanctuaries of large and influential communities bore a semi-ecumenical character. The Jewish population of "Babylonia" (Iraq and western Iran), which, in early Islamic times, constituted the largest Jewish community and the most renowned for its religious scholarship, worshiped at the (spurious) tombs of Ezekial the Prophet and of Ezra the Scribe. As the Geniza records show, these tombs were also visited by Jewish pilgrims from the farthest Muslim West, as well as by Egyptian traders on their way from, and probably also to, India. (Ezekial was the patron of seafarers.)

Here we are mainly concerned with the local shrines, intended to satisfy the religious and social needs of the surrounding population. In this respect as well, a clear demarcation line exists between the numerous smaller shrines and those that were venerated throughout a country and beyond. In the late Middle Ages the cult of saints became a mass phenomenon and, because of voluminous material on the subject, much has been written about it. A modest, but not insignificant, contribution to its history is provided by the Geniza.

During the eleventh through the thirteenth century—the classical Geniza period—the Jewish holy shrines of Egypt are never associated with a saint; the synagogues themselves were holy, although in later literary sources, both Jewish and Muslim, the places were connected with biblical figures, and wondrous legends were told about the effects of their presence there. To be sure, the veneration of the tombs of saints preceded this period by centuries. The Islamic keepers of the law condemned it as an innovation taken over—with other deplorable things—from the Jews, and the Karaites scolded the Rabbanites for following the Muslim practice of "praying to the dead." Both accusations were probably correct. In early Islamic times, the practices of the preceding monotheistic religions were partly taken over; later, the example of the majority population was followed by the minorities.

Egyptian Jews were, of course, aware that their country had been hallowed by the miracles wrought by Moses; the more sophisticated among them knew also that Jeremiah ended his prophetic career there. The sanctuary most highly venerated by the Jews of Egypt and, consequently, often mentioned in the Geniza documents was the synagogue of Dammūh, a place south of Fustat on the western bank of the Nile. What was the importance of that obscure place, the very spelling of whose name is not yet finally settled? This was the only remaining synagogue of ancient Memphis, once the royal capital of Egypt, and in Roman times still a large urban conglomerate, second in importance only to the Greek city of Alexandria; in the Byzantine era, the decimated population moved to "the Roman Fortress" on the eastern bank of the Nile. What happened to Dammūh was also the fate of the "great" synagogue of Fustat—that of the Palestinians (the Geniza synagogue). In the later Middle Ages, Fustat was largely deserted and replaced by Cairo. In a still later period, when even the halo of old age began to fade, the Fustat synagogue became a tourist attraction. In 1655 a Karaite scholar from the Crimea wrote: "All the walls of the synagogue are covered with the names of persons coming from foreign countries; some write their names with their hands, others have them incised in wood. We, too, inscribed our names." Those visitors were probably devout Jews like the scholar from the Crimea, but they could hardly be described as pilgrims. While the cities were given up, their synagogues were not, and the house of daily worship was thus converted into a site of seasonal pilgrimage.

Dammūh, according to a Muslim historian the largest place of worship possessed by the Jews of Egypt, was a rallying place for all segments of the community—men and women (especially the latter, who were happy to escape their seclusion once a year), young and old, low and high, learned and unlettered—who flocked there for edification or enjoyment or both. Sometimes Muslims were invited by friends (as was so common at the tombs of Jewish saints of Morocco in later times); even Jews who had converted to Islam could not withstand the attractions of the cherished outing.

What life was like at the visit to the sanctuary (*miqdāsh* [Heb.]) of

Dammūh can best be reconstructed by studying a lengthy statute condemning and prohibiting the abuses allegedly rampant there, a document almost certainly issued at the time of the rigorous enforcement of Islamic law and mores by al-Ḥākim (996–1021). A Hebrew preamble indicates that a rabbinical court has taken action to ensure that all abuses be abolished from the sanctuary. The measures, listed in Arabic, include the following:

1. All should attend solely for devotion. No merrymaking will be tolerated.
2. Marionette shows ["Chinese shades"] and similar entertainments are not permitted.
3. No beer should be brewed there.
4. No visitor should be accompanied by [a gentile] or an apostate.
5. No woman should be admitted except when accompanied by [a father, a husband] a brother, or an adult son, unless she is a *very* old woman.
6. The synagogue building should be respected and revered like any other synagogue.
7. Boys, or an adult man together with a boy, should not [. . .], in order not to expose themselves to suspicion and make for themselves a bad name.
8. Both men and women should take utmost care not to desecrate the Sabbath in any way.
9. Playing chess and [. . .] is forbidden.
10. Likewise games such as "watermelon and clay" and [. . .].
11. Making noise by hitting something with a bang or clapping hands is disapproved.
12. No instrumental music.
13. No dancing.
14. On Sabbath, water should be drawn from the well only when needed for drinking.
15. Men should not mix with women, nor come near them [. . .], nor are they permitted to look at them.
16. In the synagogue, women should pray in the gallery upstairs and men in the hall downstairs, as is established by ancient custom, *sunna*.
17. Visitors to the place (in times other than those of pilgrimages) should go there only for a serious purpose, not for pleasure or for something that, by deed or word, might endanger them or others or damage the compound. They should provide them-

selves with keys and not tamper with the locks, nor enter through the gardens or by scaling a wall.

18. The community has empowered [. . .] to represent them in anything concerning that synagogue—may God keep it.

The statute had no reason to mention one important aspect of the pilgrimage to Dammūh besides prayers and pastimes: The place and time when so many people flocked together provided a convenient opportunity for public announcements, especially those that had serious consequences for the persons concerned, such as bans and excommunications. This was the practice at the yearly assemblies on the Mount of Olives overlooking Jerusalem, and it was no different at Dammūh.

The findings of the Geniza seem to indicate that the great assembly could last for days, occasionally even for more than a week. A letter of 1235 to the chief justice Hananel b. Samuel speaks of "the days" (not "the holiday") spent in his company at Dammūh. A nagid (like everyone else) was supposed to be accompanied by his wife. When the widow of a nagid married her brother-in-law (who also inherited the office of her late husband), it was formally stipulated that, at the time of the pilgrimage, he could stay there with his second wife "not more than two [consecutive] days per week" (so that the prerogatives of the first wife would be sustained). The fact that it was necessary to emphasize this detail in the comparatively short marriage agreement shows how important the pilgrimage was for both communal and personal life.

Relics of saints or of the founder of the religion generated enormous interest among medieval Christians and, to a lesser degree, among Muslims as well. The desire for transportable objects of adoration was satisfied in Judaism by Torah scrolls, which were regarded as particularly "awe-inspiring and holy." One Torah scroll was—and had to be—exactly like the other; every iota of what was written in it was meticulously prescribed. How then did a scroll become holy like a relic and consequently the goal of pilgrimages? When, by outward appearances and according to tradition, it was sufficiently old, it could be ascribed to great figures of the past. An eminently knowledgeable traveler visiting the synagogue of the Palestinians in 1753 notes in his diary that they had there a holy and awe-inspiring scroll "written, they say, by Ezra the Scribe" (who brought the final version of the Book of Moses from Babylonia to Jerusalem about 2,200 years prior to that visit). The Torah scrolls in Dammūh and Ṭaṭay—a minor holy shrine—were highly venerated and in times of the breakdown of public order, as in the 1070s, were kept in the capital in the synagogue of the Palestinians.

Calls and Visits, Congratulations and Condolences

Gatherings on Sabbaths, holidays, and pilgrimages were hosted "by God"; all participants were equally bound, by law or custom, to attend; they formed a flock whose faces were turned toward the Shepherd. It is evident, however, that social obligations—meetings with purely human concerns as their object—were taken as seriously as religious duties. The rabbinical court of Fustat opined that a wife must be permitted to leave her husband's house to pursue all these activities. The many business transactions and lawsuits between women recorded in the Geniza can hardly be explained except by the assumption that women had frequent opportunities to meet, albeit not as regularly and extensively as men, who spent their lives in the bazaar and in worship, study, and communal activities as much as in their own homes.

Inquiring after the well-being of one's neighbor, keeping him or her company, and sharing his or her joy and sorrow were obligations one owed not only to others but also (and perhaps even more so) to oneself. One could not live properly without the company of congenial fellow creatures. The talmudic maxim "Company or death" is echoed repeatedly in the Geniza records. "There is no one who talks to me; death is better than this," writes a newlywed to her sister. A communal leader in Ramle who had joined the wrong party complains, "All the notables of the town keep their distance from me, they cut me and relate to me in a way which any reasonable person would regard as death." The Geniza people possessed a rich vocabulary for expressing loneliness, desolation, separation, and feeling like a stranger, an orphan, or "a lonely bird on the house top" (Psalm 102:8). The desire to retire from the world, not unknown to Moses Maimonides, was alien to them; theirs were the practical ethics of Saadya Gaon, who, in the tenth chapter of his *Beliefs and Opinions*, strongly disapproved of living as a recluse.

Most letters open with often extended expressions of yearning and longing for the addressee and the hope of being united soon under the best of circumstances and of finding him or her in perfect health and happiness. They reflect the attitude of a society that regarded intensive personal contact with one's peers as a way of life. The lists, often long, of relatives and friends to whom greetings are extended and who are mentioned by name at the end of a letter, underline this fact. If someone was ill, a visit or an inquiry after the patient's health was imperative; strong excuses had to be adduced for failing to do so. In such a case it was customary to state that one refrained from writing out of consideration that the patient might be inconvenienced by feeling impelled to answer, but we often find writers inquiring about the recipient's health and the local news.

Opportunities for parties celebrating particular occasions or achievements were numerous. In addition to the great family events of betrothals, weddings, and births, good wishes had to be extended when a person entered a new home or acquired other valuable property, when he was honored with a new title or a robe of honor, or was appointed or reinstated to an office at court, government, or in the Jewish community, when he or she was restored to good health after a dangerous illness — or when he was released from prison. The safe arrivals of overseas traders and other travelers returning home "with a happy heart and a full purse" after prolonged absence were recurring occasions for jubilant gatherings. In accordance with the practical and rather matter-of-fact character of the Geniza world, wedding celebrations seem to have been less extended, less encumbered with the magical and symbolic ceremonies that prevailed in Morocco and Yemen, although these elements were by no means absent. A person attended mainly to fulfill a social obligation (including almsgiving) and to enjoy the proceedings. Poetic creations in honor of an event, including release from prison, are in evidence, but are neither as profuse nor of the same literary merit as those common among the sophisticated Jews of Spain.

Two important types of parties not observed in Geniza times should be noted. Entirely absent are references to good wishes for a birthday, something by no means easy to explain. The exact date of a child's birth was noted, according to the Jewish and Muslim calendars (sometimes also the Christian), together with the hour and the position of the stars. The bar mitzvah, the rite of passage by which Jewish children become obliged to fulfill the commandments of their religion — in present-day Jewry an occasion for grand gatherings of family and friends, comparable almost to a wedding — is scarcely mentioned in the Geniza. The practice may have been similar to one observed in a traditional Yemenite ceremony in the early twentieth century. Since those Yemenites gave their children a strictly religious education starting at the age of four or so, there was no marked passage from childhood to adulthood worthy of an elaborate celebration. When a father noted that his boy was ready and eager to comport himself religiously like an adult, he adorned him with the prayer trappings described in the Bible (Deuteronomy 6:8) even before he reached the obligatory age of thirteen.

Hospitality in the Geniza period was religiously motivated and was

extended mainly to needy people and strangers (or to others who had
a claim to assistance), to scholars (whose learning was honored), and,
of course, to family and friends, where the motive of reciprocity was
also present. "Putting up the wayfarer" was among the religious merits
"whose dividends may be earned in this world, while the capital remains
intact for the world to come," meaning that this was intrinsically a deed
of piety for which no reward should be expected, although reward was
likely.

In general, one should remember that hospitality was often required
in times that were hard on the host himself and in places where demands
on charity were made constantly. This was true in particular of the community in Alexandria, which bore the brunt of captives brought by pirates to the Mediterranean port to be put up there and ransomed, and
of refugees, who arrived there from many parts of the Muslim and Christian worlds. In a long letter written in Alexandria in September 1212, we
read:

On the very night I am writing you this letter, there arrived here seven of
the rabbis [of France], all great scholars, accompanied by one hundred souls,
men women, and children, all in need of bread, as if we had not enough
beggars of our own here in town—we have about forty. Most of the community are in trouble because of the sluggish business, and now such a great
imposition is thrown upon them; let's see how they will tackle it.

Hospitality began before the guest arrived. Family and friends, and
in the case of a scholar or other important personage, representatives of
the community went out to meet him at his latest lodging station, or
any other place agreed upon, to welcome him and to bring him safely
through the gates of their town. At the very least, a messenger was sent
to perform this duty. Two entirely different concerns gave rise to this
procedure. At the entrance to a city, a traveler had to pay customs dues
and was exposed to all kinds of searches, in the course of which unexpected and unpleasant things might happen. Passing the gates of a city
was so dangerous that when someone got through them unscathed, he
was obliged, according to the Talmud (referring to Roman times, of
course), to pronounce a benediction of thanksgiving. When the guest
was accompanied by local people, he could at least hope to be spared
such discomfort.

Another reason for meeting a guest outside the city was to show him
respect and affection, as was the duty of the population when a new
ruler or governor arrived. Naturally this aspect of hospitality was very
cumbersome, and it was regarded as a sign of particular solicitude on

the part of the guest when he refrained from announcing the time of his arrival so as not to inconvenience his hosts. If the visitor was a very distinguished personage, this was less easily accomplished, of course. Letters of welcome, certainly containing information about the whereabouts and other details of the prospective meeting, greeted him when he was still far from his destination. In a report about his safe arrival, the proud guest would include a list of the most important of the notables who had come from the town to meet him.

It was not the practice to host guests in one's own home. The main concern was to provide the visitor with privacy, with a place belonging exclusively to him, in which he could himself receive visitors and spend his day and night as he and his company pleased. But enjoying privacy did not mean staying away from the local community. Quite the contrary: Nothing worse could be said about foreigners than that "they do not attend the synagogue service and do not visit in the houses of [respectable] people." The service was an opportunity to become acquainted with members of the congregation who routinely would invite a guest home for a meal.

Both the welcome and the departure of distinguished or particularly dear guests were elaborate affairs. People were expected to attend farewell parties. Seeing a visitor off and accompanying him as far as was feasible to his new destination were essential parts of hospitality, for which the patriarch Abraham, the paragon of a host, had set the example ("The men stood up . . . and Abraham went with them to bear them company" [Genesis 18:16]). Bidding farewell did not always conclude the duties of hospitality. One had to ensure that the visitor arrived safely at the goal of his journey. After the Fustat community had maintained a poor Palestinian woman and her infant daughter, it provided her with travel expenses down to Alexandria, where the local community was asked to assist her until she reached her final destination. In the case of a scholarly person on his way to Jerusalem, the Fustat community was instructed to arrange a collection without delay so as to enable him to join a caravan that was about to leave.

The gratitude of the guest was expressed by exuberant praise of the host and, in particular, by invoking God for blessings on him and his family. Jewish religious etiquette provided that the benedictions opening a meal were said by the host; the concluding grace was recited by the guest so that he could insert appropriate blessings on the host and his family. Another (and the most frequently mentioned) way of spreading the fame of a benefactor was to pronounce blessings upon him in public, either in the synagogue, when the holy ark was opened and the guest was called up to read from the Torah, or in warehouses serving as bourses where merchants met, or simply at social gatherings. Women, according to the Talmud, are less happy with guests than men. Because travelers were mostly male, the men in the house enjoyed entertainment, whereas the women had only more work and probably also less food, especially in the not-so-rare case of unexpected visitors. One such frightening occurrence was the arrival of an almost complete stranger in a house in Jerusalem on a Friday late in the afternoon when people had already assembled for the evening prayer, and when, for religious reasons, it was impossible to prepare additional food—at a time when provisions were scarce, at that. The women "came out [from their apartment] trembling."

Pastimes

Short "calls" and extended "visits," Sabbaths, holidays, pilgrimages, and the entertainment of travelers occupied most of the free time at the disposal of the Geniza person. There were, however, prosaic gatherings that were of considerable importance—in particular drinking bouts, sometimes accompanied by music (primarily an activity for men), and social gatherings in the bathhouse (generally a women's pastime).

Intoxicating beverages and the sounds of enrapturing music enhanced sociability. Meeting with friends over a cup of wine was a favorite pastime. The proverbial sobriety of Eastern European Jewish immigrants in the United States should not be taken as inherent to Jewish culture: in biblical times one might drink to get drunk (Haggai 1:6); joyous music, instrumental as well as vocal, was also part of banquets in ancient Israel (Isaiah 24:8–9). Wine, that "cheerer of the hearts of God and men" (Judges 9:13), and music of all kinds, which pervades the entire book of Psalms, constituted intrinsic elements of the Temple service, but were luxuries unavailable to most people in daily life. Jews generally appreciated the nutritive, medical, and convivial value of wine and made it central to sacramental ceremonies. Excessive consumption, however—especially in company—was abhorred and condemned in strong terms, from the time of the prophets of Israel down to that of Moses Maimonides.

Various wine songs are preserved in the Geniza. One of these popular poems contrasts two types of companies enjoying wine: "wise men," who came together to imbibe strong wine (a mixture of two parts wine to one part water) and weaklings, who, as recommended by the ancient sages, added two parts water to one part wine but were not able to digest even this mild mixture. Drinking parties in gardens, a standing topic in Arabic and Hebrew poetry, were common among merchants, as well as among intellectuals and government people. Important matters, such as sending a son overseas or promising a bequest, would be arranged at a drinking bout. When peace, *ṣulḥa*, was restored in a family, members came together and drank to one another's health. As in the biblical story of Joseph, brotherly love was manifested by drinking together. We learn this from a letter written in spring 1217 by the young cantor Judah b. Aaron, of the renowned al-'Ammānī family of Alexandria, in which he thanks the nagid Abraham Maimonides for settling matters between him and his uncle, the chief cantor Zadok (after he previously reported that the old man passed most of his time drinking wine, leaving Judah to manage the affairs of the synagogue).

Muslims occasionally joined Jewish drinking parties, which caused some difficulty, because wine, in view of its sacramental character, should according to law be handled only by those within the fold. When such newcomers entered, sophisticated keepers of the law would drop honey into wine. The use of honey was forbidden in the Temple service (Leviticus 2:11); consequently, its admixture converted the tabooed beverage into a regular soft drink. Maimonides ruled that the Egyptian *nabīdh,* which was diluted with honey, was not to be regarded as wine; the benediction for it was that pronounced over water. Thus, the Muslim visitors could freely partake of the beverage, as could the Jews.

Drinking parties could be dangerous in times of stress — during shortages, for example, or during the Muslim holy month of Ramadan — even in the privacy of the home, and the Jewish authorities tried to discourage them. A mother writing to her son from Aden recounts a story of three Jewish notables who had come together for a drink during the Muslim feast terminating the month of fast; when visited by a Muslim musician, they received him well. The musician reported them to the qāḍī, and the revelers were immediately set upon, beaten severely, and fined heavily. (No such incidents are known to have taken place in Egypt.) Jewish taverns, frequently mentioned in ancient Arabic literature, draw almost no attention in the Geniza documents. One enjoyed drinking and eating with specific friends, but not in a place accessible to everyone.

Tipplers in Geniza times were not, as in ancient Israel, the leaders who "were at ease and felt secure," and "were not grieved by the ruin

of the nation"; they were alienated persons, sons of well-to-do households who became addicts, wasting the paternal wealth on foreign wines
and musicians and mixing with people of dubious reputations. Drunk-
ards could, of course, be found in all levels of society. The Geniza pre-
serves a number of letters indicating family concerns with profligate sons
and the company they kept. Boon companions might enjoy each other's
presence, but they were also prone to quarrel when they did not see eye-
to-eye over a matter. A Cairene dignitary, describing a brawl in Alexandria in which the son, nephew, and son-in-law of the head cantor and
several others took part, notes that all participants were drunk, which
of course attracted the attention of the police. In a report about another
brawl, this time in a provincial town, one individual, the grandson of a
head cantor and son of a beadle, had imbibed so much that he remained
drunk even after having been imprisoned and brought before the superintendent of police. All in all, alcohol does not seem to have been a
negligible factor in Jewish life of the times.

Music was less in evidence. Music as entertainment required instru-
mentalists and singing girls who had to be hired, or kept as slaves; it
thus constituted a luxury. Jewish law, as expressed in codes and legal
opinions during the High Middle Ages, banned instrumental music
completely, in particular when it was combined with drinking bouts and
involved the presence of women. In his famous responsum on the subject, Maimonides showed himself aware of the value of music to lift the
select few to the highest spiritual experience, enhancing the service of
God; but laws, he explained, must be made for the larger community,
and listening to music thus performed made for depravity. This attitude
was by no means specific to Judaism. Islamic law displayed the same
objections to music, although musicians were quite common in Muslim
society. Still, instrumental music never entered the synagogue or the
mosque. Among observant Jews, music was officially confined to special
occasions, such as weddings or funerals, and even then it was performed
in a subdued manner.

Fulminating against instrumental music and those who listened to
it — in one case also the keeping of slave girls — was a favorite topic of
reform-minded visitors or itinerant preachers, both in the capital and in
provincial towns. Jews as players of flutes, lutes, and other stringed in-
struments or as musicians in general are mentioned in the Geniza texts.
It is possible that these musicians played mainly in the houses of well-
to-do Muslims, where they could find greater recompense. (This seems
to have been the case in some Muslim countries even in the twentieth
century.) We also find entertainers of other types, such as buffoons or

monkey trainers. Nowhere, however, do we read about the performances or other doings of these musicians and entertainers; we know
of these occupations entirely through family names retaining occupational identification.

A woman of the middle class would probably offer a cup of wine to
her visitors, but no allusion to female drinking parties or to a drunken
woman ever occurs. A *nezīrā,* a woman who had vowed to abstain from
alcohol, is noted. Temporary vows of this type were made as a sacrifice
to God (like fasting) to enhance the efficacy of prayer for the safe return
of a son or another beloved relative. The title *nezīrā,* however, implies
that the vow was made out of piety and was permanent.

For a variety of reasons, women also made vows renouncing the
pleasure of the weekly visit to the public bathhouse, which suggests the
importance that these social gatherings had in their lives. The rabbinic
decision that a husband was not permitted to deny these visits to his
wife and could not force her to live in a place that did not possess this
amenity points in the same direction. The standard price for admission
(a silver piece, for which one could buy five or more loaves of bread)
and the precious textiles and utensils used at those visits (appearing in
trousseau lists) are all noteworthy. New Moon day, which was for Jewish women a kind of half-holiday during which they refrained from
needlework and the like, seems to have been particularly suited to a
collective visit to the bathhouse. These gatherings, during which re-
freshments were consumed, might have compensated the women
somehow for what they missed by not participating in social activities
with men.

Egypt has been the classical country of storytelling since Pharaonic
times. The most interesting parts of *The Arabian Nights* were written
there during the Middle Ages. When a Jewish bookseller lent his copy
of *A Thousand and One Nights* (this title in its full form appears, perhaps
for the first time, in the Geniza) to one of his customers, it stands to
reason that the customer copied some or all of it for entertaining private
or public audiences. The Geniza has preserved illustrations from the
ancient Indian "mirror of princes" known under its Arabic title *Kalīla
wa-Dimna;* for example, a picture of "a raven holding the tail of a rat"
(accompanied by part of the story). Once fragments of fables, folktales,
adventure stories, and similar material, told in Arabic, are brought together from the Geniza collections, the extent and nature of popular
entertainment literature current in the community during the High
Middle Ages will become better known.

It is noteworthy that shadow plays—marionette theaters—are the first entertainment disapproved by the Jewish authorities in Egypt as early as the beginning of the eleventh century, far earlier than the introduction of this Indian pastime into Islamic countries is generally assumed. It was probably already of a bawdy character (as it was later), bordering on the pornographic, which made it undesirable, especially in a place of pilgrimage.

A gamut of parlor games, from the seemingly innocent play with dice described in a question addressed to Moses Maimonides, translated above, to the kingly chess, is represented in the Geniza—all forbidden if they had even the slightest resemblance to gambling. Outright gambling is strictly forbidden in Islam and Judaism. It is almost never mentioned in the Geniza documents, but we can assume that people did gamble; they simply preferred not to speak about gambling. Franz Rosenthal, describing Islam during the same period, notes that excessive gambling, though evidently not uncommon, is not frequently attested.[1]

Chess was played for money and therefore outlawed. An Arabic couplet written on the reverse side of a letter addressed to an important Jewish personage warns that playing chess may lead to the breakup of a friendship. Pigeon racing, accompanied by betting, was another common pastime that was disapproved by the authorities. It was, nevertheless, passionately pursued, so much so that we read about communal officials using the roof of a synagogue for letting their pigeons loose (pigeons were kept and fed in dovecotes and used legitimately to carry messages). Racing the birds was a Jewish sport, familiar and much condemned even in talmudic times. The passion was nourished under the influence of the Islamic environment, which was no less dedicated to this sport. A story has it that Baghdad was delivered treacherously to the Mongols, the caliph decapitated, and the caliphate terminated because the sons of the caliph and his vizier had fallen out over a pigeon race; their mutual hatred affected the fathers, and revenge took the form of treachery. In a relatively remote Islamic place like Bukhara, pigeon racing had Jewish devotees even at the beginning of the twentieth century.

Birds in general, as we remember from *The Arabian Nights* and other Arabic tales, provided much entertainment to the good people who kept them. A peculiar case is reported about the nagid Mevōrākh, who owned a parrot presented to him by an India trader that recited faultlessly two

---

1. *Gambling in Islam* (Leiden, 1975).

of the most common Jewish prayers, the "Hear Israel" (Deuteronomy 6:4) and "David's Hymn" (Psalm 145:1, preceded by 20:10). The story comes to us by way of Isaac b. Samuel the Spaniard, a member of Mevōrākh's encourage, who found it remarkable enough to mention in one of his commentaries on the Bible.

EIGHT

Social Structure

Judged by literary evidence, the Mediterranean Islamic society of the High Middle Ages was essentially urban and governed by social distinctions. This does not mean, however, that this society was cut off from the soil. Townspeople at the time were far less removed from the land than present-day urban populations, and there were no rigid distinctions between urban and rural. As the Geniza records indicate, not only the wealthy but even people of modest means often possessed farmland and administered it personally. Many lived in little towns in the vicinity of their fields. Oil, cheese, wine, and wax were produced in the districts specializing in olive growing, sheep breeding, viticulture, and bee keeping, respectively; similarly, flax, silk, and wool—the great industrial crops—often were worked on the spot into raw material or even into finished products. Thus, the medieval townsman was, as a rule, never far away from the land and was constantly involved in the primary processes of production. It is his voice, however, and only rarely that of the peasant, that we hear in the Geniza records, or, for that matter, in any records that have come down to us from the eleventh through the thirteenth century.

Urban society consisted of many different layers. The convenient division into an affluent bourgeoisie and the common people engaged primarily in manual work does not do justice to the many subtleties in the texture of the society, which we are able to observe in the Geniza records. The tone of a letter, even the formulation of a document, immediately indicates the classes of the persons concerned and by how many rungs on the social ladder they were separated. Still, this differentiation, marked as it was, had very little in common with the tightly structured world of feudalism; rather it was more akin to that prevailing in our own modern society, where the division into social classes is more a matter of fact and etiquette than of laws and institutions.

The people mirrored in the Geniza records were definitely conscious of social standing. Social inequality was natural to them, or, as they would put it, was ordained by God. Its evils were mitigated by the common service to God, by joint action for the welfare of the community, by discreet help to needy members of one's own class, and by donations made during public appeals for the benefit of others. Open conflict between social groupings was not unknown in the Geniza world.

At the apex of society was *al-ṭabaqa al-ʿaliyya,* the "uppermost stratum," which consisted of high government officials and agents, great doctors (often acting as part-time or full-time court physicians), chief judges, and leading businessmen, especially if they were learned enough to act also as community leaders—as one of our sources puts it, "the notables connected with government and well known to it." Among the Jews, such a person was normally given the Hebrew title *sār,* "prince," rendered herein as "notable." It was a small group, in which everyone knew his peer. The Geniza has preserved less material about the private life of the members of this group than any other, presumably because most of the notables lived in Cairo, the residence of the caliph, and not in Fustat (where the Geniza chamber was found) and probably also because most of their correspondence was conducted in Arabic and not in Hebrew characters.

It would be fallacious, however, to assume that the main body or lower strata of Geniza society was engaged solely in manual work. In reality the situation was far more complicated. It is true that the Hellenistic contempt for anyone who worked with his hands had infected subsequent Mediterranean civilizations, including later Judaism and Islam. But the participation of craftsmen in the development of these two religions was far too pronounced to leave that Greek prejudice unchallenged. Although we find in Judaism the notion that manual work is degrading, we find also the opposite idea: that toiling with one's hands assures bliss in this world and in the world to come. The Geniza records reveal that certain manual occupations, such as dyeing, were identified with the lowest ranks of society, but we find also people in the middle class—sometimes even the upper middle class—engaged in crafts known from other sources as despised, such as weaving. At least as far as Jewish society is concerned, occupation alone did not determine one's social position.

What, then, were the factors that assigned man his place in society?

There was first of all, his origin, his family. A member of "the good people," "the noble families," "the illustrious houses," would not lose face, even if personal misfortune deprived him of the material well-being normally enjoyed by respectable families. Thus, in a more indirect way, wealth played a decisive role in the formation of the various ranks of society. Religiosity and learning—these two attributes were interconnected in medieval Judaism, as in Islam—were additional decisive factors in determining status and establishing indispensable qualifications for public leadership. The number of pious and scholarly members in a family, along with its wealth, determined its prestige. Integrity and sound business practices were other factors that enhanced the social status of a family. They were particularly valued by a society constantly on the move and facing many risks and uncertainties.

Above all, generosity, coupled with a readiness to exert oneself for the public good or on behalf of individuals seeking help, determined the social prestige of a person and his clan. Generations after a man had died, his generosity toward the scholars and the needy would continue to be publicly eulogized during memorial services. All the year round, appeals were made and contributions solicited on his behalf.

A Geniza document speaks of five different social levels: the upper class; a bourgeoisie of businessmen, professionals, and master artisans, which was clearly divided into an upper middle class and a lower middle class; a grouping represented by the mass of urban craftsmen and laborers; and, finally, the peasants.

Were these socioeconomic groupings tightly closed castes that restricted individuals to their stations, or were there opportunities for social mobility? The Geniza contains ample material to indicate the existence of opportunities for advancement but none like those in modern societies. A son normally followed the profession of his father; he was engaged in his father's business or workshop during the latter's lifetime, either as his employee or his partner, and would take over after his father's death. Similarly in the professions, we encounter families of doctors, judges, and lower-level community servants, such as cantors or scribes. A man would be called "the son of the clan of sieve makers," "of indigo dyers," "of scarf makers," or "the son of the judge," or "the son of the doctor." About one-fourth (probably less) of the family names that have come down to us from the Geniza records are associated with occupations.

It was not always feasible, or perhaps even desirable, that all the sons (or even any sons) should do the same work as their father, and we often find a man embracing an occupation of a type different from that of his family, but of similar social status. One Muslim silk weaver, *qazzāz,* was the son of a water carrier; the sons of a man keeping poultry became vendors of dried fruit; the son of a producer (and/or seller) of sal ammoniac was a worker in silk *harīrī,* both common occupations; and the son of a scribe became a cantor. A prominent physician's son and grandson acted as merchants' representatives, a very honored position; his great-grandson returned to the medical profession. When the name of a person is followed by two occupations, the first designates his family name, or the occupation of his father, and the second his own, and often little change in status is involved, as in the combination "the money assayer, the money changer."

Nevertheless, many occupational shifts that constitute an unambiguous advancement in social status are indicated in the Geniza. We read about a physician whose father was a tuna monger, or another whose father operated an oil press; the case is reminiscent of that of a Muslim doctor, famous also as a writer, who was the son of a baker and so poor that he was unable to pay the apprenticeship fees demanded by the doctors (he later propounded the theory that medicine is better learned from books than from teachers). In short, birth determined the status of a person in Mediterranean society to a certain extent but by no means as much as it did in the contemporaneous world of medieval Europe. Native talent and good fortune enabled a man to move up to a higher level of society. Classes themselves were differentiated by occupation and wealth, but by less tangible factors as well, such as religiosity, learning, integrity, and public service. Still, occupation, together with the economic position that as a rule went with it, was the main divider of society. For practical purposes, it thus may serve as the basis of classifying various elements of society.

Craftsmen

Factories in the modern sense of the word—plants in which large numbers of wage earners are engaged in the production of great quantities of one or several closely related commodities—rarely appear in the Geniza records; the means to mass-produce particular items for public consumption were simply not available. The normal form of production was a small workshop run by a single craftsman, a family, a clan, or a group of partners, usually not more than five. Large quantities of wares, often quoted in round numbers, were handled in wholesale commerce, but as far as we can perceive, these were not delivered by a single workshop but were handpicked in a bazaar or ordered from various producers.

Only two industries seem to have operated, at least partly, in larger plants. The sugar refineries, *maṭbakh*s (lit., places of cooking), were eminent landmarks in the topography of the Egyptian capital; they are often referred to in the Geniza records and are diligently recorded by the Muslim antiquarians. Sometimes such a factory was worth well over a thousand dinars; an ordinary workshop, by contrast, could be operated with capital of less than ten dinars. In Mamluk times, sugar became an important monopoly of the sultans. Given the size of some sugar establishments, we must assume that the plants employed many laborers.

The other industrial product manufactured in plants of impressive dimensions was paper. Paper, like sugar, was sometimes mass-produced. Paper and sugar manufacturing were not local traditions, but migrated from China and India, respectively, to Persia and then to other Islamic countries. The Muslim historians tell us that paper originally was manufactured in large workshops belonging to governors and sultans. It is natural that the system of mass production continued when the bourgeoisie took over these lucrative industries from the ruling class. Unfortunately, the Geniza leaves us no evidence concerning the laborers who worked the paper plants. The documents are concerned instead with the owners and managers of the larger plants and with the partners in smaller workshops. In some state industries, skilled laborers were pressed into service against their will. Generally speaking, the Geniza is a rich source for the day-to-day life of the craftsmen. It focuses on their economic and social position and the ways in which they cooperated with one another.

Much has been written about Islamic guilds. The question is how far back in Near Eastern history we can trace the institution of organized professional corporations. The Muslim handbooks of market supervision that have come down to us from the twelfth century and that deal mainly with crafts and trades have no term which designates a guild; guilds, in the strict sense of the word, had not yet come into being. There were, to be sure, loosely formed professional associations, but organized corporations of craftsmen of the type that developed in Europe during the later Middle Ages, or in Islam during the fourteenth through the nineteenth century, are not attested in Arabic literature for the classical Geniza period.

Members of a single craft normally were concentrated in one locality, a fact evidenced from the many names of bazaars, streets, lanes, squares, and compounds (*dār*, often translated as "house") named after a particular group (for example, clothiers, tailors, perfumers, coppersmiths, turners, chest makers, woolworkers, manufacturers of leather bottles, makers of almond sweetmeats, and oil makers) or bearing the names of products such as silk, cotton, or milk, or of occupations such as spinning. Many of these names of localities in Fustat are known to us also from work of Muslim geographers and antiquarians; we possess similar data for other Muslim cities, such as Damascus. It is uncertain whether at the time of the Geniza records most of these localities were actually occupied exclusively by the crafts after which they were named. Localities in Muslim cities retained their names long after the original inhabitants had left, and particular landmarks often gave their names to geographically extended locations. All this is borne out in the Geniza documents and in many other Muslim sources.

Another indication of the geographical concentration of the various crafts is found in the Geniza lists of contributors to charity. The lists are sometimes arranged, at least partly, according to the "business addresses"—the bazaars in which persons following the same profession had their shops, or in which craftsmen working in related occupations, such as melting silver or gold and polishing the finished coins, are listed as having been solicited at the same time. Artisans exercising the same craft in a town sometimes appear as a group or as a firm. The *'arīf*, or head of a profession—insofar as such an office existed during the Geniza period—was not a leader elected by the members of his group but a supervisor appointed by the market police to assist them in their fight against fraudulent practices; the Geniza makes mention of this office rarely and only with reference to banking. The *'arīf* is known as an important figure in the formation of Muslim professions and more generally as an intermediary responsible for his tribal or group activities to the central authorities.

The Islamic guilds of the later Middle Ages had a semireligious character, as did their Christian counterparts in Europe. The Jewish corporations that later sprang up on Islamic soil—the goldsmiths and embroiderers of Fez, for example, or the *kaikjis*, or boatmen of Istanbul during the seventeenth through the nineteenth century—were similarly confined to one religious community and fulfilled specific social and religious roles in addition to their general professional tasks. But this is not the case for the Geniza community. We hear of Muslim and Jewish silversmiths and glassworkers who run shops in partnership, each group taking off its own weekly holiday—the Muslims on Friday, the Jews on Saturday. We hear of Muslim carpenters working partly as employees and partly as partners of a Jewish fellow carpenter, and even of a Jewish court inviting gentile experts in purple dyeing, together with their Jewish colleagues, to estimate the value of equipment of a workshop forming part of the inheritance of an orphan girl. Loans advanced by a Muslim to a Jewish craftsman and by a Jew to a Muslim are also in evidence.

Protecting the vested interests of the local artisans against the intrusion of foreigners—an important task of the later guilds—was entrusted during the classical Geniza period to the community at large. Several letters have been preserved in which grievances against competition by newcomers from Palestine and Lebanon were submitted to the nagid of Egypt. Conversely, we have a moving letter from a group of artisans complaining that "the Jews" (that is, the local community) did not permit them to practice their craft—under penalty of excommunication. That foreigners constituted the largest group receiving alms from the public chest seems to indicate that it was not easy for nonresidents to find work. A man from Alexandria who had fled to Fustat with his little son because he was unable to pay the poll tax writes that he did not find anyone who was prepared to employ him, even for one dirhem a day. Most of the foreigners whose occupation is indicated in the lists of persons having recourse to public charity were craftsmen.

With the exception of foreigners and disabled persons, craftsmen seem not to have suffered the curse of unemployment. Among the hundreds of requests for help preserved in the Geniza, so far not a single one has been found in which a local artisan would adduce as reason for his plight the fact that he was out of work; on the contrary, it seems that it was not always easy to get a craftsman, at least a satisfactory one. In a letter from Būṣīr in Egypt, four employers, engaged in the scutching of flax and the "beating" of hemp, compete for the services of the laborers available and snatch some away from one another.

The normal form of industrial cooperation, as reflected in the Geniza records, was partnership. Even a craftsman with small means or none would not, as a rule, become a laborer and wage earner; rather, he would enter into a partnership with one or more fellow craftsmen or with an outsider who would provide him with capital. It is indicative of the "freedom of contract" which characterizes this period that the conditions of partnership vary widely from one document to another. The normal procedure for cooperation between craftsmen consisted in capital and labor put into the partnership in equal shares, the equipment and tools also being common property. Profits and losses would be shared in the same proportion, and often a daily remuneration would be deducted from the "purse of the partnership." This remuneration might consist of cash (for example, 1½ dirhems per day), or of lunch and supper for the partners (but not their families), or might be left to the discretion of the partners on condition that it be the same for all. Sometimes one partner was unable to pay his contribution in full at the writing of a contract and promised to do so at a later date. Two documents state expressly that the working, or executive, member was not allowed to enter into another partnership for the duration of the contract, a principle inherent in industrial cooperation.

In many cases, the contributions of the partners differed with regard to the capital invested, the equipment acquired or brought into the partnership, and the work to be done by the different members. Thus, one glassmaker paid in twenty dinars; his partner did not contribute any capital, but received a personal loan of ten dinars on condition that the partner contributing the money would work only two "turns" a week, and he the rest. In a lawsuit involving three tanners in a small town of Lower Egypt, which had already been considered by Muslim courts three times and once had even reached the court of Abraham Maimonides, one partner was clearly the main provider of capital, while the two others were unable to meet their obligations. In another partnership of three, the raw materials and most of the assets belonged to all members in equal shares; for one particular debt, however, one-half was payable to one individual and one-fourth to each of the other two. In another case, one partner provided the capital, but the other, who provided the equipment and underwrote the operating costs, enjoyed special privileges.

We also hear about a "trust," a combination of two partnerships in two different cities. A successful silk cooperative in al-Maḥalla in Lower Egypt opened a store in Fustat in the neighborhood of another such corporation, lowering the prices of the product. The parties in Fustat, fearing that they would be unable to compete with the newcomers, combined with them: one of the partners from al-Maḥalla moved to Fustat and entered the workshop there, and one of the Fustat partners moved to al-Maḥalla; it was agreed that there should be only one such workshop in each city and that their respective assets should not be merged.

The short duration of some of these workshop contracts (six and a half months; one year) is paralleled by similar conditions in commercial partnerships. While short-term alliances are natural in business relations, they seem to be somewhat impracticable for running a workshop. The Geniza has preserved contracts for the continuation of partnerships, and we may assume that the short terms stipulated in the original agreements were regarded as trial periods. Partnerships between craftsmen and persons supplying the operating capital indicate the same wide variety of form as those between craftsmen themselves. There could be one or more participants on both sides (one on each side; two investors, one artisan; one investor and a number of artisans). The terms sometimes seem harsh: one craftsman was obliged to return in cash the whole sum supplied (fifty dinars out of a total of sixty-five invested) only two months after being instructed to do so by his partner. Sometimes the terms are exceptionally generous: a group of indigo dyers received two-thirds of the profit (as laid down by Jewish law) but was not held responsible for losses from government requisition, sinking of goods during transport on the Nile, or other acts of God, and was even exempted from losses of up to ten dinars resulting from the (mis)operation of the workshop. Lifelong partnerships could develop into relationships similar to or even stronger than family ties. Thus, a dyer, setting out for the holy pilgrimage to Jerusalem, makes provision for his wife and children in the event of his death, but appoints his partner as sole executor, trustee, and guardian.

We can form some idea of the craftsmen's earnings by comparing them with the wages paid to skilled laborers. A master artisan earned an average of six dirhems per day during the eleventh and twelfth centuries; unskilled workers received between two and two and a half dirhems. Payments for work done or ordered are mentioned occasionally in Geniza letters, but much more material will have to be collected and coordinated with data on the cost of living in general before any valid conclusions can be drawn.

In the light of our records, the medieval Hebrew pun *melākhā-melūkhā*, "a craft is a kingdom" (which is referred to in a Geniza letter), seems to be fully justified. To be sure, craftsmen belonged to the lower strata of the society, but a skilled and successful artisan was a respected person who was addressed as "elder" (Ar. *shaykh*, Heb. *zāqēn*), as was a merchant. Manual work as such was not regarded as degrading. A Qayrawānese trader known to us from a number of letters as a widely traveled businessman did not believe it beneath his dignity to work part-time in tailoring when business in Egypt was at a standstill.

The generally good standing of the craftsman in the Jewish society of the Geniza period has as a corollary that we hear very little about despised professions, a subject conspicuous in postbiblical Hebrew literature and discussed at length by the lawyers of Islam. According to them, a member of such a profession was not qualified to marry a girl from a good family and could even be denied the right to appear as a witness in court. Some of the occupations held in contempt by Muslim lawyers—sewer and cesspool cleaners, streetsweepers, and bathhouse attendants, for example—never appear in the Geniza records as performed by Jews. Had the community of Fustat included Jews engaged in such occupations, some of them would be mentioned in the many lists of indigent persons performing service jobs and assisted by the communal chest. The work of the cupper or bloodletter, which also was subject to disqualification according to the Muslim lawyers, was not despised by Jews: it was a subgroup of the highly honored medical profession, and prospective physicians sought to acquire surgical skills by the practice of bleeding. Members of the ruling oligarchy sometimes characterized their rank-and-file opponents as performing certain low-prestige, manual occupations: they are derided as oyster-gatherers, dyers, and cobblers in Alexandria and as potters in Fustat. Such comments, however, are rare, and with the exception of the oystermen of Alexandria, who are mentioned elsewhere in a derogatory context, it was not the occupation in itself that counted but rather the economic and social status attained. The Geniza provides a good number of examples of affluent and respectable dyers.

In a few cases, we read that an artisan bore a title indicating that he was a scholarly man. "Make these threads into a cloth," says a letter, "and send it for me to have the *ḥāvēr* bleach and tailor it before the holidays." The title *ḥāvēr*, or fellow of the academy, was given in those days only to persons who qualified as scholars, but there was nothing exceptional in a learned person being engaged in bleaching and tailoring or other manual work; in this period we even find a gaon at the head of the yeshiva in Baghdad who had formerly been a weaver, a profession ranked as despised both in the Talmud and in Islamic literature. Still, scholarship was not as common among the artisans we read about in the Geniza letters as it was in Palestine during the early centuries of the Christian era, or in the Jewish communities of Yemen as described by travelers in modern times. During the Geniza period, learning was mainly the domain of the mercantile class.

Wage Earners

Leo A. Mayer, who devoted half a lifetime to the study of craftsmen in classical Islamic civilization, defined three grades of employees: *tilmīdh*, "pupil," *ghulām*, "apprentice," and *ajīr*, "journeyman."[1]

---

1. *Islamic Metalworkers and Their Works* (Geneva, 1959), 14.

The nomenclature in the Geniza records is somewhat different. The words *ghulām,* in this context, "young man," and *ṣabī,* "boy," are generally used for a person in service of another, whether as a free person or as a slave, in industry or in commerce. The rationale underlying this designation is that one served as an employee only while young and in order to learn a craft or profession, or to acquaint oneself with local conditions.

To differentiate employees from slaves, the term *ajīr,* "hireling," was employed; the term was, however, confined to legal usage rather than ordinary speech. A journeyman would be designated by the general term *ṣāniʿ*, which means both laborer and craftsman. The word would be used to indicate a person working in a glass factory or a silk-weaving shop, but also one in service of a "bride comber," a woman who dressed brides and took care of other arrangements for weddings. Persons engaged in the highly specialized craft of perforating pearls are described in one account as *ʿamālīn*, "workmen," synonymous in the same document with *ṣāniʿ*. The difference between the ajīr and ṣāniʿ, "hireling" and "laborer," on the one hand, and the ghulām and ṣabī, "young man" and "boy," on the other, seems to have consisted not so much in the degree of ability; rather ghulām designated more transient and businesslike relations with an employer and ṣabī more permanent and personal ones.

Laborers engaged in work requiring less skill were designated by names indicating the type of help they normally provided. The most common was *raqqāṣ,* "runner," or "errand boy," which originally designated the laborer who carried the materials up to the mason working on the scaffolding, but it was also used for other craftsmen's helpers, such as carpenters, and very frequently for irregular policemen. A helper in a workshop was called *munāwil,* literally, "one who passes along or hands on," or simply ṣabī.

Domestic work was normally performed by female slaves. Therefore, we rarely hear about "servants." The word *khādim* "servant," common in the Geniza records, designates the beadle of a synagogue or a public servant in general. Sometimes it refers to the slave of a caliph, who often had an influential position. In Muslim usage the term also designated the eunuchs who served in official households or in the army. Child labor is almost never mentioned in the Geniza records. The insistence of the Jewish community on the schooling of orphans and children of the poor might have served as an obstacle to their exploitation in the labor market.

The wages and conditions of employment were normally not put down in writing, and, for that reason, references to such issues in the Geniza are mostly indirect. Moreover, the interpretation of this material is very elusive, for one must also consider purchasing power in determining the real value of wages. This, in turn, requires data on various items that were consumed, as well as data on fluctuations in currency rates. On the whole, one has the impression that the High Middle Ages were characterized by a stability of prices and wages.

According to both Muslim and Jewish law, "hire"—that is, payment for the services of a person or use of a thing—was due at the end of the period for which the payment was stipulated, normally a day for wages and a month for the rent of a house. Even when a man "hired" his divorced wife to take care of their little baby, payment would be made at the end of the month, since it was fixed at a monthly rate. While complaints by separated or divorced wives about delays in the remittance of alimony were frequent, so far no case of deferring wages has been found in the Geniza records. Sometimes a craftsman would be granted an advance, which he would return in the event that he had not carried out the work ordered. As was common with public officials, employees could be partly remunerated by their employers paying their poll tax. A Tunisian merchant mentions in a letter that he paid 29/48 dinars for the poll tax of his packer. Since, at the writing of that letter, a dinar comprised an average of 36 dirhems, and a skilled laborer earned 5 dirhems a day, the packer would have had to work two weeks (twelve working days) for his poll tax. On the whole, the poll tax caused considerable hardship for the Jews.

As for working hours, a twelfth-century manual of market supervision states (under the heading "Carpenters, sawyers, masons, . . ."): "Most workmen make an agreement about a specified daily wage, but they come late in the morning and depart before evening. Terms must be made to prevent this." This seems to indicate that medieval Eastern craftsmen did not normally work from sunrise to sunset. Since the Geniza contains references to part-time work, there must have been accepted standards in this matter. Presumably, much depended on the character and mood of the two sides concerned. In one Geniza letter, the employee of an oculist complains that his employer (who is also his relative) exploits him and does not even leave him time for prayer. Compare with this a statement in a Spanish handbook of market supervision, in which the supervisor is advised to watch that the retailers and "the boys" in the stores pray regularly. For a medieval Jew, the day normally began with the attendance of the morning service, only after which was one allowed to take breakfast; many would attend the communal service in the late afternoon as well. A young man, traveling from Mazara in southwestern Sicily, which was then Muslim, to Messina on the northeastern tip of the island, which had already been conquered by the Normans, wrote home that his father could have a good income if he emigrated to Messina, but that it was impossible to live in that town, for people there were already through with morning prayer at dawn (it should last through sunrise) and there was no communal afternoon service at all. The conditions of life, including the length of the working day, obviously varied from place to place.

The contracts for manual labor discussed thus far were all based on daily wages, even when they covered prolonged periods, such as a whole year. Such was the case with the Coptic linen-weavers of the famous industrial center of Tinnīs, who were engaged in that work all their lives, but still were paid daily. There were, however, other types of labor contracts. We read in a Geniza letter about "flax combers," who seem to have been seasonal laborers. They lived with their employer, receiving full board and half a dinar per month in cash, and were given working clothes, also valued at half a dinar. The writer of the letter complains that he had to buy clothes for one of his employees at a price far in excess of the usual half a dinar and states that he will take him back only if he accepts the usual conditions of work as other young men of his type.

Main Occupations and Professions

The Geniza records are remarkable for the great number of occupations and the high degree of specialization and division of labor apparent in them. The terms for about 265 manual occupations have been identified thus far, as against 90 types of person engaged in commerce and banking and approximately the same number of professionals, officials, religious functionaries, and educators. This total of around 450 professions exceeds by far the listed professions for all other pre-modern cities thus far known.

The records mention not only the great industries—textiles, dyeing, and clothing; metals, glass, and pottery; construction; alimentation—but also many smaller types of concerns. A few examples may serve as illustrations: makers of kohl sticks, of writing cases (in which the scribes kept pen and ink attached to their belts), mirrors, fans, spindles, sieves, combs (for hair and industrial purposes, in particular flax), manufacturers and stringers of beads of various descriptions, perforators of pearls, persons processing coral, or making woven or braided mats.

Some occupations were dominated by Muslims or Christians. Mostly, however, the reference is to Jews, and, here one should bear in mind that religious and ethnic communities used to specialize in certain professions, as did particular families and clans. Jews were prominent in the textile industry—above all, silk work and dyeing, which was a decidedly Jewish profession in all countries. The production of glass was another predominantly Jewish occupation, as was metalwork of all descriptions, but mainly silversmithing. Finally, many Jews were engaged in the food trades; the pharmaceutical profession as well was largely in the hands of the Jews.

It is, however, characteristic of the classical Geniza period, which was comparatively free of castelike separation and restrictions, that religious and ethnic occupational divisions were by no means rigid. We find Muslim silk-workers, dyers, tanners, glassmakers, or pharmacists alongside their Jewish fellow-workers. The handbooks of market supervision, whether from Spain or from the East, do not indicate that any particular occupation was confined to a certain community. Accordingly, the Geniza shows us Jews in practically every occupation, from vizier down to blacksmith and sailor. Nonetheless, their preponderance in certain occupations was a fact. The sketch of the main industries reflected in the Geniza records that follows should be taken as a cross section, rather than as a complete picture, of the immensely rich gamut of Mediterranean arts and crafts practiced during the High Middle Ages.

Textiles constituted the major industry of medieval times in the Mediterranean area. As far as the statistical data available allow us to gauge, a very great proportion—perhaps the majority—of the working population and certainly of distributors were engaged in this branch of the economy. Textiles, in a wide variety of fabrics and colors, were a highly valued product. Fantastic prices were paid for single selected pieces, the so-called *a'lāq;* this we know not only from literary sources but also from business letters found in the Geniza. Transmitted from parents to children, to be converted into cash in case of an emergency, clothing formed part—sometimes a considerable part—of a family's investment. The furniture of a house consisted mainly of various types of carpets, couches, cushions, canopies, and draperies—objects produced mainly by the textile industry. Jews played a very prominent role in silk manufacturing as well as in cotton production and dyeing. Similarly, they worked in all aspects of metal production and in the manufacture and sale of leather, parchment, and paper. Jews were active as well in the building trades, and in the production of pottery and household goods and utensils.

The Mediterranean area during the High Middle Ages was characterized by a highly mercantile economy. Still, whoever could afford it, whether a Muslim judge in Gaza, or the scribe of a Jewish court in Fustat, owned land and looked after its yields. From a query submitted to Maimonides it is evident that it was common practice for Jews to entrust their fields, vineyards, orchards, and gardens to gentile sharecroppers. Despite the glamour of the capital, many preferred to live in little towns or villages; an extraordinary number of foreigners settled in the Egyptian Rīf; at least some of them were connected with agriculture. Wealthier people invested a considerable part of their income in farming. A settlement between partners in precious stones reveals that they also owned farmland in common; one partner receives 120½ dinars in cash and the other all the flax and other crops, which proves that the land they owned must have covered a large area.

From Muslim handbooks of administration we learn that during the Geniza period even the highest officials were paid partly in cash and partly in kind—particularly in wheat and barley. We also read in a Geniza letter that a newly appointed local *mushārif*, or superintendent of revenue, received an annual salary of 180 dinars and 100 *irdabb* (about 9,000 liters) of grain. Even bribes given in the convenient form of cash were accompanied by an unspecified quantity of grain. Jewish community officials were remunerated in a similar way. Payments by the more affluent members of the community for the distribution of loaves to the needy were also made in wheat. Grain was also given on loan "like dinars," as we know not only from Jewish and Muslim lawbooks, but from Geniza letters, including one from eleventh-century Jerusalem, which speaks of grain loans. All this shows that people tried to be as close as possible to "the source of life"—bread was called "life," *'aysh,* in the local vernacular of Egypt even in the eleventh century.

A village was designated by the same word (*ḍay'a*) as a farm, which was natural, for often the entire village belonged to a single notable. The Mediterranean village, as portrayed in the Geniza documents, was entirely different from the middle and western European manor, whose lord had complete economic control and outrageous prerogatives in addition to his political authority and far-reaching juridical power. The ḍay'a was similar to the European manor insofar as its peasants were in many respects the heirs of the Roman *coloni*—legally free men who were enslaved to the soil they worked and to its proprietor. But south and east of the Mediterranean the state retained all economic, political, and juridical authority; the notable was the beneficiary rather than the master of the village.

The village, like the town, formed a rather open society. Jewish immigrants from Spain could settle in a ḍayʿa near Jerusalem in the middle of the eleventh century and operate a store there. A ḍayʿa might be large enough to have its own nāʾib or Muslim deputy judge, or a deputy police superintendent. Letters from the countryside deal with the universal topics of the state of the crops or, in a region such as Palestine, with the rain, the prices and diseases of cattle, and consignments and presents sent to town. Letters from Egypt frequently mention wheat, flax, and chickens, but also many other minor agricultural products. The contrast between town and country finds its expression in popular stories preserved in the Geniza about the Miṣrī, or citizen of the capital, and the Rīfī. A man writes in a letter, "I feel myself in relation to you like a fellah honored by a most illustrious lord of a ḍayʿa," and enlarges upon the topic in detail.

Wheat was the main grain for human consumption. Barley served as bread for the very poor, but was normally needed to feed riding beasts (and probably also for various kinds of beer mentioned in our records). As we may conclude from the quantities ordered by a scholar from a village, it was laid in stores like wheat. In Palestine it is referred to as grown in the district of Gaza. Rice was also cultivated.

In addition to wheat, the diet of the common people depended mainly on oil, obtained either from plants or from olives. Since oil, together with wax, was also the almost exclusive material for artificial lighting, its importance can be easily gauged. Because of the enormous extent of flax-growing, linseed oil was widely used, in particular for lighting. It was exported from Egypt to olive-growing Syria and to faraway Aden in southern Arabia. Edible oil was obtained to a large extent from the sesame plant, which was grown in the Nile Delta, particularly to the north, and in Palestine. Safflower, used for dyeing, also provided oil, used mainly for medical purposes. One Geniza document makes reference to the seed being sent from a village to the capital, while the red dye made from the flowers, widely used in cosmetics, was a common article in the international trade of coloring stuffs.

The olive tree, regarded as the king of all trees in the Bible (Judges 9:8), is indigenous to the Mediterranean area, but almost entirely absent from Egypt. Olive oil, however, was a vital ingredient in the diet of the population and also provided the choicest lighting. No wonder, then, that its import to Egypt was one of the great branches of the Mediterranean trade. Oil was also produced locally from imported olives. Needless to say, a wide variety of fruits were grown and sold at market. The production of wine, given its social and sacramental role, merits particular discussion here.[2]

A certain laxity prevailed during much of the classical Geniza period in the Muslim prohibition on the consumption of wine and other alcoholic beverages. A contemporaneous Muslim visitor to the Egyptian capital remarked that hardly any fresh grapes could be had there, because most of the grapes available in the countryside were made into wine. (In Egypt, unlike the more strict Muslim West, vessels containing wine were openly displayed for sale.) This report tallies with the evidence to be gleaned from the Geniza records. The large quantities of wine sold could hardly have been destined for the sole consumption of the Christian and Jewish population, especially as many people — certainly not only Jews — used to buy grapes and have them pressed and made into wine.

Unlike orchards, vineyards were legally the property of the government or its *āmirs*. Therefore, a *karrām*, or "vine grower," is not to be regarded as a proprietor of vineyards, but as one who leased them from the government and took care of them. In Spain, the legal situation was different: the Hebrew documents or formularies that have reached the Geniza from there show that private persons possessed vineyards and sold or leased them at liberty. A Spanish formulary shows how minutely the obligations of a tenant were fixed, down to the exact number of loads of manure to be used; he had to look after everything, from the amelioration of the soil and of the stock of the vines to the pressing of the grapes.

Since wine has a strongly sacramental character in the Jewish religion, its preparation has to be performed by Jews. Therefore, it is not surprising to find persons designated as "pressers (of grapes)," although this can have only been a seasonal occupation. Pressers of grapes were needed in general, as were millers. Just as people bought wheat and sent it to the miller for grinding (instead of buying flour), they also bought grapes and had them pressed or, in smaller quantities, pressed them at home. In addition to homemade wine, one could buy the much consumed beverage at the expert wineseller or, as we do, import the product from Europe.

2. The details of agricultural production are to be found in volume 1 of Goitein's five-volume *Mediterranean Society*.

Professions of Women

Woman were the laborers par excellence in the society of the classical Geniza period. Every married woman was expected to engage in some work in addition to her household chores. Therefore, marriage contracts often stated whether a wife's earnings belonged to her husband (who was under obligation to supply all her needs), whether she would be allowed to retain them, or whether they were to cover her clothing expenses. When a husband went abroad, he would earmark or deposit sums for his wife, from which she would pay rent, taxes, and her household expenditures, but would stipulate expressly not to lay claim on any earnings made by her "through work and spinning." We also read complaints about a husband illegally appropriating sums received by his wife for her work. A keen observer of life in Egypt at the beginning of the nineteenth century remarked that even upper-class women sent the products of their needlework to the market for sale.[3] A similar situation must have prevailed during the Geniza period.

A certain number of women's professions were closely connected with the lives of women. A wedding was a great affair, and the elaborate combing and dressing of the bride was confided to an expert, the bride comber, who was also evidently in charge of at least a part of the wedding reception, as she had to employ a laborer for her work. In some localities, but not universally, Muslim bride combers were employed in Jewish houses. In childbirth, a young mother was assisted by experienced women of her family, but by a professional midwife as well. Wet nurses are rarely mentioned in the Geniza records, but the oldest Muslim collection of legal opinions (the *kitāb al-Āthār* of Abū Yūsef [d. 798 C.E.]) contains the question whether a Muslim household employing a Jewish wet nurse might have its meat prepared by a Jewish ritual slaughterer in order to enable her to eat with the family without having to worry about Jewish dietary laws. A similar collection dating from the thirteenth century reports the case of a Jewish woman who nursed a Muslim boy and died leaving a child of her own; it was impossible to establish which was the Jewish boy and which was Muslim. Women doctors appear more frequently in our documents; one female oculist is also listed. These references are not to physicians who had undergone the expensive apprenticeship of scientific medicine but rather to practi-

3. Edward W. Lane, *An Account of the Manners and Customs of the Modern Egyptians (Written in Egypt during the Years 1833–1835)* (London, 1895; reprint New York, 1973), 194.

tioners, whose knowledge and skill had come to them by traditional healing practices.

Women teachers are frequently referred to. It stands to reason that they taught young girls the female art of embroidery and other needle-work; in one case it is expressly stated that the widow of a scholar was assigned two orphans to teach them the "craft" of embroidery while another person, presumably a male, would instruct them in prayer. There are also cases of women working in schools and giving regular instruction in the main subject studied there, namely, Bible reading. These may have been exceptions rather than the rule.

Textiles were clearly the main field of the female remunerative occu-pations. It is not evident whether there existed workshops that employed groups of women, or whether all work was done individually and at home. When a husband makes peace with his wife on condition that she work only at home, or when a Persian merchant writes that the (female) spinners no longer produce much of a certain material, such statements may indicate that silk was worked either in workshops or in private homes. We read about a woman unraveling the filament and reeling raw silk given to her, and of a divorced woman whose entire livelihood consisted in this type of work. In her will, a woman leaves equipment for silk weaving to her daughter; another orders silk for weaving by herself and her sister; a community statute forbids women to dye silk at home, except with the permission of the person who had farmed out the government tax for the exercise of this craft. Spinning was by no means confined to the treatment of locally obtained fibers. In addition to silk, we hear about Egyptian flax, sent in raw state to Tunisia and spun there by women living on this work.

The products of female labor were sold by female brokers. The me-dieval bazaars were normally no place for women's activities. For this very reason, it was convenient to have a female broker who visited the houses and collected and traded the threads and textiles made by women. Women designated as *wakīla,* or agent, are mentioned in com-munal lists and referred to in letters (not always in a laudatory context). Others were named after the commodity which they traded, such as the sellers of ambergris perfumes or of flour. In one case we read about a man who had inherited from his father two Hebrew Bible codices and entrusted a woman broker with their sale. She offered them "to all the elders of the community" and when she found no buyer, she fell upon the good idea of selling them to her own son at 7½ dinars, while she herself collected a brokerage fee of one-third dinar. Six years later, the original proprietor learned that one codex was allegedly worth

twenty dinars. The case was brought to court—and thus to our knowledge.

Just as the readying of the bride for her queenlike role required an
expert, so the very elaborate apparel in which the dead, especially dead
women, were buried and the treatment of the body before burial were
confided to a specialist. She was called "the washer," and since people
cling tenaciously to their local customs in these matters, it is not surprising to find in one and the same list a (female) washer for the Rūm,
or European, Jewesses (mostly refugees), and another for those of Fustat. Wailing, too, was part of the funeral and was performed mostly by
women.

The participation of women in remunerated domestic occupations is
all but absent from the Geniza records. As the maidservants doing
household work were legally slaves, it is natural that free women were
reluctant to join their ranks. Only well-to-do people could afford to keep
a slave, however, while the need for an at least temporary replacement
of the housewife must have been a frequent occurrence. In extended
families, married sons used to live with their parents and sisters and
often also with married brothers in one and the same house, so that
normally a number of women were at hand in case one of them was
temporarily incapacitated. The availability in the bazaar of freshly
cooked food of all descriptions also was of great practical importance in
this respect, and might have had its origins in the fact that families
belonging to the lower middle class and the poorer sections of the population could not afford to keep a servant.

Freewomen working as domestic help are found only under special
circumstances, notably in the houses of widowed religious dignitaries.
In his will, an old cantor leaves two dinars to a woman who had looked
after him. Another woman, who had done the same for a *rāv*, or spiritual
leader of a community, receives clothing from a public charity. A woman
of European origin who had a married daughter, writes from al-
Mahdiyya to her mother and sister in Alexandria, "I work as a servant
in any house," complaining about the weakness of her body and her old
age. In the same letter she mentions that her son had left her eight years
before and nothing had been heard from him since; her circumstances
may explain why she was forced to humiliate herself by working in other
people's houses: she was a foreigner and had no one to maintain her.
On the occasion of the marriage of her daughter, the wife of a kohen is
described as serving in the house of a judge. Somewhat more befitting
a free woman was to serve the community by cleaning a synagogue
building or school. Both the synagogue of the Palestinians and that of

the Babylonians in Fustat had a *khādima*, the female equivalent of khādim, or beadle. In one case we read about a woman serving in a *kuttāb*, or Bible school. These women received bread and clothing, as well as payment, from the community, all of which, however, smacked of charity. Service, under any circumstances, was not a proper way of earning one's livelihood in the free-enterprise society of the Geniza world.

Male and Female Slaves

Slavery during the classical Geniza period was neither industrial nor agricultural; with the exception of the armies, which were largely composed of mercenaries who were legally slaves, slaves were owned individually—by families. Slavery was personal service in the widest sense of the word, and it could carry with it great advantages, as well as social prestige, when the master served was of high rank or wealthy. In the Mediterranean area of the eleventh through the thirteenth century, slaves had to be imported from faraway countries and were expensive. If we disregard the military, slaves certainly formed only a minority of the population, unlike the situation in imperial Rome, where, according to widely held views, three-quarters of the inhabitants were either slaves or freedmen. The high value of slaves protected them and made them an object of consideration, in addition to the humanitarian laws and admonitions made in their favor by the three monotheistic religions.

The very word "slave," *'abd*, which at that time had already acquired the racial connotation of black, was regarded as improper and was replaced by circumlocutions such as "boy" and "young man." Because the same words were applied to free employees, it is sometimes difficult to determine whether a person referred to in a Geniza letter was a slave or not, particularly in the case of persons serving as business agents. The situation is complicated further by the fact that a freedman as well might be called "young man of so-and-so," even if his former proprietor had died long before. Slaves engaged mainly in household work were called *wasīf*, "servant," a word that apparently was applied exclusively to unfree persons; another Arabic root, *khadam*, normally designated service to rulers or to a community. Female slaves were never designated as *khādima*, but rather as *jāriya*, "girl." As this word as well became almost synonymous with "slave," it in turn was often replaced by *wasīfa*, "servant." Female slaves, as a rule, bore names indicative of their social station, while male slaves often had names that were also in use among the free population.

The position of male slaves was fundamentally different from that of females. In Islamic times, communities of the Middle East had become accustomed to being governed by slaves. The rulers, always distrustful of their own people, used to surround themselves with persons brought from distant regions, who knew no other attachment except to their master. The Fatimids and Ayyubids made extensive use of slaves of European, Turkish, and other nationalities for the posts of highest confidence; under their successors, the Mamluks, what had been a practice became a principle: The ruling oligarchy admitted to its ranks solely persons who had been slaves. The seeds of the Mamluk institution already appear under the Abbasids in the ninth century.

Among the bourgeoisie, male slaves were employed mainly in positions of trust; rarely do we read of male servants performing manual labor. The acquisition of a male slave was a important affair, on which a man was congratulated almost as if a son had been born to him. No wonder, for a slave fulfilled tasks similar to those of a son: He managed the affairs of his master, traveled with him or as his representative, or was in charge of the master's business, when the latter himself was out of town. The ghulām, or "young man," of a businessman would be consulted in all affairs of his master, and his movements would be reported in the same way as those of other important merchants.

Agents who were legally slaves were allowed to conduct business of their own, and some must have done very well. One document shows Durrī ("Gem"), the ghulām of a nagid, making one of the largest contributions to a public appeal. In another document, dated 1161, a ghulām gives two dinars to the widow of the partner of his master; in 1063, the "young man" belonging to the tax farmer of the market of Palermo enters into a partnership with a Jewish merchant for very high sums. Sometimes a master would perform a service for his own servant, as when a Tunisian merchant ordered old silver for himself and also for his ghulām in the notable amount of twenty-seven dinars.

While deeds of sale, gift, or bequest of females have been found in considerable number among the Geniza records, only one such document has been found with regard to adult males (there are some for minors). In it, an Indian servant named Patan Patana is sold in Fustat by a perfumer to a banker for 19½ dinars (June 1194). In the India trade, of course, the local agents, who were legally slaves, were indispensable. So far, only one deed of manumission of a male slave (as against at least six for females) has been found, although the emancipation of slaves must have been extremely common—as we may conclude from the fact that freedmen are mentioned so often. It should be noted that the act of manumission had to be made before a Jewish court, for it converted the slave into a person with all the religious duties of a Jew and enabled him to take a Jewish wife. The scarcity of legal deeds with regard to adult male slaves—as opposed to the frequent references to them in letters—might partly reflect the fact that, as a rule, they were owned only by members of the upper class, which, having its seat in Cairo, is not fully represented in the Geniza records. It is also possible that there were certain restrictions with regard to transactions in adult male slaves that necessitated that they be made before a Muslim court.

One differentiated between female domestics for personal service, those doing household work in general, and nurses. A rich bride took with her to her new home two maids (*jāriya*) and two servants (*waṣīfa*); their total value was estimated at one hundred dinars. A respectable merchant in Alexandria, whose wife had died recently, writes to his friend in Fustat that he has none to serve him and "to hand a cup of water" to his children or to himself. No help could be found in the Jewish quarter of his town; therefore, he asks the addressee to buy him a chaste slave woman to take care of his children. We find a similar request made by another Alexandrian in a letter to his brother in Fustat and by a man in the latter town writing to his father on travel in one of the countries of the Indian Ocean. In a better home there would be a *dāda*, or nanny, and a waṣīfa who did the rougher work. The nannies often became beloved members of the family.

Female slaves as domestic help and nurses of children were found in every well-to-do family. Their intimate position in the household was, however, an ambiguous and potentially compromising one. There was, of course, in this respect a deep divide between the Christian and Jewish minorities on the one hand, and the Muslim majority on the other. While Christianity and Judaism disapproved of any sexual relations out of wedlock, in Islam a female slave was at the disposal of her master, and he could own as many as he liked and his purse allowed. Judaism, in particular, regarded intercourse with female slave as a very great sin, punishable, according to some authorities, by death (see Numbers 25: 6–12). A man was not allowed to be under one roof with a female slave unless his mother, sister, or wife lived in the same house. Transgressions were punished by forced sale of the slave, the proceeds to be distributed among the poor, or by outright excommunication. We see indeed that an old man who had no one to care for him had to apply to the "mercy" of the court for permission to buy a maidservant: free domestic help was difficult to obtain.

It is only natural that the social habits of a majority should affect the minorities living among it, and the highly dependent position of female slaves in itself constituted a great temptation. No wonder that we find occasional references to such occurrences also in the Geniza records. In a query submitted to Abraham Maimonides we read about a married man with children who forsook his family in his native Alexandria, acquired a slave in Fustat, bought her beautiful dresses, the like of which his wife never had, and made off with her to the faraway Fayyūm province. An official addressing the same dignitary reports about another man from Alexandria, a kohen, who had left his newly wed wife and taken a Christian slave with him to a village in the Buḥayra province where he was a tax farmer; a ban had already been pronounced against him. There are a few queries and references to similar and perhaps identical cases, but it seems that these were unusual events. In this respect the society reflected in the Geniza records differed markedly from that of the Jews in Spain during the thirteenth century, when slave concubinage became a rampant social evil.

It is possible, however, that humane and proselytizing tendencies were involved in the acquisition and upbringing of female slaves. Thus, on her deathbed the wife of a scholar and judge frees her two slaves, who were virgins and, it seems, mere children, and provides them with housing and board for life on the condition that they remained within the Jewish fold; one of the girls, called Dhahab, "Gold," had been given by a widow to her brother a few years earlier when she was only three years old. We find repeatedly that people were eager to acquire slave girls of tender age. A trader sends his wife from India a six-year-old "maid"; a woman from Fustat asks a relative, a government official in al-Bahnasā in Middle Egypt, to buy for her "a black, freshly imported girl, five to six years old." The acquisition of maidservants at a time when they were children was done to give those future members of the household a certain measure of both practical and religious education.

The religious position of slaves varied widely among the three monotheistic religions. In Judaism, both male and female slaves were obliged to adopt a milder form of religious observances, including full observance of the Sabbath. Like other proselytes, they were initiated by baptism. According to the law, if a slave refused to be baptized within one year, he had to be resold. Maimonides ruled that slaves, once they had accepted baptism, were members of the covenant of Israel. He was followed in this by his son and successor Abraham, who states in an autograph responsum that a baptized slave was in ritual matters more trustworthy than a Karaite.

A query sent to Maimonides speaks of a Jewish bachelor who had bought a Christian "beauty" (the technical term for a prisoner of war chosen as concubine). He converted her, and she stayed with him in the house of his father, stepmother, and their three children. "But the house was vast." Denounced—for under Islamic rule a Christian was not permitted to convert to any religion except Islam—the girl contended before the qāḍī that she was Jewish, the daughter of a Jewess. This settled the affair as far as Islamic law was concerned. There remained the question of how to resolve the case under Jewish law. Maimonides, in his practical wisdom, decided that the young man should emancipate his beloved and marry her. According to strict law, this was illegal, for anyone who lived illicitly with a woman (or was suspected of doing so), was forbidden to marry her all his life. But, Maimonides adds, he already had given several such decisions in other cases involving concubines to give an opportunity to those who wished to mend their ways and to lead orderly lives. He did so, as he wrote, relying on a daring maxim of the ancient sages: "Pay regard to God by disregarding His law."

A certain latitude obtained during Fatimid and Ayyubid times as regards the religious attachment of slaves. The Islamic injunction that no one should be converted to any religion except Islam was largely disregarded. Many male and female slaves must have been converted to Judaism. In addition to the examples cited, this might be inferred from the many Jewish freedmen and freedwomen mentioned in the Geniza records. On the other hand, the Jewish authorities seem not to have insisted on enforcing the law that slaves had to be baptized, and marriages between Jews and former slave girls who had been, or who were suspected to have been, concubines, were not unheard of.

As regards the treatment of slaves, Maimonides concludes the chapter on slavery in his *Code of Law* thus: "It is both pious and reasonable on the part of a master to be merciful and just towards his slave, not to overburden him with work and not to cause him grief, and to let him share all food and drink taken by himself. . . . He should not humiliate him either by infliction of corporal punishment or even by words. . . . He should not shout at him . . . but talk to him quietly and listen to his arguments. . . ." Similar admonitions are contained in Christian and Muslim sources. But, of course, not all people were pious and reasonable. As far as our actual information from the Geniza records is concerned, male slaves, who normally acted as business representatives, are referred to in the same way as respected merchants and, when they served as personal factotums, were greeted in letters on the same terms as other members of the household, sometimes with the honorable epithet "the elder." When we find a text in which such a slave was flogged as a punishment for alleged defamation, we should not forget that even viziers were exposed to such public humiliation. There existed a strong family attachment between the master and his slave, an attachment that was even more pronounced in the case of female slaves: they were greeted in family letters and they themselves sent greetings to the relatives of their masters. Reports of slaves fleeing their owners are indeed rare. On the other hand, there are numerous accounts in the Geniza about slaves set free by their masters. These manumissions were deeds of piety and gratitude, often enacted on the deathbed.

In many cases slaves were emancipated by their masters during their lifetime, as proved by the deeds of manumission preserved and by references to freedmen at a time when their former proprietors were still alive. Rarely do we read about the specific circumstances under which freedom was granted. One case may be representative: Bahiyya, a daughter of Ibn 'Awkal, a prominent merchant and communal leader, had received from her husband a female slave of European provenance whom the man had inherited from a sister. Two documents deal with this girl, whose name was Nujūm, "Stars." In the first, Bahiyya gives her as a gift to a cousin who was married to another of her sisters-in-law. In the second, that cousin sets Nujūm free, and his wife joins him in the solemn act of manumission. Here we have the case of a slave who had already changed hands within a family three times. She was returned to the sister of the original proprietor who, together with her husband, then gave her freedom.

The deeds of manumission preserved correspond to the strict requirements of Jewish law. They state that the former slave was now entirely free, and that neither the master nor his legal representatives had any right to the person, progeny, or property of the emancipated. The freed slave was at liberty to adopt a new name, to marry a person of Jewish faith, and to do what any free person was allowed to do, including the study of the Torah. Thus, legally, the position of a Jewish freedman differed markedly from that of a Muslim. According to Muslim (and Roman) law, there remained many bonds between the former master and his freedman. The latter was called in Arabic *mawlā*, which means "the attached," while in Hebrew his designation was "freedman."

The Geniza records show us that, in real life, relationships similar to those existing between relatives prevailed between slaves and masters. In or out of bondage, the slave was a member of the family. When a

town was sacked by marauders, as happened to al-Maḥalla in the turbulent 1060s, and slaves were taken captive, we read that their masters
tried to ransom them, as they did free persons captured in war or by
pirates. (Under Jewish law, the ransoming of slaves was as much a religious duty as ransoming free persons.) Many marriage contracts and
other documents concerning marriages of emancipated women and men
have been preserved. It is reasonable to assume that the jewelry, clothing,
bedding, and household goods that constituted their dowries were at
least in part given to them by their previous masters. Even in the contract
made at her second marriage (she then was a widow), Mu'tazz, "the
one held in high esteem," is still referred to as "the freedwoman of Moses
b. Paltiel" (most probably a member of the prominent family known by
that name). Otherwise, all the conditions were the same as those in
conventional marriage contracts, and her dowry was far higher than that
of many women born free. Similar bonds of attachment existed between
male slaves and the houses of their former masters.

Jewish law did not grant the emancipator any rights whatsoever regarding the person, progeny, or property of the slave emancipated by
him. Here too, however, the influence of environment, or perhaps social
habits, was stronger than the written law. The Geniza has preserved a
long and interesting query addressed to Abraham Maimonides with the
following story: A freedwoman in a little town in Lower Egypt at her
death had left money to her friends, who did not want to accept it but
intended to turn it over to the community. Meanwhile, the son of the
master who had emancipated her (the son himself is called "her master"
in the letter), a respected and popular figure in the town, experienced
financial ruin in a matter concerning tax farming and thus laid claim on
the money due her. The head of the local community was very anxious
to accede to this request, in particular as the claimant had threatened to
apply to a Muslim court in the event that his request was refused. In his
hastily scribbled marginal answer, the nagid states that the applicant had
not the slightest rights on the estate of a person emancipated by his
father, but that there was no objection to its being turned over to him
if the women to whom it had been given consented to such a procedure—in other words, the nagid, too, favored an action in line with the
generally accepted notions. In popular usage, Jewish freedmen and even
their sons were described as *mawlās*, "attached to another," but the law
did not recognize such designations. In a court record from Fustat,
dated June 28, 1080, the freedman Mubārak (who had become a successful businessman) was initially characterized as the mawlā of Joseph
b. Joshiah, a person known from other documents; the Arabic term was
deleted and replaced by the Hebrew "freed by."

As far as we are able to discern, there were no legal inhibitions nor formal discrimination against emancipated slaves. We see them marrying free women, concluding partnerships with freemen involving considerable sums, and appearing as attorneys in court. A former slave married to a freeman would be asked by a court to give her consent to her husband's sale of a house, as would any other wife. Emancipated slaves were imbued with the social and religious notions of the community that they joined. Was emancipation always a blessing for the person concerned? Certainly, the Geniza contains lists in which freed persons receive alms and clothing from the public chest, but this happened as well when the masters of slaves died without having set them free.

NINE

Education and the Professional Class

Preliminary Considerations

Study was considered an act of devotion. To give as much time as possible to the reading and discussion of holy texts was religiously meritorious, and the reputation of being versed in them was a mark of honor, coveted not only by members of the professional class, but by any respectable citizen. No one could aspire to communal leadership without a certain degree of erudition. This popular attitude toward learning and scholarship, inculcated by the biblical commandment "This book of the Torah shall never depart out of your mouth, but you shall study it day and night" (Joshua 1:8, incorporated in the daily prayer), had a salutary effect on the whole process of education. Parents everywhere were bound by religious injunctions and the pressure of society to send their children to school, at least for a number of years. The community made strenuous efforts to provide education for orphans and the children of the poor. Adults tried to devote at least a fraction of their spare time to the regular study of the sources of their religion. The maintenance of the higher seats of learning was a concern for all; donations were solicited and collected on their behalf in countries far away, as when the Jews of Spain and North Africa contributed regularly to the upkeep of the yeshivas in Baghdad, or the Jews of southern Italy supported the scholars of Jerusalem. Honorific titles from those institutions of learning were eagerly sought after, but they were by no means awarded indiscriminately. It is noteworthy that, as far as we know, during the classical Geniza period, the title *ḥāvēr*, or member of the yeshiva, was bestowed only on persons renowned for some measure of learning.

In view of this state of affairs, it is easy to understand why there was no rigid distinction between scholars and persons in economic vocations. A learned merchant could easily become a full-time judge or teacher, while religious functionaries would sometimes do business or even engage in some manual occupation. Nevertheless, although the demarcation lines were fluid, there existed a class of professionals serving as judges, notaries, teachers, cantors, or in various other capacities. These "servants of the community," as they were called, received salaries and other emoluments from public and private funds, but their position was often precarious because of the institutional weaknesses or the vicissitudes of fortune of the organizations they served.

Secular education was the preserve of the well-to-do. There were two paths: scientific-philosophical and literary-administrative. The first prepared for the medical profession, the second for government service. The former constituted a well-organized and long-established course of studies (which originated in pre-Islamic times); training was acquired not only through private instruction and reading but partly also through public institutions attached to the hospitals. The training of the government official, the *kātib* (lit., scribe), entailed the study of Arabic calligraphy, language, and some literature, and probably also the study of some of the encyclopedias and handbooks of administration written for the use of the scribes. It was an art or technique rather than a science, and although it sometimes led to high social positions, it lacked the prestige conveyed by the study of philosophy, medicine, and related subjects. The Arabic term *ḥakīm* (learned) was the word commonly used for "physician" but also to designate a man of philosophical erudition in general.

It was characteristic of the classical Geniza period that religious and legal erudition was often combined with philosophic and scientific training. The most famous examples are the great Spanish philosopher Ibn Rushd (Averroes, 1126–98), who served as chief qāḍī in Cordoba, and his contemporary Moses Maimonides (1135–1204). Maimonides was born in the same city as Ibn Rushd, but spent most of his life in Egypt. His compendium of Jewish religious law was a magnum opus of the same high caliber as his philosophical work, and he also wrote books on medicine. The Geniza proves that Maimonides' combination of religious and secular scholarship was by no means exceptional. On the other hand, only rarely do we find in our documents a *kātib*, or government official, who is renowned also as a religious scholar. The illustrious example of Samuel ha-Nagid of Granada (993–1056), who was a vizier and general, a prolific poet and litterateur, and at the same time an authority on Jewish religious law, has no counterpart in the Islamic East.

In general, we have to keep in mind that the cultural climate varied considerably from one country to another. Of all the countries represented in the Geniza papers, Egypt was the least favorable for the pursuit of scholarly studies. Had a geniza been found in Cordoba or Qayrawān, the standards of education discernible in it certainly would have been much different from those that appear in the Cairo Geniza. Learned immigrants to Egypt by far surpassed the indigenous scholars in both erudition and number. It is for this reason, however, that the general level of culture in the Mediterranean basin is perhaps more evident from the Cairo Geniza than it would have been from a hoard of manuscripts found in a more intellectually creative but less cosmopolitan center than the capital of Egypt.

Owing to its religious character, education in medieval times was more closely connected than other domains of social life with the specific tenets, ritual, and literature of each community. In this discussion, an attempt is made to distinguish, to the extent possible, the specifically Jewish aspects of education, although inherently there is no bright line between Jewish education and general education. The details given here for one educational system prevailing in Mediterranean countries during the High Middle Ages are of great interest, however, for the study of education in that time and area in general.

Elementary Education

Elementary education was universal to a very remarkable degree, but the standards at that level seem to have been rather poor, the result of then current educational theory. Despite the enormous attention in talmudic literature to the subject of children, childhood in general was regarded as a state of imperfection. To occupy oneself with minors was almost degradation. This notion was characteristic of education as well — it was believed that knowing a text by heart must precede its understanding; as childhood was in any case only a preparatory stage, the pupil spent most of his time memorizing. The practice was not without purpose. In ancient times, when the sacred texts were only imperfectly rendered in writing, memorization at an early age was the sole means of preserving their exact reading and cantillation. This notion is the original import of the talmudic saying, so often repeated today, "The world exists solely through the breath of the schoolchildren." By the time of the Geniza records, however, refined methods of noting the pronunciation and cantillation of the biblical text had been developed, so that there was no longer any need to safeguard its preservation by memorizing. Nevertheless, the old and redundant system endured in many Oriental countries as late as the twentieth century.

The main aim of the school was to prepare its pupils to take an active part in the synagogue service. In this respect, it fulfilled a function similar to that of the Song School of contemporaneous northern Europe, in which church chant was the most prominent part of the curriculum. To be sure, the requirements of the synagogue service in those days were exacting: The Five Books of Moses (the Pentateuch) were read in their entirety from a sacred scroll, which, as today, was written in the ancient fashion without vowels or signs for cantillation; a man called up to read a section had to know it more or less by heart. Similarly, each member wishing to participate had to be fluent in the readings from the Prophets, as well as the *Targūms*, the Aramaic translations of the Hebrew Bible. A boy chanting the Targūm "on the Torah"—that is, translating into Aramaic the Hebrew lection read by an adult verse by verse—was the pride of his parents. The poetical insertions into the official text of the synagogue liturgy, whose correct chanting must have been difficult even for adults, were studied in school. The regular prayers, however, although extensive and complex, are nowhere mentioned as a school subject. The boys obviously were expected to grasp texts by listening and responding while regularly attending synagogue with their fathers. In Oriental rites, it should be noted, virtually the entire liturgy is chanted aloud (European custom favors silent reading). Christian elementary education in the East was very much like that of the Jews. A *katholikos*, the head of the Nestorian Church, reported that schoolboys learned the Pentateuch, the Prophets, the Psalms, and the liturgy; when they reached the New Testament, they left school. Understandably, the *katholikos* changed the order of the texts to be learned to better suit the specific needs of Christian education, but the texts used in the church service remained the exclusive object of study. As is well known, the Muslim elementary school, the *kuttāb*, is similarly devoted to the memorizing of the Qur'ān. It is noteworthy that the Geniza papers use the word "kuttāb" also with reference to Jewish schools.

There is one bright side to this rather dour picture of medieval elementary education. The boys had a good incentive for learning, for they could put the scanty knowledge acquired in school to immediate use. During the weekend, a father would check the progress of his son and, if the result was satisfactory, he would proudly ascend with him to the anbōl, the elevated platform in the center of the synagogue, where the boy would chant the section of the weekly lection apportioned to his father, or the Targūm, its Aramaic translation. Certain parts of the liturgy were reserved for recitation by a boy. Sometimes he would be given the honor of chanting of the whole scripture portion of a service, such as the reading of the Book of Esther—no small feat; for such an honor, a large donation had to be made to the congregation. The Geniza has preserved a lovely story from a little town in Lower Egypt, where a mother, with the help of her daughter, buys this honor for her son for forty dirhems; the father obviously balked at the price.

The syllabus of the elementary school was not universally confined to religious subjects. A well-known ruling of Hay Gaon (d. 1038) reads: "It is permitted to teach Arabic calligraphy and arithmetic in the synagogue together with the sacred law. Non-Jewish children may also study in the synagogue for the sake of good relationship with the neighbors, although this is not desirable." Since gentile children could hardly have been expected to memorize Hebrew religious texts, secular subjects must have taken up considerable time in schools. (That very issue was the subject of Hay Goan's ruling.) The caliph al-Mutawakkil, who enacted harsh measures against Christians and Jews, in 850 prohibited the admission of non-Muslim children to Muslim schools or their teaching by Muslim private tutors. Similar prohibitions appear in Arabic literature both before and after that time, an indication that confessional segregation certainly was not strictly adhered to.

References to the study of Arabic calligraphy by children are frequent, but mention of the study of arithmetic is scarce. The absence of documents on the teaching of arithmetic at the elementary stage is probably to be explained by the fact that computation was learned without the use of textbooks; so suggest the accounts found in the Geniza in which long series of numbers are added or subtracted without any apparent use of notations. Hebrew and Coptic numerals, which are used exclusively in the Geniza papers, do not lend themselves easily to written arithmetical operations; it is easy to overlook the fact that although Arabic numerals had been in use in scientific works since early Islamic times, merchants and other people engaged in economic life in the Arab world continued to use the impractical Coptic (originally Greek) signs for numbers until the modern age.

Exercise books found in the Geniza show that reading was taught in elementary schools by the tedious method of learning the individual letters (and many other symbols used in Hebrew) and their various combinations. There must have been some teachers who, like modern educators, taught reading without phonetics, using whole words and short sentences. We know this from a learned opinion, given by the renowned Spanish-Jewish scholar, Isaac b. Samuel, who served as a judge in Fustat around 1100. (The scholarly judge, of course, condemned this innovation, which was soon forgotten.) The ancient method of studying Hebrew continues to this day, as students learn to combine letters, then to form words, and then to recite whole sentences without any understanding of their meaning.

Teachers had means to make the children's first year at school more cheerful: playful exercises were used as a help to study. The teacher would draw large and elaborate calligraphic outlines of the letters, and the children would fill them in with red, brown, green and other colors; or the children would draw in various colors the outlines of letters written artistically by the teacher. The same method was followed to write combinations of letters or verses or passages from the scriptures and moral sayings. The covers of the Geniza exercise books are often decorated with drawings—in one case, eight intertwined snakes with heads of fishes or birds. Ornaments in different colors—for example, the six-cornered star of David (which at that time was not a specifically Jewish emblem) or a candelabrum with seven arms (which was)—sometimes embellish the inside. It seems that the children were sometimes even allowed to give free rein to their imagination (or did so without permission). On one page of an exercise book we find, alongside shaky, childish letters, a crude drawing of the sun and a boat on the Nile.

Medieval ideas about the art of writing differed very much from our own. Every schoolboy had to do exercises that consisted of writing the letters of the alphabet on a wooden board. These exercises were not an end in themselves, but solely a means to learn to read. Having mastered reading, pupils did not pursue the art of writing any further in the regular elementary school.

Therefore, we find in the Geniza hundreds of signatures on documents not in the cursive script used in everday writing but rather in the monumental *ductus* common in books—and mostly in very shaky and awkward shapes. These were the signatures of artisans and shopkeepers of low standing, who had not gone beyond the elementary stage of schooling. It is not surprising that a query was submitted to Maimonides about persons signing documents that they were unable to read. Documents were normally written in the cursive script, which these persons had not learned. Only at a higher stage of schooling was the art of writing taught systematically, and only future government officials, religious scholars, and merchants were trained in calligraphy. Thus, the art of writing—not of reading, which was far more widespread—was the distinctive mark of a person belonging to the professional or higher classes.

Still, not every Jewish merchant of the Geniza period, even one engaged in overseas trade, was versed in Arabic calligraphy. The writer of a letter in good Arabic style and orderly Hebrew characters asks his correspondent not to use Arabic script (as he did in previous letters). Unable to read Arabic script, the writer has to trouble a friend to read him the letters; sometimes he forgets what he has heard. We are informed that one important Muslim trader and shipowner did not know how to read or write at all. We should not, however, take letters written by a person other than the sender as evidence of the sender's illiteracy. At home, important merchants employed one or several clerks; in their travels they would ask a friend with a good hand to take down their letters. We frequently find a calligraphic letter sent from abroad concluded by personal greetings of the copyist to the addressee, or followed by a postscript in the sender's own, impatient script (which sometimes makes for very difficult reading indeed).

We can form some idea of the courses in "Arabic and Hebrew script" from the material found in the Geniza. Numerous fragmentary copies of correspondence indicate that the boys were trained in copying model letters. The artistic products of Arabic litterateurs, although not entirely absent from the Geniza, would not ordinarily have served as models; we do not in any event find their example followed in the countless letters actually preserved. Rather, the teachers must have adopted a method still practiced at the beginning of the twentieth century in Baghdad (and which, with certain improvements, is even used in contemporary schools of commerce): A teacher would ask merchants of good standing or private persons to furnish him with discarded letters that then were used by his pupils for their exercises in reading and writing. Legal deeds, on the backs of which we find all manner of writings in childish hands (such as verses of poetry or proverbial sayings), most probably served a similar purpose. Most Geniza letters are written in a good and confident style and include many conventional phrases, which also suggests that the art of letter writing was acquired through systematic study.

Each country had its own epistolary style and calligraphy. Letters from Spain are composed almost entirely in classical and very elaborate

Arabic and written in extremely cursive Hebrew characters that make for difficult reading. In Tunisia, Egypt, and Syria, a straightforward standard Arabic is used for the most part, and the script is far more similar to the type used in books, although marked differences in detail are to be noted among these three regions. The language of letters from Yemen is a more flowery (although not classical) Arabic; their Hebrew script, as a rule, is almost ornamental. Similar differences can be observed among the various periods documented in the Geniza papers. Letters written in Arabic script generally show a fairly good style; the Hebrew preambles and the many epistles composed in Hebrew usually indicate full mastery of the literary language. To attain such standards, the writers had to study the grammar and something of the literature of the two languages, demonstrating that the "Arabic and Hebrew script," mentioned in the Geniza letters as a subject studied by boys, comprised much more than mere calligraphy.

Education in general, and elementary education in particular, was affected by the relatively high price of books, all handwritten in those days, of course. In well-to-do households a newborn child would be presented with a copy of the Bible for future use. Various colophons (postscripts to manuscripts) state that the manuscript was written or bought for boys. Tender attachment to the recipient is sometimes apparent in notes on the concluding page of a manuscript (whose purchase, we should remember, required a very considerable expenditure). Private teachers provided their pupils with books, for books were indeed the teachers' "hoes and ploughshares," as Maimonides observed in a learned opinion. Donations of Bible codices were made to synagogues for the use of orphans. Still, there were not enough books to meet the requirements of educating large numbers of students. Therefore, the medieval pedagogues resorted to an ingenious expedient: They taught their pupils to read a text upside down and from the sides, so that four and more children could easily use a single book. In the Jewish community of Yemen, where medieval conditions often prevailed until the middle of the twentieth century, one would often meet persons who could read a text turned upside down with the same ease as right side up.

Life in school is illustrated in a number of Geniza letters, particularly those exchanged between parents and teachers, but occasionally in others as well. Boys had to be dressed in a seemly manner to study the Bible. This detail is often emphasized, as it is in this passage from a letter sent from Damascus in September 1127 to the writer's brother in Fustat: "Your boy Eli is happy with himself and makes happy the heart of others.

He wishes now to be sent to school [*kuttāb*]. In case you are not back in time, please send some appropriate clothing for his body and cover for his head." A turban was an indispensable part of a well-dressed person's apparel; only the lowest of the low would have been content with a skullcap.

Needless to say, boys were sometimes unruly. A teacher writes to a father that his child has been an eager student from the first day of school; another boy (the scoundrel's name is registered, of course) has broken the son's wooden writing board with the connivance of the whole class (who obviously disliked the newcomer's zeal). In a letter written in Arabic characters (so that the boy carrying the message will not be able to read it), a teacher informs a parent that his son Mūsā (Moses), having missed school for a number of days, entered class while the teacher was occupied with another boy. Assigned silent reading, Mūsā finished quickly, and, when asked to repeat his reading, swore he would never read a text more than once and ran off. The teacher ends by stating that only by repeating the biblical text four or five times can one know it by heart (which was, after all, the aim of elementary instruction). The import of this and other letters is, of course, that the parent should impose the punishment that the school is unwilling or unable to inflict. On the other hand, a father sending his two boys to school asks the teacher not to spank the older one for being late; he was studying Arabic at home and it took more time than anticipated. The father asks the teacher not to spank the little one either; he had to wait for his older brother.

With the exception of religious holidays, vacations seem not to have been customary. But it is evident from a number of passages that parents took their children with them when they traveled to attend family events or simply to visit relatives. A married woman invites her brother to her village for a month and adds, "The children, too, will have it better with me here than with you in the kuttāb." Our sources do not show to what extent the elementary school acquainted its pupils with the contents and the import of the sacred books beyond the study of the text. In any event, this was not the basic duty of the teacher; religious and moral education and the higher forms of instruction in general were left to the home. The biblical commandment that makes parents responsible for the religious education of their children (Deuteronomy 6:7; the text is included in the daily morning and evening prayers) was taken literally. The father, and in his absence other relatives, took care of the young until they were able to attend an institute of higher learning or to join the community as members participating fully in its activities. It is against this background that a traveling scholarly person writes to his wife, "Pay special attention to Eli [the youngest boy in the house, it seems], to his food, clothing, and study. Let him stay overnight with his uncle, so that the latter may teach him more than he gets from the teacher, and do not give him a poor education." Obviously, elementary education was regarded as poor without the supplementary education received at home.

The Education of Girls; Women Teachers

The Geniza papers indicate that women, unmarried girls included, attended synagogue regularly. They were confined to a separate gallery, however, which prevented them from taking an active part in the service. Since the practical aim of elementary education was preparation for participating in the synagogue service, it was natural that girls, as a rule, were not sent to school. Various letters addressed to women imply that the recipients could not read and had to rely on male relatives or acquaintances to ascertain their contents. When a woman says in a letter, "I am writing to you," it does not necessarily mean that she has done so with her own hand. At times, the handwriting of the copyist is known to us, and it is evident that the letter was dictated. Nevertheless, the education of girls was by no means entirely neglected. In an interesting letter, in which a teacher describes his difficulties with a particularly unruly boy, we read that the boy's sister also attended the school. A learned opinion of Maimonides, written in his own hand, deals with a class composed entirely of girls. The teacher is blind, and, according to the query addressed to Maimonides, the girls refuse to study with anyone except him. In a letter to the nagid, a woman entrusted with the supervision of orphan girls suggests placing two of them with a woman who will instruct them in female arts like embroidery, while a private instructor will come to the house to teach them the prayers, "so that they should not grow up like wild animals and not even know 'Hear Israel!' [Deuteronomy 6:4–9, the central portion of the daily prayers]."

If such care was taken with orphans, we may assume that even greater attention was paid to the education of more advantaged girls. Samuel the Maghrebi reports in his autobiography that his mother was one of three sisters from Basra in Iraq who were deeply versed in Jewish studies and proficient also in Hebrew calligraphy—a noteworthy accomplishment for nonprofessional people in those days, let alone a woman. The Jewish community in another Iraqi town, Daqūq, was headed by Azarya, "the son of the female copyist." In a beautiful and correctly written Bible codex from Yemen, the copyist, Miriam, the daughter of the famous scribe Benayah, asks for indulgence with regard to any short-comings; she was suckling a baby at the time. The daughter of Samuel b. Eli, the head of the Jewish academy in Baghdad during the years 1164 to 1193, was so learned that she was able to teach her father's students not only the Bible but also the Talmud. (Samuel had no son and was succeeded by the husband of his learned daughter.) In more recent times, it became common practice among Yemenites who had no son to instruct a daughter in higher Jewish subjects, presumably so that they might fulfill the commandment "You shall teach your children."

Under these circumstances it is not surprising that we occasionally find references to women teachers, mostly in lists of persons receiving emoluments or alms from the community. In most cases, the term *muʿallima,* woman teacher, probably designated a teacher of embroidery and other female arts. We possess, nevertheless, a highly detailed legal opinion by Maimonides describing the vicissitudes of a woman who took over the Bible school of her brother ("for she had a knowledge of the Bible") and trained her two sons to become her assistants. Maimonides disparaged the practice of teaching the Bible to women, per-haps illustrating that women instructors in that subject might not in fact have been unusual. When we find, in a slightly earlier period, two teach-ers called "the sons of the *muʿallima,*" it may well be that they were two sons following the profession of their mother. Be that as it may, in many cases it was the mother, and not the father, who looked after the proper education and schooling of their children.

The Economic and Social Position of Teachers in Elementary Education

Schools in the modern sense of the word—institutions comprising a number of teachers and classes of pupils, differentiated according to age and subjects—were unknown. Each teacher *was* the institution, although he or, in certain cases, she, was frequently assisted by a relative: a son by his old father, a brother by his sister, or a mother by her two sons. As in any other economic sphere, a teacher would occasionally perform the task in partnership with a colleague or would be assisted by a "young man," that is, an employee. The teaching took place in three different types of localities: in the synagogue (as in the mosque or the church); in the house of the teacher—most often, it seems, a place rented expressly for that purpose; and, among well-to-do families, in the home of the parents. There were differences between larger and smaller communities. The latter were concerned with simply having a teacher. Therefore, they contracted with an individual, promising him a minimum weekly salary—a promise not always kept. In the larger cities, where there was competition for teaching posts, synagogue buildings were given only to persons approved by the community. Furthermore, the community hired special teachers for orphans and the poor, or paid their fees. Only trustworthy persons were appointed as "teachers of the orphans." It must have been a position of honor, or we would not find persons adding this epithet to their signatures on documents. "Teachers of the orphans" are mentioned in records from Fustat, Jerusalem, Damascus, and Baghdad.

Competition among teachers was keen. A valiant woman teacher, about whom Maimonides was queried, declared in court that she was unable to leave her school (as her husband demanded) even temporarily, although her two sons assisted her, for teaching was not like any other work; if neglected for even one day, it was lost; the parents would not hesitate to send their children to another teacher. Complaints about competition by rival teachers are found in some Geniza letters. This competition also had salutary effects, as it was apt to improve the quality of teaching. Undoubtedly, in larger cities gradation existed among the various schools. When we learn in a list of communal expenses that an orphan was transferred after a few months from one kuttāb to another, it is perhaps correct to assume that his progress in the first prompted the move.

The average tuition, as several official documents tell us, was one-half a dirhem per pupil per week when the community bore the cost. Siblings attending the same school appear to have been granted a reduction. When a provincial town such as al-Maḥalla in Lower Egypt promised to pay its teacher twenty dirhems a week, it was probably done under the assumption that around forty boys would attend his school. When the private teacher in the house of a well-to-do merchant threatened to quit, his salary was raised from ten to fifteen dirhems per week, or one and one-half dinars per month. Thus, he received as much for private lessons as he would have for teaching thirty children in a kuttāb. In addition to the fees, "extras" were vowed by the communities, and presents were given to teachers at holidays—on Hannuka, for example.

Fees were normally paid on Thursday and were thus referred to in the family budget as "the school Thursday." The day was chosen so that teachers could buy provisions for the Sabbath (which began late Friday afternoon) on Thursday night. Sometimes fees were late in coming; we even read that they were once paid after the death of a teacher. Complaints from teachers about their poverty are found on more than one occasion in the Geniza papers. After the holiday vacations, when no classes were held and no fees were collected, a teacher asks for a loan of wheat, or its equivalent in cash, as he has nothing to eat. Even a prominent teacher, one who taught "the sons of the great," had to ask for an advance on two occasions—once after having spent all his savings on doctors and medications during an illness, and once after having paid the poll tax. How are we to interpret these and similar pleas found in our documents? What general conclusions may we draw about the welfare of teachers? It would appear that the economic circumstances of those who earned their living through teaching were mixed, depending particularly upon the background of the individual.

As a rule, the teachers in Egypt were foreigners—refugees driven out of their homeland by war or persecution, or other newcomers who had lost their livelihood through some personal catastrophe. It took some time for displaced persons to find suitable appointments. Not surprisingly, the communities employing them exploited their indigence. We find foreigners as teachers not only in the large cities of Egypt but also in the smaller towns. They came from all over the Mediterranean basin: France, Spain, Sicily, Morocco, Algeria, Tunisia, Tripolitania (Libya), Syria, and even Mosul in Iraq. Palestine contributed the largest number of refugee teachers; it was a center of Hebrew learning, it was Egypt's close neighbor, and, above all, it suffered from incessant warfare and devastation throughout the Geniza period. Despite the overabundant supply of potential instructors, teaching was regarded as a comparatively steady and lucrative source of income. Records expressing satisfaction with the profession are more numerous than the complaints registered above.

Since only persons with a good handwriting could become teachers, some of them, unwilling or unable to find suitable employment in education, served also as scribes—in service either to private persons or to the courts. Some, being distinguished calligraphers, were employed as copyists of books. The profession of copyist was connected with that of bookseller, and we find a number of teachers working in that field. Another profession easily combined with teaching was that of cantor, who led the community in prayer.

Although schoolteachers were not necessarily advanced scholars of religious texts, quite a number of them in the Geniza records are called *talmīd,* (scholar); a few are even described as *ḥāvēr,* a term that corresponds to doctor of law. Personal vicissitudes may have forced persons of higher education to work in elementary schools, but their presence certainly served to enhance the prestige of the teaching profession. In that respect at least, the Jewish teacher was more favored than his Muslim counterpart. The Geniza documents reveal fathers addressing teachers respectfully, not as employer to employee. The communal officials, from the nagid downward, do the same; the letters of the teachers themselves, as a rule, display not only a good knowledge of Arabic and Hebrew but also a certain degree of general culture.

The most secure indication of the comparatively high social position of the teacher in Geniza society is the fact that in many instances persons signing a document add after the names of their fathers the Hebrew word *ha-melammēd* (the teacher). No one would have done so had this occupation not been regarded as a title of honor. Nor would anyone have addressed Ephraim, "the distinguished member of the academy" and leader of the Jews at Fustat during the first half of the eleventh century, as "son of the melammēd Shemarya," had this not been a profession of some status. Perhaps because the general standard of culture was not very high among Egyptian Jews during the Geniza period, schoolteachers—by their very profession, men of some erudition—occupied a higher social position in Egypt than in other, more scholarly, Jewish communities.

Vocational Training and Further Religious Education

It was generally accepted that elementary education was to be complemented by training in a trade or profession. Because a son usually followed his father's vocation, the training could often be given by the father himself. Otherwise, a parent had to bear the expenses of this additional stage of education. Vocational schools, as far as we know, did not exist; instead, renowned craftsmen undertook to train boys in exchange for fees. As in other agreements concerning work, such arrangements with master artisans were likely to have been made orally.

Merchants, especially overseas traders, were forced by the nature of their business to use written records. Consequently, we learn more about initiation into commerce than we do with regard to manual labor. There were different ways to train a novice in business. The most common practice was perhaps to send him to a firm of high repute as a "servant," that is, an employee. Frequently a father would train his own son to be independent by having business friends send modest quantities of goods to the young man, who would deal in them for the sake of learning. Finally, since overseas business was conducted mostly through partnerships, fathers in different countries would allow their sons to engage jointly in businesses of modest size until they became experienced merchants.

Elementary school was also considered a stage preparatory to religious education. Study—the continuous reading and expounding of the Bible and other sacred texts—was a duty incumbent on everyone, and therefore could never be regarded as completed. The house of worship was thus also a house of learning, and the weekly and seasonal days of rest and prayer were devoted in the main to study. Particular care was taken to keep the synagogue illuminated during the night so that everyone who cared to could study at his desired pace and time. Since this positive attitude toward learning was widespread, it was taken more or less for granted that all Jews, regardless of their profession, pursued the study of sacred texts. As a result, the Geniza documents refer to such studies only in exceptional circumstances. Several documents portray the communal strife in the provincial town of al-Maḥalla that occasioned the exit of the dayyān Joseph, the spiritual leader of the community. In one of these accounts, a complaint is made that the study of the sacred books is being pursued in regular weekday classes; the words of the sacred law, the complainant argues, should be expounded only in the synagogues on Saturdays and holidays. (The frequency of the weekday classes is not indicated in our texts.) Another document on the subject (dated ca. 1240) mentions that, in the absence of his father (who was in hiding for political reasons), the son of a judge in Fustat gave public classes on Sunday and Wednesday nights in addition to Saturdays. The popularity of weekday classes is understandable: Monday and Thursday were the "holy weekdays" in both Judaism and Islam: the preceding nights were therefore by custom devoted to study.

In addition to formal lectures presented by scholars, there were regular and certainly shorter readings connected with the daily service. Notable in this respect is the letter of a traveling husband who tries to impress upon his wife that only knowledge acquired at a young age and continuously enlarged throughout life secures an honored position in society. (She had suggested taking a younger son out of school, apparently because the teacher was too strict). The father warmly defends the teacher and encloses a letter to him with the request to pay special attention to the boy, who is of course to remain in the kuttāb. Clearly dissatisfied with their education, the father asks his wife to have his two elder sons attend the synagogue service every morning and evening, "so that study may become habitual with them." The letter suggests that at the time and place concerned, it was customary—as is known from many other communities in later times—to conclude or precede the daily service by a short course of study, or at least, a reading by the community of several passages from a sacred, legal, or edificatory text.

Adult study was not confined to courses given in public. A scholar who has seen hard times reports that he has found favor, love, and honor in the house of Maecenas, where he gives a study course every Saturday. Ten persons attended, which suggests that the classes concluded with congregational prayer (so that the master of the house did not need to go to the synagogue for the afternoon service; he also bought books copied by the scholar). In a short (and incomplete) memorandum of the judge Elijah b. Zechariah to a notable, we learn that both the addressee and his father wished to take a refresher course in some biblical books, but felt somewhat embarrassed to frequent the judge's house for that purpose. The judge assures them that there is no need to undergo the embarrassment, since he is prepared to come to them and offer instruction. However much the notable and his father may have forgotten, the attainments of laymen must sometimes have been truly impressive.

We are able to recognize the scholarly achievements of learned businessmen in several commercial documents. On the reverse sides, the writers—merchants whose handwriting is well known to us—discuss theoretical problems or actual cases to be decided according to the sacred law. Their discussions are on a high level and do not differ in character from legal opinions written by professional scholars. These instances should not be regarded as exceptional. Many letters contain quotations from the Bible, and sometimes also from postbiblical literature, which are by no means mundane, and the poems frequently preceding letters are seldom confined to conventional phrases. Thus, the general standard of education among adults, or rather among middle-class adults, must have been high. Laymen and professional scholars differed with respect to the time that they were able to devote to their studies, as well as the scope of their reading; but the content of their studies was, essentially, the same.

The Organization of Advanced Studies

Jewish higher education in the High Middle Ages was distinguished by organization, subject matter, and method. A clear distinction must be made between the yeshivas of Palestine and Iraq (which were venerable institutions with broad constitutions and semi-legislative prerogatives), and newly created local schools of shorter duration (which mostly centered around a founder and his immediate successors). The yeshiva was originally not an educational institution—at least not for young students. It may well be that "yeshiva" is but a Hebrew version of the Greek Sanhedrin (*synhedrion:* council), frequently mentioned in the New Testament. Literally, it denotes a place in which people sit together, namely, scholars who expound the biblical text and the sacred law (actually or allegedly contained in it), issue authoritative rulings concerning the interpretation and application of the law, and decide legal and religious questions submitted to them. The yeshiva thus united the functions of an academy, a parliament, and a supreme court. To be sure, the members of the yeshiva never regarded themselves as lawmakers, for "the Law is God's" (Deuteronomy 1:17), but by deciding questions of public import by majority vote, they in fact served as a legislative body.

During the Geniza period, the yeshiva still preserved much of its original character, and in official documents it was called "the Great Sanhedrin." During most periods, three yeshivas existed concomitantly, one in Palestine and two in Iraq. The yeshiva of Palestine was called *ḥavūra*, "the Corporation," or *ḥavūrat ha-ṣedeq*, "the Righteous Corporation," referring to a group of scholars qualified to interpret and administer the sacred law who themselves lived according to its strictest standards. Originating in Hellenistic times, the yeshiva had already been in existence as an institution for over thousand years at the beginning of the Geniza period. Learned opinions on civil and ritual law, as well as the expositions of the Bible developed in these houses of learning, were collected around the end of the second century C.E and promulgated in an official corpus, called the Mishnah. The subjects contained in the Mishnah and other works from the Mishnaic period were elaborated and discussed in the yeshivas of Palestine and Babylonia (Iraq) for another two to three centuries. Finally, the material accumulated was assembled in two comprehensive collections—the Palestinian (or Jerusalem) Talmud and the Babylonian Talmud. The Talmud, a term sometimes used to include the Mishnah as well, became the authoritative source of Jewish religion and law and formed the main object of study in the Jewish schools.

Fairly detailed descriptions of the Babylonian yeshivas, dating from the tenth and the twelfth centuries, and responsa emanating from them have been preserved by the thousands. The membership of the yeshiva was limited to seventy, as was the Sanhedrin a thousand years before; there was, however, no limit on the number of scholars attached to it. The students were called "sons of a master," or "sons of the house of their master," for, unlike the scholars, they needed the guidance and supervision of a teacher. The majority of the members and scholars did not live at the yeshiva, but served as community officials, or were even engaged in trade or the professions. Twice a year, however, at the end of the summer and the end of the winter, there was a month of common study, which all were required to attend. The gaon, or head of the academy, would announce which section of the Talmud should be studied by the participants during the intervening months; during the *kalla*, as the month of study was called, the sections were expounded under his personal leadership. While teaching, the gaon was assisted by "interpreters" (*meturgeman* or *turgeman*, an ancient Near Eastern word that has found its way into English as "dragoman"). Originally, turgemans were mere broadcasters who carried the words of the master to a large audience; in the Geniza period they relayed to the gaon the questions raised by the audience.[1]

At the spring kalla, the many questions addressed to the yeshiva from all over the world were discussed by the assembled scholars. Answers could by sent by mail or with merchants who set out from Baghdad immediately after Passover. In Jewish juridical practice, these responsa fulfilled the same functions as do decisions of superior courts in present-day legal practice.

In accordance with the triple role of the yeshiva as high court, educational establishment, and legislative body, it was led by a committee of three, consisting of the gaon; the āv or "father" (the president of the court, who served as the deputy head of the yeshiva); and the scribe. The latter was in charge of formulating the answers to the queries addressed to the yeshiva, and some gaons groomed their sons for advancement to the gaonate by appointing them to this office. As a rule, in addition to the gaon, only the president of the court appears regularly in the letters in which greetings are extended from the staff of the ye-

---

1. Goitein believed that the "announcers" transmitted such questions for the gaon and conveyed his explanations because they themselves were unable to supply the answers. It is possible, however, that they were necessary because the questions and answers could not be heard in a large assembly. The practice was paralleled in the larger mosques, where announcers (*mundādī*) were employed to relay statements from the pulpit to the congregants.

shiva. He was the second in command (as he was in the centuries preceding the Christian era) and normally succeeded the gaon after his death.

Besides the gaon and two assistant dignitaries, the yeshiva was led by scholars styled *rōsh ha-seder*, or head of the row, each of whom was in charge of one of the "rows" (originally seven), in which the members of the academy had their fixed seats in order of precedence. According to the intensity and success of their participation in the activities of the yeshiva, as well as the availability of seats, the members were promoted or demoted and their emoluments increased or decreased. When, during the eleventh through the thirteenth century, Jewish houses of learning sprang up all over the Mediterranean basin, their heads often bore the title "rōsh ha-seder." Various other dignitaries of the Babylonian yeshivas appear in the letters of their heads, especially the *allūf*, or "distinguished member," a title also borne by some prominent alumni in Fustat, Qayrawān, and other cities of the Mediterranean West.

Only persons occupying a seat "in the rows" were supposed to take the floor during learned disputations. Other scholars and the students participated as auditors. They studied in an institution attached to the yeshiva called a *midrāsh*. (This abbreviated term is more common in the Geniza period than the older *bēth ha-midrāsh,* lit., "a place where the Scriptures were expounded," used in the general sense of a school of higher studies). In the letters of the gaons, the heads of these midrāshim appear regularly after the heads of the rows. They are followed by the scholars giving courses for the broader public, and the latter are in turn followed by the "group leaders."

A lower level of teacher in the yeshiva was the *tannā* (lit., repetitor), a person who knew the text of sections of the Mishnah or the Talmud with their correct cantillations by heart and who trained students to memorize them by rote. Cantillation, reciting a text in a singing matter with clear indication of short and long intervals, was of the highest practical importance. Unlike the Bible, the text of the Mishnah and Talmud at the time carried neither punctuation marks nor vowel signs. Therefore, both the pronunciation of the individual words and the correct division of a sentence into its various components depended entirely on the oral tradition, the preservation of which was much helped by the singsong accompanying the recitation. As a rule, the repetitors were not learned men; often, a blind boy with a good memory was trained to perform the task. Even great scholars, though, had occasion to seek the help of these "walking texts" to ascertain the correct reading of a difficult passage.

The Palestinian yeshiva was smaller and of less importance in the classical Geniza period than the Jewish academies of Iraq. It was governed by a board of seven, headed, like the Babylonian yeshivas, by the gaon and the president of the court. The other members, called Third, Fourth, Fifth, and so on, at the death or resignation of their superiors, moved up in strict order of precedence. Therefore, we find in the Geniza papers a person once styled the Sixth and later the Fourth, or another designated Fourth and then Third; or a scholar, first appearing as Fourth, finally advancing to the post of gaon. Sometimes, a dignitary died before he had opportunity to be promoted; his title, let us say the Sixth, would then be used by his descendants as a family name. Important documents were signed by the gaon, the president of the court, and the Third; at public appearances, the Third sat at the gaon's left and the president at his right. The Palestinian yeshiva, like the Babylonian yeshivas, was administered by an executive committee of three, mirrroring the composition of a Jewish court, which was normally composed of three persons. The office of the president of the court was a delegated authority, not an independent position. Naturally, the functioning of this office, like that of any other, depended on the strength of the person occupying it.

During the eighth through the tenth century—the period in which the Jewish ecumenical seats of learning prospered most—Iraq and Iran were among the richest countries of the Islamic realm. They contained a very large Jewish population, which was able to maintain hundreds and even thousands of scholars as community officials or as part-time students. In Palestine, the scholars, as a rule, devoted all their time to study and prayer, living either on donations sent from all over the world to the yeshiva (or to them personally) or on personal savings. The many "fellows of the academy," who lived in Egypt, Syria, and other countries of the Mediterranean, had opportunity to meet during the holy pilgrimage to Jerusalem, which took place during the autumn festivals and culminated in the great assembly held on the Mount of Olives during the Feast of Tabernacles. This assembly decided religious and communal issues and was a counterpart to the spring month of study in Iraq, when the questions addressed to the yeshivas were discussed by the participants.

After the conquest of Jerusalem by the Seljuks in 1071 and before the advent of the Crusaders, the Palestinian yeshiva moved to Tyre, then the most flourishing seaport on the Lebanese coast. After a temporary sojourn in Damascus and other places, the Palestinian yeshiva was then transferred to Fustat in 1127, where it continued to exist for most of the twelfth century, until it was replaced by the school that gathered around the towering personality of Moses Maimonides (d. 1204). Another branch had its seat for some time in Damascus. Maimonides' descendants combined the office of the head of the Egyptian Jews with that of the head of a school, in line with Muslim practice during the same period. One Maimonidean after another assumed his father's post. This endured for five generations until the middle of the fourteenth century.

In accordance with the medieval phenomenon of the "wandering scholar," common to both the Christian and Islamic worlds, the yeshivas of Iraq attracted students from many countries—even those outside the Arabophone orbit, such as France, Italy, and Byzantium. To be sure, only a fraction of the individuals who desired to pursue higher studies had the means and courage to embark on the long journey. Therefore, local schools of higher learning began to appear wherever a large Jewish community had formed; most often these schools gathered around an outstanding teacher. The Geniza records provide information about the circumstances in which these schools were founded—for example the midrāsh of Fustat.

Because of the propinquity of the Palestinian yeshiva, which relied heavily on the Jewish communities of Egypt for its maintenance, there was no strong incentive to have a separate house of higher learning in Fustat. But in the last third of the tenth century, the eclipse of the Palestinian yeshiva coincided with the prominence in Egypt of a great scholar trained in Iraq: Shemarya b. Elhanan. Shemarya, whose father had already been active in Egypt, founded a midrāsh in Fustat, an event perhaps connected with the advent of the Fatimids. Having conquered Egypt, the Shi'ite dynasty made that former province of the Abbasid caliphate the center of a great empire, as well as the fulcrum of intensive, thoroughly organized religious propaganda on behalf of Isma'īlī doctrines. At the same time and place, a Jewish convert from Iraq, Ya'qūb (Jacob) b. Killis, who had become the Fatimid vizier, personally presided over the establishment of what was later to become the famed Muslim university of al-Azhar. Shemarya's son and successor, Elhanan, reports that before al-Ḥākim's persecutions, his midrāsh had been the recipient of a government grant; he himself raised funds in Damascus and Acre from the congregations adhering to the Babylonian rite. It was as though the Alid Fatimids, in an effort to establish the centrality of their newly founded caliphate over their adversaries, the Abbasid caliphs in Iraq, had created a climate for their ambitious minority subjects to follow suit.

Elhanan himself was an ambitious man, and, as a critic recounts in a letter, had his lectures broadcast by a scholar specifically appointed for the task, a custom, prevailing in the yeshivas. Such ambition did not go unnoticed: bans were pronounced against him by several authorities, presumably because he had usurped the prerogatives of the older, well-established higher institutions. When he appeared at one of the yearly assemblies on the Mount of Olives, he was expelled. Recanting immediately, he recognized the authority of the Jerusalem yeshiva. In any event, his school was not a yeshiva, and he himself refers to it in his letters solely as a midrāsh or bēth midrāsh—a college for students.

The curriculum of "students," to be sure, was not limited by subject or bounded by time. By the injunctions of their religion, Jews (like Muslims) engaged in a lifetime of study. As we have noted, the dividing lines between continuing education and higher studies were fluid. It was natural, therefore, to find a son and his father studying together in the same midrāsh, or for a prominent physician to be styled "main speaker and prince of the midrāsh," no doubt because he often took the floor in the learned discussions during or following or a lecture.

The ecumenical yeshivas, however, were not always happy with the establishment of a local midrāsh. The letter critical of Elhanan b. Shemarya cited above emphasizes that it was not so much theoretical knowledge that was essential to the formation of a future scholar, but rather the living tradition which enabled the yeshiva to pass learning on from generation to generation; this tradition included the discussions and methods of reasoning by which the yeshiva's members arrived at their learned opinions and its judges at their legal decisions. To be sure, the methods of the yeshiva also guaranteed a consensus among Jewish scholars and a highly centralized system to make Jewish law applicable to all communities, ensuring thereby a sense of cohesion in a frequently beleaguered people.

Material considerations were also involved in attempts to preserve the authority of the academies. In one of his early letters, Sherira Gaon (in office 967–1006) decried the dangerous competition of the local colleges at a time when the Babylonian yeshivas were faced with financial disaster. "How can you believe," he writes, "that you will remain intact and that your schools will not suffer while the yeshiva goes to pieces? We are your heads, as it is written, 'Your heads—your tribes' [Deuteronomy 29:9—a pun signifying that there are no tribes where there are no heads]. How can a body remain intact when the head is sick! The body follows the head." The gaon then applies to the yeshiva the words of the prophet Haggai (1:9) said with reference to the Temple of Jerusalem, which the Jews, faced with economic difficulties after their return from Babylonia, were loath to complete: "My house lies in ruins while you busy yourselves each with his own house." It would be erroneous, however, to assume, as has so often been done, that the rise of the local midrāshim automatically meant the ruin of the ecumenical yeshivas. In fact, the opposite was the case.

The decline of and final dissolution of the ecumenical yeshivas was the result of regional developments, which no support from afar, financial or spiritual, could permanently remedy. The Abbasid caliphs, centered in Iraq from the outset of the regime in 750 C.E., had been declining in power since the middle of the ninth century. Although the caliph remained the titular head of the Islamic realm, individual provinces became nominally independent, and the army, now led by praetorians, intervened directly in the affairs of court to the point of choosing a ruler to its own liking. The capital city (and indeed the larger region of Iraq) underwent a serious decline, for the province was no longer the fulcrum of an extended and vibrant empire. By 985, Baghdad, was described by the Muslim traveler al-Muqaddasī as a city living on its past reputation. There were moments of revival, but Iraq and western Iran, which in early Islamic times had harbored the majority of the Jewish people, experienced political and economic decline from the ninth century until the Mongol invasions of the thirteenth, which brought the Iraq-based caliphate to an end. The central provinces of the Islamic world thus lost their centrality in the lives of the Jews. The prestige of the ecumenical yeshivas could not be sustained in this increasingly decentralized setting, and so they too became victims of decentralization. Palestine, the scene of incessant warfare, raids, and poorly managed government from the later part of the tenth century, also became unsuitable as a center for Near Eastern Jewry. The yeshiva situated there was forced into exile and dispersed. The growth of the Fatimids, the rival empire to the west, occasioned the migration of Jews and Jewish institutions into new lands governed by vibrant Muslim rulers. It was not lack of support by the Jewish communities of the Diaspora that brought the eclipse of the yeshivas, but rather the imposition of external factors on the former heartland of Jewish settlement in the Near East. Needless to say, the gradual disappearance of the Iraqi institutions necessitated the development of local seats of learning, which were mostly housed in synagogues (but generally not in the main hall, which was reserved for communal prayer). Why was it impossible to sustain the great yeshivas in the realm of the Fatimids—at least during those years when the rival caliphate was not beset by its own internal problems? The failure to duplicate institutions that had apparently thrived in Iraq and Palestine would seem to indicate that the decline of the ecumenical yeshiva is an even more complex story than we have been led to believe. It is a story that still awaits a detailed account.

In any case, much learning was conducted outside formal institutions. Because there were many scholarly persons without any official status, there was much opportunity for private study. A learned merchant would return in the evening to his store, and whoever wished to would assemble there and "read" with him. This occupation was in lieu of other night entertainments such as storytelling and music, also reported in the Geniza records. We even read about a young man who had just married into a Fustat family and who, in addition to attending the local midrāsh, "studied" regularly in private with a learned relative.

The organization of the Jewish houses of learning should be studied in comparison with their contemporary Christian and Muslim counterparts. Muslim higher studies lacked formal organization until approximately 1000 C.E.; each teacher constituted a school of his own. By contrast, the organization of learning in Christendom was conducted within the framework of the Church and the monastic orders. Jewish learning, with its collegial arrangements, seems to represent a middle ground.[2] Despite mutual influences during different historical periods, each system of learning—Christian, Jewish, and Muslim—seems to have developed essentially along its own lines. A more detailed comparative study of educational institutions among the monotheist communities will no doubt yield interesting results.

The Syllabus and Methods
of Higher Learning

A Jewish scholar from Iraq, writing in Egypt around the middle of the twelfth century, described the various stages of study roughly as follows: If we disregard uneducated persons, people can be classified in three categories—the broad public, scholars, and doctors of the law. The public has learned the written and the oral law, namely the Pentateuch and Saadya Gaon's prayerbook (which included as well the

2. The noted Islamic scholar George Makdisi has attempted to link the development of scholasticism in the West with the kind of learning developed in the Islamic East after 1000 C.E. (See generally his *Rise of Humanism in Classical Islam and the Christian* West [Edinburgh, 1990].) His arguments appear, however, at times strained.

religious injunctions connected with prayer and the keeping of the Sabbath and the holidays); the scholars have studied, in addition to the Pentateuch, the other sections of the Bible, as well as the "ordinances," that is, codified law (the work that the writer recommends for the purpose is of enormous length); the doctor of the law is at the highest level, a man who has made himself familiar with the Mishnah, the Talmud, and their commentaries.

While the description fails to do justice to a far more variegated reality, it brings out in clear relief the essential syllabus of Jewish higher studies of the time. A scholar was a man who had studied the entire Bible, in particular the books of the Prophets and the hagiographic books, along with the aids necessary for a proper understanding of their language and meaning. In addition, he had to know religious and civil law. The scholar was able to deliver a sermon, to write a highly literary epistle, and to serve as an assistant judge. A doctor of the law, usually a man bearing the title "member of the academy," had studied the sources of the law and the learned literature expounding them. He was therefore entitled to write a legal opinion on a question addressed to him. Only persons possessing this qualification were appointed to the posts of judges and spiritual leaders in larger communities.

We are in a position to know these courses of study in detail not only from the vast number of books and fragments of books from this period found in the Geniza, but also from the many preserved book lists, which give an idea of the libraries possessed by individual persons and the studies they presumably pursued. From all this material, the following picture emerges:

The study of the Hebrew Bible — together with its commentaries, its translations into Aramaic and Arabic (which also served as commentaries), its homiletic expositions, and the special treatises devoted to it — were the most important constituent of the general curriculum of an educated man. Closely connected with the study of these sources was the study of Hebrew grammar and lexicography and their practical application in writing letters and poems. Many fragments of translations into Arabic of the Bible, commentaries, and treatises give the impression of being notes of students and teachers rather than finished literary products. In this respect, there was a marked difference between the countries represented in the Cairo Geniza and those of central Europe, especially at the turn of the twelfth century. Just as the Christian scholars in Europe began to neglect the study of the Bible because of their preoccupation with scholasticism, so, among European Jews, the importance of Bible study (and with it the study of Hebrew language), gave way to a greater emphasis on the Talmud and cognate disciplines.

A scholarly person also had intimate knowledge of religious and civil law—a familiarity with the law itself, rather than with its ancient sources and intricate explication. Maimonides' famous *Code of Law* was not a "first," as is often erroneously assumed, but rather the crowning achievement of a long line of legal development that had begun among Jewish authorities four hundred years earlier—at the same time that Muslim scholars were trying to codify their own sacred law, and perhaps even a little earlier. During the tenth and eleventh centuries it became the fashion for gaons to write monographs on particular aspects of Jewish law. For the most part, these monographs are written in Arabic and use Muslim legal terms. The didactic character of the monographs gives the impression that they were originally composed as lectures to students, each course term being devoted to one or several special topics. Only a small number of these lecture courses are devoted to religious ritual, such as the liturgy and ritual slaughtering; the vast majority deal with civil law—subjects such as legal formularies, sale, gift, preemption, inheritance, money orders, court procedure, the duties of judges, and similar topics.

There is a good reason for this emphasis on civil law. During the classical Geniza period, Jewish legal practice continued to insist on the ancient principle of collegial courts. Even the smallest matters, as we see in the Geniza documents, were attended to by three judges. This could be achieved only if there existed a considerable supply of laymen reasonably familiar with civil law. It was to these future puisne judges that the lecture courses for everyday law were directed. In this respect as well there was a fundamental difference between the countries of the Geniza area and those of central Europe. Central European Jewish communities, at least during the twelfth century, had only limited legal autonomy. Therefore, the course of higher studies contained little applied civil law. French Jewish scholars, many of whom emigrated to the Levant shortly after 1200, were often more learned talmudists than their eastern colleagues, but because of their lack of training in applied law they made poor judges.

In the East, opinion was also divided as to whether studying handbooks of the sacred law was sufficient preparation for applying the law correctly. The controversies surrounding Maimonides' *Code of Law* are the best indication of this state of affairs. Our documents contain references to disputes of this sort. When a new muqaddam was appointed to the provincial town of al-Maḥalla, he examined the ritual slaughterer, and when he found him merely to have studied a handbook on the subject, disqualified him and relieved him of his post. But the muqaddam then promised to teach him the relevant sections of the Talmud (so that the slaughterer could function effectively in his position).

A similar controversy raged concerning the most advanced stage of higher studies. Since the completion and canonization of the Talmud, both the practice and theory of Jewish sacred law had undergone changes. These changes were largely embodied in the responsa issued by the yeshivas of Iraq and, to a lesser degree, of Palestine. Collections of these opinions appear regularly in the Geniza booklists, and, as their titles show, they were subject to different principles of organization. Either they would bear a general designation, such as "Correspondence with the Academies," or indicate the towns to which the learned opinions had been sent, such as "Answers Given to the Scholars of Qayrawān," or "Questions Asked by the Scholars of Sijilmāsa." The collections identify by name the scholars submitting queries to the heads of the academies or the authorities replying to them. Later, it became standard practice to organize the material according to subject matter. Sometimes an answer would run the length of an entire book.

Wherever feasible, learned opinions were based on detailed discussions of the relevant passages in the talmudic literature, which were usually quoted in full. There thus arose the question of whether a scholar dealing with a problem of the sacred law was bound to consult the ancient sources, or whether it was permitted — or even preferable — to base one's decision on a responsum of the heads of the academies, which, in any case, would quote the pertinent sources. It could be assumed that the material was familiar to learned Jews. Rote learning of the exact wording and cantillation of an ancient text was regarded as a prerequisite — and the only sound method — for its proper interpretation in higher studies, as it was in the elementary school. According to a letter of Sherira Gaon, the interpretation of texts was performed by the students preparing questions at home, which they would ask the teacher in class. When the students failed to compose appropriate questions, the teacher would suggest some of his own. The great responsa literature was mainly a literary product of gaons responding to young scholars who had already left the yeshiva, for the major part of the responsa preserved are answers to theoretical questions arising from the scrutiny of classical texts. The head of the yeshiva would evaluate the acumen of questions received from abroad and mark the progress made. The correspondence with the yeshiva of individual scholars or scholars of a particular city represents a continuous dialogue that includes references to previous letters, sometimes also to those of other scholars forwarded by the writers.

Dictation by the teacher or his "interpreter" was the normal procedure in the Muslim *madrasa,* but not, as far as we know, in the Jewish
schools of higher learning. There, the students kept a personal diary,
called by the ancient Hebrew term *megillat setārīm,* or "secret scroll," in
which they recorded whatever seemed worth noting. When they themselves became masters, some would continue to note their solutions of
problems, or answers to questions addressed to them, or indeed any
other scholarly matter worthy of record.

Although the most prominent contributions to Jewish theology and
philosophy happened to be made by scholars heading the yeshivas, these
subjects seem not to have formed part of the regular syllabus of Jewish
higher studies; rather, they belonged to the domain of secular education.
It was evidently thought that only those preparing themselves for the
medical profession — and therefore familiar with Greek science — stood
in need of philosophical and theological studies: Having been exposed
to another world of thought, it was reasoned that physicians required
protection against foreign influence; hence the need for proper training
in philosophy and theology. Muslim scholars similarly divided learning
into two branches: the Greek and the religious sciences.

Scholars, Judges, Preachers, and Cantors

Professional scholars normally served the community in
one or another capacity. In principle, however, it was not public service
that distinguished them and made them eligible for emoluments from
the communal chest and gifts from private persons; rather, it was the
fact that they devoted time to study which otherwise might be used for
worldly gain. It was for this reason that the community regarded it a
sacred duty to contribute to their upkeep. Under Jewish law, a town (as
opposed to a village) is defined as a place with at least ten *batlānīm,*
"persons who do not work" — men who renounce profitable occupations
(or reduce such activity) for the benefit of study and community service.
In the Geniza papers, these persons were designated as students of the
sacred law, *benē Torah,* literally, "the sons of the Torah."

Spiritual leadership in the Jewish communities of the time was naturally assigned to a ḥāvēr (a member of the yeshiva of Jerusalem) or an
equivalent degree-holder from one of the two yeshivas of Iraq. During
the Geniza period, the terms *rabbī* or *rāv* (master), which in Europe
became the usual title of a Jewish spiritual leader, in the East designated

a prominent scholar whose legal opinions were regarded as authoritative. Despite the frequent occurrence of the title "ḥāvēr" in the Geniza records, not a single certificate testifying to its conferment has thus far been found among them. No doubt such a license was a source of pride both for its bearer and his descendants and was therefore jealously guarded and never discarded in a geniza. Like many treasured items that were passed on from generation to generation, they have become lost to us. Only papers that at one point or another were regarded by their proprietors as without value have been recovered. Yet we are able to form an idea about the contents of such certificates, since references to them are found in other Geniza documents. The act of bestowing the degree was designated by the biblical phrase "laying hands upon the disciple" (Numbers 27:18), which symbolized the transfer of the spirit from the initiated to the uninitiated. (Cf. Numbers 11:17: "I shall take of the spirit which is upon you and shall put it upon them.") The certificate itself was issued in the name of the yeshiva, or, in Babylonian yeshivas, by both the secular head and the exilarch, as well as the academies themselves. The main right conferred on the new member was the license to issue authoritative legal opinions and to act as a judge. As a rule, only persons of advanced age would qualify for such tasks. Actual advancement to membership in the academy was preceded by a period of probation, during which a person was sometimes given the title "fellow designate" or "candidate." Before conferring the degree, the yeshiva considered not only the scholastic attainment of the aspirant, but also his capacity to get along well with people, particularly appropriate in the case of persons who received the title later in life after having engaged in public service.

Describing various occupations of the scholars is rendered more complicated by the fact that one official might carry out tasks normally connected to another office, while persons bearing different designations might fulfill the same function. In the early years of the Geniza period, the spiritual leader of a Jewish community often had no particular designation at all. He was referred to as "the member of academy assigned to [a particular town]." Later on, his most common title was *dayyān* (judge), since presiding over a court handling cases of civil law was the most conspicuous and authoritative aspect of his office. One should bear in mind, however, that the Hebrew term also covers decisions concerning ritual law and even theology.

As a rule, the courts sat only twice a week. Only marriage contracts and divorces were normally dealt with outside the regular court sessions. The dayyān could therefore devote most of his time to study and teach-

ing, regarded as his main duty. "Study," that is, learning in company
with other scholars, "should not be interrupted even for one hour,"
states a letter of the very prominent judge Baruch b. Isaac of Aleppo,
who was active around 1100. When he himself was kept busy with communal affairs (about which we learn from a number of his other letters),
he had his young son substitute for him in the local house of learning.
Some Geniza papers seem to indicate that students and scholars attended
court sessions as part of their regular course of study.

Sermons and public lectures were by no means the exclusive domain
of the dayyān but formed a regular part of his routine work. The large
number of books and homiletics found in the library of the "deputy"
judge of Ṣunbāt (Lower Egypt) in 1150, proves that, even in a little town,
preaching required careful preparation. Moreover, the dayyān was expected to speak at joyous occasions and at funerals, a task he sometimes
regarded as onerous.[3]

In view of the diverse aspects of the office of dayyān or ḥāvēr, it is to
be expected that some should have preferred to specialize in one field
or another. A post that particularly lent itself to specialization was that
of the preacher. While the sermons connected with the regular synagogue service were usually given by the local judge or judges, there were
many occasions for visiting scholars or professional itinerant preachers
to appear before an enlarged audience composed of the members of
more than one congregation. Visiting preachers sometimes represented
a strong moral force: When Abraham Maimonides was asked to excommunicate a preacher from Baghdad who was active in Damascus, where
he had condemned the writings of Moses Maimonides, he refused to
do so, because the man "by his discourses drew the hearts to the fear
and service of God and awoke sinners to repentance."

A successful public lecture by a guest speaker required careful preparation. Various Geniza letters illustrate this fact. One example, puzzling
at first sight, may suffice. Eli b. Amram, the spiritual leader of the Palestinian congregation of Fustat during the third quarter of the eleventh
century, writes to the head of the other congregation that he intended
to invite a distinguished ḥāvēr visiting the city to "beautify" the synagogue on the following Saturday by "a word of the Torah" and asks the
addressee—confirming what was already conveyed to him orally—to
chair the affair. He expects a definite answer so that he may go ahead in
making the necessary arrangements. The astonishing feature of this

---

3. The judge's role in supervising social services and in representing his flock before
the Muslim authorities are discussed in chapter 4.

highly elaborate letter is that it was written at all, for the offices (and homes) of the two dignitaries could not have been more than a few hundred yards apart. No doubt the letter was sent, and a written answer was expected, to make the joint venture official. The lecturers themselves took no chances and sent out personal invitations to notables and religious figures (who do not always seem eager to attend, despite the rabbinic injunction of honoring visiting scholars).

Second in importance to the office of the dayyām was that of the *ḥazzān*, or cantor, who led the community in prayer, but fulfilled many other tasks as well. The extraordinary position of the cantor in the High Middle Ages can be explained by the very nature of Jewish worship. Unlike the brief Muslim prayer, the Jewish service, like its Christian counterpart, was lengthy even on workdays, let alone on Sabbaths, holidays, and special occasions. The official service was freely augmented with poetical renditions, often the literary effort of a local *ḥazzān*, or poet. The texts of the liturgy were chanted by different participants, or responsively by two or more singers, each striving to display his musical talents. Jewish (and Muslim) sacred law provided that every knowledgeable layman was fit to lead a community in prayer, but the Geniza papers show that even small communities had a professional cantor, and often more than one. Five or six cantors or more at a time were not exceptional in the Egyptian capital during the eleventh and twelfth centuries, and two queries addressed to Moses Maimonides prove that several cantors officiated simultaneously during a Sabbath service.

A cantor had to be both literate and musical. He had to be competent in the reading of the Bible sections used during the various different kinds of services, together with their proper cantillation, which varied from occasion to occasion. He also had to be familiar with the many religious injunctions connected with synagogue worship, especially as regards the cantillation and liturgy. With the liturgy still in a very fluid state and the text of the Bible and its cantillation not yet rigidly fixed, a cantor often had to adapt to a new prayerbook.

The correct interpretation of the biblical text as provided by the Arabic translation of Saadya Gaon seems to have been known by the better cantors. A prominent cantor was also expected to be able to compose appropriate poetical additions to the service (songs for weddings and other family feasts, as well as eulogies for the dead), all in Hebrew — and in an elaborate Hebrew at that. Arabic, although freely used even in expounding the Bible or sacred Jewish law, was never admitted as part of the synagogue service (nor of family events that had a religious character). In many liturgical compositions found in the Geniza, the author designates himself as a ḥazzān or is known as such from other sources. Religious poetry itself came to be known during this period as *ḥizāna* in Arabic, or *ḥazzānūth*, the current word in Hebrew for the cantorial art.

Since the erudition needed for the composition of poems was not shared by all, a cantor eager to satisfy the avidity of his congregation for ever new experiences had to select appropriate pieces from the *diwans*, or collections, of famous poets, or receive appropriate material from friends, or rework the creations of fellow cantors. "I have left Damascus," we read in a letter, "and intend to devote myself to the calling of a cantor. For this purpose, I have borrowed the diwans of Solomon the Little [the famous Ibn Gabirol] and of Judah ha-Levi—may their memory be blessed—and made excerpts from them for my use."

Above and beyond his intellectual and musical talents it was the cantor's religiosity and moral conduct that counted. He was the "messenger" who represented his congregation before God, and "a man is judged according to his representative." These talmudic notions were fully active in the Geniza period, to judge from repeated references. This draft of a resolution recommending a cantor for permanent appointment is particularly telling. After stating that the man has been tried out on Sabbaths, workdays, and holidays (in this sequence) and has been found to conform to all the established requirements by the humility and beauty of his reading and the exactness of his rendering of sacred texts, the draft recommends him because of his "love of God, his religiosity, piety, and virtuousness, his pleasant manners, his eagerness to seek knowledge and excellence, and because he is loved by the people for his unblemished conduct, as is known to everyone."

The main source of the cantor's income—if not the major source—was conducting services at weddings, funerals, and other family events. It is difficult to generalize about the economic position of cantors. The voluminous material preserved depicts cantors of widely divergent status. There were well-to-do ḥazzānīm, others who were wretchedly poor, and again others whose fortunes seem to have been extremely unstable. The cantor and scribe Hillel b. Eli, from whose hand we have a number of personal letters, exemplifies the vicissitudes of a cantor's life. He was in service for a prolonged period (at least from 1066 to 1108) and some letters show him enjoying an honored position. But others convey a different impression, particularly one in which he complains of neglect by the community (quoting Isaiah 65:1) and of fearing the tax collector, an indication that he had fallen on bad times.

Like modern virtuosos, cantors traveled from one town or country to another to demonstrate their art and, as reward for their performances, pocketed collections made for them. Private persons would show their enthusiasm for a cantor by dropping into his hand a number of silver pieces, discreetly wrapped in paper. In Fustat one could find cantors from all over the world, including Christian Europe, Spain, and Iran. Foreign cantors appear regularly in the lists of those receiving emoluments from the community. Since the synagogue singers were so large and motley a group, it is understandable that the more serious members of the profession wished to be distinguished from their less-qualified colleagues. A fair number of cantors bore the title "expert" or "certified"; a few were even members of the yeshiva or were otherwise described as scholars. The senior cantor was officially called "the great," not only in large cities like Baghdad or Fustat, but also in provincial towns in Egypt. We also find the title "cantor with tenure"—as opposed to those of minor stature. The cantor of the private synagogue of the nagid was called ḥazzān al-majlis, "the cantor of the audience hall," to be distinguished from ḥazzān ha-keneseth, "the cantor of the synagogue." Cantors were occasionally given honorary epithets, similar in form to those borne by the members of the Jerusalem yeshiva. Such titles were conferred by a nagid or another Jewish authority and also by a local community.

The cantors, as we have seen, were busy travelers, and since they were trained in making public announcements, they were used as official envoys both by the yeshivas and the nagid. Some—perhaps many of them—engaged in commerce on their travels, for travelers in those days normally acted also as carriers of goods. Finally, there was a vast field of activities for cantors, which is perhaps more conspicuous in the Geniza records than it was in reality. The cantor was required to be a linguist. No wonder, then, that he was often entrusted with the formulation of legal deeds and court records. Countless such documents, written and cosigned by cantors, have come down to us from the eleventh through the thirteenth century. This function of court clerk led to many other kinds of employment. Cantors served as puisne judges and were charged with such minor juridical functions as visits to the homes of women who had trouble in their married life. There, the ḥazzān would take down a declaration, which would later be used in court, or receive a power of attorney; he might also be entrusted with restoring marital peace or delivering a bill of divorce (ironically, he also served as matchmaker).

In particular, it was the cantor's duty to formulate and to read out public announcements in the synagogue, including the delicate—and sometimes even dangerous—task of pronouncing the excommunication of a person, a purpose for which solemnly styled formularies were used. Furthermore, he assisted the dayyān and the laymen charged with the social services of the community in their operations—collecting funds for the ransom of captives, for example, or seeing to it that a blind man properly received the share allotted to him from the public chest. (Many lists connected with these works of charity are written in the hands of cantors well known to us.) Some cantors acted during many years as administrators of public property and as treasurers. No wonder, then, that in one document a cantor is described as being in charge of the social services and the prayer (in that order). In smaller places and in the absence of a dayyān or ḥāvēr, the ḥazzān fulfilled the functions of an all-around spiritual and communal leader and was installed or recognized as such by the central authorities. A man wishing to emphasize his loyalty to the Jewish authorities writes: "I never disobey a court [i.e., judge], and not even a cantor in a village."

In Geniza records dated between 1126 and 1226, as well as in a number of undated documents, there appear persons designated as *meshōrēr* a Hebrew term meaning either singer, chorister, or poet. The first meaning is very likely intended, although the word is used twice to mean poet in a letter written in winter 1140/41; the Arabic *shāʿir* (poet) also is attached to some names occurring in the Geniza papers. Details about the function of choristers have thus far not turned up and, unlike the *murahhiṭ,* the writer or singer of liturgical poetry, no meshōrēr is listed as receiving emoluments from the community. In Geniza documents from the fourteenth century, the family name Sōmēkh begins to appear. In Baghdad (where a prominent and extended Jewish family has borne this name from the nineteenth century onwards) the word still designates an assistant cantor who accompanies and complements the main cantor on Sabbaths and holidays. It would be interesting to know where this institution, which is known also in later, European Jewish communities, originated.

A whole group of community officials was entrusted with the implementation of the Jewish dietary laws. This venerable relic from the days of the Temple service requires some explanation. Any partaking of food was regarded as a communion with God, the giver of life, and was therefore preceded by a benediction and followed by grace. The preparation of animal food, which, according to the biblical account, man was allowed to eat only after Noah had used it as an offering, was regulated by minute injunctions, in many ways reminiscent of the ritual observed at sacrifices in the Temple of Jerusalem. The animal had to be killed in a specific, expert way with a razor-edged knife, and a benediction had to be pronounced during the operation, as was the case in Islam. Then the carcass, and in particular the lungs, had to be examined carefully and a large number of greasy substances, minutely specified, had to be removed from various parts of the body together with "the sinew of the hip" (Genesis 33:33). Finally, the meat had to guarded from being contaminated, or mixed with other meat, until it reached the consumer.

Three persons were engaged in this process: the *shohet* (in the Geniza documents most often referred to with Arabic terms), the slaughterer, who performed the ritual killing and also examined the body of the dead animal; the "picker," who identified and pulled out the impure sinews and other taboo parts; and the guard, who watched over the meat. The slaughterer, whose task carried the highest responsibility, and who supervised the pickers and guards, was appointed by the community. In larger cities, however, he is never listed as drawing a remuneration from the public chest; there he was paid by his customers, the butchers, or other private persons. On the other hand, the pickers and guards appear regularly in lists (sometimes four guards are listed at a time), for a guard also had to watch over the milking of goats and cows and the preparation of cheese, processes for which ritual purity was also prescribed.

The office of the religious slaughterer required manual dexterity to make the proper cut, as well as theoretical knowledge derived from the scholarship on the rules of slaughtering. Familiarity with the relevant sections of the Talmud was regarded as obligatory, at least by some. Moreover, a shohet had to be a trustworthy person of good conduct and acceptable to the community. It lies in the nature of such age-old ritual matters that divergent usages and "schools" developed with regard to the office. In western Europe (and of course also in America), most Orthodox Jews do not consume meat from the hindquarter of an animal, and therefore they have no need for the complicated procedures of picking alluded to above; the discarded parts can be sold to gentile butchers. In Muslim lands, the sale of discarded meat was more difficult, though not prohibited by the Muslims, and so picking was economically feasible. Determining proper procedure for certifying *kashruth* varied; matters that were perfectly harmless according to one school or "rite," were absolutely taboo in another. A Palestinian gaon exonerates two slaughterers in Fustat who have been disqualified in the strongest terms by his predecessor; after examining their case, he concludes that they are conscientious and learned persons (they are also cantors) but follow a rite different from that of their accuser. Samuel the Maghrebi, the Jewish apostate who engaged in polemics against his former brethren, heaps scorn on a Jewish scholar, who, on arriving among his coreligionists in a distant locality, refrains from partaking of their meat (so as to appear particularly strict and learned); after much dissension, the scholar ends up as their leader, and his rite is adopted. Samuel's unusually long diatribe on this subject suggests that the overemphasis on ritual taboos might have alienated many Jewish intellectuals in a century when philosophical and scientific debate was a commonplace.

The offices of cantor and ritual slaughterer were often combined—a combination made more plausible by the fact that both required a certain degree of substantive learning, and both were inherently part-time jobs. The combination of shohet and schoolmaster was rare, for the simple reason that the schoolmaster was occupied all day long with his pupils. In smaller localities, which were unable to maintain more than one or two (at most) communal officials, such combinations, which might include the cantor, were more common.

Scribes and Copyists

While knowledge of reading was fairly common, writing was an art acquired by persons with special reason for doing so, mostly, as we have seen, those preparing to become clerks, copyists, scholars, teachers, physicians, or merchants. (In Europe as well diplomatic writing formed a part of the university curriculum during the twelfth and thirteenth centuries.) Good penmanship meant composing regular and pleasing forms of letters, arranging the writing on the page aesthetically, copying with precision, and avoiding errors that would require deletions and corrections. Many persons, particularly judges, were accomplished at calligraphy and gained a part of their livelihood by this art without being designated officially as scribes. Indeed, a number of the most distinguished Jewish judges of the Geniza period also served as court clerks, as evidenced by the many documents that are unquestionably in their handwriting but signed by their colleagues. On the other hand, a number of judges were excellent calligraphers but did not engage in this profession; we have dozens of documents signed by them over a span of thirty or more years, but only two or three are written entirely in their hands, undoubtedly because no court clerk was available. As previously noted, teachers and cantors might also serve as scribes.

There were three formal categories of scribes: first, the government clerk, who was designated by the Arabic term *kātib* and was trained mainly in Arabic script, although some excelled in Hebrew calligraphy as well; second, the Hebrew scribe, who usually knew a smattering of classical Arabic and who could serve as a court clerk, as a writer of business and private correspondence, or as a copyist of books, or a combination of these functions. He was referred to by the general term *sōfēr*, a Hebrew word still common as a family name. Finally, there was the copyist proper, who was called *nāsikh*, an Arabic term applied in particular to experts in the copying of biblical texts (an occupation taken up occasionally by women). The copyists were highly valued specialists. The word "kātib" could also designate any government official, from the head of a department, or a secretary of state, down to the most subordinate amanuensis. The sōfēr was inherently a student of sacred law and therefore had claim on the support of the community and the contributions of pious individuals; we see scribes receiving both forms of funding in the Geniza records. The sōfēr was customarily paid for his services; fees seemed to vary depending on the circumstances and the financial capacities of the parties concerned.

Fees varied; to be sure, they were higher when legal action was involved. Several scribes might be involved in a given transaction. It would appear that, in those circumstances, clerks divided the fees among themselves, irrespective of who did the actual writing. Normally, at least two scribes were attached to a court and also served as its assistant members. Even in the small Jewish port community of Damietta, two persons calling themselves scribes signed a document in 989. From the still smaller town of Sunbāṭ in Lower Egypt, two documents from the year 1149, in beautiful script and well formulated, were written and signed alternatively by two different scribes, one of whom is also called "deputy"—that is, deputy judge. In a large community, such as the one in Fustat, there must always have been one chief court clerk, as the material covering about 240 years (1026–1266) indicates; in each generation, the number of documents drawn up by one individual outnumbers by far those of the other scribes connected with the same court.

The art of the medieval scribe, as evidenced in the Geniza records, deserves detailed study, but can be sketched here only in bare outline. Papyrus, the writing material most commonly used for formal documents during Egyptian antiquity, is entirely unknown in the classical Geniza period, and only a few papyrus fragments, written in Hebrew characters, have been preserved in the Geniza from preceding centuries. Linen as a writing material has turned up thus far only in documents written in India or on the India route. The practice of the Muslim scribes in Egypt (during the thirteenth and fourteenth centuries) of writing marriage contracts on linen seems not to have been imitated by their Jewish colleagues. Vellum and parchment were copiously used and, more rarely, reddish-brown leather. The main writing material, however, was paper, which is preserved in the Geniza in many different types, colors, and shapes. In general, paper was more suitable than vellum for preserving ink, and paper documents from the Geniza remain readable after more than nine hundred years. People must have been sensitive in this matter; one writer using paper of poor quality apologizes for being unable to find better.

Paper was traded in different sizes. Usually, the scribes cut the paper to size according to their needs. They were remarkably dexterous in gauging the precise length of a document or of a letter; usually only a very small part of the page was left blank. The more experienced the scribe, the better use he made of the space at his disposal. Clearly, this was a matter of taste and not simply of thrift. Blank space was regarded as aesthetically offensive. In letters, including official correspondence, more often than not the margins are neatly filled with writing. Having finished a page, the writer would continue in the right margin from the bottom to the top (and often also on the top as well from right to left); only then would he turn over the leaf to continue the text. Narrow margins were preferred in documents. Comparatively little space was left between lines (in some letters virtually none); on the other hand, the spaces might on occasion be three or four times as high as the writing. In both cases, the page gives the impression of an artistic creation, comparable to a carpet or a piece of patterned cloth.

A document was usually written on a single piece of paper in order to prevent fraudulent insertions or omissions; doing so often necessitated the use of long strips of paper. When two, three, or four leaves of paper had to be glued together, the copyist endeavored—and almost invariably succeeded—in arranging his lines in such a way that one line covered the join of two leaves so that the upper part of the letters appeared on the first leaf and the lower on the second. Sometimes, he would also write the word *emeth* (truth), or a similar expression, or sign his name on the margin across the join of the sheets, noting at the end the number of sheets and lines. With these precautions, the different leaves, if separated, could easily be identified as parts of one larger unit.

Discarded paper was reused, especially for documents, but occasionally for letters as well. This practice causes many difficulties for contemporary scholars. Recto and verso are difficult to distinguish. In reusing a sheet, moreover, the writer would cut it according to his needs; often in the process, the date and other valuable elements of the original document are lost. It cannot be emphasized enough that wherever the two pages of a manuscript do not contain a consecutive text or two different texts complete in themselves, their relationship in time, place, and subject matter can be established only by careful study of the internal evidence. Many strange bedfellows have been found together on one Geniza sheet.

Although some scribes prepared (or, as they expressed it, "cooked") their own ink, they most often bought it from a specialist. A wide variety of inks were available, evidenced by individual documents containing texts written by different persons in different places. In the declarations of allegiance to a head of the Jerusalem yeshiva made by community officials in various little towns in Upper Galilee around the middle of the eleventh century, each locality uses an ink of a different color. Generally, a viscous and intensely black ink was used. Another that now appears brown is also quite common.

Unlike the preparation of ink, the proper cutting of the pen was an intrinsic part of the scribal art. Its thickness and the resulting shape of the letters had to accord with the size of the paper, and the harmony reached in this respect (by scribes of whose work we have a sufficient number of different specimens) is often apt to evoke our admiration. Only seldom, when the scribe realized that he would otherwise be unable to finish a document on one page or a long business letter on two pages, would he exchange his heavy-tipped pen for a fine one. Not every reed would do for a good pen. Reeds growing on the shores of Lake Maryūṭ near Alexandria were particularly sought after.

Even in letters and court records, the Palestinian yeshivas and their dependencies used the ancient quadrangular script, which does not lend itself to quick writing. The Babylonian academies, however, developed a very beautiful cursive, which was eventually adopted by most Jewish communities to the exclusion of the quadrangular script; Tunisia, an important seat of Jewish learning dependent on the Babylonian schools, adopted the cursive script early on. In Palestine and Syria, a distinctive, sharp-angled script resembling a synthesis of the new cursive and the old quadrangular evolved during the eleventh century. In Spain more than anywhere else, both Hebrew and cursive acquired a flowing appearance reminiscent of Arabic script. If this theory of the Babylonian origins of Hebrew cursive script is correct, the Jewish academies parallel the role of the European universities in the development of writing.

Surviving documents and letters of the more prominent Geniza scribes are a rich source for the study of the language and style of the scribes from the eleventh to thirteenth century. Four different worlds have blended in their modes of expression. The scribes combine the precision and terseness of the jurists with the matter-of-factness apparent in the correspondence of businessmen; disciples of the great masters of synagogual poetry, the scribes were also heirs to the vast tradition of artistic Arabic letter writing. Naturally, the quality of these documents varied widely with the talents and the erudition of the individual scribes, as well as the subject matter and the circumstances of their composition: In some types of documents, such as powers of attorney and releases, the content is drowned in a flood of legal verbiage. In general, however, the legal deeds are comparatively short and remarkably free of convoluted formulations; the case, as a rule, is stated clearly and completely. In letters written by experts, the introduction, or rather the introductions—for there are often two, one in Hebrew, and one in Arabic—are mostly prolix and extended, often embellished by rhymed prose and sometimes verse (these embellishments are invariably in Hebrew). The subject matter itself, however, is usually presented straightforwardly and concisely, except when politeness prevents the writer from being too blunt, as with requests or refusals, or when the topic itself, such as a formal letter of thanks, requires artistic inventiveness.

For shorter documents, including marriage contracts for people of lower station, rough drafts were normally not made, for paper was expensive. The scribe jotted down the main facts (the trousseau for a marriage, the estate for a claim of inheritance) and then proceeded to make the clean copy. This procedure is evident from many such preserved notes and lists; many documents, moreover, show interlinear text that reflects not only the scribe's corrections of his own omissions, but also the emendations of the clients themselves. All such additions are carefully noted again at the end even of the most modest court record. Longer and more important documents were carefully drafted. The clean copy, however, was not always entrusted to an amanuensis, for "writing is like the countenance of the writer": the man in charge of a case was expected to write the document in his own hand. Better scribes rarely made mistakes, but the documents show an outspoken predilection for variety, unusual, perhaps to a modern sensibility that places high value on rigorous consistency of word usage, particularly in legal documents.

The predilection for variety may be confusing to contemporary readers, especially as regards names. Both Arabic and Hebrew names might include patronymics, proper names, names of descendants, personal or family occupations, and places of birth or adopted habitation. To add to the confusion, Jews retained both Arabic and Hebrew names. The scribes, using this elaborate system of naming, would introduce a person by one name and later refer to him by another not previously mentioned. An individual identified at the beginning of a document as Abū 'l-Faraj (an Arabic patronymic) might appear later as Joshua (a Hebrew proper name): a Japheth (Hebrew) as Ḥasan (Arabic), an ʿImrān as ʿUmayra, a Solomon as Salmān (1049), an ʿAllūn as Eli (1057), an Azhar as Yāʾīr (1072), and a Bū Najm as Hillel (1207). These Arabic-Hebrew equivalents were hardly consistent: The most common equivalent of Abū 'l-Faraj was not Joshua, but Yeshūʿā, and the Hebrew name Solomon might be rendered in Arabic by Salāma or Sulaymān or even Tamīm (which was believed to express the meaning of the Hebrew name). Variation was therefore conducive to ambiguity. An inconsistency in spelling, even of the best scribes, is equally noteworthy. Even a scribe of the caliber of Hillel b. Eli would spell the same word in two adjacent lines in two different ways.

Copyists constituted a class by themselves, although judges, teachers, and cantors also copied books. It seems strange that the work of the copyist, which required both knowledge and skill, was one of the worst-paid occupations, for the civilization of the period was decidedly bookish, and books were a much sought-after article—even in commerce. Most often, the scribe was merely a wage earner. As in other agreements on work that involved raw material, the material—in this case, the vellum or the paper—was furnished by the employer. Unlike other piecework, however, it must have been customary to remunerate the scribe partly in advance, or, as stated in one letter, to make him a "gift" against the promise to copy the book ordered. At least this custom is presupposed in the records dealing with this matter found thus far.

Scribes seem to have transmitted their art to their descendants even more frequently than was the rule in other occupations. In the colophons of books it is not uncommon to find the copyist mentioning his forefathers back to the seventh or eighth generation. Sometimes when we have a sufficient number of writings in the hands of a father, a son, and a grandson, we can trace the tradition in the writing style. It was not so much the blood relationship that counted, but the power of actual tradition. The tradition is not, however, universal: the handwritings of Moses Maimonides' son, grandson, and other descendants differ very much from his own; presumably each learned the art of writing not from his father, but from teachers using the style of their own time. But Maimonides (at his best) and his brother David have an almost identical handwriting, suggesting with a reasonable certainty that they were taught in the same school.[4]

4. The community was also served by other professionals — doctors, pharmacists, perfumers, and the like, and the Geniza documents are particularly rich in describing these professions. Such a survey, however, lies outside the scope and intent of this abridgment. For further details on these specialities, readers should consult the original version of *A Mediterranean Society* (in particular, vol. 3: 240–72). It is worth noting however, in the context of the discussion preceding, that specific professions frequently went hand in hand with others: Medical practitioners, for example, were often communal leaders learned in Jewish law; some were leading philosophers, while others were more narrowly trained specialists.

TEN

Interfaith Relations

Group Consciousness and Discrimination

Religious minorities formed a state within the state, by law as well as in fact. The adherents of another faith were not necessarily enemies, but they were certainly regarded as distinctly different. The contrast between Jews, Christians, and Muslims was profound because each of the three monotheistic religions claimed to be the sole possessor of the full truth. The very existence of other religions was a challenge or even an affront. In view of these facts, the modern term "discrimination" can be applied to the Middle Ages only in a qualified sense. When, in some modern societies, aliens are treated differently from citizens—as regards the right to employment, for example—they are, technically speaking, not being discriminated against, but are so treated because they do not share the financial and other responsibilities of citizens or permanent residents. Similarly, Christians and Jews under Islam regarded it as natural, albeit burdensome, that certain restrictions were imposed on them by the Muslim community in whose midst they lived but to which they did not belong. They too in a sense discriminated against Muslims. Thus, as a rule, they would certainly not have felt themselves obliged to provide for the poor of the Muslims or to ransom their captives. On the other hand, the minority groups lived amidst the majority; they were bound together by the same economy and were subjects of the same ruling authority. In sum, they shared similar burdens and were often exposed to a similar fate. Muslims, Christians, and

Jews formed discrete communities of their own, but in every country they shared a *waṭan*—homeland—in common.

Since the Geniza documents consist mostly of transactions or correspondence between Jews, it is natural that interfaith relations should occupy a less conspicuous place than they did in actual life. Nevertheless, various restrictions against the Jews and cases of persecution known to us from literary sources are well illustrated by the Geniza records; at the same time, our documents are also rich in details about close cooperation between the various religious groups. This complex picture should be accepted in general as a true mirror of the real and sometimes ambiguous situation. Despite limitations, the Geniza documents form a rich source of information on interfaith relations and related phenomena.

Intermarriage, of course, was proscribed by both the Church and the Synagogue, while Islam permitted a Muslim male to marry a Christian or Jewish woman. No such marriages, however, are reported or referred to in our documents. The second Fatimid caliph of Egypt, al-ʿAzīz (975–96), had, among others, a Christian wife, but in such cases the female partner normally accepted the religion of the husband. Because of Muslim dietary laws, a Muslim would not partake of a meal with a Christian family (Christians ate "unclean" animals and did not practice ritual slaughter), nor would a Jew eat anywhere outside the Jewish community (Jewish dietary laws were even more stringent than those of the Muslims). One should also bear in mind that in a Christian or Jewish house even a casual visitor would be offered a glass of wine (Jews, however, were restricted in the wines they could drink), while the Muslim middle class, at least, would shun such an open display of disregard for the prohibitions of their religion.

In view of this far-reaching segregation it is not astonishing that the Geniza letters contain practically no reference to the spiritual life of non-Jewish communities. A simple man visiting Tyre at the time of its occupation by the Crusaders adds in Hebrew to his letter written in Arabic, "The Christians here pray in open places." In contrast with Fustat, which was full of churches, but where the Christian service had to be held behind closed doors, the public ceremonies of the Crusaders aroused the astonishment of the visitor from the Egyptian capital, just as their splendor, displayed in the same town, impressed a famous Muslim traveler a few years later. The Geniza letters contain many references to Muslim festivals feasts and the month-long fast of Ramadan but only insofar as Muslim practices had an impact on economic life. Hindu business friends are mentioned with much warmth and are called "brothers," but nowhere do we find any remark about Hindu religion, whose utter difference from anything known to monotheists could not have escaped the notice of merchants from Mediterranean countries. Only at the end of the Middle Ages, when Islamic mysticism exercised a deep influence on the weakened and decimated Jewish community, is the opposition to it found in Judeo-Arabic literature echoed in the Geniza records.

Unlike Europe, where the Jews formed a single and exceedingly small group within a foreign environment, in the world of Islam the detrimental effects of segregation were mitigated by the existence of two minority groups, which, during the Geniza period, were still sizable and influential—even on the conduct of the state. The biblical term for gentile, *goy*, assumed disparaging overtones in Europe; the Geniza documents, with the exception of legal texts, do not have a word for "non-Jew" at all. In the Geniza, the term "goy," as a rule, designates a Muslim, while Christians are identified (without any negative connotation whatsoever) by the biblical word *ārēl*, "uncircumcised." In the same document a writer might use indiscriminately *ārēl* and *naṣrānī* (the Arabic term) for Christians and goy and *muslim* for Muslims. Of a dead Muslim one might write "the goy, may God have mercy upon him," just as one would say of a coreligionist.

Still, hostility directed specifically against the Jewish community was not entirely absent, as some have assumed. Geniza letters have a special word for it, significantly a word not found in the Bible or in talmudic literature, but one seemingly coined and much used in the Geniza period—*sin'ūth*, "hatred"; a Jew-baiter was called *sōnē*, "a hater." It should be noted that the phenomenon of labeling non-Jews as "haters" does not seem to have been widespread; it is mentioned only in connection with certain groups, towns, or persons. Oddly enough, the only religious group described as "haters" are the Isma'īlīs, a Muslim sect usually believed to have been intellectually subtle as regards differences of religion.

It has often been said that it is incorrect to speak about "anti-Semitism" in the Islamic world, since the Arabs, who professed Islam, were Semites themselves. This is a misunderstanding of the history of the term. The word "Semitic" was coined by a German scholar at the end of the eighteenth century for purely linguistic purposes, namely, to designate a group of cognate languages, such as Hebrew, Arabic, and Ethiopic. With the romanticizing of blood and race in the nineteenth century, the idea of a Semitic race was invented and cultivated, in particular to emphasize the inalterable otherness and alien character of Jews living in Europe. Hence the term "anti-Semitism." Although the term is perhaps inappropriate to a medieval Islamic setting, it is used here, to differentiate animosity against Jews from the discrimination practiced by Islam against non-Muslims in general. The Geniza material confirms the existence of a discernible form of anti-Judaism in the time and the place considered here, but that form of "anti-Semitism," if we may use that term, appears to have been local and sporadic, rather than general and endemic.

It is not difficult to explain Jewish "otherness" and what it implied as regards interfaith relations. To be sure, the Jews of the Geniza period did not form or belong to any specific social, economic, or occupational group, but owing to the strict observation of the Sabbath and the dietary laws, they were distinguished markedly and constantly from others in a commonly shared environment. On the other hand, both in number and in power, they fell far behind the numerous and at times very affluent Christian denominations. Therefore it is not surprising that the Jewish communities should have served occasionally as the targets of exploitation and even of assault, particularly when the Muslims themselves felt threatened from perceived breakdowns in their own society or from pressures on their society by intrusive elements. When flourishing Tunisia was laid waste by the bedouin tribes occupying it in the fifties of the eleventh century, the Jews, in addition to being visited by the same catastrophe as their fellow countrymen, were in one city menaced by the native Tunisians with extermination, although the pretext for this threat is not stated. In a time of famine in Egypt, a letter reports from a provincial town that the Jewish houses were plundered every Saturday (to add insult to injury) and its inhabitants accused of hoarding foodstuffs; in reality, they suffered the same privations as the rest of the population (and sometimes more terrible privations). Such references are, however, exceptional. As a rule, Christians and Jews suffered alike under the discriminations imposed on them by Islam. In the case of the great persecution under al-Ḥākim we learn from the Geniza that it was first directed against the Christians alone; only at a later juncture were the Jews affected as well.

Mention has been made before of the restrictions to which the Christian and Jewish houses of worship were subjected. In the decades following the disturbances under al-Ḥākim, the restoration of old synagogues and the building of a new one (in a town where its predecessor had been converted into a mosque) are referred to without mention of any opposition on the part of the Muslim government. When in the 1190s a new synagogue had to be built in Hebron because the old one was in a ruinous state, the Muslim judge declared that al-Malik al-Afḍal, the actual ruler of the Fatimid empire (to which southern Palestine then belonged) would never allow such a violation of Muslim law. The problem was solved by the synagogue being built on a plot conveniently bought from the judge, who was satisfied with the explanation that it was not actually a synagogue, but a residence. (Because Jews were prohibited from riding to worship on Sabbaths and holy days, no cluster of Jewish habitations could be without easy access to a place of prayer.)

In face of this legal situation one wonders what the Christians and Jews did when their congregations increased considerably owing to the influx of coreligionists or for other reasons. The purchase, in 882, of the Church of St. Michael in Fustat by the Jewish newcomers from Iraq and its conversion into the synagogue of the Babylonians is a case in point. The Geniza documents also report the renting of modest buildings for use as assembly halls. One example, a rather curious one, may be summarized here. A building belonging to the government was leased to the Jewish community to serve as their house of worship. The letter reporting this adds that as long as the director of finance of the town was a Muslim, the rent was low, for that pious man, as is expressly stated, did not want to be exacting with regard to a place of prayer.

Worship by non-Muslim denominations under Islam had to be inconspicuous and was confined to church and synagogue buildings. Only one exception, a privilege referred to in numerous published and unpublished Geniza letters, is known from this period as regards the Jewish religion: the yearly procession through Jerusalem and up to the Mount of Olives, which took place on the seventh day of the autumnal Feast of Tabernacles. "All the pilgrims circumambulate the gates of the Temple area and recite the communal prayer and then proceed singing up to the Mount of Olives and line up there viewing the Temple, all this with no interference." This privilege, as the source emphasizes, was not given free of charge; it was secured every year by heavy payments "to the rulers of the city and its young men."

The Christians enjoyed similar privileges, especially in the tenth and eleventh centuries. One must bear in mind that some of the Christian holidays were essentially revivals of popular ancient Near Eastern festivals; often the whole Muslim population, including the courts of the caliphs and governors, participated in full—despite the protests of Muslim religious scholars. In Fustat, the night of Epiphany, famous all over the Muslim world for its carnival-like entertainments, was enjoyed by Muslims. We know much about these popular feasts from Muslim sources, but no reference has been found thus far in the Geniza, although, to cite one example, the Christian feast of the visit to the alleged prison of Joseph in Gizeh, a suburb of Cairo, could as easily have been shared by Jews as it was by Muslims.

There was one type of religious ceremony that neither Christians nor Jews could avoid displaying in public: accompanying the dead to their final rest. Funeral processions were the target of mob attacks and of restrictions by the authorities. Around 1123, a Fatimid vizier decreed that Jewish (and presumably also Christian) funerals should be held only during nighttime — shortly before daybreak, to be more precise. Since we have from the same period a charter (dated 1138) given to the Christians of Iraq assuring them that their ways of interring their dead would be respected, we may assume that interference in the burials of non-Muslims was widespread. It is attested by the Geniza documents also for Jerusalem and Ramle, then the capital of Palestine. The wording of the Iraqi charter might have been intended to grant protection from still another insult directed against the dead of the non-Muslims: the destruction of, or the prohibition against erecting, tombstones and memorial monuments. The Fatimid vizier alluded to above tried to implement both restrictions, but his time in office was limited. In any case, there are so many references in the Geniza material to large and impressive burial ceremonies (attended by wailing women and so forth), as well as to the erection of tombstones, that the restrictions and humiliations should be regarded as intermittent rather than relentless.

The most conspicuous aspect of discrimination against non-Muslims was the obligation to wear apparel that marked them as being different from Muslims. They were forced to wear a badge of a certain color, a particular type of belt or headgear, and, in general, to be content with modest clothing as befitting a subject population. Countless references to this imposition are found in Arabic literary sources. The Geniza documents prove, however, that practice during the Fatimid and early Ayyubid periods must have differed widely from theory. Perhaps no subject is referred to so frequently in the Geniza documents as clothing, but nowhere do we find any allusion to a specific "Jewish" attire. On the contrary, there is much indirect evidence that there was none. A Jewish girl who had an affair with a Christian doctor was regarded by her fellow Jews as Muslim, which could not have been possible if her clothing marked her as a Jew. Nor can we assume that the young lady disguised herself purposely, for such an important detail would not have been omitted in a legal document, particularly since her accusers were Muslims. Accounts of Jews who had passed for Muslims similarly bear witness to laxness in enforcing the dress code, if indeed it was ever enforced on a regular basis. It would appear that when Muslim authorities were strapped for financial resources, they threatened Jews (and Christians) with distinctive dress codes and then allowed the minorities to buy their way out of that inconvenience. The situation in Baghdad (1121), described in our sources, is a case in point:

[The vizier] decreed that they should wear two yellow badges, one on the headgear and one on the neck. Furthermore, each Jew should have hanging on his neck a piece of lead weighing one dirhem [approximately 3.125 grams], on which the word *dhimmī* [non-Muslim] was engraved. He also should wear a belt around his waist. On the women two distinctive signs were imposed. They should wear one red and one black shoe and have a small brass bell on their necks or shoes to distinguish them from Muslim women. The vizier appointed Muslim thugs to supervise the Jewish males and brutish Muslim women to watch over the females, while subjecting them to curses and humiliations. The Muslims then mocked the Jews, as the mob and their youngsters beat them throughout the streets of Baghdad.

After having been treated in this way, the non-Muslims were prepared to pay the exorbitant sums demanded from them.

Aside from the regulations concerning government service (discussed later in this chapter) and those pertinent to physicians, more honored in the breach than in the observance, Islam left the religious minorities free in their choice and exercise of occupations. In this respect, the position of the Jews in Muslim countries differed markedly from that of their brethren in Europe during the late Middle Ages. The forced restriction of the Jews in Europe to a few base or hateful occupations left them with a stigma that lasted in many parts of that continent well through the end of the nineteenth century and has not been entirely eradicated even today. There was no such policy of occupational discrimination under Islam. Nevertheless, economic discrimination against non-Muslims was exercised in early Islam. In addition to the poll tax, which was often an oppressive burden, religious minorities were required to pay a double rate of customs duties, in imitation of a Byzantine law. This was a very heavy imposition, since custom duties of the time were paid not only at frontiers of countries but at the entrance of any major city. This law, however, was certainly no longer applied in Fatimid times. It was revived by Saladin and must then have been enforced for a while because several references to it from the Ayyubid period are found in the Geniza. But the Geniza records also show that Saladin himself repealed that decree, and it could not have had a lasting detrimental effect on the economic or social position of the non-Muslims.

In short, the position of Christians and Jews under Islam during the period and within the area considered here was both safeguarded and precarious. Islamic law protected life, property, and freedom and, with certain restrictions, granted Jews and Christians the right to exercise their religion. On the other hand, it demanded from them segregation and subservience, conditions that under a weak or cruel government could and did lead to situations bordering on lawlessness and even to outright persecution. During the eleventh, twelfth, and early thirteenth centuries, the protective principles of Islamic law were more conspicuous than its dark side, at least in Egypt. That was in conformity with the general character of the period, in which the predominance of a flourishing middle class and a brisk international trade favored free intercourse between the various sections of the population and engendered a certain reasonableness in behavior.

Interfaith Symbiosis and Cooperation

The massive and reliable testimony of the Geniza documents proves that Muslims, Christians, and Jews lived in close proximity to one another and to a far greater extent than could have been assumed on the basis of literary sources alone. Many neighborhoods were predominantly Jewish, but hardly any were exclusively so. Our documents contain only three references to Jewish "quarters": in Qayrawān (in the mid-eleventh century), in al-Maḥalla (in a document dated 1202), and in Mosul (in a letter dated May 16, 1237).

Our main material on Jewish settlement comes of course from Fustat, where most Jews were concentrated in a few neighborhoods situated within and bordering on the old Byzantine fortress that formed the nucleus of the Muslim city. Jewish houses were also found in other parts of the city, including some fashionable locations; one deed deals with a mansion that had once belonged to the famous vizier Ibn Killis. To the extent that documents indicate boundaries, we see that even in the Jewish neighborhoods, at least half the houses had gentile neighbors.[1] The preponderance of Christians is to be explained by the fact that Christians and Jews had lived in the Roman fortified city before the advent of Islam and remained concentrated in their old quarters so that they could be near their ancient and highly revered houses of worship. References to

1. Without attempting to exhaustively research Jewish settlement patterns, Goitein noted eight cases of Jewish living quarters bordering on Christian property, seven on Muslim property, and five on Christian and Muslim properties.

Muslims and Christians renting houses or apartments from Jews in Fustat (or Jews renting from gentiles) are common.

The close interfaith relations prevailing in Fustat are also reflected by houses and shops held in partnership by members of different religious communities. In houses in which, as it often happened, the various apartments were not entirely separated from one another, social customs could create difficulties between Jews and Muslims; Muslim custom secludes females in a separate section, a custom never accepted by the Jews. Shared living quarters caused much inconvenience to Jewish women and risked the desecration of the Sabbath; for those reasons, the Jewish authorities promulgated a statute forbidding the sale or rent of parts of houses to Muslims. Private persons, too, tried to protect their womenfolk from such inconvenience. When a notable gave a house as a gift to two brothers on condition that a certain woman be permitted to live there, he stipulated a fine of 50 dinars on the recipients if they sold the house to a Muslim during her lifetime (April 1156). A woman who had donated part of a house to the poor and a small house adjacent to it to her housekeeper stipulated that the small house should never be sold to Muslims, since this would be a nuisance for the poor (February–March 1117). Such restrictions naturally had an adverse effect on the price of Jewish property. A query addressed to Maimonides alleges that renting a part of property to Muslims reduced the price to one-third of the real value. Maimonides repeatedly insists on the strict observance of the statute, even in case of property belonging to orphans. He permits an exception solely in years of famine, when individuals were sorely pressed for income. Economic conditions could and did override. In a provincial town, most probably al-Maḥalla, it was forbidden under penalty of excommunication to sell houses situated in the Jewish quarter to a Muslim, but the prohibition was not observed. Even more telling is the fact that the charitable foundation belonging to the Jewish community found itself forced from time to time to rent rooms and apartments to Muslims and Christians. Many such cases are registered in official documents dated 1058 through 1234. Non-Jewish tenants were so common that in an account from spring of 1218 a Christian acted as a collector of the rents.

On the Islamic side, there were no restrictions on non-Muslims in their choice of domicile. This is attested both by literary sources and the Geniza papers. It was only the fanatical sect of the Almoravids of Morocco who did so. A similar decree ascribed to the Fatimid caliph al-Ḥākim with regard to Fustat was either a scholarly back-projection or a failed policy of short duration. Modern-day visitors to the *mellahs*, or Jewish quarters, of Morocco, are reminded that these places are characteristic of the later Middle Ages and not the Geniza period, which came to an end in western North Africa 120 years earlier than in the Muslim East.

Interfaith cooperation in economic matters was even closer among the various religious communities. It is significant that we find commercial partnerships between Jews, Christians, and Muslims, and even with qāḍīs. Some Muslim law schools prohibited such linkings or attached certain restrictions to them. In the eleventh century, however, the period of most of the business papers preserved in the Geniza, no such restrictions are discernible. In many cases Muslims acted as business agents (*wakīl*) for the Jews and Jews as agents for Muslims. The most common form of partnership was the *commenda*, under which one party supplied the capital or goods and the other performed the work. Many such connections were formed between Muslims and Jews, sometimes the former and sometimes the latter providing the capital. Some Islamic law schools deemed participation in one or both activities undesirable or unlawful. But the Geniza documents provide examples for each during the eleventh through the thirteenth century, and a query addressed to a Muslim scholar of the fourteenth century (answered of course in the negative with regard to Muslim participation in joint labor or investment ventures) proves that even in those late and less tolerant times cooperation between followers of different religions was in evidence.

Partnerships in workshops between Jews and gentiles were perhaps no less common than in commercial undertakings, although we hear less of them for the simple reason that craftsmen had little opportunity to write letters that found their way into the Geniza. Such partnerships made it possible for a Jew to keep his shop open on the Sabbath. The following query addressed to Maimonides is instructive in various respects: "What does our master say with regard to partners in a workshop, some being Jews and some Muslims, exercising the same craft? The partners have agreed among themselves that the [gains made on] Friday [the Muslim day of prayer] should go to the Jews and those made on Saturday to the Muslims. The implements of the workshop are held in partnership; the crafts exercised are in one case goldsmithing, in another the making of glass." Maimonides ruled that the arrangement was legal, as long as the Jewish craftsmen did not partake in any profit made on the Sabbath. The law as regards employing a gentile was, however, another matter. One was not permitted to derive any profit from the work done by a gentile employee on the Sabbath. Still, the employment of gentiles by Jews and of Jew by gentiles seems to have been common.

Were there double standards of business ethics, depending on whether dealings were made with members of one's own community or with others? Maimonides, in his *Code of Law*, strictly forbids such dealings, and the Geniza documents in fact contain hardly anything indicative of double standards in doing business. There is even evidence of an occasion when particular care was assigned to the consignments of gentile business friends, but in general, no difference is discernible in the treatment of non-Jews, nor should it be expected in a society in which, as we have seen, business connections among the members of the three denominations were frequent and cordial.

Were Muslim-Jewish-Christian relations confined to economic undertakings, or did the proximity of living quarters and close economic cooperation lead to a degree of social intercourse between the adherents of the three faiths? Particularly noteworthy are the friendly relations between the religious scholars and dignitaries of the various denominations. Throughout the Geniza letters and in the queries addressed to Maimonides and his son Abraham as well as their responsa, the Muslim judges and jurists are referred to reverently and rarely without a comment wishing them temporal or spiritual success or both. Of particular interest is a document showing that Moses Maimonides, Ibn Sanā' al-Mulk (the qāḍī of Cairo and a famous poet [1155–1211]), and a number of other Jewish and Muslim intellectuals interacted closely with one another.

On the other hand, one is left with the impression that Muslims rarely participated in Jewish communal events. There are, nevertheless, reports of extraordinary gatherings. A description of a particularly festive reading of the Esther scroll, in which over eight hundred adult males, both Rabbanites and Karaites, took part, concludes by emphasizing that Muslims, who knew of the story from their own holy book, had been present at what is for Jews always a festive occasion.

Converts and Proselytes

Although Islam objects in principle to compelling "people of the Book" to abdicate their faith, practice did not always follow theory. There were Islamic sects that did not acknowledge, even in principle, the concept of religious freedom. Two severe persecutions, marked by forced conversion to Islam, occurred in the classical Geniza period. The first was instigated by the Fatimid caliph al-Ḥākim. As in the case of the destruction of the houses of worship, his decrees seem to have been directed primarily against Christians. In 1012, according to our sources the fifth year of the measures taken against the Christians, he was still praised in a Hebrew "Scroll" as a just ruler. Later, however, his policies were extended to the Jews as well. We read, in a letter preserved in the Geniza, about Jews who had been forced to adopt Islam, while others preferred death or emigration to Byzantium, Yemen, and other countries. That persecution, however vehement, lasted for only a short period. In documents dated 1016 we already see the rabbinical court of Fustat doing normal business; in any case the forced converts were allowed to return to their religions before the caliph's death in 1121.

Far more dangerous and long lasting was the persecution of Jews by the Almohads, a Muslim sect that took root in North Africa and Spain. Their victories in the Muslim West were accompanied by the widespread killing of Christians, Jews, and dissenting Muslims. Many Jews, given the choice between the sword and Islam, abandoned their religion, and, as a Geniza letter emphasizes, the leader of the community in the Moroccan caravan city of Sijilmāsa was the first to do so. Perhaps the new converts to Islam imagined that they would soon be allowed to return to their faith, as had been the case earlier. As fate had it, the Almohads remained in power for many years, so that there developed a phenomenon of Muslim "crypto-Jews" very much similar to that of the Marranos in Christian Spain of later centuries. In both cases, conversion to the hegemonic faith did not necessarily end the risk of persecution or even death: The hardening of the religious arteries brought on by the Almohads also extended to dissident Muslims and converts to Islam.

Aside from these two persecutions, which have to be regarded as exceptional, no particular pressure to adopt Islam was exercised on the minorities during the Fatimid and Ayyubid periods, although Jews and Christians were, needless to say, encouraged to convert to Islam. Nor were the disabilities of minorities so burdensome as to cause mass conversion. There is, however, some evidence in the Geniza records that there were individual cases of persons from all ranks of society who, for whatever reason, found it more convenient to join the hegemonic religion. Persons living in a foreign country and thus uprooted from their habitual environment were particularly exposed to the lure of the ruling religion. Maimonides, in one of his responsa, calls such occurrences commonplace. Romantic love with a gentile does not seem to have played a major role in conversion.

We do find converts maintaining close relations with their former coreligionists. In the case of high dignitaries, where conversion was a matter mostly of expediency, it is perhaps not astonishing that former

Jews kept up contacts with their previous coreligionists. This is evident from the life story of the Fatimid vizier Ibn Killis. A similar situation, however, prevailed in the lower elements of society. We read about a Jewish silk-weaver employing a Jewish convert to Islam. "A red-haired renegade" is referred to in a letter as conveying a message from a relative. We hear even about a couple of converts who wanted to have their son circumcised according to Jewish practice. One does not find evidence of curses or even derogatory remarks directed at apostates. It is quite probable that converts to Islam did not have easy access to Muslim society, since the basic social unit of the urban Muslims was also the family. There is, then, the possibility that in many if not most cases, first-generation converts associated with other converts and continued to seek social and economic contacts with their former coreligionists.

Three prominent Jews embraced Islam around the middle of the twelfth century: Isaac, the son of the famous (Abraham) ibn Ezra, and a poet in his own right; his teacher, Abū 'l-Barakāt Hibat Allāh (Nethanel, "Gift of God") Awḥad al-Zamān ("The Unique") al-Baghdādī, one of the most original thinkers of the Islamic Middle Ages; and Samuel the Maghrebi, to whom reference has been made before. The stories of these conversions lie outside the scope of this book. Suffice it to say, of the three, only Isaac b. Abraham ibn Ezra, has left his mark in the Geniza records. From them we learn that he was not only the son of a great Jewish author, but also the son-in-law of another, namely the poet laureate Judah ha-Levi, whom he accompanied on his pilgrimage from Spain to the Holy Land in 1140 as far as Egypt, where they parted ways. Isaac proceeded to Baghdad, where he studied under "The Unique." A poem of his, dedicated to his master's philosophical commentary on the Book of Ecclesiastes, completed in 1143, is in fact extant. Isaac returned later to the Jewish faith, claiming in his poems that his conversion to Islam had been a sham. From the same poems it appears, however, that he had not changed faith under duress or because of an affair of heart (as a learned student of medieval Hebrew poetry was inclined to read between the lines of Isaac's poetry). Because apostasy from Islam was punishable by death, Isaac had to travel for his second change of religion to a Christian country, but he soon fell ill. His father, who in those years roamed about France, England, and Italy, rushed to his sickbed, only to watch him die.

Samuel the Maghrebi became a militant Muslim, and his book against his former coreligionists served as a main source for later anti-Jewish Muslim polemics. But Abū 'l Barakāt "The Unique" adopted Islam very late in life and possibly under duress (different reasons are given for his decision: wounded pride, the death of the mother of a sultan whom he had treated, his fear that he would be put to death if captured in battle); his daughters nevertheless remained Jewish. Since the gaon Samuel b. Eli of Baghdad quotes him in his polemic with Maimonides, Abū 'l Barakāt's apostasy may have been taken in stride by his former coreligionists.

The stability of Jewish identity that characterized the Geniza period did not last. With the catastrophic worsening of the legal and actual position of non-Muslims in the late Middle Ages, large-scale conversion to Islam became a significant problem as difficult times occasioned conversion and, with that, the potential loss of crucial numbers.

Legal circumstances worked against conversion from Islam back to Judaism. According to Islamic law, any Muslim renouncing his religion faced a penalty of death. This included, quite naturally, Jews who had converted to Islam. Any non-Muslims who persuaded or aided an apostate to return to their fold exposed themselves to the same punishment. Despite the enormous danger involved, there were, in fact, sporadic cases of Muslims attracted by Judaism, and, as two letters of Maimonides addressed to such converts show, they were usually educated persons deeply interested in religious questions. We learn also that the two converts had to leave their native lands for fear of certain death. In another letter, Maimonides rules that religious propaganda (he uses the phrase "to draw people to our religion") should be spread among Christians but not among Muslims. His reasons, however, are theological, not pragmatic: Since the Christians accept the text of the Old Testament as the unadulterated word of God, it is possible to argue with them about its interpretation; there is no such means of understanding with the Muslims, Maimonides argues, since they take the distortions found in their Qur'ān as genuine revelation.

Maimonides' favorable attitude toward proselytizing is echoed in the Geniza documents, in which converts to Judaism are mentioned far more frequently than Jews adopting Islam. Most of the converts to Judaism were, however, Christians—in particular from Rūm, that is, Byzantium and western Europe. It should be noted that conversion from Christianity to Judaism (and the reverse as well) was prohibited under Islamic law, which permitted no change of faith except to the ruling religion. Still, a Christian source tells us of a Jew who knew how to speak Coptic (which shows that he had lived in an exclusively Christian environment) and adopted the Christian faith in the latter half of the twelfth century. We have no express information about local Christians converting to Judaism.

As a rule, proselytes had to leave their domicile; many were resettled in provincial towns, at a loss of whatever income they had. Private as well as public charity took care of them, as reported in many cases from the Geniza. Of particular interest in this respect is the letter of a former cleric from Europe who expresses his gratitude to a lady providing him with bread; he adds instructions on how to prepare the bread on which he had been nourished in Europe. There is the suggestion that some Christians who converted to Judaism might have done so in order to qualify for charitable aid; proselytes frequently appear in the lists of indigents receiving bread, wheat, and clothing. There were, nevertheless, also proselytes of more affluent means.

The most impressive Geniza document on proselytism is the Hebrew "autobiography" of the Norman cleric Johannes-Obadiah, in which he describes the circumstances under which he embraced Judaism, the dangers to which he was exposed in his country after his conversion, as well as his extended travels among the Jewish communities of the Islamic world. His conversion to Judaism was no doubt due to a certain spiritual crisis, one that affected other Christians in southern Italy, where the Norman nobleman was born and educated, for he reports that, among others, Andreas, the archbishop of the city of Bari had adopted Judaism before him. He describes his conversion as the consequence of a dream he had in his youth when he was still in his father's house. In the dream, he was officiating in the church when he was addressed by a man standing at the altar who recited the following verse from the Book of Joel: "The sun shall be turned into darkness and the moon into blood, before the great and terrible day of the Lord will come" (3:4). Johannes-Obadiah, writing in Hebrew at least twenty years after the event, still quotes the words of this verse in Latin, albeit written in Hebrew characters. There was a common feeling in the Middle Ages that the end of the world was near and the Day of Judgment at hand; that sentiment caused some seekers of God to adopt Judaism, which they came to regard as the original (and thus true) form of monotheism. In any case, Obadiah is moved to comment about messianic strivings among the Jews he encountered.

The conversion to Judaism of Johannes-Obadiah begins in essence with an unsolicited repudiation of Christianity. Similarly, another cleric who converted to Judaism reports that "after having circumcised himself" and beginning to observe "the holidays of God, as they are written in the Torah," as well as the Sabbaths, he wrote fourteen pamphlets in which he assembled all "the questions and arguments" that had induced him to change his religion. He submitted his book to his archbishop

with the request to refute him. Naively he adds that if the church dignitary had only taken the trouble to read the book, he and his fellow
clerics would certainly have been convinced and would have followed
the writer's example. To fortify this claim, he enclosed six of the fourteen
pamphlets (presumably translated from Latin or Greek into Hebrew).
The anonymous cleric was put into prison and threatened with execution or with banishment to an island where he would die if he did not
repent. It is reported that one of the prison guards had an apparition
that induced him to provide for the prisoner's escape, letting him down
from a window with a rope. Needless to say, those who converted to
Judaism out of conviction were the most valuable additions to the community.

ELEVEN

Communal Jurisdiction

The Judiciary

The position of the non-Muslim minorities under Islamic rule is most clearly reflected in their judicial organization. On the one hand, their judiciary derived its authority and executive power to a notable degree from the Muslim government; criminal jurisdiction, and in particular, capital punishment were, as a rule, prerogatives of the state, and any member of the minority groups was free to apply to a Muslim judge instead of to the courts of his own denomination. Yet the wide range of cases brought before the rabbinical courts (as proved by the evidence of the Geniza), as well as the marked divergence of the Jewish judiciary, law, and procedures from Muslim practices is illustrative of the high degree of autonomy enjoyed by the minorities during the period under study.

Legal matters connected directly with religion, such as marriage, divorce, inheritance, and slavery and freedom, were the natural domain of the denominational courts. In addition, there were many good reasons that might induce a Jew or a Christian to seek justice within his own community. Religious law covered every aspect of economic and social life; pious individuals who preferred to be judged according to their own religion had no need to apply to the state courts. Practical considerations were probably even more compelling. Litigation before a Jewish court was inexpensive, no payments being required except a remuneration for the scribe who made out the documents. Application to a state authority, to the contrary, involved, in addition to fees, unofficial payments to underlings and often also costly bribes to those higher up. The members of the Jewish courts were as a rule personally known by the parties, from the synagogue or from elsewhere and in any case were regarded by them as people of their own kind. Finally, litigants themselves frequently had experience on the bench (since laymen could serve as judges), which naturally made them more inclined to entrust their cause to an authority and a procedure with which they were familiar.

Finally, the express injunctions of their own religion and the pressure of their own social group were apt to force a Christian or a Jew to apply to the denominational rather than the Muslim court. Every reader of the New Testament is familiar with the fulminating words of the apostle Paul to the Corinthians (1, 6:1–4): "When one of you has a grievance against a brother, does he dare go to law before the unrighteous instead of the saints? Do you not know that the saints will judge the world? And if the world is to be judged by you, are you incompetent to try trivial cases? If then you have such cases, why do you lay them before those who are least esteemed by the Church?" This attitude (which reveals Paul's Jewish background) remained fundamental in the Church and in the Synagogue throughout the ages and is echoed in many Geniza documents.

The Muslim and Jewish judiciaries differed substantially as to their origin and nature. The Muslim qāḍī was originally the delegate of the caliph or the provincial governor, and, like the governor and the caliph himself, never shared his authority with anyone else. He was free to consult the doctors of law or experts in any other matter, but the decision rested with him alone. His duties and prerogatives were not only judicial but administrative as well. The estates of orphans and other property entrusted to the courts were in his hands. He often combined with his office highly lucrative positions of power — controller of a particular district's revenue or superintendent of a port, for example.

Jewish law was based on the assumption that "none may judge alone save One," namely God. To avoid errors and miscarriages of justice, a court was composed of at least three men. In talmudic times, and perhaps under the influence of later Roman judicial organization, under which the delegate of the provincial governor had a position similar to that held subsequently by the qāḍī in Islam, it became a recognized principle that a person accepted by the community or authorized by the Jewish high court was entitled to render sole judgment. But even such a "generally accepted or authorized judge" was enjoined not to make use of this privilege (which infringed on God's uniqueness) but to associate others with himself. Maimonides incorporates this principle in his *Code of Law* and, as we see from hundreds of Geniza documents, it was widely adhered to in practice.

As a rule, the court records found in the Geniza bear three signatures (and very often more than three). As the names known to us or the form of the signatures show, wherever feasible, persons with learning were co-opted as associate judges. Most records do not indicate who acted as the president of the court, nor are we in a position to know this, for even in a provincial town two or more legal experts were often active at the same time. Particularly instructive in this respect is a dossier of eleven sessions of the rabbinical court of Fustat, held in 1097/98 dealing with a single litigation, in which the same judges appear again and again, but sign in different sequences. During the gaonic period of the Geniza records, that is, the major part of the eleventh century, it seems to have been customary for some presidents of the courts to sign last. This tallies with the fact that in the records preserved from the courts of the gaons—the highest juridical authority—the signatures of gaons appear regularly at the end. In reply to a query referring to this matter, the gaon Solomon b. Judah says expressly: "According to the ceremonial of the Palestinian yeshiva, those who sign first are the lowest in rank; those who sign last are the highest."

Technically speaking, the court records as a rule are not judgments, but rather "testimonies" to depositions by one or more parties or witnesses or to agreements made by (or forced upon) the parties. Since, according to Jewish law, two persons were sufficient as witnesses, we occasionally find only two signatures affixed to a document. Sometimes such a document contains the remark, "We, two out of three, sign herewith," which means that during the procedures themselves three "judges" were present. No substantial differences can be observed between records whose signatories characterize themselves as "witnesses" and those formally signed by a court. Even in the former, the final decision is sometimes introduced by the phrase "we were of the opinion," designating an action by a judge. The most prominent characteristic of the Jewish judiciary was a court composed largely of laymen, who frequently took turns at being judges, for laymen were learned in law; the courts were not always permanent but could be assembled to meet the needs of the moment, and judges could be drawn from the community. Naturally, in an orderly and developed society, no judicial organization is complete without expert judges appointed for life, or at least for some prolonged period. This was the case also in the society represented in the Geniza records. The professional judge was the dayyān, whose course of study and multiple tasks as *muqaddam*, or executive head, of a local community are discussed in chapter 3. It remains for us to define more specifically his role in the administration of justice.

With the exception of Fustat and Ramle, the administrative capital and commercial center of Palestine, a city had only one officially recognized Jewish judge. We read in the Geniza letters about "the" judge of Sijilmāsa, of Barqa in Libya, of "Sicily" (i.e., Palermo), or of Alexandria. In a city like Alexandria several Jewish professional judges were active at a time, but only the chief justice was styled "the court," whereas he would refer to the others as "my colleagues, the judges [*dayyānīm*]." Similarly, in a provincial capital, such as Damietta there would be one person of distinction addressed by his superior, the gaon of Jerusalem, as "court," two others as "judge," and still two others referred to simply as "our master," or "Mr." The title "court" is an abbreviation of "president of the court," and reflects the usage of calling the head of an institution by its name. The main prerogative of an officially appointed judge was the right to interpret the law authoritatively. This does not imply that his rulings were irrevocable; even the decision of a gaon or nagid could be contested by another scholar. As a rule, however, the community over which he had jurisdiction was bound to accept his interpretation of the law and its application to any given case. Likewise, once approached by a party, the opponents could not demand to be judged by another court, although, in principle, the choice of a court was a matter of agreement. In short, "the appointed judge has in his district the same authority as the high court of the yeshiva has over all the community of Israel."

Another confusing aspect of judicial terminology in the Geniza records is the frequent occurrence of the biblical word *shōfēṭ* for judge or leader, especially during the tenth and eleventh centuries. What was its relationship to the terms "court" and dayyān? Possibly the biblical word was revived to serve as the Hebrew equivalent of Arabic *ḥākim*, the general term for a person invested with juridical authority, whether religious or secular. The talmudic title "dayyān" carried with it the connotation of a scholar versed in all aspects of rabbinical law and lore, including ritual and theology. Thus, it could not be applied to a person who, although he might be familiar with Jewish learning, was mainly a community leader and judge in cases of civil and family law. Such a person is clumsily described in an ancient document as "one who occupies himself with the affairs of the community and considers their cases of litigation." The biblical "shōfēṭ" was a conveniently short title for such a person of authority, but, like the Arabic "ḥākim," also designated full-fledged professional judges holding official appointments. The latter usage is attested for the tenth and the first half of the eleventh centuries with regard to Damascus, Ramle, Alexandria, and Fustat, as well as Sijilmāsa. Consequently, the biblical term is also used to designate the Muslim qāḍī — sometimes in the middle of a document or letter written entirely in Arabic.

A shōfēṭ who was not a professional judge or a scholar would be in charge of a community in a smaller town. We find, however, at least three families of shōfēṭs also in Fustat; in these cases, the position was apparently a family sinecure: son, brother, and grandson, successively, held the same office. In addition, the widely dispersed Jews of Yemen were led for a lengthy period by shōfēṭs residing in Sanʿa, then, as today, the capital of the country. During the twelfth century, a time of growing religious consciousness, which was not favorable to the idea of a secular judge, the title fell into disuse. As our documents show, laymen continued to sit on the rabbinical courts after 1200, but we no longer hear about the office of shōfēṭ. The Arabic term "ḥākim" as a designation for Jewish judges (it appears in a document written as early as around 1010) is nevertheless used regularly in the queries addressed to Maimonides in the late twelfth century, as well as in his responsa.

Muslim influence is clearly evident in another term for judge, *nāʾib*, "deputy." The Muslim qāḍī, as stated, was originally a delegate of the caliph or of the provincial governor. He had no authority of his own. Thus we have in Islam the curious situation of the qāḍī who dispensed the heavenly revealed law, to which caliphs and governors, like any other Muslim, owed absolute obedience, and yet he had no independent position, but was subordinate to the state. The term "nāʾib" does not seem to refer to the relationship between judges and state authority; rather it reflects the concept that all the judges of the caliph's realm were only delegates and representatives of the chief justice at the caliphal court. During the heyday of the caliphate, the letter of appointment, say, of the chief judge of Egypt (which was then but a province of the Abbasid Empire) would state that he was installed to represent his superior (who had his seat in Baghdad) in the country of the Nile.

The Geniza records reveal that a similar situation prevailed in the Jewish community. Originally, the local judges were appointed by, and were deputies of, the gaon, the head of the yeshiva — or rather of the president of its high court. Around 1065, when the highest religious authority of the Jews in the Fatimid empire passed from the Palestinian gaonate to the Egyptian nagid, the three Jewish judges of the Egyptian capital made or approved the appointments of the local judges. These judges, as their letters show, brought doubtful cases to the knowledge of their superiors or asked the latter to deal with them in person. As with the Muslim title "qāḍī", the Muslim term "nā'īb" (deputy) was translated into Hebrew. As such, Hebrew *mishne* could designate the president of the high court of a yeshiva, who was but a deputy of the gaon—or the deputy of any other judge, Jewish or Christian.

Besides nomenclature, the Jewish judge had little in common with his Muslim colleague. In the classical Geniza period, the office of the qāḍī was a very lucrative one; it was customary to purchase the office for high sums. Unlike medieval France, however, where similar practices prevailed, the judgeship was not acquired for life. After having paid for his office, the qāḍī could be dismissed after a few years' service—even after a few days. During the four hundred years of Fatimid rule, the average tenure of a qāḍī in the Egyptian capital was five years. Only sixteen out of eighty served until their deaths; the others were discharged, often under humiliating circumstances.

By contrast, the documents signed by the appointed Jewish judges in the capital of Egypt between 965 and 1265 show a remarkable degree of continuity among legal officeholders. The average tenure of a judge seems to have been twenty-five years; the signatures of some appear for over forty years. We have to keep in mind that the preservation of dates on records (they are often effaced or torn away) is entirely fortuitous—as is, of course, the preservation of dated records—so that the actual tenure of a dayyān might have been considerably longer than that indicated by the documents signed by him. Moreover, in many cases we have definite proof of an appointed judge having been in office for a term longer than the surviving documents themselves indicate.

As far as our present knowledge goes, not one of the Jewish chief judges of Fustat and Cairo was dismissed by a gaon or nagid during the classical Geniza period. We find occasionally that a dayyān did not get along well with his flock and resigned his post. In Alexandria we have complaints about dayyānīm over three centuries, but no report about actual dismissals has been found thus far. These complaints are concerned mostly with the dayyān's strictness and overbearing manner, or, on the other hand, with his purported excessive leniency toward the common people. Charges of bribery or other forms of misconduct are extremely rare.

Arabic sources present a somewhat different picture of the Muslim judiciary. Whether we read the great Islamic theologian and teacher of ethics, al-Ghazālī (d. 1111), or the humorous stories and anecdotes of *The*

Arabian Nights, or the quasi-historical works containing the biographies of qāḍīs, we are confronted everywhere with endless charges of venality, embezzlement, and recklessness. Nor are the Geniza documents silent as regards the venality of Muslim judges, although the condemnation of certain qāḍīs is offset by laudatory remarks concerning others. The criticism of Muslim magistrates aside, the institution of the qāḍī was one of the most durable of Islamic civilization. The contrast between the Jewish and Islamic judiciaries should not be ascribed to any substantial difference in the levels of morality of the two societies but, rather, to the entirely different nature of the two offices. Representing state authority (though his judgment was, in principle, independent) the qāḍī held a position of real power that reflected a political appointment; the dayyān owed his authority to his scholarship and acumen. He was a "political" appointee only in the sense that the politics underlying his appointment were religious. The Muslim judge, as we have seen, was an autocrat who alone rendered decisions; the Jewish judge was the member of a court of three, a circumstance that could act as a check on high-handed practices.

Although there are numerous examples of judges being succeeded by their offspring, the Geniza records prove that there was a continuous healthy influx of fresh blood; at least half of the more important Jewish judges in this period were not succeeded by their sons. For example, both positive and negative evidence seems to show that none of the five sons of Aaron b. al-ʿAmmānī, the most prominent Jewish judge in Alexandria during the twelfth century, functioned as dayyān in that city after their father's death. His great-grandson is known from many documents written or signed between 1207 and 1243. He was, however, a notary and puisne judge, not a "court." Occasionally, a grandson would succeed to his grandfather's rank.

The office of notary was not as fully developed in the Jewish community as it was among the Muslims of the time. Rather, the functions of the notary were shared by versatile and learned professionals who already performed a number of communal tasks, especially those that were court related. A good many of the legal documents from Fustat (dated between 1005 and 1135 and not made out by judges) were written by six successive and more or less contemporary court scribes who also served as assistant judges. Most of them were also cantors. The records and deeds dated between approximately 1135 and 1265 were most often written by professional judges, perhaps because the general knowledge of diplomatics had declined somewhat.

Any transaction, including a marriage agreement, required only two witnesses. Therefore the parties needed only to go to a notary's office, where they made the symbolic act of purchase validating legal transactions. At that, the notary drew up the documents, signed them, and had someone else sign in addition to himself. The second signature usually betrays a man not fluent in writing, indicating a witness who is not a professional of the court. The notary would keep a diary in which he entered the main facts of each transaction, as well as the name of the witness who signed with him. In comparison with the many hundreds of court records signed by three or more individuals, deeds made out by notaries are comparatively rare.

The strength of the Jewish court—namely, the plurality of its judges—was also its weakness. Since everyone was busy with his own affairs, it was at times difficult to assemble a representative court. Most of those qualified to serve were heavily engaged in commerce and trade; often they knew the litigants from commercial transactions and were thus called upon to disqualify themselves from making a judgment, lest they be accused of favoritism. Two documents from Fustat, containing similar stories, are most telling in this respect. The first, an unfortunately incomplete court record dating from December 1016, relates that a merchant from Palermo had complained to the police that he had already waited a full month for a Jewish court to deal with his case, whereupon the head of the police commandeered the Jewish judge for a night. In the second document (dating from December 1027), a merchant from Spain was accused of having obtained from the caliphal court a rescript to the qāʾid, or commander (as the governor of the capital was styled then), as a way of obtaining legal satisfaction. The defendant explained that he preferred to be judged by a Jewish court, but that one of the three members of the court that was to judge him (after having heard his case in a previous session), had recused himself as being too busy "and other reasons." It was resolved that if the three judges mentioned would not take up the matter during the following two weeks, each party was free to apply to a government court. During the second part of the eleventh century, when Egypt benefited from a large influx of emigrants and refugees from Palestine and Tunisia, we no longer hear such complaints, at least with respect to the capital. We do, however, see a large number of qualified scholars acting as judges.

Courts exercising judgment in a wide variety of matters and consisting solely of laymen appear in the Geniza documents and in many different localities. During the gaonic period, such courts seem to have been confirmed in their office by the gaons; thus in principle the elders were representatives of the community, which was deemed the supreme judge in accordance with the biblical precept "the people shall judge" (Numbers 35:24). Against this background, an institution of medieval Jewish law that has been much discussed, but about which we know little for the period studied here, takes on particular significance: the right of a complainant who felt unjustly treated to interrupt public prayer, or to prevent its being held altogether, until his or her case was heard. This constituted an appeal to the highest authority, comparable to a man throwing himself before the horse of the caliph or governor in order to draw attention to a wrong done him. The technical term for the procedure was "to call the Jews [or Israel] for help." When the Torah scroll was taken out, the complainant would stand up on the reader's platform and delay the reading of the Torah in order to bring his case before the congregation. In one letter we even read that the writer intended to lock the Torah shrine altogether until his opponent was brought to court. Female "callers for help" are also referred to. It is, however, hardly imaginable (although not entirely excluded) that a woman would enter the men's section and address the persons assembled there. Since the Geniza has preserved eloquently styled and beautifully written appeals to the community by women, it stands to reason that, as a rule, a woman did not address the congregation herself, but her complaint was read out by her representative, be it the scribe or someone else. It was perhaps customary for the complainant to appear in the front of the women's gallery while her plea was read out below.

We are thus obliged to ask whether contemporaneous Jewish society possessed an institution similar to that of the Muslim *muftī*, or jurisconsult, an official who wrote legal opinions and rulings without acting as judge himself. As the wording of many responsa shows, the Jewish scholars cannot have been unfamiliar with the *fatwā*s, or replies, of their Muslim colleagues. Our only concern here is whether there is any indication in the Geniza records of jurisconsults who were not judges. Nahray b. Nissīm, a learned merchant whose preserved archive contains several hundred letters and accounts written by him or addressed to him, was styled "Master" (*rāv*) and "the senior member of the yeshiva." Requests from him for a fatwā (explicitly called thus in one letter) have been preserved, and there are references to other requests for responsa, but not a single court record written or signed by him that would signify he acted as a judge has yet been found. He signed, together with many others, the marriage contract of a friend in 1050 and bore witness, with the same bridegroom, on a document thirty years later. In 1055, a power of attorney was assigned to him — as was done with any respectable citizen — and a letter of his was produced in court in 1075. Nowhere, however, is there any indication that the "great Rāv" functioned as a judge. Similarly, Nahray had a teacher who, like himself, had emigrated from Tunisia to Egypt. This scholar is referred to in numerous letters from the second half of the eleventh century as "the Rāv," but here too there is no reference to that rāv as judge. It should be also noted that Maimonides, who lived for some forty years in the Egyptian capital (ca. 1165–1204), has not left a single court record signed by him in the Geniza, although many other writings of his, including about 460 responsa, have come to light.

In a number of Geniza documents Maimonides is called "the master (*rabbān*) of all Israel" and even more commonly "the great Rāv," which could be properly rendered in Arabic as "grand muftī." The ancient titles "the court," or "the judge for all Israel," were not applied to him. Rather, he was a jurisconsult — who, during certain periods, combined with this function the office of the "head of the Jews." Nahray, the Rāv, and Maimonides, were all from the Muslim West, where the rabbinate seemingly trod paths different from those of the East, whose jurisconsults also came to preside over courts; so, in any case, indicates the evidence from the Geniza.

Maimonides' son Abraham, although following in his father's footsteps, became somewhat assimilated to the eastern tradition. He was a prolific writer of responsa, but, as the Geniza evidence shows, he also sat on the court, settling even minor litigations and revising in his own hand records drafted by his colleagues or adjuncts. Similarly, Nissīm, the son of Nahray, although like his father referred to as rāv, "master" (and not as "judge"), signed, and even wrote, court records. Thus, it seems that the divorce of the office of the jurisconsult from that of the judge was characteristic of the Jewish communities west of Egypt; within Egypt (as in the East) learned doctors of law as a rule were also expected to act as a judges. Was this differentiation due to internal Jewish developments or to the influence of the Muslim environment — or both? This question cannot be answered at this time.

The Law

In reviewing the vast legal material embedded in the Geniza records, one gets the impression that it was not so much the content of the law but rather the authority administering it that gave parties the assurance that they were judged according to "the Law of the Torah."

Documents relating to family life, such as marriage contracts, bills of divorce, and deeds of manumission (which qualified the freed slave to marry a Jew) usually state that they have been made according to "the Law of Moses and Israel," or "of Moses and the Jews," or "of the Jews" alone. Even this time-honored formula contains an element of customary law. Moreover, contracts of all descriptions, including marriage contracts, often conclude with the statement that they are as valid and sound as any such contracts "instituted by our sages and in use in the world." Some eleventh-century marriage contracts even state that they are properly executed and binding, both "according to the statutes of our sages and the laws [invariably the Greek loanword *nomos* is used] of the state" or "the gentiles." These formulas, in the Aramaic language, certainly originated in pre-Islamic times. Some documents conclude, like Byzantine legal deeds, with the Greek word *akolythos*, "no objection," "without impediments"—a usage found even in Egyptian provincial towns.

"Freedom of contract"—the right of the parties to choose the conditions that met their needs best—is the most conspicuous aspect of the law that speaks to us through the Geniza records. This right applies first to commerce; the Jewish courts dealt most frequently with the "partnership according to the gentiles," that is, the Muslim brand of the *commenda*, or the "bills of exchange," called *suftaja*. "It is true," writes a gaon in reply to a query, "that our sages have said that one should not send bills of exchange, but we see that people actually use them; therefore, we admit them in court, since otherwise commerce would come to a standstill; we thus give judgment exactly in accordance with the law of the merchants." Marriage contracts, as well as other settlements made with regard to family relations, also evince an amazing latitude of provisions and a wide variety of usages. The principle of rabbinical law that "any stipulation made with regard to financial matters is valid" provided ample possibilities for satisfying the demands of the highly developed society living in the Mediterranean basin during the eleventh through the thirteenth century. On the other hand, *the* Law, that is, the religious law, also called "the preserve of God," might be administered with harsh and seemingly arcane decisions, as could be expected in a legal system that dated back to remote antiquity and often rested on tribal sensibilities. Such institutions as levirate marriage (brothers obliged to marry widowed sisters-in-law), as well as certain other aspects of family law and the law of inheritance, had their origin in an intrinsically agricultural society. The sabbatical year—the provision that every seventh year all lands lie fallow and that all debts are automatically annulled unless protected by a creditor's specific deposition in court—although an institution most inconvenient in a commercial society, seems to have been revived in Egypt by Maimonides in the beginning of the thirteenth century. In economic matters, which lend themselves to legal flexibility, the situation was of course more fluid. After the experts had given their opinions as to the legal position according to the religious law (opinions, as we shall see, that were sometimes divergent), the parties knew what they could expect from a judgment and sought agreements as favorable as possible without extensive litigation. A frustrated party could threaten to apply to a Muslim court for judgment. As far as we can ascertain, settlements were reached quickly and, as a rule, were fair and reasonable. There were, to be sure, notable exceptions.

It mattered little that Jewish law required certain symbolic formalities in order to validate legal transactions. According to Islamic law, a mere oral offer and acceptance were sufficient for making a contract binding. No doubt with an eye on Islamic law, Maimonides opens the *Book of Acquisition* in his *Code of Law* with the following words: "Title to an object is not acquired by oral agreement alone, even if witnesses testify to that agreement." He then goes on to explain in sixty-six (sometimes lengthy) paragraphs the unwieldy manner in which each type of movable and immovable property may be acquired. The reader of Maimonides' code who is not familiar with the practice of the courts as manifested in the Geniza records will conclude that Jewish law, like that of the Romans, was a peasants' law, utterly unfit for the exigencies of a highly mercantile economy. The same code, however, gives an indication of both reverence for Jewish law and a desire to make it serve contemporary needs. The sixty-six paragraphs are mooted by a single paragraph (para. 5 of chap. 5), which reads:

Real estate, slaves, cattle, and other movable property [i.e., everything] may by acquired by symbolic barter. This act is called *qinyān* [lit., purchase]. The fundamental principle of this mode of acquisition is that the transferee should give the transferor an article of however small a value and say to him, "Acquire this article in exchange for the yard or the wine or the cattle or the slave that you sold me for as much and so much." If this is done, then the moment the vendor lifts the article and takes possession of it, the purchaser acquires title to the land or the mentioned movable property, though he has not drawn them or paid their price, and neither party may retract.

In practice, a kerchief, or a similar small object was handed over by one party to the other and then immediately returned as a gift. The Judeo-Arabic *qanā*, "to acquire a right," and *aqnā*, "to confer a right," terms found in most Geniza deeds, are derived from the Hebrew. Intangible rights, such as power of attorney, were conveyed by a symbolic act called *qinyān aggāv*, "transfer adjunct" (adjunct, that is, to the transfer of land). Different forms of this symbolic act are represented in the Geniza records, from the old but rare formula of "giving" the threshold of the entrance to one's house, to the commonplace phrase of "giving four square cubits of the soil of the Holy Land," in which each Jew was supposed to have a share. Such symbolic formulas should not be mistaken as actual conveyances of land. Moreover, it is uncertain whether the symbolic act itself was always performed. When five representatives of the Great Synagogue in Alexandria (the Palestinian synagogue) acknowledged the receipt of a donation for the erection of the holy ark to the traveler who delivered it, they wrote: "We made the symbolic purchase from ourselves." What could this mean other than "We declare herewith in a legally binding form"? The document was signed by four other persons.

Criminal cases and punishment in the Geniza court records are confined almost entirely to transgressions in the sphere of religion or of community life. A religious slaughterer who was careless in the exercise of his duties was flogged and forced to make public confession in 1028, a punishment described in the document as lenient. A carpenter who let his gentile employees work on Saturday was to be flogged, according to some scholars; others wanted him to be fined and excommunicated as well. When a man declared in a public statement that he was prepared to suffer the death penalty if it were proved that he had cursed the head of the Jerusalem yeshiva, it does not by any means imply that such punishment was ever inflicted by the Jewish community on an offending member during the Geniza period. We read about a Jewish official, a cantor, in Alexandria retrieving stolen merchandise, but nothing is said about the punishment of the thief. With one exception, no reference has been found thus far to the apprehension of a culprit by a Jewish authority. There were, to be sure, Jewish criminals, but their punishment, as a rule, was the responsibility of the state authorities.

It is particularly noteworthy that sexual offenses are nowhere dealt with in the court records of the Geniza. There is occasional talk about persons suspected of having had illicit relations, but the question raised with regard to them is always whether they should be allowed to marry each other (forbidden by Jewish law), not how they should be punished. In one case, a Jewish girl is charged by two Muslims with being too intimate with a Christian physician; the document is written, as usual, in Hebrew characters, but the signatures of the three Jewish "witnesses" are in Arabic, suggesting perhaps that the case was finally to be brought before a Muslim judge (to whom the text of the accusation would be read out by his Jewish colleague). A letter calls for the expulsion from town of a man who exhibited abnormal sexual behavior (as was done with prostitutes), but no expulsion could be carried out without the assistance of a state authority.

Fines stipulated for breach of contract are often mentioned in our documents. It is therefore strange that we hear almost nothing about payments imposed by a court as a punishment. A statute promulgated in Acre around 1230 lays down the principle that any penalty imposed on a person for disrespectful behavior against a communal leader should go to the poor of the synagogue. Commercial fines called for restitution to the aggrieved party. In general, it seems, fines imposed by a Jewish authority were regarded as an extraordinary means of punishment. On the other hand, bans of various degrees of gravity, as well as excommunication, were an accepted form of punishment and were recognized by the Muslim authorities as well; such an action might be used to force a party to comply with the decision of a court or the ruling of an authority.

Excommunication meant that no person of Jewish faith was allowed to have any dealings with the punished—even to talk or shake hands with him, let alone give him food or shelter or do business with him. The man so banned was not admitted to the synagogue service and was not granted burial. In addition, the most horrible of curses were pronounced against him, some of which are actually preserved in the Geniza. Thus, the merely spiritual aspects of excommunication were commensurate in harshness with its practical consequences.

A person under ban would normally try to "cleanse himself" by acceding to the settlement or judgment originally refused by him or might seek a new agreement. As a rule, only the authority that had pronounced the ban was allowed to revoke it. We find that a man who had been excommunicated in a provincial town was advised by the court in Fustat to travel to that place and to clear his case there. Moreover, a time limit was imposed on him for this purpose; if it were to lapse, he would have to pay a fine ("to the poor") in Fustat, in addition to satisfying the claims against him in the provincial town. The penitent appeared in the court of Fustat "on the morning after the Day of Atonement," and was given a fifty-day respite.

In principle, a local community or even a scholar (normally, sitting with two others as a court) was entitled to proclaim a ban. To be effective, however, the ban had to be general, covering, as far as possible, all Jewish communities. Therefore, as a rule, an excommunication was effected by a gaon or nagid, or confirmed by him if it was first promulgated in a place over which he had no jurisdiction. During the classical Geniza period, the authorities were reluctant to make use of this stern disciplinary measure and slow in putting it into effect. The various degrees of reprimand and ban known to Jewish legal theory are represented in the Geniza records, although the distinction between them is by no means always clear or consistent. All in all, this important instrument of medieval law deserves new scrutiny in the light of the Geniza records, preferably in conjunction with the parallel institutions of the Coptic and other Eastern churches.

The law of the period was personal and not territorial. A Jew, whether he happened to be in Granada, in Jerusalem, or in some port on the Malabar coast of India, when judged by the community of Israel, was judged according to the same law. The same applied to Christians of the same denomination and to Muslims adhering to the same "school." Local custom and tradition accounted for some shades of difference, but these as a rule were small. This legal unity was a great convenience to the widely traveled Jewish middle class and contributed much to its stability and inner coherence. As we shall presently see, the court procedure itself presupposed lively international traffic.

Procedures

Naturally, procedures differed according to the character of a case and the authority before which it was brought. Nevertheless, some general trends are clearly discernible throughout. The court records preserved in the Geniza are of three main types: (1) fact-finding, consisting of depositions made by the parties; (2) questions addressed to the parties by the presiding judge or the opposing party (or both); and (3) the answers given to these questions, as well as the evidence provided to substantiate the claims. Formal judgments, quoting the legal sources and detailing the reasons for the decision made, are almost entirely lacking. Instead, a litigation is concluded (often, as stated, after long proceedings) by a declaration of one or both parties, fortified by the "symbolic purchase" (qinyān). Such a declaration is either an "acquittal," in which the parties release each other from any further obligation after the conditions specified in the document have been (or will have been) fulfilled, or an "acknowledgment," in which one party declares to owe a particular sum or another obligation to the other. Normally the terms of the payment or the fulfillment of the obligation are also specified.

It would be erroneous to assume that the courts acted merely as boards of arbitration, without recourse to statutory law. Many hundreds of legal opinions from this period indicate that conflicts in economic life, as in family matters, were decided according to rabbinical law, handled by legal experts. How, then, is the almost total absence of judgments from the Geniza records to be explained? There can be little doubt that this reflects matters of form and procedure. Wrongly interpreting or applying the law of the Torah was regarded as a very grave sin. "May God preserve me from the sin of judgment," that is, of handing down a wrong judgment, was a phrase used even in the conclusion of a legal opinion. "A judge who does not render an absolutely true judgment causes the Divine Presence to depart from Israel. If he unlawfully expropriates money from one and gives it to another, God will exact his life from him." These and similar ancient warnings, reproduced by Maimonides in his code, were taken literally by contemporaries. Therefore, in order to not expose themselves to such jeopardy, the judges refrained altogether from giving formal judgments, a procedure formulated and expressly recommended in the sixteenth century by the *Shulhan Arukh*, one of the authoritative Jewish books of law. The Geniza has preserved a tenth-century query concerning a judge who accepted his appointment on condition that he never be obliged "to give formal judgments in cases that he would decide." The Muslim judges adopted a similar attitude.

In view of these religious scruples, the decisions of the courts are in the form of declarations by the parties to litigation. Rather than stating that the court has sentenced a person to make a particular payment, the minutes contain an "acknowledgment" by that person that he owes that sum to the other party. Instead of an acquittal by a court, a party thus freed from an obligation would receive a "release" from the claimant. But we should not be misled by the seeming simplicity of this legal formality. In cases of real settlements outside the court, our documents state that "upright elders," or "peace-loving persons," or simply "those present" intervened and brought about an agreement through arbitration or persuasion. The countless "releases" and acknowledgments that do not contain such remarks have to be regarded as the result of judicial decisions.

How were these decisions reached? Attorneys, familiar figures in juridical practice during Late Antiquity are scarcely found in the courts depicted by the Geniza documents. Nor are they found in contemporaneous Muslim courts. As a rule, litigants were represented by attorneys only when they themselves were absent or otherwise unable to attend a court meeting in person. As a rule, such attorneys were not professional lawyers, although of course, for this task one preferred prominent and scholarly persons well versed in business matters (and therefore often known to us through other Geniza papers). Litigation between persons living in different localities was so common that letters of attorney constitute the type of document most frequently found in the Geniza. The appearance in court of a party together with an attorney was so exceptional that Maimonides was asked whether such a procedure was legal altogether. Maimonides answers in the affirmative but gives the other party the right to disqualify the attorney if he finds his presence disconcerting. Thus far, only one court record (dated December 1027) has been found in which the attorney's words are actually recorded. This was perhaps an exceptional case, for the attorney here is referred to not as *wakīl* (the conventional term for legal representative) but as *waṣiyy*, which, in addition to meaning "executor" or "guardian," is a general (Arabic) word for "mandatory." The attorney in question signed many Geniza documents and was probably a professional notary. In one, unfortunately incomplete, document, the attorney receives one gold piece as remuneration; most probably he represented an absentee party.

Still, many court depositions rendered in our papers are impressive in their lucidity and force, and some are indeed eloquent in their pleadings. We have to keep in mind, however, that according to both Maimonides' code and an express reference in a Geniza document, the presiding judge would recapitulate the statements made by the parties. The concise wording of the court records might thus reflect a polished literary effort rather than an oral pleading. Very often the judges found that the litigants made statements that had no actual bearing on the subject matter of the dispute. In one such case our records contain the remark: "Many statements were made which to report would lead far afield. The upshot of all that is the following." In smaller matters, the presiding judge himself would take notes—or, as is human, sometimes fail to do so. The Geniza has preserved a note by a judge to a colleague stating that he has forgotten the exact date and some of the conditions of a settlement made before them; requested data are provided on the reverse of the note.

As to evidence, statements of witnesses were often submitted in writing. The handwriting of the witnesses on the original document had to be validated by a court (local or other) so that it could be used everywhere. The validation was often executed during the same session in which the original deposition had been made. The judge would write both the minutes and the validation; the witnesses would sign the minutes, and the judge and his adjuncts would sign the validation. The handwriting of individual legal authorities seems to have been known in Jewish courts from Spain to India. Samples of signatures were kept in the archives. In smaller localities, either the validation of the local court was attested by another and more generally known authority, or the judge accepting the validation stated expressly that he recognized the handwriting of a colleague residing in a foreign country.

Two adult witnesses were required by Jewish law. In practice, frequently five, six, or more witnesses signed a testimony. In such cases, only two signatures required attestation by a court, although in many documents all the signatures, sometimes seven at a time, were validated as genuine. No fixed procedure seems to have prevailed in this matter. In the extremely frequent cases in which testimonies had not been validated by a court, each signature had to be attested by two witnesses. Owing to the lively traffic in the Mediterranean, there was no difficulty in finding witnesses in Fustat or Alexandria who could attest to the handwriting of persons living in the West. The very custom of letting as many persons as possible testify with regard to an occurrence or a legal transaction probably originated in part to make subsequent validation easier, since, as we have seen, any two signatures to a testimony were sufficient for that purpose.

Documents were widely admitted as evidence. In actual court records we indeed see records produced and used as statements of parties. Account books of merchants were also admitted in court as proof and were quoted as such in the records. Islamic law as well, although opposed in principle to the acceptance of written testimony, softened its attitude in this matter over the centuries. Depositions in court were not made under oath, as is customary today. The allegations made by the litigants sometimes differed so much from one another that they appear to be bombastic opening statements rather than attempts to report the facts. Small wonder that occasionally the payments finally agreed upon bear no relation whatsoever to the sums first claimed.

The normal procedure for a legal case of some importance would thus be as follows: First the court would try to verify the facts and define as exactly as possible the legal issues. For this purpose, the judges would hear the depositions and arguments of the parties, examine the witnesses, and study the documents submitted to them. In one case, in which the dossier has been preserved almost completely, this procedure required nine sessions held over the course of ten months. Then the parties, and if he thought it necessary, the presiding judge, would present the case as it had been formulated in court to one or more legal experts.

After receiving the opinions of the legal experts, the parties would first attempt to settle out of court. Throughout our records, there are references to multiple arbiters. As with the composition of a court, having more than one figure present was considered more conducive to equity. In a little town in the Nile Delta we find nine persons mentioned by name acting as a board of arbitration, with a circuit judge sent from the capital presiding. The circuit judge was advised by his superior to attempt a decision by himself only if arbitration failed. Many lawsuits mentioned in the Geniza records were settled by such agreements. In one letter we even find a complaint about judges "unwilling to make decisions, trying only to reach a settlement."

If the parties did not come to an agreement, often the court would not hand down a judgment immediately but would first make sure of having the support of its superiors, namely, one or more of the three chief judges in the capital, or if the chief judges themselves were preoccupied with a lawsuit, of the gaon or nagid who had appointed them. Many queries preserved by the Geniza or in the documents or responsa are veiled "feelers." Modern scholars have wondered about queries that were easily answered, since Jewish law was unambiguous regarding the issues raised. Faced with this anomaly, they are inclined to believe that the judges asking such easily answered questions were insufficiently schooled. This is, however, a misunderstanding of the procedure. The judge submitting the question was not in doubt about the answer, as can be seen from the manner in which he presented the matter; rather he sought a ruling from a higher legal authority to reinforce his own position. Therefore, we frequently find in the answers the cryptic remark, "If the case is indeed as stated in the query, the law is. . . ."

Parties unable to settle could also apply directly to the high court of the yeshiva or, later, to the high court in the Egyptian capital and, in particular, to the nagid. At that point, the higher authorities would instruct the local court as to how to deal with the case. The strange procedure of applying to a higher authority before the lower court had made its decision corresponds to some degree to the procedure of appeal, which, although not unknown, was not the established and organized course of action that it is in modern law.

A decision according to the Law often required an oath. This aspect of medieval juridical procedure is entirely unfamiliar to the modern reader. An oath in court today is a mere formality; in medieval times it was a matter of life and death, for swearing meant troubling God to be present as witness, and, as the third commandment proclaims, "the Lord does not hold him guiltless who takes His name in vain" (Exodus 20: 7). To impress the person obliged to give an oath, the ceremony was held in the synagogue. A Torah scroll was removed from the ark and clad in black; the communal bier and the ceremonial trumpet, the *shofar*, were brought in to remind those present of death and the Last Judgment, and then the oath had to be given "in the name of God and the Ten Commandments." In a document from Syracuse we read that the party giving the oath was even obliged to read the Ten Commandments aloud from the Torah scroll opened before him. A woman, too, would make a sworn declaration in the section of the synagogue generally reserved for males and hold a Torah scroll in her hands while doing so. These paraphernalia were believed to be so essential that Maimonides was asked whether an oath on a mere codex of the Bible was valid. A false oath was regarded as not only a great sin, disqualifying the guilty from serving in future as a witness, but also a disgrace that could even lead to dire repercussions for the community at large. Therefore, we find in numerous Geniza records that even when everything was ready for the oath, some well-meaning elders would intervene and arrange for a settlement.

Among the various types of statutory oaths fixed by biblical and talmudic law is the procedural "ban in general terms," *ḥerem setām*. The ban in general terms served as a kind of lie detector, inasmuch as a ban and the most awesome curses were pronounced on anyone who evaded the obligation defined in the pronouncement, as well as on anyone else who was able, but failed, to testify about the whereabouts of a particular person (should he have absented himself) or his obligation and ability to pay. There were two types of bans; the first was promulgated in the presence of the person accused of evading an obligation. When the ban was read, the accuser was obliged to answer "Amen," that is, he took upon himself the curses and the ban in case the accusation was untrue. The second was used when the whereabouts of the accused were not known. Since people were very mobile in those days, a ban might have to be pronounced in different localities and countries; it was often pronounced on holidays, when it was customary to assemble in the main synagogues. The wording of the bans had to be of the utmost precision so as not to leave loopholes by which the accused could escape responsibility. Many court records (if not most) conclude with the declaration that the parties have not made a secret deposition in another court—an action that would have rendered the validity of the undertakings considered null and void. Jewish pleadings before the Muslim courts are also a matter of concern, one that surely requires further investigation.

The handing down of a judgment did not always mark the end of a lawsuit. Its execution, even with the aid of the state authorities, sometimes caused great trouble, as we have seen. If the losing party was a notable of high standing, the court tried to give him the opportunity to save face by satisfying his opponent prior to the promulgation of the verdict. The last resort against a recalcitrant party was excommunication.

In accordance with ancient Palestinian custom, the Jewish courts in Egypt held their sessions on Mondays and Thursdays, a practice observed by various Muslim courts as well. This is attested by hundreds of records, even for the congregation of the Babylonian Rabbinites in Fustat. The original reason for this arrangement was the fact that these two days were market days in Palestine; the peasants brought their products to the town and settled their legal affairs on those occasions. The synagogue seized the opportunity for the instruction of the masses and fixed readings from the Pentateuch for these days, which thus became "the holy weekdays," honored by the pious by abstaining from food, a practice followed also by Muslim pietists.

There was a practical reason for designating Mondays and Thursdays for the sessions of the Jewish courts. Since everyone came to synagogue on those days in order to listen to the obligatory readings from the Torah, it was easy to give a case the publicity needed and to find a sufficient number of persons ready to serve as witnesses or adjunct judges. When the Palestinian yeshiva moved to Cairo, its high court held its meetings on Wednesdays and Fridays, presumably to give the judges of Fustat and Cairo the opportunity to sit together in more important cases, as we indeed see in preserved documents. The judges did not remain idle during the rest of the week: Marriages and divorces were not confined to fixed weekdays. On Tuesday, auctions of estates had to be supervised. Other business, such as making or checking inventories of estates, was also attended to on that day. Regular sessions of the court on days other than Monday or Thursday were rare, however, and sometimes a special reason for the change is recognizable in the contents of the court record. Whether the same custom prevailed in the countries west of Egypt is doubtful.

In the larger cities at least, the courts kept archives or made other provisions to preserve the minutes of the transactions. Persons who wished to substantiate claims or who had lost documents applied to courts and received from them the desired material. Most of the documents preserved are leaves from record books, as proved by the fact that reports about entirely different cases are written on the same leaf and sometimes even on the same page. Finally, dossiers of complete lawsuits have been found bearing a superscription or docket that indicates their contents; such dossiers often contain documents that one would not ordinarily expect to find in court records.

PART II

THE FAMILY
AND ITS VALUES

The community mirrored in the documents of the Cairo Geniza was bound by a religious law developed over many generations going back to ancient times. It was also influenced by a hegemonic Muslim state and society with laws and moral notions at variance with its own. Still, the Jewish community displayed social and geographical mobility and evinced creative flexibility in the conduct of its economic and public affairs. A community of this type gives rise to complex family systems, in this case systems that share major features with other societies around the Mediterranean. When thinking about his family, a man imagined not the small unit founded by himself but the larger one into which he was born. His family was, as is said in so many Geniza documents, "the house of his father." The term "father" included forefathers as well as agnates.

TWELVE

The House of the Father

Law favored the paternal family. The economic security
of a woman largely depended on what she had brought in from her
father's (or "fathers'") house. For her legal protection during her marriage she relied on her father or her brothers; she did not inherit from
her husband. Although Islamic and Jewish laws differed considerably in
some respects, both made special provisions for the widow, but if a man
had no issue his estate "returned"—in legal parlance—to his father's
house, and the wife's dowry, or at least half of it, returned to her family
if she died childless. Legal practice—although not statutory law—and
commonly accepted custom made the members of the extended family
responsible for one another. The widespread practice of marrying close
relatives, especially first cousins, had its origin not so much in economic
considerations as in the belief that such unions would provide protection
for the young couple, especially the wife, and safeguards for the honor
and continuation of discrete families.

The Arabic of the Geniza documents has two sets of designations for
the term "family," some for the extended, and others for the nuclear
family. Similarly, Hebrew *mishpāḥā*, "family," refers as a rule to the
extended family—usually one with a noble pedigree, that is, one containing a number of distinguished personalities, such as high religious
dignitaries, judges, scholars, government officials, physicians, great merchants, or other persons who have been munificent or otherwise meritorious in the service of the community. Hebrew *bayit*, "house," may
designate a man's nuclear family or his wife, but the plural, in the phrase
ba'alē battīm, invariably describes persons who are the scions of a distinguished (extended) family.

Ancestors

The Geniza records reveal that reverence for forefathers and for past generations of family found regular expression in the synagogue service. As a rule, prayers for a person, alive or dead, were said not for him alone, nor for him and his immediate relatives, but first and foremost for his ascendant and noteworthy agnates—all male, to be sure, even when the immediate object of the prayer was a woman. We possess detailed knowledge about these procedures in the numerous "memorial lists" preserved in the Geniza. The immediate occasion for these prayers was a death in the family, when at the first attendance of public prayer by the mourners, blessings were recited for the ancestors of the deceased, as well as for the survivors. A similar service was held after the first month of mourning. When the philosopher Mūsā b. Maymūn (Moses Maimonides) enumerated the seven generations of his forefathers in the colophons to his commentary on the Mishnah, he did so as a tribute to the accepted notion that such ancestry (which included four judges) added to the religious authority of his own work. It was taken for granted that a man tried to live up to the standards set by his ancestors. A letter exchanged between two high religious dignitaries states, "This document must be correct, for the father of its writer was the son of the daughter of the head of the yeshiva." The principle of hereditary public office, high or low, so thoroughly familiar to the Geniza world, was based on the same assumption and was recognized by Jewish law. In numerous requests for help, the recipient of the missive is reminded of his noble and munificent ancestors, while in letters of recommendation the person concerned is often described as of fine or illustrious stock: "There they know my forefathers, my house, my nobility, and all my family."

A man's life was perpetuated through his sons. Sometimes all the sons of an ancestor are named in the memorial lists—at times as many as six sons—but more often only the direct ascendants of the person on whose behalf the list is written are listed, along with agnates who for any reason deserved mentioning. These might include well-known or otherwise meritorious persons and those whose life had been cut short either by an early natural death—a common occurrence—or by a disaster such as the collapse of a house, drowning, shipwreck, disappearance abroad, murder, or, especially, "dying for God's sake," that is, in a religious persecution. The recounting sometimes reached back ten and more generations. In such fashion the family history remained vivid.

These pedigrees should by no means be regarded as fanciful; property deeds and other legal documents, as well as books bearing notes of their proprietors, were preserved and helped keep family records straight.

Women were never listed in the genealogies. Moses Maimonides had five brothers-in-law. Each of the brothers-in-law is listed in the joint genealogy of the two families, with both the Hebrew and Arabic forms of their names, but nowhere do we learn the names of the women of this union. It must be noted, however, that a man's status in society depended on the family of his mother no less than on the family of his father. In the genealogy of Mishael b. Isaiah, Maimonides' father-in-law, first his mother's lineage is provided through fourteen generations (her family had played an important role in Palestine, as well as in Egypt). The list goes on to indicate six generations of Mishael's paternal ancestors, known scholars, physicians, and public servants. In one doctor's *'itra,* or pedigree, the mother's lineage precedes that of the father because it included the nagid Samuel b. Hananya, one of the most prominent figures of Egyptian Jewry. But the individual to whom her reputation and that of the family accrues is always male. In wishing a father of daughters a son, one would say, "May God not wipe out the name of your fathers." By law, Judaism is inherited through the mother, but a man's extended family was represented by his father's kin and that of his sons.

Names

The cohesiveness of a family and reverence for past generations were expressed by giving newborn children the names of ascendants and agnates. As in Islam, the common usage was that a newborn child was named after his paternal grandfather, regardless of whether the old man's name was already perpetuated in another branch of the family. Unlike Christian Europe, where it became customary among Jews to name children only after deceased relatives, the firstborn male in the Judaic Near East was named after his living (paternal) grandfather in order to ensure the perpetuation of the name as early as possible. Naming the firstborn son after one's own father was a way to show him the filial piety that religion—Jewish, as well as Muslim and Christian—imposes as a sacred duty. Because young couples often lived in the father's house, as did the grandfather, the old man had daily opportunity to see himself and indeed the family perpetuated through his namesake grandson. There is also evidence that fathers named their sons after themselves, but that practice was far less common than naming a son after the grandfather. As with the customary memorial service, this may be an indication of a certain precedence for the extended family over the nuclear family.

Surnames in the strict sense of the word were known in talmudic times, and it was assumed that they might be preserved even through ten generations. Indeed, many types of family names appear in the Geniza documents. For example, an ancestor's name might serve as a family name, the practice most closely related to the custom of giving the child the name of his grandfather. A name can be identified as a true family name—and not simply as that of an ancestor—when it appears in different genealogical combinations and also is marked as such, especially by the phrase "known as." The same applies when it is preceded by Hebrew *ben* or Arabic *ibn* or when the name or names preceding it are introduced by Aramaic *bar*, all meaning "son of." Hence, Asad b. Manṣūr b. Asad is a man named after his grandfather. But "Abū 'l-Maʿālī Samuel *bar* Judah, *known as* Ben Asad," represents a notable bearing a prominent family name. In many cases it was not the name, but some special trait—physical or moral—of the person or an ancestor that gave the family its designation. And so, there are families with such names as "Blue-eyed," "Squint-eyed," "Red-haired," "With small teeth," "Long (and thin as a stick)," "Dazzler," or "Braggart."

Specific physical or moral traits of a forebear often were expressed by nicknames, which became family names, mostly under the form of "Son of a woman of [this or that character]," for instance, "Son of the Hot-tempered [woman]," "of Sweetmeat," "of the Cow," "of the Grain of Cumin." These matronymics (names derived from the mother's name) should not be taken as survivals of ancient matriarchy. Often a nickname is a mild form of a curse or a blessing: the mother, the giver of life, has a magical impact on the destiny of her son. In a magical invocation, the names of the mothers of both the supplicant and of his enemy (or his beloved, as the case may be) are mentioned (at times alongside their fathers). When Muslims wish to anger a Jewish convert to Islam, they would say to him not "You son of a Jew" but "You son of the Jewess." When a pre-Islamic, or early Islamic, warrior challenged an enemy who had cursed his leader, he would call out to him: "I am So-and-so, son of So-and-so; the name of my mother is So-and-so; curse me and curse my mother," which meant that the fight to follow was one of life and death. These nicknames could also reflect family names—witness Ibn Kammūna, "Son of the Grain of Cumin [fem.]." It appears first in a

Geniza document from 1121, a report about messianic troubles in Baghdad, when an Abū Sahl ibn Kammūna was received by the caliph and intervened with him on behalf of the Jewish community. Another Ibn Kammūna, clearly a prominent figure, died in an underground prison in Wāsiṭ, Iraq, in 1204/5. A third, bearing the title "Prince of the Efficient [Servants of the Government]," is referred to as a benefactor in a letter by the gaon of Baghdad, Samuel b. Eli, dated 1206. All these, as well as the famous oculist and philosopher 'Izz al-Dawla b. Kammūna, one of the most interesting authors of the Jewish Middle Ages (d. 1284), might have belonged to the same family. All of them lived in Iraq and were connected with the authorities in one way or another. The philosopher's son, Najm al-Dawla ("Star of the Government"), also was in the service of the state.

Family names were also derived from occupations or places of origin. "Preparer of Vinegar Sauce Relishes"—al-Kāmukhī—was borne by at least two families, one being kohens, that is, from the priestly clan of Aaron. The nonpriestly al-Kāmukhīs are represented with some regularity over two centuries by scholars, cantors, and others on the community payroll. While specific names were borne by different families, it was common for ordinary names to form the distinctive marks of families represented in the Geniza records throughout the centuries. For instance, Andalusī, "Native of Muslim-Spain," was a frequently found surname. One Andalusī family prominent in business correspondence throughout the eleventh century was headquartered in Qayrawān. The manufacture of sugar was a predominantly Jewish occupation, and the name Sukkarī, "Sugar Maker," was widespread among Jews. Yet one Sukkarī clan was active in Fustat and working in the mint and as merchants, not as sugar makers. (The first known member, who lived in the tenth century, was called Ben al-Sukkarī [*Son* of the Sugar Maker]). These patterns of naming were also widespread among the Muslims. In researching on the families of the Geniza, we can make use of surnames as indicia of social and economic history only if their occurrence is accompanied by additional corroborating information. Occupational family names reveal only that at some time in the history of the family various individuals practiced a given occupation. Similarly, a geographical attribution attached to a particular family serves to indicate that at one time the family inhabited a particular region, city, town, or more localized area; it does not mean that the individual or his family were currently residing at that place. The same is also true of Muslim family names with geographical attribution.

Three types of families tended to perpetuate themselves by adhering to the same profession or by adopting one of similar status: (1) families of religious dignitaries and scholars, both of high rank, such as judges and heads of the yeshivas, and of lower rank, such as cantors, scholars, and scribes; (2) powerful merchant houses, such as the Tāhertīs of Qayrawān; and (3) government officials and purveyors, as well as physicians, who often treated rulers and governors and thus were close to the seats of power. But here as well the data can be misleading. Judges and cantors frequently engaged in commercial activities; their sons thus might prefer business to a learned profession. The prominent representative of the merchants in Fustat around 1100, Abū Yaʿqūb al-Ḥakīm "The Doctor" (in Hebrew: Yekuthiel b. Moses ha-rōfē), bore that surname because his father, and perhaps a more remote ancestor, was a physician. Yekuthiel's son was also a representative of the merchants, but his grandson Yekuthiel b. Moses returned to his great-grandfather's profession of medicine.

Whether families from poorer segments of the population adhered to the same profession or one of similar status over generations is difficult to say at this stage of research. An analysis of the preserved lists has shown that, as a rule, the family living together was smaller in poorer houses since the boys left home to earn a living wherever they could find it. In general, the exigencies and stresses of economic life had a decisive influence on the formation and structure of families. The basic concepts of family represented one set of motivations, the economic realities quite another.

The vertical aspect of the extended family—that is, the immense significance of the patriarchs and agnates, as documented in the Geniza papers—was not unique to the Judaic Near East of the High Middle Ages. The veneration of forefathers, entailing widespread knowledge of genealogy, was the backbone of pre-Islamic Arab tribal organization. "The merit of the fathers" occupied a central position in postbiblical Judaism, and the Geniza letters show that this notion was fully alive in the High Middle Ages, referring not only to the ancestors of the community but also to the ancestors of the person addressed, including his mother. A strong sense of the duty "to make good mention" of dead relatives, especially those whose lives had been cut short, was also very much present and is to be understood as a constituent of general concepts about death, future life, and resurrection. It seems, however, that the social aspect of remembering the dead was equally strong. "Man's success depends on his social position," as one Geniza letter has it, and this was largely predetermined by his origins—by the prominence, meritoriousness, and renown of his ancestors and agnates.

Relations between Brothers

Except in letters of supplication and thanks, the Geniza people are not effusive in their expression of feelings; they can sometimes even seem businesslike. In the matter of brotherly love, however, they tend to be eloquent—even in criticizing a sibling. "He is my brother, from father and mother, even if he breaks my bones." With these words the brother of Daniel b. Azarya (gaon of the yeshiva of Jerusalem and head of the Jews in the Fatimid Empire from 1051 to 1062) concludes his bitter comments concerning the actions of his illustrious brother in ousting the Palestinian local leadership, with which the writer of the letter completely identifies himself. "From the moment he arrived here, he has humiliated every colleague and every friend of mine in a manner that is well known. Yet it is my duty to be considerate toward him and to endure everything he does to me, since no one is under a greater obligation to do so than I; may God keep him, whether he does right or wrong." In what follows, the author makes it perfectly clear that, whatever his brother's actions, he will never join his adversaries.

Similarly a judge from al-Mahdiyya writes to a brother who has emigrated to Egypt:

You wrote, dear brother, that you were much distressed by my words of reproach. But we only criticize the ones we love, and if not you, who is there that I should criticize? Have I not sworn to you time and again that you are not only my brother, but both my younger brother and my eldest son? When will this little boy, whom I made soil his feet [i.e., whom I sent on errands] and whom I punished for his misdeeds, be grown up? . . . For all the world I would not have misunderstandings come between you and me. . . . You are dearer to me than the world and all that is in it.

In the day-to-day correspondence between brothers, of which we possess a great number of documents, the writer often describes himself as "your brother, may I be your ransom," a phrase also used by parents and their children with respect to one another. The idea underlying this expression is that just as close relatives must be prepared to stand up for each other in daily life, so must they be ready to bear the misfortunes that God has apportioned to their beloved siblings. Although the Psalmist (49:8) clearly stated that God does not accept one brother as a substitute for another, the Jews of the Geniza community understood that a man must be prepared to take upon himself the responsibility for his brother's misdeeds. The metaphor of "ransom" was quite appropriate since the ransoming of captives was quite common — particularly in communities like those of Jewish traders, who traversed international boundaries.

Age demands respect. One kisses the hand of an elder brother. "My brother, master and lord" or "crown of my head" are the minimum titles of respect paid to a brother in a letter. The firstborn son occupies a similarly privileged position. In the salutation of letters he is often addressed together with his father, while his younger brothers are referred to only by number or collectively. Although the *kunya*, or honorific nickname, had long since become stereotyped and was given even to a child at birth, it had not lost its original function of teknonymic: as did the Muslims, Jewish parents called themselves father and mother of their firstborn. Even when the name of the firstborn was not mentioned, one would write, "Kindest regards to your boys, especially to your eldest." This respect was also reflected in Jewish law, which favored the firstborn and thus differed from Islamic practice, although among Muslims the firstborn male was often privileged by social convention.

Brothers and Sisters

The correspondence between brothers and sisters, which is represented in the Geniza to a far larger extent than that between husbands and wives, invites comparison with that of male siblings. The relationship of brothers to sisters did not differ in many respects from relationships between brothers; the same expressions of fraternal devotion, especially the phrase "may I be your ransom," pervade these letters. The younger brother kissed the elder sister's hand, as he did with an elder brother; she was greeted before a younger brother, and in letters to third persons, she was referred to as "my mistress," a term similar to that used for one's mother and grandmother. Men could repudiate their wives, and often did so, but a sister was a lifelong responsibility. The noble brother was the rock on which the security of a woman rested. The oldest Geniza letter preserved (eighth century?) is addressed by a sister to "my beloved and cherished brother, my hope and trust, my salvation from distress."

A woman submitting a boldly worded complaint against her husband to the nagid Samuel b. Hananya excuses herself: She has no male sibling to intercede on her behalf because her brother is considered "an unsocial, bashful young man." And so, her natural protector is of no use. Brothers held the responsibility of looking after their sisters. "You help strangers and people from outside; I, your sister, your flesh and responsibility, have more claim on your support," writes a widow in Tunisia to her brother in Egypt in a time of general disaster and personal hardship. In the Geniza letters, and also in Fatimid inscriptions, the sister is her brother's "honored dear," *karīma*, a term that in literary Arabic may designate a daughter. A brother's obligations to his sister extended to joyous occasions, as well as distressing times. A married sister thus expected to receive cash as a gift from her brother; presents were obligatory under certain circumstances — at the birth of a child, for example, when a visit from the brother was expected.

The extraordinary relationship between brothers and sisters may have had its origin in the shorter life expectancy of the times. As we learn from many deathbed declarations, fathers providing for small children often died young, and it was the brother who accompanied his sister through life: he had to look after her during her orphaned childhood, he was bound to provide her with everything she needed for her marriage, and he took her into his household when, widowed or divorced, she had nowhere else to go. Engagement contracts and other documents show that even in a father's lifetime, a brother often would represent his sister in the negotiations leading to the marriage. A variety of specific circumstances, such as the age or health of the father, might have been involved in particular cases, but this certainly was also a matter of decorum. Commenting on the story of Rebekah (Genesis 24:50), in which Rebekah's brother, not her father, confers with the messenger of her suitor, Abraham, the son of Maimonides remarks, "As is well known, fathers feel embarrassed about personally dealing with the marriage of their daughters."

The brother-sister relationship could also take a different turn. In many cases, a married woman was in an economically more advantageous position than her agnates and could serve them as a pillar of refuge. By virtue of other circumstances, she might enjoy a position of influence within the family and even beyond, and thus be able to intervene in disputes between her relatives. Finally, the code of honor demanded that a person possessing authority or power should harken to a woman's cry of help, especially that of a virtuous women; thus a sister was the natural intercessor for her brother when he was in distress. That such calls of support were not in vain is proved by numerous documents, even those related to women from less well-to-do families: When the father of a little boy was facing imminent death, his elder daughter promised him that she would take the boy to her house, bring him up at her own expense, and give him a part of the large house that she had received from her mother as a gift. (The other part most probably belonged to the father and automatically went to the boy.) The dying man expressed the wish that the property be united in the hands of his son.

Sisters would mediate in important disputes between their brothers and were helpful also in less urgent and sometimes even commonplace situations. A married woman, together with her mother, buys for her brother the highly esteemed (and highly paid for) honor of reciting the Book of Esther during the Purim holiday service. In one case, a sister illegally harbors a female slave belonging to her brother. (The master, a bachelor, had been ordered to sell the slave, since he was not entitled by law to such a possession.) "But," the local dignitary reports, "he has not offered the slave for sale, but put her up with his sister and passes most of his time there." In sum, brother and sister were considered "natural" allies in family affairs.

The Sister's Son

Affection for the sister was often transferred to her son. The sister's son looms large in the private correspondence of the Geniza. This phenomenon, like the brother-sister relation, was heavily conditioned by age distributions characteristic of the medieval period. As a rule, girls married young. By the time a woman was forty and her brother, say, thirty-five, she could easily have a son of twenty or twenty-five. Her son could become an associate of his uncle and some day—especially if the latter had no son—take over the business, preferably after marrying one of his uncle's daughters, as marriage between first cousins was preferred. (The custom was common among the Muslims as well.) In a warm letter addressed to a sister's son and mainly concerned with an unhappy, newly married young woman, the uncle reminds his nephew of the education given to him, the family obligations, and the love between them. ("Education" here means apprenticeship—whatever the occupation was.) In a deathbed declaration, a man appoints his brother-in-law as his executor but leaves money to "his sister's son" (the son of the executor). In a particularly sentimental letter, a sister's son reports to his uncle that he and his wife (the uncle's daughter) are well and healthy, but perish for longing after him and "the smell of the family." He gives regards to about twenty-five persons and, in acknowledging a letter of his uncle, states that its arrival was like the day he parted from him, meaning that the letter substituted for the uncle's presence.

Marriage with the Niece and among First Cousins

The union between a man and the daughter of his sister, censured as incestuous by the Karaites and prohibited by the Church and Islam, was regarded as most natural in the Talmud and is still practiced by some Jews, both of European and Oriental extraction. The Geniza records, however, contain only a few instances of uncle-niece marriage. We read of a thirteenth-century marriage that was about to end in divorce; another was dissolved even before the wedding. Noteworthy in this respect is the claim of the Karaite author Sahl b. Maṣlīʾaḥ (who lived in Jerusalem during the second half of the tenth century) that under the influence of Karaite scholars, the Rabbanite Jews resolved to refrain from "the licentious union" with the sister's daughter. "Mixed" marriages between Karaites and Rabbanites were commonplace in Egypt during the eleventh and twelfth centuries, and both religious groups tended to respect each other's sensibilities.

Unlike the union between uncles and nieces, marriage between first cousins was extremely common in Geniza times. Marriage between the offspring of brothers is attested more than twice as often as marriage between cousins from the female line. This difference is perhaps explained in part by the fact that we have much patrilineal, but little matrilineal, information; the father and occasionally also the grandfather of the bride and bridegroom are noted, but their mothers are mentioned only in exceptional cases. Still, the testimony of the Geniza probably reflects actual situations: marriages with the sons of paternal uncles were common Judaic practice; presumably the emphasis on patriarchy made such marriages more desirable. Such was also the case in Muslim society, where Arab tribal sentiments allowed the transfer of political authority only through the male line. *Bint ʿamm,* "daughter of the paternal uncle" in Arabic means a wife. When a man died without a political heir—that is, without male offspring—his position within the family was transferred to the oldest surviving brother of the deceased, and then, if there were no surviving brothers, to that brother's male offspring.

The pattern of marrying close kin was, of course, well established in the Hebrew Bible. Abraham, the father of the Jewish faith, saw to it that his son Isaac should marry a girl from his family, Rebekah. Isaac's wife was a daughter of his first cousin, Jacob; Isaac's son was sent by his parents to woo a cousin (Genesis 28:2). He won two sisters, Rachel and Leah, and when Ruth was married to a man from her dead husband's kin, she was blessed with the wish that she might become "like Rachel and Leah, who built the house of Israel" (Ruth 4:11). This blessing, naturally, was used in Geniza letters to convey good wishes for a wedding. Nowhere, however, does marriage with relatives appear to have been religiously motivated. Nor can the economic factors have been decisive. We hear of properties united by marriage, but any woman not related to the family could bring in houses and other valuables as dowry, receive them as gifts, or inherit them. Thus the main incentive for the proliferation of marriages with cousins and other close relatives must have been the role of the extended family and to the expectation that the husband and wife who belonged to the same kin would be considerate of each other and of the family at large; they would not expose their own people to shame. And since the expanded family was essentially conceived as "the House of the Father," the children (and children's children) of brothers were the preferred mates.

An additional reason for marriage with relatives from either the father's or the mother's side was to protect the newly wed wife, who, unless she widowed or divorced, normally was very young. It was preferable that she enter the home of people she knew and who had obligations toward her. A survey of the Geniza material seems to show that endogamy was practiced at all times and by all professional groups and segments of the population represented in the documents. It also reveals that the preferred close family relationship was no guarantee of happiness in marriage. We read about engagements that are dissolved, of hardship and even the utmost misery in marriages between cousins, as well as divorces—despite close family connections. Nevertheless, endogamy was a fact of life, based on strong social convictions.

Economic and Legal Aspects of the Extended Family

FAMILY ATTACHMENT AND CLAIMS OF THE INDIVIDUAL

In Geniza times, a household often comprised three generations and included agnates as well as cognates. Both the authorities and the private sector were prone to hold a father or brother—or an even more distant relative—responsible for a man's commitments, although strictly speaking neither Muslim nor Jewish law recognized such a claim. The widening of the nuclear family was counterbalanced, however, by the individualistic spirit of the time—the fervent insistence on acting as autonomously as possible. Internal feuds were exacerbated by close living arrangements, as well as by tightly knit economic associations. The coherence of "the House of the Father" found its physical manifestation in the family sharing living quarters or occupying adjacent or otherwise neighboring buildings. The urge (almost a moral obligation) that the members of a family should live close to one another was strongly felt ("How good and lovely it is when brothers dwell together" [Psalm 133:1]), as was the opposite and more modern sensibility of seeking escape from the supervision and encroachment of relatives. However much families tended to cluster in one or a few dwellings, there is no indication of extended Jewish family quarters—at least not in the great urban centers. The twin capitals of Egypt, Fustat and Cairo, were not the scene of mass dislocation and resettlement, the kind of urban development that might have led to large extended families taking up residence in their own discrete urban area.

Fustat was originally a Byzantine fortress, inhabited by Christians and Jews, and enlarged by an Arab tribal camp-city, into which new immigrants continuously filtered. Cairo, it is true, was a Muslim creation *ex nihilo,* but, like Baghdad, it was conceived from the outset as the seat of the court, the central administration, and the caliphal guards. Of the civil population, only persons directly connected with the court, such as higher officials, purveyors, and court physicians, were allowed to settle in Cairo—at least at the beginning.

It stands to reason that great and rich merchant families settling in the capital of Egypt, like the three Tustarī brothers who emigrated from Iran at the beginning of the eleventh century, might have acquired adjacent properties. But the ordinary immigrant did not possess the means for this manner of settlement. Settlement was ordinarily a protracted process; it took years for a middle-class immigrant to acquire a domicile commensurate with his status. In 1045 the Tunisian Nahray b. Nissīm came to Egypt; twenty years later, he was still living as a tenant in a mansion belonging to his two brothers-in-law. At a much later date, he acquired one-third of the house from one of them (the other had meanwhile died) for the considerable price of 150 dinars.

If the history of Fustat-Cairo, and indeed of all the Mediterranean cities about which the Geniza records inform us, was not favorable to settlement by clusters of extended families, the extended family itself clearly tried hard to stay together. This is proved by the numerous documents in which neighboring houses are united in the hands of a single owner or of close relatives, or in which spacious houses harbor several related families, as in the case of Nahray b. Nissīm. Since the Mediterranean house of the Geniza period—even in provincial towns—often consisted of several stories, it could accommodate several branches of an extended family. The arrangements for joint habitation were of the greatest imaginable variety. For example, a father gives an entire house to his two sons because he wishes them to stay together; the house consists of two stories with a mezzanine in between; the gift is in two equal shares, but the document defines explicitly the parts that belong to each of the two. Sometimes a house was built specifically to serve more than one nuclear family. When a father gave his daughter one-half of a house newly erected by him, he clearly was reserving the other half for himself or another branch of his family. How the arrangement worked in practice may be seen from a detailed will written at approximately the same time: To attract a desirable mate for a young daughter who was widowed and had a son, her father gave her "a large house" (as it is called in the document); he stipulated only that he and his wife, as well as his son (together with his own family), should have the right to occupy the uppermost story as long as they lived. After marrying a great merchant, the girl chose the ground floor for their domicile. The second floor was apparently rented out to a relative.

Even very low-priced houses in provincial towns could be divided up among different members of a family. A house in Ṣahrajt, worth ten dinars, is given by a brother to two sisters. In a village, a woman sells one-fourth of the one-third of a house that she owns to her son-in-law, who lives in the house and has already received a twelfth as the dowry of his wife. Besides the seller and the married couple, the woman's mother and sister and a sixth person, each owning a real (i.e., not nominal) share, live in the house.

Living in the same house did not necessarily mean keeping one household or, as our documents formulate it, "eating at one table." When a father sends his son twenty dirhems (eleven for the poll tax and nine "for the house") and admonishes him to be good company for his mother, wife, and brothers, it is evident that all of them "ate at one table." A maternal uncle and paternal aunts and uncles, greeted in that order, might have occupied other parts of the house. On the other hand, when a boy writing to his father abroad sends regards from his mother, grandmother, maternal aunts, the widow of a paternal uncle, and the maidservant, and adds, "The travel of grandfather coincided with yours so that we have become like orphans," one gets the impression that all of them formed a single household.

In general, letters to relatives express the ardent wish to be united with kin "in one locality and in one house, so that we should see one another all the time." Such conditions could lead, however, to considerable tension. Our sources indicate friction between all sorts of close relations. In one instance two brothers "ate at one table," according to a formal agreement properly stipulated in legal terms. The more modern tendency, which values separate living quarters as being more conducive to good family relations, is also evident in the Geniza papers, particularly in conditions of domicile agreed or forced upon young couples entering marriage, or in marital disputes.

JOINT UNDERTAKINGS
AND RESPONSIBILITIES

Since a son normally followed the occupation of his father and apprenticed with him or, in his absence, with an uncle or brother, occupational cooperation between a father and his adult sons, between brothers, between an uncle and his nephew or nephews, or between cousins was natural, and examples of all such partnerships are found in the Geniza documents. The legal basis for these arrangements is rarely stated expressly. When two washers of the dead, father and son, accepted a partner into their funeral business, they ceded him a quarter of the proceeds. The two appear as one party to the contract, but what arrangements were made within their extended family is not stated. In another case, two brothers, having inherited part of a sugar factory from their father, acquired the other part from their remaining brothers, the other heirs, and then took in two investors as partners. They formed one contracting party, but there is no evidence of the actual contract that bound them. (It is possible that there was, in fact, a formal agreement; it simply has not surfaced among our documents.) Nevertheless, joint undertakings and responsibilities were often arranged on an informal basis.

The character of a relationship was considered of great importance, and arrangements, particularly among families, were often based on trust. A father intent on grooming his son for independence gave him, as early as possible, some capital for doing business on his own. This might initially take the form of a preferred partnership with the son of a relative or business friend overseas. The general trend was toward keeping separate, meticulously ordered accounts.

Having cooperated in business during a lifetime, brothers and other relatives were inclined to appoint the surviving partner as trustee of their children and possessions. Members of the extended family were entrusted with guardianships because they had the moral obligation to assist relatives in need, regardless of their own situation. Besides his immediate family, an Alexandrian harbored five relatives in his house and, despite his prolonged illness, was prepared to accept two more. The debts of a relative were an obligation that the family was expected to assume. Peraḥyā b. Joseph Yijū, himself a poor schoolmaster at that time, sends forty dirhems to his youngest brother Samuel for the payment of his debts and for some personal expenses; in his letter to Samuel's creditor he writes, "God knows, I had to take them out of my mouth," meaning, I had to starve to be able to make this payment.

But brotherly affection and family honor were not always regarded as sufficient for prompting a man to act for a needy relative. Additional motives, each fitting the persons concerned, had to be adduced. The words of the prophet Isaiah "not hiding oneself from his own flesh" (Isaiah 58:7) were the *locus classicus* for the religious command that charity begins at home. Needless to say, strained relations within families could undermine traditional values and create difficulties for kith and kin, a condition attested in quite a number of documents. Whether the extended family liked it or not, the community and the government held the family responsible for its members. When a taxpayer absented himself or otherwise evaded his duties, the government sought payment from his father, brothers, or brother-in-law.

It was natural to protect the members of the family against any possible claims that might be made against them after one's death. Hence the endless releases found in the Geniza safeguarding the rights of heirs, and, where circumstances so warranted, for the lifetime of a contracting party. In these matters, the interests of the extended family prevailed over those of the nuclear family. When a man died without children, a brother or any other member of "the House of the Father" closest to him would take his estate, while his wife, who had served him all their joint life, had no share in it whatsoever. A paternal cousin as exclusive heir was not exceptional. "You are not your husband's heir; his daughters [who happened to be also her daughters] are his heirs; therefore take care and do not give their money away to others"—in such terms a widow is warned by the elders of Damietta, when, in their presence, she has given a release to the representatives of merchants who had dealings with her late husband.

The concept underlying this legal situation is brought into relief by a remarkable disposition, made by a man either while seriously ill or before embarking on a distant and dangerous voyage. His only child, a minor daughter, is declared his sole heir. His wife, designated as the child's guardian, may remain in the house as long as she lives. The wife's maintenance will come from the estate, and she may conduct its affairs without anyone being entitled to interfere (a provision which suggests that the testator had full confidence in her). But if the girl dies, the court may take over the property and maintain the widow with the proceeds; if she prefers to remarry, the court may pay her the second installment of the marital gift stipulated in her marriage contract. "The balance of the estate returns to my father's house." The word "returns" implies that a man's possessions consist in the first place in what he has inherited from his forefathers and agnates and only secondarily in what he himself has earned.

THIRTEEN

Marriage

The Nature of the Marriage Bond

In Judaism, marriage is considered the natural state for adults; the wife is the God-given companion of her husband, as stipulated in the Book of Genesis. During the classical Geniza period, the emphasis of the Mediterranean Jewish community was on reproduction: replenishing the group and, more generally, humankind. There can be little doubt that as far as marriage between young people was concerned, procreation was regarded not only as a religious duty but also as something natural and expected. But only in a very few marriage contracts of the Palestinian rite of the tenth and eleventh centuries is a stipulation preserved in which the wife declares her readiness "to become a mother of children." Moreover, as of the twelfth century, this phrase seems to have disappeared altogether. One might argue that the need to procreate was so self-evident that no good reason existed to continue the earlier practice. If so, why then was it introduced in the first place? The rabbinic interpretation of Genesis 1:28 established that the biblical injunction to multiply referred only to men. Some scholars might have concluded from this that the female partner was not obliged to participate in the process unless she had promised to do so in advance and of her own free will. In any case, the biblical quotation "they built and succeeded" meaning "be blessed with children" is found throughout the centuries superscribed over Jewish marriage contracts—Rabbanite and Karaite, Palestinian and Babylonian.

As was Eve to Adam, so were Jewish brides expected to be their husbands' companions. The documents speak of love and affection in conjugal relations, a sensibility familiar to the modern age. The Karaites, a numerous and influential section of the Jewish population during the Geniza period, were particularly explicit as to the content and scope of companionship, as can be seen from the following marriage contract:

I, Hezekiah, the bridegroom, will provide her with clothing, cover, and food, supply all her needs and wishes according to my ability and to the extent I can afford. I will conduct myself toward her with truthfulness and sincerity, with love and affection. I will not grieve nor repress her and will let her have food, clothing, and marital relations to the extent habitual among Jewish men. . . .

Sarwa [the bride] hears the words of Hezekiah and agrees to marry him and to be his wife and companion in purity, holiness, and fear of God, to listen to his words, to honor and to hold him dear, to be his helper and to do in his house what a virtuous Jewish woman is expected to do, to conduct herself toward him with love and consideration, to be under his rule, and to direct her desire toward him.

However, the vast majority of the marriage contracts preserved in the Geniza, those written by Rabbanite notaries use altogether different formulas. The usual obligations are expressed concisely: the husband undertakes to provide his wife with food and clothing, to honor her, and to fulfill the conjugal duties, as Jewish men truthfully do, and she simply declares her willingness to become his wife. Only in a limited number of documents, mainly Palestinian and from the tenth and eleventh centuries, does the bride echo the groom by promising to serve, attend, and honor him. The word "love" is never used, for love is a gift of God, not something one can promise. It is possible that the Karaite texts are closer to the idealized view of marriage within the Geniza community. Unlike the ancient Rabbanite marriage contracts, which are written in accord with ancient Aramaic formulas, the Karaite texts, written in Hebrew, a living language, were vehicles of expressing contemporaneous sentiments. Thus, the actual differences in the language and tone between the Karaite and Rabbanite contracts may not necessarily reflect widely divergent sentiments toward the institution of marriage.

The Sanctity of Marriage

Besides providing shelter for the wife and a help for the husband, as well as opportunity for companionship and procreation for both, medieval marriage fulfilled a number of other functions. It was, above all, designed to protect man from the sin of fornication, the opportunity for illicit behavior being ever present in an urban environment. "Living in Cairo without a wife is extremely difficult for blameless and chaste persons," emphasizes a Karaite husband again and again while imploring a relative to induce his wife to return to him. We are informed by a Geniza sermon that the wife is a wall around her husband; she brings atonement for his sins and peace to his domicile. The basis of this sermon is found in the Talmud, which goes so far as to say, "When a man marries, all his sins are forgiven him." The comment has no ironic intent, for the same phrasing applies to those who attain high office or convert to the Jewish faith. Indeed, marriage is thus conceived as entrance into a state of higher rank and greater responsibility. The ancient benediction recited at the betrothal and wedding gives eloquent testimony to this benefit of marriage. The benediction praises God for what He has permitted and prohibited in marriage and concludes, "Blessed be the bridal canopy and the conclusion of the marriage."

Moreover, without a proper home no Jewish religious life was feasible. The benedictions and elaborate grace accompanying meals, as well as many other religious duties, such as hospitality and care for the traveler and the poor, were best fulfilled in the atmosphere provided by a household. It seems strange, at first, that an institution couched so fundamentally in religious doctrine was not solemnized in a synagogue, or that marriage ceremonies did not require the presence of a religious functionary. The Jewish divines normally entrusted with marrying a couple represented secular authority, and the actual descriptions of marriage celebrations which we have from the Geniza period reflect their thoroughly mundane character. But even here we should not overlook the occasion's spiritual overlay. The "seven benedictions" pronounced at the ceremony and repeated at the subsequent banquet (or rather, banquets) and the superscriptions over the Rabbanite and Karaite marriage certificates all prove that the religious aspect of marriage was never completely absent from the minds of Near Eastern Jewry—or, in any event, that the celebration of marriage was imbued with religious sentiments.

Choosing a Mate

At present, we are unable to unravel the tangled threads of family politics leading to marriage that were set into motion at birth. Undoubtedly, women had much say about these matters, but their voices seldom reach us through the Geniza records. What we do know of the process leading to marriage is represented in the following summary gleaned from the available documents.

Since endogamy, especially marriage with a first cousin, was an accepted practice, the choice of a mate was largely predetermined. If a more or less suitable close relative was available and amenable, the matter was decided accordingly. In any case, the relative had precedence. How deeply these notions of the prior rights of the cousin were rooted is illustrated by the story of the India trader Abraham b. Yijū. As soon as he arrived in Aden, after a sojourn of many years in India, he offered the hand of his only daughter (together with his riches) to any son of his brother or sister—relatives who, during his absence, had been forced by the Norman invasion to leave their native Tunisia. When no reply was received, Ben Yijū settled in Aden and promised his daughter to a young man from the leading Jewish family in that town. The girl lived in the house of her future in-laws for three years awaiting a propitious time for the marriage. Then word came from his family that the eldest son of a brother of his was a scholar, hence a worthy match for his daughter. As a result, he broke his promise to the family from Aden. His action would not have been considered disgraceful, as everyone understood that "the son of my brother has more rights to her than strangers." Ben Yijū made his way to the capital of Egypt, only to find communications with his family (who then lived as refugees in Sicily) had again become severed; once more, many "strangers" asked for the hand of the his daughter. But Ben Yijū remained adamant. Finally, seven years after the initial contact, the wedding between the two cousins was celebrated.

"Marrying out," on the other hand, was an opportunity for families to widen their connections and to enhance their strength. A son of the Persian banker Sahlawayh b. Ḥayyīm, often mentioned in the Geniza records, married Mulūk, the granddaughter of Manasse ibn al-Qazzāz, the Jewish administrator of Syria for the Fatimid caliph al-ʿAzīz (975–96). A daughter of Sahlawayh became the wife of Ḥesed, better known under his Arabic name Abū Naṣr Tustarī. He was the powerful brother of Abū Saʿd, vizier to the mother of the infant caliph al-Mustanṣir (who ascended the throne in 1036), and for a short period the most influential man in the Fatimid Empire. A granddaughter of Sahlawayh also must have married out, as proved by the substantial nuptial gift assigned to her by her future husband. A good example of diplomatic marriage is offered by the scholarly and public-minded Berechiah brothers of Qayrawān (first quarter of eleventh century). They were allied by marriage both to the Tāhertīs and the Majjānīs, two powerful families in that city, at times at odds with one another, who thus found it advantageous to be linked with the pious and highly esteemed Berechiahs.

Marrying daughters out for the sake of creating useful family connections was particularly common in overseas relations. An elder brother writes from al-Mahdiyya in Tunisia, to Judah b. Moses b. Sighmār, having learned of the latter's marriage in Egypt:

I took notice of the description of your blessed and auspicious wedding and understand that God has granted you to become connected with the most illustrious and finest people, those of whom one can boast in East and West. This is more precious than the earth and the fullness thereof. Thank and praise God that He has cast your lot with the leading families of Israel. May God make . . . complete what He has given to you and make your happiness permanent, may He aid them through you and aid you through them and make you a blessing for one another. May He bless you with a male child. "May the woman who comes into your house be like Rachel and Leah. . . ." [Ruth 4:11].

Needless to say, an arranged marriage to a member of a prestigious family could also be economically advantageous. Indeed, business houses in different overseas entrepôts sought to cement alliances with one another for purposes of strengthening commercial ties and did so by means of marriage. It was recognized, of course, that blood lines and family history reflect distinctive traits, especially a capacity for learning. It was therefore desirable to marry a girl from a scholarly family in the expectation that she would produce "sons studying the Torah." In a long congratulatory letter on the occasion of the marriage of the son of one scholar with the daughter of another (whose son also was noted for his learning), the father of the groom is first praised for "the mixing of grapes of vine with grapes of vine," that is, a scholarly union. He is then assured that the young couple's offspring will live up to expectations, since "boys become like their mother's brother," and finally, that the union will be blessed because the girl is an orphan (marrying an orphan was an act of religious merit). In an extensive holograph to a dayyān and his learned sons in a provincial town, Abraham Maimonides strongly recommends a young man, probably one of his former students, as a prospective son-in-law. The young man had visited the judge's abode, but had received no clear answer. Yet, Abraham emphasizes, "he still persists in his love" (not to the girl, whom he perhaps had not even seen, but to the scholarly family). He is prepared, if required, to commit all his possessions for the nuptial gift — as recommended in the Talmud: "Sell all you have and marry the daughter of a scholar."

In a society that idealized the pursuit of religious knowledge, family connection with a scholar was sought not only by the learned but even by persons clearly lacking a scholarly education. In a letter in which the sender describes himself as "the most influential man in the community," he asks for the hand of the recipient's daughter because he wishes to follow the sages' advice to marry a scholar's daughter. Influential as he was, his profession obviously was not highly esteemed, for he suggests that should his future father-in-law wish it, he will open a clothing store. (Being a clothier was the most common occupation of a respectable merchant, whether Muslim, Christian, or Jewish.) Throughout the letter, the recipient is asked to treat the matter with utmost secrecy and to reply, if possible, at the break of dawn the next morning, for if the suitor were refused and this were to be made public, he would lose face. From various biblical quotations in the letter, it is evident that the man was a widower and father of children (probably no longer living with him), that is, a man who had gained riches and wished to enhance his position by the prestige obtained from a scholarly connection. The fact of a proposal by letter should not be misunderstood: Jewish (and Christian) girls did not remain entirely invisible beyond the narrow circle of the extended family. Girls attended synagogue services, and men chatted with women afterward, but there is no evidence that boys could speak to girls of marriageable age in the synagogue court. Rather, they would form separate groups that nevertheless managed to catch glimpses of one another. One could meet a girl in the house of relatives, and so there were opportunities to form initial impressions that could lead eventually to more enduring acquaintance and then to relationships.

The Process of Marriage

A Jewish father had the right to give his minor daughter in marriage (although such an action was disapproved by some authorities), but once she had attained sexual maturity (which was put at the age of twelve years and six months), she was legally independent. Were the betrothed a mature woman (say, someone previously married), she herself could negotiate a contract with her future husband; in this respect Jewish law differed from that of Islam. Decency and practical considerations dictated, however, that young girls appoint an experienced male to serve as their representative — usually a father or brother. Mature women, in fact, often did the same. Presumably the mother had a great say in the matter, because a substantial (or the main) part of the girl's future dowry would come from the mother's personal property.

In principle, a marriage was achieved in three stages: engagement, betrothal, and the wedding. It took place through a contract between two parties. The two parties agreed in the presence of at least two witnesses on the mutual financial and other obligations and rights, fixed a date for the wedding, and stipulated fines in the event that the agreement or the date of the wedding was not honored. This was called *shiddūkhīn* in Hebrew, and *milāk* or *imlāk* ("property conveyance") in Arabic. This legal act naturally was preceded by cautious testing of the ground, indirect and informal negotiating, and asking for the hand of the chosen mate. Betrothal constituted an intermediary stage before the consummation of the marriage in the bridal chamber of the new couple. More particularly, it was the legal conclusion and religious consecration of the marriage, by which the partners became husband and wife, although intimate relations were not yet permitted. When the relationship between the couple broke down before the actual consummation of the marriage, a bill of divorce was nevertheless necessary to terminate the relationship. That situation was not unusual; the expression "a virgin divorced after betrothal" is repeatedly found in the documents. The consummation of the marriage was legally defined as "entering," namely the bridal chamber—the event that led to intimacy. When said of the bride, it referred to entering the husband's house. Consummation was also referred to as "taking" the bride as wife; or "the procession," during which she was led from the house of her father to that of her future husband. Similar customs existed among the Muslims.

In practice, the engagement and the betrothal were often combined. The same was done, even more frequently, with the betrothal and the wedding. The latter custom became the standard practice in the centuries after the classical Geniza period. Thus, as a rule, the wedding celebration was preceded either by a period of engagement or betrothal. Sometimes, when no contractual action had been taken before the wedding, the three elements—agreement on financial obligations and other matters, formal consecration, and leading the bride home—were merged into a single event.

ENGAGEMENT

The most urgent matter to be settled was the first marriage gift, which became the bride's property on the day of the wedding. Usually a small present, forming part of the first gift, was given to the bride's family, to be retrieved in the event that the engagement was broken. Since this arrangement allowed either side to back out of the engagement (either by not giving the gift, or by returning it once given), it is easy to understand why people preferred the procedure. The time of the wedding could then be fixed. In the engagement of Sitt al-Khāṣṣa, the daughter of an India trader, to Ṣamaḥ, the son of a perfumer, the conditions imposed on the fiancé consisted of the general conditions customary in all marriage agreements made in Fustat in the twelfth century and specific ones, imposed by Sitt al-Khāṣṣa or her mother. The future wife was to be regarded as financially reliable in all matters concerning the household, and no oath could ever be imposed on her; the future husband was not allowed to take a second wife, nor could he hire a maidservant without her approval; and in case of her death without children, one half of the dowry was to revert to her father's family. The special conditions show the strong position of the fiancée's family. Sitt al-Khāṣṣa was also to have the choice of domicile — both the locality and the apartment itself. The rents from her real estate would constitute her personal property and would not be at the disposal of her future husband. Finally, both parties were subject to a fine of twenty dinars if the engagement was broken and the "symbolic purchase," which according to Jewish law confirmed legal actions, was made by the court from both the bride's mother and the fiancé.

But that was not all. Although the wedding was a full year away, the fiancé took no chances. The value of each piece of the trousseau, about 125 items, was estimated, making a total of 640 dinars, and the list was attached to the engagement document. The details about the bride's real property were also attached, although the property itself was expressly exempted from the dowry, over which the husband would have the right of disposition.

This model engagement shows us how well-to-do people arranged their affairs. They tried to avoid anything that could lead to last-minute misunderstandings between the parties; the first installment of the marriage gift was safely deposited, and the dowry was estimated and approved by the fiancé and ready for delivery. Less fortunate people were not able to contract such well-planned and tidy engagements. Most of the documents relating to marriage reveal a far less exhaustive state of affairs.

BETROTHAL

It stands to reason that an elaborate engagement agreement like that of Sitt al-Khāṣṣa and Ṣamaḥ was accompanied by a festive party. The custom was different at a betrothal. With respect to financial arrangements, a betrothal was very similar to an engagement, but in becoming betrothed, a woman also became legally married. The betrothal benediction was recited, and bride and groom drank from a cup of wine over which a blessing was said. Legal documents reflect a great variety of other customs and procedures and shed light into the composite character of the community and of its legal heritage.

An ancient example of betrothal procedures is provided by the following formulary from Fustat dated December 1027:

[The groom] declared before us: "I wish to betroth and take as wife [this woman], and here are the 'gratifications' which I shall give her." He produced three rings, one of plated gold and two of silver. We asked him, "What is the marriage gift [meaning the one given in addition to the formal, betrothal gift]?" He replied, "Twenty good gold pieces, ten for the early and ten for the late installment." We asked, "Where are the first ten?" He said, "I do not have them at present. I shall give them to her, or to a representative of hers, as soon as God has them ready for me." We went ourselves to her, and after her identity was established by two trustworthy witnesses, she legally appointed [a third individual] as her representative. Having done this, we betrothed him to her in a definite marriage bond and gave the "gratifications" to her representative. . . .

Seventeen days passed between the first and last court actions in this matter. The document shows that the bride could have acted on her own behalf; the procedures did not require her father nor any other relative to stand as her representative. The rings may once have had symbolic significance, but by that time their sole purpose was to gratify the bride and to serve as the formal betrothal gift, obligatory at the conclusion of a marriage.

An even older description of betrothal procedures, taken not from the Geniza, but from a legal enquiry sent from Qayrawān to Saadya Gaon (d. 942 in Baghdad), emphasizes the role of the father. It deals with a familiar situation—a man with more than one marriageable daughter—and raises a familiar question: with whom had the marriage been contracted? The letter states:

This is our local custom with regard to marriage: If she has come of age, she empowers her father to receive her betrothal gift; if she is a minor, he does so on his own, as approved by the sages. The congregation assembles in the synagogue which the father attends, and he receives there the betrothal gift for his daughter. This Reuben [meaning the father of the daughters] was a scholar and an old man, and scholars and others gathered in the house of study. [The old scholar prayed in a *bēth midrāsh*, or house of study.] Simeon [the groom] stood up from his seat and gave the betrothal gift to

Reuben, while the scholars from the school of the late R. Nathan were seated around. Simeon spoke up and said, "May your daughter be married to me by this ring." Those present shouted to him in Hebrew about four or five times, "Say which! say which!" but he paid no attention to them because he was abashed, standing before the congregation and the scholars.

The synagogue, it should be noted, is used here not as a place of worship but as one of public assembly and legal action. The parties involved were apparently of modest means, showing little concern about the family's prestige and the status of its members.

A betrothal document written in Fustat in summer 1007 involves a prestigious segment of society and enables us to understand why, at certain times, it was deemed desirable to keep the "betrothal" (that is, the formal marriage) and the wedding festivities separate. Here again, the daughter has appointed her father as her representative. The groom hands over to the father (standing proxy for the bride) 100 dinars and the rings, after the groom and the bride have agreed to the usual mutual obligations that they will have to fulfill once they are united under the bridal canopy. Another 150 dinars are promised as a later installment. An accompanying document no doubt contained details about the trousseau and the imminent wedding.

A purse of one hundred gold pieces was a very large sum of money; its delivery demonstrated that the contracting parties were in earnest. Tying the financial arrangements into the formal marriage left only the ceremonial and social aspects of the wedding remaining: the benedictions, the other rites, and the socially obligatory banquets. It was a reaction against the age-old experience that "there is no marriage contract that does not elicit squabbles"—the last-minute misunderstandings about details of the dowry or the marriage gift that threatened to arise when the marriage was formally contracted and the contract signed at the wedding.

THE MARRIAGE CONTRACT

Our main source for the socioeconomic conditions under which a marriage was contracted is the *ketubba,* or marriage contract. Although many hundreds of documents of this type have been preserved, no two are identical, as each was tailored to the circumstances of a particular couple and their families. Unfortunately, the Geniza ketubbas also share another common trait: the great majority of them have come down to us in tantalizingly fragmented condition.

In addition to marriage contracts proper, the Geniza contains related court records (in particular, drafts or copies of these contracts), as well as notes of judges summarizing the main points of a ketubba in preparation for the issuance of a document. Finally, settlements arranged during marital life or after the marriage's termination by death or repudiation, as well as dispositions in contemplation of death, often to refer to stipulations when the marriage was contracted. Occasionally such settlements are written on the reverse of the original ketubba.

Like any other legal document, the ketubba normally opens by stating the exact time and place of its execution. The locality is regularly defined geographically, such as "Fustat, Egypt, which is situated on the Nile River," but also administratively, by naming the head of the Jewish community to whose authority the legal action incorporated in the document was subject. Some Geniza ketubbas contain the assurances conventionally found in legal documents, namely, that in concluding the agreement the parties were in full command of their physical and mental faculties, that they were acting out of free will and had not been coerced, that the document had been executed in accordance with the strictest provisions of Jewish (and gentile) law, and so on.

The first item requiring attention is the status of the bride. She was usually described as a virgin, which simply meant that this was her first marriage. When the bride was divorced or widowed (or both), or "a virgin divorced after betrothal," this too was stated, sometimes euphemistically. Occasionally, to avoid raising unpleasant history, the bride was described as "[presently] unmarried," or among the Karaites, "the woman," or "previously married" (a freedwoman, or a captive who had been ransomed, also would be designated "the woman"); occasionally we find the name of a widow's late husband mentioned.

Such distinctions were necessary because an ancient law stipulated that the minimum obligatory marriage gift to a virgin was 200 *zūz* (silver pieces) and that to any other woman it was 100. (In the Geniza period, 200 zūz were equivalent to 25 dirhems; a woman who was not a virgin received 12½ dirhems.) For the most part, it is not expressly stated or even evident in the wording of the ketubba whether these payments of the minimum obligatory nuptial gift were actually made in silver pieces or were included in the marriage gift, which was invariably promised and delivered in gold, or equivalent property or goods. The Karaites made the same distinction, but fixed 50 silver pieces for a virgin and 25 for other brides.

These minutiae of Jewish law are helpful inasmuch as they reveal to us—even where the details about the status of the bride are lost—whether a woman was marrying for the first time. Muslim marriage contracts from this period regularly indicate whether the bride had come of age. The Karaites did the same, including the phrase "a girl able to fulfill the religious duties," for many commandments had to be observed by a married Jewish woman. In Rabbanite ketubbas, this detail occurs only sporadically, although it is found over the course of six centuries. In any case, it was redundant to specify that a bride was able to fulfill religious duties; the very fact that she had made one or more legally valid declarations in the marriage contracts constituted an indication that she had come of age.

The personal names of groom and bride are defined by those of their fathers; their mothers are never mentioned; the reason, of course, was that the name of a man's father was his family name. When the spouses are first cousins, their common grandfather is occasionally noted; longer pedigrees are rare exceptions. In one document, the bride is characterized as "of noble descent." Since numerous ketubbas from distinguished families are found in the Geniza, the fact of not reciting genealogies at weddings (unlike memorial services, at which such recitations were standard), may have been intentional, perhaps to avoid rivalry and discord between the newly united families.

Names of fathers are usually followed by the blessings to be pronounced over a dead or a living person. This detail is important, because whether or not a person was orphaned had a considerable influence on his or her socioeconomic position. Here, however, we encounter the difficulty that many of our papers are drafts of notes or enclosures, such as trousseau lists, and the clerks would not have bothered to include the relevant blessings in drafts. The occupation of the groom or his father is indicated only, it seems, when the occupation formed part of the name by which a person was known, such as Bu' l-Barakāt (the Perfumer) or Bu' l-Makārim (the Goldsmith). The patronymic and the occupational title were then followed by the parties' full Hebrew names. Occupations are also indicated in special instances, as when a cantor marries the daughter of a beadle.

In many marriage contracts—particularly the more ancient ones, which are executed according to the Palestinian rite, as well as all the Karaite ketubbas—the bride appoints a representative, whose name and those of the two persons witnessing the appointment are mentioned. The representative is referred to by the Greek term *epitropos* (appearing in many different forms) and, in Karaite documents, by the Hebrew *pāqīd,* the equivalent of Arabic *wakīl* (proxy, deputy, agent). In most other documents, especially those formulated according to standard Babylonian custom, this detail is not to be found.

The proxy mentioned in the ketubba differs fundamentally from the *walī,* or guardian, of the Muslim marriage law. "Epitropos" was used throughout the Geniza period to designate an agent appointed by a person to serve as his or her representative. By contrast, the Arabic (and later Muslim) "walī" in this context designated the male person who had power over a female unable to act for herself.

The use of two persons to witness the bride's appointment of her proxy was Jewish practice in Palestine for centuries before the advent of Islam. It is possible, then, that Karaites adapted their legal forms to Muslim models, for the detail of having the bride represented by a pāqīd appears in Karaite marriage contracts consistently and prominently. On the other hand, it is not implausible that in doing that they were observing ancient Palestinian custom to a greater extent than the majority of Jews who had adopted Babylonian usages.

Turning now to the substance of the ketubba, a note on the term itself is in order. Literally, "ketubba" simply means a written statement (on the obligations of the husband toward his spouse). Although the actual documents spell out the duties of the future wife as well (mostly in general terms), the essence of the ketubba is the husband's financial responsibility. As a result, it is the wife who receives and keeps the ketubba. Some marriage contracts describe the husband's obligations regarding the second marriage gift to be paid at a divorce or the husband's death simply as *ḥōv,* "debt," while a late document characterizes the dowry as a loan.

Under the general meaning of obligation, the term "ketubba" assumes three different meanings, two of which, strangely enough, are used concomitantly in the standard marriage contracts of the Geniza: It designates the obligatory minimum gift of 25 (or 12½) dirhems plus the sum of the second gift; it also includes the total due the wife from the husband, including various gifts and dowry, which itself is usually broken down into various items—with monetary valuations attached to each. The main part of the ketubba is followed by a list of stipulations—some long, some short—which fall into three categories: (1) general items, found in most documents, summarily called "the well-known conditions," or "the well-known conditions imposed by the daughters of Israel"; (2) fairly common items; and (3) specific items related to the special circumstances of the couple.

In the majority of marriage contracts, the "conditions" contain the postulate that the wife must be regarded as trustworthy in the conduct of her household (and sometimes other financial matters) and that no oath may be imposed on her in this matter by her husband or his heirs.

This detail dates back to biblical times, when the Israelite peasant woman held the reins of the household while her husband went out to the fields at sunrise and did not come home until sunset (Psalm 104:22–23). The God-fearing woman of valor, so highly praised in Proverbs (31:10–31), is in effect a thrifty housekeeper, of whom it is said, "The heart of her husband trusts in her, and he will have no lack of gain." (31:11) The social conditions of the Geniza period, of course, differed radically from those of ancient Israel, but the stipulation of trustworthiness was still of vital importance for marital peace and the wife's economic security. Also common are the husband's promises not to marry another wife and not to keep a maid not approved by his spouse.

Many conditions were connected with the dowry, the most common being that half of it would return to the wife's family should she die without offspring, male or female. This originally Palestinian usage became more or less generally accepted. The Karaites, interestingly, stipulated that the entire dowry of a woman dying without child should go back to her father's house. Even during her lifetime, under Karaite practice, the husband was not permitted to take any action with the dowry without informing and consulting his wife.

Not "well-known conditions" but still frequently found, are stipulations in the second category—"common items"—dealing with such questions as the domicile of the couple, whether the husband or the wife had the prerogative of choosing it, and a wide variety of other matters connected with this issue. Discussion also arises regarding whether a wife's earnings are her personal property or belong to her husband, or whether she may keep her earnings only if she uses them to pay for her clothing. The documents sometimes stipulate the condition that a husband should not travel abroad (or even outside the couple's city) without the consent of his wife and without providing for her maintenance in his absence or in the event of his death while traveling.

The third category, stipulations occasioned by special circumstances, varies greatly, as one would expect. These include the cost of the wedding, the relationship of the spouses with members of the two families, children from a previous marriage, the wife's freedom of movement, and her treatment in general. Such stipulations presuppose that each party to the marriage was aware of the other's background.

In addition to the three categories of stipulations, which reflect the realities of life in the Geniza period, there is a fourth category that may be characterized as traditional: stipulations that were common in talmudic times and were retained in the ketubbas solely according to Palestinian (not Babylonian, that is, general Jewish) usage. Most of the laws represented by these stipulations were still in force, but, for one reason or another, were no longer included in the common marriage contracts. One for instance, provided that if a wife was taken captive (which often also meant raped), her husband was obliged to ransom her—not with her dowry but with his own money; having brought her back, he was to live with her without animosity. Finally, there are stipulations concerned with religious observances (for example, in the frequent cases of mixed marriages between Karaites and Rabbanites) and, after the reforms introduced by Moses Maimonides in the late twelfth century, the so-called laws of purity. They are normally spelled out at the end of the marriage contract, and the wife is warned that if she fails to observe them she will lose her marriage gift.

THE WEDDING AND THE CONSUMMATION OF THE MARRIAGE

The date of the wedding was commonly fixed at the engagement or the betrothal. But requests for postponement because one of the two parties had not yet succeeded in obtaining the necessary funds were frequent. In addition to fines, which were usually stipulated for a delay not agreed to by the other party, we occasionally hear that the groom had to pay "alimony" to the bride for every day that the wedding was postponed after the date fixed. The favorite periods for weddings were the spring months (from March through May) and early fall (from September through November). The number of weddings for the spring months would have been far higher had not Jewish custom discouraged weddings during the seven weeks between Passover and Pentecost. Climatic reasons aside, the summer months were avoided because several members of a family, the bridegroom included, might travel abroad on business during that period. Winters, of course, could be quite cold, even in Egypt.

One preferred to hold the wedding close to the end of the week, so that there would be sufficient time for the preparations and an opportunity for an additional celebration on the forthcoming Sabbath. Approximately half of all weddings were held on Wednesday and Thursday—preferably on Thursday. Friday was not popular because the strict Sabbath period of rest, which began on Friday afternoon about an hour before sunset, left too little time for the proceedings. In addition, there might have been a desire to avoid emulating the Muslims. According to Islamic custom, the ceremonial procession of the bride to her husband's house and subsequent consummation took place on Thursday night, which is "the night Friday," the holy weekday of Islam.

Considerations of thrift caused people to hold their wedding immediately before the holidays, especially Passover in the spring and the Feast of Tabernacles in the fall, or on Purim, which was a day of merriment rather than a holy day. We even read about a wedding on the eve of the New Year's Day, which is dedicated to prayer. An examination of the cases preserved in the Geniza shows that these modest affairs were often second marriages or marriages of poorer couples, village people, and the like. Normally one tried "not to mix joy with joy," that is, not to hold a wedding close to the time of a holiday.

The festivities themselves, which took place both before and after the bride's procession to the home of her future husband, required extensive and advance preparation. Since the wedding was celebrated at home, one had to make room for the guests. The banquets for men and women were held in different rooms (or, at least, in separate sections of a room partitioned by a curtain), and both families, it seems, had to contribute to the costs. The special conditions were agreed upon long before the great event. In a betrothal agreement from fall 1140, a groom agrees to make all the expenditures for the wedding, "in respect of both women and men." A slightly earlier betrothal contract, written by Ḥalfōn b. Manasse (1100–1138), in which the groom receives one-half of a property owned by the mother of the bride, but promises to buy the bride's outfit, also stipulates that the groom will not provide a wedding banquet, "nor any of the sumptuous luxuries of the people of Fustat."

Details of the wedding ceremonies are referred to in passing in letters and documents. We read about the dyeing of the bride's hair with saffron and of her hands and feet with henna, her makeup, her ceremonial dress, and her procession to the bridegroom's house. There is also a reference to the *sīniyya,* the tray on which money was deposited for the poor and for the lower communal officials during the *hanā',* the reception for receiving congratulations. One letter speaks of the custom of the congregation ceremoniously leading the groom to the synagogue on two consecutive Sabbaths (presumably the one before and the one after the wedding day) and honoring him there by having him recite the most avidly sought-after lections from the Bible portions of the liturgy. On both Sabbaths, the cantor would sing religious poems appropriate to the occasion or specially written for the bride and groom. Hundreds of such compositions have been found in the Geniza.

The more ancient marriage contracts are occasionally signed by persons characterizing themselves as *shōshevīn,* "best man," We learn that such a relationship meant a life connection involving even the best man's family. Older ketubbas are signed by a large number of persons; thirty-six signatures are affixed to one dated 990 from Barqa in eastern Libya.

The Legal and Actual Position of the Bride

To what extent was the woman's consent to the marriage required? There is no doubt about the legal situation. A woman who had reached maturity could not be married without her consent, which had to be given before two witnesses. Most complete and better-preserved engagements and betrothal agreements (and often also the marriage contracts themselves) contain the statement that the bride had appointed another individual as her representative to negotiate and con-tract her marriage. At that stage, the choice of the mate had already been made; the question is to what extent the future bride took part in his selection. Frankly, we do not know much about this point, since our sources make little mention of it. Given the frequency of engagements broken off and betrothals dissolved, one may conclude that it was not only family politics and financial considerations but also the wishes of the young couples that influenced the final decision. Many marriage agreements say expressly, "if *she* [not her parents or another] breaks off the engagement." No doubt much depended on the nature and strength of all the personalities concerned.

According to Quayrawānese legal practice, the bride's dislike of the groom was a sufficient reason for granting her the right to demand the dissolution of the betrothal. The Jewish courts in Egypt seem to have preferred to obtain a formal declaration from both bride and groom that they were incompatible. Some Geniza letters seem to show that the choice of future mates was indeed dictated by the heart. For example, a young man from Palermo who was the business representative of prom-inent Sicilian merchants in Egypt married an orphan girl serving a great family instead of one of the wealthy daughters of the house.

In another account, a group of Karaites from Cairo came to Jerusalem and stayed there for several months, praying at the various holy sites. The group included a girl, Rebekah, and her two suitors, Abraham and Simon. The elders of the company decided for the former (no reasons given), but Rebekah preferred Simon. Abraham swore he would kill one of the two if she was not given to him. The worried elders asked the girl to remain at home, or, if she had to leave the house, to do so only in the company of a married woman. When the father in Cairo was asked his opinion, he replied that his daughter should marry whomever she wished. The elders then tried to persuade Abraham to desist from his unreasonable demand to marry Rebekah, but he remained adamant. Given the situation, the elders decided, quite reasonably, that the girl should not be married in Jerusalem at all, but that the entire matter should remain unresolved until the group safely returned to Cairo (which was to happen by "the Sabbath of Consolation"—after the termination of the period of mourning over the destruction of the Temple). At that point, Simon lost patience, and applied to a lower official of the Rabbanite community, who in return for a small payment, concocted a marriage contract showing Rebekah as legally betrothed to Simon and containing counterfeit signatures of all the Karaite elders. The fraud was easily detected, and a tremendous scandal ensued. The official lost his position and was temporarily put under ban, and Rebekah, who had become very angry, now declared that she would marry neither of her two suitors. The story is included in a letter from Jerusalem addressed to the head of the Cairene Karaite community, Aaron b. Ṣaghīr.

Marriage and the Authorities

Matters pertaining to personal status were governed by the law of the religious community to which a person belonged. The great majority of engagements, betrothals, and marriage contracts preserved in the Geniza were issued by Jewish judges or clerks known to us as community officials. As in most legal documents, the signatories appear as "witnesses," and not in their official capacity. The failure to indicate a communal authority was not accidental. According to Jewish (and Muslim) law, two witnesses were sufficient for the lawful contracting of a marriage. This principle was upheld by as late an authority as Abraham Maimonides, who, in reply to a question submitted to him, ruled that a couple who in every respect behaved as non-Jews, demonstrating their apostasy by publicly desecrating the Sabbath, but who had contracted a marriage in the presence of two Jewish witnesses, were legally married.

Such "freedom of contract" in family matters could have most undesirable consequences. We read in one document of a girl, from a provincial town, whose father was dead. When she wished to marry in the capital, the nagid sent an inquiry to the local judge asking him to determine whether there existed any impediment to the proposed marriage. The judge responded, "I learned that this girl had been engaged several times, but it is not clear to me whether a marriage was contracted with anyone of those who proposed and became engaged to her. Her mother must be carefully questioned as to the circumstances of each engagement, and if any doubts remain, further inquiries will be necessary." Had marriage registers existed in the town, or had the registration of marriage been obligatory, no such doubts would have existed.

The community had an interest in maintaining the integrity of the family, and it was natural that its authorities sought to supervise marriages—at least those of foreigners, divorced women, or more generally, of any couples whose personal status was not well known in the community. A Fustat court record from the year 1085 or so states that a man from Tiberias and another from al-Lādhiqiyya on the Syrian coast testified that a woman from the latter town had been divorced by her husband, who later married again and then died. This testimony was required for her second marriage.

During the tenure of the energetic nagid Samuel b. Hananya the procedure for obtaining marriage permits was streamlined. It consisted of three parts: (1) a declaration of two witnesses that there was nothing in the personal status of either the groom or the bride that might impair the validity of their marriage; (2) the validation of the testimony by the court; and (3) a communication to the nagid by the court that a fine of ten dinars be imposed on the groom in case any impediment should become known. To this, a request to grant the permit was attached. Three such documents (from the years 1153, 1159, and one whose date has not been preserved) have as one of the two witnesses Judah, the son of Solomon the scribe. Thus it is evident that the couples were known to the communal scribe; the testimony was a mere formality.

Under Samuel b. Hananya's successors, the text of the marriage permit—or rather, the testimonies leading up to it—were refined so as to specify that there existed neither a religious nor a civil impediment to the proposed marriage. The head of the Jewish community confirmed not only the marriage permits but also the special conditions attached to individual marriage contracts. But all this was of no avail as long as persons could legally contract marriages without applying to the authorities at all. In order to deter such anarchic procedures, especially in provincial towns and villages, anyone other than the judges appointed by the central authorities who presided over a marriage or a divorce was threatened with excommunication. Such a declaration was issued by Moses Maimonides and his court in January 1187, with regard to the judges of Damanhūr, Bilbays, and al-Maḥalla in Lower Egypt. A similar declaration for the judges of Alexandria in 1235 has been preserved.

The law recognized the presence of two lay witnesses as sufficient to make a marriage contract legal; it did not require the formal approval of a court of law. Maimonides himself recommended the use of witnesses in a situation of hardship for the parties concerned. A man sought to marry a twice-widowed woman at the time of the great famine of 1201–1202; the local judge refused to marry them because of the ancient superstition that she was a "killer wife" and might cause the death of her third husband. Maimonides ruled: "They should contract the marriage in the presence of two witnesses, which is perfectly legal. Later the document should be issued by the court, the judge feigning ignorance of what has happened [to the previous husbands]. Being strict with regard to this small offense could lead to far graver complications."

By "graver complications" Maimonides meant an application to the state authorities. Such things indeed happened, and in Maimonides' own time. A kohen, or member of the priestly family of Aaron, was not permitted to marry a divorced woman; such was the law explicitly stated in the Torah and therefore binding without exception. However, a kohen in Alexandria, who loved a divorced woman, had the unheard-of audacity to pursue his passion. Despite all admonitions, he married her before a Muslim magistrate. (An application to a Muslim judge by non-Muslims was essentially equivalent to what we would call civil marriage.) Maimonides excommunicated him in an unusually long and strongly worded document. From the wording of this ban, one may conclude that such occurrences were exceptional, at least in Maimonides' time.

Generally speaking, recourse to the more lenient Muslim courts in family matters was seen by the Jewish authorities as threatening the solidarity of the community. In Ṣahrajt in Lower Egypt a woman was charged with having "divorced her husband" with the help of the Muslim qāḍī, who also arranged an alimony for her, which the husband paid for three months. For that offense against communal discipline and religious law, the woman was reprimanded and put under ban. She went to the capital and declared before the central court that it was her husband, not she, who had brought the matter before the Muslim authority. Finally, it became evident that the two had agreed on this procedure by mutual consent. Recent research by Gideon Libson has shown that Jews turned to the Muslim courts more frequently than one might imagine. Be that as it may, family law was the domain of communal autonomy. The state authorities acted only when approached by the parties affected. It is noteworthy, however, that many marriage contracts contain the stipulation that they are "binding according to Jewish law and also to that of the state," or "the nations of the world." In family matters, the communal officials represented the authority of the state.

Child Marriage

Because a minor could not undertake legal actions, such as contracting a marriage or appointing a representative, a father could marry off his minor daughter even without her consent. The principle was unambiguous under Islamic law, but it was a point much debated under Jewish law. In principle, the father's right was upheld, but the greatest authorities of talmudic times stated bluntly, "A father is not permitted to contract a marriage for his minor daughter; [he must wait] until she has grown and says, 'I wish to marry this man.'" Nevertheless, the medieval Jewish doctors of law did not recognize this maxim as binding. Maimonides, playing both sides of the issue, concluded, "Although a father is permitted to contract a marriage for his minor daughter with whomever he likes, it is improper to do so, for our sages have disapproved of this."

The Geniza records reveal that child marriages, although quite exceptional, did occur. In a holograph, a religious authority rules in an answer to a query, "As to the one of whom you write that she has not yet reached maturity, but that her father wishes to contract a marriage for her, there are no legal grounds on which you may impede him; you must endorse the marriage. Moreover, there is also nothing to fear in this matter [from the state authorities, since this was also Islamic law]." Clearly there was some opposition to these early marriages in the community, and the local official wanted to be on safe ground. The issue of child marriages takes on added complexity in various accounts. A question submitted to Moses Maimonides tells us about a girl who was married at the age of nine and whose mother-in-law (and aunt) undertook to maintain her for ten years. This marriage was a means of providing a home for an orphan who shared a property with her mother-in-law. Marriages of very young orphaned children can be understood as intended to somehow provide them with the shelter of a home. Since marrying an orphan was regarded as an act of piety and highly meritorious, we may assume that in many cases this aim was indeed attained. Similarly, aging fathers might wish to guarantee that their very young daughters would marry into good families when they predeceased these girls.

Arranging marriages, especially when a minor was involved, could make for extremely awkward, if not tragic circumstances. A girl whose father was dead "engaged herself," as a text says, and a lavish party was given. After two months, Simon, a relative of hers who had attended the party, appeared in court and presented a document in which the father of the girl had betrothed her to him four years earlier, when she was still a minor. Neither the mother of the girl nor she herself knew anything of this; understandably, when Simon came to ask for her hand and sent two intermediaries to explain that, as her relative, he had greater right to her, she indignantly refused. Finally, she sent her maternal uncle to Simon and asked him to provide her with a bill of divorce, but he would not hear of it. And so she was trapped, since according to Jewish law divorce required the consent of the husband. The court itself was in a dilemma: The document was legally valid; in addition, honoring the will of a dead person was a sacred duty. In her distress, the mother wrote to the Muslim magistrate, who asked the Jewish judge to assemble ten of the elders of the community and thus to exercise pressure on Simon to issue the required bill of divorce. Simon gave in, but only to claim after some time that the bill had been written under duress and was therefore void. Maimonides, who ruled in this case, declared that the pressure exercised by the court was proper, while Simon's conduct constituted duress. The girl was free to marry whomever she wished. Because there is little evidence of child marriage in the Geniza records, it was, in all likelihood, not that frequent.

The Economic Foundations of Marriage

THE OBLIGATIONS OF THE HUSBAND

A mere glance at any marriage contract preserved in the Geniza shows that the foremost obligation of the husband was to provide his wife with food and clothing and to maintain her generally. Housing is not expressly mentioned as an obligation because it was taken for granted that marriage meant bringing one's wife into one's own home — either the house of the family of the groom's father or the house owned or leased by the groom himself. "By entering my house you will become my wife" was an ancient ketubba formula. In addition, the obligations included the various payments of cash: the first gift (to establish good faith) and the second gift, as well as any other stipulated gifts. The legal minimum among Palestinian Rabbanite congregations, as previously noted, was 25 dirhems for a virgin, the equivalent of the talmudic 200 *zūz*, and 12½ dirhems for other women. (The Karaites doubled these figures.) Combined, the minimum payment of the first gift and the second gift was ordinarily 5 dinars, that is, 5 gold coins (canonically, 1 dinar was the equivalent of 10 dirhems, but the actual exchange rate varied widely in place and time). In any case, it is clear that the first sum was regarded as a token of good faith; the second gift was regarded as the more significant commitment. There were also marriages in which the bridal monies came to less than the usual 5 dinars—a remarriage (to each other) by a previously divorced couple, marriage to a divorced woman or a widow (with or without children), and a marriages to an orphan or a woman of undefined status. Some marriage contracts from Cairo show that the customary minimum cash payment of 5 dinars was waived only under exceptional circumstances.

To appreciate what the payment of 5 dinars meant in real life we have to be mindful of the perennial scarcity of cash. The marriage gift entailed substantial hardship—to the wealthier because they sought to put every available dinar to work, and to the less fortunate simply because they had none. The yearly payment of the poll tax to the Muslim authorities was a nightmare for many members of the minority communities. People lived on earnings and little was left over for extras. A gift of five gold pieces, on top of the expenses for housing and other matters connected with a marriage, represented a large outlay for a less well-to-do groom. The law that obliged the groom to provide a minimum monetary marriage gift reflected a principle of the Geniza culture: that a man should not marry before he had proved his ability to maintain a household.

Did the husband's marriage gift fulfill an economic need? Did it provide for the wife in case of divorce or the husband's death? The average amount promised by the less affluent was a formidable deterrent against divorce and thus protected women from the rash actions of a spouse, since he could not reclaim the money upon parting. Nor were these sums a negligible means of sustenance, for cash, being difficult to come by, was worth more than its declared value. A young widow or a divorced women with money in hand had reasonable prospects for a new venture in marriage, provided of course that she possessed a bridal trousseau and dowry of her own. However, a husband's contribution was not always sufficient to guarantee his wife a decent living in the event of his death or the termination of the marriage. For this she needed additional means, provided by what she had brought with her from her father's house.

THE BRIDE'S DOWRY

"Give your daughters to husbands," says the prophet Jeremiah (29:6). "Is the daughter in her father's hands that he can [give her away]?" asks the Talmud (with reference to the accepted opinion that a father should not marry off the daughter as a minor, but that he should wait until she reaches her majority and makes her own choice). The answer: "Have him give her something and provide her with clothing and cover so that the young men jump to marry her."

The legal situation was as follows: The ketubba, the husband's obligation, was religious law; the *nedunyā*, an ancient Near Eastern term for the dowry, was a matter of practical wisdom and local custom. For that reason, although the Talmud includes an extensive tractate on the subject of the ketubba, there is no specific section in that vast body of legislation dedicated to the nedunyā, and very little is said about it in general. This means that material about the dowry found in the Geniza documents is hardly influenced by ancient law; rather, it reflects actual situations varying according to place, time, and individual circumstances.

The dowry and trousseau, to the extent that they included movable property, were assembled in one room. Knowledgeable men (thoroughly briefed, no doubt, by even more knowledgeable women) assessed the monetary value of each item in the presence of the groom, who then had to express his agreement with the valuation, for it was the groom who was responsible for preserving the precious objects received. The wording of documents germane to the issue suggests that the valuation of the wife's assets generally took place in connection with the wedding, or, at least, the betrothal. One court record expressly sets the date for the assessment two days before the "consecration," which denotes either the betrothal or the betrothal combined with the wedding.

A properly executed and well-preserved appraisal of a dowry provides us with a complete picture of the economic circumstances of a marriage. It lists the price of each item and, where needed, describes it by provenance, material, color, and size. The subtotals of the main groups, such as gold and silver jewelry, clothing, bedding (including hangings and carpets), copper, and other household goods, are often noted. The total of the movable assets is followed by other possessions of the bride, such as houses, one or more maidservants, and, occasionally, books. Finally, the document notes the contribution of the groom and concludes with the grand total—that is, all that will be due from him or his heirs at the termination of the marriage.

Of similar character and value, although less abundant, are documents of another type, called "dowry receipts." In times of insecurity, or for other reasons, people often found it advantageous not to include the specifics of the dowry in the marriage contract, a document read out in public at the wedding. Instead, the groom acknowledged receipt of the dowry and of his obligation to pay the second marriage gift in a separate document, explaining his doing so by his "apprehension of the vicissitudes of the time." Such receipts were written, for example, in the years of a rapacious Muslim tax collector.

The main repository of the information on the bride's dowry is, of course, the marriage contract, the ketubba, which yields many useful details. The picture of the material civilization that is emerging from the Geniza is derived largely from the ketubbas and cognate documents that describe (and assign prices to) the possessions of women, the furnishings of houses, and the implements of the kitchen. Here, however, we encounter a serious difficulty. In many parts of the Islamic world, including the countries in which the Geniza records originated, it was customary to assign fictitious, highly inflated values to the bride's property and its individual components in order to enhance the prestige of the families concerned. Descriptions left us by medieval Arabic historians speaking of donkeys carrying empty boxes in the festive procession of the bride to her future husband's house, are tangible illustrations of this custom. Nor was this an Islamic innovation: The Talmud leaves it to the discretion of the parties involved whether to list the bride's possessions in the ketubba at their real value or at double their value, and Saadya Gaon in his book of legal forms, partly preserved in the Geniza, reports that in some places the former practice prevailed—in others, the latter.

Fortunately, in most cases we are able to get at the real price. The vast majority of marriage documents originated in Egyptian capital, and there we find that when the prices were doubled, the Hebrew phrase "two dinars are worth one" was added to the list. In some cases, it is stated explicitly that the husband's responsibility is to be understood in this sense. Conversely, numerous marriage documents, including many of the most detailed and valuable ones, state expressly, "one dinar is worth one dinar, real price, no duplication." One list, after providing the real value of the entire dowry adds, "The parties asked the sums to be doubled" and gives the adjusted total. Moreover, where documents list the obligation of the husband in dinars "of full weight and worth, approved by an assayer," it stands to reason that the real worth is intended. Wherever doubt remains, we are able to check the items against those listed in documents explicitly fixing the real prices, as well as by the circumstantial evidence, including the size and appearance of the particular document, the number and type of the items listed, additional gifts of houses, conditions imposed on husband and wife, and so forth. But even lists suspected of inflated prices are not without value, for both the objects they describe and their relative values are instructive.

Besides dowry appraisals, dowry receipts, and marriage contracts, there are sundry other types of documents that describe the bride's property: agreements made when a husband granted his wife exclusive disposition of her possessions; claims for the trousseau or parts of it deposited with a third party; receipts for the return of a trousseau after the termination of the marriage, or in the case of an inheritance; and special cases, including those whose circumstances cannot be determined with certainty. The traditional sequence of the bridal trousseau's principal components—jewelry, clothing, bedding, and copper—is maintained in most marriage documents, but there are, of course, exceptions: in numerous lists the sections are headed or summarized separately, or both, but even very long lists make use of this convenience. The lists regularly conclude with a chest or trunk "and its contents," meaning the bride's lingerie.

An examination of the comparative value of these items reveals a number of socioeconomic facts. Clothing was expensive and, besides food, was the husband's main responsibility with respect to the maintenance of his wife. A wife delighted in looking after her wardrobe. Consequently, clothing was by far the main item in the bride's trousseau, a rule confirmed by only few exceptions. The second-largest group (again, principally textiles) comprised the furnishings of the house: sofas and lounges with their cushions and reclining pillows, mattresses, together with blankets and covers, curtains and other hangings, rugs and carpets. One did not sit on a chair or at a table, but on a sofa along the walls or simply on the floor. A house did not have many rooms; curtains provided privacy; wall pictures, so common in Hellenistic and Roman civilizations, were virtually absent (perhaps because of the prohibitions against graven images in Judaism and Islam, prohibitions that established different traditions of representational art); in their place, hangings beautified the home's interior. As regards bedding, the differences among social classes and among individuals were even more pronounced than with respect to clothing. A wealthy bride might bring in bedding whose value exceeded twice that of her clothing—or even that of her clothing and jewelry combined. On the other hand, the value of copper utensils and other household goods seem more uniform among rich and poor alike. About twenty-five objects appear regularly on the lists, but a single trousseau practically never includes all of them; another twenty-five or so occur only sporadically. Costly pottery serving as tableware could not be included in the trousseau (which represented a lifelong obligation of the husband) because of its perishable nature; inexpensive crockery was not brought in by the bride—for obvious reasons.

The widest divergence prevailed in jewelry and silverware. Some brides possessed none at all. Objects made of precious metals, as a rule, constitute only about one tenth or less of the total value of trousseaux estimated as being worth between 60 and 120 dinars. But in the lists of wealthy brides, jewelry is regularly second in value only to clothing; in the bridal list of a very wealthy girl, it comes first. There was a tendency to fix a round sum to the total value of the dowry. This shows that, as a rule, the bride's dowry was not simply what she possessed but what had been agreed upon, probably after long negotiation. In many cases, the individual sections as well total round sums, which points to the same conclusion. A distinct class stratification is evident in these totals — ranging from the destitute who had no dowry at all, to the wealthy with 500 dinars and more, and the very wealthy, who might bring in 1,500 dinars, as well as maidservants and parts of houses.

Occasionally we learn that a certain total was local custom. In a Hebrew document written in Fustat on June 23, 982, the son-in-law agrees to state in the marriage contract that he has received objects in gold, clothing, and furnishings worth 150 dinars, "as is customary in the ketubbas of this city." What actually was brought, however, amounted to only 50 dinars. (To make up the difference, the father-in-law gave him 20 dinars in cash and a promissory note of 80 dinars, which had precedence over all his other obligations.) This custom remained decidedly localized, of course, since more than half the brides of Fustat represented in the Geniza records brought in 10 dinars or less. By contrast a parent who belonged to a more distinguished element of society had to send off his daughter with assets worth not less than 150 dinars.

Cash never formed part of a dowry during the classical Geniza period, and evidence of the practice does not begin to show up until the fifteenth century, probably under the influence of immigrants from Spain and other Christian countries, who may have found it expedient to travel at some haste and without bulky possessions. With few exceptions, the bride's assets exceed the groom's first marriage gift — many times over. This seems natural, since the groom presumably was at the early stages of his economic independence, whereas the father of the bride was at the height of his earning capacity and her mother would either part with some of her own dowry, or pass on to her daughter movable or immovable property inherited or received as gifts. The largesse of the bride's family made it possible for their daughters to marry relatively young men, who otherwise would have had to work many years to accumulate the wealth necessary to undertake marriage. Other social considerations as well probably affected the economics of engagement and betrothal. Wealthy widows and divorced women eager to establish new alliances, relatives responsible for orphaned girls, and individuals generally anxious to arrange matrimony could offer a significant dowry as an inducement to the match.

THE ECONOMIC ROLE OF THE WIFE

In her marriage contract, the bride promised, among other things, to serve her husband. In return for this service she was compensated by her husband's gifts and his future obligation to maintain her. Consequently, a wife was bound to work, "even if she had a hundred maidservants." The Jewish legal authorities, who always tried to capture the realities of life in neat legal paragraphs, defined precisely which chores she was obliged to perform: they distinguished generally between work to be done by poorer women and by those more affluent. Naturally, the economic value of the wife's work for her husband differed widely, ranging from performing or supervising the household chores—a rather modern conception of the economic value of housework—to substituting for him in his business affairs when he was ill, to teaching the children when her husband was overburdened—for whatever reason. According to age-old custom and statutory law, spinning was one of the duties of a wife; it is mentioned as such in a marriage document from the Fayyūm.

Besides "serving" her husband, the wife could earn money working (at home or outside the house) for other people. The remarkable amount of talmudic discussion devoted to the problems of the wife's earnings demonstrates the economic importance that this source of family income had assumed in the economically strapped Jewish society of Late Antiquity. The very saying "he who expects to maintain himself by the earnings [lit., wages] of his wife, will never see blessing in his life," reveals the extent of this phenomenon. A wife's earnings belonged to her husband in compensation for the support provided by him, or, as the ancient formula has it, "her food against the work of her hands."

References to working women are extremely rare in documents dating from the tenth and eleventh centuries. They become more common during the twelfth, and are encountered with great frequency from the thirteenth onward. It would appear, however, that, as a rule, men did not—indeed could not—demand the earnings of their spouses. The benefits of the spouse's work to the husband were rather indirect. For example, there is evidence that women were responsible for maintaining their wardrobes—or, to paraphrase the rabbinic dictum: "her clothing for the work of her hands."

By the middle of the thirteenth century, statements regarding the wife's earnings are a virtual constant in the marriage contracts, an indication that working women were by this point a common phenomenon. One finds frequent statements in such contracts that the groom renounces rights to the bride's earnings. The explicit references to women's work in the later ketubbas raises a number of questions. Was there a real change in attitude toward working women in Jewish society? And if so, what occasioned that change? One can understand an aversion to women working outside the house. Contact with strangers, especially strange men, might be considered undignified. But work at home did not entail that risk. Perhaps the economic climate of the thirteenth century required the women of less wealthy families to carry their load. That is, however, a supposition that requires additional research.

One matter, though, appears to be self-evident: a wife's earnings by work could have been of substantial, even vital, value only in families with small income, for a women's wages were minimal. Among wealthier families, the wife's economic power stemmed from her property. A wife's possessions consisted of her dowry, or, rather, all that she brought into the marriage, her husband's marriage gifts (which became her personal property), and gifts and inheritances that she received during her married life. The legal rights on each of these items were defined by law; they are stated in part in the documents written at an engagement, betrothal, or wedding. The fact of women's work in Geniza times may however, reflect considerable pressure on Jewish women to leave the confines of the home for either social or economic reasons.

More surprising is the comparative rarity of stipulations in marriage contracts regulating the husband's travels away from his wife, for the husband's absenteeism is the most widespread problem of marital life known to us from the Geniza records. A conditional divorce, setting the wife free if the husband did not return at a fixed time was common practice among both Muslims and Jews. In connection with this, we note an agreement in which the husband agrees to the early deposit of the second marriage gift. This was exceptional, both as a condition and as actual practice, for a young husband normally did not possess that much money. A stipulation leaving to the wife all she needed during her husband's absence before his departure is also found only rarely in marriage contracts—again, because he ordinarily lacked the disposable income to do so. Only occasionally a condition such as "he will not travel away from her abroad except with her consent" is inserted into an engagement contract, and is included without fixing a penalty if the promise is broken. It is improbable that husbands wandered about indiscriminately; independent tradesmen and working people could hardly absent themselves from the occupations that demanded their daily presence. More likely these provisions in the marriage contracts were targeted at merchant families and their agents—drawn most often from circles that were required to spend a great deal of time away from home. Nevertheless, when economic conditions declined in a specific location, husbands might be forced to move with their families to another locality in search of employment.

Remaining Unmarried

Our documents record random cases of individual males who never married. That information comes to us usually with regard to the settlement of family estates. The only known person of prominence that we know remained unwed most or all of his life was the noble and learned India trader Ḥalfōn b. Nethanel, "the center of all leading men of his time," a peripatetic individual who frequently visited Spain and Morocco, as well as Aden and India. His unwed status was a sore point to a loquacious old relative who wrote to him:

My lord—may I be made your ransom—hurry to accomplish a matter which, if its time has passed, cannot be effected anymore, just as sowing, when its season has been missed, cannot be successfully done. May God watch over you—and present you with the choicest of human beings, who will resemble the lady, your mother, may God's mercy be upon her, so that the word of the scripture may be fulfilled with you, as it is written: "Isaac brought her [Rebekah] into the tent of Sarah . . . and Isaac found solace after the death of his mother" [Genesis 24:67].

Although marriage was a religious duty, a scholarly person who chose study as his love could be exempted from that obligation. Following the talmudic sage Ben 'Azzay, who exclaimed, "My love is Torah, let others build the world," Maimonides ruled in his *Code of Law*, "A man who loves the Torah, studying it continuously all his life, and never takes a wife does not commit a sin, provided he is not overcome by sexual desire." As so often in Maimonides' legislation, one senses a personal note. He married a woman from a very distinguished family in Egypt, where he arrived at the age of thirty, and his son and only child was born when he was forty-eight. Thus it seems that he himself tarried long before consenting to give up the life of a bachelor devoted to study. His son and successor, Abraham, must have had similar inclinations to delay marriage and fatherhood: Abraham's son and only child was born to him when he was thirty-six, an age at which, in those days, one could easily have been a grandfather. The biblical account according to which the patriarch Isaac married at the age of forty (Genesis 25:20) was understood to mean that a man should marry only after having attained spiritual perfection, while a woman marrying for the first time at forty was believed to have no prospect of bearing a child, the essential purpose of marriage.

Girls who might wish to remain unmarried had little choice in the matter—at least we have no evidence to the contrary. In fact, there is no technical word for spinster in our texts; the rare woman who never married is described as "a woman who is a girl." Nor did women, unlike females in the Christian West, deny themselves men out of spiritual considerations. The saintly virgin of Baghdad who wished not to be wed so that she might serve none but God was singularly exceptional; no other such case is known. A survey of pertinent Geniza records indicates that approximately 45 percent of all married women entered the state of matrimony a second time, that is, after having been divorced or widowed. Given the astounding frequency of second marriages, one wonders what percentage of divorced or widowed women did not marry a second time.[1] Were second marriages, while clearly common, a state entered into with reluctance? One may wish to consider the preferences of potential husbands for these widows. Men, even somewhat older men, no doubt preferred younger women—if not virgins, then certainly women still capable of bearing children. In any case, it must be noted that both in letters and in documents, especially in the lists of beneficiaries, a great number of single women appear in the Geniza.

---

1. One of Goitein's earliest and strongest impressions while doing research among Middle Eastern communities was observing how women in the prime of their lives, previously married, were leading solitary lives. He relates that, being then very young and not yet inured to the niceties of Near Eastern etiquette, he would ask in all innocence, "Why does a fine woman like you not marry again?" The reaction was invariably, albeit mostly in veiled form (and sometimes punctuated with a shudder), that, disgusted by a previous marriage, she did not desire to try it again.

Homosexuality

It is not astonishing that a society like that of the Geniza, which championed marriage and procreation as social and moral ideals, would have little tolerance for behaviors that appeared to subvert those ideals. According to the Bible, sexual relations between males were to be punished by death. It has been argued that the severity of this punishment rested on the assumption that Israel, a small nation constantly at war with stronger neighbors, could not permit a part of its male population to absent itself from the nation's social and political interest in producing offspring. It may also reflect the general prohibition on things that were "unnatural," as is found elsewhere in the Bible.

Be that as it may, the biblical abhorrence of homosexuality is echoed, if allusively, in legal and polemical literature from the classical Geniza period. The chapter on romantic love of Saadya Gaon's *Beliefs and Opinions* concludes: "[Love] is good for husband and wife. He should enjoy her company and she his. The two together 'build the world.' His passion should be spent on her with reason, in observing the religious injunctions, and in a measure preserving the mutual fondness. Anything beyond this must be avoided with all might." Although no overt reference to homosexuality is made, nor to the death penalty for pederasty, the diatribe is directed mainly, if not exclusively, against the "looking at the beardless youth" (to use a Muslim expression).

The gravity of a charge of homosexuality—and of pederasty in particular—may be gauged more precisely, however, from an account of a cantor or teacher (possibly both) in a small locality near Cairo, who was accused of having assembled young men and danced a *zuhdī* dance with them, a dance accompanied by songs of mysticism and renunciation of the world. In a sex-conscious society, any physical contact between an adult male and his younger companions was cause for suspicion. In a letter to his superior in Cairo, the accused professes himself innocent of the accusation. How serious that charge was is mirrored in the spiritedness of the author's defense: "When I learned about this matter, I became alarmed. . . . I decided to go to Cairo to clear my honor from that talk about me. . . . I wish to clear my honor against the one who told this about me. If people have indeed given witness about this, whatever I shall be obliged to do, I shall [not] dodge."

The extent of homosexual practices in Geniza society may to some extent be attested by the endeavors of the authorities to suppress it. The Geniza has preserved the statutes of Dammuūh, the Jewish holy shrine

southwest of Fustat. Among the many things prohibited during a visit
to the shrine was the attendance of unaccompanied boys, or that of a
man accompanied by a boy who was not a close relative. Even more
telling is the story of an actual pilgrimage to Jerusalem, the Holy City.
The writer reports that during the Day of Atonement, a man in a group
of pilgrims from Tyre and another in a group from Tiberias became
enamored of each other. The Tiberian made a public overture to the
pilgrim from Tyre, apparently in the synagogue itself, whereupon a fist-
fight broke out between the two groups. The local police were called
and remained in the synagogue until the conclusion of the service. Thus
far, no references have been found to lesbian practices in the Geniza.
Such activity did exist, however, and we find attestation of it in Maimonides' *Code of Law*, where he indicates that there is no formal punishment for women who indulged in lesbian sexual activity, but that
women given to such practices should not be permitted to visit one's
home and that the women of one's household be not permitted to visit
the home of a lesbian woman.

The Geniza society's attitude toward homosexuality was inevitably
affected by that of the Muslim majority within which it was nested.
Certainly, there is much evidence from medieval literary sources to indicate that homosexual behavior between Muslim men, however disapproved, was nevertheless widespread. The cult of male youths was
originally identified with a privileged, powerful class, but, as often happens with social mores, the example of the prominent filtered down and
became, if not acceptable, then arguably tolerated among other elements
of the community.

While it might be claimed that references to sexual behavior in Hebrew poetry are more a literary convention than a reflection of actual
practices, cultural diffusion nonetheless finds expression in homoerotic
allusions in Jewish belletristic texts that evoke Arabic models. The Geniza has provided us with a Hebrew *maqāma*, a rhymed short story that
may be an imitation of an Arabic original and intended to satirize Muslim practices. We are told that a cantor became enamored of a boy. To
win his favor, the cantor sold all the learned books he possessed and
gave the money to the boy, but the latter did not return his love. Then,
one by one, the love-mad cantor sold off the fifty-two weekly lections
of the Pentateuch. Finally, he went so far as to sell his prayer mantle;
still the boy did not budge. Having disposed of all the tools of his
trade—to no avail—the cantor filed suit against the boy before the rabbinical court and the elders of the community: "I have made a deal with
this boy, I have done my part, I have given all I have; but he has not

fulfilled his obligation; please let me have the well-deserved satisfaction."
The comedy ends with the discovery that the cantor was not really a Jew
but a sham convert who had come from far off in the West, where he
was notorious for similar escapades.

It seems that a segment of the Jewish intelligentsia, especially in
Spain, accepted the cult of ephebes as an essential constituent of the
civilization to which they then belonged. There exist Hebrew poems,
some found also in the Geniza, that reflect this sensibility. These poems
have generally been regarded as literary exercises composed to prove
that Jews could imitate the literary forms of Arabic, the language of the
hegemonic society. One must keep in mind that in the Muslim Near
East, the "beardless youth," who often served as a cupbearer in drinking
rallies, was not by definition an object of sexual attraction. Youthful
beauty was prized as an aesthetic ideal. This is illustrated by two strophes
of a tenth-century Hebrew poem—also from the Geniza—written in
southern Italy, a region exposed at that time to both Islamic and Byzantine influences.

> Behold ships, behold, ships coming into the port.
> Go and see what merchandise they bring.
> Beautiful girls.
> Go and see what they were sold for.
> For a barrel of straw.
> Ah, captain, you have been paid too much.

> Behold, ships, behold ships, coming into the port.
> Go and see what merchandise they bring.
> Handsome boys, finer than gold.
> Go and see what they were sold for.
> For a barrel of gold and gems.
> Ah, captain, you have been paid too little.

To be sure, these verses tell us little of homosexual practices, which
certainly did exist. Accounts that shed light on the extent of homosexuality in Geniza society or on how practices were treated outside of the
biblical moral injunctions against them are lacking among the Geniza
records themselves.

Considering the many economic and social safeguards that had to be
taken into consideration in contracting a marriage ceremony, it is not
surprising that the talmudic saying "no ketubba without squabbles" is
reflected in numerous Geniza documents. Occasions where the jubilance
of the wedding day was dimmed or spoiled by undignified haggling
over the marriage stipulations must not have been uncommon. But this

did not diminish the significance of marriage as an institution. The wedding was "the day of joy" (Song of Songs 3:11). Whenever unmarried sons are mentioned in a Geniza letter the writer adds the wish that God may keep them alive and let their father see *afrāḥhum*, "their joy." Documents recording that wish for a woman have proved elusive; the wish was rather that she should "enter her house," or "come into a blessed and auspicious home." "Making the bride happy" was, of course, the groom's religious obligation no less than a statutory requirement. The good wishes and quotations written at the head and in the margins of the marriage contracts state this emphatically. In Muslim society, female celebrants performed that function. The difference in the good wishes expressed for men and women reflects a reality: Marriage for the husband was a change of sorts, for it was thought that, together with acquiring a source of possible happiness, he took upon himself "a yoke," while essentially remaining within the same male society to which he had previously belonged. The wife, to the contrary, became uprooted from familiar surroundings and was thrown into an inevitably foreign social and physical environment. We must keep this difference in mind in turning to the study of married life as revealed in the Geniza records.

FOURTEEN

The "House" or Nuclear Family

"Baby" and "Mistress of the House"

As a rule, when a man was away from home, he did not write to his wife but rather to his mother or a male relative. In the early Geniza period (eleventh century) he would refer to his wife sparingly, if at all—inquiring after her health, making arrangements for her maintenance, or simply sending her regards. Under no circumstances would he call her "my wife"; somehow that formal expression carried too improper a sexual connotation. Instead he would send greetings to his children "and their mother," or would refer to her as "the house," "the residence," "the inhabitants of the house," or other awkward expressions. In Hebrew, where the word "inhabitants" is rendered not by a singular collective term, as in Arabic *ahl*, but by a plural, *ba'alē ha-bayit*, "masters of the house," the circumlocution sounds particularly clumsy. During most of the classical Geniza period, when writing to a relative, even to a son or a brother, one did not refer to the addressee's wife with this term, but would usually allude to her with the phrase "the one who is with you," or other indirect expressions. Even a husband writing home could say "greet my uncle [meaning his father-in-law] and the one who is with me," meaning his wife; she was then actually far away. The name of a man's wife was never mentioned, let alone that of any other woman. The correspondence of scholarly merchants of the eleventh century indicates that this taboo was taken very seriously, at least at that time.

Beginning in the second half of the twelfth century and especially in the thirteenth century, however, women are freely mentioned by name and greeted. It is not rare to read the names of a good number of women in one letter. One could now speak freely about "your wife" and "my wife," and messages by and to women become frequent. The reasons for this change are not apparent. It cannot be attributed to the weakening of religious discipline, for the late Middle Ages were characterized in that respect by strictness rather than laxity. Nor can it be explained by the immigration of French Jews and their customs to Egypt and Palestine (beginning around 1200), for that immigration was too tiny a trickle to exercise such an impact. Nor was this change necessarily confined to the Jewish community. It may indeed be one of many expressions of social transformation caused by generally worsening economic conditions and the subsequent weakening of the bourgeoisie, which had endeavored to keep up standards of dignified behavior inherited from the ruling class and the courts. This is, however, only conjecture.

Although we have few highly personal letters addressed by husbands to wives, we have no letters of this sort from wives to their husbands. The letters that wives do send to their husbands are dictated and filled with terse small details; the most a woman dares venture is a phrase like "It is strange to me that you should be in one town and I in another." We have reason to assume that women who were able to write did write personal, and perhaps even intimate, letters to their husbands. But such letters were not deposited in the Geniza—at least, none have been found.

The manner in which a man treated his wife might initially have been influenced by the fact of her youth and lack of experience coming into the household, for normally women were married in their teens. It is clear, though, that the attitude could extend long into the marriage as well. One document speaks of a wife who had borne three living children, yet her husband, on his deathbed, appoints not her, but rather her mother (his mother-in-law) as sole guardian of the children and executor of his will. As the document explicitly states, the dying man was relying on the old woman's efficiency (besides her piety and her love for her grandchildren). It is implied that he did not expect much knowledge of the world from his wife, who had not yet reached the age of twenty. Additional examples of such situations can easily be adduced. The infantilization of women may very well have contributed, along with other factors, to the marital strife that often set in soon after marriage. In any case, women were not without power, particularly as they grew older and the in-laws grew infirm or died.

As the years went by, and especially after the death of the husband's father, the mother-in-law herself would refer to the wife as "the mistress of the house," and a son writing to his mother might refer to his wife with the same epithet. Everything depended on the circumstances and the personalities involved. The path from "baby" to "mistress of the house" was a long uphill struggle, some women never succeeded in obtaining that respect. In more than a few Geniza papers, women of old age appear as harassed and miserable as they might have been in their youth. Others, especially those domiciled away from their families as a result of promises made in marriage contracts, fared better. The Geniza people believed profoundly that marriages were arranged by God, or, as they emphasized even more frequently, were a matter of luck. King Solomon in his wisdom reportedly said, "He who has *found* a wife, has found happiness" (Proverbs 18:22), but in another mood he wrote, "I *find* the woman more bitter than death" (Ecclesiastes 7:26). "Found or find?" This was the question put to a young husband by his friends some time after his wedding, meaning is the new life joyful for you or full of bitterness?

Affection and Conjugal Relations

Despite occasions for meeting in public, particularly at ceremonial functions or during family affairs, couples in Geniza times had little if any opportunity for premarital friendship. As a rule, marriage was the beginning of an alliance, not its crowning. It was not an alliance between equals, but between a master and one commended to his care. When mutual satisfaction prevailed and the wife became more and more her husband's support in the struggle of life, marriage grew into companionship and into a bond between equals—or, rather, near equals.

The Rebekah story, recited on the wedding Sabbath, relates: "[Isaac] took Rebekah as his wife. And Isaac loved her and thus found solace after his mother's death" (Genesis 24:67). The verse indicates that love was intended to be a consequence of marriage rather than its predecessor. Replacing the mother, the wife became the mature companion of her husband. When a schoolmaster living far away from home apprises his old mother of his marriage and writes that he is absolutely happy that his young wife, besides being beautiful, has all the good and noble character traits of his mother, he is stating, apparently, that his innermost desires have been satisfied. It would be interesting and, of course, most important to ascertain the attitudes of women toward the rather slow process by which they gained acceptance. Many mothers-in-law must have been very young themselves when their eldest sons married, delaying thereby the independence of their daughters-in-law. Were brides reconciled or even resigned to their fates? Did they employ strategies to subvert the authority of the husband and his family? Did they seek the comfort of other women? These are questions worthy of investigation.

What did the Geniza man seek in his wife? The usual Hebrew laudatory epithets—woman of valor, pious, virtuous, and chaste, as they were understood in those days—convey the expectations placed upon women. First, a young wife should be a Rebekah, doing willingly and effectively the work expected from her, or, as we read in one letter, "I was happy to learn that your wife is efficient, clean, solid, and doing her chores well." The term *ṣaddeqet,* "pious," included the additional nuances of charitable, lenient, considerate (toward everyone, but especially, of course, her husband). *Keshērā,* "virtuous," referred to sex and religious observances in general. *Ṣenūʿā,* "chaste," is better translated in this context as "unassuming," "knowing her place," or "one who knows to keep a secret." The beauty of a wife would be mentioned only in a personal letter addressed by a son to his mother, and even that was exceptional. Flattery of the bride's beauty in wedding songs consisted of stock phrases. We should not assume, however, that physical attraction was irrelevant; it was simply not a matter of public discourse. A wife was expected to make herself attractive to her husband by keeping her hair well combed, applying kohl to her eyes, and perfuming her body. Jewish law encourages sexual joy as well as sexual activity and endorses the wife's role as a provider of sexual comfort to her husband. That was certainly understood by the Geniza community.

A wife, in turn, expected her husband to be tender, kind, and considerate, to show her "love, approval, and a generous mind." "Treat her well, and she will be attracted to you." The husband should be a gentleman, should have *muruwwa,* "manliness," meaning the character of a man who, because he knows he has power, does not use it against someone weaker. This attitude should be expressed in presents, small and large, routine and special.

Conjugal relations were regulated by custom that had the force of law. Since they were stipulated as a duty in the marriage contract, the frequency of marital relations was discussed by the sages of the Talmud. Talmudic scholars posited a wide range of alternatives depending on the occupation of the husband and particular circumstances. They agreed, however, that for scholars once a week was sufficient and that the proper time for the fulfillment of this duty was the night preceding the weekly day of rest. Since everyone regarded himself as a student of the holy law, this measure became standard. Similar customs prevailed in Islam and Christendom. Among Muslims, Thursday night, which precedes the Islamic weekly holiday, was set aside for conjugal enjoyment, to be followed by a bath and perfuming on Friday morning — before the solemn noon prayer which all males were required to attend. In Christian Europe, in social classes adhering to traditional ways, Saturday night had a similar role. The statutory three monthly visits to their wives incumbent on Athenian husbands in the classical period implied a similar frequency of connubial relations. These customs, spread over such wide areas of time and space may at the outset have had their origins in beliefs about hygiene that in later monotheistic societies became intertwined with religious sensibilities. The Karaites regarded sexual activity on the Sabbath as a grave desecration of the holiness of the day. Therefore, in the many documents on mixed marriages between Karaites and Rabbanites found in the Geniza, the Rabbanite partner undertakes to honor the religious sensibility of his or her spouse.

The inability of a husband to perform his conjugal duties is attested in various Geniza documents. Related to that are prescriptions for satisfactory intercourse and amulets against threats from witchcraft or the evil eye; magical interference with sexual performance was taken very seriously. Matters of *coitus interruptus* and abortion apparently occupied the Jewish courts of the Geniza period less than they did their Muslim counterparts.

Because of religious, moral, and social convictions, the married wife's role as provider of sexual satisfaction was of extreme importance. This applied in particular to Christians and Jews, who did not have the legal outlet of concubinage with slave girls, as did their Muslim contemporaries. To be sure, the vast majority of Muslims were in the same situation: the purchase of a desirable concubine was beyond the means of the average man. Naturally, the sexual role of the wife greatly enhanced her position and influence. "The companion of the night is stronger than the counselor of daytime," says an Arabic proverb; more picturesque expressions were also in vogue. When a woman failed to satisfy her husband, her misery could be extreme. Many of the petty discords reported in the subsequent pages may have been rooted in reasons quite different from the issues overtly contended.

The story of the biblical Esther was well known to the women of the Geniza period, and its moral was well heeded by them. Three women, each sharply contrasted with one another, are the main characters. The proud queen Vashti, who brazenly disobeys her foolish drunkard of a husband, is dethroned and repudiated at the advice of all the counselors of the king: for if Vashti had her way, the women of the empire would all follow suit and rise up against their husbands in active rebellion. Zeresh (in the Geniza, a byword for a wicked woman), wife of Haman, the villain of the story, misleads her husband by evil advice and, indirectly, causes his downfall. Esther, on the other hand, seems always compliant; she is obedient to her uncle, to the eunuch in charge of the harem, and, of course to her husband, the king—and she is successful in everything. Because of her moral qualities and her beauty, this refugee Jewish woman can become queen of Persia, and she engineers the destruction of the archenemy Haman. Esther knows how to behave, but she is not timid. When necessary, she dares to defy the rules of the court and is prepared to suffer death. It is this type of woman, outwardly pliable and accommodating but strong and resolute in mind, who merits success in the Geniza's patriarchal society, in which men believe that they should rule the house "like a king," as Maimonides writes in his *Code of Law*. At marriage the husband remains in the safe haven of the family of his father; it is the very young wife, herself a child, who has to brave a new and often unfriendly environment and to accommodate herself to it, a task indeed worthy of an Esther.

Problems with the Couple's Relatives and Residence

It was expected that the female members of the new household would recreate the home of the husband's mother. The young wife was "the trust" given to her mother-in-law to be protected as her most precious possession. The documents themselves speak eloquently to the relationship. A young husband asks a relative (the exact relationship is not evident from the letter) to bestow upon him the "fragrance" of his mother and to become for his wife "a mother and sister." Similarly, a woman marrying a widower promises to become like a sister to the future wife of a stepson. The model relationship between mother- and daughter-in-law was that made eternal in the biblical Book of Ruth.

The Geniza husband expected his wife to live up to the image he had of his own mother; the expectation and the comparison were not always welcome. The most common complaints of a wife were that the mother-in-law was not considerate, did not honor her, imposed too much work on her, and watched her comings and goings. The relationship with the sister-in-law was even more complicated. The only females of approximately the same age with whom a young bachelor could talk intimately were his sisters. After marriage, some men would find their company more congenial than that of a new wife, especially when the sisters were older and more mature, a sentiment reflected in various reports from the Geniza. It seems, too, that the new wife at times had to live under one roof with the sisters, an additional aggravating circumstance. All this explains a considerable number of documents recounting the young wife's suffering and her endeavors to move away from her husband's family. We have noted that such situations were foreseen in many engagements, betrothals, and marriage contracts. We hear much more about them in complaints and settlements made in the course of married life.

Examples of wives refusing to follow their husbands to a foreign country are numerous. Arye b. Judah, probably a European Jew, as his name indicates, had married a woman in Cairo and wished to take her with him to Palermo, which at that time (January 1095) was under Norman domination. The young couple had visited there, but once back in Cairo, the young wife took refuge in her father's house and refused to return. Ayre swore that he could not live in Cairo and finally repudiated her in an arrangement with her father. He returned her wedding trousseau and dowry, and she restored the first marriage gift, as was the duty of a wife who declined to follow her husband "to his house."

Following a husband to another place in the same country might be just as abhorrent, and for a variety of reasons. Stipulations regulating this aspect of marriage were often included in engagement contracts and ketubbas. Young wives who were inveterate city dwellers were not always prepared to move with their husbands to a small place in the provinces, or, having made the move, could not endure remaining there. There were also women who were reluctant to go from country to city. A daughter of the dayyān of al-Maḥalla, refuses to follow her husband to the capital, for at home she is a queen; in Fustat she will be a girl from the countryside. In a similar situation, a woman from the Rīf writes to her husband, who has tarried in the capital too long (and had not written her): "You fancy that I will come to Miṣr. I shall never go there. For if I do so, we shall not live in peace with each other—may God never plant discord between us." But even inducing a wife to follow her husband from one provincial town to another might require action by the authorities. A summons to a woman asks her to appear in court and to explain why she has refused to accompany her husband (where to is not stated). As we have seen, it was her duty to do so if provisions to the contrary had not been made in her marriage contract. One can imagine the sense of dislocation that women must have felt when taken completely out of the environment in which they had been raised—all the more so given their limited opportunities for social intercourse after marriage.

The Geniza material presented thus far shows the wife relying on her own family for protection against her husband. Naturally, the battle lines were not always drawn that way. Often the wife had reason to complain about her own kin, especially when they were tardy in making good the promises stipulated in the marriage agreements. In a magnificently written Hebrew fragment, a woman named Esther appoints her husband as her proxy to sue her brother, who has not delivered what he promised in her betrothal contract. One brother even lays claim on part of a house sold by his mother to his married sister. Yemenite women of today say, "Hell with my husband is better than Paradise with family."

Possessions and Pecuniary Obligations of Husband and Wife

The economic aspects of married life were another factor that made either for cooperation and happiness or for discord and misery. As regards finances, the marriage worked well as long as mutual trust and affection prevailed between the spouses and as long as their material circumstances were not overly strained. True, the strings of the purse and of the sacks of wheat were in the hands of the husbands, and, as we learn from the letters of husbands away on travel and from many court records, they were tightly held. Male relatives or friends substituted for the master of the house in his absence; the monthly allocations of money and wheat were standardized, and they were usually modest. Ongoing expenses, such as purchases and payments for repairs, were usually made or supervised by the husband or by his male representatives. This created a high degree of dependency for the wife, but it was not necessarily always regarded as such. Husbands sometimes assumed responsibilities traditionally assigned to the wife, and there were women who did not want to negotiate matters pertaining to the household beyond the confines of the domicile.

The economic power of the husband also encompassed the wife's dowry, since he had the right to use the income from his wife's property. But this power was limited by the obligation—extended to his heirs—to restore every dinar to the dowry in the event of divorce or his death. In fact, the dowry represented a strong bond between the spouses and gave them a constant opportunity for cooperation. The bride's extensive wardrobe, bedding, furnishings, and kitchenware spared the young couple from incurring large expenses at the start of the married life. Part of the jewelry (usually a number and often a considerable number of ornaments of the same type) could be used as collateral for her husband's mercantile undertakings, but such transactions required her consent. Similarly, her houses or shares in houses, if included in the dowry, brought rent, supplementing the family budget. It should be emphasized once again that during the classical Geniza period the dowry did not consist of cash given to the husband but of the wife's property, and it remained her property, not his. Add to this the fact that the dowry was usually a multiple of the marriage gift provided by the husband, and it becomes evident that in more affluent families the dowry and other possessions of the wife made her position quite comfortable. A wife's transactions, such as the purchase or sale of a house, had to be confirmed by her husband, but her approval was similarly required when the husband sought to engage in such transactions, since his property was assigned to her. Many documents illustrating this situation have been preserved. A husband was not even permitted to remove his own furnishings from the couple's domicile, since it might constitute an attempt to evade his obligations. Explicit statements to this effect are found in our records. Throughout the centuries we read about a wife granting a loan or a gift to her husband, selling to or buying from him, standing security for him (or he for her), or engaging in other transactions—all situations demonstrating that she had a purse of her own.

A common cause of marital discord was the husband's control of the dowry. The conflict could be settled (not always permanently) by the husband relinquishing this right, in whole or in part, and the wife releasing him from any responsibility for her possessions. Such situations might arise when the wife sought to take her affairs into her own hands, when the husband went abroad for an extended period, or when the wife's family was not satisfied with his management or simply did not trust him. Then the "iron sheep," as the property entrusted to the husband was described, had to be converted into *melūg*, the wife's personal possessions.

Wife Beating

The references to beating and cursing wives in marriage contracts served as a warning to the husband that he could be forced by court action to divorce his wife (and to pay the second marriage gift) for such actions. While the frequency of such references in legal documents does not necessarily reflect the reality (wife beating is very rarely mentioned in letters), the testimony of the documents cannot be easily dismissed. Rabbis writing in medieval France and Germany were very outspoken on wife beating, branding it an un-Jewish practice. The famous Rabbi Meir of Rothenburg, Germany, went as far as to recommend cutting off the hand of a husband who habitually committed this crime, since hitting a women was a greater sin than injuring a man. Still, the practice of wife beating was not unknown in the Jewish communities of Europe; a considerable number of jurisconsults dealt with it in their legal opinions; one instance even led to the promulgation of a statute that required the culprit to separate from his wife and to support her until he reformed.

For Muslims, the situation was apparently different. The Qur'ān (5: 33) permits, or arguably recommends, beating wives who are not susceptible to milder forms of correction (although Muslim courts protected women against excessively cruel husbands). The fact the holy book of the ruling faith acquiesced in wife beating may have created a moral climate that induced some Jewish authorities in Islamic lands to take a similar view. Yehuday Gaon, the reputed author of the first post-talmudic code of law (eighth century), writes, "A wife should never raise her voice against her husband, but should remain silent even if he beats her — as chaste women do." Even Maimonides wrote in his *Code of Law*, "A woman who refuses to do her required work may be forced to do so, even with the stick." To a Provençal critic, Rabbi Abraham b. David, remarks, "I have never heard that it is permitted to correct women with a stick," meaning that he found no legal support in the sources for Maimonides' ruling. The Talmud indeed says nothing of the kind, and in the numerous Geniza records in which women bring judicial complaints of beatings, the courts invariably reprimand the husbands and occasionally impose fines on those who relapse.

If the Geniza material gives an impression that wife beating was a common social problem, it should be noted that most of the complaints concern incidents among couples from the lower strata of society.[1] Maimonides is a special case: coming from the Muslim West, with its stern mores, he was dismayed by the easygoing manners of Fatimid Egypt, and since "idleness leads to lewdness" (a maxim repeatedly quoted by him), he took a particularly hard stance — unwarranted by the law — with regard to a woman who refused to perform her (mandatory) household chores. The circumstances under which husbands beat their wives implicated issues more profound than household chores: Usually complaints about wife beating were made when there was deep discord between the spouses about their common or individual possessions.

The Absent Husband

Time and again, the Geniza documents refer to family problems occasioned by the absence of a spouse — most frequently, the husband. The material on this phenomenon is voluminous; for practical reasons, the subject is treated under two headings, although the dividing lines cannot always be clearly drawn. The first concerns absences occasioned by economic necessity, political disturbances, or other factors not directly connected with the relationship of the spouses; the second concerns absences related to marital strife, neglect, and desertion.

Traders, great and small, were forced by the nature of their occupation to travel frequently and often for prolonged periods; even craftsmen, as well as professionals such as physicians, scholars, teachers, and cantors, often had to seek their livelihoods outside their native towns. Agreements made prior to the undertaking of a voyage stated the frequency and duration of the periods of absence and made arrangements for the maintenance and other expenses of the family at home. In the case of extended travel, especially overseas, a conditional bill of divorce set the wife free if her husband failed to return at the date agreed upon. Other stipulations (in particular, safeguards for the security of the dowry and other obligations toward the wife) were included in such settlements, which it seems were made in court (and thus come to our knowl-

---

1. On the basis of his own survey of Muslim, Christian, and Jewish literary sources, Goitein was not convinced that wife beating was more prevalent in Mediterranean Islamic countries than in medieval Western Europe, nor that the legal situation within each culture was much different from the others.

edge), mostly when previous experience with the husband was not favorable. Letters, legal opinions, and court records tell us how such
arrangements and agreements worked.

Commercial travel to the Egyptian countryside (or, rather, to provincial towns) was common among the lower segments of the capital's
population. One court record illustrates such travel from the wife's point
of view. The husband had to stay at home two weeks, the period left
free by the Jewish laws of purity for intimate relations during the month.
He was not permitted to absent himself for more than a month, during
which he had to pay his wife her expenses every week. In the event of
failing to do so, he had to deliver to her the second marriage gift immediately and in full. She, in turn, promised "to attend to her house
and her work and not to go out." Contravening the agreement was
grounds for divorce.

In many instances it was not practicable to fix a term for the husband's
absence, particularly when the husband moved to another place to try
to establish himself and left his wife and children in the family home
until he was sure of the success of his new venture. This must have
happened frequently, for we often find situations in which a husband
lives in one place and his family in another, to be visited by him from
time to time. In these cases as well, the husband had to provide for the
maintenance of the family. Matters could get extremely complicated.

A question addressed to Maimonides tells of a husband who went
away without assigning anything to his wife except her own earnings
and the rent of the house (which was part of her dowry), both legal
sources of income for the husband. In debt and unable to manage, the
wife claims that the rent is rightfully hers. In another case, to avoid
ambiguities, an India trader setting out for Yemen states explicitly that
income derived by his wife from a house is hers, since he has sold the
house to her. Wives often had to sign agreements specifying in detail
the responsibilities for maintenance; such agreements protected the husband from accusations of negligence and made the wife responsible for
managing her own affairs.

Merchants, professionals, and craftsmen of the middle and lower segments of society, when setting out on a journey, hoped to sustain their
families at home with the profits made abroad. Often, however, their
hopes were not realized. Letters in which husbands excuse themselves
for tarrying longer than planned, or for sending only part of the allocations promised, or nothing at all, are legion. Unemployment, mishaps,
danger on the roads, or the failure of friends to live up to their promises
are the usual reasons given.

The Runaway Husband

A planned absence, carefully prepared by notarial agreements written before departure and made bearable by correspondence while away on travel, differed substantially from those innumerable instances where the husband simply vanished, leaving the family without sufficient support (or no support at all) and without knowledge of his whereabouts and doings. Such disappearances occurred when the husband was unable or unwilling to maintain his family or defaulted in paying his debts to private creditors or the tax collector, or both. A husband might also flee for personal reasons, such as a dangerous turn of events that forced him to go into hiding or assume a new identity, conflicts with his wife, or simply because he had found another woman.

Many examples of husbands fleeing marriage are represented in the Geniza records. This was extremely prevalent among the lower ranks of society, but not entirely absent among the higher echelons. The husband might absent himself even when he was still in town. In an appeal to the community involving an ordinary couple from a poor neighborhood, a woman asserts that her husband never stays overnight at home. But we also have an extraordinary letter from a wife to a husband who she describes as "a man of perfect character and high social rank," a letter written in excellent script and style, but reflecting a situation not dissimilar to the one just mentioned. Angry that he had to live in the family's house and also pay rent (perhaps the engagement contract had not stated that detail with sufficient clarity), the young husband sought to force the issue by staying away and coming home only for the Sabbath—when his absence could have led to a lawsuit, since love on the Sabbath night was the wife's legal right. On one occasion—the provocation for the letter—he was even absent on the Sabbath. The wife writes that the rent can be returned and that she is prepared to move with him to another place, for she has learned from the example of her sisters (who obviously had trouble with their husbands for similar reasons). She adds, however, that she will not eat (during the daytime, to be precise) until the matter is settled. The husband's hasty answer is written on the back of the letter: "If you do not break your fast, I shall come neither on the Sabbath nor on any other day." In another case, a father who was aware of the tension between his daughter and her husband sensed that his son-in-law was intent on desertion and posted a guard at the gate of the city. The fugitive was captured and brought to court together with his belongings, which he had tried to take away with him.

The search for a runaway husband could be frustrating even within the same country, as reflected by the correspondence between authorities dealing with one case. A woman in Alexandria, whose husband had fled his creditor and gone to the capital, complained that she had been deserted for so long a time that she had to maintain herself and a little girl (with special needs, it seems), and to pay her rent; she was, moreover, being sued by her husband's creditor. The Alexandrian authorities, in the most polite terms, ask their masters, the judges in Fustat, to do a pious deed by approaching the chief judge for action in this matter. On the reverse side of the document and referring to it, the judge Samuel informs the nagid that he sent several summons to the man, but since both the High Holidays (approximately September) and Hanukka (December) have passed without response from him, sterner measures are now required. The matter was of the utmost seriousness, since the Alexandrian wife asserted that her husband had married another woman and was living with her in Cairo. Clearly, the police now had to be instructed to bring the man to court by force, but only the nagid, as official representative of the state, was authorized to give that order. Needless to say, women so abandoned had little if any recourse to a social life outside the confines of their immediate family. They were thus consigned to a life that could leave them socially isolated as well as destitute.

Polygyny, Levirate, and Sororate Marriage

Although technically sanctioned by law, polygyny was not widely practiced, for the cost of maintaining households for two or more wives was excessive. Moreover, as we have seen, stipulations in marriage contracts restricting the taking of a second wife were common. Nevertheless, there were at times circumstances that made polygynous marriage necessary, circumstances that might require the permission of both the first wife and the religious authorities.

Cases of polygyny are reported or referred to in legal documents, as well as in letters found in the Geniza. The reasons given or implied include the wife's barrenness, proved after ten years of marriage; her being unfit for cohabitation; or her inability to care for her children because of insanity or other impediments, in which case the second wife undertook to look after them. There were also special circumstances that lay outside the husband's power of decision. One report concerns a government official who was obliged to have a family in Fustat while his wife lived in Damascus. Very rarely does one read about a husband running away with another woman and marrying her against the orders of the authorities. When a married man married a second wife without the permission of the first or of the authorities, he risked the ban of excommunication.

The conditions under which a wife would agree to her husband's marrying another woman were, more or less, as follows: first, a separate, fully furnished, domicile for herself, from which nothing could be removed without her authorization; second, safeguards for all the rights stipulated in the marriage contract (in one case, the first wife was paid her marriage gift under the condition that she would repay it if the second marriage were terminated); third, equal rights with regard to clothing (especially on Sabbaths and holidays) and with respect to conjugal relations; and, finally, the right to receive a divorce if she so wished. Clearly the issue of multiple wives was complicated by the economics of both marriage and divorce: divorce could be expensive—but the cost of maintaining more than one wife even more so.

Moreover, obtaining permission to marry a second wife was a very complicated matter. The story of one unhappy husband is illustrative. Having suffered for twenty years in a marriage to a severely ill woman, the husband, arriving from Jerusalem at Minyat Ghamr (probably his native town), found a suitable match for a second marriage. The local judge, who knew his story, was sympathetic, but did not dare act in so delicate a matter. Our man then went to Alexandria to submit his case to the next higher legal authority, but Anatoli, the French rabbi who was in charge there, stalled on making a decision ("You know his character and his 'dryness,'" the unhappy man writes). He therefore took his request to the highest authority, the chief judge Menahem in Cairo but was told that he had to appear in person. He could not do so because he was unable to leave his newly opened business for the time required for such an undertaking. In a letter, he asks the future judge Elijah to draw up a petition to the chief judge, which Elijah is able to do since he is familiar with the nature of the illness that beset the writer's wife and the hardships endured by the husband. (The illness in this particular case probably was mental; it was next to impossible to divorce an insane wife, since the divorce had to be accepted by her.) The writer understands that he will have to go to Cairo for the wedding (a process that would have involved drawing up various legal documents), evidence that he is hopeful for the success of his plea. On the other hand, he asks Elijah to keep the matter a secret, which seems to indicate that some hurdles still lay ahead.

An important reason for taking an additional wife in Geniza times was the obligation of levirate marriage, the marriage of the brother-in-law to the wife of a brother who had died childless. Levirate marriage was a custom in Islamic society, but only in Judaism, in that time and region, was it law. The surviving brother was free to refuse the marriage to his sister-in-law by undergoing the ancient ceremony described in Deuteronomy 25:7–9, but first the brother had to be found, and second, he had to be prepared to release the widow from the obligation. Many economic arrangements were implicated in such situations: The widow's rights, derived from her original marriage contract, and the brother's prerogatives as the heir could lead to endless chicanery and trouble before the widow was set free. Moreover, the surviving brother might be a child and, as a minor, unable to perform a legal act. In that case, the widow might be forced to wait for years until anything could be done on her behalf. The Geniza contains considerable material about these matters.

There are echoes of such conditions in Qur'ānic law, which provides that a husband cannot retake his wife after repudiating her unless she has contracted and consummated a marriage with another man. The law sought to protect the wife against a hasty repudiation made in anger. The intention was commendable, but the legal instrument created for its implementation was a disaster. Levirate marriage was well suited to the simple agricultural setting of ancient Israel, where brothers dwelled together on a parcel of land (Deuteronomy 25:5) and where a widow had nowhere else to turn after the death of her husband. It became a social monstrosity in the urban society of Geniza times. The Karaites were reasonable enough to outlaw the obligation of levirate marriage. The Rabbanite authorities of Egypt, however, ruled that levirate marriage did not override their antibigamy statute. In other words, if a man wished to marry the widow of his brother, he had first to divorce his wife and to pay all that was due her. This could leave the man destitute. Under such circumstances, the very ancient institution—designed to protect the interests of the widow and the integrity of the family and its progeny—obtained a result opposite to its intent. The problem was that levirate marriage was prescribed explicitly in scripture. For that reason, Moses Maimonides decided that levirate marriage was a religious duty and, as such, took precedence over all other considerations. Because of Maimonides' great authority, this decision prevailed, at least among Oriental Jews.

The difficult situations that levirate marriage gave rise to are impressively illustrated in a marriage agreement made between a nagid and the widow of his brother, the nagid who preceded him. The agreement was contracted on June 5, 1482, near the end of the Mamluk period of Egyptian history (during which the office of the nagid also came to an end). In accordance with Maimonides' ruling, Faraj, the widow of Yeshūʿā, son of Joseph (who also had been a nagid), married her brother-in-law Solomon under the usual conditions of equality between the two wives ("one night with this, one night with that") and the continuation of the prerogatives resulting from her former marriage contract. There was, however, an additional stipulation, necessitated by the office of the nagid: At the yearly pilgrimage to the holy shrine of Dammūh, the nagid was, of course, accompanied by his wife. It was one of the rare occasions of her public appearance. Who of the two should be the companion? Here the wife of the former nagid received some preference.

Levirate marriage, a man replacing his brother, was matched by the sororate marriage, its female pendant. That a sister should take a dead wife's place was neither law nor custom, but the actual occurrence of such unions must have been frequent, to judge from the casual way in which actions related to such marriages are reported. Apparently it was regarded as natural for a father to give a daughter to a bereaved son-in-law, even when she had already been promised, engaged, or betrothed to another man. This, too, could produce serious social and economic ramifications.

Settlements and Appeals

When husband and wife did not get along and were approaching the breaking point, both sides were prodded by the counsel, warnings, and outright threats of relatives and friends to make peace with each other. Disputes about the material possessions and claims of the two parties were one of the most common causes of marital conflict; these could be resolved by submitting the case to a legal authority. This could be done anonymously, without specifying the names of the persons concerned. How this worked is illustrated by a letter of thanks sent from the little town of Malīj in the Nile Delta to a parnās in Fustat. The mother of a newly married girl who was having difficulties with her husband had traveled to Fustat and consulted the official, who subsequently obtained a legal opinion from an acknowledged authority. She brought home with her a letter containing that opinion, which then was read out in the synagogue in the presence of the local judge, the cantors, some notables, and anyone else who cared to attend. The details of the dispute are not stated. It was noted that if the husband wished a divorce, the legal authority obliged him to pay the second marriage gift in full; this was enough to induce him to give in. "The boy cooled off [lit., broke down: Ar. *inkasar*] and kissed my head and the head of her mother [the writer's wife, who had traveled to Fustat]; those present brought about an agreement between us, and we cooled off." The legal safeguards designed to protect the interests of women were extensive and carefully delineated. In this case, the husband could not act with impunity, for the law protected the interests of his wife.

Often, if not in most cases, a wife was spared the unpleasantness of appearing in court with her husband. In numerous examples, she would appoint a brother or, in his absence, someone else to represent her. When we find that the husband as well is represented by another person, special circumstances must have been involved. In a carefully executed court record dated August 5, 1028, both wife and husband appoint their fathers as their attorneys; moreover, the fathers are made responsible for any financial obligations falling on their children. If one of the parties balks at fulfilling these obligations, "the court and the community"—twice emphasized—will permit the other side to approach the state authorities. Clearly, large sums were involved, too much to be handled by the young husband himself.

Marital strife was not the only occasion for the involvement of the court. There were many reasons why the parties might find it advisable to have their mutual agreements legalized by a notary or a judge: for instance, to forestall claims by or against heirs, to protect property in a time of general insecurity, or simply to safeguard rights that, for one reason or another, needed clarification. Settlements normally required several actions, as when one spouse made a gift of a house to the other (requiring registration before both a Muslim and Jewish authority), or when a husband ceded to his wife full disposition over her dowry or released her from a debt she owed him.

Parents and Children

The voluminous evidence preserved in the Geniza indicates a preoccupation with children, or, more correctly, with sons. When a business letter is written to a person who has no sons, the author prays that God may give him "male children studying the Torah and fulfilling commandments." When he has sons, the author prays that God may keep them, or that the father will "see their Torah," that is, success in study, "their good works, and their 'joy'"—their marriage. If they are adult, greetings must be extended to them, each in accordance with the circumstances. Even a complete stranger, writing a begging letter—and many have found their way into the Geniza—first carefully inquires about the family of the addressee so that he may insert the proper wishes for the progeny.

Procreation is an explicit commandment in the Bible, and God's law can be preserved only if it is studied and kept—now and forever. Hence the great emphasis not only on sons but also on grandsons and great-grandsons. Letters expressing the wish that fathers will witness their sons' success in study and marriage are also hopeful that they will see the same for their grandsons and great-grandsons, as happened to Joseph (Genesis 50:23) and Job (42:16). One notes as well the talmudic axiom "he who hears a lection from the mouth of his grandson is like the one who has heard it [from God] on Mount Sinai."

The precedence of "study" over "good deeds" in wishes for success of children should not be taken too literally. It is the ancient Socratic idea that one has to know what is good to be able to act in accordance with it. There is no lack of wishes in our texts that the addressee's children will grow up as righteous and honest men. The hope that a son will become a support and source of strength for his father appears frequently in letters. This wish is regularly expressed with the phrase "may God strengthen your [upper] arm through him," written in Arabic or Hebrew, and is found throughout the centuries. (The phrase originated in ancient times when, during tribal warfare, a multitude of sons was the safest protection for an aging father, but it also had its legitimate place in the urban society of the Geniza period.) Family partnerships, presided over by fathers, were the strongest business firms; craftsmen worked together with their sons, and professionals and dignitaries enhanced their prestige and influence when they had sons ready to take over their positions, which they themselves had often inherited from their fathers. The Bible verse most frequently quoted in the Geniza documents is Psalm 45:16: "Instead of your fathers shall be your sons [you will make them princes all over the country]." This is said not only in letters to high dignitaries, such as a nagid, a judge, or a great scholar like Maimonides, where it is common, but also in simple family letters. Another biblical phrase, "may [the son] sit on [the father's] chair" (1 Kings 3:6 and elsewhere), is also used in this connection, even in addressing a minor community official: in one letter, that wish is directed to a cantor for his two sons and his future grandsons and great-grandsons.

In speaking of sons (whether one's own or those of another), paternal affection finds expression in endearments; "my son, the joy of my eye" and "the dearest to me of all mankind" are the most commonly used expressions. "The lovely flower," "the blossoming rose," originally perhaps said of children, can refer also to adult sons; *muhja*, "lifeblood," is another frequently used term. The most common term of endearment to designate a son is *hamūd*, "delight," so common in fact that the Hebrew letter *h* stands in memorial and other lists simply for "son of."

We know considerably less from the Geniza records about attitudes toward daughters. No letter has yet been found in which a father is congratulated on the birth of a girl, or in which God is invoked to look after a man's daughter. At the birth of a girl, the father (or the family) is congratulated on the mother's *khalāṣ*, "deliverance"—from death or other harm in childbirth. Only once, in a letter of a sister writing to her brother overseas, are good wishes expressed for a newly born niece, and lovely things are said about the addressee's daughters. But even there, the wish is that God grant the letter's recipient something "to lift up his heart, namely, a manchild."

The absence of a similar concern with young girls went hand in hand with the socialization of women. In the house of worship, Jewish girls, like their Christian compatriots, were confined to the women's gallery. They did not actively participate in the services; they could profit individually from what they were able to take in, but they did not "study." "The men to learn, the women to listen." The religious obligation of perpetuating the faith through learned discourse did not apply to girls. From that point of view, the birth of a girl might be considered a liability: A father had to work all his life to ready an appropriate dowry and trousseau for her, and yet, once married, she would not perpetuate his line. The continuity of the family was seen exclusively in male terms: an ancient maxim, both Jewish and Arab, says, "The sons of sons are like sons, the sons of daughters are not."

A report about the death of a girl is regularly followed by the wish that she may be replaced by a boy, sometimes accompanied by the consolation that God might accept the child's death as an atonement for the father's sins. (It was believed that babies died for their fathers' sins, since they could not have committed a sin themselves.) Such disrespect for girls does not mean that they were not regarded with great affection within individual families. "I prefer girls," said Rav Ḥisdā, a prominent talmudic sage. His medieval commentators, perplexed by so preposterous a dictum, explained that Ḥisdā's sons-in-law were greater scholars than his sons. But the context suggests that the sage actually preferred girls for their own sake. Nevertheless, the medieval reaction to Rav

Ḥisdā's statement speaks volumes about societal attitudes towards women—or to be more precise, the attitudes of Jewish men. A father might adore his daughter, but in principle he understood that boys were preferred. In such fashion, the numerous indications of fatherly love and adoration for a daughter are subordinate to a societal attitude favoring men. A girl as the firstborn was nevertheless considered auspicious because she deflected the evil eye—a malign presence much feared at the birth of a son.

Bearing and Rearing Children

Attempts at family planning were not unknown in the Geniza society. An Islamic textbook on commerce, quoting a saying ascribed to the prophet Muḥammad, lauds the convenience of a small family, an attitude probably not unknown among comfortable urbanites of Geniza times. When a very young husband, who already had a daughter, is warned not to be too eager in siring children lest his quest for a boy result in producing a girl every year, we are led to believe that means were used to forestall unwanted pregnancies. Records of conception, birth, and nursing are occasionally found in the Geniza; one ought to be very careful, however, at drawing larger conclusions about family planning from such evidence, for there is a world of difference between avoiding unwanted pregnancies and birth control as social policy. Before proclaiming the existence of a "policy" of birth control during the classical Geniza period, we would have to know more about attitudes towards childbearing in different segments of the Geniza society and in different environments, and whether such practices as were used proved efficacious.

Much information about childbearing is found in letters. Women wrote freely about their pregnancies, as did their husbands, and good wishes were extended to them from their correspondents. "I am in my sixth month," writes a woman (who had a married daughter) to her maternal uncle, asking him urgently to visit, "for death and life are in the hand of God." It was not unusual for mothers and daughters to be pregnant at the same time, given that girls were married in their teens. Another woman with child asks her sister and mother to take more interest in her because of her condition. In two letters in which she makes this request she also speaks about her children, a girl and a boy. "Your daughter is well and is in her fourth month," writes a son-in-law from Alexandria to his uncle and father-in-law in Fustat and immediately adds, "We are upset because of the plague in Fustat, about which we have heard here." Given that the Geniza correspondence is filled with reports about bad health and illness, one wonders why we hear so little about the inconveniences of pregnancy or of death in childbirth. It cannot be that it was taboo to mention female distress, since illnesses of women are reported as often as those of men. There are a few references to the deaths of mothers during delivery, or shortly after, but far fewer than one would expect. Yet the risk of childbirth was great. Indeed, we have wills of pregnant women (one declaring that she was entering her ninth month) made in anticipation of the possibility of death. Two wills provide for the child, "male or female," who would survive the mother; one also gives generously to charities and relatives, and one turns the testator's assets over to her mother on condition she bring up the newborn, while the husband is released of any obligation. (The reasoning behind the latter will was, of course, that the husband would soon marry again and that a grandmother would be a better substitute for the mother than a stepmother.)

We hear little about women's physical or medical practices during the term of pregnancy and at childbirth. Women were attended by midwives and female doctors. "Son of the Midwife," "Son of the Little [female] Doctor" are family names, but we learn nothing of importance from the names themselves about the activities of the professionals who attended at childbirth. The subject of birth appears in the Geniza records mainly in connection with social events. One concern of the family was to receive in proper fashion the many women who came to see the young mother. In the case of the birth of a boy, the circumcision ceremony, following eight days later, was an important affair, second in grandeur only to a wedding. Solemn and protracted prayers were recited both on the Sabbath preceding the circumcision and during the ceremony itself. We have reports about the liturgies that were read at such "a tremendous assembly." The privilege of leading the circumcision ceremony (and of receiving the honorarium that accompanied that function) seems to refer to the recitation of prayers rather than to the actual surgical procedure. Attendance at the ceremony was a very sensitive matter of prestige for all; hence the letters of inquiry and apology sent out on such an occasion. Poems with good wishes were read out in anticipation of a reward from the happy father. A circumcision ceremony was also a good occasion for sending a begging letter; one father vows a festive meal for the poor.

The religious communities, let alone the government authorities, do not seem to have kept birth registers. The government became interested in its non-Muslim male subjects when they were old enough to be charged with the payment of the poll tax. But the proud father would nonetheless list somewhere the exact date, preferably according to the various calendars of his own and other communities known to him. The newborn is referred to neither with his Arabic nor his Hebrew proper name but, as with Muslims, by his honorific nickname, such as Abū 'l-Barakāt, "Blessed," or Abū 'l-Fakhr, "Glory."

References in the Geniza documents to nursing indicate that it was the mother rather than a professional wet nurse who attended to the children. (The paucity of references to wet nurses is curious, given that not all women were suited to nursing their offspring.) Both Jewish and Islamic law envision two years as the period normally needed for this phase of the child's upbringing, and this is confirmed by the Geniza documents. Weaning was a dangerous phase in the child's life (we should recall that the patriarch Abraham celebrated the weaning, not the circumcision of his son Isaac [Genesis 21:8]). A woman in poor health writes that she concocted a soup, cooked from two chickens, and served it as a daily replacement for mother's milk. During nursing, a woman was not supposed to perform heavy work. Thus, a husband who had given his former wife an alimony of cash and wheat while she nursed his baby demanded to be free of providing the wheat after the weaning.

Occasional notices about the upbringing of children are dispersed throughout the Geniza records. It was considered important to pay attention to the feelings of the child. When a distinguished woman in Jerusalem died, leaving a two-and-a-half-year-old son, he was claimed by his paternal aunt—none other than the wife of the gaon Elijah b. Solomon. But the prospect of the opportunities associated with growing up in a prestigious household did not sway the gaon himself from ruling that the boy should remain where he was: he would be happier in his accustomed environment. (Undoubtedly, female members of the widower's household had looked after him during his mother's final illness.) In the same letter, we read that her sister was already on her way from Egypt to Jerusalem, probably to fill the dead woman's place. A widow with a little boy in Minyat Ziftā, a town in the Nile Delta, receives a contractually confirmed promise from her future husband: He will feed and clothe the child and teach him a craft. The child will be to him like the children borne to him by the bride; he will not turn him out, or beat him, or humiliate him with words.

In letters preserved in the Geniza, fathers writing home insist that their young sons not play or be on the streets "with the boys," but spend their days in school. A father mourning a son who died at the age of six eulogizes the child for never playing in the street or at home, for running to the gate of the house to welcome the needy and share his food with them, "whether he had plenty or little," and for delighting his father with intelligent questions. (The father was a member of the yeshiva and therefore favorably disposed toward the practice, characteristic of higher learning, of asking questions about a text studied.) In a dirge concerning his daughter, a father remembers the days when he taught her the Bible: "When I remember the quickness of your mind, your knowledge of the Torah, your deeds of charity, and the gracefulness of your diction, I say, 'Would that I could listen to you again as at the time I taught you the Torah and questioned you on its knowledge by heart' and cry out, 'Let me see your countenance, let me hear your voice'" (Song of Songs 2:14).

We must assume that the parents used practical methods to implant the central importance of learning and communal responsibility in the hearts of their children. Indeed, it often seems as if young children were being trained in adult responsibilities at very early stages of their development. A most important aspect of the upbringing of children was their constant participation in the life of the adults. During the week, boys were in school, where prayers were said; on Sabbaths and holidays, they were taken by their fathers to the synagogue, and they attended services even when their fathers were abroad. Girls frequented the women's gallery with their mothers. Invitations to weekends, holidays, and family events invariably included "the little ones." And the very early participation of teenagers in economic life brought them into constant contact with the world of adults.

It is difficult to provide exact data regarding children in the economy, since our sources most often speak of "adolescents" in general terms and do not indicate their precise age. In one particular case, it was taken for granted that a girl of ten and her elder sister, who had already attained puberty, would work as embroiderers. Boys still in their early teens were thought to have the skills to engage in various commercial enterprises, but here the law could complicate the responsibilities they bore. A Karaite court decision dated 1004, for example, rules against a shrewd fifteen-year-old boy being given control of his inheritance. On the other hand, Maimonides, writing two centuries later, holds a fifteen-year-old liable for debts incurred, in accordance with the law that identifies puberty (assumed to be reached by boys at thirteen) with legally coming of age. Only certain transactions with immovable property were excluded from the adolescent's free disposition until he reached the age of twenty.

The Size of the Nuclear Family

References to children stillborn or dying in early childhood normally do not appear in our documents. Moreover, daughters are never mentioned in memorial lists and are rarely referred to in the salutations of letters; often we learn about them only circumstantially. In addition, most of our information comes from affluent families. We learn about poor families when a man complains about his large household, which he is unable to support, or from lists of paupers, where only a few members of the family live at home—in many cases certainly because the boys had to leave their homes at a very young age to seek a livelihood. Whether or not the poor had larger or smaller families than more affluent elements of society cannot be ascertained; generally speaking, such impressions have to be treated with caution.

We are best off with legal documents in which there is reason to be specific with data about children—documents such as releases, wills, settlements of inheritance claims, or inquiries addressed to authorities about these matters. They provide evidence of families with only one child, of others with five or six, and rarely, with seven or more children. The documents would seem to reflect an average number of around four, but the statistical validity of these data is problematic at best. We should keep in mind that these legal documents, while they include women, count only surviving offspring.

Appeals to the authorities, or to the community at large, in which the supplicant mentions the number of his or her children as a reason for the request, have a semi-official character and should also be regarded as fairly reliable. A community official in Acre with five daughters, but no son, complains that he has lost much of his income since the Crusaders (who had conquered the city in 1104, not long before the letter was written) no longer permit the ritual killing of animals, from which he derived a considerable part of his income. A widow who has already lost four adult sons applies to the community after her fifth and only remaining son is killed by the Ghuzz, or Seljuks. A man, apparently from Europe, leaves six hungry children—four daughters and two sons—in Alexandria after being forced to flee from the city because of debts and an unpaid poll tax. These are the highest numbers of children found in requests by needy people.

Family correspondence is another informative source, especially when it is extensive and mentions the entire nuclear family, as when a man writes from abroad to a brother and sends regards to his other siblings. A letter going overseas after the sender and recipient have been separated for a prolonged period can also be useful because the parties give each other exhaustive reports about their families. Since it was customary to recapitulate at the beginning of a letter messages previously received, we usually hear about both parties. Epistolary evidence, such as it is, would seem to indicate that the average family had five or less offspring.

Greetings in business and private letters, praises in poems, and data in genealogical lists — our most abundant sources — are of limited value in determining family size, since, as a rule, only sons are mentioned. Genealogical lists have the additional disadvantages of usually being hastily executed and exhibiting no system that accounts for agnates. Consequently, memorial lists can be used only for what they say, not for what they omit. When all is said, there is as yet no statistically valid way to break down the demographic data on the size of the nuclear household. Nevertheless, we may make at least one general observation: the Geniza people, high and low, tried hard to have as many sons as possible, but the grim realities of child mortality and changing economic circumstances put strict limitations on their hopes.

Relationships between Adult Children and Their Parents

Children who had reached maturity were expected "to serve" their parents, that is, to stay with them and to extend to them any help they needed, for it is written, "like a father who loves his son, who serves him" (Malachi 3:17). Consequently, father and mother were addressed or referred to as "my lord" or "my lady." A weaver writing to his wife, quotes his son: "My boy Manṣūr came to me and said, 'My lord. . . .'" Adult children showed reverence toward their parents by kissing their hands, or hands and feet — so the letters indicate. Mutual affection was expressed by kissing the eyes.

As might be expected, we hear about filial obligation primarily when the writer was unable or unwilling to fulfill it. A letter from Tyre tells of a young cantor who had found a job in a small Lebanese town; he writes to his parents in Alexandria, excusing himself repeatedly for being separated from them. It was not his wish, God had decreed it, for he could not find work in his native city and hated to stay idle. He goes so far as to say that he is marrying a poor orphaned girl for the sole reason that his future wife should not come from a family that would impede his returning as a dutiful son to his parents. Failure to travel to one's mother for a holiday needed a special apology. To their son's assurances of attachment, parents would reply, "You never cease to love us, whether far away or staying with us."

The mother's claim to her children's attention seems to have been regarded as even stronger than the father's. "I intended to stand before my mother [i.e., to serve her] and to acquire her religious merit," writes an old man, himself a father. The mother's honored position did not depend on her being "mistress of the house"; she might be living with a relative, but still she commanded respect. A son, sending an urgent invitation to his widowed mother, leaving her multiple alternatives for carrying out the visit, writes as follows: "You know, and everyone knows, the high regard in which you are held. Now you are even greater than when you were the mistress of the house; there is no one who does a thing except on your command." The woman's young grandson, who yearns for his grandmother, is the only attraction the writer dares to offer.

In addition to its religious value, which equated reverence towards parents with service to God — or indeed rated it even higher — there were socioeconomic circumstances that strengthened the bonds between parents and children. In their youth and early adult life, children were dependent on their parents to an even greater extent than is commonly true in our own society, and in old age the parents (especially the mother) often had to rely on their children, as much as they might wish to remain independent. Girls could not expect to make a reasonable match, to be secure in marriage, or to survive widowhood or divorce without strong financial and moral support from their parents. The very health of a sick woman frequently depended on the willingness of her father or mother to make a significant contribution to her treatment. But a son, too, could anticipate paternal assistance: the law obliged the father to arrange his son's marriage. This meant, in the first place, that the father ceded a part of his house to him, or made him a gift of a separate home in which the son would live with his new wife. The practice is illustrated in many Geniza documents.

It must not be forgotten that a father's gift was implicitly an act of generosity on the part of the mother, since a married man's property was mortgaged to his wife's ketubba and any disposition of it required her consent. A married woman could make a gift only of property that did not constitute part of her dowry. Thus, "the Mistress of Iraq," whose concern for her own funeral arrangements shows that she expected to die soon, gives one-quarter of a house to a son, another quarter to a daughter, and stipulates that her husband has the right to reside in those areas of the house (on condition he keep them in repair), while emphasizing that he otherwise has no right to them whatsoever. Stipulations granting parents rights to inhabit the premises given to a child are also found elsewhere. These types of arrangements protected all members of a given family and drew them together, but they also reduced the capacity of individual children to establish boundaries for their own private lives and that of their immediate families.

Besides the moral and material support received from parents, there was another benefit derived from them, a benefit that medieval men must have prized most highly: parental blessings, or rather, prayers. The Yemenites say "his mother has prayed for him" of a man who has succeeded in life. The biblical stories of the blessings of the Patriarchs (Genesis 27:26–29, 48:15–20, 49:1–28) reminded everyone of the power of paternal intercession. But children were not regarded as worthy of praying for their parents: they had not yet accumulated enough merits to be worthy intercessors. Although children in the Geniza often ask their parents to pray for them (or have their parents' assurances that they are doing so), the reverse does not seem to be the case. An ancient Palestinian prayerbook, found in the Geniza, instructs children to include their parents in their private supplications for forgiveness, but the official prayer for the dead, the Kaddish, now so prominent a part of the synagogue service, assumed that function only in late medieval Christian Europe. In Geniza times, the Kaddish was a solemn doxology, including a prayer for the living—in particular, for the spiritual leaders of the community.

Wishes that children should be like their parents and more virtuous, more successful, or more renowned (sentiments expressed in letters both to parents and to children) reflect more a desire for a better worldly existence than the religiosity of parents. This is evident from the wording of the wish and also the biblical reference to it—the words spoken to the dying King David: "May God make Solomon's name more famous than yours and make his throne greater than your throne" (1 Kings 1:47).

"When your son is grown up, let him be your brother"—this Arabic maxim, which has Hebrew and ancient Near Eastern antecedents, is reflected in the Geniza correspondence between parents and children. Since sons entered economic life early, they soon became the helpers, collaborators, or partners of their father, or took over their responsibilities altogether, a fact frequently reflected in the Geniza sources—and in great detail. But, as in all societies, fathers and mothers often had reason (or believed they had reason) to be dissatisfied with their sons' behavior, or gave voice to the expectation that their sons would be idle or fail to live up to their responsibilities. Occasionally, friction between children and parents came into the open. "I was sad when I learned that you quarreled with your father—but he is your father!" we read in a personal letter to a man who is otherwise praised for his actions and described as noble and worthy of the traditions of his family. Quarrels between parents and children appear fairly tame and rarely reflect estrangement. This does not mean that serious rifts with strong animosities did not arise, but in general, families tried to hush up conflicts. Lawsuits between parents and children were rare and were clearly regarded as outrageous. The cause of animosity was often tied to the complex financial arrangements of inheritance, made even more complex because of safeguards to protect the wealth of women. The situation was different as regards stepchildren: fathers who remarried often left male offspring older than their young wives—a situation that invited obvious disputes.

Foster Children

Adoption in the strict sense is unknown in both Islamic and Jewish law. But persons called "foster child," *rabīb*, of a man or a woman, are mentioned in the Geniza records frequently. Often we are able to ascertain that they were stepchildren; sometimes we cannot. We have, however, clear examples of persons rearing children with whom they had no natural connection whatsoever. In a time of great calamity, probably at the beginning of the Crusader period, when many female prisoners had to be ransomed and cared for, one woman, herself a mother of three girls and two boys, reportedly took a little girl into her house and brought her up "in order to acquire a religious merit."

The record of an actual adoption proves that the Jewish courts had considerable experience in these matters. The wife of a stranger died sixteen days after she had given birth to a girl for whom the bereft father was unable to provide. He "sold" her for five dinars to a prominent lady, who agreed to raise her. (According to both Jewish and Islamic law, no free person, whether one-day old or of maturity, could be sold. The word "sold" was here used so as not to put the unhappy stranger to shame for having given up the child.) The father promised to allow the foster mother complete freedom in the girl's education; he would never demand the return of the girl, nor even come near the place where she resided. He would have no claim on any gains made by the girl or on any other income accruing to her from the house of her benefactors, from a marriage gift, or from compensation given to her for a disgrace or an injury inflicted upon her. If the girl died, no claim of negligence could be made against the woman. An incomplete last sentence seems to say that the father promised restitution of all her expenses to the foster mother if the girl, when grown up, wished to return to her father's family.

The informal adoption of *parents* is a common feature of the Geniza correspondence. Just as a man would address a friend to whom he was not related as "my brother from both father and mother," so would he call an older person on whose guidance, advice, or support he counted, "my father," *wālidī* (lit., my progenitor) and himself "your son," using even the term of endearment *ḥamūdō* (Heb.), "your delight." (This form of address, familiar from the Bible [2 Kings 2:12, 5:13, 6:21, and elsewhere] and the ancient Near East survives in present-day Arabic.) It is not, of course, legal adoption that is at issue here: rather, this extension of family terms to human relationships in general (the term ʿamm, "paternal uncle," is another example) is an indication of the intensity of feelings toward the family itself.

Widowhood

We read much about widows in the Geniza documents but little about widowers, undoubtedly because husbands were better able to sustain the loss of a spouse. A husband's social and economic status was hardly affected by the death of his wife. If not otherwise stipulated, he was heir to her dowry and other possessions and was freed from the obligation of paying the second marriage gift. The domestic chores could be carried out by the women of the household, and a household was composed mostly of female relatives. Besides the wife, there might be a mother, a sister, a grandmother, and an aunt. In their absence, a maidservant or an elderly hired freewoman performed the work, or the husband might take a second wife soon after the first had died, especially if he had children.

For the wife, however, the death of her husband was often a disaster. She lost her support and even her domicile and could rely only on the remainder of her dowry, her other possessions, and the promised second marriage gift. This might leave her with uncertain and insufficient assets. Indigent widowhood was a calamity for the woman concerned and an imposition on the community. It is for this reason that so many Geniza papers contain complaints of widows or describe actions to improve their lot. On the other hand, widowhood or divorce freed a woman from the yoke of marriage. She was now free to act on her own in financial as well as other matters; for instance, she could marry whom she liked and often on conditions that she herself imposed. The well-to-do widow or divorced women is a social figure prominent in the Geniza records. But freedom was sweet only if fortified by adequate means.

At marriage, a husband mortgaged all his possessions, "even the coat on his shoulders," and after his death his estate went to the "debts" he owed his wife: her second marriage gift and her dowry, the income that he had been entitled to use for the duration of the marriage. In reality, this agreement frequently proved to be unenforceable simply because the husband was unable to guarantee the payments. Consequently, when the end of life approached, we find settlements made in which the size of the second marriage gift was reduced, sometimes to half the original amount, or even less. The reductions involved concessions on the husband's side, usually formally granting the wife the status of "trustworthiness," which protected her from being troubled by heirs and courts with demands to render account of any of her husband's property that she might hold.

The frequency of such occurrences induced husbands to make deathbed declarations of what sums they still owed their wives from their marriage contracts a very common practice. Moreover, it was customary to provide the wife a gift additional to the payments due her; often this was done on the condition that she remain unmarried, at least as long as the children were young and had not themselves married. That being so, the children would be protected until they themselves were launched. In wills to a second wife we find legacies made to children from a previous marriage. Sons from a previous marriage were inclined to be suspicious of their stepmother; stepmothers figure in a number of lawsuits brought by the offspring of a deceased father.

"I give," and "I will," were terms used in deathbed declarations when the husband left all his possessions to his wife because their total value hardly covered what he owed her. Other than in these circumstances, we rarely read of a husband making his wife the sole heir, for if she remarried and died, the estate would go to another man—possibly at the expense of his offspring. A husband could, however, appoint his

wife as his executor during his final illness; such declarations are sometimes preceded by her appointment as his caretaker or guardian. A notable leaves to each of his three minor daughters 100 dinars for their
trousseaux, and his two sons receive the balance of his property. His
wife (whose father is still alive) is to be executor of his estate and guardian for his children ("to bring them up and to look after their affairs").
No court has a right to supervise or to restrict her actions, nor can a
court or her children, upon coming of age, "impose an oath on her,"
that is, sue her to give an account of her actions.

In another disposition, a man contemplating his death appoints his
wife as executor (and guardian of an only daughter) giving this reason
for such confidence: "She understands the child's circumstances better
than others, she is more experienced, and she has more compassion for
her." In each instance, it was expected that the wife would not inherit
at the expense of the children. Among people of modest circumstances,
the wife took care of her husband's affairs during his illness and after his
death until the courts, the statutory guardians of fatherless children,
came in and clarified the legal position.

The widow as well was often in need of protection. When a widow
was not granted the status of executor or other special privileges by her
husband, she was likely to encounter difficulties. As soon as her husband
died, she ceased to be "the mistress of the house"; everything in the
house now passed into the possession of the legal heir—a son, a daughter, a brother, a paternal cousin of her late husband, or someone else.
To be sure, she could claim debts against the estate of the deceased, but
people often were tardy in living up to their commitments, especially
towards a creditor in a weak position, such as a widow. This attitude
toward a widow's claim is already expressed in an ancient law of the
Israelite peasants: "Payments for torts are made with the best field, debts
are paid off with fields of middle quality, and for the wife's ketubba,
with the worst." To mitigate the law, the marriage contracts preserved
in the Geniza normally contain the stipulation that after the termination
of the marriage the wife is to be compensated with "good gold dinars
of full weight," that is, with the choicest of her former husband's possessions. Only two documents have been found thus far in which the
groom agrees to pay his second marriage gift in dinars "of the worst
sort," using the legal term occurring in the ancient law cited. But the
attitude persisted and is even expressed in wills in which the husband
assigns to his wife the price of objects difficult to sell or of limited value,
such as household goods or books, while objects of more value are made
available to other beneficiaries.

Before a widow could obtain anything from the heirs, she had to show which of her late husband's possessions were "under her hand," so that these assets could be offset against the heirs' obligations. If not otherwise stipulated or agreed upon, she had to confirm this by taking an oath that she was hiding nothing, the so-called oath of the widow. The courts went to great lengths in this respect, locking away everything in the house and inquiring not only about small pieces of furniture and kitchenware but even about the wife's earnings from work during her husband's lifetime, which were legally his.

Uncertainty or outright ignorance of the law could have disastrous consequences. One woman had permitted her husband to give a house belonging to her personally (and not part of her dowry) as collateral for a debt. She had acceded "to do him a favor" and "to have a quiet life with him," after he had coaxed and pressed her to accept what appeared to be a temporary measure. But when the husband died without having paid the debt, even the great judge Menaḥēm b. Isaac b. Sāsōn, was forced to rule that her property was forfeited. To protect a woman from such uncertainties, we find husbands and heirs making legal documents as explicit as possible.

Complaints about heirs who did not pay a widow her due or did not honor the term of the agreement are, of course, found in the Geniza, but less often than one would expect. More common are releases in which the heirs declare that they have no further claims against the widow and in which the widow declares that she has received all that is owed her. Many such documents have been preserved. Expressly or by implication, the releases show that they were preceded by lawsuits, sometimes of long duration. A trousseau list, written with a thick pen and greyish ink, in which each somewhat faded item is gone over with a fine pen and black ink, looks as if it accompanied such a release, whether for a widow or a divorced women we cannot know.

After her claims had been recognized by the heirs and the courts, the widow had to overcome another hurdle: collecting the sum assigned to her. Except for the wealthy, a man's assets consisted mostly of partnerships, other forms of investment in business ventures, promissory notes, and the like; there were, of course, often counterclaims, frequently giving rise to protracted litigation. The majority of widows about whom we read in the legal documents of the Geniza were mothers of minor children. The courts, in their endeavor to preserve the property of the children, entrusted it to executors or administrators (if that had not been done by their father) and assigned alimony of mere subsistence level to the household of the widow. But even these scarce means of livelihood were often not delivered on time, or in full; sometimes they proved totally insufficient. A widow with adult sons usually lived with one of them, a fact documented in numerous family letters and legal documents. Living with a married daughter was less common, but not as rare as one would be inclined to assume in view of the popular prejudice against residing with a daughter.

Special arrangements had to be devised to provide women from a second marriage with a domicile. For well-to-do people this presented no difficulty, since they normally possessed several houses or units within houses. Poorer people had no such choices. A widower who was about to marry but who had a grown son stipulated that his new wife could stay in his house after his death but that he would not be able to provide her with separate "widow's lodgings," a privilege normally expected under such circumstances. Grave conflicts could ensue when the legal situation was not clearly stated as it was in that document.

Most of the women forced to have recourse to public welfare were widows. The term "wife of" in the lists of those receiving bread, wheat, clothing, handouts of money, and other benefits, means "widow of"; most of the single women with children registered in those lists must have belonged to this category. A particular benefit granted to them was the right to live in a house belonging to the community (for which, however, a rent had to be paid); in one document we even read about a house occupied, with one exception, solely by women, comparable with the Muslim houses of widows known from later times. Many more single women than men were "exposed" to public welfare.

Divide

"God hates divorce," says the Bible (Malachi 2:16). One is not surprised to find the Geniza courts expending much effort to settle matters between husband and wife before granting them a divorce. "Take with you some of the elders, go to her, talk to her heart, and reason with her; hopefully they will make peace with each other." Such attempts to urge reconciliation are found during all the phases of the judicial process leading to divorce. But the ample references to these matters in the Geniza documents proves that divorce was much more common in those times than among Jewish families in Europe and America until World War II.

What could occasion so many references to divorce in a society that disapproved of repudiating the bonds of marriage? First marriages were normally arranged by the parents or other relatives in order to form an additional link in the connections existing between the two parties through family or occupational ties. But what happened to the wife when those ties themselves became strained or severed altogether? In a long letter from Jerusalem, containing much news, we read: "The member of the High Court, R. Ḥayyīm, behaved in an ugly way toward his brother-in-law. The matter ended up with the latter separating [from his wife], but God provided the girl with a replacement better in every respect: religiosity, means, and scholarship; these days she is entering her new house."

The extreme mobility of the Geniza society was another factor that undermined the unity of the family. Young men of all walks of life often had to leave their wives for months and years, and wives usually were not prepared to follow them to foreign ports. Separation caused by travel was apt to lead to divorce. In a lengthy letter, mostly in rhymed prose, Joseph ha-Kohen b. Solomon Gaon, writing from Jerusalem or Ramle, informs the Jewish chief justice of Aleppo that it has taken seven months to find the husband whose wife, a resident of the Syrian city, demanded a divorce; the bill has been made out and entrusted to a man who will deliver it to the woman.

Mobility had another negative effect. It resulted in marriages, probably often hastily concluded, between persons from different localities who were not compatible. There are indeed numerous examples of such marriages ending in the divorce courts. Some of the Geniza court clerks, recording divorce proceedings, mention the places from which the parties hailed; the majority do not. Had all clerks adhered to the custom of noting the parties' countries of origin, perhaps the deleterious effects of mobility on marital life would be even more evident. All said, a bad marriage was a disgrace, for divorce never remained a secret for long, but terminating such a marriage was preferable to the shame that it might bring to the families concerned and, in particular, the husband.

As regards divorce, the dominant position of the husband was sealed in Islamic and Jewish law by his right of unilateral repudiation. Ancient Near Eastern (and Jewish) law knew more humane forms of separation. The Aramaic marriage contracts of the Jewish community of Elephantine in Upper Egypt, written in the fifth century B.C.E. provide the wife with a right to initiate divorce proceedings similar to that of the husband. Traces of such legislation are found in the Talmud, and Mordechai A. Friedman's painstaking study of the marriage contracts according to Palestinian custom found in the Geniza has shown that its last vestiges were still alive well into the eleventh century.[2] Whether caused by the broader social environment (Iranian or Muslim), or by an excessively literal and generalizing understanding of a passage in the Bible ("when . . . he writes her a bill of divorce . . . and sends her out of his house" [Deuteronomy 24:1]), the overwhelming testimony of the Geniza documents proves that only action on the part of the husband could formally terminate a marriage. The courts could coerce him, but if he remained obstinate, or could not be found, the wife was condemned to the life of "a widow whose husband was alive," which was worse than the life of a true widow, for she could never marry again.

The law required that, to be rendered valid, the bill of repudiation had to be received by the wife. Many such documents preserved in the Geniza confirm, on the reverse side, that "it has got into her hand." How fastidious the authorities were in this respect may be surmised from two reports about the delivery of the bill: the first, an official document describing the event; the second, a letter advising the addressee of how the delivery was performed. At least three men acted, two serving as witnesses and one as the actual deliverer. The official document tells us that the three entered the hall of the woman's house while she was sitting in an adjacent room; the proxy of the husband entered the room and put the bill into her hand while the two others looked on. The letter describes four persons, including a *ḥāvēr*, or member of the yeshiva, waiting on the landing of a staircase behind a door. The wife opened the door, and the writer put the bill into her hand, but took it back in order to keep it in a safe place. The same meticulous attention to detail was observed when the husband was present at the delivery.

In reality, the acceptance of the bill of repudiation by the wife, required by the law, was more than symbolic. In many, if not most cases about which we have detailed information, one gets the impression that it was the female partner who sought the divorce, generally, to be sure, by renouncing what was due her. In such a fashion women could in effect initiate divorce, but at a very high price: namely, giving up elements of her dowry or perhaps relieving the unwanted husband of responsibility for the second marriage gift. Divorce might also prove expensive when the husband sought to repudiate his wife, for she could insist on his fulfilling the obligations of the marriage contract. The price of the second marriage gift alone might break him. And so, divorce could be acrimonious, involving extensive and time-consuming legal action.

2. *Jewish Marriage in Palestine*, 2 vols. (Jerusalem, 1988).

Two basic documents were needed to make a divorce legal, or rather, to enable the partners to remarry: a declaration from the wife that she had received all due her from the marriage contract or other financial dealings with her husband (including alimony in the event that she was pregnant or had children from him) and the formal bill of divorce given by the husband, a brief, standard document called a *get*. The wife's declaration is usually referred to by the Arabic term *barā'(a)* "release," which, in informal speech occasionally seems also to designate the *get*. When the husband had counterclaims, as so often happened, he had to acquit his wife. A mutual release seems to have been the standard procedure. The bill of divorce was of tremendous religious significance. It was commendable that a divorced woman marry again, but for a married woman to be with another man was a mortal sin; that piece of paper made it permissible for her to belong to someone else.

Divorce did not sever the relations between the two spouses completely. Payments to the woman could be made in installments, and the remittance of child support looms large in the Geniza records. One might also remarry a divorced spouse, a practice confined largely to the less-affluent elements of society. It would appear, based on current knowledge, that when the divorced husband approached his former wife with a plea to consider marriage again, she would hold out for a larger marriage gift than before. Where less-affluent husbands were able to obtain the means to provide these gifts remains to be discovered.

Remarriage

We have many details about the second marriages of women, for a marriage contract normally indicates whether the bride was previously married, and, in many cases, whether she was widowed or divorced, or both. Nothing comparable exists on the male side. A husband's previous marriage is implicit in a marriage contract only when children from that union are mentioned. Otherwise, references in deathbed declarations, in letters, or in combinations of data constitute our sources. The most urgent reason for a single person with children to marry again was the need to provide orphans with a mother or father. Contracts in which the bride or the groom agrees to bring up the other's children, or in which both parties provide for their offspring from a previous marriage, are frequently found in the Geniza. The number of widowed or divorced fathers marrying a second time must have been infinitely larger than the number of mothers. The evidence for this is the fact that we have next to no references to fathers making, or trying to make, arrangements for their orphans (except through remarriage, as just noted). On the other hand, we have an abundance of reports about unmarried widows or divorced women raising children.

Being married was the preferred state of an adult. Remarrying after a previous marriage had been terminated was therefore the natural thing to do. Single fathers with children were far less numerous than single mothers, but we have no demographic data to gauge what percentage of the male population entered matrimony more than once. No direct statements displaying social prejudices against second marriages, especially against a woman formerly married, have been found in the Geniza. To the contrary, a father suggesting to his son a choice among three girls explicitly mentions a divorced women, and a woman in Jerusalem who remarried soon after her divorce is hailed as having made a good exchange. Marriages with widows and divorced women (particularly the latter) were far more common among the poor than among the more affluent. Occasionally, we find widows who assert that they do not wish to marry again being forced to do so by their dire economic situation. In a somewhat enigmatic letter, the widow of a physician, a distant relative of the nagid Samuel b. Hanaya, implies that she will be compelled to marry against her will (apparently to a man beneath her station) unless the nagid assists her in redeeming half of her house, which has been mortgaged against a debt.

Regard for the children's welfare has been noted as a main reason for a second marriage, but the same consideration could have the opposite effect: a single mother might prefer not to remarry in order to dedicate herself exclusively to the upbringing of her small children; marrying without sufficient safeguard for the children was disapproved. Two letters from the same pen tell of a widow with children intending to marry a man of ill-repute. The judge warned her: "You will be his slave." She replied: "I wish to be his slave." The writer reporting this summarizes the situation: "She has set her mind on marrying and has forsaken her children."

The legal impediment that prohibited individuals from remarrying before being cleared by a release from the previous spouse is echoed in precautions intended to protect children. When a widow wished to marry, her son had to free her from the widow's oath, if that had not been done before. Jewish (and Eastern Christian) law prohibited a woman who had had illicit relations with another man from marrying him. We hear very little about such matters in the Geniza records, however. The most frequent mention of such difficulties concerns men taking up with maidservants whom they later wish to marry.

The popular belief that a woman widowed twice was "a killer" and should therefore not be permitted to marry a third time is mentioned in the Talmud and was adhered to by some judges in the Geniza period, much to the objection of Maimonides, who was particularly concerned about younger widows, even those who lost more then two mates. To soothe the scruples of those who were apprehensive about contravening the authority of the Talmud, Maimonides recommended the practice commonly accepted in Spain. Following the Jewish authorities there, he ruled that the couple should marry outside the court in the presence of only two witnesses and then report to a judge, who would legalize the union post facto and arrange for the religious ceremony.

A considerable number of second marriages listed in the Geniza documents seem to be contracts between two aged persons who have decided to form a common household: she brings in little and he promises even less. These were probably working people — engaged in such work as they could find and were able to do — or people living on public charity, or both. But this interpretation, like the broader question of poverty in Geniza society, needs further study.

Procreation was the concern of both first and second marriages. The Geniza tells us of husbands who sired more children in their second than in their first marriages — or vice versa. It depends, of course, on the circumstances, such as the age of the spouses and the duration of the unions. The same is to be said about compatibility. When marrying for a second time, the prospective spouses certainly had more advance opportunity to get to know each other than had been the case earlier, although second marriages were also arranged between persons in different places who probably had never met.

Heirs and Orphans

The orphaned child — that is, a child whose father (or, of course, whose father and mother) had died — was not the only successor to property. First, the Muslim state had to be reckoned with. Immediately after the death of a non-Muslim, the Office of the Poll Tax and the Estates had to be informed. Formal death announcements found in the Geniza date from the second half of the thirteenth century. It is doubtful whether so rigorous a procedure was followed in Fatimid times, when a greater leniency toward minority groups prevailed and the government was reluctant to interfere in the affairs of its subjects. That left the legal handling of estates to the religious authorities of the non-Muslim communities. The interference of the government was feared at all times; bans were pronounced and fines imposed on persons applying to Muslim courts in cases of inheritance. Not until the thirteenth century did the Muslim authorities formally assert jurisdiction, thus securing for themselves whatever portion of an estate they could lay their hands on. There was the inheritance tax, but also the share claimed by the government from heirs who allegedly could not be found, or from persons who bequeathed their possessions for charitable purposes—an indication that they had no legal heirs. In such fashion the Muslim authorities brought Jewish practice in line with the more stringent laws of Islam, while at the same time increasing state revenues.

A Muslim source reports that Saladin (r. 1171–93), whose accession ended Fatimid rule, was approached by the Jewish authorities with the request that their longstanding right to deal with the estates of their coreligionists, especially those whose heirs were absent, not be taken from them. Saladin consulted the doctors of Muslim law, who confirmed that the demand of their Jewish counterparts was justified. Whatever Saladin's ruling in that matter (it is not known), shortly after his death, the Muslim authorities acted rather high-handedly with regard to Jewish estates, a practice that was symptomatic of a general deterioration taking place at the time in the condition of non-Muslim minorities.

Before turning to the matter of how the claims of heirs were handled by the authorities, some special cases of inheritance must be considered. According to Jewish law, a husband inherited from his wife, but a wife did not inherit from her husband. We hear surprisingly little discussion of this issue in the Geniza records. Probably agreements made at the marriage, or thereafter, took care of the wife's successor. It was considered natural for a husband to turn his wife's estate over to their children. When a man sues his mother-in-law to recover his late wife's estate, alleging misappropriation, the document emphasizes three times that the dead woman was "the mother of his children"; it is in the children's name that the demand is made. That concern for the offspring is reflected in all levels of society.

It is characteristic of a period of transition like that of the Geniza that ancient laws and notions continue to exercise their force as new ideas come to the fore. One example is the legal and social position of the firstborn son, to whom Jewish law gave a double share of the estate and who was treated by the family and outsiders with special respect. A mutual release contracted among the firstborn, his younger brother, a stepbrother, and a stepmother thus stresses the privilege of primogeniture on no fewer than three occasions. The parties declare that the agreement has been entered into freely, not imposed by a court, and that it has been confirmed by a Muslim notary. In this case, the young man, (the son of a butcher) received only eleven dinars, but the principle of primogeniture had triumphed.

An ambivalence prevailed with regard to the inheritance of daughters. Here it must be noted that daughters appear in numerous documents as sole heirs or receiving equal shares with sons. From the tenth through the beginning of the thirteenth century these matters were handled as though no outside interference was anticipated. When interference did occur, the interested party applied, or was expected to apply, to a Muslim court. Nevertheless, fathers continued to exercise the right to distribute their possessions equally among their children, thus creating a tension between older law and custom and contemporaneous reality. Among the numerous detailed documents that deal with female inheritance, none indicate that the daughter's claims did not accord with the law of the majority population. We may assume that, during the eleventh and twelfth centuries, daughters who were the sole offspring were regarded as having the same rights to their fathers' estates as sons. The egalitarian spirit is reflected as well in the numerous cases in which males and females receive equal shares in wills, or other forms of gifts, from relatives near and distant.

In the thirteenth century, when the government began to meddle more and more in the estates of the minorities, a father might leave one third of his estate to a daughter and two thirds to a son (both minors) in order to forestall lawsuits before the Muslim magistrate when his children came of age. In Islamic law, a female inherited one half of a man's share.

If a father had sons and daughters, the distribution of property depended on the circumstances. When the daughters were married, it was assumed that their dowries and the gifts (such as a house or a part of it) received at the wedding represented their share in their father's possessions. They did not inherit; at most, they received a small legacy as a token of love. If they were unmarried or minors, the father earmarked fixed sums for their dowries, or instructed his wife or a son to bear the expense. The heir was obliged to see to it that the orphaned girls were

married in accordance with their station. The courts—the guardians of
the orphans—watched over the fulfillment of this obligation. Although
the ancient law of inheritance, which discriminated against daughters,
seems to have been at variance with the egalitarian trends of the Geniza
period, the preferential attitude toward males had its place in that society. The majority of females were either minors, who were in need of
a male guardian, or married women, who, having received a fair share
of their father's inheritance, still saw their financial affairs administered
by male relatives.

The actions of the courts and other agencies with regard to the
administration of estates and their distribution were probably not
very different from those of other societies that have a mercantile economy and a fairly well organized juridical system. Immediately after a
person's death, his possessions were inventoried and sealed by the court;
the Geniza reports one case in which this was performed before the
burial and another in which seals were placed on the belongings of a
rich goldsmith on the day of his demise. A third case has Moses Maimonides ordering the registration of all that was found in the house of
a dead physician during a holiday week, when normally no legal documents were written. It is evident that inventories were made soon after
death.

The widow's mandatory declaration or oath that she did not hold
any of the belongings of her husband was another measure of precaution. It was matched by the confirmation of the heirs, which
released her from all claims in this respect. These measures were
only the first step in the endeavors of the authorities to preserve an
estate for its legal heirs and legatees. Usually not all of a man's possessions were kept in his house, and often they were not fully or properly
listed.

A common device of the courts was the promulgation of "a ban in
general terms" against anyone who held possessions of a deceased person without returning them or who failed to report knowledge of them.
A letter from Alexandria, written around 1080, reports that on the Monday and Thursday following a death, the local Jewish judge pronounced
a ban against those who knew of a document or an account book noting
the assets of the deceased, or of things he had deposited with anyone.
The ban was to no avail; nor was a similar "warning" issued by a judge
of al-Maḥalla to return books (it seems of a bookseller) for the benefit
of the decedent's orphans.

Since business was international, a ban was not confined to one place
or country. A ban on behalf of a merchant who had died in Egypt was

proclaimed in all provincial towns of Palestine and in Jerusalem on the peak day of the pilgrimage to the Holy City, when the ban would be widely heard. In these and other instances from the eleventh and twelfth centuries, bans were applied only when warranted by the circumstances; by the thirteenth century, however, they had become almost commonplace. The reasons for that change are not clear.

When an inheritance was not problematic (the inheritance uncontested, the collection of assets assured), or when minors were not involved, the courts did not seek to intervene—at least that seems to be the testimony of our sources. One should not argue that the Geniza documents had no reason to make mention of inheritance taxes simply because these taxes were collected by the Muslim authorities. The poll tax, too, was levied by government agencies, yet the Geniza is replete with information about it. The intervention of the Muslim qāḍī was widely dreaded: once he had laid his hands on the estate it was difficult to retrieve it. He would raid the estate under whatever legal pretext he could find, and bribes were a matter of course. In any case, the Jewish authorities had no intrinsic right to impose an inheritance tax and thus had no reason to interfere in the process of succession unless specific circumstances made that necessary.

When an inheritance was contested, the first duty of the courts was to determine the legal heirs. Such cases were presumably complicated, but we have little evidence to describe the process of establishing heirs. Sometimes the instructions given by the testator were ambiguous, or a document that was not legally binding might designate additional heirs; in either case, the decision was in favor of the legal heir. When the various claims had been established, either by mutual consent or by litigation, often before both Muslim and Jewish authorities, the heirs appeared in court and released each other from any future obligations. These procedures were not essentially different from those regarding conventional debts or deposits and acknowledgments of their payment or receipt.

Conversion to Islam was not widespread during the classical Geniza period. Therefore we hear very little about Jews who had embraced Islam succeeding to an inheritance. According to a well-known principle of Islamic law, "the adherents of different religions do not inherit from one another," but the Fatimids were Shi'ites, who gave individuals who had converted to Islam special rights to the estates of their non-Muslim relatives: a Muslim could inherit from an "infidel," but an infidel could not inherit from a "believer."

The Administration of the Possessions of Orphans

In addition to the actions taken for the protection of any heir, the first duty of the judge was the appointment of a guardian or guardians for the minors, unless that had already been arranged by their fathers. A classic case is represented by a detailed and complete Hebrew court record from spring 1026, fortunately complemented by a document in Arabic written thirteen months later. Together, the two documents give us a clear picture of a case involving the courts and the inheritance of a minor. The Hebrew record concerns a minor, four years old; the Arabic document deals with his elder siblings who had come of age but were not yet able to take care of their financial affairs. The court did not act of its own initiative. Yeshū'ā b. Ṣedāqā (possibly the orphans' maternal grandfather) "and others" remonstrated against the inactivity of the authorities and demanded the appointment of a guardian, since the orphans' father had died intestate. In the Arabic document, the minor's siblings appointed their maternal uncle Joseph b. Yeshū'ā as their representative (July 1027). But "the judge and the elders" took another course of action with regard to the minor. They appointed Eli b. Japheth, "known as Bar 'Adī," but not otherwise described, as guardian, with the banker Solomon b. Saadya b. Ṣaghīr as his supervisor. The assets collected were to be deposited with the latter, and he and the judge had to approve any payments to be made from the child's estate. "The judge is the father of the orphans," is a talmudic maxim often cited in our documents. There are numerous instances in the Geniza documents of court interventions on behalf of orphans.

A *cause célèbre*, represented in the Geniza by at least six documents, involves persons from different countries, religions, and professions. An Andalusian merchant residing in Fustat, Samuel (in Arabic, Isma'īl ha-Levi b. Abraham) felt his end approaching and assembled "a large crowd" of Karaite and Rabbanite Jews, as well as Muslims qualified to testify, before a qāḍī. In their presence, he appointed a Baghdadi with the family name Nīlī and a banker as guardians of his only son Abraham. A man whose grandfather was called Yazdād, that is, from a family native to Iran, was chosen by him as their supervisor. A Rabbanite judge was also present. The guardians were Rabbanites, the supervisor probably a Karaite. They were given complete freedom of action, were not obliged to make accounts, nor could any oath be imposed on them. Two fragments of the official document serving as the legal instrument for these appointments are extant. They are entirely in Aramaic, not in Arabic, which seems to indicate that the office of supervisor of guardians might well have been pre-Islamic.

Three documents show how the guardians fulfilled their task. The first two are letters to former partners of the deceased. The writers emphasize that they have taken the guardianship upon themselves solely out of compassion and affection for the orphan (that is, not for any compensation) and expect a similar attitude from the recipients, whose piety and probity were lauded by the dead merchant. Following a court order, the partners are obliged to transport the movable assets of the partnership to the guardian's place or, if that proves too difficult, to bring the equivalent in cash. One letter concludes with the admonition: "Live up to your reputation."

The third document, an extended Hebrew court record, shows the effect of the guardian's action. A merchant known from other sources as commuting between Tunisia and Egypt had a partnership with the deceased Andalusian worth 1,043 dinars, part of which had reverted to the latter during his lifetime. A careful examination of the papers and account books showed that 136½ dinars were still owed the Andalusian. The sum was delivered to the guardians, and the partner was released from his obligation to the orphan on condition that he be prepared to honor it if the orphan, having come of age, asked him to do so.

The affair did not end as harmoniously as it started. The orphan, Abraham b. Samuel al-Andalusī, was declared of age in January 1026 and began to make trouble. At his instigation, the guardians were forced by the government to produce their accounts; a Jewish court threatened them with flogging. (It is uncertain whether the threat was carried out.) In December 1027, Abraham again brought them before a court and demanded that a balance still due be delivered; they refused unless a proper release were given by Abraham before a Jewish judge and a Muslim qāḍī, and declined to produce additional accounts, since they had been expressly exempted from this duty by the orphan's father. A committee of three, headed by Samuel ha-Kohen b. Ṭalyūn, head of the Babylonian congregation of Fustat, was to look into the matter, but nothing came of it.

The next document is dated December 18, 1027; in the intervening time something else had happened. A legally recognized court, composed of the heads of the two congregations and a third person, Samuel, "the Delight of the Yeshiva," was to end the affair either by mutual agreement or by imposing a decision on the parties. Many outsiders came, complaining about the nuisance caused by the young man's public appeals in the synagogues and elsewhere, but "the Delight" recused himself as being busy "and [for] other reasons." The session was adjourned for two weeks at most, and the guardians were warned not to bring Abraham before a Muslim court. When one of them remarked that it was Abraham who had approached the governor (*qā'id*) with the request "to assemble the Jews" to consider his cause, he retorted that he had done so because he wished to have a decision according to Jewish law.

Unlike the case just described, most of the others are represented by a single document; examined together, they describe a fairly consistent practice of the courts regarding the care of orphans: The judge retained constant supervision, although this duty was not always exercised in an efficient manner. The attorney who was to retrieve the estate, the guardian with whom the child was entrusted, and the keepers who held the orphan's assets might be replaced by others if the judge saw fit, or rather, if he was asked by a complainant to do so. Preserving the remaining capital seems to have been the foremost concern of the authorities. If feasible, it was put into the hands of more than one person; the guardians had to provide collateral, usually real estate, sometimes also guarantors. No remuneration was expected for this service. Support was proportional to the amount of the estate, but was always modest. When the support of the orphan had to come out of his capital, each payment had to be approved by the judge or his representative. The red tape often caused great hardship, since the authorities did not always act promptly when the widow or the guardian approached them with the request to release the amounts approved. At maturity (boys at thirteen, girls at twelve and six months) the orphan was given legal possession of the estate, but the court "and the elders" retained actual supervision until they were satisfied that he or she was able to make use of it responsibly.

A lengthy draft describes in detail the appointment of the trustee of the court ʿUllā b. Joseph as *wakīl*, or representative, of an infant in Damietta whose father had died in Fustat. First, the choice of the wakīl is elaborately justified: ʿUllā was pious, reliable, eager to do good works and to exert himself for others, and to gain merit before God; he was knowledgeable in the ways of business and cooperative with others, experienced in dealing with tough customers in and out of court, and trained in the pursuance of lawsuits. ʿUllā was reminded that his task would be merely a deed of charity; he could not do otherwise but accept it. The legal powers and obligations of the executor were specified and accepted by him, especially his duty to regularly make account with the judge on all that was accruing to the orphan and all that was to be expended on his maintenance, and make the sums received available to the court upon request. His office would come to an end at the orphan's maturity.

A widow, contemporaneous with ʿUllā, complained to the nagid Mevōrākh that her brother-in-law, who had been appointed by her late husband as executor of her children's estate, was too weak to deal with a hard bargainer like "The Doctor" (the representative of the merchants, Abū Yaʿqūb al-Ḥākim), a business partner of the deceased. For the sake of God, the nagid was expected to spend an hour of his precious time in dealing with this matter, for "he had the wisdom of an angel of God" (2 Samuel 14:20). The personal intervention of the nagid was needed, for the law made it obligatory to carry out the will of a dying man; the judges for that reason had been reluctant to take the office of the executor from the uncle of the orphans and to entrust it to someone else.

The transfer of orphans' capital from one trustee to another was an easier matter and would appear to have been a common practice of the courts. Samuel, "the Master of the Discerning," served as "guarantor" for a banker in al-Maḥalla in whose keeping orphans' money had been deposited. Under circumstances not specified, Samuel handed over the amount to another trustee, who was advised not to make any payments from it except on written order from the court.

It is assumed that one who held money belonging to orphans would make some profit with it, part of which would be used for their maintenance. The undertaking of the holder to return the amount in full implies that the orphans participated in the profits, not in the losses. That was the law. The degree of security demanded from a man entrusted with an orphan's property depended, of course, on his financial circumstances and on his standing in the community. Measures of precaution were taken even when close relatives were placed in charge of the estate of fatherless minors. An old woman appointed by the court as guardian of her grandchildren received cash and utensils left by her son; she mortgaged her home as collateral. As this was not enough to guarantee the welfare of the children, another son of hers agreed to be her guarantor. The matter was different when a person was appointed as executor and guardian by a testator. In such a case, much depended on the strength and authority enjoyed by the local judge. When a man died in Bilbays (Lower Egypt) in the spring of 1217 leaving a wife, an adult son, and a minor boy, seals were placed on the contents of the house so that the property could not be disposed of. But when the judge wished to proclaim the customary "ban in general terms," the elder son, an affluent merchant, protested, "God has not put me in a position where I need to take anything from the share in the estate of his father from the orphan, my minor brother." The share of the orphan, according to him, was 80 dinars, which was to be kept by him until the boy came of age. Moreover, as an act of charity, for which he hoped to be rewarded by God in this world and in the world to come, he would provide his brother with food, clothing, and anything else needed at minimum value of 15 dirhems per month. This would mean about 4 to 4½ dinars over a year against possible profits to be made from the 80 dinars. Since no security was given for the principal, this was obviously an undertaking of no great religious merit.

There are cases in which a dying man appoints a wife, a son, or a brother as plenipotentiary executors, explicitly or implicitly freeing them from the supervision of the courts. Despite such provisions, courts did intervene. The general procedure seems to have been that immediately after a death the customary precautions for safeguarding the rights of heirs—and in particular orphans—were taken, but as soon as the legal position was cleared, much depended on the circumstances, including the power wielded by the authorities dealing with the case.

When orphans possessed real estate, the courts, according to the circumstances, either converted it into gold or tried to preserve it, even if keeping it in repair required spending most of the cash left to the children. The most eminent experts on housing would be consulted and their advice followed, whereupon the trustee would be advised to release the amount agreed upon. If property was conspicuously luxurious, or belonged to a person connected with the government, it was always in danger of attracting the attention of rapacious tax collectors, with the usual catastrophic consequences. In one such case, the executor had to spend 220 dinars in order to "get back" the property, which he then sold for 300 dinars.

Often the cost of supporting an orphan was to come out of the capital deposited on his behalf with a guardian or a trustee. In such a case, court supervision was particularly rigorous. The cost had to be kept as low as possible, and each withdrawal from the principal had to be approved. When the orphan came of age, the trustee was ordered to deliver to him the balance of the estate. This balance was arrived at by subtracting the sums spent for the orphan's maintenance from the amount deposited with the judge.

The material presented thus far shows how the administration of estates by courts affected the lives of minor heirs. But before considering the lot of orphans specifically, it is perhaps proper to ask how the handling of cases of inheritance by the courts influenced the economy of the Geniza society in general.

As a rule, the courts acted only when they were approached. True, the sealing of the property of a deceased was customarily done immediately after his death and at the initiative of the authorities. Presumably it was effected in connection with the burial, in which a religious notable, or his representatives, participated. But once that was done, it was up to interested persons or public-minded notables to initiate further action. When an orphan resided with its mother, a grandmother, an uncle, or a grandfather who had not been appointed as executors, the property could not be touched until someone was selected for that office by a court. When the executors and their supervisors or guarantors had been selected, the most difficult part of their job was to assemble the minor heir's estate, a process often exceedingly difficult not only for him but also for anyone who had dealings with the deceased. Since a minor did not have legal standing to act on his own behalf, the trustees of his estate had to guarantee that they would be liable if the dead man's debtors or partners were sued by the orphan when he came of age. Often a contested property had to be left untouched until a settlement or decision had been reached, or even until the minor was legally entitled to act on his own behalf. An especially serious cause of delay in the freeing of an estate was the frequent disagreement between judges or jurisconsults about the rights of the parties concerned.

The Lot of Orphans and Stepchildren

Because husbands so often abandoned their families, many children were in effect orphaned when their fathers were still alive. The situation was so common, in fact, that the Arabic language had a special term for it: *aytām al-aḥyā*, "orphans whose parents are still alive." In a list of beneficiaries at a communal distribution of wheat "an orphan whose parents are alive" appears as a legal term, meaning that the minor was eligible for public charity to the same extent as a true orphan. In most Geniza texts that mention fatherless children, the youngsters reside with their mothers. The boys would pass their days in the Bible school; if the family was indigent, the fees were paid by the community to individual teachers, or there were special classes for orphans, admission to which was free. Orphans who went to work often did so at an early age. Girls kept their mothers company, learning or perfecting the techniques of spinning, weaving, and especially embroidery, while a teacher—paid by the community if necessary—came to the house to provide a minimum level of religious education. Girls as well became wage earners at a young age. When a judge in the town of Malīj in Lower Egypt reports to his superior in Fustat that "the little orphan girl does embroidery every day," he means that she works in other people's houses.

When a widow died, her children normally found shelter in the house of a relative, the father's brother being the natural choice. In this matter, too, the courts acted as the orphans' guardians. We find one orphan put in the house of a person not characterized as a relative even though a paternal uncle was still living. When a widow in a small locality died, leaving a girl of three (together with a small house), the judge in the capital, among other questions, asked for a report on who had taken the orphan in and cared for her. A high authority refuses to give a small boy to a woman who claims to be his next of kin, but orders him to stay in the house in which he lived before his mother's death.

When the family was not able or willing to provide a home, or when no appropriate relatives were available, the orphans were placed in the care of a trusted family, preferably that of a teacher or cantor, or the widow of one. Lists of indigents receiving handouts from the community contain such phrases as "the orphans of the house of the cantor," "the teacher and the orphan girl who is with her," or "the orphans with the sister of Abū 'l-Faraj, the son of the astrologer."

Numerous Geniza letters are cries of help for orphans and their mothers lacking food and clothing, and sometimes even a proper place to live: the father had died leaving nothing, the rations fixed by communal charity were insufficient, and, not uncommonly, the payments due from estates under the administration of the courts had not been made in time or in the requisite amounts. Such pictures of misery are often topped by the woeful excuse that the mother was unable to work because of illness ("your maidservant's eyes are sore and have been bandaged for the last forty days") or general incapacity.

There is no mention of an orphanage in the Geniza. The number of orphans remaining after the relatives had done their duty was small and did not call for the creation of one. Moreover, the notion that children belonged in a house with a family — even if it was only an adopted one — was too strong to permit placing orphans in a barracks-like location. The so-called orphanages erected by Muslim rulers in a later period were often nothing but training schools for future soldiers.

Destitution and misery seems to have been regarded as the inevitable lot of orphans and their mothers — and not only those from poor families. In an appeal to the community, an unnamed widow and mother of four, who had taken on loans that she was unable to repay, asserts that she and her children had never before "uncovered their faces" by asking either private persons or the public for support. It is not difficult to imagine what might have happened here. Real estate belonging to the family had dwindled in the process of succession, and what remained was ruined by lack of repair. The cash left to the survivors had been eaten up, if not lost, by the negligence or dishonesty of the administrators. Since the widow had seen better days, credit had been extended to her—until it became evident that she could make no repayment. We read also about a widow who was imprisoned, undoubtedly for debts she was unable to pay; in that case a Muslim judge was involved.

Orphans who were cared for were generally well treated. There was a hope that they would evolve into productive members of society, but the great care that the community took for the schooling of orphans certainly had a practical motive as well: to keep them off the streets and away from mischief. Payment for professional training may have been limited to the sons of deceased community officials. Since facilities for organized charity were not easily available in provincial towns, indigent widows with small children frequently moved to the capital, as is amply proved by the detailed lists of beneficiaries of the communal chest. This explains, perhaps, why funds were collected for orphans in the capital, rather than in the Egyptian countryside. The heavily burdened community of Fustat was forced to devolve some of its obligation on the congregations of the Rīf.

The orphaned girl was the poorest of the poor. Since the position of the wife depended largely on the strength of her own family and the wealth she brought into the marriage, the female orphan's prospects were bleak. Her natural refuge was a position as a domestic in a friendly household, but people seem not to have been eager to employ orphans, and we read little about it in the Geniza records. For understandable reasons, the community insisted that orphan girls be married as soon as possible. That being so, it was not practical for a household to employ a domestic who would leave precisely when she became fully capable of carrying out her duties. One preferred slave girls for domestic work. It is in this light that one must understand an emphatic passage in Maimonides' *Code of Law* in which he declares that the keeping of slaves means sin and iniquity, day in, day out, while employing orphans and the poor turns every hour into a good and meritorious deed.

Sometimes an orphan serving in a household would attract the attention of a visitor, especially if he was a traveling stranger, whose family was far away and could not guard him against marrying a penniless orphan. In such situations, people were quick to offer excuses: "Your son has done nothing wrong. He was ill, suffering pain, and had no one to look after him. Therefore he decided to hire an orphan girl who would take care of him. Later he married her on condition that, when he preferred to return to his country, he would divorce her." In this case, the girl gave birth to a boy who died. A female relative who reports this to the family back home adds: "It was all his doing. You accuse me in vain. Have I married him to my own daughter?"

The eagerness of the community to get rid of unmarried orphan girls might have disastrous results, especially in small towns in which the surveillance of the courts was lax. Sometimes the girl was married before she was prepared to perform what was expected of her. She also might be given to an unworthy stranger, as, for example, when an orphan and her child were deserted by a husband from the Egyptian capital, who disappeared together with the little money she had saved. A man from Aleppo was betrothed to an orphan in Cairo, promising to marry her after a month. The month became three, and then six, and at the end, the girl had to be content with 5½ instead of 10 dinars, imposed by the court as the fine for nonfulfillment; otherwise the man would not have given her the bill of repudiation required after a broken betrothal. A lonely orphan who had been married to an unworthy man for ten years, describes her plight to a nagid in an eloquent letter, possibly written in her own hand. The man lived on what she earned, and when she refused to go on with this any longer, he gave her a bad name. She was prepared to buy herself free by renouncing her second marriage gift, on condition that a ban in general terms be pronounced against anyone impugning her honor; this request was turned down by the judges. She now approaches the nagid himself, asking him to free her "from a hell which only God knows."

Even in families with means and prestige, an orphaned girl could not always be sure that her relatives would exert themselves on her behalf. But we also find substantial gifts to an orphan so that she might marry, and when the women of the community brought together the outfit of a poor orphan bride, they made an effort to provide her with something to make her happy on her wedding night. Marrying an orphan was regarded as a deed of great religious merit.

Children without mothers are rarely the subject of Geniza documents. Female relatives in the house, occasionally also domestics, would carry on where the deceased had left off, until the father, by remarriage, had given his children a new mother. But established practices must have existed for the care of motherless children whose fathers possessed no means for their upbringing. In two documents, motherless children are

entrusted to two women living together who raise (but do not financially support) the orphans as a charitable deed. The children, especially
the girls, probably were regarded also as being (or as capable of becoming) a help to their elderly foster mothers; in one case, the children were
accompanied by a maid who clearly was. One of the documents contains
no financial arrangements. In that text, two women, apparently not related to each other or to the widower, agree to join in bringing up his
daughters "in friendly companionship"—a phrase used in marriage contracts and elsewhere for the relationship between husband and wife: if
one of them breaks that agreement, she will be committing a sin before
God. The record was read out to them and they confirmed it by the
usual "symbolic purchase."

Marriages of widows and widowers (or divorced persons) with offspring still in the household could often complicate family life. As a
result, provisions for the children of previous marriages were written
into marriage contracts. Promises for the good treatment of the stepchildren are found mostly in the ketubbas of poor couples. "The groom
agrees to bring up the son of his spouse [a divorced woman] in his
house; he will provide this orphan with food and clothing and teach
him a craft. The boy will be to him like the children whom he will have
with his bride; he will not drive him out of his house, nor beat, nor
humiliate him." This we read in a marriage contract from the provincial
town of Minyat Ziftā, written in summer 1110. The divorced woman
received one dinar as immediate, and five dinars as her second marriage
gift—a mere trifle. She renounced all her claims in favor of her boy.

Agreements like these were not always included in marriage contracts
because they were clearly taken for granted. When a man was reminded
on the day of his wedding that his future stepson, when grown up,
might wish to sue his mother for the inheritance of his natural father,
he drew up a document in which he declared: "I have brought this
orphan up, he is my relative from my father's and mother's side [one of
the boy's parents was a relative of that man's father and the other a
relative of his mother], and love him more than anyone else. All you
[the court] ask me to do for him [meaning, permitting him to sue his
mother], I will do." Moreover, he agreed to provide the boy with food
and clothing as long as the bride remained his wife. The document,
which supplements the marriage contract, proves that the groom had
found it unnecessary to include his obligation to support the boy in the
marriage contract itself. Frequently a young orphan possessed an estate
inherited from his father when his mother entered a new union, and
that estate had to be regulated.

A widowed father might remarry to provide his children with a mother's care. But here as well express stipulations to that effect are rarely included in marriage contracts and, again, only in those of people with limited means. Instances where both spouses had children from a previous marriage also must have been frequent. In the case of a well-to-do merchant, the sons of the two spouses from former unions were well provided for. In setting down the details concerning a couple that seeks to marry, a judge notes casually, "His children are with her, and her boy is with him until [the boy] marries." In an engagement contract, a future stepfather agrees to supply his bride's daughters with food for five years (unless they marry before that period), but not with clothing; the bride, in turn, will look after his sons—one an adolescent, and another five years old. (The bride owned a house in which the couple was expected to reside.) A man's stepson or stepdaughter would be called "the son [or daughter] of the wife," and this designation could become a personal or family name. A common designation for a stepchild from either father or mother was *rabīb(a)* "foster child," for instance, *Ibn imra'at al-Wāsiṭī rabībuh,* "the son of al-Wāsiṭī's wife, his foster son." One wonders whether the term *rabīb(a)* was not also used of a person brought up in a house without being the stepchild of one of the spouses.

The question remains of how in fact Geniza society did provide for its orphans. The answer must be, first, that their care was certainly regarded as a religious commandment of the highest order; both the community and individuals were eager to earn merits by this deed of charity. Nevertheless, the condition of fatherless children and their widowed mothers was apparently difficult, given the frequent mention of their sufferings in our sources. The reason for this was partly the weakness of the economy and the looseness of the juridical and communal organization. The individual's strength derived from his or her family, and when the family was impaired by the death of the father—particularly in the male-centered society of the Geniza—the survivors became weakened, if not more gravely compromised. Orphans without means had to be plucky if they were to survive. Quite a number of articulate orphan girls brought their claims before the highest authorities or even to the community at large, despite the shame it brought upon them. For human charity, as the prayer has it, "is scarce in providing, but plentiful in causing shame."

FIFTEEN

The World of Women

The men who left us their writings in the Geniza believed that "the princess's place is in the innermost corner of the house"—that women should be confined to the narrow circle of the family. Whether and how far the actual experience of these men tallied with their ideas about the role of women in society is the topic of the study undertaken in this chapter. The existence of a distinctive male society does not preclude the formation of female groups within or alongside the world of men. How deeply, then, were women integrated into the male environment? To what extent did they identify with the world of men or live lives apart from it?

Men were supposed to know only the women of their own household or extended family. Consequently, a woman appearing in court or before a notary was introduced, in principle, by the phrase "after we have taken [proper] cognizance of her," a phrase never mentioned in connection with men, since it was taken for granted that men knew one another. Since the phrase is rendered not only in Arabic and Hebrew, but also in Aramaic, the language spoken in southwestern Asia before the advent of Islam, it is reasonable to assume that the practice was pre-Islamic. One suspects, however, that the phrase is often added only out of reverence for traditional attitudes, not because the judge or his associates in fact did not "know" the woman before them. This assumption is confirmed when we find the phrase repeated on the second day of a lawsuit after a woman had already testified in the presence of the same court the day before, or when three men talk a girl into a marriage, assuring her that they know her well; when she has agreed, and the formal betrothal has been contracted, the clerk again notes "after having made proper cognizance of her." It appears, all in all, that the juridical practice based on the notion that women were known only to their own menfolk did not quite correspond to reality. This is not surprising, since women—rich and poor, single and married—were involved in economic activities that required their presence in the offices of notaries and in courts. These were places frequented by men, since legal actions required public postings and aroused curiosity. The recovery of women's voices from the male-scripted documents of the Geniza nevertheless requires some imaginative forays.

The Message of Women's Names

We might choose a name today because it sounds attractive, or because it is traditional in the family or has some other importance for us; but as a rule we pay no attention to its meaning, which in most cases is unknown to us. In the Geniza community, to the contrary, female names were living words, each with a distinctive and widely recognized connotation. The meaning of a name and the frequency of its occurrence are therefore plausible indicators of what a woman wished for her daughter and, by implication, for herself. The large number and wide variety of first names given to females at birth immediately attract attention. No specific female first names predominate in the Geniza records surveyed thus far; no one name occurs more than twenty times; only eight names occur ten times or more. The average recurrence seems to be two to five times, and many names occur only once. A number of nicknames were given to women during their lifetime and were used and reused by their descendants as family names.

There exist rich and well-known onomasticons for ancient Israel and pre-Islamic Arabia. The equally abundant treasure of female names in the Geniza period, however, derives from neither tradition; indeed, it is entirely different. Biblical and other Hebrew names are noticeably absent among the Jewish women of Egypt. In the rare instances where they do appear, it can be shown that the family originated in Palestine, Tunisia or another North African country, Spain, Byzantium, or Western Europe, where biblical names were occasionally given to females. The startling absence of biblical names would seem to demonstrate, assuming that women were responsible for naming girls, a chasm between the popular local subculture of the women and the worldwide Hebrew book-culture of the men. The dichotomy is emphasized even more by the entirely secular character of the female names, which, with very few exceptions (confined to upper-class, mostly Karaite families), do not contain any reference to God or other religious concepts. One must therefore reckon with the possibility that the absence of biblical and theophoric names among women was originally not a matter of free choice or female preference but a taboo imposed by males, and in fact became an accepted custom in the course of time. All this, to be sure, is conjecture.

Names from Arabic classical or popular narratives also are seldom found. To be sure, one encounters Laylā, the heroine of the stories of the love-mad poet Majnūn; ʿAblā, the beloved of the great warrior ʿAntara; ʿĀtika, the favorite wife of the caliph ʿAbd al-Malik; and Bānūqa, the boyish daughter of the caliph al-Maʾmūn. But it is highly unlikely that these names were taken directly from Muslim narratives. These names were probably chosen by Jews because they were in general use, as is true in choosing names today. Perhaps the most surprising aspect of female nomenclature in the Geniza records is the prevalence of the ideas of ruling, overcoming adversity, and victory. Most of these names are composed with the word *sitt*, "mistress," "female ruler," originally an honorary title added to a name that became the personal name of a girl, given to her at birth. The word *sitt* was often omitted, so that strange forms of female names result. One encounters, for example, ʿAmāʾim, "Turbans," abbreviated from *Sitt al-ʿAmāʾim*, "She Who Rules over the Turbans," namely, the men. A girl belonging to the class of government officials was called *Sitt al-Kuttāb*, "Mistress of the Clerks," shortened to *Kuttāb*, "Clerks"; the daughter of an important merchant, *Sitt al-Tujjār*, or *Tujjār*, "Merchants," designating one of the leading elements in society. Similarly there are names meaning "Lords," "Notables," and more frequently "Kings," *Mulūk*. Female names sometimes reflect cities, or peoples. We thus read several times of a *Sitt Baghdād*, "The Mistress of Baghdad," or simply *Baghdād*; the same holds for Iraq (*ʿIrāq*), the Muslim West (*Gharb*), Byzantium (*Rūm*), and the Persians (*Furs*).

Names describing their bearers as ruling "The House" (*Dār*), "The Household" (*Bayt*), "The Family" (*Ahl*), or "The Clan" (*ʿAshīr*) are also frequent. A most common female name in the Geniza records is *Sitt al-Kull*, "She Who Rules Everyone," paralleled by *Sitt al-Jamīʿ*, which means the same, *Sitt al-Nās*, "Mistress of the Notables," *Sitt al-Zamān*, "Mistress of Her Time," and *Sitt al-Aqrān*, "Mistress of Her Peers." The names *Sitt Aʿadāhā*, "Mistress of Her Enemies," and *Sitthum*, "Their Mistress," are particularly noteworthy.

The group of names describing a woman as ruling over certain types of people is matched by another composed of *Sitt* with an abstract noun. Here again the idea of eminence is found throughout. The most common names of this type were *Fakhr,* "Glory," *Thanā',* "Praise," *'Izz,* "Fame," followed by similar notions, such as *Ri'āsa,* "Leadership," *Naṣr,* "Victory," *Naẓar,* "Control or Supervision," *Ma'ālā,* "Excellence," *Ghalb,* "Victorious" or "Overcoming," and so forth. Telling names in this context are *Qā'ida,* "General," *Wazīra,* "Vizier," and *'Alam,* "Standard [at the head of an advancing troop]." *Labwa,* "Lioness," not found in pre-Islamic Arabia, probably also belongs to this category.[1]

How shall we explain these female names, which constitute almost 70 percent of those mentioned in our sources? It should be noted that the proud names presented above were not unique to Jewish women. The image of the powerful woman is one that appears time and time again in wisdom literature and belletristic texts of the Near East. Women were often viewed by men as "stronger than riches, wine, wisdom, and kings." That does not mean, however, that women were viewed as competing with men—let alone competing successfully; open competition with men led to humiliation, as it did in the story of Solomon and the Queen of Sheba. Like the biblical Queen Esther, a woman had to show her strength in other ways. Indeed, some names reflect the demure side of women. Bashfulness, the allegedly intrinsic characteristic of women, is represented by the names *Ḥayā'* and *Khafar.* But names reflecting the expected character of women are less common than one would anticipate. More often we find the opposite: *Dalāl,* "Coquetry," "Taking Liberty With Someone," "Boldness"; there is *Fā'iza,* "Successful [with men]," *Khulla,* "Lover," *Haziyya,* "Favorite," *Mawadda,* "Love." The names *Mūnisa,* and, even more remarkable, in the masculine form *Muwānis,* "Good Company," "Intimate Friend," probably also contain a wish that women so-named might succeed in marriage. As an Arabic (and Judeo-Arabic) saying has it, "Enchanted by his beloved [wife], a man neglects his [male] companions."

Chastity and Fertility, regarded by men of the period as the most praiseworthy attributes of a woman, are all but absent from the female onomasticon of the Geniza. Many men are called "Pure," *Ṭāhir* (Ar.) or *Ṭāhōr* (Heb.), or "Chaste," *'Afīf,* but comparable female forms have not

---

1. Goitein found in the Geniza frequent occurrences of girls' names such as *Turfa,* "Cherished Gift" (also in the plural *Ṭuraf*); *Ghāliya,* "Precious"; *Munā,* "Wishes Fulfilled"; *Mu'ammala,* "The One Hoped For"; *Ghunya,* "Gain"; *Yumn,* "Good Luck." He surmised that this might reflect a female protest against the male preference for boys. There was a common notion among men that girls represented unfulfilled wishes, dashed hopes, and a financial drain on the family.

come to light. Perhaps these traits were taken for granted by women: It was their lot, imposed on them by God, to be faithful to their husbands and to bear them children, and there was no point in expressing that as a specific wish embodied in a name. But that their menfolk should remain pure and chaste was indeed a deep concern for mothers, since concubinage with slave girls was the most dreaded source of marital conflict.

Names designating "noble lineage," such as *Nasab, Nisāba*, and *Ḥasab*, were common. *Karīma*, "noble, distinguished," had in the Geniza period the additional meaning of "sister" (unlike modern Arabic, where it means "daughter") and is found as a female name also in a Muslim marriage contract of 1028.

There is no need to survey here names found everywhere and in all societies. We all greet the newborn as dear and beloved, hence the name *'Azīza*, "Dear," and many other derivatives from the same or similar roots. "Pearl" and its synonyms were as common then as they are today. Beauty was prized, and since *nomen est omen*, numerous names describe the newborn as a paragon of beauty, especially the extremely common *Sitt al-Milāḥ*, "The Fairest of the Fair," often abbreviated as *Milāḥ*. It was expressed in many ways: simply and directly, such as *Jamīla*, "Beautiful"; by numerous variants of the notion of light, including "Moon," in the early period, and "Sun" in later Geniza times; or by the names of graceful animals (in particular, "Gazelle,") or trees (especially "Cypress"). Since Turkish slave girls were renowned for their beauty, Jewish mothers called their daughters *Turkiyya* or, as a sign of particular affection, *Turayk*, "Little Turk" (in the masculine), or *Khuzayr*, "Little Khazar" (a Turkish people, some of whom converted to Judaism).

Many names were common to males and females. These names most express general notions and wishes, such as "Blessings," *Baraka;* "Good Tidings," *Bushr;* "Gift," *Hiba;* "Well-being," *Salāma;* "Happiness," *Sa'āda;* "Long Life," *Baqā;* "Substitute [for a child that had died]," *Khalīfa;* and "Beauty," *Zayn*. Several names expressing the idea of eminence, mentioned above, such as "Glory," "Praise," "Victory," appear also as male names, but then mostly preceded by *Abū*, "Father [meaning Possessor] of." The same applies to feminine forms of male names, such as *Maymūna*, "Good Auspice," paralleling *Maymūn*, made famous through Maimonides (*Mūsā b. Maymūn*).

Genealogies were confined to the male line. Women were identified by the name of their fathers, not of their mothers. We are therefore not in a position to know whether female names were transmitted in a family as male names were—among men, the firstborn male grandchild was often named after his paternal grandfather. In similar fashion, a woman from Qayrawān writes to her brother traveling abroad that a girl was born to one of their brothers "and I called her by the name of my mother, *Surūra* [Happy]." Thus, this girl was named after her paternal grandmother. We find the same in a contemporary family chronicle from southern Italy (where the names, of course, were not Arabic but Latin or Hebrew) in which a girl is named *Cassia*, like the mother of her father. One can hardly draw a reliable conclusion from this limited sample, but it stands to reason that the custom — unknown in biblical times — of strengthening the family attachment of a newborn male by giving him the name of an ancestor or other relative was observed in the Geniza period also with regard to girls.

Historical Antecedents

To put the women's world of the Geniza period in its proper historical context, some of its antecedents must be considered, if only in the barest outlines. The women of ancient Israel, as they appear to us in the Hebrew Bible, were disadvantaged by polygyny and all of its ramifications, but they played a far more vital role than their female progeny in postbiblical times. In the agrarian society of the ancient Israelites, the wife was "man's helper, his counterpart" — that is the proper translation of Genesis 2:18. He produced the food; she made the clothing. He was in the field — tilling the soil from daybreak to sunset, or deliberating with the elders "at the gate," or sometimes participating in combat. She ran the house — planning, storing, buying and selling, spinning and weaving, and dispensing help to the needy and advice to whomever sought it. Echoes of this view, along with more critical assessments of urban women, persisted during monarchical times; the movement of the political center of Israelite life to towns and cities is reflected in the praise of the woman of valor in Proverbs 31:10–31, as well as in the many negative statements of that book. Love among the Israelites is portrayed in the Bible as robust and passionately expressed. Joseph was the manifest favorite of his father Jacob because he was the son of his beloved Rachel. "Am I not better to you than ten sons?" the barren, but preferred Hannah is consoled by her husband (1 Samuel 1: 8). The wife was her husband's "companion" (Malachi 2:14). Hence the many and unforgettable portraits of women presented by the Hebrew Bible.

Marriage in biblical times, unlike marriage in Geniza period, carried the impression of permanence. "Your clan will be mine; your deity will be worshipped by me. Where you die, I will die, and there I will be buried; even death will not separate me from you." This is the vow of the bride (Ruth 1:16–17, in which the attachment to the dead husband is extended to the bereaved mother). A wife who left the house of her father and clan became a member of the husband's family. This severance from her original kin was so strict that a woman of the progeny of Aaron, when married out of the priestly clan, was no longer permitted to partake of the sacrificial meal restricted to the descendants of priests, and her parents and siblings were not allowed to "defile themselves" by following her bier. She, in turn, agreed to be buried in the common tomb of her new family. The husband's vow also stressed permanence: "I betroth you to me for eternity, I betroth you to me in equity and justice [you will get all due to you] in love and mercy [and more than that], and I betroth you to me in steadfastness [a reiteration of the everlasting character of the marital bond]" (Hosea 3:19–20; here said by God to Israel).

Israelite religion was, however, hardly egalitarian. A woman could enter the Temple and pray, as Hannah did, but the immediate service of God was reserved for male priests. Women could be possessed by God's spirit; they could become prophets, like Miriam, Deborah, and Huldah (2 Kings 22:13–20). The very last prophet mentioned in the Bible by name, No'adya ("Meeting with God"), was a woman (Nehemiah 6:14). But they were exceptions. In the sanctuary, men alone were permitted to officiate. The reason for this may have been the obsession with ritual purity (endangered by the woman's monthly menstrual cycle), an obsession shared, to be sure, by other ancient peoples. The oracle of Delphi in Greece, was a woman prophet, but the priests were men.

The missionary spirit accompanying the religious revival preceding and following the Babylonian exile affected women as well as men. In all the teaching and other public assemblies, women were expressly mentioned among those present, even prominently (Ezra 10:1; Nehemiah 5: 1, 8:23, 12:43). Women became the protagonists for the salvation of their people, such as Esther in the Bible and Judith in the apocryphal book named after its heroine. The mother of the seven Maccabean martyr brothers, who died after encouraging her sons not to yield to idolatry (Second and Fourth Books of the Maccabees), is the prefiguration of the woman-saint dying for her faith.

Nevertheless, the trend unfavorable to the participation of women in the community's religious life became strengthened by a powerful new

son, and do not separate them from her, for she is fond of her and I have willed the Sudanese nurse to her. However, the younger slave girl, ʿAfāf, shall be given to [my elder daughter] Sitt al-Sirr—but nothing else—and this only after our debts to Abū Saʿd and others have been paid. Cursed be he who acts against my dying wish. . . .

It is highly probable that the ill woman had written this letter with her own hand. Her mother had been a pious woman—ʿābida in Arabic—and it is therefore not surprising that she gave her daughter a religious education, which included reading and some writing. The writer's elder daughter, Sitt al-Sirr, had obviously gone astray, and the mother had therefore disinherited her. Thus, the mother was all the more eager that her younger daughter receive an education, which would lead her on the right path, and that she not appear in public—which the elder daughter apparently was doing much too often.

It seems that the writer's sister was more akin to Sitt al-Sirr than to the pietists in the family. Therefore, the writer uses the strongest form of entreaty—a curse—should the request be refused. Another interesting feature is the writer's order that the younger girl not be separated from her old Sudanese nurse, because the little one was fond of her. Obviously, she had more confidence in the educational capabilities of the old slave than in those of her sister. Education was costly; teachers of the elementary stages of Bible study and of calligraphy, letter writing, and arithmetic were paid, although the higher education was normally free. The letter does not contain any concluding formula, not even the word shālōm, "peace," an indication that it was probably not dispatched. Perhaps the writer, in reading through what she had written, backed off when she realized that she had twice pronounced a curse.

A World within a World

"Women are a nation by themselves." This popular maxim, quoted in the Talmud, expresses man's inability or unwillingness to understand his womenfolk or to let them participate in his own pursuits. (The female counterpart, "Men are locked chests," is more optimistic: if you find the key, the chest can be opened.) The question of whether this attitude was reflected in the society known to us through the writings of the Cairo Geniza must be answered to a large extent in the affirmative. Man's foremost duty—his very reason for being—was to study God's teachings, leading to the fulfillment of His command-

influence: Hellas. The Greeks, who thought deeply and systematically about life, came up with divergent viewpoints on the issue. Aristophanes and Plato, each in his own way, visualized the possibility of almost complete equality between men and women, but Greek society did not. The conviction that women were inferior, biologically and mentally, became the dominant trend, with the practical consequence of excluding them from participation in the pursuits of men. With the Hellenization of the Mediterranean world, this conviction resulted in the deprivation of women of their right to a proper education. The Jews were one of the peoples affected by this influence.[2] In any case, by the talmudic period, certain prejudices against women were deeply ingrained.

Studying and expounding the Scriptures became the very core of rabbinic Judaism, as it developed in the centuries before and after the destruction of the Second Commonwealth (70 C.E.). Discussion of women's roles gave rise to such expressions as "the woman's wisdom is for the distaff, no more" and "better to burn the words of the Torah than to give them to women." The propitious beginnings of female participation in the religious revival at the beginning of the Second Commonwealth were stifled by a new spiritual situation. Popular Greek scientific theory combined with ancient Near Eastern prejudices to reduce the stature and activity of women. Something similar happened in Islam. Muḥammad, in his missionary zeal, addressed women frequently and strove to enlist their participation in his new faith. He also bettered their lot by legislation. But when the Arabs moved their tribal societies from the desert environment into the agrarian and urbanized areas of the Near East—areas settled by societies marked by an antifeminine bias—the reforming spirit of Islam became blunted. In Judaism, the exclusion of women from the study of Scripture, which was the main expression of piety, inevitably had a degrading effect. Ironically, the inscriptions in the synagogues of antiquity show women as frequent donors, and the zeal of women in helping their husbands and sons to acquire religious learning is highly praised in the Talmud. Rabbi Aqiba, the most popular of the talmudic sages, is reported to have said to his disciples, pointing to his wife, "Mine and yours is hers."

The socioeconomic character of the Jewish community, and with it the position of its women, also changed markedly in postbiblical antiquity. Farming still was prominent, both in Babylonia-Iraq and in Pal-

2. This view of the deleterious effects of Hellenistic civilization, propounded by Goitein and others, needs to be looked at more critically.

estine, but the process that converted the Jews into an almost exclusively urban population was already in full swing. It was completed in early Islamic times, during the seventh through the ninth century, an eventful period that remains largely obscure as regards the Jewish experience.

The women of the Geniza world cannot be regarded as if all were of the same society and social standing. The Iraqi and Iranian communities, with their Persian traditions, insisted on strict seclusion and subordination of women. But the migration of Jews—to Syria-Palestine, Egypt, Tunisia, and even more distant regions—gave rise to a somewhat changed outlook toward women, and the emerging affluence of various families afforded women of means some measure of hitherto unknown independence.

Visitors to Egypt from the religiously strict and zealous Muslim West were shocked by the easygoing ways of the Egyptian capital, where wine was publicly sold and women enjoyed much freedom—so much so that a popular legend was invented to explain how it came to be that the Cairene women were so haughty. When, by God's decree, Pharaoh and his hosts were drowned in the Red Sea, the slaves of the dead Egyptians approached the widows, proposing marriage. The widows agreed but on one condition: that the Egyptian husbands always be slaves of their wives. The account concludes: "Have you ever made a deal with a Copt? When you are sure that the matter is settled, he says to you, 'Wait, first I must go home and consult my wife.'" (The Copts referred to here are not necessarily Christians, as one might suppose, but indigenous Egyptians.) The Muslim women of Fustat were deemed notorious for their licentiousness: "Every wife [there] has two husbands," exclaims Muqaddasī, the great Muslim traveler from Jerusalem. (Needless to say, the people of the Holy City were "the most virtuous of all mankind"—at least according to our learned traveler.)

Rabbinic Judaism took shape mainly in the strict religious milieu of Iraq, the world of the Babylonian Talmud and the gaons, and was codified by Moses Maimonides, who came to Egypt from the equally strict Muslim West. On the other hand, the Babylonian scholars, living within a highly developed economy, were inclined to a certain pragmatism, which led to progressive legislation in family matters. Similarly, Maimonides was able to mitigate the effects of his rigorously codified religious law through gentle guidance and admonition. The decisions of the judges preserved in the Geniza generally appear to us as practical and humane, but they could not dissipate the strictures of sacred texts and widespread social notions that the Geniza world had inherited about women from Late Antiquity and early Islam.

Women in Economic Life

The Geniza documents tell us virtually nothing about working women during the tenth and eleventh centuries. By the twelfth century, women are seen entering the workforce, and by the thirteenth, women who have to work in order to make ends meet become a significant concern. This is partly explained by the progressive impoverishment of minority groups, or perhaps of the population at large, and partly also by the loosening standards of social custom, as men grew less reluctant to expose their wives to the outside world. The professions open or specific to women were limited, however, and brought only small income. Women's possessions were mainly acquired through gift, dowry, or inheritance, and in many cases, also through communal charity. It was precisely this derivative character of their participation in economic life that constantly brought women in contact with the world of men.

Many widowed, divorced, or deserted women lost their struggle for a decent livelihood, if indeed they ever had one. They could not sit at home, awaiting assistance. They had "to uncover their faces," as the phrase went—to show themselves in public in order to secure their rights or obtain a minimum of sustenance. To be eligible for public welfare, a person had to be registered; these registrations were frequently checked and changed. The semiweekly distributions of bread and the occasional handouts of wheat, clothing, and cash were not delivered to the home, but had to be picked up at the synagogue compound. All this required much moving about and unavoidable contacts with the men in charge of supervision, registration, and distribution.

Those in charge of public welfare were only a small segment of the male world with whom single poor women ordinarily had contact. It was their fellow poor whom they constantly met while making use of the communal services. The lists show that women and men mixed freely while receiving their distributions.[3] This seems to strengthen the surmise that numerous marriage contracts may have been contracts of convenience between indigent old men and women to form a common household. As we have seen, they had much opportunity to meet one another.

Private charity was different. The Geniza contains countless begging

3. When Goitein started to study the organization of public welfare in the Geniza documents, he expected to find separate lists for men and women and the sexes assigned separate days for the collection of food, clothing, and cash. Nothing of the kind was found.

letters written or dictated by men, but none by women. Women appealed to the heads of the community, to judges or welfare officials, and, naturally, also to members of their own family, but not to strangers. Considerations of decency closed this avenue of economic support to women; charity could not be solicited in the impersonal way permitted men.

To be sure, there were women who could fend for themselves, if need be. Women of all classes appear in the Geniza documents owning immovable property. They receive as a gift or donate, inherit or bequeath, buy or sell, rent or lease a variety of real estate—houses (more often parts of houses), stores, workshops, flour mills, and other types of urban properties; we also see them taking care of their properties' upkeep. This prominent aspect of the female role in the Geniza economy deserves closer study.

When it is said of a girl that she "enters her house," the reference is not to a house that she herself owns but to the domicile of her husband, which generally was on the premises of his family home or otherwise provided by him. Yet, to some extent, the husband's house was morally hers, because she was to become "the mistress of the house" and to take charge of its management. It was also legally hers, since the house—like all other possessions of the husband—was, as stated in the marriage contract, mortgaged to his obligations toward her. In early deeds of sale, the wife is mentioned first as the seller, even when the property at issue was not brought into the marriage by her. In one document, it is expressly stated that the house was inherited by the husband from his father; the mention of the wife indicated that she had lifted her mortgage from the real estate sold and would lay no claim on it after her husband's death or divorce. The wife's mortgage rights could become grim reality when the husband had no other means of discharging his obligations toward her.

In some instances, an apartment brought in by the bride, either as part of her dowry or as her personal property, served as the residence of the young couple. But this was the exception, since, ideally and normally, the husband provided the family's domicile. The primary purpose of providing a woman with real estate was to grant her enduring economic security, which would make her financially independent. This is self-evident in the numerous cases in which a woman possessed more than one piece of property. It must be assumed that real estate was seen primarily as an investment and that properties did not normally serve their owners as living quarters.

In numerous documents we see women vigorously taking charge

of their properties. Sitt Naba', "Lady Excellence" of the renowned Am-shāṭī family, leased two of her properties, one an orchard with a modest building, and another, a qāʿa, or one-story house, overlooking the Nile, for a period of seven years against a rent of 52½ dinars, that is, 7½ dinars per year. The tenant was not required to pay rent but to put the two properties into good repair. By the time of the document's writing — the spring of 1231 — three and a half years had passed; the repairs had been successfully completed, an upper story had been added to a modest building situated in the orchard "with her permission and consent," and the townhouse had been renovated. Sitt Naba' now declares in court that the tenant may keep the properties for another four years, may gather the fruits of the orchard for himself and sow there what he likes; and if she sells one of the properties, or both, she will restore to the tenant the balance remaining from the rent already paid, plus his ex-penses. Throughout the document it is Sitt Naba' who speaks; at the end, her husband confirms her actions.

Women regularly appear in the Geniza documents buying and selling slaves, but these transactions should not be regarded as commercial ac-tivities. To be sure, slaves, like houses, represented a financial invest-ment, but they were required for domestic service; such matters inevi-tably fell within the purview of women. Whereas male slaves acted as business agents and aides to traveling merchants, female slaves — those changing hands were often minors — were groomed for service in the house of the purchaser — almost like children. Thus a widow, who ob-viously did not foresee that she might one day need her help, sold a young girl for the considerable sum of 18¾ dinars; another women ac-quired a slave child from her husband, born, most likely, in the house during the husband's previous marriage. When a mother sold her son a *mamlūk* (a male slave of European extraction) no doubt the reason was that the slave, having been the business agent of her father or husband, had come into her possession by way of inheritance or as part of her second marriage gift; she had no use for him, since it was not customary in Jewish houses to keep male domestics.

Because women often possessed commercial experience, we fre-quently find them appointed as legal guardians of their children and executors of estates. The Geniza records provide instances not only of wives performing these functions but also a mother-in-law, a grand-mother, and a sister-in-law. When a women who happened to be the daughter of a scribe and the wife of another acted as guardian for her two daughters, as well as executor, the estate she had to manage was probably very limited in size. In the document that details the circumstances, she receives books and Torah scrolls (probably copied by her late husband) which had been deposited with a physician. In a post-script, she is warned that the items are not hers, but rather the property of her daughters, the heirs. A communal official in Malīj informs his superior in Fustat that "last week" a man died after appointing his wife as guardian of his minor son and executor of his possessions. He further indicates that the deceased had investments with the banker Ibn Shaʿyā and goods with the Tustarīs—two of the most prominent names in the commercial world of Egypt during the first third of the eleventh century. It is likely that in this particular case the management of this estate required someone experienced in business matters; that the wife was appointed guardian over this significant wealth is a testament to her business acumen. Sometimes a wife took care of her husband's affairs during his final illness. Hence, the deathbed declarations that no claims could be made against her by the heirs of the husband, in particular with regard to actions taken by her during his illness. On rare occasions, a wife managed whatever business or workshop a man possessed. When a man appears in court and declares that he has no claims against his wife "with regard to any dispositions she made in my house and all she managed for me," that situation probably reflects her direct involvement in commercial affairs.

Despite notable cases such as these, the roles played by women in economic life were restricted. A women invested mainly in real estate, lent money, entered into partnerships; she also sold and bought textiles, jewelry, and other items included in a trousseau or dowry. But she was not in the mainstream of the economy—the large-scale production and exchange of goods. Moreover, a married woman, insofar as she did not ordinarily possess means outside the shared property of the nuclear family, depended usually on her husband, and in his absence, on his male relatives—even her own sons—or their business partners or friends. This dependence on the men might have been humiliating and occasionally even precarious. Still, many women, married and unmarried, had some means of their own and made varied use of them, which made contacts with men outside their own family unavoidable.

Women in Court

Whether, as a matter of regular practice, women were free to fight for their rights in person or had to rely on others—that is, whether they were represented in the courts, Jewish or Muslim, by men or acted on their own—is a question that begs an informed answer. Muslim women are regularly portrayed in Arabic literature appearing in courts to plead their cases. Similarly, it is noteworthy that when two women come to the rabbinical court of Fustat in December 1132 to settle a sale of property, they are accompanied by their husbands. But the men play a secondary role; the women act, the husbands only confirm the transaction after its conclusion.

Two conflicting notions governed the participation of women in court sessions: One was the sacred principle that no party to a dispute should be heard by the judge without the other hearing every word said. The other was that the woman had to be protected from the court discussion, a protection that was imperative if she was noble or aged, and thus not in the habit of mixing with people in public, or if she was grieving over a loss. In either circumstance, two witnesses would come to her house and take down her declaration. She also might not appear in court because she was young and inexperienced, or otherwise incapable of legal action, whereupon a representative (ordinarily a relative) would take up her cause. Much depended on the circumstances—more specifically, on the character of the litigation. In general, however, the demands of justice and proper procedure triumphed over consideration—or, rather there was no need to be considerate, for the women were generally neither weak, nor inexperienced, nor overly shy or too haughty to appear in public.

Women giving security or safeguards to and for others were normally expected to do so in person, and many such actions are recorded in the Geniza records. To be sure, there are numerous cases in which women did not sue in person but appointed a representative, generally a relative or a communal official. One particular reason for a woman to employ the services of a representative was to sue a close relative, such as a brother or a husband. That they did not appear in court to plead on their own behalf does not constitute a restriction exclusive to women: men also absented themselves. A variety of reasons compelled a person to make use of a proxy: The party sued might be unavailable; real estate or other matters that required action in a Muslim court could give rise to prolonged contention; often the legal case was too complicated to be pressed by an ordinary person. In all such instances, no difference between men and women with respect to representation is discernible in the Geniza documents.

A woman appointing a proxy could do so in court, as when Ḥasnā ("the Belle") bt. Ezekiel b. Masʿūd al-ʿAqrabānī appointed a cantor, who probably served also as court clerk, to sue the daughters of Isaac ha-Kohen, the butcher. Isaac had taken possession of a house left to her by her father. Teenage girls, who were supposed to be shy (and certainly often were), were spared the embarrassment of making declarations in public. One such representation is documented in the Geniza: the appointment of a maternal uncle as proxy by two siblings who had come of age but were still too young to take care of the estate of their father. The boy made the appointment in court, after the judge had explained to him what the action involved. Several persons—certainly acquaintances of the family—two of whom are mentioned by name, were sent to the house to take depositions from the girl, and then, in court, they put her declaration on record. The Geniza evidence has shown that, with the exception of teenage girls—those "pearls still hidden in their shells"—women were as active as men in court proceedings.

Women and Travel

A good many men were engaged in commercial activities requiring travel within a country and, to a large extent, beyond its borders. Consequently, overland journeys and seafaring occupy a prominent place in the Geniza records. The day-to-day activities of women, on the other hand, did not require extensive travel away from home. Rather than accompany their husbands, some women preferred to stay in their native towns, where they felt protected by their families. The occasional—indeed in certain circles frequent—separations of men and women had a profound impact on family life. The issue of who traveled is, however, not so simple. Owing to the population's general mobility, even closely knit families could become dispersed, a situation that provided many opportunities or pretexts for visits—by women as well as by men. The Geniza documents show that women did travel for a variety of reasons and to a larger extent than we would expect.

A woman in Fustat married to a man from Alexandria was obliged to visit her in-laws in the Mediterranean seaport for one month (but not more) during the course of a year. The couple would pass the month of the High Holidays (which included seven days of complete work stoppage and five half-holidays) with the husband's extended family. These family visits, requiring travel for holidays and even weekends, formed a conspicuous aspect of social life in Geniza times. Women frequently had to travel unaccompanied by their husbands, and often for prolonged periods, to visit a married female relative in another town expecting a baby, or recuperating after delivery, or who was ill, or suffering in an unfamiliar or unfriendly environment. Another common occasion for female travel was a visit to a holy shrine, or even to the city of Jerusalem. When a woman is called "the pilgrim," we may assume that it was because she had made the journey to Jerusalem alone, perhaps as a widow, but in any event unaccompanied by a husband. For, unlike Islam, in Judaism this honorific epithet was not normally applied to a person who had made the pilgrimage.

The *kabīra*, the old lady, or "dowager," was the female traveler par excellence. She kept the extended family together and could get away more easily than the younger women in the house. Having arrived at her destination, a kabīra would be in no hurry to return, a situation seemingly reflected in a letter in which a mother staying with her son is requested in the most urgent terms to hurry back to her husband, who is seriously ill and could die at any moment. A postscript adds, "Otherwise you will feel regrets when regrets will be of no avail." Clearly other letters asking her to return had been sent previously.

Women living outside the capital had another reason for travel: the need to appeal to a higher legal authority. A Muslim book of responsa tells of a woman who tried to flee from her village to Qayrawān, to seek justice in a dispute with her husband. Similarly, several Geniza records that show provincial women appearing before a court in Fustat might well concern individuals not resident in the capital who had come there to argue their cases in person. Other documents explicitly illustrate such situations. For example, a women from Ṣahrajit, who had been banned because she had allegedly "divorced her husband" before a Muslim judge, appealed to a higher authority, and the mother of a newly married girl in Malīj brought home from the capital a legal opinion which restored peace to a family that had been divided by marital strife.

Travel could, of course, be dangerous and often was. Exposing women to the dangers of sea travel was always a matter of concern, and yet, by Geniza times, sea travel for women was not unusual. For the most part, these were married women who did not stay home as most women did, but accompanied their husbands or traveled to join them in a foreign country. Single women traveling overseas, even those who had never been married, are mentioned in the Geniza records as a common occurrence. When some Christian ships were taken by Muslim freebooters, the Jewish captives brought to Alexandria included the wife of a physician, accompanied by her husband, another married woman, and a girl. Unmarried girls had the opportunity to brave the dangers of sea travel because overseas marriages were much sought after by the mercantile class. Such marriages were arranged by fathers seeking to cement commercial alliances or simply to provide suitable mates for offspring whose access to suitable partners might be limited. The contracting parties were in any event interested in the success of the match. Perhaps some girls liked the idea of being married overseas, or perhaps, to some extent, the spirit of overseas adventure that inspired the teenage sons of the Geniza traders inspired their daughters as well. Naturally, the girls did not travel alone. But men as well, on sea and on land, normally traveled in the company of friends.

A Muslim handbook of market supervision orders captains carrying women in their ships to set up a partition between them and the men. A Greek savant humorously describes how a very devout Jewish sea captain from Alexandria went so far as to put up a dividing screen on his boat—to the chagrin of the male travelers, for the girls were comely (404 C.E). Such arrangements have not yet been found in a Geniza text. Female passengers had to carry their marriage certificates (or similar identity papers) with them when they traveled in the company of their husbands; otherwise, the couple could incur unpleasant experiences. The bravest of all female travelers were those needy women who did not accept their dire lot, but set out to try their fortunes elsewhere. For example, a deserted woman from Acre came, via Jaffa and other places, to Fustat together with her son; she then went off to Malīj in an effort to find her husband, and finally returned to the capital to secure her rights.

At Home

Much of the work traditionally associated with the household was in fact often performed by others outside the home: Grain was stored in the house, but the handmill, the eternal symbol of female servitude, is almost never referred to in the Geniza inventories of household implements. One brought one's grain to mills, found throughout the city. Bread, the main fare, could be bought in a market. If the dough was prepared at home, the actual baking was done in a bakery nearby. In general, food was simple, and since fuel was expensive because of the

scarcity of wood, one preferred during weekdays to bring home prepared food from the bazaar. Washing and cleaning cannot have been too
burdensome; the heavier textiles were taken care of by professional
cleaners. Spinning and weaving, the labors theoretically incumbent on
all women, are hardly ever mentioned, except with regards to individuals
who were professional weavers.

The rearing of children, too, was perhaps less exacting than one might
imagine. Women were praised for their eagerness to give their boys a
good education, or scolded for neglecting them, but complaints about
"the pains of raising children," to use a talmudic phrase, are practically
absent from the Geniza. Troublesome boys were packed off to school,
even in poor homes (since the community took care of the fees), whereas
girls were expected to take care of their younger siblings or to make
themselves useful in other ways. Boys entered the labor force at an early
age and girls usually married in their teens. Most households included
more than one female adult, and all middle-class families normally possessed a maidservant.

The occupation most frequently referred to in the Geniza records in
connection with women is embroidery, and here we should remember
that even among Western cultures not too long ago there was not a
single piece of household linen or lingerie that was not embroidered or
otherwise embellished. This preoccupation with decorative work inspired a continuous search for new models. Inventiveness was a standard
for comparing one's own work with that of others and a quality to take
pride in; the steady and quiet work also had a soothing effect. Embroidery was a luxury, produced by one's own efforts; it constituted
the female counterpart to the modest amount of leisure obtained by
the bourgeois male and used by him for his spiritual and other pursuits.

Trousseau lists describe comparatively few items of bedding and
clothing as embroidered. This may mean that the pieces of the trousseau
that were bought in a bazaar were usually plain. It was left to the future
housewife to adorn her pillows, linen, and personal wardrobe in the way
she chose. Men's clothing as well could be richly embroidered, but the
texts seem to indicate that this was done by professional embroiderers,
not by housewives. As the trousseau lists show, even a middle-class bride
often brought into the marriage numerous pieces of clothing of the same
type; wealthier girls acquired quite bewildering quantities. Clothes were
kept in beautifully decorated trunks or chests; to preserve those pieces
it was necessary to take them out from time to time and expose them
to air. Great pride was taken in the beauty of one's wardrobe. Women

were, no doubt, preoccupied with their extensive bridal trousseaux. Although the total cost of the trousseau was noted in the marriage contract as a liability of the husband, its individual items could be and were often exchanged, with his consent, for more desirable items. The services of agents and brokers could be used for this purpose, but the Geniza women insisted on their right to do so in person; while the daily household errands were performed by a servant or by the husband, who regularly went to the bazaar, the selling and buying of textiles was the pastime of the woman of the house.

There were many other occasions for leaving the house, as is evident from documents detailing the struggle of wives for their freedom of movement. The most suitable place for a respectable woman was the synagogue. On the Sabbath, when all work, whether household chores or embroidery, was forbidden, women could attend the synagogue service. There, a woman could hear her father, brother, husband, or son recite a lection from the Bible or sing a portion of the liturgy — she might even have bought such an honor for him. She could watch the proceedings, especially the opening of the holy ark, when the Torah scrolls were taken out and God was near — so near that the most secret wishes of the heart could be conveyed to him, so to speak, in person; or she could listen to discussions about communal affairs, which took place during the service. Then, coming down from the women's gallery through the "secret door," she might enter the synagogue courtyard for a chat with members of the community and friends of the family.

Visits to the public bathhouse were similarly frequent (normally once a week) and of even wider social significance. Less regular, but probably more time consuming, was attendance at wedding celebrations and visits at childbirth and mourning, also expressly included in the lists of proper occasions for a woman to leave the house. Finally, and perhaps most frequently, women went out to see their families and female friends, and, in return, expected to be visited by them.

"Tell me what you do, and I will tell you who you are." We would like to know what the women did when they got together for social occasions, but for the most part little is known about the society of women. We can imagine that they exchanged social pleasantries; no doubt, they also talked about their purchases and sales. Some might also play chess, the delight of that beautiful and wicked Jewish woman in *The Arabian Nights* who defeated her Christian paramour so often that she had won all his possessions. But we have no idea at all of how women, speaking to other women, accounted for the world arranged for them by men.

The Independent Woman

The enticing chess player mentioned previously is a paradigm of the independent heroine in certain types of longer stories found in *The Arabian Nights*. Such women became independent, either because their husbands absented themselves frequently and for prolonged periods, or because they had divorced or been widowed and inherited riches from fathers or other relatives. As the Geniza documents and other sources of the period sources prove, these women could be found in all layers of the society. Usually we know them only from the transactions that they made or the cases they litigated. But there were also forms of independence that were expressed outside of legal matters. Throughout the centuries, we find women (occasionally described as Nazirites) vowing to abstain from wine and other intoxicating beverages, which in those days must have been a very trying vow, since bread and wine were staples of the diet. We may surmise that the vow, like that taken by Karaites living in Jerusalem, also included abstinence from meat, the idea being that as long as the Temple was in ruins, and God was not honored with the obligatory libations of wine and sacrifices of meat, His servants should not enjoy such luxuries either. One woman described as a Nazirite (there were male Nazirites as well) made private donations for orphans and the communal chest; another gave a house to the community for charitable purposes; the son of still another female Nazirite is found in an ancient list of those receiving bread. We do not learn what induced them to make the vow nor what it meant to them.

The following letter is written by a mother—the daughter of a pietist woman—coming to grips with her own mortality. The writer of the letter wants her own daughter to receive *ta'līm*, formal instruction, so that the child may emulate her pious grandmother. Believing that her own days are numbered, the writer asks her sister to attend to this, but the sister clearly inspires her with little confidence.

This is to inform you, my lady, dear sister—may God accept me as a ransom for you—that I have become seriously ill with little hope for recovery, and I have dreams indicating that my end is near. My lady, my most urgent request of you, if God the exalted indeed decrees my death, is that you take care of my little daughter and make efforts to give her an education, although I well know that I am asking you for something unreasonable, as there is not enough money—by my father—for support, let alone for formal instruction. However, she has a model in our saintly mother. Do not let her appear in public, and do not neglect her Sudanese nurse, Sa'āda, and her

ments. Women (in principle, because of their chores) had fewer obligations, and were therefore exempted from study. To use a Greek notion, the woman was the *banausos*, the drudge, who by definition, did not enjoy the privilege of liberty and leisure required for learning. As a rule, women were uneducated. Of the letters found in the Geniza, a few dozen at most were sent by women; it is likely, but not absolutely certain, that they were personally written by women; often women could read but not write.

It seems that women of all classes knew the basic Hebrew prayers, but that in itself did not constitute much learning. Girls from prestigious families, circumstances permitting, certainly received some formal instruction. The twelfth-century author Samuel the Maghrebi recounts that his mother and her two sisters knew how to read and write Hebrew and Arabic. Samuel emphasizes writing because even among men the art of writing was acquired only by certain classes of people. In the poorer sections of the population there was the *mu'allima*, the female Bible teacher, usually a relative of the teacher who owned the school. She fulfilled the double task of assistant, probably taking care of the smaller boys, and manager, dealing with the mothers bringing their children to school.

The level of literacy in Geniza society was not essentially different from that in other literate societies of the same period—that is, if we disregard faraway Christian Europe with its nunneries and their princely abbesses. More detailed comparisons with societies closer to the Geniza world are difficult, because too little research has been done on the women of medieval Islam or those of the Oriental Christian communities. What we know concerns mostly the women of the ruling classes. The few women saints and visionaries mentioned in the Geniza have many counterparts in Islam.

The prominence of women in the affairs of Fatimid Egypt and Zirid Tunisia is remarkable. 'Azīz, the first Fatimid caliph to reside in Egypt for an entire reign (975–96), was married to (among others) a Christian woman who was so influential that she obtained the appointment of her two brothers, one after the other, as patriarchs of the Melchite Church. Her son, the mentally disturbed al-Ḥākim (996–1021), became his father's successor. Al-Ḥākim's sister, Sayyidat al-Mulk, "The Mistress over the Kingdom," was suspected of having engineered his murder, and she ruled the country after his death for four years. Originally a slave girl of the Jew Abū Saʿd al-Tustarī (who later became her "vizier"), the Sudanese mother of the caliph al-Mustanṣir (1036–94) held power while her son was a minor. Al-Mustanṣir himself, on his deathbed, put the Imamate—the religious and temporal leadership of the empire—into the hands of his sister, who then swore allegiance to al-Mustaʿlī, the youngest and therefore, most malleable, of the seven sons of her dead brother. Al-Muʿizz (1016–62), the most splendorous ruler of Zirid Tunisia was brought up by his aunt Mallāl, also known in the Geniza papers as al-Sayyida, "The Mistress," or "The Ruler." She acted as regent until her death in October 1023; there were other prominent women as well in the Zirid court. The role of women at the courts of eleventh-century Egypt and Tunisia was so conspicuous that Ibn ʿIdhārī, the noted historian of the Muslim West, dedicates a special chapter to the topic.

Women in public affairs could not escape the attention of the subject population—in particular the circles of the higher government officials, physicians in attendance, court purveyors, and others who had direct access to the men in power. These contacts were, in turn, extended to their womenfolk. When the mother of the nagid and court physician Mevōrākh is praised in a dirge for having placated the ire of the ruler, this influence probably was exercised through the women of the court. In a legal settlement, the daughter of a late government official is warned not to use her relations with either the government or persons connected with it to impair the rights of her stepson. In a letter from the Ayyubid period, some women are asked to use their good relations with the wives of some close servants of the sultan to secure a particular benefit.

The influential position of women of the higher class seems not to have been matched by spiritual fame. Neither literary texts nor documentary evidence from the Geniza contain a single piece of religious writing attributable with certainty to a woman. Tens of thousands of pieces of liturgical poetry have been preserved in the Geniza, but we never hear of a female poet. (A Jewish woman writing Arabic poetry in Spain is known through a Muslim source.) A woman's voice was not to be heard in the synagogue; thus, there was no "seat in life," no incentive for the creation of a religious poem by a woman. It is also true that the more important families tried to live in Cairo, the residential city, far away from the Geniza chamber. Still, the dearth of any Geniza documents relating to religious literature created by, or even for, women cannot be taken lightly. The Arabic and Hebrew folktales found in the Geniza are pastimes and mostly belong to the international stock of entertainment literature. In any case, most of these tales, as their contents show, cannot be classified as women's lore.

Men and women clearly occupied different inner worlds. Still, common interests created many occasions for men and women to meet and perforce made for similar attitudes. To some extent, women lived in seclusion, but men might be secluded as well. A respectable merchant sat in his house or his office in the bazaar, while brokers and agents did the auctioning and haggling. The nobler a woman, the more she had claim to being served by persons doing her errands, but there was no strict segregation within the household; the Jewish houses in Fustat described in the Geniza documents, with few exceptions, had no women's quarters. There was privacy, but no forced separation.

As noted earlier, the participation of women in the community's economic life, though limited and derivative, brought them into frequent contact with the world of men; religion as well served to bind men and women together: The presence of a synagogue was the first prerequisite in a woman's choice of residence. Women regularly attended services; they donated Torah scrolls for the service, oil and books for study, and houses, the rents on which supported the upkeep of synagogues. There was no God to turn to other than the God of men. The husband was the priest in the house. His officiating at the benedictions before and after a meal and at other ceremonies was essential for the spiritual comfort of the female members of the household. Milton's "He for God only, she for God in him" is valid also for the Geniza society.

This should not be understood to mean that the women's contact with the world was made solely through her husband (as was assumed for Athenian wives in the time of Pericles). Within the world dominated by men there was another world created by women for themselves. The Geniza women were of a very sociable nature; they constantly flocked together, whether in the women's gallery in the house of worship, the bathhouse, the bazaar, in gatherings on happy and mournful occasions, or through the visits of friends and relatives. No wonder that a woman—even a young woman—could become "dear to the family and the town." The Geniza woman was not the slave of her household. She had a life beyond her family. Unfortunately, we have no detailed picture of how women themselves envisioned that life.

Sexual Mores

The Muslim injunction of *satr al-'awra*, the covering of the private parts of the body—which for women meant almost the entire body—was not merely a matter of religious ritual; it reflected a strong social attitude of the common people, who took religion seriously. The more the affluent and the influential felt themselves secure in their wealth and power, the more they loosened their tongues and secluded their wives. The littérateurs, who frequented the courts of the princes and palaces of the rich, have provided us with abundant and uninhibited reports about sex as it was discussed and practiced in those circles. At the other end of the social spectrum, the people who were not *mastūr*—literally, not "covered," that is, not protected by wealth, family, or social standing, in short: not respectable—had little power to seclude their wives, and no cause to restrain their own tongues. Their voice, or in any case what is represented as their voice, is heard in the later versions of *The Arabian Nights* and in similar literature.

The sexual mores of the majority of the urban population—the great masses of skilled craftsmen and artisans, respectable shopkeepers, middle-class merchants, and lower bureaucrats—are less well known. Medieval historians had little opportunity to speak of what we might term "the middle class." Books of entertainment, if systematically analyzed according to the social groups that they address, will give us a better picture of medieval sexuality, but more work is still to be done in this respect. Much is to be expected also from a careful perusal of Islamic religious literature, since many who wrote these texts came, as did the people of the Geniza, from families engaged in crafts or commerce, or were themselves involved in such occupations. Literary works not withstanding, we should like to hear the unmediated voice of the so-called common man speaking privately of his own daily concerns—not *voicing* opinions but revealing them inadvertently.

In this respect the Cairo Geniza is able to make a modest contribution, despite the fact that respectable persons of the lower and middle classes were extremely reticent about sexual matters. At the height of the classical Geniza period, the eleventh century, none would have dared to commit to paper even an expression with so harmless a sexual connotation as "my wife." One did not write "my wife," *zawjatī*, but "the one who is with me," *man 'indī*, or similar (and sometimes exceedingly awkward) circumlocutions. The Geniza has preserved more than 250 letters addressed to Nahray b. Nissīm, a merchant banker from Qayrawān, who had settled in Egypt. We are thus able to follow his fortunes for a full fifty years, from 1045 through 1095. Many of the letters were written by close relatives and friends and often contain references to matters other than business. But nowhere are greetings extended to his wife, and, needless to say, Nahray himself never mentions her in his own letters, of which we have about twenty-five. From the letters, we know the names of his son and his daughter, we hear much about his mother

and something about his sister—but not the wife whom he survived. We know her name only from a legal document written after his
death.

The Geniza contains innumerable details about a woman's wardrobe
and ornaments but practically nothing about her physical appearance.
When a young schoolmaster living far away from home apprises his
mother of his marriage, he assures her that her prayers have been heard
and that his young wife possesses all the wonderful qualities of character
that he has always admired in his mother. This is expressed in Arabic,
the language in which the body of the letter is written. The additional
praise of the girl, namely, that she is very beautiful, is expressed in Hebrew, as if there were some doubt about the propriety of what was being
communicated.

For such matters as sex and family life, our information comes mainly
from Egypt itself and, in particular, from its ancient Islamic capital,
Fustat. That in itself may present a skewed picture of sexual mores, for
the simple reason that life in the cosmopolitan center was different from
that in the provinces. Fustat was often censured in the Geniza documents by visitors and newcomers from other Muslim countries (including Moses Maimonides) for the reputed licentiousness of its inhabitants.
Sexual mores also differed among the different religious elements of the
population. The seclusion of women was far stricter in Islam than in
Christianity and Judaism. Christian and Jewish women were required
to cover their hair and to dress modestly, but they were not obliged to
veil their faces, and they could talk to a man of another family without
incurring opprobrium. This contrast is beautifully illustrated in a legal
question submitted to Moses Maimonides. A Jewish family and a Christian family might live in one house, an arrangement that was in fact
quite common. When the Christian family embraced Islam, the letter
emphasizes, it caused no end of inconvenience to the female members
of the Jewish household. It was taken for granted in the Judaic world
of the Geniza records that a male unrelated to the family could come
into a home and discuss matters with the woman of the house in the
absence of her husband. Since women were very much involved in economic matters, there was ample opportunity for such encounters.

Muslims were uneasy about admitting women to public services in
the mosque. In contrast, the churches and synagogues of Fustat had
women's galleries, frequented by married and unmarried women alike.
The entrance to the gallery was through a so-called secret or women's
door, the *bāb al-sirr* or *bāb al-nisā'*, located on a street different from
that on which the main gate opened. (The same special entrance for

women was found in many large private homes.) But in the synagogue court, men and women mixed freely. A woman writing (or dictating) a letter to a man could mention what they had discussed "when we met last Saturday in the synagogue. . . ." Thus, the basic attitude toward the seclusion of women was not the same in the minority and majority populations.

For most of the Jewish community represented in the Geniza, sexual satisfaction had to be obtained through marriage. Marriage was instituted by God, not only for procreation but for the partners to find full sexual satisfaction without being forced to seek it illicitly. That attitude toward marriage reflects ancient Near Eastern wisdom, as it is expressed, for instance, in an often quoted passage from the Book of Proverbs (5: 15–21): "Drink water from your own cistern . . . rejoice in the wife of your youth. . . . Why should you become infatuated with a stranger?" A Geniza sermon in praise of marriage describes the wife as a protecting wall surrounding her husband. A man imploring his wife to return to him, after she has fled to her relatives, assures her that, in the future, she will be the queen and he the slave, for "living without a wife in Cairo is very difficult for blameless and chaste persons." An adult man without a wife was regarded as living in sin, and it was not easy for him to find an apartment for himself alone. Widowers, unlike widows, rarely remained unmarried.

Legal documents and letters indicate that the night of the Sabbath (Friday night) was set aside for the fulfillment of the conjugal obligations a husband owed his wife. In the Talmud this was only a recommendation — and then only for scholars. Among the Rabbanite majority of the classical Geniza period, however, it had become a general observance that could be claimed in court as a minimum conjugal requirement. The Karaite Jews, who recognized only the Bible as their guidance, took an opposite stance: sexual intercourse was regarded by them as a desecration of the holy day. In the numerous cases of mixed marriages, most often a Karaite woman marrying a Rabbanite man, the sensibilities of the wife had to be honored. Indeed, the sensibilities of women were generally respected. "Living together without mutual consent is like prostitution." Divorce was often sought by, and granted to, wives. The fact that about 45 percent of all women whose cases are known to us from the Geniza were married more than once should teach us that marriages were often dissolved.

Proven cases of adultery involving married women are known only from Alexandria, a city of "loose mores," and only in special circumstances, for example, when some petty merchants tried their luck in faraway India and were forced to remain there for years. Scandals ensued, but, as far as we know, nothing happened to the women involved except that they produced healthy babies. One of these children sent greetings to a brother out in India, as one letter sarcastically remarks. Elsewhere, we read only about allegations of adultery (sometimes not entirely unfounded): A luckless woman, who has run away from her husband, reports that her father-in-law suspected her of having an affair with a brother-in-law, but she mentions it only as an absurdity exemplifying the extent of the family's hateful treatment of her. A story is reported by a cantor who served as spiritual leader for a small congregation in a provincial town in a letter seeking advice from his superiors in the capital. A young couple lived in the house of the husband's mother, who had remarried. After her death, the stepfather began to visit the apartment of the young woman often enough to arouse the suspicion of the community; some were prepared to bring the matter to the attention of the police. Summoned by the cantor, the man promised to stop these visits and to pay a modest fine of two dinars if he failed to honor his commitment. A similar promise was broken repeatedly by a Karaite who visited a married woman of his community, using frivolous language and making indecent overtures. Brought before the assembly of the elders, the woman argued that she discouraged those visits and had complained about them to her husband and the authorities of the community; whenever the man came in when she was alone, she asked an aunt to stand watch. In the presence of the accused, however, she changed her testimony, stating only that she disapproved of the visits. Finally a group of Karaite women testified that she was a person without blemish. At the next prayer service, a solemn ban was pronounced on anyone who had positive knowledge about the affair and did not deposit it in court. The carefully written record of four pages is fittingly headed by the superscription "In the name of Him Who knows the secrets" (Psalm 44:22).

Concubinage with a slave was legal under Islamic law, as it was under the Hebrew Bible. In postbiblical times, however, when concubinage with foreign women was viewed as menacing the very character of Jewish religion, opposition to the practice became intense; the same attitude took root in Christianity. To choose a female according to one's own taste and to have complete disposition of her might be preferable to having a wife selected by others—a wife who, moreover, was constantly watched and protected by her family. But circumstances called for restraint. First of all, concubinage was expensive. To purchase a simple maidservant required about twenty gold pieces (a sum almost sufficient for the sustenance of a modest family for a year). An attractive slave could cost four or more times as much, and if she was a trained musician, even more. Since three-quarters of the Jewish male population were unable to produce twenty dinars in cash as the first marriage gift, only a small minority could have been in a financial position to afford a concubine. Moreover, if the girl was a Muslim (or claimed to be), her non-Muslim master could be fined or suffer more severe punishment. Finally, whenever the Jewish (and probably also the Christian) authorities were strong enough, they forced the owner of a concubine to sell her, a painful experience, both sentimentally and materially, especially when, as an act of atonement, the proceeds of the sale were distributed among the poor. We are not informed about the prevalence of concubinage among the affluent Jews with domiciles in Cairo, for they do not leave us any writings in the Geniza of Fustat.

References to prostitution are also extremely rare. We have some sporadic and not unequivocal notes concerning the seaports of Acre, Alexandria, and Aden, perhaps also Cairo; only one case is known for Fustat, but the word "prostitute" in that instance seems to be used in a general pejorative sense. A member of the highly respected Ibn Sighmār family was suspected of having an affair with a Muslim woman; he had already paid a fine of 120 gold pieces, an enormous sum, and had been imprisoned for a month and a half at the writing of the letter reporting the scandal to someone in Qūṣ, in Upper Egypt. Twelve court records were written in this matter. Clearly the woman involved was an unusually independent woman.

The world of the learned and religious merchants, which provides the bulk of the Geniza correspondence, presents a different problem. These merchants were engaged in the Mediterranean trade (the Indian trade as well, although to a lesser extent) and were regularly absent from home for months, a year, or even more. Notable in this respect is the absence in the vast corpus of writings of references or allusions to concubinage with a slave girl or to a visit to a house of prostitution. That still leaves us with the question of how individuals removed from their families over long periods of time sublimated or satisfied their most basic sexual needs. Whatever the case, they had to fall back on the community and its institutions. Ultimately, it was the strong sense of community engendered among the people of the Geniza that allowed their society to cohere, to prosper, and in times of crisis to pull together.

Addendum

Genizah Studies in the United States:
Its Past and Future Links to
Near Eastern Historiography

In the fall of 1953, S. D. Goitein arrived in the United States to study the numerous Geniza documents in Philadelphia. He had by then decided to devote his scholarly energies to the India trade, a subject that attracted his serious attention a few years earlier when, investigating the interplay of Jewish and Islamic law, he came across some Geniza records referring to a lawsuit. The case involved a merchant from Tripolitania (present-day Libya), who, while conducting business in India, had lost part of the merchandise entrusted to him by colleagues from Tunisia and Egypt. That discovery alerted Goitein to the potential importance of the Geniza to the social and economic history of the Mediterranean. And so, Goitein took a year's leave from the Hebrew University where he was director of its prestigious Institute for Asian and African Studies and accepted a visiting professorship in Arabic and Islamics at Dropsie College, a Philadelphia-based institution offering advanced degrees in Hebrew and cognate studies.

Goitein was by nature an extremely curious person who, despite his meticulous Germanic ways, was always open to new experiences and ideas. The burden of teaching and research in Philadelphia notwithstanding, he attempted to see something of his host country. He accepted a number of invitations to lecture and to visit different universities, among them the University of Michigan, which had a long history of scholarly involvement with the Near East.

As cultural chairman of the Jewish student organization and as a major in the university's Department of Near Eastern Studies, I had the privilege of inviting the distinguished visitor from Israel and also serving as his campus guide. For me, it was the beginning of a lifetime of informal mentoring. I do not recall many of the technical details of his conversations with the faculty, but I very well remember that he was favorably impressed with the university and its facilities. I believe that impression of American higher education was reinforced by visits to other seats of higher learning. He was particularly moved by the energy and financial support that universities in this country invested in student life and the ample time that they provided for research-oriented faculty.

In 1957, the opportunity to return to Philadelphia presented itself once again. Julian Obermann, who had taught Arabic and Islamics (among other subjects) at Yale, had retired, and Franz Rosenthal, Obermann's counterpart at the University of Pennsylvania, was recruited to take over for him in New Haven. That left open a position for a senior Arabist to replace Rosenthal. The University of Pennsylvania, which had for many years sought out distinguished scholars in Arabic and Islam, turned to Goitein, and he accepted their invitation of a permanent appointment. Goitein's decision to leave the Hebrew University, with which he had been associated from almost its very founding, came as somewhat of a shock to his Israeli colleagues. His decision to leave Israel — he had come to Mandatory Palestine as a committed Zionist in 1923 — still occasions speculation. Goitein himself always maintained that his administrative obligations in Jerusalem simply would not have left him time to plunge into his new project. Time certainly must have been a factor in his decision. The truth is that when he arrived in Philadelphia to accept his Pennsylvania appointment, he was already approaching his sixties, an age that would discourage most people from heroic scholarly exploits; but Goitein was, as all who knew him quickly discerned, a most unusual individual and scholar.

In Philadelphia, Goitein proceeded full steam with his Geniza studies, expanding the original project on the India trade (which he never completed) to a more comprehensive project that led eventually to *A Mediterranean Society*. For Goitein, the picture that emerged from the diverse and fragmented texts which he examined so thoroughly was that of a whole society embracing Jews and others. When asked to describe his vocation after he had immersed himself in the Geniza documents, Goitein shied away from conventional labels that reflect the breakdown of current scholarship into various disciplines and subdisciplines. Instead, he declared himself a "sociographer," a long-forgotten technical term resurrected from the academic vocabulary of the 1920s. For Goitein was, despite or perhaps because of his extraordinarily broad learning, a generalist—albeit a generalist whose erudition was breathtaking, as any random conversation with him was bound to reveal. The unusual scope of the Geniza materials forced Goitein to acquaint himself with the minutiae of many fields and subfields required to reconstruct the living community of medieval Jewry and its neighbors in the lands of Islam, a heavy intellectual burden that grew heavier with time.

Eventually, he saw the need to share the workload of the project, and thus he began to train specialists to handle the various subfields of Geniza studies, areas of scholarly concern that were arousing the curiosity of reflective historians broadly interested in the history of the Muslim Middle Ages. He became a sort of talent scout, coopting young scholars with already established reputations and encouraging them to apply their craft to the problems of the Geniza. It was not an overwhelming sense of modesty that drove him to acquire associates (although he often preferred to address himself, I thought somewhat self-mockingly, as "Mr. Goitein"). If he turned to others for assistance it was because he was above all a person of uncompromising scholarly standards and integrity. He simply could not cover the entire waterfront by himself. A particular moment comes to mind. He was telling me of his early training in Talmud. As did the enlightened parents of many bright and enterprising orthodox Jewish boys in Germany, his parents never farmed him out to the rabbis of a prominent yeshiva—the traditional school for study in Talmud and related subjects; instead, he was given over to a private tutor. He studied classical Jewish texts rigorously, rising at dawn to take instruction with his mentor, or in later years, to study his "daily page." He was no slouch when it came to Jewish legal texts—quite the opposite. Indeed, unlike some present-day scholars, he was sufficiently learned to appreciate the limitations of his own talmudic learning. Hence, when Mordechai Friedman, a gifted young talmudist, came to study with him, he quickly steered him to the Geniza's legal materials. In similar fashion, he recruited students and parceled out to them specific projects that were beyond his established areas of expertise. By then he simply lacked the time or energy to take on every aspect of Geniza research.

These associations with younger scholars and students bore fruit. Working informally with Goitein, or under his supervision, a coterie of newly shaped "Genizologists" were able to reconstruct the realia of bridal dowries, trace the intricate legal situation and social status of Jewish women in a polygynous society, and recover a large range of highly complex commercial arrangements—not simply as they are described in legal handbooks, but as they were actually practiced by Jews and Muslims in local, regional, and international settings, ranging from India to southern Europe. There is, to be sure, an enormous amount of work yet to be done. There are currently a number of ongoing projects on the social and economic history of the Geniza world ranging from the publication of women's correspondence to the economy of the Rīf, the hinterland of Egypt. In addition, there is the present research into the literary texts of the Geniza, some quarter of a million fragments.

At the outset, not all scholars had the imagination to see the potential of the Goiteinian enterprise. When the first volume of his magisterial study was published in the late 1960s (a hefty work that he subtitled *Economic Foundations*), it occasioned a number of conflicting opinions: An Arabic book surveying Western scholarship on the world of Islam—published in Libya no less—dismissed Goitein as someone who had forged a career examining the remains of a rubbish heap. While, in a manner of speaking, this actually reflected the truth, it is abundantly clear that the Libyan's assessment was not intended to be ironic or complimentary. A less tendentious review by a leading medievalist of Western Europe, celebrated for an acidic tongue and equally acidic pen, gave Goitein high marks for the breadth of his technical learning, but admonished him for what may be described as a lack of analytical insight when it came to economic history, as if the insights required to study medieval Europe and those relevant to an understanding of a Mediterranean economy controlled by the Muslims are in all instances complementary. A scholar actually learned in the subject matter of Goitein's book found it enormously important to the study of medieval Jewish society, but wondered to what extent one could relate Goitein's findings to the world of contemporaneous Muslims, a caveat that was fully answered to the critic's satisfaction by the publication of the subsequent volumes.

In time, Goitein's work was more fully appreciated for both the scope of its enormous learning and the wide range of topics that it opened to serious review. One notes in that respect the unofficial assessment of the two leading historians of the Islamic Near East in the United States. While taking a constitutional in the streets of Princeton, New Jersey, one fine day, the two pillars of Islamic history waxed philosophical about those works of twentieth-century scholarship that had and would continue to have the greatest impact on the way Islamists "do" Near Eastern history. They both agreed, and very quickly at that, that among the many books published within the current century, the most important historical work had been Goitein's *A Mediterranean Society*, which was in effect not only a ringing endorsement of Goitein's prodigious effort, but of the importance of Genizology in general. The study of the Geniza for a more broadly based Near Eastern history has become even more important as the current generation of Geniza scholars has turned more deeply into the vast array of issues raised by these unique sources.

Any critical assessment of the present and future relationship between Geniza studies and a more broadly defined historiography of the medieval Near East has to address several queries: To what extent are the medieval Jewish communities described in the previous pages self-defined by their own cultural artifacts and institutions? To what extent must they be defined by a detailed knowledge of the hegemonic Muslim community in whose midst they dwelt? To rephrase that question: Can we understand the organizational structure and internal dynamics of medieval Jewish communities in the lands of Islam, to say nothing of their vibrant intellectual life, without direct access to the pervasive Islamic culture of the Middle Ages? Related to that, are we obliged to reverse the trend of our thinking and ask whether the recorded activities of the Jewish communities are useful—indeed essential—to a larger understanding of medieval Islam? It is abundantly clear from the cumulative evidence presented and discussed in *A Mediterranean Society* that the Jewish communities of the Geniza world were inextricably linked to the larger and dominant communities in whose midst they dwelt. That being the case, promoting Geniza studies should be a major desideratum for all historians of the medieval Near East, regardless of their special interests. That would also hold true for scholars more generally interested in Islam, Judaism, and Christianity, as well as specialists in economic, social, and religious history.

All (save perhaps our Libyan colleague) are likely to agree that, because of the growth of Geniza studies, the Jewish communities of the Islamic world have become an extremely fertile area of historical research that ought to attract a wide following. The range and number of items is absolutely staggering when we consider the paucity of similar material describing contemporaneous Muslim society. To be sure, there are literally tens of thousands of pages of historical writing in Islamic languages that record the dramatic events of the Muslim Middle Ages. Strewn among the memorabilia of the times, there is much compelling material concerning politics and the growth of political institutions. But, for all the richness of the detail, there is something disquieting about the accounts of the medieval Muslim chroniclers. If anything, the tale that they tell is too richly textured; one could argue that it is also too compelling. For as told by Muslim historians, the story of the medieval Islamic world is a history that has been discovered, embellished, and when necessary, invented in an effort to enhance the public images of those whose patronage floated a fair share of the larger enterprise of historical writing. The portrayal of the past is so often tendentious as to raise the most serious doubts concerning the basic historicity of specific episodes, if not the larger events that frame them.

Those who are interested in recovering elements of the medieval past have also to consider the didactic nature of Arabic historiography, that is, its moralizing tone. For medieval Muslims, history was the recording and interpretation of events on the basis of individual or collective behavior and, relatedly, the values that reinforce behavior. The larger realities that furnish the means and occasion of individual or group action are of decidedly less interest, as are the minute details of quotidian life — the very stuff of the Geniza. It is safe to say that the medieval chroniclers would have been bemused by the historians of the *Annales* school, with their emphasis on *longue durée,* and certainly disdainful of modern social science, with its elaborate and highly antiseptic modeling based on accumulated statistical data. For the chroniclers, the sum and substance of what transpires between individuals and groups is the sum of their moral rectitude and, more often than not, their moral failings. This is not an analytical sensibility that satisfies the needs of present-day historians, who see situations as governed by circumstances that we might wish to describe (in a moment of epistemological recklessness) as objective realities.

In short, medieval Arabic historical writing is a history that should have been, or, rather, a history that was or might have been. Moreover, it is, as some would say, largely a history of elites written by the hired pens of the elite or members of the religious establishment. How can modern historians control this material to recover varieties of experience that fall outside the world of the court, the military, and more generally, the privileged households of important clients and patrons?

Admittedly, Muslims also wrote letters, as did the Jews of the Geniza world. There are indeed numerous references in the Muslim chronicles and belletristic works to exacting methods of keeping records, be it private accounts or those of state and regional bureaucracies. There are even handbooks for scribes employed in government service. However, few of the actual documents have been recovered or even quoted at length; those sources that have been recovered remain largely unread.

One can scarcely imagine how many individual items the state and regional archives might have contained, let alone private records and correspondence. For all intents and purposes, the Geniza texts, the bulk of which range from the eleventh to the thirteenth centuries, constitute the only researched documentation that paints a broad and more or less systemic picture of daily life for that period. Nor is there anything comparable to the Geniza for the four preceding Islamic centuries; it is only at a later time that Near Eastern historians have access to detailed and wide-ranging Muslim records comparable in some instances to those of the Geniza. But these records, by coincidence found in Mamluk Egypt, remain largely unexamined. Only the later Ottoman archives have been given their deserved attention.

There are, assuredly, Arabic coins, inscriptions, and administrative and literary papyri for the earlier periods. But the numismatic and epigraphic material is highly schematic, and the papyri, however valuable, are highly fragmented and confined to a single region, that is, Egypt, where the arid climate allowed for their preservation. At last count, there were about one hundred thousand listed papyrus fragments in Arabic, but less than a handful of scholars with the skills to read and analyze them. When the largest known private collection of these papyri was put up for sale, no antiquarian bookseller was willing to broker the lot because there were no experts available to prepare even a preliminary catalogue. Only the Libyans expressed an interest in the collection, or so it was reported. They were prepared to purchase it sight unseen, not because the documents retained for them any scientific value that they could then share with the scholarly world; to the contrary, they were interested in acquiring the material so that they could destroy it, as they considered the papyri to be documents that had been recently fabricated by skilled Israeli Arabists to undermine the foundations of Islam. (It would appear that the reported presence of alternate readings of Qurānic passages had caused the Libyans consternation.) In truth, such slight variants were well known among medieval Muslims, who cited them freely; they are found, for example in early Qurān commentaries. Be that as it may, to the best of my knowledge the documents still remain in a bank vault in Liechtenstein, covered with feathers from the chicken crates in which they were smuggled by their owner out of Egypt.

In contrast, there are some 250,000 literary fragments in the Geniza and tens of thousands of documents, including fairly large archives in a relatively good state of preservation. Moreover, while the Jewish materials were admittedly deposited in a single location, the texts themselves document an extraordinary range of activities involving Jewish communities widely dispersed from India to the Iberian Peninsula and as far north as the French city of Rouen. That is to say, unlike the Egyptian papyri, the Geniza offers us a perspective and geographical sweep as broad as could be hoped for by a historian of the medieval Near East.

Among the various subfields of medieval Muslim history, perhaps the one most enriched by the Geniza is the history of the Mediterranean economy, a subject dealt with tangentially but in some detail in the preceding pages. One could indeed claim, and with justification, that no general economic history of the Geniza period can be produced for a discriminating scholarly audience without direct access to the Jewish materials. For example, during my researches on medieval Baghdad, an effort that continued on and off for a period of over twenty years, I was able to identify, after a thorough search of Muslim materials, both in published texts and manuscripts, some thirty professional occupations, and, at best, I could establish the general location of the workshops and/ or retail establishments—this in a city of perhaps a half a million inhabitants or more, a city that is probably the best described of all medieval Muslim urban centers. In contrast, the Geniza yields references to more than 450 occupations. Furthermore, the Geniza documents and letters allow us to reconstruct in detail complex aspects of production and marketing and, beyond that, the economic infrastructure that regulated, however informally, vocational training and the conduct of commerce and trade. No doubt, certain professions were typical only of the Jews; various occupations were subsumed by the Jewish educational establishment and religious hierarchy—teachers, cantors, rabbis, beadles, ritual slaughterers and the like—positions that often overlapped, as they did in other times and in other Jewish communities. But in so many other professions, what is described for the Jewish community must have had its parallels among the Muslims and also the Christians. Indeed, there are many Jewish texts that bear testimony to business relationships with non-Jews involving the special hiring of agents and, more generally, partnerships and transactions. The Mediterranean trade portrayed in the Geniza was, in every sense, a multiparty undertaking involving, as we would suspect, all segments of the commercial community, often working cooperatively with one another and informally with the state authorities and their representatives. The intricacies of these arrangements are, at best, hinted at in the Muslim literary sources, which because of their limitations have to be scanned for mere snippets of information—tidbits so small or indigestible that they often overwhelm our capacity for analysis. Similarly, other aspects of daily life, hitherto known from vague references in the Muslim chronicles and belletristic texts, are vividly described in great detail in the Geniza. There are extended references to architecture, household furnishings, jewelry, clothing, cooking wares, and other appliances, all of which were utilized by Jews and Muslims alike. The Muslim sources, particularly the belletristic texts, also refer to the realia of daily life, but scarcely in such detail. For example, we know of unusual treasures possessed by various caliphs; there are lengthy passages and even an entire book devoted to valuable objets d'art. Some of the more famous items are even illustrated. However, the Geniza goes well beyond that insofar as it allows us to recover the realia of the households of the poor, as well as those of wealthy families and elements of the populace that fell in between.

Occasionally, one finds in medieval Arabic sources somewhat detailed descriptions of buildings, but such descriptions are usually confined to mosques and palaces and are, in any case, few and far between. Even Baghdad and Fustat-Cairo, the two cities best described in the Arabic geographical and historical sources, remain very much of an enigma when it comes to the smaller details of toponymy and topography. It is true that extensive archeological digs in Fustat have yielded a pattern of medieval housing for various neighborhoods that should be of extraordinary interest to historians. It goes without saying that the archeological evidence would be significantly enriched if it were to be juxtaposed with the documentary evidence from the Geniza. Unfortunately, most Islamic field archeologists are unable to interrogate the Geniza texts first hand. Lest I appear too harsh on those who actually dig for a living, I should point out that historians are rarely appreciative of the importance of Islamic archeology to their own concerns. Where courses in Islamic art and archeology are available to historians of the medieval Near East, they are rarely, if ever, elected by them. Such failures of communication between scholars in different disciplines are most unfortunate. Reconstructing the physical setting of medieval communities is certainly a key to capturing the daily workings of their society.

More than anything else, the Geniza allows us to reconstruct the pattern of private lives, at times over many years, and down to the smallest details. Our sources are exceptionally rich in describing an entire population previously known to us largely from legal materials and popular literature. I refer to the world of contemporaneous Jewish women. The picture that emerges from the Geniza is much different than that which we would have imagined based only on legal and literary sources. That is made quite clear from the recent work of Gideon Libson on the legal status of Jewish women in the Gaonic period, research that graphically illustrates the numerous and unexpected options that Jewish women exercised in domestic matters. In this instance, Libson was able to draw upon his expertise in Islamic law as well as his broad knowledge in Jewish practices, an indication that the Jewish world of the Geniza resonated strongly to the dominant Muslim culture in whose midst Jews dwelt. We ought not be mislead, however. As a rule, historians should exercise caution when comparing Jewish and Muslim societies. Regarding the social and economic status of women, we have to be extremely wary of applying what we learn of Jews from the Geniza to the general condition of Muslim women in their own society. Indeed, the Geniza itself indicates how much freer Jewish women were in so many respects, especially in setting the agenda of their social obligations. Similarly, we should look for differences between Jews and Muslims as regards the broader aspects of communal responsibilities. Unlike Muslim society, which relied heavily on individual acts of charity, the Jewish communities, in keeping with time honored customs, were heavily organized to handle individual and communal distress. In that respect, they share much in common with Jewish communities today.

Obviously, the two cultures, Jewish and Muslim, were most likely to intersect when it came to material life and matters of the economy to which we have previously referred; above all, it was the relationship of the Jewish communities to established authority, be it the centralized Islamic state or its regional representatives, that drew the cultures into close proximity. As regards formal relations between Jews and the Muslim authorities, the Geniza is most instructive. Historians of the medieval Near East, whose researches are most often based on Muslim literary sources, have much to learn from the Jewish documentary record. At best the Jews are shadowy figures in the pages of the Muslim chronicles, geographical writings, and belletristic texts. Aside from Muḥammad's early and sustained conflict with the Jewish tribes of Arabia, an elaborate story which the Muslim sources relate in considerable detail, there is little mention of the Jews or the pattern of their settlements in the lands of Islam — be it in rural areas and small towns or, as increasingly became the case, the place that Jews came to occupy in the diverse urban environment. If I may be permitted to return to Baghdad once again. In the extensive literature dealing with the topography and toponymy of the great Abbasid capital, I was able to find only two references to possible Jewish neighborhoods: a so-called Qanṭarat al-Yahūd, or "Bridge of the Jews," a place whose location is indicated, but whose pattern of settlement is not described, and the Darb al-ʿAwn, a place where Jews were said to have lived, but about which nothing more is revealed. (I believe that I heard Moshe Gill say that he had found an additional brief reference or so.) The point is that for the most part one would hardly know, based on Muslim sources alone, that there was in fact a Jewish community of any consequence, let alone vitality, in the greatest of all Muslim cities, let alone in so many other locations within the lands of Islam.

Nor do the Muslim sources tell us in detail about daily contacts between Jews and Muslims, or of the more formal relations between representatives of the tolerated Jewish minority and the centralized authorities. We have, based on the Muslim sources, virtually no idea of the extent to which the authorities actively intervened for their own narrowly defined purposes in the actual conduct of the Jewish communities, or to what extent they were invited to do so when fractiousness among Jewish communal leaders demanded an imposed solution to internal Jewish conflicts. The Muslim sources relate, albeit ever so briefly, the rare occasions when Jews were subjected to discriminatory legislation that remained on the books but was hardly ever invoked, but the specific context for such action is often omitted. Muslim writers have absolutely nothing to say about the cumulative effects of more limited hardships imposed on the Jewish communities, namely, the burdensome taxation commonly referred to as the poll tax, a levy that in times of harsh economic conditions, could be devastating.

In effect, the Geniza documents have forced us to reassess the relationship between the Muslim authorities and their Jewish subjects, at least for the periods covered by the materials at hand. Above all, it is largely through the Geniza, particularly the economic materials, that we can gain a real insight into what made Fatimid society cohere at the outset and for some time thereafter as a relatively tolerant polity, a regime that encouraged economic expansion and that was marked by many elements of what may be described as a fledgling civil society, albeit without any of the formal institutions that allowed the civil societies of Europe to take root and prosper. Similarly, the continuous record of Jewish documents allows historians of the Near East to more accurately describe the incipient collapse of that tolerance as the Fatimids succumbed to internal and external pressures. It was as though the conditions of the Jews in the Fatimid Empire served as a barometer of the general condition of the Muslim body politic. In such fashion, the Geniza adds vivid color to the sepia description of medieval Muslim chronicles—that history all too often written from both the perspective and the sites of centralized authority.

There is another area where the Geniza allows us a particular insight in how to better do Islamic history, an area that has thus far eluded extensive discussion: the language of Arabic historiography, particularly the technical vocabulary that often confuses present-day historians, or, in any case, those historians of the medieval Near East who still remain grounded in texts. Compared with other Near Eastern languages, Arabic features an expansive vocabulary whose individual items generally reflect a wide semantic field. Hence the pithy expression, oft repeated, that every Arabic word has at least five basic meanings: the conventionally accepted meaning (the first item in the lexicon), the opposite, something related to a curse, something related to a blessing, and, last but not least, something linked to the behavior of a camel or its anatomy.

While intended as a humorous quip, the statement trumpets an undeniable truth, that is, the richness of Arabic, a language made even richer by a never ending need for more elaborate ways with which to praise friends and defame enemies. Humor aside, there is a reality of which we should take note, namely, the extraordinary elasticity of many frequently used technical terms. Although we possess enormously detailed medieval dictionaries and a number of highly specialized lexicons, tracing the path of Arabic words and expressions can be exceedingly vexing. Arabists lack the equivalent of the *Oxford English Dictionary*, with its detailed philological history and its representative illustrations of evolving usage. Many medieval words and expressions remain all too obscure, even to the most learned and experienced Arabists. The gap between the historian's working vocabulary and the wide range of meanings that could be attributed to so many words were we able to place these words in specific contexts is probably far greater than suspected.

These observations about lost meaning in Arabic historical (and indeed other) writing are not entirely conjectural. The elasticity of technical terms in Arabic is amply illustrated by materials from the Geniza. Unlike the literary sources utilized by historians of the medieval Muslim world, the Geniza materials are often dated or datable. Were that not bounty enough, the handwritings of individual scribes and prominent writers are also identifiable, thus allowing for chronological precision even when the documents are undated. Moreover, the material is linked to specific locations throughout the Mediterranean basin and beyond. This unique and carefully researched body of texts confirms that various technical terms, retained over generations and even centuries, may reflect different meanings at particular locations and moments of time. The Geniza also allows us to trace the introduction of entirely new terms according to chronology and region. Checking and cross-checking these documents and letters, we discover as well that at given times seemingly discrete words were, in fact, interchangeable, thus clearing away much confusion. In sum, unlike the Arabic lexicons, the texts discovered in Cairo enable us to establish more closely the provenance and shelf life of specific terms, with all that that implies for more accurate historical readings.

Despite all that can be learned from the Geniza, it continues to remain, by and large, *terra incognita* to historians of the Islamic world. This is particularly true in the United States, where the current system of educating historians of the medieval Near East, even in the most prestigious institutions, is not nearly as broad based as it was a generation or so earlier. There was a time when historians of the Near East, many of them trained in departments of Near Eastern languages or oriental studies, were required to undergo rigorous philological training. In addition to extended instruction in Arabic, departments obliged them to study other Near Eastern languages and civilizations; it was not uncommon to find Islamists familiar with a broadly based history of the region, its languages and its cultures. That is not so today.

All too often, students of Islamic history, now mostly trained in history departments, study an Islam that was seemingly created *ex nihilo* in seventh-century C.E. Arabia, a civilization that is studied, for the most part, without drawing detailed attention to the rich cultures of the region that preceded it or were contemporaneous with it. Ironically, that narrow vision contradicts what the early Muslims themselves say about their culture and its relation to the broad monotheist history of the Near East. For the present, most historians of the Islamic Near East have, at best, a passing acquaintance with Geniza studies. I would assume that many have taken the opportunity to peruse *A Mediterranean Society;* but few have read the five volumes from cover to cover; and only the rare individual has mined the text for all that it has to offer. The same is no doubt even more true for the various specialized monographs and articles based on Geniza materials.

Strangely enough, Judaica specialists have been remarkably slow in appreciating the cornucopia represented by the Geniza, particularly the materials that bear directly on the social and economic condition of the Jews of Islamic lands and their relationship to the Muslim ruling authorities. Generally speaking, the vibrant history of the Jews in Islamic lands remains—in the United States at least—a shamefully neglected area of study. It is significant that most of our Geniza specialists were not educated at the leading departments of Jewish studies, nor did they learn their craft at rabbinical seminaries, nor do any of these religious or profane institutions retain on their faculties scholars specifically trained and recruited to teach the history of Near Eastern Jewry as a

separate field of enquiry with distinctive methods and a curriculum of
its own.

Rigorous instruction in Near Eastern Jewry is all too often offered
by scholars whose original research interests and formal academic appointments were outside the recognized centers of Jewish studies. These
include scholars who were recipients of a traditional Jewish education
in their youth and who retained a scholarly interest in their own tradition, although their formal graduate training was in Arabic and Islamics.
This group of Jewish Islamists, along with the coterie of Judeo-Arabic
scholars specifically trained by Goitein—who was, you will recall, recruited by the University of Pennsylvania to be a Professor of Arabic
and Islamics—represents the central core of investigators in what has
become a long neglected field.

There is perhaps no more pressing agenda for Jewish studies in the
United States than that of creating the critical mass of scholars necessary
to make the history of medieval Near Eastern Jewry a viable academic
enterprise, one that can play an integral role in the current curriculum
of Jewish learning, and, more generally, in the teaching of Islamic history. To accomplish that we will have to recognize the centrality of the
Arabic language and Islamic studies in educating the next generation of
medieval Jewish historians. For not only was the world of the Geniza
an Arabaphone site; it was a world whose constituents, Jews and Christians among them, were shaped directly by the civilization of Islam.

General Index

Aaron b. al-ʿAmmānī, 312
Aaron b. Ṣaghīr, 367
Abbasids, 33, 82, 270
ʿAbd. *See* Slaves
ʿĀbida (pious woman), 459
Abraham b. ʿAṭāʾ, 86
Abraham b. David, 394
Abraham b. Samuel al-Andalusī, 429, 430
Abraham b. Yijū, 353
Abraham Maimonides, xix, 51, 90, 92, 131–32, 143, 183; on freedmen, 246; and Judah b. Aaron, 215; as judge, 315; on marriage contracts, 341, 367; marriage/fatherhood of, 380; on marriage to scholar, 354; pietist movement of, 200; on public service, 110; on slaves, 243–44; on synagogue seating, 153, 196; on visiting preacher, 277
Abraham the Pious, 200
Abūʾl-Barakāt ("The Unique"), 302–3
Abūʾl-Barakāt Judah ha-Kohen, 166–67
Abūʾl Ḥusayn al-Tinnīsī, 65
Abū ʾl-Rabīʿ Solomon b. Joseph b. Gabbay (Abraham the Pious), 200
Abū Manṣūr. *See* Samuel b. Hananya
Abū Naṣr Tustarī, 353
Abū Saʿd al-Tustarī, 165, 166, 353, 460
Abū Yaʿqūb al-Ḥākim, 338, 431
Aden, southern Arabia, 123, 235
Adoption, 413–14

Adultery, 465–66
Age group conflicts, 102–3
Aḥdāth (armed force), 177
Aḥmad b. Ṭūlūn, 20
Al-Aḥnaf (Arab chieftan), 65
Ajīr (hireling), 230
Akolythos ("no objection"), 316
Aʿlāq (select textiles), 233
Aleppo, 21; synagogue of, 59
Alexandria, 31, 110, 111; adultery in, 465–66; despised occupations in, 229; female slaves in, 242, 243; funeral services in, 157; Fustat's relations with, 43, 44–45; hospitality in, 212; Jewish judges in, 309, 311; muḥtasib office in, 176; names to identify, 43; qāḍī's role in, 173; runaway husband in, 398; social services in, 128–29; tax burden in, 105; topographic terms in, 48
Alimony, 114, 127, 231, 364
Allūf (distinguished member), 266
Almohads, 37, 38, 301
Almoravids, 37, 38, 298
ʿAmālīn (workmen), 230
ʿĀmil (director of revenue office), 171, 181, 187
Amṣār (garrison towns), 48, 57
Anatoli, Rabbi, 399
Anbōl (reader's platform), 147–48, 252
Ancestors: on marriage contracts, 361; on memorial lists, 334; names as tribute to, 335–36; and occupational specializa-

Mediterranean Sea, 31; three great regions of, 27–28; trade routes on, 31–33, 35

A Mediterranean Society (Goitein), xi, xiii, 289n, 470, 481; abridged version of, xvii–xx, xxi; assessment of, 472–73; *Economic Foundations* volume of, 472; original design of, xiv–xv

Megillat setārīm (personal diary), 275

Megilloth (scrolls), 17

Meir, Rabbi, 394

Melākhā-melūkhā ("a craft is a kingdom"), 228

Melamméd (Hebrew teacher), 261

Melūgg (wife's personal possessions), 393–94

Memorial lists, 16, 157, 334, 335, 410

Menahem (chief judge in Cairo), 399

Menaḥēm b. Isaac b. Sāsōn, 417

Merchants: "freedom of contract" of, 316; marital absenteeism of, 379, 395, 467; in overseas marriages, 455; qāḍīs as, 174; scholarship of, 263, 271; vocational training by, 261–62

Meshōrēr (singer, poet), 281

Meshōṭetē layla (night watchmen), 117. See also *Ṭawwāf*

Meturgeman (interpreter), 265

Mevōrākh, Nagid, 64, 97, 165, 193, 431, 461; and beadle's post, 116; and muqaddam position, 107, 109; parrot of, 218–19

Meyer, Eduard, xxii

Mezōnōt. See Bread

Midrāsh (school of higher studies), 266, 268–70

Midwives, 237, 406

Migdāl (reader's platform), 148

Milāk (property conveyance), 356

Minbar (reader's platform), 148

Mint, caliphal, 55, 168, 176, 177, 180

Miriam (daughter of Benayah), 258

Mishael b. Isaiah, 335

Mishnah, 264, 265

Mishne la-melekh (deputy to the ruler), 165

Mishpāḥā (extended family), 333. See also Families

Miṣr (term for Egypt), 42. See also Egypt

Misṭāḥ (open space for dyed materials), 133

Morocco, *mellah* of, 298–99

Moses, synagogue of. See Dammūh shrine

Moses b. Paltiel, 246

Moses Maimonides, 52, 90, 92, 96, 135, 142, 249, 268, 364, 426, 447, 464; ancestorship of, 334, 335; on attorneys, 322; on charity, 123–24, 144–45; on child's debt, 408; on employment of orphans, 435; on funeral services, 157–58; on hereditary readers, 156–57; on house sales, 298; and Ibn Sanā' al-Mulk, 300; on instrumental music, 216; as jurisconsult, 315; on lesbianism, 382; on marriage, 368–69, 370, 379, 400; marriage/fatherhood of, 379–80; on muqaddam's authority, 109–10; on number of elders, 101; on partnerships, 299; on piyyūṭ, 156; on proselytizing, 303; on public service, 92, 139; on ritual bathing, 152; on Sabbath pastimes, 203–4; on slaves, 243; on statutes, 95; on synagogue compound, 150; on validation of contracts, 317; on widows, 423; on wife beating, 394–95; on women's Bible instruction, 258; writing style of, 288–89

Mosque, the, 57–58, 146–47, 153, 158

Mothers: and adult children, 411–13; bearing/nursing children, 405–6; education role of, 256–57, 456, 458–59; family names from, 336; informal adoption of, 414

Mothers-in-laws, 386, 390–91

Mount of Olives procession, 267, 294

Muʿallima (woman Bible teacher), 258, 460

Mubārak (freedman), 246

Muftī (Muslim jurisconsult), 58, 174, 314

Muḥammad the Prophet, 153, 446

Muhja (lifeblood), 404

Muḥtasib (market superintendent), 175–76, 177, 178

Al-Muʿizz (Fatimid caliph), 32

Al-Muʿizz b. Bādis of Tunisia, 86, 461

Munādī (herald), 117

Munāwil (workshop helper), 230

Muqaddams (community leaders): appointment of, 88, 108–9; authority of, 108–10; elders and, 101; emoluments of, 109, 136–37; in factional conflicts, 103–4; foreigners as, 107–8; as rōsh ha-qāhāl, 111; use of term, 106–7

Muqaddar (something valued), 140

Al-Muqaddasī, 270

Murahhiṭ (singer of liturgical poetry), 117, 281

Muruwwa (manliness), 388

Muṣādara (requisition), 188

Prophets, the, 251
Prostitution, 467
Puisne judges *(na'ib)*, 107. *See also* Jewish judges
Purim, 365

Qāḍīs (Muslim judges), 172; authority of, 307, 310; bribing of, 173; documentary criticism of, 311–12; Jews' appeals to, 191–93; other occupations of, 173–74; tenure of, 311; wālī's duties and, 177–78. *See also* Muslim courts
Qāhāl (congregation), 95. *See also* Congregation
Qālūs market, 55–56
Qalyūb, 170
Qanā (to acquire a right), 317–18
Qanāts (water conduits), 61–62
Qantarat al-Yahūd (Bridge of the Jews), 478
Qāṭn (permanent resident), 184
Qayrawān, Tunisia, 22, 43–44, 84, 95
Qayṣāriyya (market hall), 55–56
Qayyim (administrator of synagogue), 111
Qinyān aggāv (transfer adjunct), 318
Qōdesh (community chest): administrative cost of, 136; administrators of, 126–27, 132, 134–35; centralization reform of, 135; derivation of term, 126; property donations to, 132–33; public funding of, 125–26, 128, 129–30; revenue farming by, 135–36. *See also* Charitable donations; Charitable foundation properties
Quffa (basket), 128
Quppā (basket), 128, 129
Qur'ānic law. *See* Islamic law
Qūs (Upper Egypt), 111

Rab' (area or residence), 48–49
Rabbanites: Babylonian, 19–20, 22–23, 326; conjugal duties of, 465; Karaites' relations with, 76–77, 97, 194–95, 207, 343; *khaālifa* of, 77; on levirate marriage, 400; majlis meetinghouse of, 159; marriage contracts of, 350, 351, 361; Palestinian, 19–22, 371; rayyis of, 87; two branches of, 19–20
Rabbī (master), 275–76
Rabīb(a) (foster child), 438
Ra'īs al-Yahūd (head of the Jews), 85–86. See also *Rayyis*
Rallier *(ḥāshir)*, 177, 181, 186
Ramadan, 215, 291

Ramle, Palestine, 44, 95, 159
Ransom: of prisoners, 122–23, 124, 143–44, 212; and "ransomed brother" metaphor, 339–40; of slaves, 246; of wives, 364
Raqqāṣ (runner), 89, 176, 181, 230. *See also* Police services
Rāv (master), 275–76
Rav Ḥisdā, 404–5
Al-Rāya (high command area), 48
Rayyis (head of the Jews): appointment/installation of, 88; functions of, 87, 89–91; *nagid* title of, 85–86; origins of, 87–88; social services role of, 127, 129; status/emoluments of, 92
Reading without phonetics, 253
Reali Gymnasium (Haifa), xii
Release documents, 14
Remarriage, 380, 421–23, 437–38
Repudiation, bill of, 371, 419–20. *See also* Divorce; Divorce, bills of
Reshūth (taking permission) custom, 84
Residential areas. *See* Houses
Responsa, 17
Rīf (the province), 45–46, 234
Rīfī (farmland), 45
Ritual baths, 151–52
Ritual slaughterer *(shoḥet)*, 137, 273–74, 282–83, 318
Rosenthal, Franz, 218, 470
Rōsh ha-keneset (head of the synagogue), 110, 111
Rōsh ha-qāhāl (head of the congregation), 110–11
Rōsh ha-seder (head of the row), 266
Rub' (fourth or quarter), 49
Rub' al-kanīs (synagogue compound), 150
Ruins, 52–54
al-Rūm (The Land of the Romans), 28, 35, 113
Runciman, Steven, 50

Saadya Gaon, 153, 210, 271–72, 278, 358, 374, 381
Sabbath: cantor's role on, 278; and conjugal duties, 388–89, 465; derāsh of, 154; disapproved pastimes on, 203–4; Muslim influence on, 202; piyyūṭ poems of, 154–56; Scripture readings on, 153–54, 156–57; social status element of, 157
Sabbatical year, 316–17
Ṣabī (boy), 230
Ṣaddeqet (pious woman), 388

Index of Scriptural Citations